MORAL DESPERADO

Moral Desperado

A Life of
Thomas Carlyle

SIMON HEFFER

faber and faber

TO MY DARLING WIFE

This edition first published in 2012
by Faber and Faber Ltd
Bloomsbury House, 74–77 Great Russell Street
London WC1B 3DA

Printed and bound by CPI Group (UK) Ltd, Croydon, CR0 4YY

A CIP record for this book is available from the British Library

ISBN 978–0–571–28836–6

CONTENTS

ILLUSTRATIONS

ACKNOWLEDGEMENTS

The modern scholar of Carlyle has the great good fortune to have, thanks to the editors of the *Collected Letters of Thomas and Jane Welsh Carlyle*, the greatest possible advantage in seeking to find, interpret and judge a vast collection of essential biographical material. To them – Clyde de L. Ryals, Kenneth J. Fielding, Ian Campbell, Aileen Christianson and Hilary J. Smith – my debt is incalculable. Professor Campbell also offered his expert opinions at a late stage, for which I am especially indebted to him. Similarly, for letters in their possession, I must thank the Master and Fellows of Trinity College, Cambridge, the Most Hon the Marquess of Northampton, the British Library and, above all, the National Library of Scotland, whose Manuscript Room staff could not have been more helpful.

I must also thank the Cambridge University Library for the use of its facilities and for the loan of books long out of print. Many others helped me by finding books or other material, and by providing hospitality on research trips, and other essential assistance. I am particularly grateful to Mark Amory, Maurice Cowling, Martin Edmunds, Giles Gordon, Robert Gray, Mr and Mrs Neil Hamilton, Christopher Howse, Noel Malcolm, Mrs Ferdinand Mount, Miss Juliana Nedelkovska, Mr and Mrs J. Enoch Powell, Dr Anne Ridler, Stephen Robinson, Christopher Silvester and Miss Virginia Utley. Modern authorship is impossible without the help of a technical genius to advise on the mysteries of word-processing, and I am indebted to Miss Fiona Graham for her unstinting help in this respect.

Four people read the manuscript at various stages and provided invaluable suggestions for its improvement. For their great sacrifice of their time and energy I am grateful to Hywel Williams, John Patten, Andrew Roberts and Mme Radoslaw Sikorski. I have acted on much of what they told me, but all mistakes, misprisions and misconceptions are mine alone.

My greatest debt, though, is to my wife, Diana. Mrs Carlyle was almost killed by thirteen years of Frederick the Great; it was my most earnest hope, while writing this book, that Mrs Heffer would not be almost killed by three years of Carlyle. She has, in appropriately heroic fashion, borne the burden of having to live with Carlyle for all that time, and has been utterly indispensable to me. This book would not have been possible without her; unlike Carlyle, I have no need to wait for the light of my life to go out before I realise its strength.

Great Leighs, Essex
5 January 1995

'My dearest Clough these are damned times – everything is against one – the height to which knowledge is come, the spread of luxury, our physical enervation, the absence of great *natures*, the unavoidable contact with millions of small ones, newspapers, cities, light profligate friends, moral desperadoes like Carlyle, our own selves, and the sickening consciousness of our difficulties: but for God's sake let us neither be fanatics nor yet chalf blown by the wind but let us be ὡς ὁ φρονιμος διαρισειεν and not as anyone else διαρισειεν.'

Matthew Arnold, letter to Arthur Hugh Clough, 23 September 1849

'Ernst ist das Leben!'

Friedrich Schiller

'As Religion is the only bond and life of societies, so the only real Government were a Hierarchy.'

Carlyle, letter to Gustave d'Eichthal, 9 August 1830

'A well-written Life is almost as rare as a well-spent one.'

Carlyle, 'Jean Paul Richter'

Introduction:
Death and Assassination

THOMAS CARLYLE died at his Chelsea home at half past eight on the morning of Saturday 5 February 1881, in the third month of his eighty-sixth year. He had originated no great philosophy, nor possessed conventional literary gifts, yet he died the most influential man of letters of his day. The twentieth century has come to ignore him, even though it is impossible to understand the Victorians without understanding Carlyle first. He wrote little after 1865, but right up to the end scores of young men and women came to his terraced house in Cheyne Row to hear him talk; they were rarely required to say anything. Politicians, critics and historians had their minds altered by him, but it was in literature that he made his greatest impact. He had been the friend, and at times inspiration, of Dickens; an intimate of Tennyson, Browning, Leigh Hunt, Ruskin, Lecky, Froude and (before a long estrangement) John Stuart Mill. A quarter of a century before his death George Eliot, no great admirer, had written:

It is an idle question to ask whether his books will be read a century hence; if they were all burnt as the grandest of Suttees on his funeral pile, it would be only like cutting down an oak after its acorns have sown a forest. For there is hardly a superior or active mind of this generation that has not been modified by Carlyle's writings; there has hardly been an English book written for the last ten or twelve years that would not have been different if Carlyle had not lived.[1]

His influence had moderated since 1855, when Eliot was writing; but his status as prophet was unmatched by any other. 'For many years before his death,' wrote the critic R.H. Hutton, 'Carlyle was to England what his great hero, Goethe, long was to Germany – the aged seer whose personal judgments on men and things were eagerly sought after, and eagerly chronicled and retailed.'[2] It is easy to forget how important the struggles with faith and dogma were to the Victorians; and Carlyle, above all, had been seen as one who had sought – not entirely successfully – to liberate a generation from the chains of dogma.

Nor had Carlyle been a hero to England alone. His work as a propagator of Teutonic culture since the 1820s, through his discipleship of Goethe, his support of Prussian expansionism and, above all, his biography of Frederick the Great earned him the adulation of Germany. Americans had read him voraciously since Ralph Waldo Emerson championed him in the 1830s, while he was still struggling for recognition in England. On Carlyle's death Walt Whitman, the prominent American poet and man of letters, wrote that 'as a representative author, a literary figure, no man else will bequeath to the future more significant hints of our stormy era, its fierce paradoxes, its din, and its struggling parturition periods, than Carlyle.'[3]

The Dean of Westminster, Arthur Penrhyn Stanley, visited Cheyne Row immediately after Carlyle's death to persuade Mary Carlyle, Carlyle's niece and companion since 1869, to have her uncle buried in the abbey among others of the highest rank in English letters. She refused, knowing Carlyle (who had spent his life abjuring what the twentieth century would call 'the establishment') would have had none of it. The Scotch peasant had willed that his remains be returned to Dumfriesshire and interred at Ecclefechan, where he had been born in December 1795.

Stanley, in his sermon at the abbey the day after Carlyle's death, paid the first public tribute, and set in train the troubled progress of Carlyle's posthumous reputation. He took as his text Matthew xiii:24, 'The Kingdom of heaven is likened unto a man which sowed good seed in his field.' After disquisiting upon Socrates, St Paul, Luther and John Wesley he came to Carlyle. Like these men, he said, Carlyle had been 'one of the gifted few' who had been 'a new light in the world'. Stanley lamented that the sage had turned down the honour of resting finally in England's Parthenon:

It may be that he will not be laid, as might have been expected, amongst the poets and scholars and sages whose dust rests with us in this Abbey; it may be that he was drawn by an irresistible longing towards the native hills of his own Dumfriesshire, and that there, beside the bones of his kindred, beside his father and his mother, and with the silent ministrations of the Church of Scotland, to which he clung amidst all the vicissitudes of a long existence, will repose all that is earthly of Thomas Carlyle.[4]

Stanley (who was wrong about the Church of Scotland) admitted he was speaking 'only of him [Carlyle] and of his best self', almost the only application of the principle of *de mortuis* seen in the aftermath of his death. He continued that 'all the world knows how the words and deeds of former times became in his hands, as Luther describes the Apostle's language, "not dead things, but living creatures with hands and feet".' This was a reference to *The French Revolution*, which made Carlyle's name in 1837; to *Past and Present*, which in 1843 had held up the feudal glories of the abbey of twelfth-century Bury St Edmunds as an example to an England ravaged by the Poor Law; to *The Letters and Speeches of Oliver Cromwell, with Elucidations*, in which Carlyle hero-worshipped the last strong man to govern England; and to *Frederick the Great*, a six-volume epic that took Carlyle twelve years to write, which helped undermine the health of and ultimately kill his wife, and which took him from a robust (if hypochondriacal) middle age into a wretched, lonely dotage. But Stanley understood well the other side to Carlyle's character; indeed, a side contained in all Carlyle's writings right from his earliest days, whatever their notional purpose:

It was customary for those who honoured him to speak of him as a 'prophet'. And if we take the word in its largest sense he truly deserved the name. He was a prophet, and felt himself to be a prophet, in the midst of an untoward generation; his prophet's mantle was his rough Scotch dialect, and his own peculiar diction, and his own secluded manner of life. He was a prophet most of all in the emphatic utterance of truths which no-one else, or hardly anyone else, ventured to deliver, and which he felt to be a message of good to a world sorely in need of them.

Carlyle had set himself up as prophet, with a certainty that peppers all his work, from his first writings. This was despite the fact that, in one of his earliest essays, he had lectured pompously against the trade of prophecy: 'It is no very good symptom either of nations or individuals, that they deal much in vaticination. Happy men are full of the present, for its bounty suffices them; and wise men also, for its duties engage them.'[5]

Carlyle was wise, after his own fashion, but he was certainly not happy for much of his life. Until the death of his wife in 1866 his main miseries had been those of a martyr to dyspepsia. Until his early forties he had been depressed by a fight for recognition. Then, paradoxically, once famous he had been aware that only a select few were actually listening, a few who did not include the politicians and prelates who might bring about changes to the society he so abhorred. There is also the clear implication of some of his friends and of his biographer, the historian James Anthony Froude, that he was impotent throughout his forty years of marriage. Whether because of that, or because of his addiction to work and need to preach, his wife had little of his attention. After her death he was paralysed by guilt at what he discovered (from her letters and journals) to be the effect of his behaviour towards her.

He had spent the second half of his life repudiating what Stanley called in his sermon 'the whole drift and pressure of modern days towards exalting popular opinion and popular movements as oracles to be valued above the judgment of the few, above the judgment of the wise, the strong, and the good'. Carlyle had become the embodiment of the reactionary movement in England against parliamentary and social reform. In his works, starting with The French Revolution, he pleaded against further progress from feudalism, and from leadership by a natural, non-democratically chosen aristocracy. In his most angry exclamation against post-Chartist England, he observed that 'it is the everlasting privilege of the foolish to be governed by the wise; to be guided in the right path by those who know it better than they. This is the first "right of man".'[6] Carlyle had been reviled in 1850, when the Latter-Day Pamphlets damaged his reputation for humanity (Mill, among others, had taken exception the previous year to Carlyle's pamphlet on emancipated slaves, the *Occasional Discourse on the Nigger Question*).[7] However, by 1881, with organised Labour agitating for extensions of the franchise to all men and the prospect of socialist representation in clear view,[8] in at least one respect he appeared to have been successfully prophetic.

The acceptance of democracy as a fundamental human right by the thinkers and politicians of the twentieth century has made Carlyle seem irrelevant, even offensive. The harm has been intensified by Carlyle's failure to offer anything original instead of democracy, save a retreat to feudalism. The desire for originality is one reason why Marx, an infinitely less humane and more dangerous man than Carlyle, enjoyed such popularity until the late 1980s. Hitler (who had Goebbels read him *Frederick the Great* in the bunker during the Russian advance on Berlin)[9] made Carlylean authoritarianism a foul-smelling concept. Today, the rule of a leader unanswerable to an electorate is synonymous with oppression, destruction and even genocide. Nor can one say that Carlyle was a Christian, believing in an authoritarian society based on Christian principles and practice; he is best described in Maurice Cowling's thoughtful phrase as 'a post-Christian'.[10] Carlyle did, though, believe in a divine order in which man took his appropriate place, and was accountable inevitably to God rather than to a dictator. Stanley explained this concept in his sermon thus:

The whole framework and fabric of his mind was built up on the belief that there are not many wise, not many noble minds, not many destined by the Supreme Ruler of the universe to rule their fellows; that few are chosen, that 'strait is the gate and narrow is the way, and few there be that find it.' But when that few appear, when the great and good present themselves, it is the duty and the wisdom of the multitude to seek their guidance. A Luther, a Cromwell, a Goethe, were to him the born kings of men. This was his doctrine of the work of heroes; this, right or wrong, was the mission of his life.

Carlyle's religion is at the root of his moral and political teachings. Seldom is his creed stated clearly; yet everywhere it permeates insidiously. He was unconcerned with the practicalities of politics; that political action should be moral was everything. Stanley said that 'he never, during the whole course of his long life, took an active part – never, I believe, even voted – in those elections which, to most of us, are the very breath of our nostrils.' Carlyle's concept of duty, which he saw as the highest aim of man in serving God, would not have been served by striving to choose whether Mr Gladstone or Mr Disraeli should have the right to govern England badly.

II

Stanley's encomium was echoed in the next day's newspapers. *The Daily Telegraph* said that 'in every corner of the earth where our tongue is spoken multitudes will be sorrowing for the death of an inspiring teacher whom most of them have never seen, a fiery-souled Prophet whom most of them have never known, but whose words have left upon their lives and hearts an indelible imprint ... on the first half of the present generation, and, for that matter, on every thinking man and woman during a certain stage of mental evolution, Mr Carlyle's writings have exercised a vast influence.'[11] *The Times* devoted a leading article to him. 'No such individuality has been felt in the Republic of English letters since the grave closed over Dr Johnson,' it said. Its obituary claimed that 'no recent man of letters has held in England a place comparable to that which for at least a quarter of a century has been his without dispute, and authors of all kinds and all schools will feel that they have lost their venerable *doyen*. A great man of letters, quite as heroic as any of those whom he depicted, has passed away amid universal regret.'[12] Remembering the angry middle age, *The Times*'s obituarist, Sir John Mac-Donnell,[13] was not too soft on his subject. 'His criticisms were often grotesque caricatures. They abounded in contradictions, and it was always pretty clear that Mr Carlyle found it much easier to rail at large than to suggest any working substitutes for the systems he despised ... harsh and crude judgments are to be met with in almost every page, and much of the teaching, so far as it is intelligible and consistent, is preposterous and impracticable.' The obituarist blamed Carlyle for prompting a host of second-rate imitators ('They have not always copied the sound sense which made atonement and which controlled all that he did') and broadened the charge-sheet to say he was 'responsible for much in modern literature which it is not pleasant to look upon'. Despite these criticisms, which were the beginning of the snowball of contumely against Carlyle that was to roll itself up in the years ahead, the conclusion gave the orthodox, laudatory view:

To whom has he not been a salutary teacher? Kingsley, Froude and Ruskin have sat at his feet, and a host of others, scarcely a leading mind of our time excepted, have felt his influence. Wherever, in truth, men have turned their minds for the last quarter of a century to the deep relations of things his spirit has been present to rebuke frivolity, to awaken courage and hope. No other writer of this generation ever cast so potent a spell on the youth of England ... What Hazlitt said of Coleridge was true of him – he cast a great stone into the pool of contemporary thought, and the circles have grown wider and wider.

The funeral was on the following Thursday at Ecclefechan. Carlyle had viewed his destination after death as 'the Eternal Silence'. There was no ceremony, and the event appropriately took place, as *The Times* put it, in silence.[14] The occasion was private, attended mainly by Carlyle's family. His brother James, a farmer, led the mourners, who included his sister's husband and four nephews. Froude, a constant companion for the last twenty years, had travelled from London with the coffin. Another historian, William Lecky, was there too, along with the prominent scientist Professor John Tyndall. The cortège arrived at Ecclefechan station just after ten o'clock on a cold, dull morning. Snow lay on the ground. The mourners lingered at the station for two uncomfortable hours until the hearse was ready to leave. On the way to the kirk the cortège passed through small crowds of villagers. On arrival, the flower-strewn polished oak coffin was taken to the north-west corner, which had been enclosed by iron railings ten years earlier at Carlyle's request. *The Times*'s reporter tells us that 'a shower of rain fell' as the coffin was lowered into the grave.

III

Before Carlyle was cold in that grave the assault on his reputation began. On the same day the funeral was reported in *The Times*, a correspondent under the pseudonym of 'Common Sense' attacked the paper's obituary.[15] 'Carlyle was emphatically a man of genius; he had imagination, humour, wit in no stinted measure; honesty of purpose, courage, energy and an intense, although often misdirected, sense of right and wrong. But he was not an original thinker, nor a sound moralist, nor a good writer, nor a safe guide.' The letter laid down what became the ruling themes of criticisms by anti-Carlyleans in the century ahead. His style was 'simply execrable'. His belief in 'power, might, volition, force' was immoral. Such ideas as he had were derived from Jean Paul Richter, Novalis and Swift. He was a bad critic, for failing to appreciate that Goethe's *Wilhelm Meister* had been added to by Eckermann to make it up to the required number of pages (Carlyle had said this work 'coheres so beautifully within itself').

The Spectator, delivering judgment on its former contributor the next day, took the attack a stage further. It regarded Carlyle as having been, in his last years, principally a form of entertainment. 'The Chelsea shrine, as was well known, gave out only one sort of oracles, and that sort was graphic and humorous denunciation of all conventional falsehoods and pretentiousness, or what was presumed to be conventional falsehood and pretentiousness.'[16] The writer added that 'Carlyle in his greatness was ever more disposed to sympathise with the great organs of the destructive, than with those of constructive force.' An effort was made to find some good in him ('His teaching was incessant that the reconstruction of society was a far greater work than the destruction of the worn-out shell which usually preceded it'), but this was half-hearted. 'Unfortunately, in his own time, there was hardly any species of reconstructive effort which could gain his acquiescence, much less his approval.' The conclusion was that Carlyle, in his extreme mis-anthropy and apparent hatred of the world, forfeited any right to be taken seriously; however, he did disturb those who discounted him into recon-sidering their own outlooks. Whitman, in his obituary for *The Critic*, said that:

He has lit up our Nineteenth century with the light of a powerful, penetrating, and perfectly honest intellect of the first class, turn'd it on British and European politics, social life, literature, and representative personages – thoroughly dissatisfied with all, and mercilessly exposing the illness of all. But while he announces the malady, and scolds and raves about it, he himself, born and bred in the same atmosphere, is a mark'd illustration of it.[17]

The Spectator rebuked him for his religion, and for his impatience with those who could not see that the 'Hebrew old clothes', as he called them, of orthodox Christianity, were worn out. The conclusion was, though, reverential, reflecting too the importance of the mid-Victorian intellectual tumult about faith:

Carlyle was far the greatest interpreter our literature has ever had of the infinite forces working through society, of that vast, dim background of social beliefs, unbeliefs, enthusiasms, sentimentalities, superstitions, hopes, fears, and trusts, which go to make up either the strong cement, or the destructive lava-stream, of national life, and to image forth some of the genuine features of the retributive providence of history.

The Spectator also made the first posthumous attempt to praise Carlyle as a political thinker. It reflected that 'we doubt whether any writer of his time has produced a more powerful effect, both good and bad, on the political tone and creed of thinking men, or done more to destroy that blind belief in mere institutions, whether aristocratic, or plutocratic, or democratic, which was at one time the equivalent for a political creed.'[18]

For the first half of Carlyle's life it had seemed doubtful (not least to him) whether he would ever break into the world of letters. The second half had been spent in London; Carlyle had used the force of his idiosyncratic opinions, rather than more usual means of ingratiation, to establish himself. Where more conventional methods had been used in his climb he owed most to the social skills of his wife, a doctor's daughter from Haddington, near Edinburgh. Although during their marriage (as often during their courtship) her private feelings for him were mixed, she was his champion in public. Once Carlyle made his reputation, his views were sought on the great issues of the day – reform, the American Civil War, colonial government or instability in Europe. This was not always deemed by the liberal establishment to be beneficial. 'In relation to the attack of Prussia and Austria on Denmark,'[19] the *Spectator* article contended, 'there can be little doubt that Mr Carlyle's eager admiration of Prussia, and of the Prussian drill-system, did very much to reconcile those Englishmen who had fallen under his influence to one of the earliest and most cynical of the acts of international violence for which the last twenty years of the history of Europe have been remarkable.' This was a common thought, *The Athenaeum* talking of 'fighting the good fight of liberty against tyranny, Christian kindness against Carlylism'.[20]

A rare defender of Carlyle was the anonymous obituarist of the *Saturday Review*, which had been no supporter of his. 'Though his conception of the moral order of the world may be called dynamic,' the obituarist wrote, 'unfriendly critics who accused him of deifying force were wholly mistaken. He was never tired of asserting the right of a hero to compel the obedience of ordinary men, but always on the condition that he was a hero, and not a vulgar despot. His own judgment in the selection of heroes was not infallible, but it excluded mere tyrants and usurpers.'[21] This distinction, which the writer illustrates by comparing Carlyle's distaste for Napoleon with his admiration, in *Past and Present*, for Edmund King and Martyr, has been lost on most of the critics who have followed him.

IV

The worst blow to Carlyle's reputation was, though, delivered by his own hand. It also complicated the assessment of him by his successors, for it caused his roles as prophet, philosopher and 'moral desperado' to be, for a time, overtaken by prurient interest in his relations with his wife and in his failings of rampant self-pity and introspection. He had entrusted Froude, then at the height of his powers as a historian and a friend of Carlyle's from the 1850s onwards, with two great tasks. First, he was to edit and publish reminiscences Carlyle had written of his father, wife and several friends and acquaintances. Those of his father had been written at the time of James Carlyle's death in 1832. The others were written in the months of intense and bewildering grief after Mrs Carlyle's death in April 1866. Froude had been told by Carlyle to do as he would with the raw materials given him, and he opted (after much internal struggle) for scholarly honesty. The result was that the self-indulgent, self-pitying narrator who emerged was very different from the public image of Carlyle. The book also challenged the boundaries of polite taste, allowing out as it did emotion without much restraint.

Andrew Lang, reviewing the work in *Fraser's Magazine*, wondered whether the tone was the result of an incipient bitterness in Carlyle's blood, 'a deposit, perhaps, of many centuries of hereditary poverty and ill-rewarded toil.'[22] Lang was prepared, just, to give Carlyle the benefit of the doubt on the evidence of the *Reminiscences*. 'Posterity will regard him with deep sympathy and reverence, as one of the greatest of literary forces; thwarted, like Byron, by selfwill; torn, like Swift, by *saeva indignatio*, and all his life vexed, almost physically, by a fierce hunger and thirst after righteousness.' *The Spectator* regarded the book as 'impressive',[23] but was shocked by the 'picture with almost a permanent scowl on it' painted of the author. 'A tone of moroseness runs through almost the whole of the *Reminiscences*,' the article continued. The reviewer detected bitterness and jealousy throughout the chapter on Carlyle's friend Edward Irving, one of the few men to whom he had looked up, saying the writing showed 'that grudging, ungenerous, peasant side of him ... This is not a pleasant thing to say of a really great man, so recently dead.' That was not all. 'This morose criticism, though so freely poured out as it is, never seems to be painful to him ... this book betrays a profound and almost intolerable deficiency in charity.' As well as having this failing, Carlyle had made himself a sitting target by setting himself up as the arch-persecutor of cant. He complains in the *Reminiscences* that having to spend two weeks in Kew as a private tutor when in his twenties was intolerable.[24] This brings down a torrent of abuse from *The Spectator*'s reviewer:

The man of genius, who has taught us all to rectify our lives by diminishing our insatiable demand for happiness almost to zero, and being even thankful to get hanged, if that is what will best serve the purpose of Providence, was evidently no very stern practiser of his own principles, when even banishment for a fortnight to Kew with a brilliant and affectionate pupil was intolerable to him.

Froude inevitably attracted blame, notably from old friends of Carlyle such as David Masson, for allowing private thoughts and expressions to be made public, and making the sage seem a hypocrite. He held his tongue. The second of the great tasks with which Carlyle had entrusted him – the writing of his biography – was still under way. It was only when the attacks on him increased from the mild to the vituperative, after the publication of his four-volume life of Carlyle, that he felt he had no option but to defend himself, at least to his and Carlyle's close circle.

Froude's *Life of Carlyle* is one of the great biographies in the language. It was, like the *Reminiscences*, frank and candid, not least about the marital relations of Thomas and Jane Carlyle. It has its inaccuracies; and Froude, like all biographers, had to be selective in his use of material. It is the selection of that material that has attracted much of the criticism against Froude. In his preface he wrote that 'Mr Carlyle expressed a desire in his will that of him no biography should be written. I find the same reluctance in his Journal. No one, he said, was likely to understand a history, the secret of which was unknown to his closest friends.'[25] That last point one must take to be a reference to the unusual marriage of the Carlyles. Carlyle's mind, as expressed in his will, was however changed before his death. Froude continues:

Carlyle knew that he could not escape. Since a 'life' of him there would certainly be, he wished it to be as authentic as possible. Besides the Memoir of Mrs Carlyle, he had written several others, mainly autobiographical, not distinctly to be printed, but with no fixed purpose that they should not be printed. These, with his journals and the whole of his correspondence, he made over to me, with unfettered discretion to use in any way that I might think good.

Froude had, in fact, censored the *Reminiscences*, notably over a quarrel the Carlyles had had that ended in physical violence, leaving Jane with blue marks on her wrists; but even that had been suppressed only after the greatest soul-searching.[26] In his preface, Froude explained what had motivated him:

If I had studied my own comfort or the pleasure of my immediate readers, I should have produced a portrait as agreeable, and at least as faithful, as those of the favoured saints in the Catholic calendar. But it would have been a portrait without individuality –

an ideal, or, in other words, an 'idol', to be worshipped one day and thrown away the next. Least of all men could idealising be ventured with Carlyle, to whom untruth of any kind was abominable.

He appears not to have restrained the truth too often in the *Life*. He further justified himself by quoting Carlyle's own precepts, laid down in his review of Lockhart's *Life of Scott*:

The English biographer has long felt that if in writing his Man's biography, he wrote down anything that could by possibility offend any man, he had written wrong. The plain consequence was, that, properly speaking, no biography whatever could be produced. The poor biographer, having the fear not of God before his eyes, was obliged to retire as it were into vacuum; and write in the most melancholy, straitened manner, with only vacuum for a result ... there was no biography, but some vague ghost of a biography.[27]

So Froude wrote the book he felt the sham-hating Carlyle would have wanted. He might have borne in mind, too, another thought from the review of Lockhart: 'How delicate, decent is English biography, bless its mealy mouth!' Froude laments that neither John Forster, Carlyle's close friend and intended executor, nor Carlyle's brother Jack was alive to be consulted. None the less, it is hard to see how Froude, believing as he did what Carlyle would have had him do, could have acted any differently and still have maintained his integrity.

While none of Froude's biography shocks today, its effect on Victorian England was seismic. The public, led by some of Carlyle's family, were plunged into moral outrage. Even disciples, reading the innermost thoughts of their master in the letters and journal extracts Froude included in his work, found themselves repelled by aspects of Carlyle. Ruskin, writing to their mutual friend Charles Eliot Norton, said:

Carlyle's letters, like all the words of him published since his death, have vexed me, and partly angered, with their perpetual 'me miserum' – never seeming to feel the extreme ill manners of this perpetual whine; and, to what one dares not call an affected, but a quite unconsciously false extent, hiding the more or less of pleasure which a strong man must have in using his strength, be it but in heaving aside dust-heaps.[28]

Froude, once more a target for obloquy, drafted what became his slim and understated volume *My Relations with Carlyle*. Froude's family found his defence of his conduct, written in 1886, in his papers after his death in 1894. When the *New Letters and Memorials of Jane Welsh Carlyle* were published in 1903, the malignancy of the attacks on Froude's reputation contained in the introduction to the work (written by Sir James Crichton-Browne, who had been Carlyle's physician) and in the footnotes (written by Carlyle's nephew Alexander) were such that Froude's family felt no option but to publish his side of the story. Crichton-Browne's and Alexander's thesis was that Froude's judgment was so poor he had not appreciated how neurotic Jane was. He had taken at face value complaints by her about Carlyle's conduct that should have been dismissed; he had more or less invented the idea of Carlyle feeling remorseful after her death, and seeking to atone for his guilt by having Froude publish his private papers. Anyone reading the papers with even mild disinterest can see that Alexander Carlyle and Crichton-Browne had less regard for the truth than Froude, and the motivation they had to defend the memory of a great man cannot excuse the virulence of their attacks on his biographer. Crichton-Browne's quality as a doctor was, to say the least, dubious, to judge from the indiscreet, improper and superficial account he gave of Jane's health in 1897 (thirty-one years after her death), in which he concluded in the most patronising terms that she was 'hereditarily disposed to nervous disease' and mentally ill.[29] Jane may well have been mentally ill; but Crichton-Browne, in his partisanship, never asks whether Carlyle contributed to that illness. Froude discerned what a selfish and at times vile man Carlyle had been. His only crime was to share this insight, in remarkably tactful terms, with the rest of us.

Froude recalls in *My Relations*[30] that he had been shocked to discover what he called the 'tragedy of life in Cheyne Row' as revealed in Mrs Carlyle's papers, and in Carlyle's *Reminiscence* of her (written in a similar state of shock, Carlyle having read for the first time his wife's deepest thoughts on their forty years together). He had realised he could not write an anodyne biography, particularly since Carlyle's own revelations of his character in the *Reminiscences* would have exposed the mendacity of a hagiography.

He had sought advice from Carlyle about how to handle the *Reminiscences*. 'He said I must do as I pleased. He never gave me any order. Then and always he avoided giving any order ... I made up my mind to the worst. The whole story must come out now.'[31] When the *Reminiscences* were published, Froude recalled they were 'received with a violence of censure for which I was wholly unprepared'.[32] As work was well advanced on the *Life*, the reception must have been doubly unnerving for him. Five, more conventional, biographies were published within nine months of the sage's death, by Wylie, Nicol, Conway, Shepherd and Oswald.[33] After such a deluge of anecdote and opinion, most of it unexciting and unexceptional, the public's plate appeared to be becoming overloaded. 'Those who profoundly move the men of their own time,' observed a *Spectator* reviewer, after wading through the last three of these works, 'are not, perhaps, the original thinkers of the world, so much as the thinkers who bring original thought home to the multitude.'[34]

The first two volumes of Froude's work, covering 1795 to 1834, were published in April 1882. *The Spectator*'s reviewer, motivated additionally by snobbery, detected the same foul qualities as had prevailed in the *Reminiscences*. Carlyle emerged as so dreadful that 'a man more absolutely destitute of that "charity" which, in St Paul's words, "suffereth long and is kind, envieth not, vaunteth not itself, is not puffed up, doth not behave itself unseemly, seeketh not her own, is not easily provoked, thinketh no evil," cannot easily be imagined, and probably never yet lived, than the proud and scornful peasant of genius whom Mr Froude's pages delineate.'[35] For the moment it was not Froude, but his subject, who suffered. In a longer notice of the two volumes a fortnight later, *The Spectator* concluded that Froude had done his task 'perfectly'.[36] The Carlylean creed, defined as a faith in God, a belief in duty, a scorn for middle-class morality and institutions, now seemed 'a very vague and ambiguous sort of gospel'. The review concluded that 'of grave desire to redeem mankind by persuading them to accept even this message, of passionate craving to find others possessed with the same creed, of eager spiritual sympathy with those who preached anything at all analogous to it – and there were many contemporaries who did so – we can find no trace at all. Therefore we deny Carlyle the name of a prophet.'

In a leading article, *The Spectator* attacked what it called Carlyle's 'prophetic misanthropy'.[37] It also attacked Froude for having brought it to the notice of the world, as if scholarship and truth would have been better served by covering it up. 'Mr Froude remarks with a sort of pride that probably Isaiah himself was not a very pleasant or accommodating companion, and intimates that in this respect prophets who denounce the shortcomings of their countrymen are apt to be very much alike,' the leader-writer sneered. The tone of criticism is very much one of a class – the educated, orthodoxly Christian middle class – that had had enough of having its moral and intellectual shortcomings pointed out by Carlyle and now reinforced by his disciples, and was determined (in the light of the new evidence of the sage's own failings) to get its own back. 'If the prophetic faculty is supposed to include the power of really spurring man on to higher life and work, we doubt very much whether it be consistent with a nature of such unmixed aggressiveness as Carlyle's.' Carlyle was seen as a ranter, and a destroyer. He was exposed as a man without humility, without any will to encourage or inspire his fellow men to make the world better, but keen only on the sadistic joys of denunciation and ridicule. Worst of all, said *The Spectator*, he was not marked by 'any of that genuine love for man, in spite of all his weakness ... which alone has power to cast out that weakness, and to make him conscious of the mighty stores of strength to which, if he will, he may yet have access.' Anticipating those who, more than half a century later, would align Carlyle with Hitler, the article went on:

His desire was to purge the earth of its weaklings – and he accounted amongst weaklings many who knew far better than himself what the proper and normal strength of the smaller and more habitual elements in our nature really is – not to lift the weaklings into a life of comparative strength.

One who had long held a low opinion of Carlyle, and who had not hesitated to express it in the sage's lifetime, was Anthony Trollope. The *Latter-Day Pamphlets* had prompted him to caricature Carlyle as Dr Pessimist Anticant in *The Warden*. In 1851 he wrote to his mother:

I have read – nay, I have bought! – Carlyle's *Latter-Day Pamphlets*, and look on my eight shillings as very much thrown away. To me it appears that the grain of sense is so smothered up in a sack of the sheerest trash, that the former is valueless. He does not himself know what he wants. He has one idea – a hatred of spoken and acted falsehood; and on that he harps through the whole eight pamphlets. I look on him as a man who was always in danger of going mad in literature and who has now done so.[38]

This was hypocritical of Trollope. As soon as *The Warden* catapulted him to fame in 1854 he sent his publisher a manuscript called *The New Zealander*, which sought to address the condition of England question. It was rejected by Longman's reader with the observation that 'all the good points of this work have already been treated of by Mr Carlyle, of whose *Latter-Day Pamphlets* this work, both in style and matter, is a most feeble imitation.'[39] Trollope's Dr Anticant 'cannot write English', and 'began the great task of reprobating everything and everybody, without further promise of any millennium at all'.[40] Trollope's animus against Carlyle was nurtured for another three decades and when, shortly after Carlyle's death and not long before his own, he was writing his *Autobiography*, he ranted once more:

If [Carlyle] be right, we are all going straight away to darkness and the dogs. But then we do not put very much faith in Mr Carlyle, nor in Mr Ruskin and his other followers. The loudness and extravagance of their lamentations, the wailing and gnashing of teeth that comes from them, over a world which is supposed to have gone altogether shoddywards, are so contrary to the convictions of men who cannot but see how comfort has been increased, how health has been improved, and education extended, that the general effect of their teaching is the opposite of what they intended. It is regarded simply as Carlylism to say that the English-speaking world is growing worse from day to day. And it is Carlylism to opine that the general grand result of increased intelligence is a tendency to deterioration.[41]

Perceptions of Carlyle had come far in the months since Dean Stanley's eulogy. None the less, in the autumn of 1882, there was much attention paid to the unveiling of Boehm's statue of him on the Embankment at the bottom of Cheyne Row, where he still sits staring across the Thames to Battersea Park. Professor Tyndall[42] made a speech to a small crowd of Carlyle's friends, and casual passers-by. Conscious of the difficulties into which the posthumous reputation was sailing, Tyndall likened Carlyle to a mountain, standing tall and strong despite its peak being covered in mist. Robert Browning was present, Ruskin absent due to illness, Froude simply absent. The money for the statue had been raised from friends and admirers by a committee led by the Dowager Lady Stanley of Alderley. Froude had not subscribed to the fund, donations to which had stopped almost dead when the *Reminiscences* were published.

Froude himself did not escape for long. In May 1883 Mrs Margaret Oliphant, long a friend of the Carlyles, went into print in the *Contemporary*

Review attacking Froude for his representation of the Carlyles' marriage. The literary establishment, and even Carlyle's own family, became divided on the question, and sides were vigorously taken. The conclusion was that both biographer and subject had something to answer for. 'We blame Mr Carlyle even more than we blame Mr Froude,' was how *The Spectator* put it.[43] When the two final volumes, covering Carlyle's life in London from 1834 until his death, were published in October 1884, the bilious attacks on both Froude and his master resumed. Since the volume covered the most attritional years of the Carlyles' marriage, and the years of Carlyle's self-immolation in grief and self-pity that followed it, the scope for further offence and hypocritical outcry was vast. Masson, in one of the kindlier remarks, referred to the posthumous reputation of his friend as being 'that monotone of grimness, gloominess, misery, and self-pity which runs so interminably through Carlyle's soliloquisings and journalisings'.[44] Carlyle, in the reviews, was abused for his style and the shallowness of his thought; Froude for allowing it all to be made public. *The Spectator* reviewer lost patience with both of them. Quoting an attack on Jeremy Bentham, the radical utilitarian philosopher, made in a letter, he tells his readers:

We ought to remember, of course, that all this was not written for publication, and that Mr Froude alone bears the responsibility of publishing these freaks of intellectual ill-temper. Still, it is simply impossible that a man who gave the rein to his intellectual self-will in such a style as this, could have been a trustworthy guide on subjects of the highest import. Carlyle maimed his intellect by the riotous indulgence he gave to his self-will.

V

Within four years of Carlyle's death his journey from literary colossus to hypocrite had been completed. Worse, the process had been accomplished in such a way as to take his biographer and most trusted friend down with him. Froude, however highly strung, was a scholar of distinction and a man of integrity. Under Carlyle's influence he, too, had abandoned traditional religious forms, thereby putting himself under suspicion in the eyes of polite society for reasons other than of his biographical practices.[45] It is fortunate that modern standards allow him to be recognised as a great biographer, and his work as a monument to truth. But if his reputation has been restored, Carlyle's seems never to have recovered. This is true not only in terms of his personal life, but also of his intellectual. He emerged from Froude's biography as a man mightily superior about his own creed, and deeply condescending towards others – which he inevitably described as 'cant'. Carlyle had had what he felt was his own revelation of the truths of spirituality in Edinburgh in 1821; it is recalled in the Everlasting No, the Centre of Indifference and the Everlasting Yea of *Sartor Resartus*. Those who had not had such an experience, but who merely copied the orthodox Christian beliefs of others, were worth little in Carlyle's estimation. He was convinced he had seen the ultimate religious truth, one far from the worn-out clothes of Christianity, and he tended to mock those (like his friend John Sterling) who did not have the same insight.

Such superiority did not go down well with Carlyle's audience, few of whom possessed the intellectual confidence to question their beliefs, and the nature of their own faith, that he had employed to question his. Even the intellectually confident were repelled by his arrogance. 'Carlyle is abundantly contemptuous of all who make their intellects bow to their moral timidity by endeavouring to believe Christianity,' John Stuart Mill wrote in his diary on 22 February 1854. 'But his own creed – that everything is right and good which accords with the laws of the universe – is either the same or a worse perversion. If it is not a resignation of intellect into the hands of fear, it is the subornation of it by a bribe – the bribe of being on the side of Power – irresistible and eternal Power.'[46]

A reading of Carlyle's translation of *Wilhelm Meister* suggests he had imbibed his spiritual view undiluted from Goethe. But he was an instinctive attacker of orthodoxy, a cast of mind under-represented in the intellectual movement of the mid-nineteenth century. The smell of anarchy in his approach to religion did not endear him to the highly conformist generation of educated men that survived him; nor could they stomach his absolute certainty that he was right to feel that while God was everywhere, Christ was nowhere. Froude said that 'to him God's existence was not an arguable probability, a fact dependent for its certainty on Church authority or on apostolic succession, or on so-called histories which might possibly prove to be no more than legends; but an awful reality to which the fates of nations, the fate of each individual man bore perpetual witness.'[47]

Had Carlyle sought to communicate this faith he might not have seemed so antipathetic. But it was a selfish faith, incapable of mass communication. Even if the creed had been communicable, Carlyle was so lacking in persuasive skills (as opposed to those of loud and rigid insistence, which he had in abundance) that he would have been the last man able to pass it on. All that could be transmitted was the message of the importance of every man fending for himself, of experiencing his own Everlasting No, Centre of Indifference, and Everlasting Yea. He tried to clarify this further in the first lecture *On Heroes* in 1840:

By religion I do not mean ... the church creed which he professes, the articles of faith which he will sign and, in words or otherwise, assert; not this wholly, in many cases not this at all ... but the thing a man does practically believe (and this is often enough without asserting it even to himself, much less to others); the thing a man does practically lay to heart, and know for certain, concerning his vital relations to this mysterious Universe, and his duty and destiny there, that is in all cases the primary thing for him, and creatively determines all the rest. That is his religion.[48]

David Masson rejected the common label of 'mystic' for Carlyle, but described him rather as a 'transcendentalist'. He defined this as 'the very opposite of what we call a Secularist. He is the opponent of that system of philosophy which "apprehends no farther than this world and squares one's life according," that system which regards the visible universe of time, space, and human experience as the sum total of all reality, and existing humanity in the midst of this universe as the topmost thing now in being.' Beyond this, for the transcendentalist, was 'a supernatural world, a world of eternal and infinite mystery, invisible and inconceivable, yet most real, and so inter-connected with the ongoings of the visible universe that constant reference to it is the supreme necessity of the human spirit, the highest duty of man, and the indispensable condition of all that is best in the human genius.'[49] This not only aptly describes Carlyle's theism, but also why he held history to be so important as a living continuum rather than a dead past.

While Carlyle's wide erudition had, in his youth, caused him to fail to believe in the Christian miracles, the Darwinian (and other) developments of science in his old age did not cause him to challenge the notion of the creation that had underpinned his theism. This, as we shall see, is just one of the forces that divides him from Nietzsche. However, he also became a powerful force, unwittingly, for secularisation. Engels, having read *Past and Present*, concluded in 1844 that 'Carlyle sees that Christianity, whether Catholic or Protestant, declines irresistibly. If he knew the nature of Christianity, he would see that after Christianity no other religion is possible.'[50] Carlyle is not quite so explicit as that in the work, but Engels's is a legitimate interpretation.

In 1858 Carlyle attempted, in response to a letter from W. Lattimer, a Carlisle cork-cutter, to outline what he regarded as the spiritual essentials. Lattimer had sought advice on the upbringing of children, and Carlyle replied that teaching a child prayers 'might have a very good effect, on one proviso (but this a rigorous one), That the father himself completely believed in them.'[51] Honesty was all: 'we are all "bound to speak the truth" to our fellow creatures,' he wrote; though with regard to the gospel of silence, in which he profoundly believed, he added that 'all men are entitled at least to keep their thoughts *dumb* when they please ... there is a far deeper veracity than that of the tongue.' His adherence to honesty made the established Church and its superstitious creeds impossible for Carlyle; the Catholic Church he regarded as even worse.

An article published by the *St James' Gazette* within days of Carlyle's death said that 'It is obvious that from an early age he entirely ceased to believe, in its only true sense, the creed he had been taught.' The article goes on:

The line he took up was that Christianity, though not true in fact, had a right to be regarded as the noblest aspiration after a theory of the Universe and of human life ever formed: and that the Calvinistic version of Christianity was on the whole the best it ever assumed; and the one which represented the largest proportion of truth and the least amount of error.

Carlyle's faith was simple.

First, he believed in God; secondly, he believed in an absolute opposition between good and evil; thirdly, he believed that all men do, in fact, take sides more or less decisively in this great struggle, and ultimately turn out to be either good or bad; fourthly, he believed that good is stronger than evil, and by infinitely slow degrees gets the better of it, but that this process is so slow as to be continually obscured and thrown back by evil influences.

God is not, though, in Carlyle's writings, to be confused with the Father of Christ.

God in his view was not indeed a personal Being, like the Christian God – still less was He in any sense identified with Jesus Christ ... The God in which Mr Carlyle believed is, as far as can be ascertained, a Being possessing in some sense or other will and consciousness, and personifying the elementary principles of morals – Justice, Benevolence (towards good people), Fortitude, and Temperance – to such a pitch that they may be regarded, so to speak, as forming collectively the will of God. That there is some one who – whether by the earthquake, or the fire, or the still small voice – is continually saying to mankind '*Discite justitiam moniti*'; and that this Being is the ultimate fact at which we can arrive, is what Mr Carlyle seems to have meant by believing in God.

Froude, while understanding the faith perhaps better than the *St James' Gazette* writer, because of his intimacy with the believer, states clearly that 'he did not believe in historical Christianity. He did not believe that the facts alleged in the Apostles' creed had ever really happened. The resurrection of Christ was to him only a symbol of the spiritual truth.'[52] Froude, sounding Darwinian, claimed it had been all right to accept that Christ was 'believed' to have died and 'believed' to have risen 'in an age when legend was history, when stories were accepted as true from their beauty or their significance ... it was not so now.'[53] The basis of religious belief, in an age of growing knowledge, had to be renegotiated, and Carlyle had started that process.

Thirty years after Carlyle's death the question of his beliefs was addressed by W.S. Johnson, who said:

Carlyle's religion, as visible to us in the early essays, is neither dogmatic and ecclesiastical, nor vaguely benevolent and humanitarian. It is not allied with theology on the one hand or with socialism on the other. It has been called pantheistic, but pantheism is a vague term and may mean anything or nothing. Religion for Carlyle consisted in a clear perception of, and a deep reverence for, what he calls the Divine Idea of the World. The perception everywhere of a divine power and presence, manifest in the moving of the stars and in the smallest blade of grass, through which as through a window man may look into the infinite, the recognition of the miraculous in what men are pleased to call the common, and of the supernatural in the natural, these are its essential modes.[54]

Also on Carlyle's theology G.B. Tennyson, in his magisterial book *Sartor Called Resartus*, wrote:

If the real world presented by the poet-philosopher is an invisible one, what is the visible world? It is, of course, a symbol. It represents the invisible world. For this reason Carlyle equated the Divine Idea with the Open Secret. The Divine Idea is invisible and not physically verifiable. But the Open Secret is visible to anyone who will look; it is the manifestation of meaning in the real world. Meaning is what Carlyle is ever seeking; so he readily seizes upon that which makes the open secret open – physical phenomena – as a means of reaching the Divine Idea. Everyday reality is a symbol of the greater reality. By realistic signposts the poet can lead the reader to the perception of the truth.[55]

In *Sartor Resartus* one sees the clearest exposition of this idea, as Teufelsdröckh, echoing Carlyle himself, seeks to find meaning and understand God, and ultimately finds God in everything. Harrold, in his study of the influence of German thought upon Carlyle, had no hesitation in defining Carlyle's God as, simply, the God of Calvin, 'immanent and transcendent ... believed to be terribly present everywhere at every moment, testing, judging, rewarding, punishing.'[56] Carlyle's idealised society had religion at its heart, governing the relations between men. Never is he so crude as to describe religion simply as a means of social control, by which the fear of divine punishment influences behaviour. Some of his disciples, notably Sir James Fitzjames Stephen,[57] however saw that as one of his main teachings, the strength of religion giving men the moral confidence to acclaim the rightness of good against the wrongness of evil.

When, in 1874, Carlyle wrote a letter to one who had enquired about his religion, it provoked *The Spectator* to rebuke him for setting a bad example to his followers by making them pantheists. The magazine had long been suspicious of Carlyle for the way in which he would use 'the eternities' or 'the immensities' when others would say 'Almighty God'.

He did not perhaps *fully* believe in God – the most difficult thing in the world, we admit, though the most necessary – and he could not dismiss the thought of a personal ruler; so he invented an answer to the question, 'God or no God?' which was in effect what he himself calls the answer 'Yes, *though* no' ... the true answer being evaded and deferred. And the effect of the Carlylian paraphrase for God was, in our opinion, much more disastrous to the numerous devotees of Mr Carlyle, than a blank assertion that the answer was 'unknown and unknowable'. It enabled people to do exactly what Mr Carlyle has always most severely condemned – clothe themselves in an unreal costume of sentimental awe which was neither piety nor its negation.[58]

The Spectator felt it had detected signs of a willingness to suggest there might be a God as understood by the Church of England, which it found satisfying; though it criticised Carlyle for vanity and lack of humility in not going the whole way. As usual, they had misunderstood him. He died as he had lived since 1821, a theist and a post-Christian.

VI

When the thinkers of the twentieth century came to reappraise those of the nineteenth, Carlyle suffered by comparison with his fellows. There was no one quite like him, however hard Ruskin had tried to emulate his master. Being *sui generis*, Carlyle at least retained a curiosity value. Ruskin was a better writer,[59] and a more sophisticated architectural and art historian than Carlyle was a political or military one. It is ironic that Ruskin's neo-Carlylean attempts at tackling the 'condition of England question' should have been so misappropriated and misunderstood as to make him a hero of the twentieth-century Left. Mill and Arnold were more practical political philosophers than Carlyle. Mill's doctrines in particular were to grow in relevance in our own century, as the magic of socialism wore off and its fundamental illiberalism was exposed. His judgment of the central importance of liberty to individuals in a free and prospering society was at an opposite extreme from Carlyle's, whose views on this matter have been wilfully misunderstood none the less. Arnold remained in high regard for his poetry, and in higher regard still for his accomplishments as a literary critic. Yet Carlyle, it seemed, had nothing to offer to posterity. His religion was that of an idiosyncratic fanatic. His prose style was barbarous. His political views were proto-fascist. In the civilised world of the late twentieth century, there was simply no call for him. Indeed, far earlier, on the centenary of his birth in 1895, *The Spectator* reflected that 'Carlyle's writings are passing through a period of that almost extravagant depreciation to which dogmatic teachers of Carlyle's angry type, who are never tired of repeating half truths in a positive and rather peremptory key, are especially liable ... he has flashed all manner of brilliant lights upon character and history, but he has not found for us any coherent code of wisdom, or any valuable avenue to religious truth.'[60] Carlyle would not, to judge from his writings, have meant to find such things for those who read him; what he seems quite clearly to have been doing was urging them to think for themselves, and to find these things for themselves.

The Times, on the same occasion, wondered in a leading article 'how many persons will today remember without prompting that this is the centenary of the birth of Carlyle'.[61] The article continued:

Some fifteen years have passed since his death, and in that period has taken place a great change in opinion as to his work and place in literature. The servile imitators of his dialect and private catchwords are gone. So also are most of his intimate friends and the band of illustrious men of letters who called him master. Many who in youth felt his spell survive ... let them take their bearings towards him today, and they will find that, instead of being moored close to him as they once were, they have drifted far apart. Nor is all this solely the inevitable correction of contemporary exaggeration and calmer judgment following the heated praise of youth, the repugnance of his artificial style, with its grotesque gesticulations and uncouth reiterations and exclamations, the effect of the dead weight of an obsolete jargon, and of the ephemeral pamphleteering character of much of his work ... the few years that have passed since he died have been a solvent of his fame. They have been a revealer of his central weaknesses.

The leader-writer argued that Carlyle was irrelevant to the youth of the age, who wanted a more orthodox religion. His writings were 'extinct volcanoes'. He had not been capable of crossing the chasm dug by Darwin, but had been happy to stand and rail in a superior, mocking fashion at those who had. Carlyle had showed at the end of his life that he had 'learned and unlearned nothing since he wrote his *Heroes and Hero-Worship*'.[62] Carlyle's approval of the strong man, the argument simplified as 'might is right', was attacked too. More seriously, the leader-writer doubted Carlyle would have had a mind open enough to cope with the intellectual developments since his death, such as those represented by Ibsen and Nietzsche. One has to concede, certainly, that Carlyle finding himself able to enjoy *Hedda Gabler* or *Ghosts* requires too much of a leap of the imagination; but why one should condemn him for that is unclear.

In 1903, once Froude's family had published *My Relations With Carlyle*, Sir James Crichton-Browne and Alexander Carlyle (who had started the argument with their poisonous comments in the introduction and notes to the *New Letters and Memorials of Jane Welsh Carlyle*) published a 'rejoinder' to it entitled *The Nemesis of Froude* (echoing Froude's own controversial religious 'cry of pain'[63] of the 1840s, *The Nemesis of Faith*). The purpose of this odious work of lies, distortions and self-delusions was 'to show ... Mr Froude was wrong, that he believed a myth, betrayed his trust, and must himself take the place of the man he so unmercifully pilloried.'[64] Froude's little book ran to forty-one pages, plus appendices such as Carlyle's will: Carlyle's nephew's and physician's rebuttal to 169 pages of rhodomontade. The burden of their assault, predictably, concerned Froude's decision to tell the truth, and took as its basis undeniable occasional (and minor) inaccuracies by the biographer, many of which stemmed from misreadings of Carlyle's spidery handwriting. The authors betrayed themselves to non-hypocrites in the following passage:

The frank biography is unquestionably desirable; but even the frank biography has its limits, and has not hitherto been held to include details of physiological functions or stenographic records of every unguarded and hasty word ... in every human life there is a highest and a lowest which even the frankest biography should leave untouched.[65]

Sadly, it was thirty years before this vicious attack on Froude was adequately repelled. First, the dishonest view of him (and, therefore, of Carlyle) was inflated and sustained by the one-dimensional six-volume life by David Alec Wilson, published between 1923 and 1934. This was the extended sequel to Wilson's book of 1898, *Mr Froude and Carlyle*, which had assassinated Froude's reputation, accusing him of sloppiness and venality (Wilson contended, without any evidence, that Froude had only spent so much time with

Carlyle over more than twenty years because he had made the conscious, and potentially profitable, decision to be his Boswell). It was, of course, greatly in Wilson's commercial interests to attack Froude, a point inadequately appreciated by reviewers at the time. Wilson was more accurate in his minor detail than Froude (having taken decades rather than months to write the work, this was only to be expected) but he still refused to see the truth about the Carlyles' marriage. And, like Froude, he robbed Carlyle of his greatest virtue, his sense of humour. The tables were finally turned in 1930, when Waldo H. Dunn exploded the cant of Wilson, Alexander Carlyle and the others who had sought to assassinate Froude's character. In a work dedicated to finding out the truth about the controversy, Dunn published the fact that Alexander Carlyle had refused him access to the relevant papers, whereas the Froude family had given him unrestricted help. He also proved that Alexander knew about, but did not publish, letters of Jane's in which she referred to the miseries suffered as a result of her husband's relationship with Harriet Ashburton, with whom Carlyle had enjoyed a close friendship for fifteen years. Although the final exposure of Alexander's humbug and down-right wickedness – for he had ruthlessly lied in an attempt to destroy Froude's reputation and credibility – helped rehabilitate Froude, Carlyle himself, and his own posthumous reputation, were but spectators in the matter. 'I think,' Dunn concluded, 'it is doubtful whether any other man of letters in Great Britain of equal ability has been the object of such bitter misrepresentation as has Froude.'[66]

Seeming a museum-piece, with nothing to say of importance to the modern world, Carlyle fell into desuetude in the twentieth century. Such influence as he continued to have was negative; in 1914, Millais's portrait of him in the National Portrait Gallery was slashed by a militant suffragette, presumably for reasons of Carlyle's anti-democratic tastes. Otherwise, with the exception of a handful of specialist scholars producing new editions of some of his works, Carlyle became ignored. Writing in 1917, the former Liberal cabinet minister John Morley, who as a young man had sat at Carlyle's feet, defined the problem:

You walked away from Chelsea stirred to the depths by a torrent of humour. But then it was splendid caricature: words and images infinitely picturesque and satiric, marvellous collocations and antitheses, impassioned railing against all the human and even superhuman elements in our blindly misguided universe. But of direction, of any sign-post or way out, not a trace was to be discovered, any more than a judicial page, or sense of any wisdom in the judicial, is to be found in his greatest pieces of history. After the grand humorist's despair was over, it was a healthy restorative in passing homeward along the Embankment to fling oneself into the arms of any statistician, politician, political economist, sanitary authority, poor-law reformer, prisoner-reformer, drainage enthusiast, or other practical friend of improvement, whom genial accident might throw in one's way.[67]

Whereas the general reader of the twentieth century did, from time to time, regard many of his contemporaries as having something to impart of practical value, all it could see in Carlyle was a figure of fun, and at times (as when considering his views on democracy, race and authoritarianism) not even that. However, in America and, for less savoury reasons, Germany, he continued to merit closer attention.

As English literature became a more popular industry in our universities, so Carlyle came up against academics who found his political views repugnant and his style unforgivable. One of the few voices raised in his support – and a half-hearted one at that – belonged to the first Professor of English Literature at the University of Cambridge, Sir Arthur Quiller-Couch. 'I grant you,' he wrote, 'that the claim to possess a style must be conceded to many writers – Carlyle is one – who take no care to put listeners at their ease, but rely rather on native force of genius to shock and astound. Nor will I grudge them your admiration. But I do say that, as more and more you grow to value truth and the modest grace of truth, it is less and less to such writers that you will turn ... they one and all offend against Art's true maxim of avoiding excess.'[68] But Art was no concern of Carlyle's.

Mrs Carlyle's letters, many of which had been published by the Great War, attracted great interest, and served largely to confirm her husband's status as something between freak and monster. In the aftermath of the war against Carlyle's beloved Germany, some of the criticism became hysterical. Norwood Young, writing in 1927, blamed the Great War (which started thirty-three years after Carlyle's death) partly on him:

There would have been no eagerness for war in Germany but for the military prestige of Prussia, which was based principally upon the Frederick legend which Carlyle had helped to disseminate. No doubt Blucher and Moltke were remembered with satisfaction, but the name of Blucher recalled Prussian defeats at the hands of Napoleon, and Moltke's victories had been too easy to arouse the greatest enthusiasms. It was the fable of Frederick, surrounded by enemies, beating off their huge forces, defying the world, that gave Prussianised Germany the conviction that its army was unconquerable, that victory was certain. These were the views which Carlyle spread over the world. Without them there would have been no world war.[69]

Kaiser Bill may well have followed Frederick's example in finding spurious justifications for marching through neutral countries to attack his rivals. However, to suggest as Young does that Carlyle's failure to expose Frederick's chicanery of 1756 that launched the Seven Years' War gave Wilhelm II the opportunity to try the same trick again is too preposterous to require further attention; but it none the less illustrates the depth of Carlyle's unpopularity even before the rise of Hitler.

Such revisionist interpretation, and the further damage done to his image by the bickering of his legatees, left Carlyle trussed up and ready for the attentions of our universities. They wasted no time in dealing with this man who felt that 'the nigger question' was best answered with a 'beneficent whip', and that democracy was no way to run a country; stylistic and literary considerations do not come into it. In his epic *History of Western Philosophy*, published in 1946, Bertrand Russell placed Carlyle in awkward company, in a progression that ran 'Fichte, Byron, Carlyle, and Nietzsche, into Hitler'.[70] Some years earlier, in 1930, H.J.C. Grierson had addressed this point specifically in his lecture *Carlyle and Hitler*. Grierson had, though, made the point that Carlyle was no respecter of ruling elites, but rather that his own opposition to democracy was that of a 'sansculotist'.[71] Grierson developed his point by reference to the concept of the hero as being religious-based; Masson had written in 1885 that in Carlyle's view 'your reverence for those fellow creatures that seem worthiest of reverence is invoked expressly on the principle that they were servants of God and may be regarded as manifestations of God. The real God who made them, and who made you, still fills the universe; and it is He that is walking on the wings of the wind.'[72] Grierson distinguishes Carlyle from Nietzsche, quoting the latter describing the former as 'at bottom ... an English atheist who makes it a point of honour not to be so':[73]

Might is right, says Carlyle, because in the long run, if it is not also right, the might will prove delusive ... if the power you rely on is not a power in nature you must fail; if you make a mistake your airship will fall; or, to speak religiously, if you are violating the fundamental instinct of justice, if you are not acting in accordance with God's Will, you must be defeated. Nietzsche, accepting from his first teacher Schopenhauer the doctrine that there is no providential order in the world, no law revealed and sanctioned by a power external to man, obedience to which is rewarded, disobedience punished, as set forth so clearly in the Book of Deuteronomy, that we are our own guides and create our own values, Nietzsche takes the step and declares Might is Right.[74]

This demonstration of how Carlyle had a religious-moral dimension absent from Hitler's thought, and that by implication Hitler followed Nietzsche rather than Carlyle, is convincing. Grierson clarifies this point when he continues:

Ultimately, it [Might] is the only Right, imposed on the mass, *das Gesindel*, by the superior class and accepted by them. If morality becomes something different, then it is a kind of miasma rising *from* the mass and paralysing the strong, the authentically good, a device by which the Will to Power that is in us all, directed by the priest, the strong in craft though wanting nobility and courage, succeeds in restraining the strong and noble, dragging all down to the anarchic level of equality ... Christianity especially has been one long conspiracy of the weak against the strong, exalting the so-called virtues of humility, meekness, pity, over the natural and essential virtues of strength, pride, and courage. Nietzsche indeed pushes the superiority of the great man to all morality so far ...

Carlyle's moral dimension, and its inclusion of a recognition of divine justice, while not at all Christian, was within a religious framework. Hitler had no moral dimension nor an orthodox conception of justice, let alone one within a religious framework.

Grierson claimed that the failure of the main powers at the end of the Great War to devise an order that prevented the coming of Hitler was an example of the chaos and lack of leadership that Carlyle had said would come from 'democratic control'. Grierson, though, was not representative of popular academic opinion. Fortunately, a distinguished group of specialist Carlyle scholars survives in Britain and America and continues, in monographs and occasional lectures, to present the positive significance of Carlyle to his own, and to our, century. Elsewhere, among non-specialists, academic opinion seemed, by the second half of our century, to have become uniformly hostile. Writing in the *Pelican Guide to English Literature* in 1958, G.D. Klingopulos dismissed Carlyle as 'frequently unreadable'.[75] Paul Turner, in his volume of the *Oxford History of English Literature*, found something to be said for the early Carlyle, but execrated the later as 'a bore, endlessly repeating the same prejudices, in a style that had gone stale'.[76] Mr Turner, who seems like so many modern interpreters of Carlyle to be unable to judge his subject in the context of the nineteenth as opposed to the twentieth century, seems to fail to appreciate the deliberately polemical tone of much of Carlyle's more extreme writing, and fails altogether to discern his sense of humour; but then humour is not high on the priorities of any of our great departments of English literature, except sometimes unintentionally.

Carlyle has, in the estimation of many academics, become a mere footnote to nineteenth-century writing. However, he has in recent decades become better known for writings that were never intended for the public. His wife is now reckoned, justly, as one of the finest letter-writers of the nineteenth century, and he not far behind her. Their complete correspondence is being collected and published jointly by Duke University in America and Edinburgh University – a project that has already taken thirty years, and is only up to the late 1840s. It is the single most important contribution to the study of Carlyle and to the maintenance of his reputation as a serious thinker of massive influence. The revival in interest in the Carlyles as letter-writers was started by Lady Bliss, who in 1950 published her selection of Jane's letters, and later a selection of Carlyle's letters to his wife.

An exception to the detractors of Carlyle in general academia has been the Cambridge historian Maurice Cowling. Unlike, one suspects, many of Carlyle's modern critics, he has a deep knowledge of what Carlyle actually said. Having correctly understood Carlyle's religion, and avoided being sucked into the blind alley of denouncing Carlyle's politics, Mr Cowling has instead found new meaning in Carlyle's thinking. 'Carlyle did not anticipate the expansion of science and secular universities, and he missed the tension which has been endemic in England between high thought and low thought. But about the replacement of a Christian priesthood by a secular priesthood of writers and thinkers, he was prophetic and deserves the most serious consideration.'[77] Also John Kenyon, writing in 1983, undertook a thoughtful revaluation of Carlyle as a historian, though like many modern critics was distracted by the style ('reminiscent of some modern American prose avowedly written under the influence of drugs').[78]

Ironically, since Carlyle has been rebuked so hotly for his style, it is that feature of his writing that commends him to a lay audience today, when his religious thought is incomprehensible and his political thought unacceptable. Writing in 1956, Peter Quennell said Carlyle owed what good reputation he had to 'his skilful and sensitive handling of the English language, to a prose style in which the voice of the literary artist is constantly making itself heard beneath the prophet's grumbling bass.'[79] Quennell surmised that *The French Revolution* was Carlyle's most enduring work, not because it made any great contribution to our understanding of the subject but because modern readers liked 'the headlong sweep of the narrative, enlivened by a series of brilliant miniature portraits of revolutionary men and women.' Digressing into politics, Quennell noted how, in the era of consensus politics that followed the Second World War, Carlyle's opposition to *laissez-faire* was vindicated. In the last decade of the twentieth century, after the fall of socialism across the world, Carlyle's opposition to markets seems, suddenly, by far the most hopelessly wrong part of his doctrine. However, if the Russian experience is any guide, the short-term consequences of the move to *laissez-faire* that he predicted were absolutely right.

VII

There is no question but that Carlyle has had a long and damaging fall from the pedestal he occupied at his death. How far this fall is the fault of his beliefs and doctrines has been overstated, usually by those determined to do him down because of what they think were his politics, not because of his literary or philosophical merit. Those who have quarrelled over Carlyle's corpse, and those who have been determined to ally him with twentieth-century movements of varying degrees of repellence, and of which he had no inkling, have been the agents of his undeserved decline. Yet it remains that he was one of the bravest thinkers of his era. He was also among the most seminal; George Eliot's point about the pervasiveness of his literary influence was obvious at the time she made it, and should be again now. All the greatest stars of the Victorian literary firmament came into Carlyle's orbit at some stage; so did many historians, theologians, philosophers and, more grudgingly, politicians. Hundreds of thousands of people bought and read his books; his works were considered indispensable to the late Victorian educated classes. He took the accepted learned style of English prose and revolutionised it, inventing words (like 'environment') where none meeting his needs existed. Without understanding Carlyle one cannot properly understand the Victorian era, and without understanding that era we cannot understand where, culturally, we have come from. No one from his time cries out for rediscovery and reappraisal as urgently as he does.

This biography is intended also to be a reinterpretation of Carlyle's writings, with special attention paid to their political thought. Carlyle's political thought was, to use a twentieth-century term, sociological. The most political of his writings (such as *Past and Present*, *Latter-Day Pamphlets* and *Shooting Niagara*) were about social control. Carlyle was not a conservative. What he saw of the socio-political system in the mid-nineteenth century he despised, and saw no point in conserving. What alarmed him was that all change seemed to take the country further away from the neo-feudalist or autocratic models he had decided were, because of their essentially religious base and their place in God's natural order, its best hope. To his disgust, the materialism advocated by the utilitarians had distorted man's relationship with God. Only Robert Peel, of the British political leaders of his lifetime, was to inspire him (though he did show a sneaking regard for the Duke of Wellington).

He may well have abjured the politicians and political system of his day, but none the less his arguments for trying to improve society were political. He may have expressed the hope that change could be effected by religious influences, but he never showed any optimism about that. Yet for all his earnestness, sternness and frequent selfishness, Carlyle was a humorous and, to his family especially, a kind man. If he is estranged from polite society today, it is because his humour is misunderstood, and his candour undervalued in a world based on avoiding truths wherever those truths are uncomfortable.

Carlyle died without bequeathing a philosophy because he never intended to construct one. All he set out to do was to describe things as he saw them. He often saw them more clearly than anyone else, and his inability to dissemble meant he relayed these truths to his audience without moderation, shading or tact. Often, his audience could not see where they were going because he had not properly communicated to them the details of the road they were on. For, as we shall see, Carlyle was throughout his life intensely self-obsessed. It was enough of a struggle for him to manage to make things explicable to himself. If others could not follow his meaning, he never had the time or the patience to help them.

I

Educating Tom

1795–1814

THOMAS CARLYLE was born at Ecclefechan, a small town on the road between Glasgow and England, on 4 December 1795. His family name came from the town of Carlisle fifteen miles to the south-east, just over the border. W.H. Wylie, one of Carlyle's earliest biographers, traced the family back uncertainly to 'Crinan, Abthane[1] of Dunkeld, whose son, Maldred, married Beatrice, daughter of King Malcolm II.'[2] He claims the family were of the same stock as the Lords Carlyle of Torthorwald. By 1795 Carlyle's branch of the family (if branch it be) survived in circumstances far removed from those of its alleged warrior forebears. The Carlyles were numerous in the area. The church at Hoddam, near Ecclefechan, had many Carlyles in its graveyard, as did the churchyard at Ecclefechan itself.

Thomas was named after his grandfather, an itinerant joiner, who had watched the Highlanders pass through Ecclefechan in 1745, and had been at Dumfries when they returned, defeated, from Carlisle. He died aged eighty-four in 1806, when Carlyle was ten. Old Thomas was, his grandson tells us,[3] an accomplished street-fighter, and he trained Carlyle's father, James, and his brothers in the art. The family were peasants who found most of their meat by hunting. James (like his three brothers) was apprenticed to a stonemason in 1773, when he was fifteen. He became highly skilled. The house in the main street of Ecclefechan, where Carlyle was born and which still stands, was his father's work. The family (who had let the downstairs rooms to a baker) did not live there long, but moved around the area while James plied his trade. By his skill he improved his family's prosperity, and the hunting expeditions Carlyle recalled from his childhood were undertaken for amusement rather than sustenance. Carlyle's mother, Margaret Aitken, was James's second wife. The first, Janet, a kinswoman, had died in 1792. She had been just twenty-five, and in a marriage that lasted just over a year gave James his first son, John, who later emigrated to Canada and died there in 1872. As a child Carlyle discovered a tress of Janet's fair hair in a secret drawer, cut off by his father when she had been delirious with fever and near to death. The discovery gave him, he wrote, 'a certain faint horror';[4] not unlike the feeling of weird curiosity that visitors to the Carlyle House in Cheyne Row have now, when they see locks of Thomas and Jane Carlyle's hair preserved in a display-cabinet.

James and Margaret married on 5 March 1795; he was almost thirty-seven, she twenty-three. Thomas was born nine months almost to the day later, in the distinctive arched house that still stands in Ecclefechan's main street and which his father and uncle had built in 1791 at a cost of £119 15s 5d. His mother told her daughter-in-law that Carlyle, as an infant, had been a 'lang, sprawling, ill-put-together thing',[5] and that he had been 'gey [very] ill to deal wi'.' He was the first of nine children, four boys and five girls, all but one of whom survived to adulthood.[6] Throughout his life, Carlyle's regard for his father was immense. 'I consider my father as one of the most interesting men I have known,' he wrote the day after news of James's death reached him.[7] 'He was irascible, choleric, and we all dreaded his wrath. Yet his passions never mastered him, or maddened him; it rather inspired him with new vehemence of insight, and more piercing emphasis of wisdom.'[8] Above all, the earnest and industrious tone of James Carlyle's life, which placed work and duty at the apex of man's responsibilities, informed his son's entire philosophy.

James's attitudes had their roots firmly in Calvinism. The Carlyles were Burgher Scotch Seceders, members of a sect that had left the Free Kirk in 1740. Then, in 1747, the seceders quarrelled among themselves over the swearing of the Burgess Oath, which hardliners believed endorsed the corrupt establishment from which they had seceded. These became the Anti-Burghers, their opponents the Burghers. Carlyle described the seceders as 'a Free Kirk making no noise', a sect that had 'walked out of its stipends, officialities, and dignities, greatly to the mute sorrow of religious Scotland'.[9] No time was spent discussing secular controversy; all energies instead were devoted to considering God's Law. As well as imbibing from his parents the Calvinist doctrines of the work ethic and of the Bible as a guide to personal morality, Carlyle was imbued with the Church's idea of God trascendent. This stayed with him throughout his life, whatever his theological vicissitudes.

His mother was barely less influential than his father. 'To us the best of all Mothers,' he said, 'to whom for body and soul I owe endless gratitude.'[10] His childhood seems to have been of almost unbroken happiness, spent roaming the fields and observing nature, and moving freely and curiously among the quiet, industrious, God-fearing people around him. Ecclefechan was principally agricultural; the weaving trade, the other staple of the local economy, was conducted in primitive conditions. The earliest memory Carlyle shares with us[11] is of his sense of 'loss and remorse' at throwing his own little brown stool at his half-brother, and breaking it, to be soothed and comforted by his father; Carlyle was barely two years old. G.B. Tennyson, reporting that Carlyle's first words were allegedly 'What ails wee Jack?' when his baby brother was ill says that it is an 'unlikely story' with 'a certain appropriateness ... for Carlyle's great labour was to be ascertaining what ailed the world and broadcasting his findings'.[12] He soon encountered the unavoidable griefs of life 200 years ago, such as the death of his little sister, the shock of seeing her being measured for her coffin, and the sustained grief of his mother after the bereavement. He inherited the stoutness of both his parents' constitutions. He had no serious childhood illness, nor, indeed, an adult one. The dyspepsia that would dog him from his twenties onwards would seem to have been psychosomatic, a consequence of his only detectable weaknesses being mental rather than physical.

At five his father was teaching him arithmetic, his mother (with less success) reading. Once he could read (his mother, who could not write, had tried to teach him to recognise letters, but outside help was needed before he could) he did so voraciously. His instruction in writing, too, had to wait for his first elementary tuition outside the family home. Mrs Carlyle herself did not learn to write until later in her life, in order to be able to write to her absent son. Carlyle's first intellectual talent was with numbers. 'Tom,' his father told him, when he was ten, 'I do not grudge thy schooling, now when thy Uncle Frank owns thee to be a better arithmetician than himself.'[13] A 'wise man' of Ecclefechan, James Bell, warned James Carlyle not to have his son educated, because he would grow up 'to despise his ignorant parents'.[14] James ignored this advice, and he and his son proved Bell wrong.

Carlyle attended both a private and a parish school in Ecclefechan, and a day school at nearby Hoddam. He was judged 'complete in English' at about the age of seven, and told he would have to 'go into Latin' or waste his time.[15] Every Sunday the family's religious observance took place at the Ecclefechan meeting-house, the only Burgher Seceder church for miles around; he recalls in the *Reminiscences* that one family made a thirty-mile round-trip, in all weathers, from near Carlisle.[16] The Burgher Seceder minister, John Johnston, taught Carlyle Latin privately, to give the boy his passport into higher education. Then, on 26 May 1806, Whit Sunday, James Carlyle took his son to Annan Academy, six miles away, to begin formal schooling. The aim of this Calvinist forcing-house was to prepare large numbers of boys, at relatively low cost, for entry to university. In this it succeeded, whatever its other failings, though the entry requirements for the university at Edinburgh were not, at that time, especially high. Carlyle embarked upon the adventure with optimism, though this was not to last. 'It was a bright morning, and to me full of moment; of fluttering boundless Hopes, saddened by parting with Mother, with Home; and which afterwards were cruelly disappointed.'[17]

Carlyle was unsettled by the transition from the seclusion and loving attention of a family home to the rough outside world. Indeed his temperament, already volatile, seems permanently to have been changed for the worse from the moment he went to school. He was bullied by his schoolfellows (until, in atavistic style and against the moral command of his mother, he hit them back) and thrashed by his schoolmasters. In these regards he was no different from many of his fellows, just less well prepared for it. Hinterschlag, the name by which Carlyle refers to Teufelsdröckh's school in his semi-autobiographical work *Sartor Resartus*, roughly translates as 'blow on the back-side'. One must be cautious when relating events in *Sartor* to Carlyle's life. In his remarks on Althaus's biography of him in 1866, Carlyle commented that '*Sartor* is quite unsafe for details! Fiction *founded* perhaps on fact – a long way off.'[18] In *Sartor* Carlyle caricatured his schoolmasters as men who 'knew syntax enough; and of the human soul thus much – that it had a faculty called memory, and could be acted on through the muscular integument by appliance of birch rods'.[19] In real life the English master and guiding force of the academy, a tobacco-chewing black-toothed rigid-Seceder pedant called Adam Hope, showed a sophistication that went beyond mere physical punishment:

Self-delusion, half-knowledge, sham instead of reality, could not have existed in his presence. He had a Socratic way with him; would accept the poor hapless pupil's half-knowledge, or plausible sham of knowledge, with a kind of welcome, 'Hm, hm, yes;' then gently enough begin a chain of inquiries more and more surprising to the poor pupil, till he had reduced him to zero, to mere *non plus ultra*, and the dismal perception that this sham of knowledge had been flat misknowledge with a spice of dishonesty added ... the poor boy had to sit in his place, under arrest all day, or day after day, meditating those dismal new-revealed facts, and beating ineffectually his poor brains for some solution of the mystery, and feasible road out.[20]

Carlyle spent three years at what he called this 'doleful and hateful' place,[21] the suffering alleviated only by weekends at home. He was not exposed to Hope very often, though engraved upon his memory was the study made of Sallust with him. He recalled the black teeth showing through 'a settled humanely-contemptuous grin', which seemed to say: 'Nothing *good* to be expected from *you*, or from those you come of, ye little whelps; but we must get from you the *best* you have, and not complain of anything.'[22] Yet Hope it had been who had prepared Edward Irving (who was to be the greatest influence on Carlyle's life towards the end of his time at Edinburgh, and beyond) for his later triumphs. The pedagogues were the least of his troubles, however; his schoolfellows were worse. Sixty years later he recalled that 'unspeakable is the damage and defilement I got out of those coarse unguided tyrannous cubs, especially till I revolted against them, and gave stroke for stroke; as my pious mother, in her great love of peace and of my best interests, spiritual chiefly, had imprudently forbidden me to do.'[23] This passage from *Sartor* confirms the misery of his schooldays:

Green sunny tracts there are still; but intersected by bitter rivulets of tears, here and there stagnating into sour marshes of discontent. 'With my first view of the Hinterschlag Gymnasium,' writes he, 'my evil days began. Well do I still remember the red sunny Whitsuntide morning, when, trotting full of hope by the side of Father Andreas, I entered the main street of the place, and saw its steeple-clock (then striking Eight) and *Schuldthurm* (Jail) ... I was among strangers, harshly, at best indifferently, disposed towards me; the young heart felt, for the first time, quite orphaned and alone.' His schoolfellows, as is usual, persecuted him: 'They were Boys,' he says, 'mostly rude Boys, and obeyed the impulse of rude Nature, which bids the deerherd fall upon any stricken hart, the duck-flock put to death any broken-winged brother or sister, and on all hands the strong tyrannise over the weak' ... He wept often; indeed to such a degree that he was nicknamed *Der Weinende* (the Tearful).[24]

Those who would make much of the 'might is right' philosophy of later years would do well to see it, to start with, in this context. In the same passage, the 'editor' of *Sartor* – a device Carlyle uses to interpolate his own, often humorous, voice – adds that 'Only at rare intervals did the young soul burst forth into fire-eyed rage, and, with a stormfulness (*Ungestüm*) under which the boldest quailed, assert that he too had Rights of Man, or at least of Mankin.'

Also in 1806 he almost drowned, an event recalled in a letter to his brother Jack twenty-six years later, the memory prompted by Carlyle's riding past the spot where his mother had dragged him out of the water by the hair; he swore to her that he would never bathe in deep water again.[25] Eventually he made some friends, and his natural intelligence and curiosity spurred him on to put the difficulties of the place behind him. In simple academic terms the exercise was a success, for he passed without any difficulty into the next stage of his education. He learned French, Latin, algebra and geometry, and had a grounding in literature. Life was not entirely miserable. His success with numbers made mathematics enjoyable, and he described his teacher, Morley, as 'an excellent Cumberland man, whom I loved much, and who taught me well'.[26] The school maintained, in his religious instruction, the Burgher Seceder faith in which he had been brought up. Already at this time the *raison d'être* of Carlyle's schooling was becoming clear to him, as it had from the start been to his parents: that he would become a minister of the cloth. It was at Annan in 1808 that he first saw Edward Irving, who had left two years before Carlyle arrived. Irving was returning to visit his old school from his studies at Edinburgh, where he, too, was destined for the Church.

An effect of Carlyle's upbringing, both at home and at school, was that his personality was not repressed. His father was noted as a man with plenty to say, and Carlyle inherited this trait. The editor of *Sartor* tells us that little Diogenes Teufelsdröckh, the semi-autobiographical hero of the book and Carlyle's *alter ego*, 'could perform the miracle of Speech' by the age of fifteen months.[27] Perhaps Carlyle shared this precocity. The very existence of the Burgher Seceder sect was a gesture of adamant self-will against the Free Kirk, so the seceders themselves were not self-effacing or timid people. When he reached university his loquaciousness marked him out from his fellows; once he reached London it, in the form of the monologue, was to become his trademark.

II

In November 1809, when not quite fourteen, Carlyle went to Edinburgh University. The Scottish educational system was radically different from the English, and the age at which Carlyle began his studies was typical. Nor, because of the availability of cheap schooling in Scotland, was it unusual that he, and many other sons of peasants, should go to university. Once there, it was intended he would work towards ordination, fulfilling for his parents an ambition common among their class, and regarded as a main end of education. There were, though, sacrifices to be made by him and his family. Only one of his younger brothers – Jack, who became a doctor – followed him to university; the others were trained to farm. Seen off from Ecclefechan on a dark, frosty morning by his parents, who went the first few steps of the way with him before turning back, Carlyle walked there from Dumfriesshire, a journey of nearly eighty miles. There was no question of affording transport over that long distance. The sentimentality and sensitivity of Carlyle, important features of his character to which many of his critics, in searching for evidence of his inhumanity, have seemed oblivious, are never more clearly seen than in his recollection of this leave-taking in the *Reminiscences*.

He accomplished the hike in three days with a companion, Tom Smail, who was starting his second year at university. Carlyle enjoyed hard physical exercise throughout his life, but had dour memories of this first great excursion. Smail, 'a very innocent, conceited, insignificant, but strict-minded orthodox creature, for whom knowing him to be of no scholarship or strength of judgment, I privately had very small respect',[28] trudged a few paces ahead of Carlyle throughout, saying little or nothing. Carlyle goes on in the *Reminiscences* to describe his companion as 'thoroughly insignificant, conceitedly harmless', but says they maintained a loose friendship for his first two years at Edinburgh.[29] On the last day they walked twenty miles, reaching the city in early afternoon. They found a clean, cheap lodging in Simon Square, one of the poorer areas, but close to the university. Edinburgh University had none of the grandeur of Oxford or Cambridge at this period, when, for example, Byron was at Trinity. The old part of Edinburgh, where Carlyle's lodgings and place of study were, had become a backwater since the development of the Georgian squares north of Princes Street in the late eighteenth century. It had a high incidence of disease and crime. But since the university existed to provide a cheap, rigorous education for the sons of the poor, as well as for those with better resources, these conditions were quite normal.

Immediately upon arrival, Smail took Carlyle for a guided tour. It included a visit to the High Court, 'such a scene of chaotic din and hurlyburly as I had never figured before.'[30] Carlyle acquired a taste for this form of theatre, and attended regularly in the five years of his studentship. He came to recognise the leading advocates and judges, among them Francis Jeffrey, a future Lord Advocate whose literary interests brought him and Carlyle together in the 1820s.

Carlyle embarked upon the standard four-year arts course, learning Greek as an early priority. In his second year he took his Greek further, but diversified into mathematics and logic. His existence was, though, stark. David Buchanan, a New South Wales MP, recalled a meeting in the 1860s with a Dr

Nicholson, who had known Carlyle at Edinburgh, and who gives us a clear account of what life was like:

> Dr Nicholson . . . informed me that he was a student with Mr Carlyle at the Edinburgh University, and that they lived together in lodgings, along with another young student, and that the whole three slept in the same bedroom. Dr Nicholson added that Mr Carlyle took the dux prize in the mathematical class, and that their other bedroom companion took the second prize; but he observed that while Mr Carlyle seemed to master the subject without much effort or application, the other lad laboured at his problems with desperate zeal, sometimes sitting up all night at his task.[31]

Carlyle verified the details to Buchanan in 1869, though denied he had found mathematics as easy as Nicholson suggested.

Though he soon made friends with a few other children of his class, and occupied himself by reading avidly in the university's library and in the circulating libraries, there were few indulgences. Ecclefechan was well served by networks of carriers. Using these, Carlyle's family could send provisions to their son, so he could subsist more cheaply than if relying on other sources. His laundry was sent back and forth by the same means. The Carlylean scholar Ian Campbell, describing the nature of an Edinburgh education at this time, writes of one of Carlyle's contemporaries who went mad after living on porridge for three months; there were some worse off than Carlyle.[32] At least, as Froude points out, such restricted means prevented undergraduates indulging in the vicious temptations the city had to offer. Lack of money (both on the part of the students and of the under-endowed university) also meant the terms lasted barely half the year, with much of the summer and autumn left free for those children who would be needed to help their families bring in the harvest. For Carlyle, whose family did not seek to earn a living on the land until 1815, his long vacations provided an opportunity for still wider reading.

Carlyle seems to have learned more by his own efforts than through formal teaching, with which he was not impressed. Since the fees of the university were only about three guineas a year, it was not too surprising that the quality should have been comparatively low. By the time he completed his studies, at the age of eighteen, Carlyle was probably as well educated as many eighteen-year-old English public schoolboys of the time; he had, though, completed his university education, whereas they were but starting theirs. He had read prodigiously widely at university. Within weeks of going up he had started Robertson's *History of Scotland*, Cook's *Voyages*, Gibbon, Shakespeare, the *Arabian Nights*, Congreve, Hume, *Gil Blas* and *The Spectator*.[33] In the following year he went more deeply into the novels of the previous century, as well as dabbling in philosophy. For all Carlyle's educational self-help, however, Edinburgh had its share of distinguished minds. He admired Professor Leslie (later Sir John Leslie) who taught him mathematics, and who had published his *Elements of Geometry* shortly before Carlyle arrived at

Edinburgh. Dugald Stewart, the renowned Professor of Philosophy, had just vacated his chair. For his classics teacher, Professor Christison, Carlyle had contempt. Christison 'had never noticed me while in his class, nor could distinguish me from another "Mr *Irving* Carlyle", an older, considerably bigger boy, with flaming red hair, wild buck-teeth and a scorched complexion, and the *worst* Latinist of all my acquaintance'.[34] Carlyle was right to have fond memories of Leslie, for it was he who helped Carlyle secure a dominie's post in Kirkcaldy in 1816.

In *Sartor* there are more clues about Carlyle's feelings towards his university, though they must (as with those relevant to Annan) be treated as only part of the truth. Teufelsdröckh conducts his studies in 'an atmosphere of Poverty and manifold Chagrin'. The editor quotes Teufelsdröckh's own reminiscence:

The University where I was educated still stands vivid enough in my remembrance, and I know its name well; which name, however, I, from tenderness to existing interests and persons, shall in nowise divulge. It is my painful duty to say that, out of England and Spain, ours was the worst of all hitherto discovered Universities ... Had you, in Crim Tartary, walled-in a square enclosure; furnished it with a small, ill-chosen library; and then turned loose into it eleven-hundred Christian striplings, to tumble about as they listed, from three to seven years; certain persons, under the title of Professors, being stationed at the gates, to declare aloud that it was a University, and exact considerable admission fees, – you had, not indeed in mechanical structure, yet in spirit and result, some imperfect resemblance of our high seminary. I say imperfect; for if our mechanical structure was quite other, so neither was our result altogether the same: unhappily we were not in Crim Tartary, but in a corrupt European city, full of smoke and sin.[35]

How far all this was true of Edinburgh, and how much of it can be attributed to Carlyle's outlook being damaged by the struggle he was starting (as he read more widely) to have with his faith and his whole psychological balance, one can only conjecture. Certainly, the experience of the wider intellectual life of a university affected him deeply, though he did not participate in any of the formal intellectual societies. The most profound effect was seeing he was not suitable for the Church. He fretted about how best to tell his parents, who had made such sacrifices for him to this end, of this change of heart. His university life became in his memory the years that led up to the time when he would 'sink into spell-bound sleep, under the night-mare, Unbelief; and, in this hag-ridden dream, mistake God's fair living world for a pallid, vacant Hades and extinct Pandemonium'.[36] William Allingham, in his diary, tells us of Carlyle distressing his mother by asking her, when home for the first time from university in 1810, 'Did God Almighty come down and make wheelbarrows in a shop?'[37] It was the start of his apostasy, which took ten more years to complete.

'Goethe drove me out of it, taught me that the true things in Christianity survived and were eternally true; pointed out to me the real nature of life and things – not that he did this directly; but incidentally, and let me see it rather than told me,' Carlyle told Allingham more than sixty-five years later. Certainly, few of Calvinism's theological or moral certainties had survived the assumption-questioning of the Scottish enlightenment. Edinburgh had been at the heart of this process in the late eighteenth century, and in Carlyle's time at university was still suffering from the hangover. Another passage in *Sartor* displays his resentment at these lingering influences, which seemed to have caused him much pain in the way that they forced him to question his simple faith. Also, Carlyle's often-expressed disdain for the eighteenth century, as a time of moral and religious decadence, can be traced back to the shock of the years when he was first away from the mores of Annandale:

We boasted ourselves a Rational University; in the highest degree hostile to Mysticism; thus was the young vacant mind furnished with much talk about Progress of the Species, Dark Ages, Prejudice, and the like; so that all were quickly enough blown out into a state of windy argumentativeness; whereby the better sort had soon to end in sick, impotent Scepticism; the worser sort explode (*crepiren*) in finished self-conceit, and to all spiritual intents become dead. – But this too is portion of mankind's lot. If our era is the Era of Unbelief, why murmur under it; is there not a better coming, nay come?[38]

Yet Carlyle's earliest discovered letter,[39] written to his university friend Thomas Murray in June–July 1813 when he was seventeen years old, reveals an alert, amusing, sociable and gossiping youth with a taste for the sarcasm for which he was already noted. Carlyle recalls meeting an acquaintance of his and his correspondent's travelling through Ecclefechan. The traveller had been ill, and Carlyle found him weak with hunger and poverty on his way to London. Carlyle provided for him, saying (as he told Murray) 'it is my duty and I will assist thee to the utmost of my power.' A similar compulsion, to do what he felt God had decreed to be his duty to the deserving poor, prompted him, thirty years later, to write *Past and Present*.

Carlyle did not take a degree: few undergraduates did, though, his disciple David Masson argues, Carlyle had reached the standard of master of arts.[40] Once he had finished his basic education in 1813 he had not yet decided to abandon the ministry; but mathematics was still his greatest interest. He recalled in 1866 that (thanks to Leslie's influence) from about 1813 to 1820, when he cast it aside and hardly thought of it again during his remaining sixty years, 'geometry shone before me as undoubtedly the noblest of all sciences; and I prosecuted it (or mathematics generally) in all my best hours and moods.'[41] In the spring of 1814 he conducted a detailed correspondence in the columns of the *Dumfries Courier* about its mathematical problems column. He was much amused, too, by the downfall of Napoleon, who benefited from an early display of Carlylean sarcasm,[42] but great world events increasingly take second place in his thoughts to his personal predicament. After November 1813 he kept his options open by attending the classes at the Divinity Hall in Edinburgh, the beginnings of the slow means (which could have taken him up to seven years) to qualify for ordination. The painful bridge of whether or not he believed would only be crossed once the influences of the next two or three years had done their work on him, and steered him towards another, more public pulpit.

2

'My Conduct is Absurd'

1814–21

IN THE SPRING of 1814 Carlyle returned to Ecclefechan. 'I felt,' he recalled three years later, 'as if I had been leaving the fountain head of all knowledge and good humour.'[1] It was a comfort, though, to be with his family. As he was to say to his brother Alick, 'we Carlyles are a clannish people; because we have all something original in our formation, and find, therefore, less than common sympathy with others; so that we are constrained as it were to draw to one another, and to seek that friendship in our own blood which we do not find so readily elsewhere.'[2]

By the time he left Edinburgh Carlyle was a tall, thin, clean-cut youth with thick brown hair, handsome, and with a physical appearance that would change surprisingly little until he grew his beard in his late fifties. He was in need of earning a living, pending his decision on whether or not to pursue the ministry. He soon obtained, by a two-hour competitive examination (and with the help of a recommendation from Leslie), a place as mathematical master at Annan Academy, with, as he put it, 'some potential outlook on Divinity as ultimatum (a *rural* "Divinity Student", visiting Edinburgh for a few days each year, and "delivering" certain "Discourses"; six years of that would bring you to the Church-*gate*, as four years of continuous "Divinity Hall" would.'[3] Before leaving Edinburgh he had delivered what was to be the first of only two such discourses, on the text 'Before I was afflicted I went astray.' He recalls it as having been 'a very weak and flowery sentimental piece'.[4] He also notes, however, an obvious problem with his ecclesiastical ambitions. 'I never had the least enthusiasm for the business, and there were even grave prohibitive doubts more and more rising ahead.' As Masson points out,[5] the instruction at Divinity Hall was under the auspices of the established Church of Scotland, and there is no record of his non-conforming parents objecting to such a course of learning.

However unenthusiastic Carlyle was about the Church, he was hardly keen on returning to the place he was to caricature as *Hinterschlag* either: the best he could say for it was that his salary of £70 a year relieved his father of the need to support him. His family were about to move into farming, to a 'wet, clayey spot called Mainhill' a few miles away.[6] Carlyle said this change was made because the mason's trade had declined 'when universal Poverty and Vanity made *show* and *cheapness* (here as everywhere) be preferred to Substance; when as he [his father] said emphatically honest trade "was done".' It would be some time before the farm was running efficiently enough to allow his family to support him as generously as they had. So, whether Carlyle liked it or not, it had to be Hinterschlag.

He manifestly did not like it. He had an innate urge to teach and to guide others, but not in this way. 'I was abundantly lonesome, uncomfortable and out of place there,' he said.[7] It was 'not a gracious destiny, nor by any means a joyful; indeed a hateful, sorrowful and imprisoning one'.[8] He was anti-social, gauche and frustrated, and found consolation only in books. He had few friends, naming only Mr and Mrs Church, of Hitchill, and the Reverend Henry and Mrs Duncan, of Ruthwell, as his companions at that time. His manner did not endear him to others. 'Far too sarcastic for a young man' was how he himself, half a century later, assessed his personality as a youth.[9] Thomas Murray, his university friend, and he corresponded sporadically, though he implored Murray to write more often to help relieve his feelings of isolation. No women had yet come into Carlyle's life, though Murray teases him in a letter[10] about the possible affections of a Miss Merchant of Edinburgh, who had 'felt keenly' Carlyle's absence. Carlyle, for his part, advises Murray to make the lady's acquaintance better. He recalls[11] having read out to Miss Merchant 'one of the very best jokes' in *Tristram Shandy*, and educing melancholy rather than humour from her. Carlyle had a keen sense of humour, and it may be considered an even more redeeming feature than his abundant humanity; though, to modern sensibilities, it is often just as invisible as that other quality.

Not wanting to lodge at the academy – the unhappy memories of childhood and grim realities of the present were presumably enough without that – Carlyle took a furnished room in the town at the house of a merchant called Kennedy, for 4s 6d a week. He was teaching six hours a day, and in the late summer became tutor to two of the sons of Lieutenant-General Alexander Dirom, who had taken a house in Annan. Once the school holiday came in August Carlyle had no rest, but concentrated on the Dirom boys, to whom he was teaching Greek, Latin and mathematics. Sitting in Annan and reading the *Edinburgh Review*, which brought home to him the vibrant world from which he was exiled, he became immersed in depression. He managed to motivate himself, however, to read widely in some of the minor European literature of the recent past. It included Sotheby's translation of *Oberon* by the German romantic poet Christoph Wieland, a foretaste of what would become Carlyle's intellectual obsession in the years ahead. The rest of his reading seems to have had less long-lasting effects: *Exiles of Siberia*, by the Frenchwoman Sophie Cottin, a translation of Tasso's renaissance poem *Jerusalem Delivered*, Fénelon's *Lives of the Ancient Philosophers* and, from nearer home, Beresford's *The Miseries of Human Life* and the poems of the eighteenth-century impostor Richard Savage, who was befriended by Dr Johnson while attempting to trumpet the supposed injustices of his estrangement from his alleged aristocratic birthright. By about the end of 1814, he had read Scott's *Waverley*, which had been published in June of that year, and was much admired by his friends at Edinburgh. 'By far the best novel that has been written these thirty years,' Carlyle told Thomas Murray in December 1814.[12]

Within a matter of weeks he had grown to hate schoolmastering, to the point where he felt that he 'would prefer to perish in the ditch, if necessary, rather than continue living by such a trade'.[13] His requests for friends to write to him take on a note of desperation ('Direct to me at Annan Academy – *quick*,' he implores Robert Mitchell, another Edinburgh contemporary and Dumfriesshire boy, on 18 October 1814).[14] He visited Edinburgh during his Christmas vacation, but it was just a brief respite from drudgery. He felt a lack of inspiration, a lack of ideas, but it did not stop him writing extensively in his letters to Murray and Mitchell of the latest philosophical disputations, as presented to him in the pages of the *Review*. Hume, in particular, caught his attention, with Carlyle finding Hume's powers of reasoning compelling even if he did not agree with his arguments. It was in the essays, Masson reminds us, that Carlyle first encountered the notion of 'hero-worship'.[15] Napoleon's escape from Elba and return to France distracted him briefly, but he was still complaining to Murray, at the time of Waterloo in June 1815, that 'the most disagreeable circumstance, in a Tutor's life, is his want of society.'[16] His friends were keen to see him in Edinburgh again once his school duties were over in August, but apathy had taken over even that prospect. 'I naturally dislike locomotion,' Carlyle wrote to Murray on 22 August, ironically, given what turned out to be his life-long habit of exercise, 'and when I came to reflect on the hardships of a solitary excursion of eighty miles, I was obliged to lay aside my scheme.'[17] By now wallowing in a mixture of self-pity and inanition, Carlyle decided instead to stay in Ecclefechan 'in a state of vegetation or torpor.'

There were diversions nearer home, or so he thought. When he heard that Francis Jeffrey was due to come to plead in court at Dumfries, he cancelled all other arrangements in order to witness the spectacle. Jeffrey, however, did not show. Instead, as autumn drew on, Carlyle had to return not just to teaching, but also to consideration of his supposed studies for the cloth. He was due in Edinburgh in December to read an exegesis, or discourse in Latin, at the Divinity Hall on the subject '*Num detur religio naturalis?*', or 'Is there a natural religion?'. He told Mitchell, not without sarcasm, that his exegesis was 'truly a most delectable production',[18] and using the good offices of Murray managed to have another student 'persuaded' to give up a place to read out an exegesis on 22 December in favour of Carlyle, for which Carlyle owed a bottle of whisky to those who had done the persuading.[19] However,

Carlyle also gave Mitchell a broad hint that his pastoral ambitions were coming to an end. 'You will ask me,' he writes in the same letter, 'why, since I have almost come to a determination about my fitness for the study of Divinity, why all this mighty stir – why this ado – about "delivering" a thesis – that in the mind's eye seems vile – and in the nostril smells horrible. It is not because I have altered my sentiments about the study of theology: but principally because it came into my head, to try what sort of essay upon natural religion, I could make.' Mitchell, beginning a career as a schoolmaster, had also just decided to abandon the idea of taking Holy Orders, though Carlyle advised him to continue with the presentation of discourses in the Divinity Hall in case he changed his mind. Carlyle would shortly feel no need of such insurance for himself.

Sitting on the top of a mail coach, he went to Edinburgh on 19 December. He recalls in the *Reminiscences*[20] that he had gone 'with great pleasure,' which, given the dullness of his life in Annan, was no doubt true; but he told Mitchell a few weeks later that it had been 'a dull pilgrimage'.[21] It was certainly not a pleasant journey. Carlyle, while sitting outside, was snowed upon, and found none among his fellow passengers to provide him with good company. The two women of the party he dismissed as 'both seemingly exceeding vain as well as stupid'.[22] Resting for the night at Broughton[23] he made, in the circumstances, the adventurous decision to leave the coach-party the next morning and make his way on foot. He left at four o'clock (about five hours, on almost the shortest day of the year, before daylight) and trudged along tracks in 'truly an Icelandic scene,' through drifts of snow several feet deep. At Noblehouse[24] he found a fellow Edinburgh divinity student, Thomas Clark, who introduced him to a walking companion. Carlyle grudgingly agreed to this companionship because the man seemed 'sufficiently inoffensive,' though 'he did turn out to be a very shallow man'. In time the man tired, and Carlyle happily left him behind, reaching the city at seven o'clock that evening. 'I was never more happy at seeing Edinburgh.'

The next morning he delivered his discourse, feeling it superior to the other he heard on that day, by one Samuel Caven. 'He says an infinite deal of nothing,' Carlyle told Mitchell.[25] He stayed in the city for Christmas, using the week there to seek out old friends. He went to the house of a half-cousin of his called Waugh, with whose father he had boarded while at school in Annan. Here he first met Edward Irving, whom he had seen in his schoolroom at Annan seven years earlier. Irving had by this time become a successful dominie, in Kirkcaldy, though his strict methods (he was, unlike Carlyle, a firm adherent of corporal punishment for schoolchildren) had brought him into controversy with the parents of some of his charges. Before moving to Kirkcaldy Irving had taught in Haddington, home of Jane Welsh, Carlyle's future wife, and had been her tutor.

The first meeting between Irving and Carlyle was unhappy. Irving, very much the great man among his fellow expatriates from Annandale, domineered Carlyle ruthlessly, quizzing him about events at home. They were, Carlyle recalled,[26] events 'of which I knew little, and had less than no wish to speak'. Irving was annoyed by Carlyle's reticence, and eventually attacked him with the abjuration, 'You seem to know nothing!' Carlyle, who despite his comparative lack of self-confidence was unwilling to take such handling quiescently, fought back with 'Sir, by what right do you try my knowledge in this way?' It seems the others present were amused at Carlyle taking Irving down a peg, and Irving himself was a little wounded by it. It was a good way, though, to ensure he did not forget Carlyle.

II

Carlyle returned to Annan in January 1816. His depressions, brought on by spiritual and social isolation, deepened. By July he is writing to Mitchell to say that 'I have been extremely melancholy during the last six weeks, upon many accounts.'[27] He had had two weeks in bed with a bad throat, during which he lost his voice; a blow to him, but no doubt a relief to those around him. Nothing pleased him. He had read, and cast aside in moral disgust, Chesterfield's *Letters to his Son*. Even Addison and Steele's *Spectator* could not rouse him. Burdett, in his book on Carlyle,[28] throws into the equation his view that Carlyle's condition was not helped by raging sexual frustration – 'thwarted virility', as he more tactfully expresses it, making a comparison with Browning before he met Elizabeth Barrett. There is no evidence for such a view, just as there is no evidence (other than the circumstantial) for any suspicions about Carlyle's sexual activity. There are, though, many occasions in the decade between 1816 and Carlyle's marriage when it would be tempting to make such a guess at part of the reason for Carlyle's ill-temper and moroseness. However, such supposition is based on the belief that Carlyle was much like other young men, which he plainly was not.

Mitchell had tried to suggest a form of escape for them both, by going to France. Carlyle squashed this ruthlessly. 'First, how are we to get to France; second, how are we to live in France; and third what good will living in France do to us?'[29] In any case, a new horizon had opened for Carlyle, if he could find the enthusiasm for it. The much-derided Christison, his classics professor from Edinburgh, had written to ask whether he would be interested in a position as teacher of the parish school at Kirkcaldy, the Fife town where Irving lived. Christison had head-hunted Irving for his school, and was urged by Leslie, who knew Carlyle far better than he did, to extend this invitation. The offer was worth £100 a year, and Carlyle was to go to Kirkcaldy in August to discuss the prospects. He told Mitchell he would be staying at home; and, in any case, in an early expression of his intensely moral political opinions, Carlyle wondered whether France, 'inhabited by fierce rev-olutionists and rascally marauders and flimsy aristocrats – all sweating under foreign and arbitrary yoke – would be a fit place for an honest man to dwell in.'

Irving was back in Annan during his school holidays, and the two dominies met at the house of of old Adam Hope, their former master, whose wife had died. There were no hard feelings.

At first sight he heartily shook my hand; welcomed me as if I had been a valued old acquaintance, almost a brother; and before my leaving . . . came up to me again, and in the frankest tone said, 'You are coming to Kirkcaldy to look about you in a month or two: you know I am there; my house and all that I can do for you is yours; two Annandale people must not be strangers in Fife!'[30]

Carlyle warmed to Fife and its people. He saw St Andrews for the first time, and developed a deeper relationship with Irving. He was particularly impressed by Irving's library, to which he was granted free access (Carlyle, throughout his life, had a soft spot for those who could afford large collections of books, and who would allow him to read them). Though they would be rivals, Carlyle was persuaded to make the move north. The prospect of Irving's friendship made the difference; it caused Carlyle to look back upon the time in Fife as the happiest chapter of his youth. No other man, indeed, was to have so profound an effect on Carlyle as Irving in the next five years. No wonder, when recalling him half a century later, Carlyle should have said:

[He] was a brother to me, and a friend . . . Such a friend as I never had again or before in the world . . . he was the sun in my firmament, where all else had become so wintry . . . Irving's influences on me were manifold . . . we were in constant correspondence, he knew all my secrets.[31]

Promising to return in a couple of months, Carlyle went back to Annan to work out his notice. On 14 November 1816 he set out for Edinburgh, the first instalment of his journey to Fife. Yet again it was a journey made vile by the elements, this time wind and rain. Once in Fife he underwent a ceremony of introduction to the Burghers of Kirkcaldy, and found a furnished room (for six shillings a week) opposite the parish school. When his term started, on 25 November, he had twenty-seven scholars in his charge. He also set about tackling Irving's library, demolishing Gibbon at a volume a day for twelve days, devouring Hume, and then ploughing through the French classics. He did not seek new friends, but diverted his spare energies into reading. Froude quoted Carlyle as having said his first two favourite books were Hudibras and Tristram Shandy;[32] but now he was becoming more sophisticated. Gibbon abetted him in the process of losing his faith. He told William Allingham fifty years later that he had 'studied the Evidences of Christianity for several years, with the greatest desire to be convinced, but in vain. I read Gibbon, and then first clearly saw that Christianity was not true.'[33] Elaborating this to Masson, he said that Gibbon had caused 'the extirpation from his mind of the last remnant that had been left in it of the orthodox belief in miracles.'[34]

Even though Carlyle, with his customary grace, would soon be dismissing Kirkcaldy to Mitchell as 'this long and dirty town',[35] he was happier. He also told Mitchell that 'I am sufficiently comfortable, and feel less spleen and ennui than I used to do at Annan.' Britain itself was just sinking into the depression and repression that followed the Napoleonic Wars, and Carlyle noted the feelings of his neighbours against 'the hardness of the times'.[36] The country was beginning to change at a revolutionary pace in more ways than one. In the ten years between the 1811 and 1821 censuses the population of Britain rose by seventeen per cent, from twelve to fourteen million. Wages, which had risen steadily in real terms since the start of the Napoleonic Wars, were now beginning a downward progress that would not be stopped until after the repeal of the Corn Laws in 1846 – three years after Carlyle had railed against the economic and social conditions in England in *Past and Present*. The political establishment was unsteady, the King mad, his son the Prince Regent dissolute and disliked. High stamp duties, of 4d on a news-paper, limited the circulation of opinions hostile to the Tory government of Lord Liverpool. A rash of prosecutions for seditious libel, and for the defa-mation of the King and his ministers, also occurred in 1817, as another means of encouraging conformity. A fall in demand immediately after the war led to a great rise in unemployment, exacerbated by the reduction in manpower of the army and navy. Sporadic rioting, and disturbances even among the middle classes, fed the Tory establishment's fear of the mob. In 1817 par-liament suspended Habeas Corpus and passed bills forbidding potentially seditious meetings; this was two years before Peterloo and the Six Acts. Although Carlyle commented little on it at the time, these repressive, auth-oritarian measures were only the start of the economic and social injustices that were to create the climate in which the Chartist movement, and Carlyle's career as a polemicist, would later flourish. And, in the authoritarian means Liverpool took to stifle dissent, he was coming as close to the Cromwellian model (of which Carlyle was to become the nineteenth century's greatest supporter) as anyone since the Lord Protector.

Carlyle went to Edinburgh in March 1817 with a view to enrolling at the Divinity Hall and continuing his studies; but the effects of Gibbon and others were now asserting themselves. The professor, Dr William Ritchie, was too busy to see him, being embroiled in a row on that day about the library. Carlyle seems to have had his spiritual view crystallised by that moment of squabbling. 'The Official Person, when I rang, was not at home; – and my instant feeling was, "Very good, then, *very* good; let this be *finis* in the matter," – and it neatly was.'[37] He wrote to Mitchell that 'we ought to be somewhat sorry for the Divinity-Hall; but our grief need not stop here. If we follow its members into the world, and observe their destination, we shall find it very pitiful.'[38] Irving had been made a licenciate of the Church in

1815, qualifying for presentation to a living, and was pursuing his ambitions zealously. Though he exerted great influence over Carlyle in these years, on this matter he did not.

Carlyle rationalised his decision to Mitchell thus:

With the exception of the few whom superior talent or better stars exempted from the common fortune, every Scotch Licenciate must adopt one of two alternatives. If he is made of pliant stuff, he selects someone having authority before whom he bows with unabating alacrity for (say) half-a-score of years, and thereby obtains a Kirk: whereupon he betakes him to collect his stipend, and (unless he thinks of persecuting the Schoolmaster) generally in a few months, falls into a state of torpor, from which he rises no more. If on the other hand, the soul of the Licenciate is stubborn and delights not to honour the Esquires of the district – heartless and hopeless he must drag out his life – without aim or object – vexed at every step to see surplices alighting on the backs of many who surpass him in nothing – but their love for gravy.[39]

This is not the whole story. Carlyle's religious doubt, extensively catalogued in *Sartor*, was about more than the injustices of ecclesiastical patronage; but no doubt it was as good a reason as any to offer to his friends. He simply could not believe what he read in the Bible. God was plausible; the Resurrection, miracles, and other myths and legends were not. 'No church,' he wrote in 1866, recalling this crisis, 'or speaking Entity whatever, can do without "formulas"; but it must believe them first, if it would be honest!'[40] He retained the simple Calvinist view of God as a force commanding duty, with man bound to perform duty according to his station; it is the idea of religion as a means of social control which was to dominate much of Carlyle's later writing.

Carlyle was still pursuing scientific interests, including a new interest in astronomy, and in one letter gives a hint of a link between this fascination with science and the erosion of his faith. Having read Bailly's *Histoire de l'Astronomie Moderne*, he notes how the new perception of the Earth's insignificance had prompted fears that people would be tempted away from Christianity. Carlyle had read a work by another Scot attempting to defend the old religious truths in the light of scientific progress. *A Series of Discourses on the Christian Revelation, Viewed in Connection with Modern Astronomy*, by Thomas Chalmers, and found it unconvincing. 'His best argument seems to be, that as it is in the scriptures, we have no business to think about it at all,'[41] he told Mitchell. 'Christianity itself is only supported by probabilities; very strong ones certainly, but still only probabilities.'

In the summer of 1817 the usual calm of Carlyle's family was badly disrupted. His mother became ill with a fever. Carlyle remembered his mother's illness as the only time he had seen his father lose control of his emotions, when her suffering 'seemed to threaten the extinction of her reason; we were all night desperate, and ourselves mad,' he wrote in the *Reminiscences*.[42] 'He burst, at last, into quite a torrent of grief; cried piteously, and threw himself on the floor, and lay moaning.' The effect on Carlyle was immense; the scene made him aware of 'what unknown seas of feeling' were to be found in a man, not just in his father, but in himself. This recognition deepened his own sensitivities, and made him both more troubled by his own feelings and vulnerable to new influences, like the impact of German transcendentalist thought, that were soon to come upon him. It would intensify the sense of spiritual struggle that was now overwhelming him.

Although in such crises Carlyle had his family to draw comfort and support from, he was coming to depend heavily on Irving's friendship in a way he seems to have depended on no other before. In Kirkcaldy, when he could be torn away from Irving's library, the two of them made frequent visits by the ferry across the Firth of Forth to Edinburgh, mainly to visit university friends. They undertook what seemed to Carlyle in retrospect to be rather dangerous little voyages along the Forth, on one occasion (retailed in the *Reminiscences*)[43] returning to Kirkcaldy so long after dark that their friends thought they had been lost at sea. They went on great summer walking tours together too, the first, in August 1817 (once Margaret Carlyle had recovered from her illness), to the Trossachs, returning home via Loch Lomond and Glasgow. As well as the spectacular scenery, which deeply impressed him, Carlyle saw for the first time steamers on the water off Greenock. Two other schoolmasters went with them; one, James Brown, was like Irving a former tutor to Carlyle's future wife.

Despite what distractions he could make for himself, he quickly became as depressed by schoolmastering in Kirkcaldy as he had been by it in Annan. By the spring of 1818, less than eighteen months into his post, he was having thoughts of moving on, influenced strongly by similar feelings on the part of Irving. 'My existence is marked by almost nothing, but that silent stream of thoughts and whims and fantasies that never ceases to pervade the mind of every living man,' Carlyle told James Johnston at the end of April.[44] He entered once more into a period of apathetic disillusion, no longer enjoying the trips to Edinburgh, but hating the boredom of Kirkcaldy. He began to devote his mental energies more and more to finding a purpose in his life now that he had renounced the Church. Since he claimed that 'the men with whom I meet are mostly preachers and students in divinity'[45] there seemed to him no escape from the life he had given up. Indeed, all Irving's talk of giving up schoolmastering was with the view of going to Edinburgh (which Carlyle now decided he disliked) to find work as an itinerant preacher (which Carlyle had decided was no life for him).

'My conduct,' he wrote to Mitchell at the end of May 1818, 'is absurd ... I am assaulted by those feelings of discontent and ferocity which solitude at all times tends to produce.'[46] He tried to overcome them by throwing himself more deeply into mathematics and physics ('I am now pretty well convinced that a body projected from the earth with a velocity of 39,000 feet per second will never return'), but that gave only temporary relief. He started to write poetry, a poem from about this time, 'Tragedy of Night-Moth', being his earliest creative work extant. Carlyle was a hopeless poet, a weakness that can be seen in his later translations of the German masters.

In August he, Mitchell and Johnston had a walking tour of the Lake District, taking in Grasmere and Ullswater. He set off with his self-confidence at a painfully low ebb. Three days before leaving he wrote lachrymosely to Thomas Murray that 'with most young men, I have had dreams of intellectual greatness, and of making me a name upon the earth – they were little else but dreams. To gain renown is what I do not hope and hardly care for, in the present state of my feelings ... My prospects are not extremely brilliant at present.'[47] None the less, it is clear (though whether Carlyle himself realised it is hard to judge) that much of his restlessness was provoked by under-fulfilment. He was becoming a fervently ambitious young man.

III

After his walking tour, Carlyle went home briefly to Mainhill. Farming was not a financial success for James Carlyle. Once back at Kirkcaldy, Carlyle sent his father a banker's draft for £15 to help supplement the family income. The family were, however, better off than had James Carlyle remained in the building business, which was suffering worse than agriculture. Carlyle found his school reduced to a mere twelve scholars, thanks to competition from a newly opened establishment. 'The people's rage for novelty is the cause of it,' he complained to his father. Since his rival was 'very ignorant and very much taken to drink' there could be no other reason.[48] His father had already had to endure his son rejecting the profession for which he had been destined. Now Carlyle told James that he was 'very much tired' of schoolmastering, and would be hunting for 'some other way of making my bread'. He was frustrated by his profession's 'mean contradictions and poor results'.[49] Irving had made up his mind to leave, which, with the fall in the numbers on Carlyle's roll, tipped the balance. ' "It were better to perish," as I exaggeratively said to myself, "than continue schoolmastering".' He toyed with the idea of becoming an advocate, or even an engineer, but realised that he could not yet give up teaching altogether. He suspected that (with the aid of the £70 he had saved) he could survive a year in Edinburgh, making up his earnings with some private tuition. He asked his father to advise him urgently, but his mind seems to have been made up from the moment he returned to Kirkcaldy. Quoting Lucian, he told Mitchell that 'when the Gods have determined to render a man ridiculously miserable, they make a schoolmaster of him.'[50]

Carlyle was in deep torment. He tells Mitchell, in the letter just quoted, of his living in 'a dense repulsive atmosphere ... of deeper feelings, which I partly inherit from Nature, and which are mostly due to the undefined station I have hitherto occupied in society.' Carlyle was a hierarchical figure, and this is the first evidence of it. 'If I continue as a schoolmaster, I fear there is little doubt that these feelings will increase, and at last drive me entirely from the kindly sympathies of life, to brood in silence over the bitterness into which my friendly propensities must have changed.' His problems were not simply social, or professional, or material; they were also becoming spiritual, and he was on the slope downwards to the crisis of faith retailed in *Sartor* as the Everlasting No. On 23 October he asked the Magistrates of Kirkcaldy, who administered the school, to accept his resignation. At the end of the month they did. Irving left a couple of days later, and Carlyle's only other companion, a schoolmaster named John Pears, was due to leave the following week. Carlyle was, though, prevailed upon to reconsider by a Kirkcaldy banker called William Swan. Swan was a man Carlyle respected, and was later to be of great help to him, smuggling in German books for him in bales of flax from Holland. He offered Carlyle £120-£150 if he would stay another year and run a school Swan wanted to found. The scheme came to nothing, and so at the end of November Carlyle followed Irving to Edinburgh.

Looking back from the late 1860s, Carlyle saw the period that began with the return to Edinburgh as 'my four or five most miserable, dark, sick and heavy-laden years'.[51] Elsewhere in the *Reminiscences*, he recalled the 'huge instalments of bodily and spiritual wretchedness in this my Edinburgh Purgatory'.[52] He was to see Irving make a success of his career in the Church, while he himself lurched from one crisis to another. He had a little money – perhaps £100 – but was to find it fast disappearing. Despite Irving's companionship (and Irving went beyond the call of duty with Carlyle, involving him as far as he could in his own social life and introducing Carlyle to people he thought might stimulate him), he was lonely. He was unsure of what to do and could not apply himself properly to any calling. He was losing the religious faith in which he had been brought up. As a result of all these pressures, his health began to suffer. 'My long curriculum of dyspepsia,'[53] and long periods of sleeplessness because of internal torment and extreme sensitivity to noise, had begun.

Though Carlyle decided to devote his time to study – mineralogy was his first object – he had more pragmatic intentions. His ambition was sufficiently well developed for him to seek hack-work from booksellers. He was helped in this by a recommendation from Dr Henry Duncan, the minister of Ruthwell who employed Mitchell as tutor to his children, to Dr (later Sir) David Brewster, the Edinburgh encyclopedia publisher, that Carlyle would be a useful man to write articles for him. On his arrival in Edinburgh, however, Carlyle's over-sensitive spirit underwent further disorientation. Once installed in poor lodgings he wrote to Mitchell:

Conceive to yourself a person ... loosened from all his engagements with mankind – seated in a room in S. Richmond St – revolving in his altered soul, the various turns of fate below – whilst every time that the remembrance of his forlorn condition comes across his brain, he silently exclaims 'why then the world's mine oyster; which I (not with sword, as Ancient Pistol) will open' – as best I may: and you will have some idea of my situation.[54]

Carlyle was not entirely unhappy. As well as being reunited with friends he quickly found some work, teaching spherical trigonometry and astronomy for two hours a day to a young officer of the East India Company, whom Irving (too busy preaching) had passed on to him. He subsequently found another hour teaching geometry to an English gentleman, which with his other engagement brought him in six guineas a month. He reacquainted himself with Professor Leslie, with whom he discussed mathematics, and used Duncan's introduction to Brewster to meet the publisher. It was to be a longer association than either of them could have suspected. In 1866, in his eighty-fifth year, it was Brewster who, as Principal of Edinburgh University, introduced Carlyle when he made his Rectorial Address.

As in his student days, Carlyle's family supplied him with laundered clothes and food via the carrier from Ecclefechan. He complained to his mother[55] that he was living in accommodation that was both unpleasant and expensive. He had seen fifty possible lodgings, only one, even more unpleasant than South Richmond Street, any cheaper than where he was. 'Surely you thought,' he said to his mother, 'five years ago, that this troublesome washing and baking was all over.' The change of scene, the anxiety he was now feeling about the future, and the difficult circumstances in which he was forced to live took their toll upon his health. He first notes his affliction with dyspepsia in November 1818.[56] In his book *Mr Carlyle – My Patient*[57] Dr James L. Halliday suggests most of Carlyle's illnesses were attributable to the repression in his personality and emotions caused by his strict upbringing, his need to please his mother and his fear of his father; yet Halliday also quotes Sir Richard Quain, Carlyle's doctor in his declining years, who in 1895 wrote in the *British Medical Journal* that his patient's dyspepsia 'was fully accounted for by the fact that he was particularly fond of a very nasty gingerbread'.[58]

Still star-struck by advocates, Carlyle thought again about a career in the law. However, he was deterred when he learned it would cost 'several hundreds' to train for this calling. While in Edinburgh, though, he sporadically attended law lectures at the university when he had the opportunity, partly for intellectual stimulation, partly to keep his options open. The gamble taken in throwing up his post in Kirkcaldy began to sink in, and the anxiety and dyspepsia were aggravated. He told James Johnston, 'till not very long ago, I imagined my whole duty to consist in thinking and enduring. It now appears that I ought not only to suffer but to act.'[59] His sense of urgency increased when he was reduced to an hour a day of geometry, bringing in a mere two guineas a month. Leslie suggested he try his luck in America, a thought Carlyle, so close to his family as he was, quickly dismissed.

A great, but potentially refreshing, change came over Carlyle at Christmas 1818, when he returned to Fife with Irving. He made his first serious romantic attachment, with a former pupil of Irving's, Margaret Gordon. They had met earlier that year, and he made a point of seeing her on his return to Kirkcaldy. She could not reciprocate his affections. Carlyle had found her 'the brightest and cleverest' of the young ladies of Kirkcaldy, and lamented in the *Reminiscences* that his poverty and her aunt's disapproval made a deeper relationship impossible.[60] He was much taken with her, and when recalling her in the *Reminiscences* could still construct a powerful picture of her attractions: 'She was of the fair-complexioned, softly elegant, softly grave, witty and comely type, and had a good deal of gracefulness, intelligence and other talent.' Carlyle claimed in the same passage that he had hankered after her romantically for three or so years, and even half a century later still felt 'goodwill' towards her. She, however, married 'some rich insignificant Aberdeen Mr Something,' Alexander Bannerman, who after service as a Whig MP became Governor of Nova Scotia. She and Carlyle never spoke after 1819, though Carlyle saw her in the early 1840s twice in the street in London, 'when her eyes (but that was all) said to me almost touchingly, "Yes, yes; that is you!" '[61] He told Johnston[62] that the festive excursion had been the happiest of his recent life, and one can surmise this was because of the affection she showed him. It is fair to suppose, given the semi-autobiographical nature of *Sartor*, that she was the prototype of Blumine, Teufelsdröckh's inamorata.

There was still, despite this diversion, the matter of earning a living; which Carlyle settled he would do most readily by writing. His teaching had dried up altogether, other new interests he found hard to sustain, so he turned once more to books for something to do. With no money to buy them, and Irving's library more or less exhausted, the only place Carlyle could feed his addiction was the university library. Obtaining books from there involved making a request to a librarian, who would return in an hour or so with the book or, more often than not, with the news that it was unavailable. His extensive leisure did, though, prompt what was to be a study of greater enthusiasm, and longer-lasting significance, than anything he had so far tried: that of the German language. His interest in German thought had been excited by the *De l'Allemagne* of Madame de Staël, but it could not be pursued without knowledge of the language. His teacher was another Dumfriesshire man, Robert Jardine, for whom he performed the reciprocal service of teaching French. Within three months Carlyle had the grammar sufficiently mastered to read German books with a dictionary; one of the first was a history of Frederick the Great, lent him by Irving.

The squalor of South Richmond Street soon became too much for him. In February 1819, after three months there, he left, horrified by 'vermin of various sorts, which haunted the beds ... together with sluttishness and a lying, thievish disposition with which [his landlady] was afflicted'.[63] He once more faced a trudge around dirty, expensive lodging houses. Demoralised, he persuaded an old university friend, Edward Hill (Irving's cousin) to take him in at his lodgings in Carnegie Street. There Carlyle had his own, clean room for 8s a week, 3s 6d less than Mrs Davie had charged, and he found Hill 'harmless'. Hill, indeed, had apparently been in awe of Carlyle for years because of Carlyle's sharp, sarcastic tongue; and had, in the preceding years, addressed him in puerile terms in letters as 'Dear Dean' or 'Dear Jonathan,' supposedly comparing Carlyle with Swift. Having moved, Carlyle's luck looked up. Dr Brewster, at last, found work for him. His first commission was to translate a scientific paper by Baron Jacob Berzelius from French into English, for publication that June in the *Edinburgh Philosophical Journal.*

Carlyle's crisis of faith was deepening. A passage in a letter to his mother of March 1819 gives the clearest hint yet of his rejection of orthodox Christianity:

I am rather afraid that I have not been quite regular in reading that best of books which you recommended to me. However last night I was reading my favourite Job; and I hope to do better in time to come. I entreat you to believe that I am sincerely desirous of being a good man; and tho' we may differ in some few unimportant particulars; yet I firmly trust that the same Power who created us with imperfect faculties, will pardon the errors of every one (and none are without them) who seeks truth and righteousness, with a simple heart.[64]

Carlyle knew how much his decision not to be a clergyman had hurt his parents. Incapable of lying, he none the less could not involve them in the full details of his loss of faith too. He reassured his mother that he was applying himself hard – up at five or six each morning, at his books. But he felt his physical health declining the longer he had nothing useful to do, and in May decided to retreat to Mainhill for the summer, with a mountain of books, to improve further his grasp of German. He had just read the *Confessions* of Rousseau, who was to come to represent for Carlyle all he loathed about the hedonistic eighteenth century. His first reaction was mild in the light of the obloquy he would pour on Rousseau as he became older; he contented himself with writing to Mitchell that the *Confessions* 'should teach a virtuous Briton to be content with the dull sobriety of his native country'.[65]

Though Carlyle had become so content, and had rejected the prospect of emigration, his friend James Johnston sailed for New Brunswick that June. Carlyle had planned to see him off from Liverpool, but as his sailing was delayed they had a short walking tour in Cumberland and parted at Workington. Carlyle was depressed at losing one of his few confidential companions, probably for ever (as it turned out, Johnston was back within three years); but, none the less, a few leisured and well-fed weeks spent with his family restored his health and, to an extent, his spirits. He knew, however, he could not stay at Mainhill indefinitely, and had to devise a project to see him through the winter. Also, he now found the society of Ecclefechan outside his family beneath him intellectually and socially ('the people in our neighbourhood are mostly peasants, and display the sentiments and habits usually met with in that race of men,' he told John Fergusson, a dominie he had befriended in Edinburgh the previous winter[66]). He missed his companions:

the nearest geographically, Robert Mitchell, was an eight-mile trek away. There is little in his letters that takes us away from introspection, though in that same letter to Fergusson he raises a theme that will recur twenty years later, and form the basis of the first phase of his social criticism – the further impoverishment of the lower classes by the government, on this occasion by the levying of a tobacco tax.

Carlyle's family that summer was not as serene as it had been. His father had come to accept, though not perhaps understand, the withering of his son's faith, and that he could no longer believe in the formulas of the Church. He realised his son's belief went no further than the Old Testament. Carlyle's mother was, though, deeply hurt by this, and her son's consequent absence from family prayers. She bade him read the Bible and, when he had finished, to start reading it all over again. Eventually they were to reach a *modus vivendi*, but not before much grief had been caused. Carlyle's letters to his mother at this period reflect the intense guilt he felt at not being able to conform to her religious standards. Writing in 1866, in his commentary on Althaus's biography of him, Carlyle recalled that 'finding I had objections, my Father, with a magnanimity which I admired and admire, left me frankly to my own guidance in that matter, as did my Mother (probably still more lovingly, tho' not so silently).'[67] Thirty years earlier he had noted, on his father's death, that when James had heard his son's decision not to go into the Church he had 'respected my scruples, my volition, and patiently let me have my way'. His son was never, though, in any doubt about the inner grief this concealed.

In early November 1819, after six months in the country, Carlyle walked back to Edinburgh. He was without Irving, who had been invited to take an assistant preacher's post in Glasgow the previous month. Carlyle, with this example of success before him, had resolved to make a go of studying law, choosing to cross the bridge of financial sacrifice when he came to it. He found a new lodging in Richmond Place, at 6s a week; he stayed but three weeks, though, moving to Bristow Street by early December. He found intelligent society at Edinburgh still unsettled after the Peterloo massacre, which had occurred at Manchester ten weeks earlier, when more than 50,000 people had marched in favour of political reform, and hussars armed with sabres had killed 11 and wounded 400 of them. He noticed worsening poverty, and it was rumoured that at Glasgow a rising such as those seen in England was being prepared. He saw thousands of soldiers march out of Edinburgh towards Glasgow, but the radicals there did nothing.

He resumed attendance at law classes and, having come from Dumfriesshire so recently, decided not to return home for Christmas. It was as well, for he found there was no vacation in the law school. He reassured his mother, in a letter just before Christmas, that hard study and hard exercise were keeping his spirits up.[68] He did, however, find the lectures dull, and his inability to stick at anything was coming to the fore again. He wrote an article about Alfred Gautier, the scientist, which he sent, unsolicited to Francis

Jeffrey at the *Edinburgh Review*, signalling that his new enthusiasm for the law had not killed his literary ambitions. Irving told him he must force his way into the columns of the press, and become known, before he could hope to obtain well-paid and regular employment as a writer. 'Find vent for your notions – get them tongue,' Irving wrote to him on 28 December. 'Upon every subject get them tongue.'[69] He also told him, prophetically, that 'known you will not be for a winning attaching accommodating man, but for an original, commanding and rather self-willed man.' Irving urged him to persist with contributions to both *Blackwood's Magazine* and the *Edinburgh Review*. As always, Carlyle was deeply influenced by what Irving said. His friend's work in Glasgow had proved a great success, so his advice carried more weight than before.

The winter of 1819–20 was the hardest Carlyle had known. Apart from a cold and the usual dyspepsia he survived it well enough. He completed his review for Jeffrey, though did not expect it to be accepted; and indeed it was not. Radical disturbances continued, and Edinburgh became more febrile. There was a flurry of drilling and training by the militia, fearing an uprising in the Scottish capital. Carlyle found the whole spectacle disgusting. There was further alarm when the Cato Street conspiracy (a plot to assassinate the cabinet at a dinner in February 1820) was uncovered, and even one as apparently cynical as Carlyle was shocked by the idea of assassination (though the last Prime Minister, Spencer Perceval, had been shot dead in the lobby of the House of Commons just eight years earlier). Writing to his brother Alick, Carlyle developed his theme about the behaviour of the governed being conditioned by that of their governors. 'Some pity should be mingled with our abhorrence of the frantic conspirators,' he wrote. 'Well-founded complaints of poverty, one might almost say starvation, met with indifference or cold-blooded ridicule on the part of the Government, very naturally exasperate the ignorant minds of the governed, and impel them to enterprises of a desperate nature.'[70] If Carlyle's theory of how an aristocracy or natural governing class should behave was rooted in any particular experience, it was in this spectacle of what he regarded as the wilful misgovernment of England, and the distress caused to the lower classes by it, in 1820.

Soon, though, his mind was diverted by the chance of some modest literary work. Brewster offered him the chance to write (for very low fees) articles for his encyclopedia. This was to be Carlyle's main outlet for the next three years. He began with a life of Montesquieu, and one of Lady Mary Wortley Montagu. Other Ms, Ns and Ps were to follow: Dr Moore, his son Sir John Moore, Montaigne, Monfaucon, Newfoundland, and the Elder and Younger Pitts to name but a few: several of them are collected in the *Critical and Miscellaneous Essays*.[71] They are factual and without any of the opinionation of Carlyle's later writings, and as such stylistically unremarkable, though pleasant and easy to read. They do, though, reveal a fluent and attractive writer with a good grasp of language and of his material.

The fluency was deceptive. Now he had achieved his ambition of writing professionally, Carlyle did not find it easy. He told Alick that 'I do not get on very quickly in these operations; but this is like my apprenticeship as it were; in time I shall do it far more quickly.'[72] Now he had his foot on the bottom rung of the literary ladder, he put the law (with which he had become discontented) behind him. 'Law, I fear, must be renounced,' he wrote to Mitchell.[73] 'It is a shapeless mass of absurdity and chicane, and the ten years, which a barrister commonly spends in painful idleness before arriving at employment, is more than my physical or moral frame could endure.' In the same letter he made it clear he is not content with compiling 'wretched lives' for Brewster; but he saw it might be the start of something better. He was twenty-four, and could not afford more false starts. He was also writing reviews of scientific tracts for the *Edinburgh Philosophical Journal*, which Brewster ran too, so it was not all hack-work.

At the end of April 1820 Carlyle went back to Mainhill again, via Irving at Glasgow, where he spent ten happy days. Irving introduced him to many of his Glasgow friends, who treated Carlyle warmly. Once more, Edinburgh was boring him. He wrote to Johnston in Nova Scotia that the visitor to the city was 'disgusted probably with the most feeble drivelling of the students – shocked at the unphilosophic spirit of the professors – dissatisfied with the smoke and the odour and everything else in or about the city.'[74] Shortly before Carlyle left Irving, his friend elicited from him 'by degrees, in the softest manner, the confession that I did not think as he of Christian Religion, and that it was vain for me to expect I ever could or should.'[75] That night Carlyle stayed alone in an inn at Muirkirk. Leaving at four o'clock the next morning he walked all the way to Dumfries, a distance of fifty-four miles, arriving at eight o'clock in the evening. He spent the 'mournful' journey brooding.[76] In his confused and rootless state he was even having third thoughts about teaching, entertaining the suggestion from an academy in York that he might go there as mathematical master – though not, he insisted in a letter to the man who had made the suggestion, Robert Allen, to sit for ten or twelve hours of the day as 'an usher'.[77] Nothing came of this. Instead Carlyle made his most important intellectual adventure yet, into Goethe, starting with *Faust*, which transfixed him. He told Irving:

I wish Goethe were my countryman, I wish – O, how I wish – he were my friend. It is not for his masterly conception of human nature – from the heroes of classical story down to the blackguards of a Leipsic alehouse – that I admire him above all others; his profound sentiment of beauty, his most brilliant delineations of all its varieties – this gayety of head and melancholy of heart, open all the floodgates of my sympathy.[78]

He added that Irving should persist in his own studies of German, because 'these people have some muscle in their frames'. He himself was preparing to read through all of Schiller's plays during the summer, unconsciously paving the way for what, within five years, would be his first book. At about this time the influence of the German language, with its declamations and sonorities, begins to be detected in his hitherto simple, educated Scots style. His letters (except to his family, which retain a touching simplicity of tone) begin to sound high-flown and rather pompous, marking an important development in what the world would call 'Carlylese'. He was also, under the added influence of German thought, coming to his spiritual crisis. In a letter to Robert Allen he disquisited: 'Is happiness our being's end and aim? All men believe so.' The Germans he read confirmed for him the concepts of work and duty, familiar from his Calvinist upbringing, as man's chief aim. They repudiated the shallow values of sensualism and self-indulgence of the eighteenth century that had so disgusted Carlyle.

At Mainhill he felt his health improving. His relations with his family improved too, and much of his energy was diverted to intellectual stimulation and encouragement of his younger siblings. At tea-time he would have theological disputes with his mother, though 'I did learn at length, by judicious endeavour, to speak piously and agreeably to one so pious, without unveracity on my part.'[79] He received another offer of employment from Allen, this time as travelling tutor to an educationally sub-normal boy in the North Riding of Yorkshire. Carlyle sought further details, hinting that £100 a year might be enough to make him change his mind about teaching. Clearly Allen (whose letter in reply is missing) had hopeful news of the salary, because Carlyle was prepared to make the three-hundred-mile round trip to York to see him. This trip eventually happened in October once his potential employer, a Mr Hutton, had promised to meet Carlyle's travelling expenses. Carlyle was glad he made the trip, for when seeing the house where he would have to live and work he was immediately deterred from the idea. In a letter to William Graham, an old friend of his family's, he remarked that 'the situation seemed scarcely preferable to manufacturing oakum in Botany-bay. The creature to be tutored is a perfect Sooterkin; a placid, rickety thing, with a head not larger than one of your tea-cups, two dead glassy eyes ready to drop from their yellow sockets, a carcass corresponding to this superb capital ... any good lively orangoutang would have formed a more eligible companion than such a monster.'[80] He had not found the rest of the family much more appealing. Carlyle was amused by Yorkshire, particularly by the accent of the people, and gives examples of the speech in his letter to Graham in the most condescending manner. At least his difficulties had not deprived him of his sense of humour.

IV

Having passed his customary six months with his family, Carlyle went back to Edinburgh in November 1820, sitting on the roof of a coach rather than walking all the way there. He found lodgings in Carnegie Street, again the best of a bad lot. However his landlady, a Mrs Robertson, the widow of a

Perthshire schoolmaster, was, he felt, the best he had ever had. He had little to look forward to other than writing for Brewster. Perhaps as a result of his anxieties he plunged into ill-health, suffering with his bowels, and became subject to a regime of pills, castor-oil, porridge and exercise. He became subject, too, to immense frustration, but this only deepened his resolution to sort things out. 'I feel determined,' he told Alick in December 1820, 'to find something stationary – some "local habitation and some name" for myself ere it be long.'[81] He believed he would succeed, and was prepared to do anything (though preferably writing) in order to do so – except school-mastering. However, he added in his letter to Alick that he would even contemplate that 'rather than stand here in frigid impotence – the powers of my mind all festering and corroding each other, in the miserable strife of inward will against outward necessity'.

His deepening anxiety about religion reawakened guilt about his mother. He wrote to her apologising 'for the poor way in which alone I have hitherto been able to reward your truly maternal love and care of me'.[82] He was depressed by his failure, at the age of twenty-five, to make a definite way in the world. Faith was at the heart of his problems. 'I respect your religious sentiments,' he told his mother, 'and honour you for feeling them, more than if you were the highest woman in the world without them.'

He took on a little tutoring, which brought him four guineas a month. He became involved in a plan with Brewster to launch a review, but the idea was stillborn, causing him more disappointment. Instead, he conceived a project to translate Schiller's *History of the Thirty Years' War*, but Longman's of London rejected him (pointing out that a translation had already been made). Throughout the next twenty years, while he was making his name as a writer, Carlyle was handicapped by the fact that hardly any publishers shared his enthusiasm for German thought and letters. He passed Christmas in Glasgow with Irving, who took pity on him and urged him to stay awhile; but Carlyle was driven on by the desire to be productive, and went back to Edinburgh directly the holiday was over. His rest had improved his health, but not his idea of what to do next. Consequently, within a few days of returning to the city hypochondria (and he was the first to admit that he was a hypochondriac)[83] took over. His letters reveal sharp changes of mood: pessi-mism and optimism alternating, as well as more physical changes. Having written to Alick on 2 January to say he was in better health, he wrote to his brother Jack on the ninth to say it had worsened.[84] He decided his lodgings were too cold, so spent much of January looking for (and eventually finding) supposedly warmer ones. In fact it took two moves until he was settled, back in Carnegie Street. He was feeling very sorry for himself. 'This raw open weather is against me,' he wrote to Jack, 'and bodily disorder – embodied now in a most refractory state of the digestive process – cramp my exertions and almost entirely forbid study.'[85]

With little to occupy him, he divided his time between reading, walking and eating, subsisting still mainly on produce sent up by his mother. As January passed into February his bowels began to play up, he pumped himself full of dubious patent remedies and laxatives, and his demeanour worsened. 'I have scarcely been one day right, since I came back to this accursed, stinking, reeky mass of stones and lime and dung,' he told Jack on 10 February. 'Today the guts are all wrong again, the headache, the weakness, the black despondency are overpowering me. I fear those paltry viscera will fairly dish me at last.' He sank into self-pity. 'I am grown a very weak creature of late. The heart longs for some kind of sympathy: and in Edinburgh I find little of it.'[86] His family were alarmed by such news, and wrote advising him to come home at once, to be looked after properly. Carlyle was wont, though, to pour out his miseries in letters, and forget he had ever done so when he woke up the next morning feeling better. He was surprised, when they wrote back, that he could have disturbed them so. Masson, in his corrective of Froude, argues that the documentary evidence Froude found in letters and journals about Carlyle's obsessions with his health and other psychological problems made him get these factors out of proportion, and forget that Carlyle did not often seem so gloomy to those who came into contact with him. The fact was, though, that hypochondriac wretchedness was to dog Carlyle all his life, and he and his wife would eventually seem to be in competition in the matter.[87]

None the less, a week or so later Irving was sufficiently worried about him to take him away from Edinburgh, to stay at Kirkcaldy for a long weekend. The sea air bucked him up quickly; he returned to the city not recovered, but perhaps less melodramatic about his condition. He set to work again for Brewster, an article on Jacques, Baron de Necker, who had been French finance minister at the time of the revolution. Such hack-work went slowly. He found a couple of hours' teaching a day, to keep him from utter penury.

Irving, who seems at every crucial moment in Carlyle's early development to have been there opening doors for him, now opened the most important door of all. Visiting Carlyle in Edinburgh at the end of May 1821, he took him on a walk to Haddington, fourteen miles to the east of the city, to introduce him to Mrs Welsh, whose daughter Jane Baillie Welsh had been his pupil. Irving had had strong feelings for Jane, feelings that were apparently reciprocated. However, Irving was promised to Isabella Martin, daughter of the minister at Kirkcaldy, so nothing could come of this passion. After this excursion, however, Jane was to find a new suitor.

'I was supremely dyspeptic and out of health, during those three or four days,' was Carlyle's recollection. 'But they were the beginning of a new life to me.'[88]

3
Courting Jane
1821–26

JANE BAILLIE WELSH was nearly twenty when she met her future husband. Her father had died two years earlier, suddenly of typhoid, contracted from a patient. Her personality and activities were still dominated by this event, though she was emerging from the gloom; her mother, by contrast, seems still to have been unhinged. Having pressurised her parents to have her natural curiosities satisfied by learning, Jane had been well educated. As well as having Irving as a tutor, she had gone to school in Haddington, and to an academy in Edinburgh.

Jane was a handsome young woman, unlike the cadaverous late photographs of her by which her image is now best known. Her friend Geraldine Jewsbury described her as 'extremely pretty, a graceful and beautifully formed figure, upright and supple, a delicate complexion of creamy white with a pale rose tint in the cheeks, lovely eyes full of fire and softness, and with great depths of meaning. Her head was finely formed, with a noble arch, and a broad forehead ... her voice was clear, and full of subtle intonations and capable of great variety of expression.'[1] It is no wonder, when one recalls that these physical accomplishments were matched with a sharp tongue, wit and desire for learning, that Carlyle should have been smitten, like other men before him. Apart from Irving and Carlyle Jane had many other suitors, so much so that she would occasionally sign her letters to Carlyle 'Penelope'. As well as her beauty, she had an arresting lineage: descending from John Knox on her father's side and, allegedly, William Wallace on her mother's. Although Carlyle was, and appeared to be, a highly educated man – he spoke in a Dumfriesshire accent, but not in dialect – the social gap between Jane and him was vast.

His future mother-in-law also made a strong impression on him. He found her 'beautiful, a tall aquiline figure of elegant carriage and air,' but one whose severity of dress and manner 'repelled' him.[2] Jane, though, was charming, which made him feel 'true joy'. He was overwhelmed by his surroundings. He had never seen a finer apartment than the drawing-room at Haddington, and was at a loss to express himself. Irving drew him out, anxious his hostess should not misinterpret his shyness as rudeness. Carlyle found a useful means of beginning a correspondence with Jane, by sending her a reading list mainly of French and German history. His first letter to her was remarkably forward, stating prophetically that 'unless Fortune treat me even worse than usual – I am destined in process of time to know you far more intimately.'[3] He also showed early signs of proprietorialism, bidding her not to overwork as it would endanger her health, 'which I will not allow you ever to endanger on any account'. As an act of ingratiation this first letter would be remarkable in anyone. Coming from one as brusque and self-centred as Carlyle, it is a revelation, showing what an impact Jane had had upon him.

A further event at about this time was of as much significance as this meeting, and may for all one can tell have been prompted by it. Carlyle's biographers differ over whether it was June 1821 or June 1822 that he had his religious experience in Leith Walk, Edinburgh (David Masson pinpoints the exact spot as 'just below Pilrig Street'[4]), that became the Everlasting No of *Sartor*. The improvement in Carlyle's demeanour as seen through his letters in late 1821 (which may just be down to Jane's influence, of course), suggests that Froude's original contention about the earlier date is right. Carlyle's nephew Alexander (who had a vested interest in impugning Froude's judgment) doubted this, placing the experience a month or two later than Froude, or even in 1822. Clubbe agrees with 1822, saying that Carlyle's notes to Althaus would seem to confirm this.[5] But, as readers of the *Reminiscences* know, Carlyle's excellent memory sometimes let him down by a year or so. Indeed, in the very notes on Althaus that Clubbe takes as apparent proof of the 1822 date, Carlyle claims that 'In 1822, it must have been, that I first went to Haddington'; when, as all other documents prove, it was 1821. One can just as easily adduce this as evidence that the visit to Haddington and the experience in Leith Walk happened in the same year.[6]

After his experience, Carlyle became not so much a happier man as a more balanced and philosophical one. His fears about loss of faith had been conquered, and he was on the path to discovering his theistic alternative. A corner had been turned. The prelude to this religious transformation was three weeks of sleeplessness. In his comments on Althaus Carlyle says:

Nothing in '*Sartor*' thereabouts is fact (symbolical myth all), except that of the '*incident in the Rue St Thomas de l'Enfer*,' – which occurred quite literally to myself in Lieth [sic] Walk, during those 3 weeks of total sleeplessness, in which almost my one solace was that of a daily bathe on the sands between Lieth [sic] and Portobello. Incident was as I went *down* (coming *up* I generally felt a little refreshed for the hour); I remember it well, and could go yet to about the place.[7]

Since Carlyle directs us so explicitly to *Sartor* on this point, which is crucial to our understanding of his religious and psychological development, the specific passage deserves quotation at length:

Perhaps the miserablest man in the whole French Capital or Suburbs, was I, one sultry Dog-day, after much perambulation, toiling along the dirty little *Rue Saint-Thomas de l'Enfer*, among civic rubbish enough, in a close atmosphere, and over pavements hot as Nebuchadnezzar's Furnace; whereby doubtless my spirits were little cheered; when all at once there rose a Thought in me, and I asked myself: 'What *art* thou afraid of? Wherefore, like a coward, dost thou forever pip and whimper, and go cowering and trembling? Despicable biped! What is the sum-total of the worst that lies before thee? Death? Well, Death; and say the pangs of Tophet too, and all that the Devil and Man may, will or can do against thee! Hast thou not a heart; canst thou not suffer whatsoever it be; and, as a Child of Freedom, though outcast, trample Tophet itself under thy feet, while it consumes thee? Let it come, then; I will meet and defy it!' And as so I thought, there rushed like a stream of fire over my whole soul; and I shook base Fear away from me forever, I was strong, of unknown strength; a spirit, almost a god. Ever from that time, the temper of my misery was changed; not Fear or whining Sorrow was it, but Indignation and grim fire-eyed Defiance.

Thus had the EVERLASTING NO (*das ewige Nein*) pealed authoritatively through all the recesses of my Being, of my ME; and then was it that my whole ME stood up, in native God-created majesty, and with emphasis recorded its Protest. Such a protest, the most important transaction in Life, may that same Indignation and Defiance, in psychological point of view, be fitly called. The Everlasting No had said: 'Behold, thou are fatherless, outcast, and the Universe is mine (the Devil's)'; to which my whole Me now made answer: '*I* am not thine, but Free, and forever hate thee!'

It is from this hour that I incline to date my Spiritual New-birth, or Baphometic Fire-baptism; perhaps I directly thereupon began to be a Man.[8]

This final rejection of Christianity, and the discovery of the self-confidence to search for the new theology, is consistent with the comparative optimism of the later letters of 1821. Yet Carlyle was still not beyond some whining sorrow, then or ten or twenty years later. The struggles of this time were not kept to himself, but shared with friends. Writing to him in December 1834, William Graham compared Carlyle's then peace of mind with memories of the Edinburgh years. 'Have I not seen you,' Graham wrote, 'say in Leith Walk, baited by a legion of atrabilliar Devils and their nameless auxiliaries?'[9]

Whether his new-found interest in Jane improved or worsened his health is debatable. In his first letter to Alick after his return he reverts to type, retailing the guzzling down of Epsom salts, but claims to be getting better. Jane's reply to his first letter, however, unsettled him greatly. She wrote back curtly, in response to his gushing prose, 'To Mr Carslile [*sic*], with Miss Welsh's compliments and very best thanks.'[10] He took the hint, and whereas his first letter had been addressed to 'My dear Friend', his second was to 'My dear Madam'. Ingratiating himself ruthlessly, he volunteered that 'upon the whole, I suppose, you did well to treat me so'.[11] But he teased her, saying that but for the cold 'compliments' there would have been 'a hundred thousand things' he would have told her. None the less, he concluded with a desperate plea to be allowed to serve her, by sending her books if in no other more interesting way.

This elicited an only slightly less curt reply, returning books he had lent her, and informing him that she had sacked her German tutor. Carlyle seized this opportunity. Would she like him to take over her German tuition? He did not, though, quite appreciate how easily shocked some young women can be by certain enthusiasms of tone, and it might have been better had he not added that 'some sunny morning, about the first of August, you are to find me beside you, at breakfast, when you least expect it.'[12] Her reply this time was not entirely discouraging. Her mother was not sure they would be there for his proposed August visit, but he could call on Miss Welsh in Edinburgh in late July to discuss the prospect of German tuition. Suddenly, Carlyle was able to report better health. Nor was this just because of Jane. He was working hard, writing avidly for Brewster in addition to his part-time teaching, and thus was his mind taken off his bowels.

He called on Jane, urging her to embark upon Goethe. He persuaded her to make verse translations, promising to do the same himself, so that they could exchange the results. She found the task difficult, almost beyond her. He then returned, later than in recent years, to Mainhill for the summer. There was no prospect of travels with Irving, whose increasing success was keeping him in Glasgow. So Carlyle confined himself to study of German literature, his hack-work, and increasingly passionate letters to Jane, with pleas to her to write to him encoded in German postscripts her mother could not read. Jane promised (in a letter she begged him to burn, so guilty was she at deceiving her mother) that they would meet to read Schiller and Goethe to each other, but not yet.[13] Carlyle's passion for Goethe was raging, and he sat one evening and stared at the poet's portrait for hours. At least it took his mind off Jane.

In early November he went back to Edinburgh, and to the familiar business of searching for suitable lodgings, which took him most of his first weekend there. He found a backroom in a house in Jamaica Street, hoping it would be quiet. However, he was once more plagued with noise, thanks to the vast building works at the nearby Royal Circus. Nor was this all he had to endure. Shortly before being forced to quit his lodgings, he complained to Alick of the racket made by 'dog fights, cat-squallings, carpet beatings,' as well as the masons, and the coughing of a little girl nearby dying of consumption.[14] He would have to move several times before finally settling, after Christmas, in Leith Walk, which was quieter and enjoyed better air. He was about to lose Irving's companionship, however, as his friend had been invited to London effectively to audition for a job as a preacher. It was a job that would have far-reaching implications for both Irving and Carlyle.

His hack-work was making him feel more prosperous, and on his return Brewster gave him a banker's draft for fifteen guineas. Carlyle immediately sent his parents a gift of a pair of spectacles each; his father's made of silver. Jack reported that, when the gift arrived, his father had exclaimed: 'What in the name o' wonder tempit the fallow to lay out his money i' buying him sic gran' silver spectacles', but was none the less moved to tears by the gesture, which he felt was 'a kin' o' rewaird for the expence 'at his edication has cost me'.[15] Brewster had also given him a substantial project to work on, and to maintain his income, a translation of Legendre's *Elements of Geometry*.

Jane at last asked him to call on her at the end of November, where their intellectual intercourse was resumed. She was warming to him, telling him the following month that 'your attention in supplying me with so much amusement and edification deserves from me the strongest expressions of gratitude.'[16] The pressure from her neurotic mother, and Jane's own alarm at the passion shown by Carlyle, soon brought their courtship to the first of its many crises. Stealing a few moments from the maternal glare at the very end of the year, Jane wrote:

Oh Mr Carlyle how I am plagued with you! Why will you not let me live at home in peace? By what right do you extort from me promises which after sober reflection I find it as painful as imprudent and difficult to fulfil ... You say there is no harm in our correspondence and I believe it. But assuredly there is harm in disobedience and deceit, the only means through which it can at present be maintained ... What have you done to me to merit such a sacrifice? What proofs of regard have you given me, greater than I can command from every fool who comes in my way?

My friend, before you draw so largely on my gratitude do something for my sake. Render your friendship as honourable in the eyes of the world to my Father's child as it is already honourable in her own eyes to Jane Welsh and then you may exact as your due favours you have as yet no claim to ask. Oh Mr Carlyle if you wish me to admire – to love you (admiration and love is with me the same feeling) use as you ought your precious time, and the noble powers that god has given you, and waste no hours or thoughts on me – And do not laugh at fame – It is indeed a name – perhaps an empty name – but yet it is the object of no low ambition, and ambition is the crime of no low soul –

I will not write again – do not urge me least [*sic*] you wear out my patience and with it my esteem.[17]

Even though she said she would not write again, she none the less in the same paragraph asked Carlyle to send her the review of Goethe's *Faust* that he was writing for the *New Edinburgh Review*. No wonder Carlyle saw no reason not to persist with his suit.

II

In addition to the modest writing commissions he was now able to secure, Carlyle had an offer, through Irving, to become the tutor to the fifteen- and thirteen-year-old sons of an Anglo-Indian family, the Bullers. Irving had been approached by Mrs Buller, the wife of an Indian judge, after he had given a trial sermon at the Caledonian Chapel in Hatton Garden, London. She sought advice on what to do with Charles, the fifteen-year-old, who had just left Harrow and was too young to go to an English university. Irving advised her to put the youth and his brother in Carlyle's care in Edinburgh. He had no trouble selling Carlyle, of whom she had not heard, to Mrs Buller; though Irving did concede that Carlyle 'had seen little of life, and was disposed to be rather high in humour, if not well used'.[18] Having been assured by his friend that the family were pleasant, and being tempted by the impressive salary of £200 a year, he accepted for a trial period, until July. Even when offered, by Irving's future father-in-law, John Martin, the editorship and a share in the profits of a Dundee newspaper, Carlyle did not retreat, not least because his opinion of journalism was even lower than that of teaching.

He must have been a shock to this grand family. Jane wrote cruelly to her cousin Eliza Stodart that despite Carlyle's formidable mind, principles and spirit, he also had a 'want of elegance' that had led to him kicking the fire-irons on a visit to Haddington and making 'puddings in his teacup'.[19] The relationship with the Bullers was, though, happy. For the first six months, until the whole Buller family moved to Edinburgh, the boys boarded with a clergyman, and Carlyle taught them in the mornings and early evenings. He found Charles 'a most manageable, intelligent, cheery and altogether welcome and agreeable phenomenon,'[20] though found him occasionally guilty of 'levity and inattention'.[21] His younger brother Arthur was similarly pleasant, though not quite so quick-witted, partly because of slight deafness. The tutor and his pupils struck up a happy relationship, which was to last for life. Carlyle was impressed by how Charles was a far better classicist than he was. He put Charles into the Greek class at Edinburgh University, to ensure he was properly taxed.

Jane now often wrote imploring him to tone down his over-ardent protestations of friendship. He seemed incapable of doing so. She told him that 'I will be to you a true, constant and devoted *friend* – but not a Mistress – a Sister – but not a Wife – *Falling in love* and marrying like other Misses is quite out of the question – I have too little romance in my disposition ever to be in love with you or any other man; and too *much* ever to marry without love.'[22] 'Very satirical,' her suitor replied.[23] 'It was once reckoned generous, I believe, to "crush the haughty, but spare those who cannot resist": however, I do not complain.' He took the attack to her. 'In spite of the ridicule which you cast on me, or rather in part because of it, I am coming out to see you shortly.' He went in early February, and spent much of the visit reading German with Jane. His iniquities this time included scratching the fenders: 'I must have a pair of carpet-shoes and hand-cuffs prepared for him the next time,' Jane wrote to Eliza Stodart. She added that 'his tongue only should be left at liberty his other members are most fantastically awkward.'[24] Carlyle had been received coldly and formally by both mother and daughter; it was a year before he visited again, and then at the express invitation of the two women. At the time that invitation was issued, in February 1823, Jane told him that 'my Mother took it into her head when you was [*sic*] last here to dislike you with all her heart – as my regard for you increased her's seemed to diminish in an inverse ratio.'[25]

Still undeterred by his reception, he wrote to Jane 'from the heart' on 13 February 1822 saying he was a wreck as a result of his emotional trauma, and begging encouragement for his suit.[26] She found this 'the most *tasteful* Epistle I ever, in my life, received', though if this response excited Carlyle he would have been quickly disillusioned by her sarcasm. She found the letter harmonious because he was playing a tune, the same old tune he had played to her over and over again, and she was becoming rather bored with it. 'Is it possible Mr Carlyle? Can a man of your genius and learning find nothing with which to entertain a young woman of an inquisitive spirit besides these weary, weary professions of regard, and apologies for making them?'[27] Teasing him, she agreed she would let him admire her, but she would be grateful if he would, in future, do so in silence; and that was not the end of her ridicule: 'You are not my *Friend*, you are not my *Lover* – In the name of wonder, Sir what are you? – Oh! – I had forgot – "A wreck!" – "a perfect Wreck!!" – For Heaven's sake Mr Carlyle be, *if you can*, a *Man* – if not try at least to seem one.'

Initially he took offence in his reply, telling Jane he hardly saw the point of pleasantries. However, he added a postscript the following day exclaiming, 'what a fool I am! Today your letter seems an excellent letter, and you the kindest creature in the world for sending it.'[28] He was obsessed to the point of losing his critical faculty, and deeply unhappy. He begged Irving (and Irving complied against his better judgment) to write to him and explain how he saw him. Part of Irving's reply is lost, but in the part that survives he tells his friend to avoid ranting and other extremes of temperament. Otherwise, he would be deprived of the warmth of wider friendships, and female love.[29]

Whatever he told Jane about being wrecked, he continually claimed in his correspondence with his family that his health was getting better; in March, however, he told another friend he was 'not unfrequently on the verge of being sent to pot entirely, by the worst of stomachs'.[30] His literary work was progressing. His linguistic and mathematical abilities made him the ideal translator of Legendre's *Geometry* for Brewster, which occupied him during the spring of 1822. It earned him £50 which, despite the affluence he had supposedly entered into as a result of the Bullers, he claimed badly to need due to a shortage of ready money. He even asked Jack to lend him £5 or £10 'for a month or two' until the cash-flow improved.[31] Five pounds arrived promptly. His mother was still keeping him in food, clothes and other requisites, so he was hardly wanting.

After a short *froideur* with Jane in the spring of 1822 he detected some hope in what she wrote to him, and sought to make a new entreaty of a different sort. He exhorted her to use her genius to write a novel, suggesting Boadicea as a possible subject; in his role as Jane's tutor, he was sending her fiction to read, much of it French, but also the likes of Washington Irving.

She became less sarcastic, but laced her increasingly affectionate letters continually with pointed reminders about what she considered to be the appropriate form for their relationship. They exchanged poetry (mainly verse translations), a form for which he had less feel than he thought. Intellectually stifled by Legendre, Carlyle too looked for a creative project, and told Johnston he was 'fermenting some villainous cookery about the "Commonwealth-times" which in due season I hope to make the nation drink of.'[32] He had been reading Milton and works about Cromwell voraciously to develop his knowledge of the period. It was to be brought to fruition nearly a quarter of a century later.

He found time, once the days became warmer, for a sea-bathe every day in between his lessons and his work on Legendre. His contentment was such that he asked whether his experimental period with the Bullers could become a permanent arrangement. They were satisfied, and the children had a high regard for their tutor, so the matter was swiftly concluded. Carlyle regarded his situation as a not unpleasant way to earn a living until he made his name as a writer; he had finally found the sense of vocation that allowed him to decide on a career. He told his mother in June 1822:

I have also books to write, and things to say and do in this world, which few wot of. This has the air of vanity, but it is not altogether so. I consider that my Almighty Author has given me some glimmerings of superior understanding and mental gifts; and I should reckon it the worst treason against him to neglect improving & using to the very utmost of my power these his bountiful mercies.[33]

Carlyle went in early August to see his family at Mainhill, before taking up his permanent appointment with the Bullers on 7 September. He took particular care to be out of Edinburgh for George IV's visit in August, seeing the King (or, as he later said, 'whom though called and reckoned a "King" I, in my private radicalism of mind, could consider only as a – what shall I call him?'[34]) as a misbehaving aristocrat of the sort that, he would later argue, had helped undo the seams of English society. Carlyle found both Buller parents affable, though felt uncomfortable at their grand house with its 'apparatus of servants and apartments and formalities'.[35] He was impressed that they treated him as an equal, and had no 'airs'; yet it was with relief that he returned to his simple lodgings each evening, to his books and his pipe. He wrote to William Graham of the Bullers' excellence, yet added that his exposure to them had made him 'the more thankful ... that Providence did not create me "a person of quality" '.[36] It is not a pleasant facet of Carlyle's character that he should, both in his letters and in his attitude to the Bullers, show consistent ingratitude. They acted with consideration to him, in return for which, self-obsessed as he was, he usually found something of which to complain.

Later that autumn Jack, who was starting training as a doctor, came to share Carlyle's lodgings. Carlyle promised his brother, to whose company he was looking forward, that they would not get in each other's way, as Carlyle was out all day, and often until nine in the evening. He also found Jack a little teaching to do, of arithmetic to two girls, to earn him two guineas a month for sustenance.

Carlyle had sought to be allowed to visit Jane at Haddington before he had gone to Annandale, but had been forbidden. They had no contact until his return to Edinburgh in September, when he wrote begging her not to cut him off. Jane had gone to Fort Augustus with her mother, and was feeling culturally deprived; at any rate, she was glad to hear from Carlyle, and wrote to tell him so. Some of the remarks in her letters from her Highland tour will have given him cause for concern. Having first told of how she could easily have fallen in love with a handsome soldier at Fort Augustus, she wrote on her return to Haddington to tell, at great length and in some detail, of a Mr Benjamin Bell 'about six feet two – rather slender and very graceful,' whom she coyly termed 'my new friend.'[37] Carlyle would, though, have been relieved if he had managed to read to the end of this great paean to Bell, for Jane noted with obvious regret that he was off to Germany and Italy, and would be away eighteen months. None the less, Carlyle said in a letter of inordinate length to 'my beloved pupil' that he regarded Bell with the 'jealous leer malign,'[38] which should have struck home. Referring to some verses Jane had enclosed, Carlyle sarcastically continued:

Did he write these verses? If so, he seems young at the art like us, but not without powers of doing better: dactyls are always difficult to manage, and his accordingly are but a kind of flash in the pan – no damage is done; but the other piece has a sort of swaggering *pococurante* [little-caring] air about it which looks more like genius and truth, and answers greatly better. Except the last stanza, they are good. If he is only about twenty years of age or so, he may cultivate poetry with considerable hope: if nearer thirty I advise him never to write another line.

While making no progress on his projected book on the Civil War, because his work on Legendre dragged on, Carlyle was offered £150 to write a short life of Milton, with notes on his poems. He almost accepted, but it was not the book he wanted to write. Nor was it only literary openings that came his way. In November Alexander Galloway, a professor at Sandhurst and another of Brewster's contributors, alerted Carlyle to a forthcoming vacancy at the military academy for a mathematical professor. He did not reject the idea out of hand, but was concerned that it would pay him less – £180 – than he earned from the Bullers, would be less congenial, and allow him less freedom. The two eldest Buller boys were now at college, and did not require Carlyle's superintendence until the afternoon; and his only other duty was to break from that at 3.30 p.m. to dine with Reginald, the youngest brother, whom he did not teach. He asked Galloway for more information, and thought seriously enough of it to let Jane know of his possible candidature. His name eventually went forward, but in February 1823 he learned he had been unsuccessful.

Carlyle's communications with Jane were becoming warmer, so much so that in December 1822 he wrote that 'if you do not grow more cross with me soon, I shall become an entire fool. When I get one of those charming kind letters it puts me into such a humour as you cannot conceive.'[39]

III

The new year saw Carlyle in a state of customary moroseness. He observed that it was always the saddest time of year for him, for 'one thinks with pain that so many more days have passed away forever, and been marked by so very small a portion of improvement.'[40] He had, though, made a successful excursion into creative writing, and had sent Jane a copy of the tale that was to be published in 1831 as 'Cruthers and Jonson', which she read in between Rollin's *The History of the Arts and Sciences of the Ancients* and the plays of Schiller that Carlyle had set her.

'Cruthers and Jonson' is the story of two schoolfellows from Hoddam, a school Carlyle himself attended near Ecclefechan. After a particularly acrimonious fight in which Jonson is badly beaten, he returns home to fetch a gun with which he intends to shoot Cruthers. He is stopped by the dominie from doing so, and threatened with expulsion. Cruthers intervenes on his enemy's behalf, and the two become lifelong friends. Both become farmers, but one takes the Jacobite side in the rebellion of 1745, while the other keeps out of the fray. Jonson, the Jacobite, is captured in Cumberland after a last-ditch attempt at resistance and thrown into Carlisle jail. He is sentenced to be beheaded. News of his fate reaches Cruthers, who rushes to the jail to see what comfort he can bring his friend. He spends what is supposed to be Jonson's last night on Earth with him in the condemned cell. When morning comes the jailer bursts in, apparently to take Jonson to the scaffold. However, he in fact brings a reprieve from George II, who has decided that further bloodshed will serve no purpose.

Jonson keeps his life on condition that he surrenders his property and goes into exile. He sails for Jamaica where he is befriended and employed by a planter, whose beautiful daughter he marries. There is a note of wistfulness in Carlyle's tone as he recounts the ease with which Jonson's suit was accepted:

My own admiration is, how in the name of wonder Jonson ever got her wooed! I should have thought it the most hopeless task in nature. Perhaps he had a singular skill in such undertakings: at any rate he throve. The cynosure of neighbouring eyes, the apple of discord to all bachelors within many leagues – richer many of them and more showy men than Jonson – preferred Jonson to them all.[41]

Jonson's exile is lifted by George III and he returns, with his wife, to re-purchase the estate he had had to surrender. They all live happily ever after. It is a simple tale, and one feels that as a narrator Carlyle does not make the best of his material. The work is short on human insights, for which the subject gives plenty of scope, and one senses that Carlyle, lost in cerebration, had not developed a good eye for detail. It is certainly instructive to compare the narrative skill of this short story with that of *Sartor*, written seven years later. What is clear from the earlier work, though, is that Carlyle had developed a pure, unpretentious literary style, again at odds with the robust, ejaculatory diction that was to become his trademark.

Jane found the tale enjoyable, rereading it so often that she told Carlyle she could almost say it by heart. Carlyle, in the meantime, encouraged her into more challenging study, notably Gibbon and Sismondi, both of whose histories had been highly stimulating to him. He urged her, unsuccessfully, to write, suggesting either an essay on Byron (in whom they had a shared interest) or Madame de Staël. Relations between Jane and her suitor may have been improving, but those between suitor and prospective mother-in-law were strained. He solicited the right from Jane to visit her at Haddington, and she – ever more keen about such a visit – sought to propitiate her mother in order to have this allowed. Eventually, in mid-February, Jane managed to have her mother agree to a visit. 'What Generalship it has required to bring matters to this point!'[42] she told him.

A tone of affection for and intellectual dependence upon him was now creeping into Jane's letters. The visit was infinitely more successful than its predecessor. Mrs Welsh was hospitable and Jane warm to him. He took the shrewd step of propitiating the mother by seeking to interest her in some of the reading he was setting for Jane, and successfully tempted her towards French literature. He was in a state of ecstasy on his return to Edinburgh. His mind was set upon marriage, not least because, under the programme of reading he had set Jane, her mind had sharpened and expanded since he had last met her – 'almost doubled in power', he told her.[43] He sent her two volumes of Madame de Staël's *Delphine*, and promised to find a copy of the *Decameron*. He had some reservations about its 'impurities,' though added that 'I believe ladies do read the work whenever they can: Mrs Buller speaks without hesitation of having perused it in French.'[44] He led her astray into the anti-Christian (as he had found them) parts of Gibbon, and deep into Goethe, which she found difficult, but which was fast becoming her tutor's religious and philosophical underpinning.

Their intimacy grew, and he began to address her in his letters as 'My dear Jane' rather than 'My dear Friend'. He started to worry that the Bullers, who had been threatening for weeks to go to the country, would leave Edinburgh before Jane made a visit there in April, and take him with them. He became ill with anxiety and frustration. He felt he detected a moroseness of tone in Jane's letters, where once there had been flippancy. His own affliction was easily understood. It had been a bitterly cold winter, and he was sleeping especially badly. Unintentionally funny is his description, in a letter to his mother, of the lengths to which he was prepared to go to get some sleep. 'I fell upon the notable device of sleeping with my finger squeezed upon my ear, which I find to be the most effectual method of excluding sound, of any hitherto devised. It cost me many efforts to accomplish using myself to this expedient; but now I am quite trained to it, and practise it whenever any of the neighbours chooses to be noisy.'[45]

He was about to embark on his first large-scale literary project, a life of Schiller, and was overwhelmed by the enormity of the task. Irving, now making a name for himself in London, had put the idea his way, saying the London Magazine would publish it in parts if it was worthy. It did not begin auspiciously. Shortly after he had started it he branded it a 'farrago', and such was his despair that he claimed to have been on the point of burning the manuscript three times.[46] By the middle of April he was viewing it with a little more confidence, contemplating that the work would have to be in three parts. Once he finished the first he sent it to Jane, asking her to read it 'with the eye not of a friend, but of a critic'.[47] 'The thing is absolutely execrable,' he added. 'I have written as if I had been steeped in Lethe to the chin.' Looking back on it in 1867, Carlyle still regarded the book as 'nothing considerable of a work even to my own judgment, had to be steadily persisted in, as the only protection and resource in this inarticulate huge wilderness, actual and symbolical. My Editor I think was complimentary; but I knew better.'[48] He had waited with growing impatience for Jane and her mother to make their longed-for visit to Edinburgh, and they arrived at the very end of the month, three weeks before he was due to go to the country with the Bullers.

Jane's mother remained an obstacle to their activities, and this frustrated Jane as much as it did Carlyle. They were able to meet four times during the Welshes' truncated stay, and in all that time have only an hour alone. Jane told him, in a letter written after their arrival in the capital, that she had 'a thousand things to say to you which must remain unsaid as long as I am forced to cut my sentences by rule,' but raised his hopes of her mother's possible departure, alone, for Dumfries within days.[49] Carlyle urged her to occupy herself with Wilhelm Meister until they could spend time together, for he longed to discuss it with her; the idea of translating it, which was to be his next project after Schiller, was already being formed, and would be embarked upon the following winter. Their plans were thwarted yet again, though. Mrs Welsh decided that Jane must go to Dumfries with her, and there was no chance of a further meeting. 'It is impossible to say how much I am vexed,' wrote Jane.[50] Meanwhile, the Bullers were packing up to leave for Kinnaird, on the Tay in Perthshire, and Carlyle was to follow them within days. He was miserable, having planned to spend the days the Bullers had given him off entirely with Jane. There was no hope of that now, so he obtained permission from Mr Buller to go home to Mainhill for a few days before resuming his tutorial duties.

He wrote desolately to Jane, taking the brake off his intentions towards her. 'This visit of yours has been sadly marred ... I dreamed of it pleasantly for three months . . . I still keep looking forward to a glorious time, when we shall feel independent of other people's arrangements, and to be to one another all that Nature meant us to be.'[51] He bade her cheer up, and not quarrel with her mother, and ended with the imprecation: 'Forget me not, my Dearest! Farewell and love me! I am your's forever and ever.' His 'beloved Jane' no longer sought to correct his strong emotions towards her. In tracing her warming towards him, one finds in equal measure her longing for an ally against her mother, and the deep attraction Carlyle's mind held for her.

Carlyle was at Mainhill for a little over a week, and then went to Kinnaird to join the Bullers. He was housed in great comfort in a large room in another, almost empty, house on the estate the Bullers had rented. There was perfect peace all around him, interrupted only by the song of the birds and the distant sounds of the river. He fell into a routine that allowed him the afternoons and most of the evenings free to do his writing. It should have been an ideal place to rest and work, but he recalled later, in his journal, that: 'My health, in spite of my diligent riding, grew worse and worse; thoughts all wrapt in gloom, in weak dispiritment and discontent, wandering mournfully to my loved ones far away.'[52]

Jane wrote to assure him he was her best friend, and that they would be 'friends for ever', but also to tell him that she had given a local doctor, Alexander Fyffe, reason to believe she might accept a proposal of marriage. She intended no such thing, and wrote to Carlyle confessing her mistake, and seeking advice on how to extricate herself from the implicit arrangement. Carlyle told her the fault lay with Fyffe, and advised her to forget about it and him; easily done since Fyffe was now out of the country. There was obvious relief that she was not minded to accept such proposals from other men, but that was his only consolation. He claimed to be idle and unmotivated, and wrote to her that 'my life here is the most unprofitable and totally inane I ever found it. I think of little or nothing else but you; and that not like a man of sense, but like a foolish boy. I read none, I do not translate three pages of Goethe a week. Good heavens! am I growing mad?'[53]

He poured out to Jane, in the same letter, his worries and fears for the future; whether simply to unburden himself, or as a ploy to extract more sympathy from her, one cannot be sure:

I form ten thousand plans of future conduct, but each is weaker than its forerunner, each is rejected in its turn. I am also fast losing any little health I was possessed of: some days I suffer as much pain as would drive about three Lake poets down to Tartarus; but I have long been trained in a sterner school; besides by nature I am of the *Cat* genus, and like every Cat, I have nine lives. I shall not die therefore, but unless I take some prudent resolution, I shall do worse. I often think of leaving these Bullers entirely; going home to my true-hearted Mother, for a year; and then, with recovered health, fronting the hardest of the world once more. The people treat me with extreme consideration, the young men love me and are worth some love in their turn; but their way of life threatens to prove inconsistent with my very pitiful health, my employment is without vexation but it leaves my best faculties *un*employed, leisure hours must be devoted to exercise; thus I accomplish nothing, but waste the flower of my existence – in earning daily bread. Absolutely this will not and shall not do . . .

In July he negotiated a month's holiday, and went to Mainhill. After a worrying silence of three weeks he received a kind letter from Jane, who had been travelling about Scotland. She had had unpleasing members of her family inflicted on her by her mother, keeping her away from her German studies; and she wrote both to Carlyle and to Eliza Stodart telling how she had seen, on the opposite bank of a river, Benjamin Bell, who had taken her fancy a year earlier. She clearly was not as committed to Carlyle as he was to her, for she wrote to Miss Stodart that 'to have met him "*eyes to eyes, and soul to soul*," I would have swam – ay, swam across, at the risk of being dozed with water gruel for a month to come.'[54] She stated her conviction that 'something must come out of all this', based on the superstition that she had last seen Bell on her twenty-first birthday, and next saw him on her twenty-second. The conviction would have crushed Carlyle had she expressed it to him.

While at Mainhill he rode every day to improve his health, though the weather was consistently wet and cold and further depressed him. He prepared to return to Kinnaird on 17 August, and as he did so heard that Irving was about to come back from London, in order to marry Isabella Martin in Kirkcaldy in October. Boyd, the Edinburgh publisher, gave him firm encouragement to translate *Wilhelm Meister*. This propelled Carlyle to try, unsuccessfully, to step up his work to ten pages a day, settling down to his translation at six every evening, as Boyd wished to start printing in November. For the moment, he put *Schiller* to one side. He told Jane that *Meister* was a book 'I love not, which I am sure will never sell, but which I am determined to print and finish.'[55] This was at some variance with the memory he had of first reading the book two years earlier, when he wandered the Edinburgh streets on the evening he finished it thinking it 'grand, surely, harmoniously built together, far-seeing, wise and true: when, for many years, or almost in my life before, have I read such a book?'[56] Harrold, in his peerless work on the German influence on Carlyle, suggests that *Wilhelm Meister* was among the most significant books in Carlyle's intellectual development:

He sought the stimulating power of a great personality, and found it presented in Goethe himself, and its cultivation set forth in admirable detail in *Wilhelm Meister*. He had fought with the demons of skepticism and suicidal despair; and Schiller's triumph and Goethe's progress from Werther to the serenity of the *Wanderjahre* and the second part of Faust showed him that his problems had been other men's problems and had been solved.[57]

Carlyle's greatest problem was physical and spiritual loneliness, and his German books helped solve it in a way more prosaic, less profound works of

English writers could not. Not only did the ideas of Goethe and others help
him conquer his sense of isolation, they also gave him self-confidence. He
resented the intellectual limitations of translation, which gave him little scope
to use more than a small part of his mind. Irving, who had by now made a
great (but controversial) reputation as a preacher in London, had taken the
first part of *Schiller* to a publisher called Taylor, and persuaded him to bring
it out in book form. If it was a success, there would be opportunities for
Carlyle to express himself rather than others.

Jane was, as usual, the recipient of his frustrations. An especially unrestrained outpouring ('we are one heart and soul forever') at the end of
August[58] provoked her to clarify her own feelings. She said it had 'troubled'
her because 'you no longer regard me as a friend, a sister; but as one who at
some future period may be more to you than both – is it not so?'[59] Some of
the old, waspish, Jane showed through. 'Is it not true that you believe me, like
the bulk of my silly sex, incapable of entertaining a strong affection for a man
of my own age without having for it's [sic] ultimate object our union for life?'
She realised, appropriately, that the warmth she had showed him 'might
mislead you as to the nature of my sentiments', and added that she was
'startled to find our relation actually assuming the aspect of an engagement
for life'.

She admitted she loved him, but as she would have loved him had she been
his sister. She could not contemplate marriage without 'disgust' (to be fair to
Carlyle a general, and not a specific, disgust).

Your Friend I will be, your truest most devoted friend, while I breathe the breath of
life; but your wife! never never! Not though you were as rich as Croesus, as honoured
and renowned as you yet shall be.

You may think I am viewing the matter by much too seriously – taking fright where
there is noth[ing] to fear – It is well if it be so! But, suffering as I am at this very
moment from the horrid pain of seeing a true and affectionate heart near breaking
for my sake, it is not to be wondered at tho' I be overanxious for your peace on which
my own depends in a still greater degree – Write to me and reassure me – for God's
sake reassure me if you can! Your friendship at this time is almost necessary to my
existence. Yet I will resign it cost what it may – will, will resign it if it can only be
enjoyed at the risk of your future peace . . .

Carlyle took this well, to judge from his reply. 'Your letter has,' he told her,
'set me a-thinking about matters which, with my accustomed heedlessness,
I was letting take their course without accurate investigation.'[60] He even
told her that 'you have put our concerns on the very footing where I wished
them to stand,' a triumph of tact over reality. He acknowledged she would
not wed, and he told her he would not either; so, in diplomatic fashion,
he had left both their options open. Yet he protested undying love, and
begged to be readmitted to Haddington. He was not prepared to give up
easily.

IV

The Bullers were so pleased with Carlyle that they decided to stay at Kinnaird for the autumn and winter. They saw no need for Arthur to go to Germany when he could have so good a German education from his tutor in Perthshire; and Charles was as well educated as he could be at any college. Carlyle planned to have his translation of *Meister* written in time for him to have a leave of absence to oversee its printing in Edinburgh before the departure south. The plan was to go to Cornwall, where the Bullers had their seat, in the spring of 1824. Jane seemed tamed by his latest letter to her, writing back fervently 'Oh how I do love you my own Brother! I even wish Fate had designed me for your wife,'[61] hardly sentiments geared to dowse the flames of his passion. This prompted him to reply that 'my noble Jane illuminates and cheers the desolation of my thoughts as with the light of a summer's dawn' and that 'we will never part,'[62] which was effectively a return to the *status quo ante*.

Carlyle's work on *Meister* was interrupted in mid-October, when John Taylor, editor of *The London Magazine*, wrote demanding the second instalment of *Schiller* without delay, as he had imprudently printed the first without giving consideration to its successor. Taylor lauded the work, though Carlyle dismissed his praise as 'essential oil'.[63] He had another, more welcome distraction. Irving – whom Carlyle was about to visit, at the home of James Johnston, on his honeymoon – had written to Jane suggesting that both she and Carlyle should spend three months of the following summer with him and his new wife in London. Jane was ecstatic at the idea, and wrote to Carlyle that this would be 'the happiest, happiest life that my imagination hath ever conceived'. She said she and he would be 'in the same house for months! together in our occupations, together in our amusements, always together! no duties to interfere with the duty of loving each other!' For good measure she added, 'I know the noblest heart in Britain' (by which she meant Carlyle) 'loves me.'[64] She hoped he would not go to Cornwall instead. What was he to make of this blowing hot-and-cold?

He did, inevitably, write back with equal fervour, welcoming the prospect of being able to show 'you by words and deeds a thousand times a day that I loved you more than any thing beneath the sky'.[65] Indeed, Carlyle's only reservation (apart from the uncertainty of whether his obligations to the Bullers would allow him to go) seemed to be what effect prolonged exposure to Irving might have upon him. He joked that Irving seemed to suggest he would undergo 'some strange development of genius' merely by being set down on London's streets, and that if he were to have the chance to converse with Coleridge and De Quincey he would 'soon learn to speak in tongues'.[66] This was a prophetic way of putting it, for Irving's ultimate degeneration was to come after he imagined some of his congregation had received the gift of tongues, which he associated with possession by the Holy Spirit.

Carlyle finished his first draft of the second part of *Schiller* by early November, and then set about what he regarded as the depressing task of rewriting it. He made slow progress, feeling tired out after his day's teaching. Moreover, it was mid-November, and *Meister*, of which he had not done a stroke for five weeks, had to be ready within three months. He told Jane his life was 'miserable', and that he planned abandoning his work with the Bullers because of the depressing solitude of Kinnaird.[67] This remark was made in frustration that he had not enough time to finish his literary projects; the Bullers treated him exceptionally well. He thought his health might recover if he went to Annandale, but it is hard to believe he would have been any better looked after there than at Kinnaird, where the Bullers had doctors on call for him. On 21 November he completed the second part of *Schiller*, and sent it to John Taylor in London, with the most unsalesmanlike 'I am sorry to have kept you waiting for this worthless article.'[68] Despite the agonies of composition, Carlyle told Taylor he had other similar projects in mind, notably lives of Alfieri, Voltaire and Rousseau.

His letters take on, at about this time, a self-pitying tone not seen since before he met Jane. She was now writing him letters of similar hypochondriacal self-indulgence, each feeding off the other, setting a tone for their marriage. He went to Edinburgh in November to see Jack, studying medicine there. He wrote imploring to be allowed to visit Haddington, and the request was granted. It was not an entirely satisfactory occasion. He found her miserable, and this distressed him.

With the new year arrived the proofs of the second part of *Schiller*, which he found it intensely troublesome to correct. His morale, though, was helped by a note in *The Times* of the first part. He recalled in the *Reminiscences* that this notice 'I remember to have read with more pleasure ... and as the *first* public nod of approval I had ever had, than any criticism or laudation that has ever come to me since. For about two hours it had lighted in the desolations of my inner man a strange little glow of illumination: but here too, on a little reflection, I "knew better;" and the winter afternoon was not over when I saw clearly how very small this conquest was, and things were in their *statu quo* again.'[69] It was, though, the first smell of fame in a lonely and, he believed, unrecognised life, and at the time it felt good for his self-esteem. 'The natives in this Gothic district ... begin to look upon me as a youth of parts superior to what they had suspected,'[70] he told his brother Alick.

At the same time he had to write the third part of *Schiller*, and he was expected in Edinburgh on 10 February to oversee the printing of *Wilhelm Meister*, on which he had done little work now for nearly three months. He managed, though, to finish the first third by mid-January, and sent it to Boyd, his publisher. *Schiller* was causing him grave difficulties, and he was now rewriting his earlier rewritings with growing futility. The work all too clearly betrays what, in terms of Carlyle's *oeuvre*, it is: the bridge between hack-work and more considered literary endeavour, and the hurried circumstances of its composition and tortured mind of its author explain why this is so. He finally finished it in the first week of February, shortly before leaving for Edinburgh and a three-month sabbatical from the Bullers. The first part had appeared the previous October, the second in January. The last section was serialised in three parts in July, August and September 1824, and brought out as a book by Taylor in 1825.

As the start of Carlyle's *oeuvre* the work is important, but in truth the low estimate he himself had of it does not seem to have been unduly modest. It is an easy book to read, thanks to the clarity of his style. The numerous translations of Schiller's verse Carlyle made for the book are also valuable guides to how poor his idea of poetry was. His renderings are lifeless and unimaginative. The work is also distinguished from Carlyle's later biographical writings by the tone of simple reverence Carlyle adopts towards his subject. In the case of Cromwell and Frederick the Great this becomes, instead, fanatically partisan, though no less entertaining for that.

The book is not without its insights, not least into the character of Carlyle. There are similarities between the poet's rigid schooldays and Carlyle's which seem to attract the author's special sympathy. So, too, do accounts of Schiller's ill-health and the weakness of his constitution. The loving tone of Carlyle's concern for his subject suggests a lonely man reaching out for a fellow sufferer. In examining Schiller's solitude, Carlyle understands precisely the problem. He writes that 'for a man of high qualities, it is rare to find a meet companion; painful and injurious to want one. Solitude exasperates or deadens the heart, perverts or enervates the faculties; association with inferiors leads to dogmatism in thought, and self-will even in affections.'[71] When Schiller left Stuttgart, at the age of twenty-three, he was not unlike Carlyle, at more or less the same age, leaving Kirkcaldy to seek a new start:

The future was indeed sufficiently dark before him. Without patrons, connexions, or country ... without means, experience or settled purpose, it was greatly to be feared that the fight would go against him. Yet ... he was now a free man, free, however poor; and his strong soul quickened as its fetters dropped off, and gloried within him in the dim anticipation of great and far-extending enterprises.[72]

Carlyle allowed his own personality to creep in at the start of Part II, reflecting, no doubt, the pressure under which he felt at the time:

If to know wisdom were to practise it; if fame brought true dignity and peace of mind; or happiness consisted in nourishing the intellect with its appropriate food, and surrounding the imagination with ideal beauty, a literary life would be the most enviable which the lot of this world affords. But the truth is far otherwise. The Man of Letters has no immutable, all-conquering volition, more than other men; to understand and to perform are two very different things with him as with every one. His fame rarely exerts a favourable influence on his dignity of character, and never on his peace of mind: its glitter is external, for the eyes of others; within, it is but the aliment of unrest, the oil cast upon the ever-gnawing fire of ambition, quickening into fresh vehemence the blaze which stills it for a moment ... Far from being the most enviable, his way of life is perhaps, among the many modes by which an ardent mind endeavours to express its activity, the most thickly beset with suffering and degradation. Look at the biography of authors! Except the Newgate Calendar, it is the most sickening chapter in the history of man.[73]

Schiller also contains the germ of Carlyle's highly allegorical concept of the use of history. 'In the hands of the thinking writer,' he opines, 'history has always been "philosophy teaching by experience".'[74] Another seed for the future is the 'heroism' Carlyle detects in Schiller's fight to continue work while ill.[75] Perhaps because of the self-indulgence of much of the book, one never really comes to terms with Schiller, and certainly one gets scant grasp of Schiller's ideas; and of the small details of his life there is very little. In an embarrassed footnote,[76] for example, Carlyle mentions that Schiller left a widow and two children, but that he knows nothing of them. Revising the work for the People's Edition in 1872, Carlyle partly atoned for the absence of basic biographical detail by appending his own extensive translation of a work by Ernst Julius Saupe, a German schoolmaster, about Schiller's parents' household. A harsh critic of himself, however, he knew that he was still far from finding either the subject matter or the proper means to express himself as he knew he must.

V

As soon as Carlyle arrived in Edinburgh and found lodgings, in the first week of February 1824, he made efforts to see Jane. She was in town with her mother and they met, though she appears to have been in an ill-humour and the event was not a success. She wrote to him immediately, apologising, and offering 'a whole dozen of voluntary kisses at the earliest opportunity ... I assure you I never offered such liberal terms of reconciliation to mortal man before.'[77] She was now signing herself 'Yours for ever,' and her mother was sending greetings to Carlyle through her, so he had every reason to hold out expectations again following the irruption of the previous autumn.

His time was now entirely devoted to *Wilhelm Meister*, of which he tried to translate sixteen pages a day. He intended to spend the third month of his leave at Mainhill before going to meet the Bullers in London. The plan was then that Carlyle should go on to Looe in Cornwall, though he was far from sure he would want to, especially if Jane stuck to her resolve to visit the Irvings in London. Away from the calm of Perthshire he could not sleep, and had to dose himself with sleeping-draughts, which made him feel ill all day. In the evenings Jack helped him correct the sheets coming from the printer of the first part of *Meister*. In addition to his earnings from the Bullers he had made £180 from *Schiller*, with a like sum to come from *Wilhelm Meister*, so he was financially better off than at any time in his life. He was worried that the printing of *Meister* was proceeding so slowly that he would be detained in Edinburgh long after he had to be in London, but decided he would not submit to the tyranny of his printers. Rejecting an opportunity to go to Haddington, he finished his translation of the second third of *Meister* and then went to Mainhill at the end of March, slightly earlier than he had planned, to complete the work. He bade Jane endure better his absence by persisting with Goethe, whom she did not enjoy, even when reading the proofs of Carlyle's translation. Carlyle tried, without success, to make her appreciate the romanticism of his writing and especially of Goethe's characterisations. However, his persistence was beginning to bear fruit. She was becoming more and more dependent on him. When she had not heard from him because of his hard work, she wrote chiding him, claiming she was sick at heart for his neglect of her.[78]

He sent Boyd the last manuscript pages of his translation on 8 May, after six weeks' work at Mainhill. He planned to relax and visit old acquaintances, but the shock of moving from intense labour to idleness gave him a sore throat, which confined him to the farm. As soon as he was better he had to go to Edinburgh briefly to superintend the printing of these last sheets. Jane was now begging him to go to Haddington before he left for England. He eventually went at the end of May, staying for five days. They spent almost every moment together, and Carlyle left more than ever convinced that he had to marry her. He wrote her a passionate letter, for which she rebuked him, not because she did not welcome such feelings (those days were past) but because of the difficulties if her mother saw the letter. Providentially, she did not.

Carlyle returned to Edinburgh on 3 June. He was suddenly wealthier, as the £180 payment for the first edition of *Wilhelm Meister* had arrived. It was a welcome subvention: five days later he left by steam boat for his first visit to London, where he was to stay with the Irvings in Islington. Such travel was a novelty, and he reported back to his mother on the voyage down the east coast, and up the Thames. Nothing in his life had prepared him for what he saw. 'It is an astounding sight: on approaching the city, its dense masses of grim smoky buildings, its forests of masts, and the sound as of a million of hammers as if proceeding in louder and fainter notes from many-handed labour, give a strange impression of the bulk and bustle of this mighty place.'[79] He was with the Irvings for little under a fortnight, before moving with Charles Buller to lodgings on Kew Green.

He had never presumed to correspond with Goethe, but when the three volumes of his translation of *Meister* were ready he sent a set to him. He wrote that he hoped one day to meet his master, so that he might 'pour out before you, as before a father, the woes and wanderings of a heart whose mysteries you seemed so thoroughly to comprehend and could so beautifully represent.'[80] Carlyle's coming to London had brought him into contact with other literary figures. Through Irving he met Coleridge, 'the Kantean metaphysician and quondam lake poet', holding court on Highgate Hill. He found Coleridge physically unprepossessing and lazy, but with 'a good soul, full of religion and affection'.[81] However, Carlyle's judgment (to be developed to venomous lengths in his life of John Sterling[82]) was that meeting Coleridge was 'unprofitable, even tedious'. He gave him a copy of *Meister*, which the *Scotsman* and the *Examiner* had just praised ('the translator appears to have performed his task admirably'[83]), and which had caused J.G. Lockhart, in the notoriously harsh *Blackwood's*, to congratulate Carlyle on his 'very promising debut'.

London's novelty soon wore off. In little more than a fortnight Carlyle had decided it was 'unspeakable' and a 'great desart of brick', whose sheer size he could not comprehend.[84] The sight of the poverty, far worse than anything in Scotland, shocked him, and sowed the seeds of *Chartism* and *Past and Present*: 'Children were puddling in the gutters, ragged, wild and careless: it made me sad to think that most of them were breeding for the hulks and the gallows!'[85] he wrote to Alick. He took advantage of being in London to seek new opinions on his health, meeting a chemist friend of Irving's called John Badams, who promised to design a new regime for him. This advice was easier for him to take than that offered by the last doctor he had consulted in Edinburgh, who had told him to give up tobacco. 'Gave it instantly and strictly up,' Carlyle recalled. 'Found, after long months, that I might as well have ridden sixty miles in the opposite direction, and "poured my sorrows into the long hairy ear of the first jackass I came upon," as into this select medical man's.'[86]

The success of *Meister* led him to propose to Boyd that he should translate the sequel, *Wilhelm Meisters Wanderjahre*. The background against which he could do this work was in doubt, however. His arrangement with the Bullers was not working out. Charles was ready for Cambridge, and the two of them seem to have agreed in early July that there was little they could achieve together in Kew Green. Mrs Buller had also become an irritant, not least because of her desire to move around continually. Before it was settled that Charles would go to Cambridge (for which she wanted the family moved to Hertfordshire) the plan had been to go to France in October. So Carlyle and Mrs Buller met, and agreed to end the relationship. Charles tried to persuade his tutor to stay; but Carlyle was now, in a minor regard, a man of means, and in no mood to show any gratitude or loyalty. He wanted to devote himself to literature, for which calling he had received some minor acclaim, and he did not need or want the Bullers to employ him. 'Their family was ruining my mind and body,' he wrote to his mother, unfairly.[87] 'But,' he recalled, 'the question, What to do next? was not a little embarrassing, and indeed was intrinsically abstruse enough.'[88]

Not only had he no job (though he had proofs of *Schiller* to revise, and negotiated with John Taylor its publication as a book), but also nowhere to live. He left Kew, and the Irvings were glad to take him back under their roof in Islington. He was not there long. The dislike he had formed for Kew and the little drama of the end of his life with the Bullers had stimulated his hypochondria. He went to Birmingham, where Badams (himself a former martyr to dyspepsia) lived, to undergo his 'regime' for six weeks. This included wine before dinner, soft eggs, tea and gallons of castor oil, and entailed living with Badams (who, as an intelligent bachelor, was grateful for Carlyle's company, and continually told him what a 'philosopher' he was). They quickly became friends, and in the interests of Carlyle taking more exercise went on explorations of Birmingham together, on foot and on horseback. He found the town full of 'sooty artisans',[89] and was overwhelmed by the concentration of noisy manufacturing industries there.

Carlyle, once settled in with Badams, wrote to Jane to tell her how much he still depended upon her. He put the most passionate sentiments in German, as a defence against her mother. Jane was overjoyed to hear from him, not least because Mrs Welsh had just invited another potential suitor to stay at Haddington, and he had alarmed Jane by pressing his suit upon her in a vigorous, not to say over-emotional, fashion. So overwrought did the man, a Mr Gilchrist, become that he took to bed with a fever, and had a fit when the letter from Carlyle ('his favoured rival,' as Jane tactfully put it)[90] arrived. He soon dropped his idea of marrying her.

The visit to Badams made Carlyle feel much better, though whether this was because of the superiority of the regime or through a placebo effect one cannot tell. He certainly believed in Badams enough to recommend the regime to his mother, who does not appear to have needed this advice. In the last week of September he returned to London, and immediately complained of feeling ill again. He moved in with the Irvings and worked on the book of *Schiller*, planning to go back to Scotland by Christmas. He hoped for more translation work, despising the prospect of journalism, which seemed the only alternative; he regarded a man like Hazlitt who earned his living in this way as 'a miserable scrub of an author, sharking and writing articles about town,'[91] and had no desire to emulate him. He degenerated into remarkable ill-humour. Irving, who had been a better friend to him than he deserved, but who was, admittedly, becoming rather pompous, he found a bore. His baby son was 'a squeaking brat', and Irving had a sister-in-law staying who had had the effrontery to question 'in a mincing, namby-pamby tone' whether Carlyle really was as ill as he made out.

Irving sought to cheer up the ingrate by taking him with his wife and a friend, Kitty Kirkpatrick, an heiress with £50,000 and with whom Carlyle (much to Jane's distress) was much taken, on an excursion organised by Mrs Strachey, Mrs Buller's sister. They went first to Dover, which Carlyle liked, and from whose cliffs he stared each day at France. Then, in mid-October, on a whim, Carlyle, Kitty and Mrs Strachey's husband went to Paris for a fortnight, Carlyle's first trip abroad. He had failed to tell his family he was going, and the sudden interruption in correspondence from him caused his mother great distress.

Carlyle found the French decadent; they indulged in eating, gambling and generally pleasuring their senses to an extent he had not imagined before. On his way to Paris he saw the cathedral at Beauvais, which did not impress him. His first sight of Paris did: 'A huge bowl, or deepish saucer of seven miles in diameter, not a breath of smoke or dimness anywhere, every roof and dome and spire and chimney-top clearly visible, and the skylights sparkling like diamonds: I have never, since or before, seen so fine a view of a town.'[92] His subsequent experiences did not disappoint. 'Paris proved vastly entertaining to me,' he recalled.[93] He went to the Tuileries, the Louvre (where he came across King Charles X, 'a swart, slightish insipid-looking man, but with the air of a gentleman,'[94] on a progress), saw King Louis XVIII lying in state at St Denis, saw Talma in Voltaire's *Oedipe* at the Théâtre Français, and managed to spend £5 in his fortnight there. He introduced himself to the elderly Legendre, whose geometry he had translated, 'the only man of real note with whom I exchanged a few words.'[95] Legendre took him to meet other French intellectuals. As well as seeing the conventional sights, he went to the morgue to see laid out the corpse of 'an old grey-haired artisan whom misery had driven to drown himself in the river.' He told Jane, in a letter, that he regarded the dead man as 'stretched in silence and darkness forever', a hint of Carlyle's depressive religious understanding. 'I think I never felt more shocked in my life,' he observed. 'To live in Paris for a fortnight is a treat; to live in it continually would be a martyrdom.'[96]

In early November the travellers returned to London. Despite entreaties to stay with the Irvings, Carlyle chose instead to take good lodgings nearby for 16s a week. The main impediment to his staying with his friend was the infant Edward, about whom Carlyle continually complained in his letters, because of the three-month-old child's lack of consideration in keeping him awake. He also found Irving's displays of affection towards the child 'piteous to behold.'[97] What emotional or psychological defects this suggests in Carlyle we can only conjecture. Once re-established in solitude, he meditated self-pitifully upon what to do. Short of a great project, he divided his time between reading, writing letters, making translations of Schiller (he was negotiating with Brewster about translating the complete works) and taking exercise. He told Jane he had decided he had to have a house of his own, and it is clear he was coming to the point when, ignoring her earlier injunctions, he would ask her to share it. Another important consideration was the expense of board and lodging; he was now spending two guineas a week. Jane had inherited a farm in Scotland, Craigenputtock, from her father. Hearing of Carlyle's plans to strike out on his own, she hinted to him in a letter that he might move there.

His stay in London was prolonged over Christmas 1824 and into the new year. He was correcting the proofs of *Schiller*, and the slowness of the printers in providing him with them was holding him up. London was exerting an increasing fascination over him, and he spent much of his free time exploring it. In a letter to Alick he inadvertently reveals that fascination, and (in one of his finest pieces of descriptive writing) depicts a London familiar from the novels of Dickens, twenty years later:

You are packed into paltry shells of brick-houses (calculated to endure for forty years, and then fall); every door that slams in the street is audible in your most secret chamber; the necessaries of life are hawked about thro' multitudes of hands, and reach you, frequently adulterated, always at rather more than twice their cost elsewhere; people's friends must visit them by rule and measure; and when you issue from your door, you are assailed by vast shoals of quacks, and showmen, and street-sweepers, and pickpockets, and mendicants of every degree and shape, all plying in noise or silent craft their several vocations, all in their hearts like 'lions ravening for their prey'. The blackguard population of the place is the most consummately blackguard of anything I ever saw. Yet the people are in general a frank, jolly, well-living, kindly people.[98]

The literary life exerted no hold over him. He ridiculed Coleridge and De Quincey for their vice and indolence; they were all the literary life he could find. While he still recognised Irving's kindnesses to him, he no longer felt comfortable in his old friend's company. Irving had changed since marriage, not just because of his wife, but because of the way he was being unhinged by religious fanaticism. From further afield, though, Carlyle received the stimulation he needed, and, indeed, the greatest recognition he could have wanted. In mid-December a letter dated 30 October arrived from Goethe in Weimar, with two books of verse. He apologised for not having acknowledged earlier the gift Carlyle had made him of his translation of *Meister*, and thanked him for it and for the work he had done. 'It was almost like a message from Fairy-Land,' he told Jane.[99] There could be no finer proof of his feelings for her than to send her the letter from Goethe; so he did, and she was suitably overwhelmed.

VI

At the start of 1825 Carlyle was making his plans to return to Scotland, to fulfil this urge to settle down. It had to be Scotland, 'among my fellow creatures … one hates to be a *foreigner* anywhere.'[100] In this same letter, to Alick, one detects the root of the philosophy propounded fourteen years later in *Chartism*. He had come to despise Londoners because of their materialism: 'With them it is money only that can "make the mare to go." Hence Cash! cash! cash! is the everlasting cry of their souls. They are consequently very "hard characters".' He also (displaying an attitude that was drastically developed by the time of *Latter-Day Pamphlets*, a quarter of a century later) told his brother how he had been, with Elizabeth Fry ('as much like an angel

of Peace as any person I saw'), into Newgate jail, and there seen further pre-
Dickensian horrors:

But oh! the male felons! The two hundred polluted wretches, thro' whose stalls and
yards I was next carried! There were they of all climates and kinds, the Jew the Turk
the 'Christian'; from the grey villain of sixty to the blackguard boy of *eight*! Nor was
it their depravity that struck me, so much as their debasement. Most of them actually
looked like *animals*; you could see no traces of a *soul* (not even of a bad one) in their
gloating, callous, sensual countenances; they had never *thought* at all, they had only
eaten and drunk and made merry. I have seen as wicked people in the north; but it
was another and far less abominable sort of wickedness. A Scotch blackguard is very
generally a thinking reasoning person; some theory and principle of life, a Satanic
philosophy, beams from every feature of his rugged scowling countenance. Not so
here.[101]

With these horrors on his doorstep, Carlyle was certain to turn down another
offer from the Bullers, now settled at Shooter's Hill, to take Arthur Buller
under his tutelage. Moreover, he was about to put into execution the main
phase of his plan to settle down. On 9 January he wrote to Jane formally
proposing marriage. He took up her hint of the land she needed tending, and
asked why they should not both do it. 'Will you go with me, will you be my
own forever?'[102] He told her that literature, their shared love, could not sustain
them alone; but that if they were to farm, they could build a happy and
relatively comfortable existence. He told her what she knew well, that she was
frustrated and bored living with her mother, and being chased by a succession
of small-brained suitors. He exalted her, but quickly returned to earth: 'I
must . . . avoid romance; for it is an earnest practical affair we are engaged in,
and requires sense and calculation, not poetics and enthusiasm.' He may have
been trying to impress her that he was not light-headed, but that he genuinely
had a plan for her welfare. She should, perhaps, have seen in his protestations
of reality the *ernst ist das Leben* ('Life is earnest') attitude that was to serve as
his motto, and would make her life in the years ahead at times intolerable.

He set out his prospects to Jane, assuring her that many couples subsisted
on slenderer means than they would have; there would not be the style at
Craigenputtock that Jane had been used to in Haddington, but such would
be their happiness that it would not matter. He promised her that the peace
and exercise of country living would restore his health, and that he would
never 'degenerate into the wretched thing which calls itself an Author in our
Capitals, and scribbles for the sake of filthy lucre in the periodicals.' He would
stick to grand, respectable literary projects. He begged her to accept, to help
him fulfil his destiny; and then waited anxiously for her answer.

She replied almost immediately, making light of her 'joke' that he should
farm Craigenputtock; yet levity was not her pre-eminent feeling. She was
greatly perplexed by his entreaty, and realised she could no longer, with
equanimity, hold him at arm's length. So she admitted. 'I love you – I have

told you so a hundred times; and I should be the most ungrateful, and injudicious of mortals if I did not – but I am not *in love* with you – that is to say – my love for you is not a passion which overclouds my judgment ... In short, it is a love which *influences*, does not *make* the destiny of a life.'[103] Further, she set out some conditions for marriage; she would not marry if it were to leave her financially worse off, a condition Carlyle would find it hard to meet. And she added that 'I conceive it a duty which every one owes to society, not to throw up that station in it which Providence has assigned him; and having this conviction, I could not marry into a station inferior to my own.' Jane was the least pompous of letter-writers, and so it is no surprise when, in this letter, she tells Carlyle that her words had her 'mother's sanction', and had presumably been dictated to her. She gave him hope, though: 'Think of something else ... to glide over the inequality of our births and then we will talk of marrying.'

Carlyle wrote back on 20 January. He thanked her for her candour, and assured her he was not hurt or angry. This drew a waspish retort, when she answered him, that she had done nothing for him to be hurt or angry about. He reaffirmed how his prospects of happiness were entirely tied up with her, and how, with or without her, he had to change the direction of his life. Hinting heavily that such a change might be easier with her, and having told her at great length how wretched he was, he invited her to think the matter over again. He also made it clear to her that farming Craigenputtock was no joke, and that he and Alick would like to become her tenants. *Schiller* was now printed; he decided to return to Scotland.

Jane, perhaps at a slight remove from her mother, now wrote to him that 'not many months ago, I would have said it was impossible that I should ever be your wife; at present I consider this the most *probable* destiny for me; and in a year or so, perhaps, I shall consider it the only one.'[104] She explained away the discouraging tone of her earlier letter by saying it was written after a sleepless night and with a headache; but she had clearly been shocked by Carlyle's suggestion that he would go his own way without her, if necessary. 'How could I part from the only living soul that understands me?' she protested. 'I would marry you tomorrow rather.' Though no strict engagement was made, Jane regarded herself as Carlyle's fiancée from this point. 'My own Jane!' he replied. 'You *are* a noble girl!'[105]

VII

Thus, in this exchange of letters between London and Haddington, did Carlyle bring his three-and-a-half-year courtship of Jane to its crucial point. Another twenty-one months were to pass before they were married, and her eccentric acceptance of his proposal was only the start of further confusions. Jane insisted Craigenputtock could not be farmed; so Carlyle wrote to Alick to ask him to find a suitable farm for them. It was, in fact, Carlyle's father who found, at a leasehold cost of £100, a farm at Hoddam Hill, three miles from Ecclefechan and in sight of Mainhill. Carlyle did not intend to do much farming. His desire to translate Schiller's works was growing, and some booksellers, Taylor and Hessey, had offered him £100 for a life of Voltaire; and he had decided to teach himself Spanish. At the end of February he went north via Birmingham, where he underwent Badams' regime again for three weeks. He rode a lot, and Badams offered him a horse on which to ride to Scotland. Carlyle declined, going instead by coach, via Manchester and Carlisle. He stayed two months at Mainhill, until he could take possession of the farm at Hoddam on Whit Sunday. Mainhill was overcrowded, so his mother and two of his sisters came to live and work at Hoddam too. Carlyle's devotion to his family, his desire for a change, his longing for peace and quiet to restore his health and his capture of Jane all conspired to make the next year the happiest of his life; even though – or perhaps in retrospect because – he hardly saw Jane. Four years after starting the process not just of courtship, but of spiritual discovery, with the Everlasting No, Carlyle had now reached the Everlasting Yea.

An early reunion with her, though, was much on his mind. He went to Edinburgh at the beginning of April and then, when she bade him, to Haddington. He stayed but a couple of days, returning later in the month (once he had persuaded a publisher to be interested in the series of translations that would appear in 1827 as *Specimens of German Romance*) for a longer visit. Most of their time together was spent discussing German literature; little, unfortunately, the practicalities of their future. They did agree, though, that Carlyle should be relieved of the embarrassment of marrying an heiress. Jane had been left all her father's property. Her mother was dependent upon her. Later in the summer, Jane transferred ownership to her mother, to make it clear that marriage to Carlyle would not in any way affect her mother's domestic arrangements.

Carlyle was much distracted, and the business of embarking upon his translations was held up both by his longings for Jane and in the confusion and activity that preceded his move to Hoddam. By early June he was settled in, and it was quickly established with Mrs Welsh that there would be no 'impropriety' in Jane visiting Carlyle and his family there.[106] 'Your arrival in these parts promises to form a sort of epoch in our domestic history,' Carlyle told her. 'All hands are waiting for you with a sentiment compounded of terror and delight.'[107] Before she arrived, Carlyle was already sure his health and well-being had been restored. Writing to Mrs Anna Montagu, whom he had met through Irving in London, he said that 'I am happy, perhaps too happy, happier than I have been for many a year.'[108] Nor was his composure disturbed by a confession from Jane that she had once loved Irving; Jane's composure was, though, affected by his delay in replying to her letter announcing this piece of ancient history; she was beside herself with anguish lest Carlyle call off their marriage. There was, though, nothing that could shake Carlyle from his resolve, least of all this profession of something he had probably long suspected and discounted.

Jane had been expected in mid-July; by the end of August she had still not come, having to fit in with her mother's arrangements. The Carlyle family, heavily prepared, were increasingly anxious. So concerned was she at the impression her delay might be making on her future in-laws that she wrote to Carlyle's mother to confirm she would be arriving on 1 September. Even this did not go as planned. Carlyle rode out to meet her coach that evening, and she was not there. Next morning he had a note to say she was at a nearby inn, so he went to find her. She stayed at Hoddam until 19 September, 'happy, as was very evident, and making happy,' as he later recalled.[109] 'Her demeanour among us I could define as unsurpassable; spontaneously perfect. From the first moment, all embarrassment, even my Mother's as tremulous and anxious as she naturally was ... fled away without returning.' The visit was, he said, 'a clear success on all hands.' Jane met all of Carlyle's family. They did much riding about the scenes of Carlyle's idyllic childhood, and he introduced her to some of his friends. Both were sad when she had to return home, and Carlyle immediately became ill – so ill that a projected visit to Jane (who was still in Dumfriesshire, staying at Templand with her grandfather and aunt) in early October had to be postponed until later in the month. Alick Carlyle's interest in Craigenputtock was taken seriously, and he offered Jane's mother £215 a year for it – a substantial sum – but he was not the highest bidder, and failed to secure it.

Irving was in Scotland, and met Carlyle in Annan soon after Jane's departure. Irving's son, about whom Carlyle had been so vituperative, had died of whooping-cough a few days earlier at Kirkcaldy, where his wife was staying with her parents while giving birth to a daughter, nine days before the other baby's death. Carlyle was impressed with the way in which Irving had borne his loss, sustained by his belief in the gospel, a belief of a type and fervour that Carlyle felt made his friend strange, and which he could not understand. Irving had suggested to Carlyle that he seek an appointment at London University, then in its infancy.

At this point the engagement ran into some squalls. After Carlyle had left Templand, where Mrs Welsh was also staying, his future mother-in-law (who Jane felt had been waiting to get this off her chest for weeks, as she prepared for the day when she would lose her daughter) denounced him to Jane. She felt Carlyle had 'bewitched and poisoned'[110] Jane's mind. Jane fought back, reminding her mother that Carlyle would, with her consent, become her son-in-law. After a day-long sulk Mrs Welsh wrote to her daughter telling her she had lost her sense of duty, and that she had only agreed to her marrying Carlyle once Carlyle had made a name for himself. What she had seen of Carlyle since then had not caused her to like him more. Jane had told her mother she was going to marry Carlyle, and all future complaints could be made in that certain knowledge. Her fiancé was not especially perplexed.

'Her views of me and my connection with you I cannot greatly blame; they coincide too nearly with my own.'[111]

Now settled in and enjoying isolation at Hoddam, Carlyle's thoughts turned once more to his career. He continued to read German with a view to translating it, and was anxious to embark on the sequel to *Wilhelm Meister*, the *Wanderjahre*. Translating filled the winter months for him, but he looked for the inspiration to write an original work of his own. On 4 December he turned thirty, and planned to go to Edinburgh to see Tait, his publisher, and, perhaps, Jane; but he became more and more reluctant to leave Hoddam, and it was the New Year before he travelled. He took with him the first of his completed translations for Tait, but did not see Jane. Her mother's state of mind would not have made such a trip tactful. Instead, Carlyle wrote that 'we must take up house, Jane, at no distant date in some way or other!'[112] Yet he was not sure where that house would be. His return to Edinburgh had been miserable, since the unfamiliar noise had stopped him sleeping. He had looked in Morningside, then as now a genteel suburb, and thought of taking a house there. However, marrying Jane was now becoming more urgent to him than achieving domestic perfection in other, more material, regards. 'Who knows,' he wrote to her on 21 January 1826, 'but by this time twelve-month we may be married!' After nearly five years of courtship, his wish was, indeed, to be realised in that time, but not without further difficulties – even though Jane and her mother had more or less made up their quarrel.

Carlyle returned to Hoddam in early February to find his family perplexed. Both properties – Hoddam and Mainhill – were in doubt because of troubles with landlords. Carlyle's father had, however, found another farm at Scots-brig, nearby, and was negotiating for the lease. The plan was to merge both establishments, but the new menage could scarcely accommodate a newly married couple too. Since Jane had rejected the idea of their living at Craig-enputtock, another option had to be decided upon. Both of them became miserable at the apparent hopelessness of their situation, and Jane compounded things by reminding Carlyle, in a letter of 16 March, that her mother (no helpless old lady, but still in her forties) was 'looking forward to my marriage with a more tranquil mind, in the hope that our separation is to be in a great measure nominal, that by living wheresoever my Husband lives she may at least have every moment of my society which he can spare.'[113] She ruled out going to Annandale for this reason, but asked Carlyle to consider coming to live in Edinburgh with her and Mrs Welsh. 'My mother would like you,' said Jane, hopefully. 'Oh assuredly she would if you came to live with her as her son.' Carlyle was not having it. 'Your plan is bright as the May Morn on one side: but (alas for the conjunction!) there are many buts.'[114] He did not say no at this time, because he was thinking of a painless way of letting her down, or hoping that she would change her mind.

He applied himself to his work more assiduously than for months. He translated *Wilhelm Meisters Wanderjahre* ('The Trampship' as he called it) and wrote a short biographical essay on Goethe as an introduction to it. Carlyle's father took the lease on Scotsbrig, leaving it to Carlyle for his use until the lease on Mainhill expired in May 1827. The house at Scotsbrig needed almost complete rebuilding, so there was little scope for taking Jane there as his bride and hoping to find somewhere else before the family had to move in from Mainhill. This, though, was not how Carlyle saw it. He tried to persuade her that the joy of living with him in Annandale would more than compensate for the physical privations she would have to endure; then they might leave for Edinburgh in the spring of 1827. 'I had taken no distinct account of your Mother,' he admitted. 'I merely remembered the text of Scripture: "Thou shalt leave father and mother, and cleave unto thy husband, and thy desire shall be towards him all the days of thy life".'[115] He thought her mother might come to Dumfriesshire and spend time with Jane's grandfather at Templand, so as to be nearer. He dressed up these robust sentiments in paragraphs of flattery about Mrs Welsh. His gamble paid off.

Jane wrote back that 'you and I are *soon* to be the happiest pair of people in all Annandale!' Mrs Welsh had agreed to let Jane marry Carlyle in his existing circumstances, and to live in Annandale; and she would, indeed, move to Templand, 'and visit us often as may be.'[116] Mrs Welsh herself appended a conciliatory note to the letter. Carlyle was sufficiently elated by the news to write on 14 April to Jack, now a doctor in Edinburgh, that he expected to be married that summer. However, trouble intervened again. The sitting tenant at Scotsbrig was reluctant to leave; and, in any case, Carlyle's parents (whom he had not hitherto thought to consult) said they doubted the efficacy of Jane moving into Scotsbrig. He was also horrified at the prospect of Jane's mother coming to visit them there in what would be the rudest of surroundings and the barest of comforts; and there was also a class problem. 'It would astonish her to see this same household. O No my Darling! Your mother must not visit mine!'[117] Mrs Welsh offered to furnish a house for the bridal couple in Edinburgh, but Carlyle turned the offer down, not just out of pride, but for the practical reason that by that time in the year, not long before Whitsunday, only the dross of houses was left untaken. Also, he was too poor to support them in Edinburgh; Annandale was affordable. So they were back without a plan, and he asked Jane to meet him in Edinburgh to discuss what to do. He told her he would live almost anywhere, so long as it was quiet.

She had no solution to offer. She suggested that, if money were a problem, the match could be postponed. Carlyle planned to go to see her at Haddington, for he was expecting a large parcel of books from Germany that he might have to collect from Edinburgh; but they were sent on to Ecclefechan, and since they provided him with eight weeks' work of reading, selection and translation he had no excuse to go on travels. He was quick, however, to dismiss Jane's suggestion of postponement. His next plan was that the Welshes' family home at Haddington, which was to be empty once Mrs Welsh went to Templand, could be lent to the married couple for a year while they sorted themselves out. He asked her to decide whether she would rather have him as her husband quickly, or pass up the idea of living with him at Haddington. Jane was horrified at the idea. 'To imagine for a moment I would not live anywhere on earth rather than in this vile Haddington! What a surprising *inhuman* scheme!'[118] The only other option, if it were possible, would be finding a cheap house in Edinburgh.

Prompted by this suggestion, Mrs Welsh took immediate action; she rented, for Carlyle and Jane, a house at 21 Comely Bank, Edinburgh. It had a rural aspect, overlooking fields, while being a short walk from the town; and it was relatively quiet. Mrs Welsh offered to pay the rent of £32 a year, but Carlyle, despite Jane's insistence that they accept this help, would have none of it. Haddington was not an option; in order to provide some money for Mrs Welsh, the house there was to be sold, and indeed was sold at the end of May. At about the same time Carlyle moved into Scotsbrig, which he found to his liking; it was to be the last chapter of his life as a single man. Once there, his marital home in Edinburgh now settled, he and Jane began to contemplate the ceremony itself. 'I agree with you in heartily recoiling from it,' he told her in the middle of June 1826. 'Pity indeed that we could not both fall asleep, and awaken married in each others arms! It would be infinitely finer and far less trouble.'[119] She replied that 'this marriage, I find, is like death',[120] so at least they were at one. They agreed on October as the date of their match.

Carlyle continued to divert himself from these horrors with his translations, of which he sought to do ten pages a day. He would look back on these times as 'a pleasant, diligent and interesting summer; all my loved kindred about me for the last time, hottest and droughtiest summer I have ever seen.'[121] Throughout July he was buried in Richter, not only earning a living but also broadening his knowledge of German literature, and its influence on his thought. By early August proofs of *German Romance* began to come from Tait, his publisher, in Edinburgh, and these occupied him for much of that month, while Jane and her mother were preparing the house at Comely Bank.

The women then went to Templand, where Carlyle visited in early September to discuss final arrangements. The banns were read – or 'proclaimed', as the Scottish custom has it – shortly afterwards. He went to Dumfries to have a new suit made, and attempted to chase his publisher for £200 with which to start married life; but Tait had gone to London, and the best Carlyle could do was, with great reluctance, borrow £50 from Alick. The wedding was to take place at Templand, and Carlyle had to plan the journey from there to Edinburgh after the ceremony. He thought they might travel there in a stagecoach with Jack, but Jane squashed that suggestion; they would hire a chaise, and Jack would make his own arrangements. The bridegroom gave in on all points; otherwise, the faint air of dread risked blowing up into one of grave irritation and anger. Carlyle warned Jane, a fortnight before the day, that 'we take this impending ceremony far too much to heart. Bless me, have not many people been married before now?'[122] She calmed down somewhat, and in a letter to her aunt a week before the wedding gave a positive estimate of the man for whom she was going through this ordeal: 'Not a great man according to the most common sense of the word, but truly great in its natural, proper sense – a scholar, a poet, a philosopher, a wise and noble man, one who holds his patent of nobility from Almighty God ... Will you like him? no matter whether you do or not – since I like him in the deepest part of my soul.'[123]

If this was how Jane saw it – the acquisition, at the age of twenty-five, of a fine man as her husband – for Carlyle the match had more profound implications. In notes on her letters of this period, made forty years later, he gave his view of what it meant, a view analogous with the end of the Everlasting No of *Sartor*:

A grand and *ever*-joyful victory getting itself achieved at last! The final chaining-down, and trampling home, 'for good', home into their caves forever, of all my *Spiritual Dragons*, which had wrought me such woe and, for a decade past, had made my life black and bitter ... I found it to be, essentially, what Methodist people call their 'Conversion', the deliverance of their soul from the Devil and the Pit ... and there burnt, accordingly, a sacred flame of joy in me, silent in my inmost being, as of one henceforth superior to Fate, able to look down on its stupid injuries with pardon and contempt, almost with a kind of thanks and pity. This 'holy joy', of which I kept silence, lasted sensibly in me for several years, in blessed counterpoise to sufferings and discouragements enough.[124]

They were married at Templand on 17 October in a quiet ceremony, with just Jack there to support Carlyle; they had come up from Scotsbrig the previous evening, and stayed at an inn. The bridal couple drove off in the hired chaise after a wedding breakfast, and arrived at Comely Bank that evening to begin their married life.

4

Marriage and Retreat

1826–29

IT HAS BEEN ASSUMED that the central fact about Carlyle's marriage to Jane Baillie Welsh was that it was not consummated. We do not know the truth. They had no children, at best circumstantial evidence. In his *apologia pro libro suo*, Froude wrote that Carlyle had intended no biography of him should be written because 'there was a secret connected with him unknown to his closest friends, that no one knew and no-one would know it, and that without a knowledge of it no true biography of him was possible.'[1] He never told Froude his secret. Geraldine Jewsbury, who became Jane's most confidential friend, was told something; delicacy did not prevent her from telling Froude there had been a problem, though it did prevent her from telling him precisely what it was. 'When she heard that Carlyle had selected me to write his biography,' he wrote, 'she came to me to say that she had something to tell me which I ought to know. I must have learnt that the state of things had been most unsatisfactory; the explanation of the whole of it was that "Carlyle was one of those persons who ought never to have married".'[2] It may have been the case, or it may have been Froude choosing a suitable euphemism for the problems of Jane's sexual frustrations, when he adds that 'she had longed for children, and children were denied to her. This had been at the bottom of all the quarrels and all the unhappiness.' Froude had supposed the Carlyles had agreed not to have children because, by the time they were wealthy enough to support a family in comfort, Jane was past child-bearing. Geraldine made it clear to Froude that this was not so and that 'Mrs Carlyle never forgave the injury which she believed herself to have received. She had often resolved to leave Carlyle. He, of course, always admitted that she was at liberty to go if she pleased.'[3]

Froude, in his little book, makes plain his belief that Carlyle was impotent. He cites as evidence the tale of the morning after their long-awaited wedding when Carlyle 'tore to pieces the flower garden at Comely Bank in a fit of ungovernable fury'. There is no evidence that Carlyle, nearly thirty-one when he married, had had any sexual experience; but equally there is no evidence that he had not. Froude says the wrecking of the flower garden 'shows that

Carlyle did not know when he married what his constitution was.'[4] Certainly Carlyle's extensive courtship correspondence with Jane gives no hint of carnal interest or longings on his part, but then it would not have been considered proper to do so. But it cannot even be detected latently; what he most wanted was intellectual and spiritual companionship, someone to appease his fear of loneliness, someone to be with him to give his life meaning. Sexual relations do not appear to have played much of a part in his plans, which perhaps explains the shock of what happened. Froude did not imagine he had mis-understood this point. 'It is as certain as anything human can be certain that what she related to me was what Mrs Carlyle had related to her, and to all who knew Mrs Carlyle that is evidence enough.'[5] Less reliable was the testimony of Frank Harris, who alleged that in 1876 he had walked with Carlyle to the spot in Hyde Park where Jane had died, and Carlyle had taken off his hat in the rain and bowed his head in penance. Hugh Kingsmill, Harris's biographer, reported that Carlyle 'had never, he confessed to Harris, consummated his marriage. The body part, he pleaded, seemed so little to him.'[6] Harris further claimed that Carlyle proved inconsolable on this point, and stood crying, again and again, 'ma puir girlie!' When Harris, in 1911, published his account of this touching scene he was critically crucified, with some justification; much of Harris's recollections on other matters read as the work of an over-active, sensationalist imagination, and there is no reason to suspect his memories of Carlyle are any different. Certainly, there is no good reason why Carlyle should have opened up to a casual acquaintance like Harris about his intimate problems when better-known, and more trusted friends were told nothing.

Alexander Carlyle, the sage's nephew, dubiously claimed (in one of his many efforts to discredit Froude) to have found evidence of sexual relations. A letter written at the end of the fifth year of Carlyle and Jane's marriage, on 14 September 1831 when Carlyle was in London trying to find a publisher for *Sartor*, includes the imploration to Jane to 'take every care of thyself ... there is more than thy own that thou carriest with thee.' As the editors of the letters point out,[7] Alexander Carlyle interprets this in his attack on Froude as proving a belief by Carlyle and Jane that she was pregnant; something they could hardly have imagined if they were not having sexual relations. To support him there were family memories of Jane packing baby clothes, and baby clothes were found in her drawer at Cheyne Row after her death. Nothing else in the *Letters* or *Reminiscences* substantiates the view that she might have been pregnant. Dr Halliday, in *Mr Carlyle – My Patient*, takes advantage of post-Freudian techniques to surmise from Carlyle's writings that he was anally fixated, homosexually inclined (notably in his relations with Irving), had married someone who by looks and disposition was sexually ambiguous, and was a sado-masochist. The psychiatrically unqualified must draw their own conclusions. Wilson, in his assault on Froude, concludes from a little poem sent to Jeffrey by Jane that Jane was physiologically prevented from having children; but the poem could just as easily be interpreted, by one not partial to Carlyle, as hinting at his impotence. The stanza Wilson quotes reads:

> God speed thee, pretty bird; may thy small nest
> With little ones all in good time be blest.
>   I love thee much;
> For well thou managest that life of thine,
> While I; Oh, ask not what I do with mine!
>   Would I were such![8]

Despite the gloomy report Froude gives of the start of the marriage, Carlyle wrote in good enough spirits to his mother, on the day after he wrecked the flower garden, to tell her that while still 'dreadfully confused' he also felt 'far happier than I have ever been.'[9] He admitted he had been 'sullen' the day after his wedding, 'sick with sleeplessness, quite nervous, *billus*, splenetic.' They had made basic domestic arrangements. Carlyle would give Jane two pound notes each Saturday, with which she would keep his house. As Geraldine Jewsbury notes, in the reminiscences of Jane that provoked Carlyle's own, 'until she married she had never minded household things; but she took them up when necessary, and accomplished them as she accomplished everything else she undertook, well and gracefully.'[10] Marriage brings responsibilities to both parties; but to Jane it brought not just responsibility, but the squashing out of some of her individuality, subjugating herself to the austere regime of her husband.

After a week of marriage he wrote to Jack that he was still 'tinged with gloom'[11] about his new state, mainly through lack of sleep. There is a sadder undertone to the letter. Carlyle begged Jack to come to see him that he might talk to Jack 'about many things, *ut cum fratre, ut cum medico*' – as a brother and as a doctor. It might be wrong to conclude that this was to discuss sexual difficulties; Carlyle stresses in the same letter that (perhaps as a result of these anxieties) his dyspepsia had made a fearful return; and he had also given up tobacco, which had further worsened his temper. For the first few weeks of their marriage Jane had to put up with his constant hypochondria, which, so Carlyle says, she bore cheerfully – 'the best of all wives: I declare I am astonished at the affection she bears me.'[12] He amused himself with reading, writing and walking, and before long there were notes creeping into his letters of greater spiritual satisfaction, once the upheaval of the change had been overcome. In letters to his family he is full of praise for his wife, and reports improved health by the end of the year. He was, later, to look back on the first months at Comely Bank as the happiest of his married life.

He was finishing his *German Romance* for the press, and sending off to Germany for more books and literary reviews. It was still not clear when they would be published, for the book trade had been hit severely by the economic recession, and Tait was waiting for better times. Carlyle was still longing to write a book of his own, and by the end of 1826 had started to contemplate his unfinished and, until after his death, unpublished autobiographical novel *Wotton Reinfred*. He knew, though, that while the economic conditions were so bad he would struggle to make a living by his pen, particularly with a fiction so deficient in imagination, so badly constructed and so poorly written as *Wotton* ('an isolated man ... amused only by studies of philosophy and literature'[13]) turned out to be. He remained proud; when, at Christmas 1826, his mother-in-law sent them £60, he sent it straight back, noting the kindness of her gesture. Provisions were sent, and gratefully received, from Scotsbrig, however; and Jane was becoming a good cook, making the most of the ingredients donated by her husband's family. Carlyle had fewer scruples about accepting help from his kin, because he had helped them in the lean times, and had been largely responsible for Jack's being able to complete his medical studies.

Living in Edinburgh brought its own diversions. The Carlyles entertained often, usually at tea-time, and soon had met the cream of Edinburgh literary society. 'We give no dinners and take none,' Carlyle wrote to Alick in February 1827. 'Only to some three or four chosen people we give notice that on Wednesday nights, we shall *always* be at home, and glad if they will call and talk for two hours with no other entertainment but a cordial welcome and a cup of innocent tea.'[14] However, it was through one of the friends he had met in London, Bryan Procter, that he made the most important Edinburgh literary connection. Procter gave him a letter of introduction to Francis Jeffrey, the great advocate whom Carlyle had watched and admired while a student fifteen years before. Jeffrey was now running the *Edinburgh Review*. Carlyle, who had stopped thinking about *Wotton Reinfred* and had started writing it at the end of January, held on to the letter until he felt the time was right to meet Jeffrey. In the *Reminiscences* he claimed that 'nobody except Jeffrey seemed to either of us a valuable acquisition'[15] of all the people they met in Edinburgh in the early months of their marriage, though he had wished to know John Wilson – the reviewer 'Christopher North' – better, 'but he would not let me try.'

In February the *German Romance* was at last issued, and Carlyle waited to see whether it attracted any favourable attention. Once his book came out he delivered Procter's letter to Jeffrey at the advocate's house in George Street, and met with a kind reception. Jeffrey spent twenty minutes kindly cross-examining Carlyle about his writings, and concluded with the exclamation 'we must give you a lift!'[16] Yet Carlyle did not, even after this pleasant meeting, hold out much hope of Jeffrey having time for him: 'I am sorry the man is so immersed in Law,' he wrote to his mother. 'Otherwise, we might even become friends.'[17] Deeply grateful that Jeffrey should want to help, Carlyle none the less displayed admirable reserve. He did not jump at Jeffrey's offer to introduce him to Sir Walter Scott, and others in the Pantheon of Scots literature whom Carlyle might want to know. When Jeffrey offered him a chance to write for the *Review*, Carlyle bade him read the *German Romance* first, to see what sort of writer he was; no one could accuse him of being pushy. Luckily, the first notices were impressed with the work of the translator and his choice of translations. Sensing that his new discovery was somewhat shy, Jeffrey made a point of returning Carlyle's call quickly, presenting himself on one of the Wednesday evenings at Comely Bank. 'The intimacy rapidly increased,' Carlyle remembered. 'He was much taken with my little Jeannie, as he well might be.'[18] Before long the Carlyles and Jeffreys were firm friends, and they would on Sundays go walking together in the woods on the shores of the Forth.

As well as commending him to Jeffrey, this reputation that Carlyle was acquiring caused another firm of publishers, Hunt and Clarke of London, to react positively to a suggestion that he should translate Goethe's memoirs, of which three volumes had appeared between 1812 and 1814; however, again because of the economic conditions, they suggested a decision to start be postponed a few months. Thus the problem of a substantial project to occupy – and pay – Carlyle was still not solved. He stuck to writing his novel in the mornings, giving the work in progress to Jane to read each afternoon while he went out for his walk. A pattern was set that would last for much of their married life, and reach its nadir during the writing of *Frederick*: Carlyle, despite his longing for the companionship of marriage, was already subjecting Jane to periods of numbing solitude and neglect.

As the Carlyles' economic prospects showed no sign of improving, so the idea of Craigenputtock was raised again. Although their life in Edinburgh had been interesting, Carlyle longed for the country, and felt the farm could be made to pay. He wrote at the end of March 1827 to Alick, asking whether he would come in on the enterprise with them. Alick was interested, and in April Carlyle made his first journey away from Jane to go with Alick to see the farm. The tenant, one Blacklock, was making no money and paying no rent, a situation Carlyle felt he and his brother could reverse because of the complete lack of talent of the tenant. If Blacklock did not pay his rent he could be evicted, and Carlyle felt this would be the best outcome. His mother-in-law, by Jane's decree *chatelaine* of the estate, agreed, saying that Blacklock deserved 'no mercy – far less delicacy.'[19] He received none, being victim to a whole day of hard bargaining with the Carlyle brothers, after which a rent was exacted, along with a promise to be out of the farm by Whitsunday. Carlyle was delighted to have made the deal. 'O Jeanie!' he wrote to his wife. 'How happy we shall be in this Craig o' Putto!'[20] A year, though, would elapse before they went to live on the farm.

Before he had left Edinburgh Carlyle had sent Goethe copies of his *Life of Schiller* and *German Romance*, in the last of the four volumes of which was the translation of *Wilhelm Meisters Wanderjahre*. He told Goethe of how his translations had secured for his master a wider public in Britain, and was sufficiently forward to enclose some domestic news, about his marriage, on the grounds that 'my young wife, who sympathises with me in most things, agrees also in my admiration of you.'[21] Such was her admiration that she had made Goethe a purse, 'the work, I can testify, of dainty fingers and true love' which Carlyle also enclosed. Within a month Goethe briefly acknowledged the letter and its appendages, inflaming the Carlyles' excitement by announcing that a longer letter, and a packet, would be dispatched in due course.

Despite planning to go on the land, Carlyle's mind was not entirely closed to other possibilities. In a postscript to a letter of May 1827 to Henry Crabb Robinson, a founder of University College London, Carlyle noted he had seen advertisements in the papers for professors, and wondered whether such a post, either in moral philosophy or rhetoric, might be suitable for him. Irving tried to dissuade him, mainly on the grounds that the university had an insufficiently strong religious basis. Carlyle was becoming wary of Irving, but wrote to Jack that 'I do honestly believe there is much worth among his failings, much precious truth among all this cant.'[22]

II

Carlyle now took another crucial step in his career, succeeding in publishing his own thoughts rather than translating those of others. Jeffrey asked him to write an article on Jean Paul Richter for the *Edinburgh Review*, which he set to at the beginning of June, while Jane was intensifying her own study of German. It meant that *Wotton Reinfred*, for which Carlyle's enthusiasm was in any case waning, was put to one side. Jeffrey started to call on the Carlyles at Comely Bank, and became especially fond of Jane. He asked Carlyle to write another, more substantial piece to follow his work on Richter, an article entitled 'The State of German Literature'.

Shortly after Carlyle had finished his first article the promised packet arrived from Goethe. It included Goethe's poems in five volumes, two other books, two medals (one of Goethe, the other of his parents), and a wrought-iron necklace with a gold likeness of Goethe in it for Jane. Still more important for Carlyle, the covering letter included high praise from his hero for the *Life of Schiller* ('the accurate insight into the character and distinguished merit of this man, which you have thus acquired is really admirable, and so clear and just as was hardly to have been expected from a foreigner'[23]), and for Carlyle's critical faculty in *German Romance*. Nor did this appear simply to be Goethe flattering an admirer. David Masson quoted this passage of contemporaneous comment in his *Carlyle Personally*:

'It is admirable in Carlyle,' said Goethe to Eckermann [his assistant and friend] in July of that year, 'that in his judgments of our German authors he has especially in view the mental and moral core as that which is really influential. Carlyle is a moral force of great importance; there is in him much for the future, and we cannot foresee what he will produce and effect.' Goethe here struck the keynote. It was the depth and strength of the moral element in Carlyle's constitution that was to impart to his literary career its extraordinary importance and its special character of originality.[24]

Goethe also told Carlyle in his letter that a translator was 'a prophet to his people,'[25] a remark whose import may be judged from Carlyle's subsequent sense of mission; in what he said to Eckermann Goethe may have seen this, certainly in identifying Carlyle as a 'moral force'. Carlyle wrote back in gushing tones to thank his master for the gifts, and, in response to a polite enquiry from Goethe about his past, Carlyle provided a rare moment of spiritual autobiography:

Your works have been a mirror to me; unasked and unhoped for, your wisdom has counselled me; and so peace and health of soul have visited me from afar. For I was once an Unbeliever, not in Religion only, but in all the Mercy and Beauty of which it is the symbol; storm-tossed in my own imaginations; a man divided from men; exasperated, wretched, driven almost to despair ... But now, thank Heaven, all this is altered; without change of external circumstances, solely by the new light which rose upon me, I attained to new thoughts, and a composure which I should once have considered as impossible.[26]

Jeffrey was not entirely uncritical of Carlyle's first effort for him, but praised him highly too, telling Carlyle he was 'a man of genius.'[27] Like all of Carlyle's early writing, 'Richter' is most remarkable for the clarity and simplicity of his style in comparison with his later work. It shows, too, a rigorous literary critical faculty, though little intuitive thought or great insight. The lack of these qualities may explain why Carlyle found Jeffrey a little reserved about the piece. In any case, the slight coolness ensured that Carlyle tried harder with his next commission, 'The State of German Literature'. 'Richter' does give clues, however, to students of Carlyle about its author's development. Carlyle says of Richter's philosophy that 'it springs not from the forum or the laboratory, but from the depths of the human spirit; and yields as its fairest product a noble system of Morality, and the firmest conviction of Religion.'[28] He adds:

Independently of all dogmas, nay, perhaps in spite of many, Richter is, in the highest sense of the word, religious. A reverence, not a self-interested fear, but a noble reverence for the spirit of all goodness, forms the crown and glory of his culture. The fiery elements of his nature have been purified under holy influences, and chastened by a principle of mercy and humility into peace and well-doing. An intense and continual faith in man's immortality and native grandeur accompanies him; from amid the vortices of life he looks up to a heavenly loadstar; the solution of what is visible and transient, he finds in what is invisible and eternal. He has doubted, yet he believes. 'When, in your last hour,' says he, 'when in your last hour (think of this), all faculty in the broken spirit shall fade away and die into inanity, – imagination, thought, effort, enjoyment, – then at last will the night-flower of Belief alone continue blooming, and refresh with its perfumes in the last darkness.'[29]

This passage begins to answer the questions about the influence of German thought upon Carlyle, for the sentiments could just as validly have been expressed about his own religious outlook. Harrold, in his definitive book on this aspect of Carlyle, noted that 'Richter ... supplied the memorable image, the impassioned tone, which was necessary for Carlyle's acceptance of any abstraction.'[30]

After almost a year of marriage, in which Carlyle had done little remunerative work, money was becoming very short. There was an element of farce in this. He had to write, in heartbreaking fashion (for he always wanted to give what help he could to his family), to Jack to tell him that he could not find £7 Jack needed to help him further his medical studies in Munich, because Jeffrey had given him a banker's draft without telling him which bank it was to be presented to: and Jeffrey had gone away. Carlyle waited to hear whether London University would offer him a trial, which he was prepared to embark upon despite Irving. The rhetoric chair to which he had originally aspired was no longer in prospect, and of the two that were – English literature and moral philosophy – Carlyle aspired to the latter. He sought a reference from Dr Henry Duncan, a minister at Ruthwell, whom Carlyle had known for more than a decade through university friends. Duncan agreed to recommend Carlyle for the moral philosophy post provided the religious base of the morality being taught was Christianity. This provoked a letter from Carlyle to Duncan, unfortunately lost, which the recipient found 'heart-moving and most embarrassing,' and which forced him to conclude that Carlyle's Christianity 'is not the Christianity of the Bible, nor, I trust, of the 19th Century.'[31] Therefore Duncan could not push Carlyle for the post, and the Carlyles began to contemplate more seriously the plan to move to Craigenputtock with Alick. It was not the end, however, of his attempt to secure the professorship. He asked Jeffrey to intercede with Lord Brougham, the Chancellor of the University, but this was not successful. Jeffrey said he had not liked to press Brougham on the matter until Brougham had come better to know Carlyle's writings, so Carlyle sent him the as yet unpublished paper on German literature. It was to no avail. Jeffrey did not succeed with Brougham (not that he seems to have tried very hard), and the moral philosophy chair was not immediately filled.

By mid-October 1827 Carlyle had written 'The State of German Literature'. As with his previous article it was unexceptional, an erudite review of two books on this subject just arrived from Germany, though published between 1819 and 1824. Carlyle criticises the author of both works, Franz Horn, for his 'affected style,'[32] which should amuse those who recall the development of Carlyle himself. There are, too, some hints of themes to be more broadly examined in his own writings. In pleading with his readers not to hold poverty against a poet he exclaims: 'God forbid that the time should ever come when he too shall esteem riches as the synonym of good! The spirit of Mammon has a wide empire; but it cannot, and must not, be worshipped as the Holy of Holies.'[33] This is a seed of the idea of the 'cash nexus,' though it echoes the lack of materialism and willingness to make sacrifices that had characterised Carlyle's own upbringing and family life. Perhaps more significantly, bearing in mind his own subsequent assumption of the mantle of prophet, he quotes approvingly Fichte's notion of the 'Divine Idea' pervading the visible universe (close, again, to his own conception of religion). Carlyle, never more clearly defining the new 'secular priesthood' of the man of letters, writes that:

To the mass of men this Divine Idea of the world lies hidden: yet to discern it, to seize it, and live wholly in it, is the condition of all genuine virtue, knowledge, freedom; and the end, therefore of all spiritual effort in every age. Literary Men are the appointed interpreters of this Divine Idea; a perpetual priesthood, we might say, standing forth, generation after generation, as the dispensers and living types of God's everlasting wisdom, to show it in their writings and actions, in such particular form as their own particular times require it in.[34]

That work completed, Carlyle embarked on the 'Life and Writings of Werner', for the *Foreign Review*, for which he was paid £47. Its editor, William Fraser, had written to him in September inviting him to contribute, following a recommendation by Procter. This absorbed him as autumn became winter, and both he and Jane, after a happy first year of marriage, subsided into ill-health. There were consolations, though, in the reactions to 'The State of German Literature'. De Quincey, the opium abuser whom Carlyle (following a brief acquaintance in London) ridiculed whenever the opportunity arose, had given it a favourable review in the *Saturday Post*, and it received other good notices. Shortly afterwards De Quincey called on the Carlyles in Edinburgh, bringing his two children with him and staying until midnight. He inspired some pity in Carlyle, who lent him Richter's autobiography, recently sent to him from Hamburg.

Carlyle's mother and sister Jean came to Comely Bank to stay during December, and Carlyle, fighting a sore throat, showed Mrs Carlyle the sights of the capital, or as many as the weather would allow them. When they could not go out he and his mother sat and smoked together, and she read his works in the *Edinburgh Review*. After a fortnight – which Carlyle said were the first two weeks' idleness in her life – she became anxious to go home. She left at New Year, though Jean stayed on with her brother and sister-in-law. Her visit to them was the first time she had been outside Annandale. Carlyle, meanwhile, had a new project to contemplate, the possibility of the chair of moral philosophy at the University of St Andrews. Jeffrey, again, and some of Carlyle's other friends encouraged him to apply; but he was to have no more success than with the London chair. Money was still a problem, and was a significant incentive for him to seek the post. On 30 December he wrote to his publisher, John Taylor, to ask about the sales of *Schiller*, and to see whether a second edition might not be possible. Taylor replied gloomily that he still had 650 of the first on his hands.

Carlyle did have one trump card, however, in his quest for the St Andrews post. In January 1828 he wrote to Goethe, asking tactfully for a testimonial that he could present with his application. He also asked Procter, who had done him great service already, not only to give him a reference, but to seek one from Basil Montagu, a noted London literary figure with whose wife, Anna, both Carlyle and Jane frequently corresponded; Carlyle had met the Montagus through Irving, as he had Procter. Brewster, his first publisher, Jeffrey, John Wilson, the reviewer and academic, and Mr Buller sent encomia for him, and there was 'a most majestic certificate in three pages from Edward Irving.'[35] The election for the chair was not to take place until the spring, but Goethe's ringing, poetic testament did not arrive before late March, when it was too late. 'I may well regard him as a man who would fill a Chair of Moral Philosophy, with single-heartedness, with purity, effect and influence,' he wrote from Weimar, 'enlightening the youth entrusted to him as to their real duties, in accordance with his disciplined thought, his natural gifts and his acquired knowledge, aiming at leading and urging their minds to moral activity, and thereby steadily guiding them towards a religious completeness.'[36]

While he waited to hear from St Andrews, Carlyle set to writing about Goethe's *Helena* for the *Foreign Review*. It is a pedestrian piece of Goethe-worship, and one that (in the verse translations Carlyle attempted of his master) demonstrates again his own severe limitations with poetic forms. Another packet arrived from Goethe in February, containing a dozen or so volumes of his works, and a letter and medals he asked Carlyle to pass on to Sir Walter Scott, whom Carlyle did not know. It was not until April that he wrote to Scott, hoping that in his role as an 'Ambassador between two Kings of Poetry'[37] he might have a chance to make Scott's acquaintance. Scott, much to Carlyle's chagrin, did not even acknowledge the letter; and so Carlyle wrote curtly to him in May, enclosing the medals in a letter given to Jeffrey to deliver to him. Masson, an authority on both Scott and Carlyle, surmises that Scott was too punctilious to have snubbed Carlyle; he details how busy Scott was at the time to support his view that he accidentally forgot to read the letter.[38]

His sister Jean's visit, prolonged beyond February, gave his wife a companion while he turned obsessively to his work; Jane was not always to be so lucky. Money was coming in at last, and he was able to send more to Jack in Germany, continuing his selfless funding of Jack's medical training that had started years earlier when his brother went to Edinburgh. The Carlyles would not need too much material wealth to survive at Craigenputtock, though Carlyle himself was showing signs of regret at having to leave the city. However, the final decision was made to settle in Dumfriesshire on Whitsunday, as it was felt it would benefit Carlyle's health, 'and for the sake of cheapness.'[39] In late March Carlyle went to Scotsbrig to see his family, and from there made visits to Craigenputtock, which was having minor renovations.

On his return, Carlyle set to work on a substantial article on Goethe for the *Foreign Review* in which he seeks to persuade a largely uninterested public of the great merits of his master. The *Dichtung und Wahrheit*, for example, he accuses the reading public of having censured without displaying 'any insight into its proper meaning.'[40] Throughout, Carlyle is agog that a man revered by all educated Germans can be so little noted by the British. He attributes this to a failure of the British to appreciate the supreme intellectual struggles through which Goethe had been. He contrasts the artifice of much late eighteenth-century writing with the 'fire' of Goethe; and he makes one of the first of many attacks on the decadence and shallowness of the preceding century, rebuking Voltaire for finding religion 'a superfluity, indeed a nuis- ance.' He observed, though, that Voltaire's disciples soon rediscovered the value of religion, when they remembered that 'being a great sanction to civil morality, [religion] is of use for keeping society in order, at least the lower classes, who have not the feeling of honour in due force; and therefore, as a considerable help to the Constable and the Hangman, *ought* decidedly to be kept up.'[41] It was ironic that this discovery should take place, but it presaged the great liberal dilemma of the nineteenth century, with which Carlyle would continually taunt his intellectual opponents: that to give liberty to the hitherto subject classes may be theoretically desirable, but the practical effects on the privileged classes can be horrific.

The German culture of the late eighteenth and early nineteenth century, of which Carlyle took Goethe to be the apogee, was in his view of principally religious significance. Yet, ironically, although Goethe wrote often of religion – some of the longer passages quoted by Carlyle in his long article deal with Goethe's analysis, in *Wilhelm Meister*, of the different sorts of religion – it is widely accepted that this cultural tradition was the foundation of the existentialist philosophy of the later years of the nineteenth century, a philosophy that had Nietzsche as its principal exponent. The self-confidence of the German people after the era of Frederick the Great was reflected in the vigour, and the radical thought, of their literature. This self-confidence imbues Goethe's works, and allows him to find the transcendentalist solutions to religious dilemmas that Carlyle, lacking such confidence, had failed to formulate. That explains why Carlyle, on discovering Goethe's creed, was so bowled over by it, and felt such an urge to bring the message of his master to his own benighted people. The *Sturm und Drang* ('storm and stress') move- ment of those times was one that sought new experiences, new realities, for their own sake, and sought to challenge stale and orthodox feelings. As in Carlyle's own education and outlook, the boundaries between arts and sci- ences, natural and supernatural, were aggressively broken down.

But it is in religion that Carlyle felt German culture had the most to teach a society in which the standard interpretation of the Christian message had, to his mind at least, become inadequate and even wrong. He picks out the explanation of the unity of the 'three religions' from *Wilhelm Meister*, and in it we can discern the central importance, to Carlyle's mind, of the German movement. The three religions were the Ethnic, or national religion, 'which depends on Reverence for what is Above us'; the Philosophical, or 'Reverence for what is Around us'; and the Christian, 'Reverence of what is Beneath us.' The message is that Christianity is a part, not a whole; that, to those who followed merely the Christian religion, God had become synonymous with it, when, in fact, he was much more, above one and around one. This essay is Carlyle's ultimate attempt to persuade his readers by direct means of the significance of the culture he had taken to his heart; in future, its insidious presence in his works would continue the process by more subtle means.

This was to be his last work in Edinburgh. Comely Bank had been re-let by its landlord, and there was no turning back on the plan to go to Craigenputtock. Doubly so, indeed, as the word came from St Andrews that, despite the panoply of good references, Carlyle had failed again in his bid for a professorship. Many of their friends, the Jeffreys chief among them, had tried to talk them out of this scheme to go to live miles from anywhere. They would not be dissuaded. In mid-May 1828 they packed all their belongings on to half a dozen carts, stayed for a few nights with the Jeffreys in Moray Place, and then started south.

III

The renovations were still in progress when the Carlyles arrived, which upset Carlyle's routine, concentration and, inevitably, health. In the *Reminiscences* he recalled the house, on which an extra storey was being built, as being 'a bewildering *heap* . . . for some time after.'[42] Once finished, it was an impressive heap. In the advertisement Carlyle placed in the *Dumfries Courier* of 5 March 1834, to advertise that the house was to let following their decision to move to London, its facilities were listed: 'Diningroom, Drawing-room, Library, 4 Bed-rooms, small dressing-room, Servants' apartment, Kitchen, with all appurtenances; and, for offices, in an enclosed court, Fuel-house, Gig-house, Mangle-room, Stable of 4 stalls.'[43] By the time they left the farm to embark on their career in London, the silence and solitude had altered their characters and strained their marriage. They were not, however, alone. Alick was farming the land, and they had a servant, brought from Edinburgh, as well as other helpers. Jane found the arrangement surprisingly satisfactory, writing to Eliza Stodart on 28 July, two months after moving in:

We . . . see a distinct prospect of being more than tolerably comfortable. This solitude is not so irksome as one might think. If we are cut off from good society, we are also delivered from bad; the roads are less pleasant to walk on than the pavements of Princes Street but we have horses to ride; and instead of shopping and making calls I have bread to bake and chickens to hatch – I read, and work & talk with my husband and never weary.[44]

She also had her mother near at hand, at Templand, and could ride over to visit her. On her horse, called Harry, Jane (a good horsewoman) took herself off frequently for rides, not least because Carlyle, obsessed with his work, did not seem greatly to desire her company. Carlyle, though, was less sanguine. The weather in their first summer there was bad, and delayed the building of the new house that Alick needed – consequently prolonging the disruption. In the first three months there he managed only to write a short paper on the eighteenth-century German classicist Christian Gottlob Heyne for the *Foreign Review*, though at the end of August he embarked on a substantial article on Lockhart's life of Burns. Both pieces reflect a greater self-confidence, a readiness by Carlyle to let out his natural, robust humour. Heeren, whose *Life* of Heyne he was reviewing, is ridiculed for the high-flown sentimentality with which he describes his subject's death; though Heeren goes little further in his reverence of Heyne than Carlyle in his of Goethe.

Carlyle was getting into the habit, which would become obsessive in London when driving himself on through *Frederick*, of matching his writing with bouts of lone riding to clear his head. Though, as Carlyle wrote to Goethe, Craigenputtock was 'six miles from *any* individual of the formally visiting class,'[45] he and Jane were not without occasional companions. In early October Jeffrey, his wife, their daughter and maid came to stay three days, Jeffrey bringing with him proofs of the essay on Burns. He had edited the piece drastically, which angered Carlyle, and caused him to try to unedit it. In the end, it was published according to Jeffrey's judgment on style and content, so much so that Carlyle told Jack he could not bear to look at the finished piece. One wonders how much the clarity of these early writings is down to Carlyle's as yet uncorrupted style, and how much to his being accompanied through life by a good editor, such as he did not have – or such as would not have dared take issue with him – later on. He considered not writing for the *Review* again, though was anxious not to end his friendship with a man who had been a useful and willing patron. Jeffrey, with an eye to commercial success, tried to coax Carlyle out of his 'German mysticism.' Carlyle suspected, probably rightly, that this was simply a way of Jeffrey nudging him into 'Edinburgh Whiggism, Scepticism and Materialism.'[46] The uncomplicated Calvinism of Carlyle's upbringing, and the Germanic transcendentalism that modified it, always insulated him against the attractions of David Hume, the ultimate Edinburgh Whig and sceptic. Neither this doctrinal difficulty, nor the filthy weather at the time, marred the visit, in which the Carlyles revelled in sophisticated conversation after four months of ruder pleasures. 'He talked from morning till night,' Jane wrote to Eliza Stodart about Jeffrey.[47]

Jane took enthusiastically to her new role as a rural housewife. As well as the Jeffreys, other visitors came to see them in the early months at Craigenputtock, including Mrs Welsh and Carlyle's father. Jane learned to bake bread and to perform all the other menial household chores for which they kept a servant, but which the servant was not always available to perform. She also helped out in a token way with feeding chickens and rearing pigs. For intellectual exercise she taught herself Spanish, in tandem with Carlyle, and together they read Cervantes in the evenings. They also planned and planted shrubberies to improve the look of their farm. Having finished with Burns, Carlyle turned to a series of commissions for the *Foreign Review* as winter drew on: first an article entitled 'German Playwrights', on the recent low-grade dramatic output of some thought (though not by Carlyle) to be great German dramatists. There were in prospect articles on the German romantic poet and novelist Novalis and on Voltaire, for subsequent editions of the *Review*. Carlyle felt isolation to be the right environment for a 'philosopher,' as he termed himself in a letter to Eckermann, Goethe's assistant.[48] The other lasting effect of Carlyle's isolation was the growth of his misanthropy. Although he joked in a letter to De Quincey that he and Jane had talked about forming 'a sort of Colony here, to be called the "Misanthropic Society",'[49] it is from around this time that Carlyle's deep pessimism about his fellow men, which was to creep out in *Sartor* and to become a theme of the works of the decade after 1840, begins to take root.

After Christmas, as winter deepened, so did Carlyle's depression. His sister Margaret had fallen ill with severe intestinal problems, and her family feared the worst. She recovered enough to come to Craigenputtock the next summer, but Carlyle was told by his wife to expect the recovery to be temporary; it seems Margaret had cancer. Also, the unrelenting process of article-writing was beginning to irritate him, though there was little else to do. The supposed benefits to his mental and physical health that the move had been designed to provide were not emerging.

'German Playwrights' appeared early in 1829, and exhibited the first signs of the distinct style of the mature Carlyle, with its rhetorical questions, apostrophe, hyperbole, bathos, prolixity and heavy humour. One example will suffice:

Of the fact, at least, that such a superior demand for dramas exists in Germany, we have only to open a newspaper to find proof. Is not every *Litteraturblatt* and *Kunst-blatt* stuffed to bursting with theatricals? Nay, has not the 'able Editor' established correspondents in every capital city of the civilised world, who report to him on this one matter and no other? For, be our curiosity what it may, let us have profession of 'intelligence from Munich,' 'intelligence from Vienna,' 'intelligence from Berlin,' is it intelligence of anything but of greenroom controversies and negotiations, of tragedies and operas and farces acted and to be acted? Not of men, and their doings, by hearth and hall, in the firm earth; but of mere effigies and shells of men, and their doings in the world of pasteboard, do these unhappy correspondents write.[50]

Long having despised journalism as a trade himself (and probably despising it all the more because his own article-writing was bringing him perilously close to it), he also used this essay to mount a further assault, jesting that 'it is a well known fact in Journalistics, that a man may not only live, but support wife and children by his labours in this line, years after the brain (if there ever was any) had been completely abstracted, or reduced by time and hard usage into a state of dry powder.'[51] It is a sentiment shared by many twentieth-century press proprietors, and is one of Carlyle's more minor claims to the status of prophet.

He worked slowly at a comparably bilious attack on Voltaire, and at an article on Novalis. Voltaire he had written by the end of the winter, and was published in the April 1829 number of the *Foreign Review*. It is not just Carlyle's sense of humour that shines through again, but also a pomposity and pride in what he now considered to be his established calling as a *littérateur*. The essay begins with the assertion that 'could ambition always choose its own path, and were will in human undertakings synonymous with faculty, all truly ambitious men would be men of letters.'[52] He believed true power was the 'promulgation of thought,' so literature outshone all more temporal definitions of this quality. Voltaire, as was suggested in the earlier article on Goethe, was the epitome of the moral sink of the eighteenth century. 'No philosopher, but a highly accomplished trivialist,'[53] was Carlyle's judgment on him, provoked by what he felt was Voltaire's selective and insufficient regard for truth. His religious understanding, too, disgusted Carlyle: 'He ardently, and with long continued effort, warred against Christianity, without understanding beyond the mere superficies what Christianity was.'[54] The essay is less important for what it says about Voltaire than for what it says about Carlyle's view of the eighteenth century. His description of the court of Louis XV is the finest set-piece in his writings of this fundamental intellectual belief, in which he compares that age with that of the Roman Emperors: 'external splendour and internal squalor . . . Instead of Love for Poetry, there was "Taste" for it; refinement in manners, with utmost coarseness in morals; in a word, the strange spectacle of a Social System, embracing large, cultivated portions of the human species, and founded only on Atheism.'[55] It was a society that had deserved the cataclysmic revolution that, within a generation, it got.

He and Jane longed for letters from Edinburgh friends, informing them of what was going on in the world, and especially treasured were new books. On excursions to Dumfries Carlyle could find hardly any books at all, and the lack of literature to stimulate him was becoming intensely frustrating. He and Jane entered into the routine of riding the thirty-seven miles to Scotsbrig to see his parents, and to stay for three or four days, when he had finished a piece of work; or they would go to Templand, fourteen miles away, to see Jane's mother: 'and then back to work and silence,' he recalled.[56] Their regime seems to have been almost unbearably austere, though in the *Reminiscences* he claimed that 'we were not unhappy at Craigenputtock; perhaps they were our happiest days.'[57]

IV

In this solitude Carlyle was prolific. His review of an edition of Novalis's writings appeared in the *Foreign Review* in July 1829; the previous month the *Edinburgh Review* had published the most important work, in terms of the flowering of his intellect and the development of his reputation as a social commentator, that he had so far produced. 'Signs of the Times' was not Carlyle disquisiting yet again on the German romantic impulse; it was Carlyle on the state of his own land. It was mainly the result of Jeffrey's trying to persuade him that he had to make his name more widely known, and he would not do this with articles on German literature. Carlyle had wanted to travel in England to see how things were, but the plan was defeated – as a similar one to visit Weimar and see Goethe had been – for want of money. He was still paying out for Jack, who was instead making the foreign journeys as he furthered his medical education, and who wrote tantalisingly to Carlyle about life in Germany.

'Novalis' was significant in that it represented an attempt by Carlyle to rebut the accusations of 'mysticism' made against him for his love of the German romantics. He was not entirely successful, for in parts the review is distractingly vague and prolix. Carlyle describes Novalis's transcendentalism (to which he was not immune himself) as 'the most serious in its purport of all philosophies propounded in these latter centuries.'[58] He sought to substantiate this by saying that the effect of this philosophy on morals and religion was 'of almost boundless importance.' Carlyle, nodding at Kant, says that 'if time and space have no absolute existence, no existence out of our minds, it removes a stumbling block from the very threshold of our Theology.' He goes on to give as good a religious self-definition as one can find in his works:

For on this ground, when we say that the Deity is omnipresent and eternal, that with Him it is a universal Here and Now, we say nothing wonderful; nothing but that he also created Time and Space, that Time and Space are not laws of His being, but only of ours. Nay, to the transcendentalist, clearly enough, the whole question of the origin and existence of Nature must be greatly simplified; the old hostility of Matter is at an end, for Matter is itself annihilated; and the black Spectre, Atheism, 'with all its sickly dews,' melts into nothingness forever.

There is the root here of the spiritual self-confidence that underpins the Everlasting Yea in *Sartor*, which he was little more than a year away from starting to write. He concluded the review with an expression of the hope that, as a result of his discussion of these theories, 'mysticism . . . should, like other actually existing things, be understood in well-informed minds.'

'Signs of the Times' – which took its title, at Irving's suggestion, from St Matthew's gospel – is a bridge between Carlyle's eclectic religious belief and his political philosophy. It was written in the year of Catholic emancipation in Britain and amid growing clamour, at home and in Europe, for political reform. It is a cry against mechanism, by which Carlyle means all structures, systems and institutions that have superseded individual faith and, in effect, the transcendental mysticism of such faith. This is the seed of his faith in heroes, and of his cynicism about modern society's capacity to organise itself effectively without heroes to govern it. Nature was being subverted by machines, which had an effect not just on industrial production, but on man's spiritual relations. The turbulence caused by the lust for political change was, he wrote, 'the sign of a mechanical age.'[59] In a sonorous preview of his later arguments, he sarcastically adds: 'Give us a reform of Government! A good structure of legislature, a proper check upon the executive, a wise arrange- ment of the judiciary, is *all* that is wanting for human happiness.' It was written in a spirit of untrammelled pessimism about Britain at the end of the dissolute reign of George IV: 'The King has virtually abdicated; the Church is a widow, without jointure; public principle is gone; private honesty is going; society, in short, is fast falling in pieces; and a time of unmixed evil is come on us.'[60] Or, as he would later write, properly linking his creed with his politics, 'all power is moral.'[61]

This is an assault on utilitarianism, a complaint that the age had rejected the likes of Socrates, Plato and Hooker, the type of philosopher who, unlike James Mill, Bentham and Adam Smith, 'inculcates on men the necessity and infinite worth of moral goodness, the great truth that our happiness depends on the mind which is within us, and not on the circumstances that are without us.'[62] Such materialism disgusts him. 'It is no longer the moral, religious, spiritual condition of the people that is our concern, but their physical, practical, economical condition, as regulated by public laws. Thus is the Body-politic more than ever worshipped and tendered; but the Soul-politic less than ever.' He despised the modern state for forsaking its paternalistic duties, and behaving instead 'like an active parish constable.' His opposition to the cash-nexus is soon apparent, though expressed less articulately and succinctly than he would later manage; he laments that 'profit and loss' have become the main motives for human action, whereas a higher form of inspiration moved philosophers and great artists of earlier times. Carlyle seems to imagine the profit motive had been invented only in his own times, a lack of understanding that dulls the force of his argument.

He asserts the superiority of the 'dynamical' over the mechanical – 'dynami- cal' meaning reliance on inspiration from man's soul rather than from external systems or institutions or economic incentives – by taking a religious example:

How did Christianity arise and spread abroad among men? Was it by institutions, and establishments and well-arranged systems of mechanism? Not so; on the contrary, in all past and existing institutions for those ends, its divine spirit has invariably been found to languish and decay. It arose in the mystic deeps of man's soul; and was spread abroad by the 'preaching of the word,' by simple, altogether natural and individual efforts; and flew, like hallowed fire, from heart to heart, till all were purified and illuminated by it; and its heavenly light shone, as it still shines, and (as sun or star) will ever shine, through the whole dark destinies of man. Here again was no Mechanism; man's highest attainment was accomplished Dynamically, not Mechanically.[63]

No wonder Carlyle, in later years, should be astonished by Darwin, whose ideas such passages as this seek to pre-empt; and no wonder, with beliefs such as these, reeking of his intoxication with German romanticism, he should come to view democracy as an interference by temporal and material institutions in the Divine order, the denial by the mechanical ballot-box of the individual dynamical inspiration of the hero. 'Mechanism,' he wrote, 'has now struck its roots down into man's most intimate, primary sources of conviction.' Thus had the immorality of this age been formed. 'The truth is, men have lost their belief in the Invisible, and believe, and hope, and work only in the visible; or, to speak it in other words: This is not a Religious age.'[64]

Watching, as Arnold and his contemporaries would more ostentatiously watch for themselves a generation later, the tide going out on the 'sea of faith,' Carlyle argued that 'Unbelief, which is of a still more fundamental character, every man may see prevailing, with scarcely but the faintest contradiction, all around him; even in the Pulpit itself.'[65] He called for religion once more to be 'a thousand-voiced psalm from the heart of Man to his invisible Father, the fountain of all Goodness, Beauty, Truth, and revealed in every revelation of these,' instead of the 'wise prudential feeling grounded on mere calculation; a matter, as all others now are, of Expediency and Utility,' with religion being a matter of profit and loss like everything else.

There are other 'signs' of Carlyle's mature thought in the piece: most notably, he raises the idea of the 'secular priesthood,' that 'the true Church of England, at this moment, lies in the Editors of Newspapers.'[66] The secular, non-feudal society he saw developing was no longer as susceptible to influence by ministers of religion or theological evangelists as it had been; its new influences were leading articles. The editors who wrote them 'preach to the people daily, weekly; admonishing kings themselves; advising peace or war, with an authority which only the first Reformers, and a long-past class of Popes, were possessed of; inflicting moral censure; imparting moral encouragement, consolation, edification; in all ways diligently "administering the Discipline of the Church".' Carlyle saw that as 'the printed communication of Thought' had never had such importance as at that time, the power of the writer was immense. It was why, as he had several times said, he wanted to write; and the idea grew, until it formed the basis for one of the lectures in *Heroes*. And another of his core beliefs, in strength or might, is laid out here too: he says of poetry that 'beauty is no longer the god it worships, but some brute image of Strength; which we may call an idol, for true Strength is one and the same with Beauty, and its worship also is a hymn.'[67] Had Carlyle never written another word after 'Signs of the Times,' it would not have been too difficult to discern in this short article the foundations of his outlook and principles.

5

Sartor:
'That Divine ME'

1829–31

BEFORE HE WROTE 'Signs of the Times' Carlyle's literary experience was mainly confined to his role as a practised author merely of critiques about the works of others. Now he had made the leap of publishing creative thought of his own, he had started the shift of style and subject matter that would soon result in the construction of *Sartor*. The writing for reviews was to last for some time yet, though Carlyle lost an important champion in the summer of 1829 when Jeffrey was invited to become Dean of the Faculty of Advocates in Edinburgh, and passed the editorship of the *Review* to MacVey Napier. In August the Carlyles saw the Jeffreys, and from the fact that Jeffrey neither mentioned the *Review* nor his successor Carlyle felt he would not be welcome back in those pages; and it was nearly two years before he again wrote there. However, he and Napier formed cordial relations, thanks to Jeffrey. When Carlyle did work for him he was glad Napier did not butcher his prose in the manner Jeffrey had done.

There was still no shortage of ideas, no shortage of books arriving from Germany that Carlyle wanted to review. Carlyle wanted to write on Richter again, which he did, and Fraser wanted him to write a life of Luther, which he did not. If there were to be a longer project, Carlyle preferred it to be a history of German literature; though had he not been able to do that, he was prepared to consider the Luther offer. All work was conducted in a less than perfect atmosphere, as Carlyle's health and spirits remained poor. In the early autumn there was relief from the isolation, when he and Jane went to Edinburgh. They began to feel financial pressure, and Carlyle devoted much energy to chasing up his debtors. He was peeved when Fraser postponed his article on Richter in the *Foreign Review*, for he needed the £50 fee. He set to work on an article about Schiller for Fraser, while seeking some way to make the leap from being an essayist to a writer. Goethe had sent him a copy of the Goethe-Schiller correspondence, which Carlyle was able to use as some original material for his work.

He kept at this task, which became harder and harder for him to proceed with as the days darkened, through November and into December, when the first heavy snows made life still more tiresome, and he and Jane still more isolated. It was a hard winter, and in February 1830 Jane wrote to Eliza Stodart expressing a longing to see green fields again, and not 'this wide waste of blinding snow.'[1] Carlyle longed to make a start on his history of German literature, but could not do so until more books, ordered from London, arrived. He even wrote to a friend, David Aitken, a clergyman at Minto with a substantial library, to beg the loan of some books so he could start on this great project. Loneliness, too, was a problem, and almost every letter he sent contained an imploration to the recipient to come to visit them at Craigenputtock. Jack, now returned from Germany, briefly came to see his family in Dumfriesshire at Christmas. However, much to Carlyle's regret, he soon left for England, where Carlyle, through Badams, had attempted to find him a medical practice. Jane, whose tolerance of exile was lower than her husband's, spent much of the Christmas and New Year period in bed with a sore throat. There were fears that it was diphtheria, which further disrupted her husband. Nor could medical help be summoned easily, not simply because the nearest doctor was at Dumfries, but because the snows made reaching the farm so difficult. Mrs Welsh, who came to nurse her daughter, could hardly reach them.

There was eventually an improvement in Carlyle's fortunes. In mid-January 1830 Whitaker's, a publisher with which William Fraser was associated, offered Carlyle £100 per volume for a four-volume history of German literature, and shortly afterwards an invaluable packet of books arrived on loan from Aitken. James Fraser, who had just established *Fraser's Magazine*, also wrote to Carlyle (at the suggestion of William Fraser and of Irving) to ask him to contribute. Another entreaty that winter had come from Jeffrey, begging the Carlyles to end their isolation and return to Edinburgh. Carlyle wrote to say that, for reasons of economy, he could not consider such a move unless he had a steady income of £100 a year. Jeffrey, to show his commitment to the Carlyles, offered to provide Carlyle with that sum if they would return to Edinburgh. Though Jeffrey was acting in accordance with the same charitable principles that Carlyle showed towards his family (Carlyle was still funding Jack, and had had to make subventions to Alick for the farm), and would have shown towards others had his finances allowed, pride would not permit him to accept the offer.

In the *Reminiscences* Carlyle noted that this 'annual sum, had it fallen on me from the clouds, would have been of very high convenience at that time: but which I could not, for a moment, have dreamt of accepting as a gift or subventionary help from any fellow mortal.'[2] He claimed, in the same passage, to have declined the offer 'at once, in my handsomest, gratefullest, but brief and conclusive way,' though his actual letter is missing, probably destroyed by Jeffrey's daughter in a fit of rage when she read some of Carlyle's ungenerous remarks about her father in the *Reminiscences*. However, Carlyle quotes himself as having said that 'Republican Equality [is] the silently fixed law of human society at present; each man to live on his own resources, and have an *Equality* of resources with every other man; dangerous, and not possible except through cowardice and folly, to depart from said clear rule.' Jeffrey tried twice more to change Carlyle's mind, without success; and Carlyle also suspected (and this is precisely the type of remark that would have offended Jeffrey's family) that the gesture had been made not just out of generosity but also from a conscious decision of Jeffrey's that he wanted to perform a 'fine action.' We have only Carlyle's possibly irrational suspicions to substantiate this. He did borrow £100 from him when his cash-flow had been interrupted, and recalled the joy of being able to pay the sum back within a few weeks. However, in May 1830 he had to seek a second loan, this time of £60, and repayment could not be so swift, much to Carlyle's distress.

The winter was passed planning the history of German literature, and Carlyle tried to gird himself to go to Edinburgh to find the additional books he needed. However, April came and he had still not made the trip, telling Henry Inglis (a lawyer some ten years his junior whom he and Jane had met while at Comely Bank) in a letter that he had spent his time instead 'in the service of worthless taskmasters, Discontent, Biliousness, Indolence and the Devil.'[3] He decided the excursion could wait until he had written the first volume, which was to be about German mythology, including the *Niebelungen Lied*. Jack, now in London, was able to send up some volumes to his brother. Carlyle worked remorselessly, for Jack, who had seen Fraser, told his brother that the material for the first volume was expected in May. Fraser was still keen for him to write the life of Luther, and another publisher's editor, the Reverend G.R. Gleig, tried to persuade Carlyle to write a popular German history. Carlyle saw that such a project was too much for him, though he did offer to write a volume specifically on Frederick the Great. For the moment nothing impeded his existing project, with which Goethe, writing from Weimar, offered to help.

Once summer came Carlyle's spirits rose. He wrote to Anna Montagu in early June of 'how like [Craigenputtock] is to the ideal existence I was wont to dream of ... a dwelling-place remote from Green-grocerism of every kind.'[4] Jane's health had recovered, and with the better weather she set out once more to improve the garden, planting furiously. He revived his earlier idea of travelling to Weimar the following winter, partly to meet Goethe and advance his researches, partly to be away from the bleakness of Craigenputtock, and to travel there via London and renew old acquaintances. The plan was to come to nothing. He was soon to suffer the worst blow of his life so far. Several of his aunts and uncles had died in the previous year, but death was to strike closer to him than ever. His sister Margaret, whose cancer had been in remission, entered upon her last, awful illness, and died on 22 June 1830, aged twenty-six. At midnight on the 21st Carlyle and Alick had received a summons to ride over to Dumfries, where Margaret had a week earlier been taken to hospital; but by the time they arrived at four o'clock in the morning they were too late. 'That day ... is to be counted among the painfullest of my life,' he wrote in 1866, after his wife's death.[5] That evening, he recalled 'having at last reached the silence of the woods, I remember fairly lifting up my voice and weeping aloud, a long time.'

II

Carlyle noted that his mother bore the bereavement heroically, and he himself had been too busy helping with the funeral arrangements to allow himself to be indulgent in his grief. His father took the blow hardest. For Carlyle, this grave event put in perspective a more temporal, but none the less frustrating, setback. Whitaker's, his publisher, had realised the market for books on German literature was hardly buoyant, and told Carlyle they were uncertain when, if at all, they might be able to publish his *magnum opus*. Jack, in London, sought to find out from William Fraser what the prospects were, and found that they were bleak. Carlyle bore no animus against Fraser, who had been driven almost to nervous collapse by the pressures of business, and who felt the deepest regret at having to let his author down. Within days Carlyle was starting, unsuccessfully, to hawk the manuscript around other publishers, starting with Tait in Edinburgh. Undaunted, Carlyle embarked on the second volume, not realising that none of this work would be published until seventy years after his death.

He made other plans. In August he at last replied to James Fraser's letter of earlier in the year soliciting contributions for his magazine. He sent him the tale of Cruthers and Jonson, asking him to publish it only 'on condition that you MENTION TO NO ONE who the Author is.'[6] Thus far, Carlyle's work had been published in books and journals where it was not the custom to give the author's name (although it could be discovered on enquiry of the journal concerned, if the author chose to make contact with a correspondent) and his fame was to be confined to those who knew him until the *French Revolution* came out attributed to him in 1837. Another article, which Carlyle called 'Thoughts on History', and which indeed appeared (like 'Cruthers and Jonson') in the magazine, under the title 'On History', was sent too, as were fragments of his poor poetry, which Fraser none the less found space to slip in over the succeeding months. The establishment at Craigenputtock also made a great advance; Carlyle and Alick paid £10 for a gig, which would make easier their travelling around Dumfriesshire.

Also in August, out of the blue, Carlyle received a parcel of books from some Saint-Simonians in Paris, who had read and enjoyed 'Signs of the Times' when it had been reprinted in the *Revue Britannique*. Saint-Simon himself had died in 1825, leaving behind a band of disciples to develop his variant of socialism. Described by one critic as a creed that 'combined a highly rationalistic analysis of society with something approaching religious mania,'[7] Saint-Simonianism sought the emancipation of women and the improvement of conditions of the workers by preaching a gospel of universal love. The creed had been spurred on by the revolution of the previous month in Paris. Carlyle wrote back in flattering terms. He had seen that the constitution of European society could not long endure. He was sympathetic to the creed because it was based on sincere religious faith, and because he too was shocked by what he knew of the conditions in which the poor, during the depression of the 1820s, had been forced to live. He confided in his journal that someone with £200,000 a year earned the same as 6,666 ordinary men, and yet all he usually did for the money was 'kill partridges'.[8] He said he found 'little or nothing'[9] to dissent from in the books he had been sent, unsurprising since they conformed with his view that the eighteenth century had been a moral and religious disaster, while the priority for the nineteenth was to rebuild society on a religious basis. 'Religion is the only bond and life of societies, so the only real Government were a Hierarchy,' he told them, outlining some themes of his life's work. The historian Theodore Zeldin unwittingly gave another clue to Carlyle's infatuation with this cult when he described the Saint-Simonians as 'in some ways, a new aristocracy'.[10] Saint-Simon shunned democracy, extolled duty, and believed in a natural class of leaders; he and Carlyle could have been made for each other.

The ideas gained from the Saint-Simonians were to imbue *Sartor*, which Carlyle was now close to conceiving. In a letter to Goethe later that month Carlyle asked his master for his opinion on Saint-Simonianism, and Goethe replied promptly that Carlyle would do well to give the society a wide berth. Carlyle did, however, continue to receive their literature, and to correspond with Gustave d'Eichthal, who had made the initial approach to him. D'Eichthal, a member of a wealthy Parisian-Jewish banking family, had started to correspond with John Stuart Mill in 1829, and Mill had warned him that an organised ideological sect like the Saint-Simonians was not designed to attract ordinary English men and women. Others were less tolerant, haranguing the creed for its apparently absurd economic and social ideas when some Saint-Simonian 'missionaries' came to England in search of converts in 1831. Both Carlyle and Mill successfully kept a distance from them when the sect's leaders were tried for a series of offences, including outraging public morality for advocating free love, in 1832. Carlyle's association with the sect was, in the light of his later philosophies, bizarre.

Carlyle continued writing his history of German literature until he reached the Reformation, and then put the manuscript away to await the time when, he hoped, it might be commercially profitable to return to it. In September 1830 he started to write *Sartor*. The idea had come to him – initially while visiting his mother-in-law at Templand – that the institutions and forms of everyday life were merely clothes in which people chose to dress up reality. Moreover, they were clothes that disguised the significance, or 'open secret' of reality – that God was immanent in everything. Goethe had sent him his *Farbenlehre*, or theory of colour, in which he used a similarly abstract idea to construct a philosophy. The new project raised his spirits, and he wrote to his mother that, after three weeks of work, it was coming on 'wonderfully well.'[11] He added that 'what it is to be I cannot yet tell, whether a book or a string of Magazine Articles; we hope, the former, but in either case, it may be worth something.' To Jack he wrote:

What I am writing is the strangest of all things: begun as an article for Fraser; then found to be too long (except it were divided into two); now sometimes looking almost, as if it would swell into a book. A very singular piece, I assure you! It glances from Heaven to Earth & back again in a strange satirical frenzy whether *fine* or not remains to be seen.[12]

As the days shortened, Carlyle adopted his by now familiar winter routine and winter melancholy; walks in the 'ghastly solitude' of Craigenputtock alternating with 'impetuous' bursts of writing.[13] It was as well he had this new task to occupy him, for as well as the problems of the spirit there were also material difficulties. In October he begged Jack to see whether Fraser had published any of the pieces Carlyle had sent him in August, for he desperately needed the money, following the financial shock of the aborted deal on the history of German literature. 'Am I happy?' he asked, rhetorically, in a letter written from the 'grave-like silence' of his farm to Anna Montagu.[14] 'My theory was and is that the man who cannot be happy (as happy as is needful) wheresoever God's sky overspans him, and men forbear to beat him with bludgeons, deserves to be and will always be, what one calls miserable.' They received more visitors, the Jeffreys coming from further afield (and Jeffrey still troubled by Carlyle's 'earnestness'), and Carlyle's father staying for a fortnight in October.

Initially, Carlyle thought *Sartor* (or 'Teufelsdreck' as he referred to it until 1833, when he changed the title, and the spelling of the name of the hero to 'Teufelsdröckh') would make a pair of articles for James Fraser. He sent the paper, under the title of 'Thoughts on Clothes,' to Fraser, only to write to Jack in London a few weeks later to beg him to retrieve it, hoping it had not been printed. As he brooded on the work during the winter, he decided it would make a book. Until he could transform the article into the work he wanted, all the labour he was putting into it would bring him no return: so he had to seek other ways of earning money. He offered Napier an article on Moore's life of Byron, steering clear of matters German. However, Napier rejected this, saying Jeffrey had already offered to review the work and, if his legal duties precluded him from doing so – the new Prime Minister, Lord Grey, had appointed him Lord Advocate when forming his pro-reform ministry in November – there were two others with a better claim than Carlyle. Macaulay ended up writing the review, now best remembered for his observation that 'we know no spectacle so ridiculous as the British public in one of its periodical fits of morality.' In the article Macaulay attained a standard of invective and polemic Carlyle would wait another decade to emulate, and then without the attendant subtleties. Ironically, Napier had a German theme to suggest to Carlyle instead, and asked him to review the *Historic Survey of German Poetry*, by William Taylor.

The Carlyles had hoped to have a visitor, Henry Inglis, for Christmas, but he had to go to London to search for his sister, who had been abducted there by a woman in a carriage, and who was found safe the following month. Jane celebrated the season with her traditional sore throat, but professed to Eliza Stodart in a letter that her spirits remained good; however, she surmised that had she just returned from Edinburgh she would have found the isolation intolerable.[15] It was worse for her than for Carlyle, who shut himself away for most of the day writing. As ever, he paid little attention to her frustrations. She made visits to Templand when the weather allowed, and dreamt of going to Edinburgh.

By mid-January 1831 Carlyle had finished the review of Taylor, and sent it to Napier with the imploration that 'the next subject you give me may be an English one, at least no German one. On that last business I have said enough for a year or two.'[16] Napier thought the article excellent, even though Carlyle had confused William Taylor with another, which necessitated some hasty rewriting on the proofs. Carlyle begged to be allowed to write an attack on fashionable novels, notably those written by Edward Bulwer, only to be told by Napier that Bulwer was a friend and reviewer, and there would be no attacks on him in the *Edinburgh Review*.

He sent Jack in search of the first draft of *Sartor*, currently with Fraser. 'I can devise some more biography for Teufelsdreck; give a second deeper part, in the same vein, leading thro' Religion and the nature of Society, and Lord knows what,' he told his brother.[17] Morale was low. The first draft, 'slightly altered would itself make a little volume first (which would encourage me immensely),' Carlyle added, 'could one find a bookseller, which however I suppose one cannot.' The manuscript was retrieved, and Carlyle set to expanding it. Before sending it back Jack had shown it to Irving, who had agreed with its comments on religion and society and found the character of 'Teufelsdreck' amusing. Jack endorsed this opinion, which helped motivate his brother in Dumfriesshire.

Carlyle had to look for other subjects for articles to support himself and Jane. He was aware of the political developments in London, as the reform ministry started about its work, but was in no position to comment upon them from Craigenputtock. His next essay work was, in fact, an extract from his aborted German literary history, about the *Niebelungen Lied*, which he sold to the *Westminster Review*. Although the work he had done on that history had in effect dislocated his career for a year, it was not after all entirely wasted. J.G. Cochrane, editor of the *Foreign Quarterly Review*, asked Carlyle to send him a paper he had offered on the German legend of Reynard the Fox, also culled from the history. Carlyle offered Cochrane a larger section of German literary history, to include Reynard, but expanded under the title of 'German

Literature of the Fourteenth and Fifteenth Centuries.' Anxiety about money, while he waited for news that his review articles would be accepted (which they were), interfered with his creative writing; and a savage snow-storm cut off Craigenputtock for more than a week at the end of January. Alick, who had married the previous year, could no longer make a living farming Craigenputtock, and was preparing, with his brother's encouragement, to cut his losses and set up elsewhere. The prospect of losing Alick's society, though, depressed Carlyle further; as the new tenant, one Joseph M'Adam, prepared to move in, Carlyle lamented that there was now no creature within fifteen miles to whom they could talk.[18] And Jack, in London, was also on hard times, unable to find patients for a practice, and trying to sell review articles on medical and scientific subjects, with help from his brother. However, Carlyle was determined that the work that would be *Sartor Resartus* would be his salvation: it would give him a 'pulpit', from which he could expound his world's view. 'I see a busy summer before me,' he told Jack at the beginning of March 1831, 'and therefore no unhappy one.'

He worked night and day on *Sartor*, his confidence in it sufficient to tell his family what he was doing. That it was radical in form and content he did not doubt, for he told his mother to 'ask no account of it, for it is inde-scribable.'[19] He had made a plan, which he would stick to, to finish the book by the autumn and then to take it to London in search of a publisher. By the end of March he had completed four chapters, and his enthusiasm showed no sign of waning. The same could not be said of the cash account, for by April Carlyle was down to his last 7s, though he was awaiting payment for some of his articles. Because of this poverty, and his obsessive attention to his work, he was able to write to Jack in June that, apart from a visit to Scotsbrig, he had not left Craigenputtock since January. The book, however, was progressing well, and he told Jack it would be finished in July.[20]

'It will be one of the strangest volumes ever offered to the English world,' he added, perhaps foreseeing the difficulties this eclectic quality might give him when he sought a publisher by concluding: 'whether *worth* anything is another question.' As the book neared completion he began to develop his plan for the visit to London, to try to sell it. He suggested to Jack that he might even decide once in London to send for Jane and settle there. He could no longer see any point in their isolated farm. 'This place is as good as done: not even the best advantage, that of living in any pecuniary sufficiency, for I never was as poor,' he wrote.[21] That was the fault of editors not paying him properly, and he forgot how much poorer they would be if he had had to find rent. With typical selflessness, though, he asked the editor of the *Westminster Review*, which had just published his piece on the *Niebelungen Lied*, to send the payment to Jack, who was virtually destitute. Jack had been to see Jeffrey to ask whether the Lord Advocate could help him find a job, and Jeffrey had offered him a gift of £20; like his brother before him, Jack could not accept the lawyer's charity, and having taken a draft for the money returned it to

Jeffrey uncashed. Jeffrey promised to look out for a post for Jack, as he had also just done for Carlyle, who had written to him saying that, in order to further the idea of settling in London, he was willing to work 'at ANY honest thing whatsoever.'[22] The anxiety was making Jane ill. Even Carlyle noticed this, and it partly explains why he should have been so anxious to get to London and seek to improve their fortunes.

III

No work of Carlyle's better reflects his native genius, or his sense of humour, than *Sartor*. Fantastical to the point of incomprehensibility to generations of readers, it is hardly surprising that those who in 1831 saw the manuscript of what Carlyle still called 'Teufelsdreck', after the professor of his creation who had invented the clothes-philosophy, found its innovative tone and structure baffling. They either did not detect the joke Carlyle was trying to play upon them, or if they did they resented it. No one was to see its commercial possibilities. *Sartor* provides a guide to Carlyle's early understanding of religion, society and politics, on which he built in his later works. A problem with it was that no one quite knew what it was. Some critics were taken in by Carlyle's joke, and complained they could not find out anything else about the professor. Carlyle himself described it as 'a kind of didactic novel'.[23] Insofar as it is fictional, that is more or less what it is; the serious philosophic points it makes count against this definition, though. G.B. Tennyson, in his masterful analysis of the work, says simply that 'Victorian readers accepted *Sartor* primarily as a moral document.'[24] It was to have profound religious influence; as a vehicle for Carlyle's sub-Goethean, transcendentalist, post-Christian creed it was read avidly by the circle of Matthew Arnold, Arthur Hugh Clough and Froude in the Oxford of the 1840s. Carlyle took a consciously religious approach to the book. In an exhaustive analysis in *The Victorian Sage*, John Holloway has demonstrated the numerous rhetorical allusions to the Bible in Carlyle's text, though the smell of the Old Testament pervades all his writings.[25]

If in his tone Carlyle has a model it is to be found in Swift, Sterne and Fielding, whose satires he had read as a younger man. The strange, often violent images and metaphors in which he expresses himself may be redolent simply of his tortured digestion. The targets of his satire are unbelief and mechanism, themes already familiar from his published work. The age of literary conservatism into which he tried to launch *Sartor* had buried such robustness of humour, and could not cope with it from this novice. An age preoccupied with its own material concerns, now symbolised by the reform agitation, had little time for Carlyle's new and predominantly Germanic versions of spirituality.

'Up to this hour,' says the narrator in *Sartor* in an early chapter, 'we have never fully satisfied ourselves whether it is a tone and hum of real Humour, which we reckon among the very highest qualities of genius, or some echo of mere Insanity and Inanity, which doubtless ranks below the very lowest.'[26] This confusion remains throughout the work, as the narrative alternates between the philosophical profundities (and self-indulgences) of the semi-autobiographical sequences, and the sometimes laboured, sometimes subtle jokes of the narration. Carlyle's style throughout is fresh, never lapsing unintentionally into orotundities or the monologic rant of some later works. His characterisation of Teufelsdröckh is brilliant in its simple vividity. The radical structure of the work allows him to claim that the manuscript of *Die Kleider, Ihr Werden und Werken [Clothes, their Origin and Meaning]*, by Diogenes Teufelsdröckh has fallen into his hands as an editor. All he is doing is relaying a philosophy, a search for faith, distancing himself from it where necessary, as if Carlyle lacked the self-confidence to take immediate responsibility for some of his own thought. He has a fictional base to illustrate his points. The version of the professor's opinions Carlyle presents is, literally, the patching of the tailor – *Sartor Resartus*. This also allows stylistic experiments, with the straightforward prose of the editor contrasting with the abrupt, quizzical and apostrophic style of Teufelsdröckh. The style creates much scope for humour, too, as Carlyle laces Teufelsdröckh's prose with excessive exclamations, biblical syntax and increasingly absurd compound phrases like 'humano-anecdotical' and 'cabalistico-sartorial.'

John Stuart Mill, who before meeting Carlyle had expected him to be a Germanic bore, found instead a man whose immersion in German culture had not destroyed his objectivity about it. On one level *Sartor* is also a satire on the earnestness of German letters and thought: Carlyle's all too conscious humour, his highlighting of the pomposity of Teufelsdröckh, the mock-serious translations of obscure German words in the text and the relentless depiction of the earnestness of life at Entepfuhl ('Duckpond') and Weissnichtwo ('Knownotwhere'), is a successful attempt to display how ridiculous Teutonic seriousness is to the British. Yet *Sartor* draws in equally serious fashion on the thought that made Germany so earnest: the religious creed that German ideas had helped Carlyle to formulate is at the heart of the work in the semi-autobiographical passages; and the book is Carlyle's attempt to offer this means of faith to an era passing through social and spiritual upheavals, and struggling for want of an adequate conception of God. By pointing, however obscurely, to his own German influences, and by showing how his understanding of what constituted reality had been altered by the transcendentalism of Goethe in particular, he hoped to help his readers to a means of fulfilling that need.

No polemical work of Carlyle's shows more direct influence from the German than *Sartor*. Anyone who had closely read 'Signs of the Times' would not have found this philosophical departure too surprising. Harrold argued that the whole idea of emblemism in *Sartor* was derived from Schelling, and that the idea, prevalent throughout the book, of 'man's indwelling divinity' supporting the moral progress of society through the greater spiritual attainments of man, came from Fichte.[27] The attack on materialism is renewed in *Sartor*, the clothes or other symbols concealing religious truths that men simply wanted the wisdom to strip away the covers from and have revealed. This idea of a body of truth being concealed beneath a literal or metaphorical vestment was first raised in his essay on 'The State of German Literature'. It is the basic Carlylean idea of God immanent in everything, most essentially in the soul of man himself, and everything – clothes, officials, institutions – being disguises concealing that immanence. Teufelsdröckh says that

All visible things are emblems; what thou seest is not there on its own account; strictly taken, is not there at all: Matter exists only spiritually, and to represent some Idea, and *body* it forth. Hence clothes, as despicable as we think them, are so unspeakably significant. Clothes, from the King's mantle downwards, are emblematic, not of want only, but of a manifold cunning Victory over Want ... Men are properly said to be clothed with Authority, clothed with Beauty, with Curses, and the like. Nay if you consider it, what is Man himself, and his whole terrestrial Life, but an Emblem; a Clothing or visible Garment for that divine ME of his, cast hither, like a light-particle, down from Heaven?[28]

The point about clothes as disguises for reality (which earlier critics, like Henry Larkin, regarded as the central thesis of the book[29]), or as symbols of authority, is better developed into the idea of spiritual relations a little later on:

Man is a Spirit, and bound by invisible bonds to *All Men ... he wears Clothes,* which are the visible emblems of that fact. Has not your Red hanging-individual a horsehair wig, squirrel-skins, and a plush gown; whereby all mortals know that he is a JUDGE? – Society, which the more I think of it astonishes me the more, is founded upon cloth.[30]

Soon, we encounter the idea in its widest application, where it should become clear that the entire clothes philosophy is a religious metaphor, a test of spiritual insight:

Nothing that he sees but has more than a common meaning, but has two meanings: thus, if in the highest Imperial Sceptre and Charlemagne-Mantle, as well as in the poorest Ox-goad and gipsy blanket, he finds Prose, Decay, Contemptibility; there is in each sort Poetry also, and a reverend Worth. For Matter, were it never so despicable, is Spirit, the manifestation of Spirit: were it never so honourable, can it be more? The thing Visible, nay the thing Imagined, the thing in any way conceived as Visible, what is it but a Garment, a Clothing of the higher, celestial Invisible, 'unimaginable, formless, dark with excess of bright?' ... Happy he who can look through the Clothes of a Man (the woollen, and fleshly, and official Bank-paper and State-paper Clothes) into the man himself.[31]

Other familiar themes of Carlyle's make an appearance, notably his use of the supposed power of the press as an indication of the secularisation of society. The professor complains that ' "the Journalists are now the true Kings and Clergy: henceforth Historians, unless they are fools, must write not of Bourbon Dynasties, and Tudors and Habsburgs; but of Stamped Broadsheet Dynasties, and quite new successive Names, according as this or the other Able Editor, or Combination of Able Editors, gains the world's ear." '[32] The first of the work's three books is devoted to the rough outline of the philosophy and its related ideas, and displays Carlyle's narrative originality when, as editor, and in a mystical way in keeping with the tone of the book, he suddenly finds six paper-bags that contain biographical details of the professor.

The second book is devoted to this biography, and the reader is asked to understand the man that he might better understand the work. While still laced with appropriate mystical inventions, what follows is largely autobiographical. Carlyle as editor has already told us of Teufelsdröckh that a 'tendency to Mysticism is everywhere traceable in this man,'[33] and we know he speaks of himself. Much of what Carlyle writes reveals a coming to terms with himself, and with the unhappiness of his own past. There are the 'fever-paroxysms of doubt'[34] that seize Teufelsdröckh as they did Carlyle when he was forced to abandon his plans to enter the Church; there is the need for 'the dead letter of religion' to 'own itself dead'[35] before a new faith can be embraced. In Blumine, object of Teufelsdröckh's unfulfilled love, there is Margaret Gordon, who also went off and married a worthy but dull man of a higher station.

This book contains the three chapters central to the whole work. 'The Everlasting No' sees Teufelsdröckh confront the terrors of unbelief, when utterly in despair, as Carlyle had been in Leith Walk. In an echo of 'Signs of the Times,' the professor protests that 'Soul is not synonymous with Stomach' and that, for man, 'Faith is properly the one thing needful.'[36] And, through Teufelsdröckh, Carlyle gives the best possible expression of his feelings at the nadir in Edinburgh ten years earlier:

In the midst of their crowded streets and assemblages, I walked solitary; and (except as it was my own heart, not another's, that I kept devouring) savage also, as the tiger in his jungle. Some comfort it would have been, could I, like a Faust, have fancied myself tempted and tormented of the Devil; for a Hell, as I imagine, without Life, though only diabolic Life, were more frightful: but in our age of Down-pulling and Disbelief, the very Devil has been pulled down, you cannot so much as believe in a Devil. To me the Universe was void of Life, of Purpose, of Volition, even of Hostility: it was one huge, dead, immeasurable Steam-engine, rolling on, in its dead indifference, to grind me limb from limb. O, the vast, gloomy, solitary Golgotha, and Mill of Death! Why was the Living banished thither companionless, conscious? Why, if there is no Devil, nay unless the Devil is your God?[37]

Typically, Carlyle as 'editor' immediately follows this passage of the deepest personal emotion with a dig at Teufelsdröckh, accusing him subtly of hypochondria. Whether because he could not stand the unalleviated wallowing in memories of self-pity, or whether he had obtained a better perspective on himself than previously, Carlyle is careful to exploit the structural freedom given him by the invention of the editor to modulate the tone of his treatise, from grave seriousness to high humour. As the narrative moves on through the other two central chapters, 'The Centre of Indifference' and 'The Everlasting Yea,' these variations persist, though the tone becomes progressively more serious. Quoting Goethe, Teufelsdröckh reminds us that 'it is only with Renunciation (*Entsagen*) that Life, properly speaking, can be said to begin'[38] – uncoincidentally, shortly before the famous imprecation to 'Close thy *Byron*; open thy *Goethe.*' This self-denying, or rather self-flagellatory, view, is then developed further. 'Love not Pleasure; love God. This is the EVERLASTING YEA, wherein all contradiction is solved: wherein whoso walks and works, it is well with him.'[39]

This sentiment stays with Carlyle throughout his works, underpinning his moral view, and leading to the extreme moral position of some of the writing of his middle period. Whatever the Germanic influence on *Sartor*, and however much Goethe had helped him to find confidence in himself and in the view of spirituality that he had developed, the Everlasting Yea owes as much, if not more, to the Calvinism of Carlyle's upbringing.

The third and last book of *Sartor* reveals more of Teufelsdröckh's thoughts, clarifying the idea of clothes as symbols, disquisiting on the nature of society and the relationships between people who live in it, showing practical applications of the philosophy. The professor makes what is probably the central pronouncement of the whole philosophy, that 'it is in and through *Symbols* that man, consciously or unconsciously, lives.'[40] He cites military banners, regal coats of arms, and vestments of religious sects as such symbols, but there is more to his argument than that. In each of them a 'Divine Idea' is seen to shine through, such as the ideas of duty or heroic daring in military banners. It is tangential to the clothes philosophy, but without doubt another means of Carlyle expressing the immanence of God in everything; the ultimate expression of his belief that he had created a post-Christian creed out of a fundamentally romantic work of fiction. To convey the message of God's immanence, Carlyle had not only to redefine the material, but also the abstract. He believed a barrier to man's appreciation of God's immanence was the limited experience of time and space that man had; therefore, the eternal nature of time and space had to be made clear to man, as forces that had neither beginnings nor ends. In his later historical work, notably *The French Revolution*, he seeks to make history relevant by depicting it as part of such a continuum, in which all his readers were living and would continue to live. In *Sartor*, in the chapter 'Natural Supernaturalism', he says that 'Yesterday and Tomorrow both are. Pierce through the time element, glance into the Eternal ... believe that Time and Space are not God, but creations of God; that with God as it is a universal HERE so it is an everlasting NOW.'[41]

God is omnipresent as that 'indwelling divinity' in men's souls; once men see that, they see Him in all around them.

Carlyle also uses this part of the work for another attack on utilitarianism, his thought identical to ideas and expressions in 'Signs of the Times'. ' "The Soul Politic having departed," says Teufelsdröckh, "what can follow but that the Body Politic be decently interred, to avoid putrescence! Liberals, Economists, Utilitarians enough I see marching with its bier . . ." '[42] He accuses these same Liberals and Utilitarians of working to 'destroy most existing institutions of society.' Indeed, he argues that because religion has deserted it and been replaced by what he would come to term the cash-nexus, society was extinct; but one day, he hopes, God will be recognised and, phoenix-like, society will rise again. In such passages *Sartor* is a primer for Carlyle's later work, with early rumblings of his principal political doctrine. 'Fools!' cries the professor. 'Were your Superiors worthy to govern, and you worthy to obey, reverence for them were even your only possible freedom.'[43] He outlines thoughts on kingship similar to those in *Heroes*, arguing that 'he who will be my Ruler, whose will is to be higher than my will, was chosen for me in Heaven.' This is fundamental to the anti-democratic impulse in Carlyle's thought.

The last part of the work is the least felicitous, the most ponderously written and the most obscure, but it takes us closer to Carlyle's own developing world view than any other part of *Sartor*. Carlyle seems to have been aware of this, for he asks:

Can it be hidden from the Editor that many a British Reader sits reading quite bewildered in head, and afflicted rather than instructed by the present Work? Yes, long ago has many a British Reader been, as now, demanding, with something like a snarl: Whereto does all this lead; or what use is it?[44]

He answers that, in utilitarian terms, it leads to nothing, but for those able to see the spiritual message once the clothes-screen is removed, it leads 'into the region of the Wonderful,' where the reader will see and feel 'that . . . daily life is girt with Wonder, and based on Wonder, and thy very blankets and breeches are Miracles.' Carlyle cannot allow this profound reflection of his own religious beliefs to pass without a joke, so the editor adds that he hopes the reader will recognise this profit to be had from the work, and 'nay, perhaps in many a literary Tea-circle wilt open thy kind lips, and audibly express that same.' Certainly, no one who wishes to see the intellectual force behind Carlyle's subsequent works can afford not to read *Sartor*.

IV

Carlyle left Craigenputtock on 4 August 1831 at two o'clock in the morning, taking with him the manuscript of *Sartor* and an introduction from Napier to Longman's, the publisher. Napier had also given him some advice, namely that the London books market was so depressed, and that even steady publishers like Longman's were saving their money for better times. He at last paid Carlyle the money owed him, thirty-five guineas, which came in time to stave off penury. Carlyle went by sea to Liverpool, and thence, after a weekend with Jane's uncle John Welsh in that city, to London by coach. Jane missed her husband dreadfully, regular visits from his family doing little to ease her isolation. A few days after Carlyle left, she went to her mother at Templand. He missed her too, his letters to her full of endearments to his 'lovekin', 'goodykin', 'wifiekin' and 'screamikin'. Life for them was not entirely *ernst*.

Having moved in to share Jack's lodging in St Pancras, he went at once to Jermyn Street to see Jeffrey and his family. Although Carlyle had the letter of introduction to Longman's, Jeffrey persuaded him that John Murray was a better publisher. Therefore, Carlyle took a letter from Jeffrey to Murray, who had published Byron, with the manuscript, begging him to read it urgently. The letter, Carlyle told Jane, said 'that I was a genius and would likely become eminent,'[45] and added that Jeffrey wanted to talk to Murray about the book. Eventually Carlyle found Murray in, and the publisher pledged to start reading the book immediately, promising an answer a week later. Carlyle renewed old acquaintances while he awaited the decision. Mrs Montagu rebuked him for not having brought Jane, and told him of the decline into dissoluteness and ruin of Badams. Other old friends, such as the Bullers, had fled London for fear of becoming part of the cholera epidemic sweeping Europe. He was asked out to see the Stracheys at Shooter's Hill, where he was given an introduction to the great reform debate; all, like Mrs Montagu, were sad not to see Jane. And he made some new acquaintances, notably William Godwin, the radical philosopher and Shelley's father-in-law, who told him that literary life in London had declined in recent years; a trip with Irving to Highgate to see Coleridge never happened, because on the September evening they had set aside for the trip it rained heavily.

Irving was away when Carlyle arrived, so it was some time before they met. His beliefs and preachings had become steadily more unorthodox, bringing him into trouble with the Scottish established Kirk, which was beginning the process to have him removed from his pulpit. Carlyle described him to Jane as having been forgotten by the 'intellectual classes,' but taken up by the 'fanatical classes,' which went straight to the heart of the problem.[46] He urged Carlyle to bring his wife and settle in London, and Carlyle made it clear he was considering such a move. But the acceptance of *Sartor* was crucial to this. Carlyle was distressed by the religious aspect of Irving, whose ministry was now degenerating into the gift of tongues. Carlyle called it, in a letter to Jane, 'a positive belief that God is still working miracles in the Church – by hysterics.'[47] Such talk, along with that of casting out devils, left Carlyle cold; and he noted it was mainly women who succumbed to Irving's supernatural style, 'the crazed weakliest of his wholly rather dim and weakly flock.'[48] He regarded Irving as being 'deep in Prophecy and other aberrations,'[49] and as keeping the company of 'ignorant conceited fanatics,' though on secular matters he was ahead of Carlyle. London was discussing nothing other than the Reform Bill, to which Irving was far more hostile than Carlyle. From the vantage point of the *Reminiscences*, Carlyle admitted his views had subsequently followed Irving's.

Carlyle went to see Longman's, but found them so uninterested in him that he did not feel it worth while bothering them with *Sartor* if Murray rejected it. When the appointed week had elapsed Carlyle went back to Murray, to find he had left for the country. His clerk assured Carlyle that Murray would be writing to him, though Carlyle was sufficiently unimpressed to write that evening to Jane and describe Murray as 'the Dog of a Bookseller.' Carlyle found some distraction not just in the society of others, but in new experiences. On the evening after he failed to see Murray he went for the first time to the House of Commons – the old building, which burned down in 1834 – to see Jeffrey. The chamber was

far smaller than I expected, hardly larger than some drawing-rooms you have seen, with some four ranges of benches rising high behind each other like pews in a church gallery; an oval open space in the middle, at the farther extremity of which sits the Speaker in what seemed a kind of Press (like our wardrobe, only oaken); opposite him is the door. A very narrow gallery runs all round atop, for reporters, strangers &c...[50]

When he lived in London, Carlyle made no habit of visiting parliament. However, the image of that reporter's gallery, with its inhabitants communicating events there to 'twenty-seven millions, mostly fools',[51] came to be a symbol in his later writings of what he disliked about democracy: those deliberating in the chamber having to modify their words and deeds for public consumption, the public being given a superficial account of the proceedings, and government being less effective and less convincing as a result.

Next morning he went back to see Murray. The publisher told him that, because his family had been ill, he had not yet had the chance to read the manuscript. Carlyle reminded Murray, in plain terms, of the agreement between them; and Murray promised Carlyle he would read the work by early September, a promise Carlyle doubted 'this Blockhead'[52] would keep, so he took the manuscript away in disgust. He realised the truth of what Napier had told him, and saw there were no other prospects of finding a publisher. James Fraser had told him he would publish *Sartor*, provided Carlyle paid him £150; something Carlyle would not have considered, even had he had such resources. The frustration of his intentions for this trip, of which he had had such high – and unrealistic – hopes, left him 'bilious and sad.'[53]

In desperation, he let Longman's look at the manuscript for two days, but held out no hope that they would publish it. In this he was correct. However, he was unshakeably confident about the value of *Sartor*. 'My persuasion that Teufk. is in his place and his time here grows stronger the more I see of London and its philosophy,' he wrote to Jane.[54] 'The Doctrine of the Phoenix, of *Nat. Supernaturalism* and the whole Clothes Philosophy (be it but well stated) is exactly what all intelligent men are wanting.' Jeffrey asked to see the manuscript of *Sartor* once Longman's had done with it, that he might read it carefully and make specific recommendations to Murray. Despite his anger with that publisher, Carlyle, who had little choice, agreed. Distracted by politics, and fearing the difficult progress over reform might lead to revolution, Jeffrey could not attend to it quickly, and kept Carlyle waiting. Though Jeffrey found some of the opening pages dilatory, he none the less wrote to Murray, asking that the two of them might meet to discuss it.

Carlyle wrote to Jane suggesting she might join him in London for the winter. One can only conjecture that the thought of his returning to the desolation of Craigenputtock having failed to find a publisher for *Sartor* would have been more than he could stand. He had decided to allow the book to be published even if the publisher failed to pay him for doing so, so keen was he for recognition. There was enough money from his review articles to sustain them in this adventure, which he computed would cost 45s a week. And, if London palled, the Bullers had invited both Carlyles to Cornwall. One burden, at least, was removed from him. Having supported Jack for so long, he was glad to hear he had been appointed travelling physician to the Countess of Clare, on a salary of 300 guineas a year, plus expenses. Jeffrey had secured him the post; at least he was able to help one member of the family. Carlyle himself grew irritated with Jeffrey to the point of resentment, embarrassed that he had not the £60 to pay back the loan made him fifteen months earlier. It is hardly attractive of Carlyle that he made it plain to Jane that he tolerated Jeffrey only because, in those days before the penny post, the Lord Advocate was able to supply him with franked letters for him to use to write home.

There were others worse off than he was. He went to see Badams at the end of August, and found him in terminal decline; he met the essayist Charles Lamb, whom he described as 'a miserable, drink-besotted, spindle-shanked skeleton.'[55] References to Lamb in the *Reminiscence* of Jane, thirty-five years later, showed no growth of charity on this subject, and attracted Carlyle much posthumous opprobrium. 'A very sorry pair of phenomena,' he said of Lamb and his sister. 'Insuperable proclivity to *gin*.' Carlyle was becoming increasingly disgusted by the literary men of London. 'They are the Devil's own vermin, whom the Devil in his good time will snare and successively eat,' he told Jane.[56] One such, William Empson (Jeffrey's son-in-law), however offered to introduce Carlyle to John Stuart Mill, of whom Carlyle had heard enough attractive reports to be willing to make the acquaintance. He was not disappointed, telling Jane that he and this 'gifted and amiable youth' (Mill was then twenty-five) had had 'four hours of the best talk I have mingled in for long.'[57] Carlyle had been aware of Mill's work before coming to London, having in early 1831 read and approved of a series of anonymous articles of his under the title 'Spirit of the Age'. He later told Mill that, when he read them, he had said to himself 'here is a new mystic,' and decided to discover who the author was and to find him on coming to London.[58] For his part, Mill claimed that Carlyle, in his earlier writings, had provided 'one of the channels through which I received the influences which enlarged my early narrow creed.' Writing long after their friendship had been breached by Carlyle's militant objections to liberalism, Mill took care to add that 'I do not think that those writings, by themselves, would ever have had any effect on my opinions.' He also claimed to have found Carlyle's early articles full of 'insane rhapsody.'[59] Carlyle was usually level-headed about his friendships, but the flattery he, in his struggle for recognition, received from so attractive a figure as Mill quite turned his head, and they quickly developed an intimacy. Mill was, in many respects, the first proper 'secular priest' of Carlyle's acquaintance.

The stimulation Carlyle received from London society also deepened his political pessimism. Reporting to Jane on his view of the coronation procession of King William IV and Queen Adelaide on 8 September, he regarded the others watching with him as '70 or 80 thousand woodenheads,' the King and Queen as 'foolish wax dolls', and the whole spectacle as 'the ghost of the Past perhaps taking final leave of a world, where as body or as ghost it has now walked for some three thousand years.'[60] Such was the significance of the approaching democratic revolution.

However repellent Carlyle thought he found London, it offered him social and intellectual stimulation of a sort he had been starved of for three years; hence his entreaties to Jane to come south for an exploratory visit. He found his reputation was greater than he had imagined, and even that he had some younger acolytes, not least because of 'Signs of the Times'. Such recognition cheered him. Jane was persuaded of the benefits of coming, not least because the depressive tone of Carlyle's letters to her was making her anxious for his health. He began to make plans for her journey, and for their winter in London. Realising he could not exist without making some money, he wrote to Napier in Edinburgh offering his reviewing services.

Carlyle's belief that he would allow *Sartor* to be published for nothing was soon put to the test. Jeffrey convinced Murray that he ought to print 750 copies on the half-profits system, which meant Carlyle was paid nothing but received nothing either. He would, though, retain the sole copyright. 'A poorish offer, Goody,' he told Jane, 'yet perhaps after all the best I shall get.'[61] None the less, he tried one further publisher – fruitlessly – to see whether someone would pay him. Having failed, pinning Murray down was hard. In mid-September 1831 Carlyle thought he had wrung an agreement out of him that the work would be published at the beginning of 1832; the reform agitation had, Murray claimed, made it pointless to try to publish books at that time. But no sooner had the first proof-sheets arrived than Carlyle received a curt letter from Murray. The publisher claimed he was under the impression that he had had first refusal of the manuscript; he was not aware that another publisher had already rejected it and, that being so, he would have to gain a second opinion on its merits. Carlyle was stung, and wrote back saying that if Murray wanted to back out of the bargain they had struck, he was welcome to do so. The printing was stopped. Carlyle wrote to Jane at Liverpool, where she was staying with her uncle *en route* for London, to say that Murray had 'behaved like a Pig,' and acknowledging the painful truth that 'Dreck cannot be disposed of in London at this time.' Murray claimed he was only trying to avoid the professional embarrassment of having to compete with a rival for a work he thought was his to do as he pleased with. Carlyle never forgave him, commenting in the *Reminiscences* thirty-five years later that 'stupider man than the great Murray, in look, in speech, in conduct in regard to this poor Sartor question, I imagined I had seldom or never seen.'[62] When Murray returned the manuscript to Carlyle in October, he sent with it the critical report of his 'taster'. It is this, along with other readers' opinions, that Carlyle appended to *Sartor*, not being above saying 'I told you so to those publishers who had once looked down their noses at him.

On 1 October Jane at last reached London, to be met at the Angel, Islington, by Carlyle and Jack, who was about to leave for the continent with Lady Clare. Jane came laden with provisions from Annandale, and not in especially good health. More ominously, she brought a letter from Carlyle's father to him and Jack in which, for some reason sensing mortality, the old man had written that 'I am a frail old sinner that is very likely never to see you any more in this world' and that 'I feel myself gradually drawing toward the house appointed for all living.'[63] Shortly before Carlyle left for London, he had seen his father and been offered two sovereigns of the old man's, a gesture which caused his son to think he was 'fey', or under the power of the fate that controlled his life, and therefore being swayed into making uncharacteristic gestures. The letter was further, and as it turned out accurate, confirmation of this.

Carlyle quickly moved himself and Jane from Jack's lodging into more comfortable ones in Ampton Street, in St Pancras, where they could better receive visitors. One of the first invited to meet Jane after her arrival was Mill. He had been as taken with Carlyle as Carlyle had with him, telling John Sterling (who would not meet Carlyle for another four years) that his new friend was 'a man who has had his eyes unsealed, and who now looks round him & sees the aspects of things with his own eyes, but by the light supplied by others.'[64] He also described Carlyle as 'a great hunter-out of acquaintances.' Apart from social activity, Carlyle had work to do. Napier asked him to write a review of Thomas Hope's *An Essay on the Origins and Prospects of Man*, and this was soon published as 'Characteristics'. The one difficulty was that

Carlyle could find no copy of Hope anywhere, not even at the publisher's. He was becoming distracted by politics, as the Lords, on 8 October, rejected the Reform Bill, causing it to be postponed another six months and the crisis prolonged. 'Poor country!' he wrote to Jack. 'Millions in it nigh starving; and for help of them, Talk, Talk, and nothing but Talk!'[65] *Sartor* had not been abandoned, but the delay meant the book trade would not revive until the following year, further depressing Carlyle.

Jane took to London well, enjoying meeting Carlyle's new friends, though distressed at seeing the state into which one of their old ones, Irving, had fallen. A short exposure to the true believers in Irving's house 'speaking in tongues' sent her home in tears. She warmed to Mill, acquitting him of the utilitarianism of his upbringing, and thinking him a mystic, like her husband. Carlyle, though, found mysticism being superseded more and more by concern at the worsening political situation. The ideas aired later on in *Chartism, Heroes, Past and Present* and the *Latter-Day Pamphlets* were being formed by the good fortune of his being in London, mixing in political circles, as the postponement of reform caused further severe civil unrest around the country. He wrote to his mother in November 1831 of

a country agitated with political discontent, with economical embarrassment; the lower orders, straitened by want, exasperated by disappointment, all ready for *any* kind of change, whether by revolt or otherwise; nowhere any Wisdom, any Faithfulness to give them counsel ... Nevertheless there is always this strong tower of Defence, that it *is* of God's ordering; that not a hair of our head, of the very meanest head, can fall to the ground without his command ... God is great; God is also good: this is the sum total of all the Wisdom I could ever learn.[66]

When the Reform Act was passed the following year, and the problems by no means alleviated, Carlyle's pessimism was proved right. Partly as a result, he set on a career of pointing out the fallacies of democracy and other attempts to interfere with God's order. What he saw in London in 1831–32 was vital to the growth of that belief.

6

Out of Exile

1831–34

LATE IN NOVEMBER 1831 Carlyle wrote to MacVey Napier in Edinburgh that he was 'busy with an *Article* intended for you, which I have entitled CHARACTERISTICS.'[1] He had eventually tracked down Hope's *Essay on the Origin and Prospects of Man,* and coupled it in his review with Schlegel's *Philosophical Lectures,* something to which he was much more temperamentally disposed. The result was an important, but diffuse, exposition of Carlyle's views on belief and unbelief, utilitarianism and materialism, and other vices he perceived in society, and with which those who had read his unsigned, but now distinctive, pieces would already be familiar. There is a significant rebuttal of an accusation yet to be made, that he believed 'might is right'. 'In all even the rudest communities, man never yields himself wholly to brute force, but always to moral Greatness,' he wrote. 'As the crown and all supporting keystone of the fabric, Religion arises.'[2] Reflecting the Reform Bill agitation, he stigmatises 'Vote by Ballot' as the 'dyspepsia of society',[3] an affront to its natural course; and he makes clear his estrangement from Christianity by observing that 'the Christian Religion of late ages has been continually dissipating itself into Metaphysics; and threatens now to disappear, as some rivers do, in deserts of barren sand.'[4] Considering the stimulation Carlyle had had in London, the piece seems tired and clumsy, showing little evidence of his having much new to say, and him trapped in the usual, narrow, German perspective. He told Jack it was 'a sort of second *Signs of the Times*',[5] when all he had to say had been said in the first. When Napier received the work he described it as 'inscrutable', a euphemism for 'unintelligible'. Carlyle rejoined that his own fear had been that the work might have been 'too *scrutable*', and he told Jack that 'it indicates decisively enough that Society (in my view) is utterly condemned to destruction, and even now beginning its long travail-throes of Newbirth.'[6]

Luckily for him, his next articles were to take him away from these confines, into biography and the new edition of Boswell's *Life of Johnson,* which he spent December and January reading. However, the winter of 1831–32 was also to be one of painful personal distractions. He could find no work to supplement his reviewing, though he sought lecturing or teaching posts, and he was in despair. He felt there was 'no hope' for *Sartor*,[7] though his former pupil Charles Buller was enthusiastically reading the manuscript. Jane was constantly ill with colds, and he too spent much of January trying to shake one off. They both lived in fear of the cholera epidemic reaching London. However, minor or feared horrors were soon put into perspective by a greater blow. On 24 January, Carlyle found Jane in tears reading a letter from his sister Jane at Scotsbrig, telling them of the death of his father two days earlier, having been taken ill with a cold six days before that. He was seventy-three. 'The stroke ... as yet painfully crushes my heart,'[8] Carlyle wrote to his mother. He was distressed not to be able to attend the funeral, and withdrew to spend 'hours in solemn meditation, self-examination, and thoughts of the eternal'.[9] His grief was profound, and he believed it visible in the tone of his review of Boswell. He passed on the news to Jack, in Rome, telling him to 'mourn not more than is unavoidable; lay the matter solemnly to heart, and study to turn it to good.'[10] Writing his *Reminiscence* of Irving more than thirty years later, Carlyle recalled how he had, at this time, 'sat plunged into the depths of natural grief; the pale kingdoms of eternity laid bare to me, and all that was sad and grand, and dark as death, filling my thoughts exclusively, day after day.'[11] Jane helped him to bear up by pampering him with kindness and tenderness.

He took practical steps to expiate his grief. He shut himself away and for four days wrote what became the first of the *Reminiscences*, in which, denied the chance to bid his father farewell, he compensated by recalling the goodness and greatness of the man. Until the day of James's funeral he and Jane saw no one, except for Irving, who came with his wife on the day of the burial. They prayed together, though this event disturbed Carlyle. He found Irving's mind 'crippled and weakened', full of 'inane babble about tongues'.[12] The calamity helped them decide when to return to Scotland, and they set early March as the date, Carlyle hoping to have finished his article on Boswell for Fraser by then.

Once this blow was absorbed, intellectual life continued. Carlyle sought a commission from Napier to write on the *Corn Law Rhymes* of the Sheffield steel-worker Ebenezer Elliott, which he had borrowed from Mill and liked. Napier agreed, albeit cautiously, because of the radicalism of Elliott's attacks on the system that fixed corn prices for the benefit of landowners irrespective of the effect on the people. Leigh Hunt, having read 'Characteristics', sent the anonymous author a copy of his *Christianism: or Belief and Unbelief Reconciled*, and Carlyle wrote back in gratitude, identifying himself and saying how much he would like to meet Hunt. As Carlyle was to find when, two years later, they became neighbours in Chelsea, Hunt was not the most organised of men. He took nearly a fortnight to reply, but said he had been acquainted with Carlyle's work since reading the translation of *Wilhelm Meister*, and would indeed call on Carlyle one morning in Ampton Street, his and Jane's St Pancras lodging. As if to prove his keenness to meet Hunt, Carlyle immediately wrote and asked him to come at six o'clock the next evening, to take tea with Jane and him. Hunt came, and Carlyle was struck by his congeniality; and also by the pecuniary difficulties Hunt and his family were in.

As the Carlyles prepared to start north, they at least had the consolation of knowing that their winter in London had widened their range of friends in a most helpful way. This was to reduce the isolation of their last two years in Scotland, as Carlyle now had the likes of Mill and Hunt with whom to correspond. The prospect of such society was to influence strongly their decision to move to London two years later. The piece on Boswell was finished, and Carlyle and Fraser decided to divide it into two, with the shorter introductory piece, 'Biography', appearing in the April number of *Fraser's Magazine* and the main piece on the *Life of Johnson* following in May.

'Biography', while remaining a vehicle for Carlyle's prejudices at the time (there are further assaults on 'mechanism') shows some interesting features of his developing style. Having disquisited on fictitious biographies, he compounds the joke by quoting at length from one of his own inventions, Professor Sauerteig, to support his own arguments. There are some serious points, however, about good biography, namely that it should reflect reality; and later on, after Sauerteig (which literally means 'leaven') has had his say, Carlyle concludes that the 'English' cannot write biography, the only exception being Ayrshire's Boswell.

The essay is important for more than what it says about Carlyle's understanding of the *Life of Johnson*. He spells out his aversion to the school of historical writing that he subsequently caricatured as 'Dryasdust', using the name of a mythical pedant invented by Sir Walter Scott; and in discovering this loathing, we come to understand much about the development of Carlyle's own writing style, and why he chose to write his next significant work, *The French Revolution*, in the way he did. The main essay is one of Carlyle's most impressive pieces of early writing, free of mystical 'rhapsodising' but instead comprising an intelligent and original discussion of the editing of this great work, with thoughts on the author and his subject. Carlyle's humanity, as well as his sense of humour, comes through in his descriptions of both Boswell and Johnson; it shows Carlyle to have been what from his letters is also clear, a shrewd judge of human nature. There are also signs of Carlyle's abilities of characterisation that would be seen, unevenly, in *The French Revolution*. He shares with his readers a phrase he had long used privately to convey contempt for shallow bourgeois respectability, 'gigman' and 'gigmanity' – literally, that class that could afford to own a gig. In a footnote to the review Carlyle said that society naturally divided itself 'into four classes: Noblemen, Gentlemen, Gigmen and Men'.[13]

In justifying his view of the greatness of Boswell's writing, Carlyle composes a passage that typifies what would, in his own historical works, become the definitive anti-Dryasdust, realistic style:

The Mitre Tavern still stands in Fleet Street: but where now is its scot-and-lot paying, beef-and-ale loving, cock-hatted, pot-bellied Landlord; its rosy-faced assiduous Land-lady, with all her shining brass-pans, waxed tables, well-filled larder shelves; her cooks, and bootjacks, and errand-boys, and watery-mouthed hangers-on? Gone! Gone! The becking Waiter who, with wreathed smiles, was wont to spread for Samuel and Bozzy their supper of the gods, has long since pocketed his last sixpence; and vanished, sixpences and all, like a ghost at cock-crowing. The Bottles they drank out of are all broken, the chairs they sat on all rotted and burnt; the very Knives and Forks they ate with have rusted to the heart ... All, all has vanished ... Of the Mitre Tavern nothing but the bare walls remain there: of London, of England, of the World, nothing but the bare walls remain...[14]

This, he says, is history, for Boswell's work with its attention to the minutiae of everyday realities 'will give us more real insight into the History of England during those days than twenty other Books, falsely entitled "Histories", which take to themselves that special aim'. He derides the grand school of historical fact, protesting that 'the thing I want to see is not Redbook Lists, and Court Calendars, and Parliamentary Registers, but the LIFE OF MAN in England: what men did, thought, suffered, enjoyed; the form, especially the spirit, of their terrestrial existence, its outward environment, its inward principle; how and what it was; whence it proceeded, whither it was tending.'[15] The style that became known as 'Carlylese' originated in this desire to convey robust, conversational immediacy in presenting historical detail; but once employed in *The French Revolution*, Carlyle was unable to shake it off. In this essay we see its first clear emergence, the first departures from the regular prose of the works up until then.

The essay finished, the Carlyles left for Birmingham at eight in the morning of Saturday 24 March 1832, the day after the Reform Bill passed again through the House of Commons. The first leg of the journey and the stop at Birmingham were pleasant, but Carlyle had to ride outside to Liverpool. They recuperated there for a few days with Jane's uncle, John Welsh, before taking the steamer to Annan. Craigenputtock was in need of maintenance before they could move back in, so they went to Templand.

II

Hardly had they returned when word came from Weimar that Goethe had died on 22 March, two months to the day after Carlyle's father. 'Alas! Alas!' he wrote to Alick, 'I feel as if I had a second time lost a Father: he was to me a kind of spiritual Father.'[16] Despite the distractions of the farm at Craigenputtock, and of house-painters, Carlyle was meant to be at work on the *Corn Law Rhymes*. However, he set this aside for a few days, and in homage wrote 'The Death of Goethe', published in the June number of the *New Monthly Magazine*, edited by Edward Bulwer, whom Carlyle had met in London. The 'Death' firmly establishes Carlyle's view of his master's heroism, a theme to be developed more extensively in the lectures of 1840.

To impress Goethe's greatness upon a sceptical British readership, Carlyle argued that he had 'made a new era in literature',[17] and had been, like the true poets of antiquity, a seer, 'for he *sees* into this greatest of secrets, "the open secret"; hidden things become clear; how the Future (both resting on Eternity) is but another phasis of the Present: thereby are his words in very truth prophetic; what he has spoken shall be done'.[18] The 'open secret' was 'the godlike Mystery of God's Universe', and it was a secret into which Goethe had let Carlyle. Goethe's achievements, as set out by Carlyle, formed an agenda for his pupil's career: 'This man, we may say, became morally great, by being in his own age, what in some other ages many might have been, a genuine man.'

Once he had finished this he decided to write a longer piece on his works for the *Foreign Quarterly Review.* Such was the enormity of his subject, and so overwhelmed was Carlyle by it, that he had rare difficulty composing the piece, which occupied him until early July. He also had to finish the piece on the *Corn Law Rhymes*, which he dispatched fairly quickly, and which was published in the *Edinburgh Review* of July 1832. The essay is significant for what it shows us of Carlyle's concerns for the people suffering under the inhumane economics of driving up the price of corn to benefit the aristocracy who grew it while starving those who needed to buy the bread made with it. We learn far less about Carlyle's capacity as a critic of poetry. Despite the literary failings of the Rhymer, Carlyle praised him because he was 'genuine'.[19] Carlyle's early thoughts on what he would call 'the condition of England question', which he would address in *Chartism* in 1839 and in *Past and Present* in 1843, are set out clearly:

Mournful enough, that a white European Man must pray wistfully for what the horse he drives is sure of, – That the strain of his whole faculties may not fail to earn him food and lodging . . . is it not frightful as well as mournful to consider how the widespread evil is spreading wider and wider? Most persons, who have had eyes to look with, may have verified, in their own circle, the statement of this Sheffield Eye-witness, and 'from their own knowledge and observation fearlessly declare that the little master-manufacturer, that the working-man generally, is in a much worse condition than he was twenty-five years ago.'[20]

Carlyle does not yet develop his criticism of the cash-nexus, but does allude to the problems of leaving economic welfare to the markets and to chance, as opposed to earlier feudal provision. His analysis, as far as it went, was flawed, for if ever anything militated against markets, it was the Corn Laws.

He argues that England's hopes rest on the likes of the Rhymer, on people able to summon up the heroic voice and exert leadership, since the established leaders have been corrupted by self-interest and stupidity. 'All Reform except a moral one will prove unavailing,' he wrote. 'Political Reform, pressingly enough wanted, can indeed root out the weeds . . . but it leaves the ground *empty*, ready either for noble fruits, or for new worse tares!'[21] This reform, he says, will be accomplished only by providence sending good strong men like the Rhymer to undertake it, 'to disseminate Goodness; literally to *sow* it'. His longing for the 'Good Man' was, though, to prove unfulfilled, however loud and often he cried for him, and however angry he became in his frustration. When he wrote this review Carlyle had only the sketchiest knowledge of how bad things really were. The following year he read in *Blackwood's Magazine* an article by John Wilson that depicted the suffering of children in Lancashire factories, quoting from the report of the Select Committee on Factory Children's Labour of 1831–32. He was horrified to read of the sixteen-hour days, the inhalation of cotton dust and the corporal punishment endured by such children, 'without prospect of rest, save by speedy death'.[22]

This political exercise completed, he returned to Goethe. In the longer essay on his master's works he shows he has lost his sureness of touch. He chose, for no obvious reason, to quote extensively from the imaginary Professor Teufelsdröckh on the rightness of hero-worship, when it would have been less embarrassing simply to state the views as his own. The writing is prolix, reflecting the compositional difficulties of the piece, and Carlyle has little new to say. He further advances his theory of hero-worship, saying reverence for the great should be 'a chief aim of education', and gives the distinct impression that hero-worship in general, and in his case worship of Goethe in particular, was by way of a substitute for Christ for those who could not (like him) bear the Christian religion;[23] yet this Christian antipathy contrasts with a remark made to his brother Jack a few months later that 'the completest profoundest of all past and present Antigigmen was Jesus Christ.'[24] He tediously attacks reform, and gigmen, and in neither case convinces us that Goethe has much direct bearing on either point. Carlyle's writings often tell us more about him than about his subject, and this is a notable example. He echoes his own life in his description of Goethe's, telling of scepticism that was eventually conquered. The fundamental point about Goethe, however, is this:

The question, Can man still live in devoutness, yet without blindness or contraction; in unconquerable steadfastness for the right, yet without tumultuous exasperation against the wrong; as an antique worthy, yet with the expansion and increased endowment of a modern? is no longer a question, but has become a certainty, and ocularly visible fact.[25]

The article was not a success. His editor, Cochrane, wrote to him after it appeared to report that almost all the reactions to it were unfavourable. His eccentric insertion of Teufelsdröckh's thoughts into the piece was particularly attacked. Not one to take criticism kindly, Carlyle confided in his journal that Cochrane was 'what we might call an *editing Pig*, as there are learned Pigs, &c.'[26] Yet Cochrane had only confirmed what Carlyle himself had thought. 'Now,' he wrote to Mill late one night during the writing of the article, 'is the sad season of dubitation and dislocation when the woodenheaded must sit biting his pen, and see nothing before him but the nakedness of the land.'[27] Another benefit of his having made friends such as Mill, whose intellect he profoundly respected, was that their letters to him praising his work gave him a significant lift at such times. Mill was particularly taken with the article on Boswell, and wrote to Carlyle to tell him that 'you I look upon as an artist, and perhaps the only genuine one now living in this country.'[28]

Life was, though, comparatively easy for the Carlyles. When summer came he was reunited with his widowed mother, who came to stay at Craigenputtock for a fortnight, and whom Carlyle was relieved to see in strong spirits. She had been sustained by her religion, and Carlyle, tactfully putting his own feelings aside, joined her in Bible readings. Material things were more settled too. The demand for review articles had taken away worries about money, and as his fame rose so did his earnings per article. In the autumn, once paid for 'Goethe's Works', he was at last able to repay Jeffrey, which relieved him greatly. Fraser, for example, doubled what he had used to pay him, so successful had the piece on Boswell been.

Once Carlyle had started to bury Goethe, his mind began to range more widely. He wrote to Napier at the end of May asking for books about Count Cagliostro, the eighteenth-century Italian charlatan and alchemist, or for a copy of Casanova's memoirs. Jane, whose health had been poor throughout the winter, started to feel well again once back in Scotland, and she seemed to find Carlyle more agreeable too. Writing to Eliza Miles, with whose family they had lodged in Ampton Street, she said that 'my Husband is as good company as reasonable mortal could desire,' and described their happy routine of morning rides and breakfasts together before Carlyle spent the day at his desk.[29] They had hired a woman servant to make life easier for Jane, who was greatly amused when the minion allowed mouse-droppings to find their way into Carlyle's porridge.

One problem Carlyle found in working at Craigenputtock, after the facilities he had enjoyed in London, was the shortage of books. In letters he starts complaining about the lack of public libraries, a cause that was to lead, once he settled in London, to his own role in establishing the London Library. Mill offered to lend him books by post. He gratefully accepted, his first list of requests including recent works by Charles Babbage, the mathematician. He was preparing an article on the eighteenth-century French *philosophe* Denis Diderot for the *Foreign Quarterly Review*. The subject was some way outside his field of expertise, and thus his need for books was acute. He managed to find the twenty volumes needed to do justice to Diderot, and in mid-August told his mother he was reading them at the rate of one a day.

By the end of the summer, the contentment of being back in Scotland conflicted with the sense of comparative isolation after the winter in London. Carlyle wrote to Mill begging him to be a more regular correspondent, saying he and Jane were in 'a starving state' for want of news. 'Were you to tell me only that you had met such a one at such a time walking in the Strand "with his hat upon his head," you have no notion what I could make of it on the moors!' he told him.[30] He told Mill that 'sometimes there are weeks in which one does not speak a word to any other mortal,' with the exception of Jane. He took himself out for rides, either with Jane in their gig on summer afternoons, or on his own on horseback. He went to Ecclefechan late in August, finding it changed, a new main road opened and hardly anybody alive whom he knew. He had the diversion, too, of being summoned to serve on a jury at Dumfries in September, though he was cross that it had taken so many men to give up their work to find a chimney-sweep guilty of stealing an ass worth a pound. Now Jane was better the two of them wanted to go to Edinburgh, both for books and for society, but the writing of 'Diderot', which dragged on, meant that he could not contemplate the trip before November at the earliest.

Jane wrote to Eliza Stodart in early October to ask whether she could look for a house in Edinburgh, large enough to accommodate the Carlyles and a maid, that could be rented for the winter. Eliza wrote back to say she had found something Jane might feel suitable. Life in London had had its effect on Carlyle. 'The grim prospect of another winter in this solitude is too frightful for my husband,' Jane wrote, 'who finds, that it is absolutely essential for carrying on not only his craft, but his existence to hear from time to time a little human speech.'[31] Their isolation, even before winter set in, was further enforced by the raging of cholera through Dumfries. While Jane filled her days reading and sewing, Carlyle made use of the time to finish 'Diderot' which he told Mill was 'a wearisome straggling affair', while despising the fears of his neighbours about the epidemic. 'The people all in panic,' he noted on 1 October. 'Fools!' He reflected that the people were, fortunately, 'too eupeptic, hardworked and stupid' to worry much about the contagion, and blamed the authorities for stirring up such panic as there was, scaring people by creating medical boards to control the situation. None the less, a significant proportion of the Dumfries population – 422 people out of 13,000, or just over 1 in 30 – died from the disease. Before he realised the extent of the casualties ('rather an alarming proportion', he admitted to Jack once the worst was over),[32] Carlyle saw it in a wider context. 'What is there new in cholera? Death has not been new here for the last six thousand years.'[33] Yet Carlyle was anxious for the welfare of his uncle, John Aitken, who lived in the town and from whom he had not heard. He wrote agitatedly on 16 October to him, imploring Aitken to write back – 'tell me only that you are all spared alive!' Carlyle's intolerance of the emotional indisciplines of others did not always extend to himself.

His debts paid, and with plenty of work being offered, Carlyle was becoming more self-confident, and his inherent vociferousness was not being restrained by humility: which might explain his more frequent lapses of charity. His letters begin to be peppered with more offensive remarks about the 'Able Editors' queueing up to employ him, and about others of whose positions he is contemptuous – such as Jeffrey, whom he derided as now 'walking in the vain show of Parliamenteering and Gigmanity'.[34] For all the attentions of the editors, though, he was frustrated at not finding a publisher for *Sartor*, for until then he could not find the heart to consider new work. Jane's grandfather died at Templand on 16 November, and after the funeral the Carlyles made plans for the trip to Edinburgh. It was decided to spend Christmas in Dumfriesshire and then head north. Carlyle was subdued by a cold he claimed to have caught from having cut his hair too short; by way of warming him, and in response to hints dropped throughout the autumn, his mother sent him thick woollen underwear as a present, and a protection against the Edinburgh frosts ahead. Eliza Stodart having found them a house in the suburb of Stockbridge, they arrived on 7 January 1833, intending to stay three months.

III

'It is an excellent Floor of its sort,' Carlyle wrote to Jack once he and Jane had taken up their lodgings. 'Two really dashing Rooms, with three Bedrooms, Kitchen and all *etceteras*, for £4 a month.'[35] Carlyle, energised at the prospect of renewing old acquaintances, set out into society. He soon saw Bradfute, a bookseller friend, Napier and Brewster, and found the city in a tumult after the recent general election, in which the Whigs had swept the country. 'The whole struggle is poor and small,' Carlyle told Jack, explaining his lack of involvement. 'In *thought* I am the deepest radical alive in this island, but allow it to rest there, having other to do.'[36] He wrote in his journal the day he arrived of creative frustrations he had to alleviate. 'Have long been almost idle; have long been out of free communion with myself. Must suffer more before I can begin thinking. Will try to write; but what? but when?'[37]

Something was stirring in his mind, despite this negativity. His reading on Diderot had set him thinking about the moral decline of the eighteenth century, and how, in France, it culminated in revolution. In his lengthy review of Diderot's life and works, Carlyle inveighed against 'the Apostle Denis',[38] and blamed the fault of eighteenth-century society on atheism. He pronounced that France before the revolution (Diderot himself had died in 1784, too early to see the fruits of his philosophy) had 'fallen into rottenness, rainholes and noisome decay', and the 'shivering natives resolved to cheer their dull abode by the questionable step of setting it on fire'.[39] Having painted a picture of Diderot's hedonistic and faithless life, Carlyle laments his influence on France, where he became the 'head and mystagogue'[40] of the *philosophes*. 'A much smaller destiny would have been desirable,' adds Carlyle, helped by hindsight. It was bad enough that Diderot had been an atheist; but, worse, he was a 'proselytising' one.[41] He had furthered the view that in the French system of thought – like the 'mechanical' that Carlyle had already attacked – there was no scope for a divinity, because logic demanded proof, and there could be no proof. He had chosen 'to anchor himself on the rock or quagmire of Atheism – and farther, should he see fit, proclaim to others that there is good riding there'.[42]

With Goethe's help, Carlyle points out Diderot's error, the error that took France to the abyss. He and his circle had looked for God 'everywhere outwardly in physical Nature, and not inwardly in our own Soul, where alone he is to be found by us'.[43] He saw the age of Diderot, and what followed it, as one of the Goethean conflict between belief and unbelief; if belief won, the world would once more be uplifting; if it lost, the world would be a sham. But if anything angered Carlyle more than atheism, it was 'faint, possible Theism', which he felt was underpinning English religion at the time, and which had to be eradicated. He had more regard for atheists, who at least were not hedging their bets. With its moral certainties and anti-utilitarianism, it was no surprise that, when published, the piece was profoundly disagreed with by Mill; it was the first sign of his intellectual parting from Carlyle, which fifteen years later broke their friendship altogether. Carlyle was beginning to see the great liberal paradox; his instincts were that it was better not to give people freedom if they used it in so destructive a way as those empowered in France in 1789 had used it by 1792–93. This is what would ultimately divide him from Mill. However, when Mill, later in the year, began to write attacks on the Whig government in the *Examiner*, Carlyle returned to the theme, finding common ground. 'The true Atheist,' he told Mill then, 'in these days is the Whig; he worships nothing but respectability . . . the Tory is an Idolater, the Radical a wild heathen Iconoclast: yet neither of them strictly are "without God in the world": the one has an *infinite* hope, the other an infinite remembrance: both *may* be men and not gigmen'.[44]

The study of Diderot had been, as it turned out, the best intellectual groundwork for his next great project. Once settled in Edinburgh he wrote to Mill that he had also been reading Thiers's *History of the French Revolution*, which he had found 'rather a good book'. One feature missing from the work, however, stimulated his interest. He described it to Mill as 'the private biographical phasis; the manner in which individuals demeaned themselves, and social life went on, in so extraordinary an element as that'. Boswell had had this knack; so too would Carlyle in his next great work. As he read Thiers he was struck by how 'man stood there, with all the powers of Civilisation, and none of its rules to aid him in guiding these'.[45] He begged Mill to send him any other books he knew of on this subject, and wanted especially to know more of Danton, Mirabeau and Napoleon. This project would overtake his studies into the history of the Scotch Church, with which he had been desultorily occupying his time.

The Carlyles' sojourn in Edinburgh began unhappily. Alick wrote soon after their arrival to announce the death of his baby son. Both Carlyle and Jane went down with colds. Jane was to worsen in health throughout the winter, something her physician brother-in-law attributed, much to her anger, to her not having enough to occupy her mind. However, Carlyle's spirits were lifted by the access he had to libraries. He spent his days searching and finding new forms of intellectual stimulation. Being in Edinburgh made him feel more strongly that Craigenputtock could never prove a satisfactory home for him and Jane. He resolved that, as soon as circumstances permitted, they must move permanently. Carlyle knew he would have to be more certain of his financial circumstances before he could make a decision. He also wanted to make no move before the autumn, when Jack would return from his duties with Lady Clare in Italy. Dr Irving, the keeper of the Advocates' Library at Edinburgh, suggested Carlyle apply for the chair of practical astronomy at Glasgow, which was thought about to be vacant. But, despite his scientific grounding, Carlyle could not seriously have entertained such an ambition. He did, however, hint to Jeffrey that he would not mind strings being pulled, a sign more of his desperation to leave Dumfriesshire than of belatedly finding a vocation.

Since October, when he finished 'Diderot', Carlyle had written nothing. He had found books on Cagliostro, and in early February broke his silence by beginning to write a piece for Fraser about him. As always now, he was racked with doubt about what he was doing, confiding self-pityingly in his journal of 13 February that it was 'a thankless, fruitless, nigh foolish labour' that was undermining his health.[46] Once the work was nearly complete, Carlyle spoke of it to Mill as 'a long half-mad kind of story'.[47] He was feeling no more enthusiastic about writing for some of his other outlets. He had met Napier and found him dull, and was further disinclined to write for the Review because of how badly, and slowly, it paid. Further exposure to Napier hardened his view because, as he told Jack, Napier lacked 'common honesty'.[48] Carlyle let one or two of his Edinburgh friends, notably Henry Inglis, read the manuscript of Sartor, but was no nearer finding a publisher. He resolved to save £60 and publish it at his own expense.

Edinburgh had provided relief from solitude, but little else. A month before they were due to return home, the Carlyles moved lodgings because they had started, in their permanent psychosomatic illnesses, to be irritated by the noise there. As well as being weighed down with hypochondria, Carlyle found the intellectual climate unappealing, full of 'Scepticism, Dilettantism, Whiggism'.[49] He felt too radical for his old friends, like Wilson or Jeffrey, and he was not too sad when the latter left Edinburgh to take up his place in the new reformed parliament. Carlyle felt their friendship, which had been rocky ever since the move to Craigenputtock, would never consist of more than politeness. Despite the odd flash of generosity, Carlyle's letters contain more and more slighting remarks against his benefactor.

Instead, he tried to cultivate newer friends. He wrote to Leigh Hunt begging him to come either to Edinburgh before the Carlyles left in April, or to make the sea-voyage north to visit them in the spring at Craigenputtock. Oppressed by money worries, Hunt was reluctant to come. However, he offered instead (to Carlyle's chagrin) to send the eldest of his eight children, a youth of twenty-one, who was ill and in need of a change of air. Having grown apart from his Edinburgh friends, and with Jane ill from the neuralgia that would dog her to the grave, his best intellectual activity was in letters to such as Mill, who was providing him with more books on the French Revolution, and Hunt. Depressed by 'Cagliostro', which he had to complete to earn the forty guineas for the winter's expenses, he diverted to some more random thoughts on history, and sent these to Fraser as an interim submission in lieu of 'Cagliostro'. Fraser published them under the title 'Quae Cogitavit' in May 1833, and they appear in the *Critical and Miscellaneous Essays* as 'On History Again'.

When the time came to plan the journey home Carlyle was looking forward to Craigenputtock with surprising enthusiasm. Edinburgh had in the end so disillusioned him that, when and if he came to making a permanent move from Dumfriesshire, it would have to be to London. His stay in the Scottish capital had impoverished him both materially and in spirit. On 18 April, three weeks before he and Jane returned home, he wrote to Mill that the winter just ended had been 'among the saddest (from ill-health outward and inward) I have known for long'. Even their leaving of Edinburgh did not go smoothly; they missed the coach to Thornhill, which they were taking to visit Jane's mother at Templand on their way home, by three minutes, and had to stay another two days. Once they did leave, Jane caught flu on the journey, and promptly infected her mother. Her mild illnesses were now becoming more dramatic, ushering in thirty years of predominantly, and self-indulgently, ill-health. 'Such headaches I never witnessed in my life,' said Carlyle of Jane's state on reaching Thornhill. 'Agony of retching . . . and of spasmodic writhing, that would last from twenty-four to sixty hours, never the smallest help affordable.'[50] He would become callously inured to such suffering before long. 'Oh what of pain, pain, my poor Jeannie had to bear in this thorny pilgrimage of life.' As he admitted in the *Reminiscences*, he did not discover how great her suffering had been until after she had died.

IV

Once home, Carlyle's thoughts turned again to *Sartor*. It had become like a blockage, and until it was freed he could not write another book. He decided to ask James Fraser, with whom his relations were good, to publish it in instalments. He admitted to Jack that 'want of diplomacy'[51] on his part had not helped achieve the book's publication in the past, so he was planning to use all his reserves of tact to persuade Fraser now. He made the approach in a letter of 27 May 1833, in which he reminded Fraser of the existence of the work, and told him of his decision to have it serialised. 'Your magazine is the first I think of for this object,'[52] he wrote, and added:

It is put together in the fashion of a kind of Didactic Novel; but indeed properly like nothing yet extant. I used to characterize it briefly as a kind of 'Satirical extravaganza on Things in General'; it contains more of my opinions on Art, Politics, Religion, Heaven, Earth and Air, than all things I have yet written ... the ultimate result, however, I need hardly premise, is a deep religious speculative-radicalism (so I call it for want of a better name), with which you are already well enough acquainted in me.[53]

With brazen salesmanship, he then sought to convince Fraser of the 'astonishment' his readers would feel once they had digested *Sartor*; and begged to be told, as soon as possible, whether Fraser would take the gamble. With unprecedented flattery, he added that the last issue of *Fraser's Magazine* was the best for ages. In one respect, the next, at the end of June, was probably even better. It included a likeness of Carlyle by Daniel Maclise, the earliest we have of him, and a brief note of him, describing him as the foremost German scholar in the land.

Both Carlyle and Jane improved in health and spirits as the summer, which was to be their last at Craigenputtock, went on. Fraser accepted his proposal for *Sartor*, and they agreed on the 'whimsical title'[54] by which *Teufelsdreck* or *Teufelsdröckh* has since been known. 'Cagliostro' preceded it in *Fraser's*, in the July and August numbers. This article tediously reiterated Carlyle's loathing for eighteenth-century attitudes and morals. However, it contains fine examples of his invective style that bring out, better than anything he had previously published, his sense of humour, based heavily on irony. It also shows Carlyle to be an attractive writer of history.

The Carlyles once more were alone. He thought occasionally about politics, writing to his friend Mrs Austin in London that 'the signs of the times are quite despicable in England, nothing but a hollow, barren jarring of Radicalism and Toryism.'[55] Jack had returned for a summer holiday, and they visited Templand and Scotsbrig; but promised visits from Mill and even from Hunt's son did not materialise. Despite his thoughts of abandoning a literary life, Carlyle concentrated on reading about the French revolution, which had now become his main project. Jack was not with them long, returning by steamer to Liverpool at the end of August. However, just after he left, the Carlyles had a surprise American visitor who would remain a friend for life: Ralph Waldo Emerson.

Emerson, who at thirty was nearly eight years younger than Carlyle but who had an equally well-developed transcendentalist philosophy, had been touring Sicily, Italy and France, and in Rome had met the Saint-Simonian Gustave d'Eichthal, with whom Carlyle had been in correspondence. D'Eichthal gave Emerson introductions to both Mill and Carlyle, and on 28 August the American, having travelled through England to Edinburgh, the Highlands, Glasgow and back to Annandale, arrived at Craigenputtock. It was a thrill to the Carlyles to meet this intelligent stranger. 'The most amiable creature in the world,' said Carlyle in a letter to Jack.[56] 'A singular apparition here, on a to me nigh inconceivable errand,' he wrote in his journal.[57] Emerson, who regarded Carlyle as 'the latest and strongest contributor to the critical journals',[58] stayed a night with them, leaving the next day in pursuit of Wordsworth before going to Liverpool and thence to Massachussetts.

Emerson, at the start of a career as a poet and essayist that would make him one of the great men of American letters, recalled the meeting with Carlyle in *English Traits*, leaving a rare documentary glimpse of the Carlyles in their Scottish wilderness. He described Carlyle as 'a man from his youth ... as absolute a man of the world, unknown and exiled on that hill-farm, as if holding on his own terms what is best in London.'[59] Emerson gives us a detailed physical description too:

He was tall and gaunt, with a cliff-like brow, self possessed and holding his extraordinary powers of conversation in easy command; clinging to his northern accent with evident relish; full of lively anecdote, and with a streaming humour, which floated everything he looked upon.

Emerson and he went for a walk, and talked mainly of books. Carlyle had encountered few other topics of late of which to speak, except his pig, which he praised highly. 'He worships a man that will manifest any truth to him.' Emerson also found himself treated to a lecture on the evils of British political economy, which he characterised as 'the selfish abdication by public men of all that public persons should perform'.[60] He quoted Carlyle as saying 'governments should direct poor men what to do'; and Carlyle made it clear that he was planning to move to London.

'The only true enemy I have to struggle with,' he told Jack, with reference to the effect renewed isolation was having upon him, 'is the unreason within myself.'[61] By early September he was in a black mood, unable to write or think constructively, once more wallowing in the depression that would return again and again in the years ahead. Jane – whether as a result of this or not – went for a week to visit Moffat, a fashionable Scottish resort, with her mother and a cousin. Carlyle wrote to her that this 'seven days of the utterest solitude' he would experience would allow him valuable time to improve his temper. 'I am determined to be heroical, and cast the Devil out of me.'[62] He walked miles each day while Jane was away, and made a trip to a house at Barjarg, a few miles away, where the owner, Godolphin Hunter Arundell, had a fine library compiled by his great-uncle. Carlyle had needed a library as much as anything during his time at Craigenputtock; now, only a few months before he was to leave, he had found one. He managed to persuade the Reverend John Hunter, the owner's uncle, to allow him to use it, and soon began to make regular visits there for reading. Along with the books Mill regularly sent, this library helped turn Carlyle's mind away from self-absorption and towards more profitable subjects, notably France and the revolution. 'It is properly the grand work of our era,' he wrote to Mill. 'To me, it often seems, as if the right *History* (that impossible thing I mean by History) of the French

Revolution were the grand Poem of our Time; as if the man who could write the truth of that, were worth all other writers and singers.'[63] Carlyle was determined to take this place for himself, though knew well how much more reading he would have to do before he could hope to have enough information to do the job thoroughly. He begged Mill to assist him in finding the books he would need.

He chose to prove to himself that he could compose just the sort of exciting narrative he felt was lacking from almost all historical prose. For his subject he chose the affair of the Diamond Necklace, in which Jeanne de St Rémy de Valois, wife of the self-styled Comte de Lamotte, had in 1783 sought to swindle a jeweller out of a necklace under the pretence that Marie-Antoinette was willing to buy it. Marie-Antoinette herself was implicated – though subsequently exonerated – and such interest as there was in the subject lay in who was or was not to blame. Like 'Cagliostro', the work was a useful prelude to the main work on the revolution. Though he spent much of October reading books from Barjarg, he could not find what he needed, and so wrote to Henry Inglis with a list for him to procure in Edinburgh. Before even starting to write 'The Diamond Necklace', though, he received a setback, the editor of the *Foreign Quarterly Review* telling him that nothing original remained to be said on the subject, so he would not want to publish it. None the less, Carlyle had written the first draft by the middle of November, and put it away in a drawer until someone was interested. He was not much minded to write for no profit, and so dismissed an idea he had had to write an essay on the Saint-Simonians, for which he could also find no buyer. He did, though, take 'The Diamond Necklace' out of the drawer before Christmas, and polish it up. Fraser eventually published it, but not until 1837, and only then on the back of the success of *The French Revolution*.

As winter deepened Carlyle's thoughts turned again to travel, a prospect made more attractive by the fact that he and Jane were enjoying a rare period of good health. He longed to go to Paris again, to help with his revolutionary studies, but it could not be afforded. All money was put aside to help achieve the aim of moving from Craigenputtock. Carlyle was writing nothing, but as *Sartor* was now being serialised in *Fraser* he at least had an income, though not, he felt, an appreciative audience – 'the Public seems to receive him with fixed bayonets' he told Henry Inglis the following year.[64] With no travel, indeed with almost nothing else except visits to and from family, to distract them, the Carlyles spent the Christmas and New Year period reading extensively, and thinking of a future away from Craigenputtock. The few surviving letters from Jane at this time reflect a self-pitying tone about yet again declining health, and a feeling of loneliness as deep as Carlyle's; she had far less recognition from the outside world than he did. She had written to Henry Inglis at the end of November begging him to come to spend Christmas with them, which can only be interpreted as a sign of distress at being so much in the company of her miserable husband. The years of solitude had not helped their marriage, though as soon as they were apart, even for the shortest time, the old sentimentality returned to their letters.

V

Carlyle found throughout his time at Craigenputtock that his friends were not always assiduous correspondents, which partly explains why it was not until January 1834 that he learned of the death of Badams the previous September. He wrote to Jack that 'Badams was among the men that I loved most in the world,'[65] Carlyle never having forgotten the kindness he had received in attempting to solve his digestive horrors. The news came at a time when Carlyle's most important friendships were under stress. Irving's religious manias had disabled him materially, mentally and physically, and he would not survive the year. The breach with Jeffrey now threatened to widen to a point where it could not be bridged. In his desperation to escape Craigenputtock, Carlyle once more entertained ambitions of an astronomical professorship, this time at Edinburgh. He admitted later that he had got into 'considerable spirits' at the prospect, his lack of true self-knowledge leading him to fancy himself 'in the silent midnight interrogating the eternal Stars'.[66] As this post was in the gift of the Crown, Carlyle sought help from the Lord Advocate. The answer he received was described by Carlyle as 'a kind of polite Fishwoman-shriek',[67] Jeffrey telling him his doctrines were 'arrogant, antinational and absurd'; and, in any case, Jeffrey had the post earmarked for one of his former secretaries. Carlyle did not complain, apparently realising the truth of what Jeffrey said: 'I feel it very wholesome to have my vanity humbled from time to time.'[68] None the less, the friendly relations of old would never be rebuilt.

The events of the previous winter had, in any case, made Carlyle feel he would no longer enjoy living in Edinburgh. So when, by the middle of February, he and Jane had decided that they could not stay another winter at Craigenputtock, the only solution was a move to London. Their servant, Grace, had told them she wished to leave their employment once summer came, and Carlyle saw this as the last straw: unlike most of the staff they had had she was a good servant, and they were not hopeful of replacing her. Jane began to make enquiries of London friends about houses; Carlyle had heard from Leigh Hunt, who had just moved to Upper Cheyne Row, that Chelsea was attractive. In Scotland it was the custom for houses to be exchanged at Whitsuntide, so Carlyle resolved to find somewhere in London by May. Despite the problems of going south to settle – leaving Carlyle's elderly mother and family, and Jane's family, and finding the money to live in London – their course was set.

He was especially apprehensive about telling his mother of his plans. 'Except in the little circle of my own kindred, I know of no soul out of London, whose society cheers or fortifies me,'[69] he wrote to Mill on 22

February 1834. 'Life here is but a kind of Life-in-Death, or rather one might say a Not Being Born,'[70] he told Jack, confiding in him his deep anxieties at moving, but expressing his belief that he would find work enough to sustain them. 'Thousands of sillier fellows than I flourish in it,' he added. His attitude was not entirely of levity. He also told Jack he felt this would be 'the last chance I shall ever have to redeem my existence from Pain and Imprisonment, and make something of the faculty I have.' Hunt had told him his house was to be had for thirty guineas a year. Carlyle had £200 to tide them over the first year, until he had made some money, so he felt that, in economic terms, the move could be made. At the beginning of March, the tenancy of Craigenputtock was advertised.

One of their London friends, Mrs Sarah Austin, found them a house at 4 Holland Street, Kensington, and Carlyle was sure they would take it: so sure that he wrote to Inglis on 28 April advertising it as his new address. The prospect, however, fell through a couple of days later. Carlyle wrote to Hunt asking him to look out in Chelsea, and decided to go south on his own to try to find a decent house before Whitsuntide, planning to send for Jane later. He stopped any pretence of work altogether during this time of uncertainty, and what intellectual exercise he took amounted to reading Homer. On 8 May, having said sad farewells to his wife, mother and brothers he started south, by steamer to Liverpool, where he spent two nights with Jane's uncle John. He then travelled by stagecoach, sitting outside in the rain, through a day, a night and half of another day down to London. He managed to lodge at their old rooms in Ampton Street, St Pancras, and once settled went to Bayswater to see Mrs Austin, and to embark on the business of finding a house. He believed that the English had the Scots system of the Whitsuntide change-over, a point of which Mrs Austin disabused him; there had been no need for him to rush to London at all. He particularly regretted this mistake for Jane's sake, for she had been left (with Alick's help) to do all the packing and shipping of their belongings. They brought with them mainly furniture inherited from Jane's father, much of which is still to be found at the Carlyle House in Chelsea. What was not worth shipping she set about selling, though the proceeds were less than they had hoped, since their family asked to buy some of the stuff, and Jane lacked the heart to complain about the uncommonly low prices they offered.

There were worse disappointments. Walking through Kensington Gardens, as he described it to Jane, 'there starts from a side-seat a black figure, and clutches my hand in both his: it is poor Edward Irving! O what a feeling! The poor friend looks like death rather than life; pale and yet flushed, a flaccid, boiled appearance; and one short peal of his old Annandale laugh went thro' me with the wofullest tone.'[71] Irving, accompanied by a nurse, had been sent out to the relative rurality of Kensington by his doctor; he had barely six months to live. He asked Carlyle to visit the next day, but when he did he found Irving out. Within a couple of weeks Carlyle did find him, and they spent two hours together. Carlyle thought his friend had much improved in health, and he was hopeful that the worst was over.

He went to find Hunt to enlist his help in the search, but found him out. This did, however, give Carlyle the opportunity to meet the rest of Hunt's family, who were in a typically disorganised and anarchic state, reminding him of a clan of gypsies. He chose not to linger, but returned to Chelsea the following day, and this time found his friend in. They went out looking for houses. He told Jane:

Chelsea lies low close by the side of the river; has an ancient, here and there dilapidated look; the houses apparently a tenth cheaper; some market articles, especially coals said likewise to be cheaper. I liked it little; and, to say truth, cared not be so near the poetic Tinkerdom.[72]

None the less, within weeks he would be living within yards of Hunt's 'Tinkerdom'. They combed Brompton and Kensington as well, and found nothing. At the end of this fruitless day Hunt gave him dinner; the next morning Carlyle was tramping about again, still without success, though finding the time to renew his acquaintance with Buller and Mill. The latter, Mrs Austin told him, had become romantically involved with Harriet Taylor, a young married woman of twenty-seven (Mill was a year older), and as a result Mill have become lost to his friends. He also saw Fraser, who was perplexed by the unpopularity of *Sartor*, and was not forthcoming with offers for Carlyle to write further. Carlyle was too preoccupied with finding accommodation to worry about that.

He asked Jane to come and share his lodgings, that they might continue the search together, and that he might have the benefit of her judgment on the qualities of their next home. While waiting for her reply he did not rest, walking himself lame day after day, and progressing further north, through Regent's Park and Camden Town. Eventually he went back to Hunt and Chelsea, and saw the house that was to be his and Jane's for the rest of their life, in Cheyne Row, just down towards the river from Hunt's. So impressed was he with this house that he modified his objections to living 'within a gunshot' of the Hunts. 'Tho' tinkerish-nomadic, I find the Hunts are not intrusive.'[73]

Carlyle sent Jane a full description of the premises, and of the environs, and told her how close they would be to all their friends. She wrote that she was preparing to start for London, by steamer and coach. Recalling the discomfort of his own journey, he told her to rest at Liverpool until she was sure she was fit enough to continue. He also advised Jane to collect Bessy Barnet, who had been a servant of the Badamses and was now to work for the Carlyles in London, from Birmingham on her way down. He had arranged for the house in Chelsea not to be let until Jane arrived, so begged her to come as speedily as she could. On 4 June 1834 she arrived at last, having borne the journey well. The life in London could now begin for both of them.

7

Revolution in Chelsea

1834–37

As soon as Jane reached London the matter of where to live was settled. She saw, and approved, the house at 5 Great Cheyne Row (now 24 Cheyne Row), Chelsea; she had worried that being by the river they might be prone to 'damp and unwholesome' fogs,[1] but this proved not to deter her. She agreed it was nearly twice as good as anything else they could get for their money. They moved in, with Bessy Barnet, on 10 June 1834. Thanks to its preservation, first by the Carlyle's House Memorial Trust from 1895, and then by the National Trust since 1936, the house today is much as Carlyle described it to Jane after he had seen it, with the obvious exception of the soundproofed room that he had built at the top in the 1850s:

The House itself is eminent, antique; wainscotted to the very ceiling, and has been all new-painted and repaired; broadish stair, with massive balustrade (in the old style) corniced and as thick as one's thigh; floors firm as a rock, wood of them here and there worm-eaten, yet capable of cleanness, and still with thrice the strength of a modern floor. And then as to room . . . Three stories besides the sunk story; in every one of them *three* apartments in depth (something like 40 feet in all; for it was 13 of my steps!): Thus there is a front dining room (marble chimney-piece &c); then a back dining room (or breakfast-room) a little narrower (by reason of the kitchen stair); then out from this, and narrower still (to allow a back-window, you consider), a china room, or pantry, or I know not what, all shelved, and fit to hold crockery for the whole street. Such is the ground-area, which of course continues to the top, and furnishes every Bedroom with a dressing room, or even with a second bedroom . . . a most massive, roomy, sufficient old house; with places, for example, to hang say three dozen hats or cloaks on; and as many crevices, and queer old presses, and shelved closets (all tight and new painted in their way) as would gratify the most covetous Goody. Rent £35!²

Jane – 'Goody' – had impressed upon Carlyle the importance of finding a house with space for crockery, and he had fulfilled her main wish. The terrace in which the house is set, according to a stone in one of the other houses, was erected in 1708, and was now owned by a Mr William Morgan, of Pope's Head Alley. The Carlyles took the house initially for a year, with an option to renew.³ They ended up spending 'two and thirty years of hard battle against Fate' there together, and Carlyle himself another fifteen besides.[4] The visitor today sees the same dark wainscotting, the same piano and oval table in the front room, and many more features that Carlyle notes from their earliest days there; and the details of Tait's famous picture of the Carlyles in that room, *A Chelsea Interior*, painted in 1857, are immediately recognisable.

On the day they moved in they took a carriage from their lodgings, through Belgrave Square, to Chelsea, accompanied by Bessy and a canary called Chico that Jane had brought from Scotland. The bird started to sing in Belgrave Square, which they took as a good omen; however, the creature was to peck a hole in the head of his mate, and kill her. Two hours after their arrival the furniture, which had come down by canal from Liverpool, turned up in Pickford's van. Carlyle was relieved that little damage had been done to their possessions, and that the whole operation had cost him under £20. He reported all this to his mother in the first letter from their new home, advising her additionally that 'Chelsea is an "unfashionable place"; that is the secret of it: a quality, as you may well imagine, rather in its favour with Anti-gigmen like us.'[5] 'Gigmanity', he suggested to his brother Jack, had saved £10 a year, for that was what he supposed the rent would have increased by had Chelsea been fashionable.[6] In one regard, though, he was to be disappointed. He told his mother that Chelsea had 'air and quiet hardly inferior to Crai-genputtoch'. He wrote, however, on the eve of the great expansion of London and the de-ruralisation of the western suburb. Noise, and the means of escaping from it, were to become obsessions. Living west of the City, with its smoke blown east by the prevailing westerly winds, clean Chelsea certainly was, and Carlyle intended to make the most of sitting out in the small garden attached to the house, with his pipe. He spent 6s on tools to use to smarten up the garden, and £1 2s 6d on a shower-bath to be set up in their kitchen, so that he and Jane could 'splash' themselves daily;[7] he reported every domestic development faithfully to his family in letters, and prayed for the railway to be finished, so his mother could make the trip south to visit them and see the scene he described.

As Thea Holme has detailed extensively in *The Carlyles at Home*, the servant problem was to dog the Carlyles throughout their life in London. Initially, though, Bessy proved a paragon, 'the orderliest, cleverest servant we have ever had'.[8] So impressed were the Carlyles with her that they settled for her to have tea with them each Sunday, where they would share with her 'perhaps a few chapters of good reading'; they were undeflected by an allegation spread by Mrs Montagu that Bessy had for years been Badams's mistress, and not simply his housekeeper. Now that she had found someone so reliable to share the domestic burden, Jane was uplifted by the change. She wrote to her mother-in-law that it had been 'a great cause of thankfulness' and that 'my husband will be healthier and happier than he has been for long years.'[9] The relative smoothness of their new existence allowed Carlyle the leisure to make final plans for his next project, *The French Revolution*.

He quickly noted there had been no improvement in the publishing trade. Fraser, to whom he offered a series of articles on the revolution at £10 a sheet, was not interested. The shock with which his readers had received *Sartor* still worried him; only two people, Emerson and a Catholic priest, Father O'Shea of Cork, had bothered to write to say how much they had enjoyed it; some had written in threatening to cancel their subscriptions if much more like *Sartor* appeared. Nevertheless, Fraser agreed to publish Carlyle's book under the 'half-profits' system, which would effectively mean Carlyle would get nothing. It was not clear where his living was coming from while he undertook this massive project. Mill was planning to launch a magazine, the first number of which finally arrived in April 1835 as *The London Review*, and Carlyle hoped he might profit from that, perhaps even by becoming its first editor. It soon became apparent that he was not in the running for the post. Perhaps as a result he realised there was, for him at least, no great future in periodical writing; he sensed, rightly, that his name counted for something in that milieu, but that once those launching reviews had used him to help them start, their interest in him dwindled. There was, he felt, another prospect. Jane and he took advantage of London by going out in the evening to lectures, and Carlyle began to think that he might make a living in this way too.

His natural gregariousness, suppressed for so long in Dumfriesshire, was given full rein. His former pupil Charles Buller, now a Member of Parliament, became a special favourite, and Carlyle predicted that if his health held up (which, as it turned out, it did not) he would do more good in parliament than anyone. Hunt came for tea once a week, sometimes staying to take porridge with them for supper and to listen to Jane play Scotch tunes on the piano. Underemployed, he was always available for a walk or talk with Carlyle. Hunt was especially fond of Carlyle, whom he described as 'one of the kindest and best, as well as the most eloquent of men'. He did, though, find Carlyle's moral stringencies hard to stomach, complaining that 'in his zeal for what is best he sometimes thinks it incumbent on him to take not the kindest tone, and in his eloquent demands of some hearty uncompromising creed on our parts, he does not quite set the example of telling us the amount of his own.' Hunt's life was so disorganised and profligate that it would have been no surprise that Carlyle found much in it to moralise about. But Hunt did spot in Carlyle the deep pessimism that was to come out so clearly in the works.

Mr Carlyle sees that there is a good deal of rough work in the operations of nature: he seems to think himself bound to consider a good deal of it devilish, after the old Covenanter fashion, in order that he may find something angelical in giving it the proper quantity of vituperation and blows; and he calls upon us to prove our energies and our benevolence by acting the part of the wind rather than the sun, of warring rather than peace-making, of frightening and forcing rather than conciliating and persuading.[10]

Carlyle for his part found Hunt 'an innocent-hearted, but misguided, in fact rather foolish, *un*practical and often much-suffering man'.[11]

Mill too was a frequent visitor, sometimes bringing hwith him is mistress Harriet Taylor, for whom Jane developed a fascination. Carlyle longed to renew his old relationship with Irving, but a further visit to him found him – and Mrs Irving – in severely bad health, Irving's lungs being seriously affected. There was no hope of recapturing the spirit of former days. In fact, in early September, Irving left London altogether, and embarked on a convalescent trip around the English countryside. Before he did so he came to Cheyne Row for his first – and last – visit, 'toward sunset', as Carlyle remembered it, on a 'damp, dim' day.[12] He had come on his bay horse, and stayed only fifteen or twenty minutes with them in their ground-floor room. 'You are like an Eve,' Irving had told Jane, 'and make a little Paradise wherever you are.'[13] In his memorial essay on Irving, Carlyle recalled that on this occasion 'friendliness still beamed in his eyes, but now from amid unquiet fire.'[14] When he left, Carlyle stood on his steps and watched him turn the corner on his horse, never to see him again.

However, Carlyle had not just come to London to socialise. By the end of July work on *The French Revolution* was already well in hand, the preparation for and writing of it taking up all his working hours. He spent much time in the library at the British Museum, enjoying the eight-mile round trip for the opportunity it gave him to stroll in the summer sunshine, smoking a cigar (though he lamented the absence of hills on his walks). Mill had lent him about a hundred books. He planned to have a manuscript ready for Fraser by the following spring, always an optimistic goal even if events had not turned out as they did. Fraser wanted to publish it in March, deemed a good time as parliament would be sitting and 'fashionable society' would be in town. The construction of this great work of history was a challenge to Carlyle to prove he could make history more interesting than the 'dryasdusts' whom he castigated. 'It is part of my creed,' he wrote to Emerson, 'that the only Poetry is History, could we tell it right. This truth (if it prove one) I have not yet got to the limitations of; and shall in no way except by trying it in practice.'[15] 'The Diamond Necklace' had, thus far, been his only (unpublished) attempt to establish his own genre, though the tone he would take had been clear enough in some of his reviews, such as 'Cagliostro'.

That summer Fraser's serialisation of *Sartor* finished, having netted its author £82 1s. He presented Carlyle with fifty-eight stitched-together copies, which he dispatched (at Fraser's expense) to friends. Being among literary men spurred him on in his next work, not because they were an inspiration, but because they were 'duds' than whom he could do better.[16] As the novelty of London wore off he became more reflective, telling Alick at the end of August that he had had 'a pensive, sometimes a sad, yet a sweetly-tender summer'.[17] Jane, though, felt her husband 'rapidly mending of his Craigenputtoch gloom and acerbity', even adding that 'he is really at times a tolerably social character and seems to be regarded with a feeling of mingled terror and love in all companies.'[18]

In September he started to write his book. Progress was slow, and for ever interrupted by the need to go to the museum to root out an obscure pamphlet. As well as having to gather research materials, the nature of the work created stylistic problems. It is really from this time that proper 'Carlylese' can be dated. It was a more conversational and emphatic, less formal style of prose, mimicking the monologues he was becoming noted for ranting out at his visitors. Eventually he was satisfied with the approach he was taking. 'After two weeks of blotching and bloring have produced – two clean pages!' he wrote to Jack at the end of September.[19] 'But my hand is out; and I am altering my style too, and troubled about many things; bilious too in these smothering windless days.' Nor, as he told Jack, was he setting himself any modest ambitions for the work: 'It shall be such a book! Quite an epic Poem of the Revolution: an Apotheosis of Sansculottism! Seriously, when in good spirits, I feel as if there were the matter of a very serious Work within me; but the task of shaping and uttering it will be frightful.'

Most of their friends had gone away for the late summer, not to return until October, so Carlyle had nothing, except a summons to sit on a coroner's jury after an old woman had died on an omnibus, to distract him. The first of their domestic troubles came at about this time. Bessy decided she was distraught with grief for Badams, and went to Birmingham to live with her mother. Within a few weeks Mrs Montagu had supplied them with a girl called Jane from Lancashire; the servant problem had started.

II

Jack, in Italy with Lady Clare, witnessed the eruption of Vesuvius that September. Carlyle, on 16 October, watched the fire that destroyed the old Houses of Parliament. The Reform Act had not improved public perceptions of politicians. Carlyle recorded that the crowd around him was 'quiet, rather gratified than otherwise; *whew'd* and whistled when the breeze came as if to encourage it'.[20] They had felt the fire was a judgment on the Poor Law Bill, which would have an effect of concentrating the indigent in workhouses and dividing up families; 'a man *sorry* I did not anywhere see.'

Being in London, and partly through his association with Charles Buller, Carlyle started to take a closer interest in politics. Not long after the fire, the Whig ministry resigned, and Carlyle feared the ferment that would take place if another election had to be called. Again through Buller, he began to attend Radical meetings, 'but there is,' Jane told his mother, 'no fear of his getting into mischief – Curiosity is his only motive.'[21] Certainly Carlyle was not interested in organised politics, but it is unlikely that curiosity was all that motivated him. His anger at the incompetent way in which the country was being run has already been documented, and would grow. However, the main target of the radicals – Sir Robert Peel, who was just forming his first ministry – was to become greatly admired by Carlyle. On 21 November

Carlyle attended a meeting organised by Buller that drew a crowd of 2,000 people, and enjoyed the denunciations of Toryism. However, his incipient loathing of democracy was already coming through. 'Toryism or Radicalism, it seems to me all things are going *to the howe pot*,' he wrote to his mother, using the slang for 'bottomless pit'.[22]

The stimulation of being in a great city helped his work. By the last week in October he was on his fourth chapter of *The French Revolution*, and Mill had lent him another fifty books on top of the cartload already provided; it was lucky for Carlyle that Mill's own intentions of writing a book on this subject, which had caused him to accumulate so many books about it, had never been fulfilled. This fourth chapter, in his original draft, dealt with the storming of the Bastille. However, nearly a month later he wrote to his mother that 'I am not getting the *Bastille taken* so readily as I expected.'[23] Fraser had read 'The Diamond Necklace' (which Mill so enjoyed that he was minded to publish it at his own expense), and agreed to publish the piece, though not until Carlyle's *magnum opus* was available.

As he and Jane prepared to spend their first Christmas in Chelsea some bad, but not unexpected, news reached them. Irving had died at Glasgow on 7 December, aged forty-three, three days after Carlyle's thirty-ninth birthday. Carlyle had seen Irving's father-in-law in London during the autumn, and had heard his friend was weakening, even though no doctor could find any trace of disease in him. The news shocked Carlyle. Fraser asked him to write a short piece on Irving for the next issue of his magazine. Carlyle did this quickly, though endured a rancorous exchange with Fraser, who decided to rewrite the piece in a manner Carlyle found offensive. It appeared as a short, unpretentious tribute and testament of friendship, most valuable especially for the insight into Carlyle's mature feelings for the man who was once his best friend. Supposedly quoting, somewhat archly, 'one who knew him well', Carlyle said that 'but for Irving, I had never known what the communion of man with man means.'[24] Carlyle did not gloss over the problems with Irving, implying he had been killed by the 'foul incense' of fashion,[25] by what he termed the 'poison of popular applause', by a craze that had driven him mad with alternate burst of mania and disappointment.

He and Jane promised themselves that Christmas would be jovial, since previous ones had been solitary, dour affairs. But the day after they made this resolution Jane's new servant poured boiling water over her mistress's foot, scalding it so badly that Jane was confined to the house for five weeks, unable to walk. She had to be carried about by Carlyle who, given his wife's indisposition, had the perfect excuse to stay at home and concentrate on work. He now realised *The French Revolution* would fill two volumes rather than one, and with hardly a break worked on at it over Christmas. By mid-January he felt three volumes would be necessary – and so it turned out. He would breakfast at nine and work till two; go walking until four, when darkness fell in mid-winter; and then, after dinner, would spend the evening reading.

It was a clear, still, bitter cold December, and Carlyle enjoyed his walks especially, wrapped up in a new brown cloak. By the turn of the year, though, his spirits were low. On 1 January 1835 he noted in his journal:

Twelve o'clock has just struck; the last hour of 1834, the first of a new year. Bells ringing (to me dolefully); a wet wind blustering; my wife in bed (very unhappily ill of a foot which a puddle of a maid scalded three weeks ago); I, after a day of fruitless toil, reading and re-reading about that Versailles '6th of October' still. It is long since I have written anything here. The future looks too black round me, the present too doleful, unfriendly; I am too sick at heart (wearied, wasted in body) to complain – even to myself. My first friend Edward Irving is dead; above three weeks ago, I am friendless here; or as good as that. My Book *cannot* get on, though I stick to it like a bur.[26]

This unattractive self-pity seems to have been no more than the consequence of delayed grief about Irving, estrangement from his family, the usual misery of mid-winter, his sick wife and, above all, the unexpected difficulties he was having with *The French Revolution*. He did have friends, but none that could replace his family, with whom he remained closer than ever, despite the miles that separated them. He told Jack ('with your brotherly affection and trueheartedness, you are one of the best possessions I have') that Mill was probably the man dearest to him, but 'so theoretic a man, and like a printed book, I never open myself to him'.[27] Moreover, they saw each other only once a fortnight. Despite living round the corner from him, Carlyle claimed in a letter to Alick at the end of January 1835 that he had not seen Hunt for three months. 'There was no quarrel . . . but I believe the poor man is very miserable, and feels shocked at my rigorous Presbyterian principles; in short is afraid of me!'[28]

Carlyle's gloom was deepened by what he observed of life around him, a state of mind that led to the great philippics of the 1840s. He had an indefatigable sense of moral superiority, which did not help him to mix. 'The longer I live among the people,' he told Jack, 'the deeper grows my feeling (not a vain one: a sad one) of natural superiority over them; of being able (were the *tools* in my hand!) to do a hundred things better than the hundred I see paid for doing them.'[29] Carlyle could not but believe that an apocalypse was coming, and he waited righteously for it, expecting the failure of the governing classes would, as in France, be punished by revolt. His political judgment was not always of the best. A general election was held throughout January, which would result in Peel struggling throughout the winter to retain power, only to have to surrender it to Melbourne in April.

For all his complaints of difficulties in writing, he finished the first volume of *The French Revolution* in mid-January. He admitted he was writing in a bad humour, 'without hope of it, except being *done with it*'. He looked ahead with pointlessness, feeling that even if his work were a success, it would result in being besieged by editors (able or otherwise) to write for their reviews for the six months or so after its publication; and then they would forget him. His political feelings began to drive him towards the search for heroes that

Carlyle's mother, Margaret Aitken: 'how often do I find, with an unspeakable tenderness of recollection "That is *thy Mother's* now; that thou got from thy poor Mother, long ago!" '

Carlyle's birthplace, Ecclefechan, with guidebook notes by the Sage.

*room where I was born; to the middle of that Arch was my Father's House, Village of Ec-clefechan, 4 dec 17 95. – T. Carlyle (Chelsea, 5 July, 1871) –

TOP LEFT The first likeness of Carlyle, aged 36, 1832.

ABOVE Edward Irving, Carlyle's first best friend, not speaking in tongues.

LEFT Johann Wolfgang von Goethe, Carlyle's first hero.

Samuel Laurence's crayon drawing of Jane Welsh Carlyle, made in about
1838 when Jane was 37.

A likeness of Carlyle's most brilliant pupil, Charles Buller, made in 1844, when he was aged 38.

BELOW LEFT Alexander Carlyle, a younger brother, whose problems at making a living in the depressed 1830s and 1840s led to his emigration to Canada, whence he continued his lifelong correspondence with Carlyle.

BELOW John Stuart Mill, pictured in middle age, by which time he and Carlyle were no longer on speaking terms.

ABOVE Harriet Martineau, pictured in 1844: Carlyle's first encounter with feminism.

RIGHT Leigh Hunt, Carlyle's Chelsea neighbour, pictured in 1850.

Harriet, Lady Ashburton 'had fallen deeply in love with Carlyle ... Carlyle had behaved nobly ... Lord Ashburton was deeply obliged to him'.

Richard Monckton Milnes, later Lord Houghton, to whom Carlyle was close in the 1840s.

ABOVE Arthur Hugh Clough, whom Carlyle led out into the desert, and left there.

Oliver Cromwell, Lord High Protector of England, 'the last glimpse of the Godlike vanishing from this England'.

Matthew Arnold, who for all his contempt for 'moral desperadoes like Carlyle' seemed to learn much from him.

BELOW Charles Gavan Duffy, pictured in 1848 between stretches in gaol for promoting Irish nationalism, and at a time when he was forming his friendship with Carlyle.

RIGHT Carlyle painted by Tait in the early 1850s, not long before the acquisition of the Sage's beard.

Geraldine Jewsbury, with whom Jane sought refuge in Manchester at the height of the difficulties in her marriage to Carlyle, and who became the root of the rumours about the Carlyles' sexual practices.

BELOW LEFT John Forster, friend and adviser to Carlyle, friend and biographer of Dickens, historian and man of letters in his own right.

BELOW Charles Dickens pictured shortly before his death: 'a most correct, precise, clear-sighted, quietly decisive, just and loving man; till at length he had grown to such recognition with me as I have rarely had for any man of my time.'

would dominate the middle years of his creativity. Charles Buller was involved in the scheme to settle South Australia, under a Colonel Napier. Carlyle thought this was the same Colonel Napier who had distinguished himself in the Peninsular War, 'actually a man (not the sham of a man) with a strong head, a valiant heart; a "clang in him as of steel" '.[30] So he strode off one January night to find Buller and demand to be introduced to this hero, only to be told that the Napier Buller knew was the hero's brother. Carlyle saw the absurd side of what he had done, and confessed all to Jane. None the less, he had declared 'everlasting war with Shams', so this would not be the end of his pursuit of men who were 'actually men'.

Once the first volume of *The French Revolution* was finished, Carlyle calculated he would have the other two finished by the end of May; which was as well, because he and Jane had money enough only to last them a few months beyond that. Part of the problem was, as always, his generosity to his kin. A year before coming to England he had lent Alick, a victim of the agricultural depression, £140, which there was no prospect of having back quickly. In writing his book he was slow because he was determined to be accurate, a consideration he felt had not troubled his forerunners. His political thoughts were also distracting him, and in early February he broke from his main work to write some thoughts on education, something the English have always taken less seriously than the Scots. He was shocked by reports of mass illiteracy, feeling this condemned many to exist in a 'semi-barbarous state', unable to contribute to the civilising process.[31] In contrast to the popular image of Carlyle as a heartless anti-democrat, this paper reveals a concern – and an unhelpfully sentimental one at that – for the indigent:

Such a state of matters, were we not used to see it daily, would fill us with sorrow and amazement. For each untaught individual it is a tragedy. His life passes, and will not return, and he has never lived. To mutilate his body, to annihilate half the strength of his body, were small matter: but his soul has never opened her eyes; on him spiritual life never dawned, no faculty was unfolded but animal instincts, and some mechanic ingenuity as of beavers: he has issued from Eternity and returns to Eternity with a man's gifts in him, yet so like the beasts that perish!

The editors of the *Collected Letters*, who publish this piece for the first time, correctly point to the raising of themes about improving the lot of the poor otherwise thought to have been first voiced in *Chartism*, four years later, or *Past and Present* in 1843. As in those works, Carlyle is not advocating a socialist solution, but argues that if responsible government does not provide some form of education for these people they will fall prey to such elements of socialism as trade unions and other radical political associations. He defined the problem:

Their old guides and commanders (Clergy, Gentry and such like) are becoming distrusted; class after class of them is getting dismissed from the actual guideship; the popular mass feels more and more that it can trust only to its own guidance, that all other guidances mistake the griefs it labours under, or wilfully misinterpret them, and refuse any answer but coercion.[32]

From this, it led on that a man can rule only if he can convince the people of his being right, an idea solemnised and institutionalised by the Reform Act; effectively denying the people true leadership, but supplying them only with leadership on their terms, a self-contradiction. Extending his view about religion being a means of social control, Carlyle now says that secular education can, if necessary, perform a similar function. These ideas are central to Carlyle's thought throughout the rest of his life, though seldom expressed as unprovocatively as here. So, early on in the democratic experiment, he suspended judgment, arguing that the idea of letting the people decide would stand or fall according to the wisdom the people themselves showed. When, after writing *The French Revolution*, he returned to this theme, and made it the be-all and end-all of his political philosophy, he had abandoned optimism. In allegorical terms, *The French Revolution* addresses these points too, showing France's fate as leading inevitably from the abdication of responsible government by the traditional governing classes. Carlyle was only half right, however; the governing classes in France and England were not analogous, and his condemnation of clergy and gentry was stronger than was realistically deserved.

In his essay on education, Carlyle appeared to resign himself to the continuance of the democratic process. He argued that it was important to have the new electors properly educated, that they might better perform the important task delegated to them by the Reform Act. But Carlyle doubted the ability of the state to provide this service, and called for leaders among the people to organise 'educational associations' instead; one such had already been established in Glasgow, and one was, he felt from what he saw around him, urgently needed in London. He felt the essence of any education would be to make a child religious, and was sure higher morality would allow greater social control. Given his own peculiar religion he suggested, hopefully, that teaching should simply communicate religion 'by the sacred contact of heart with heart ... the grand requisite is a true-minded devout schoolmaster.'[33] He pleaded for an end to sectarianism, as it was, in his view, an irrelevance compared with the grand vision: 'There are properly but two Sects in the world: the believing and the unbelieving.'[34]

He returned to his great work in low spirits. In February 1835 he told Emerson he was thinking of another way to earn a living; considering he was in his fortieth year, this seems a breathtaking show of defeatism. He complained that he fitted neither of the 'grand Categories under which all English spiritual activity ... must range itself',[35] namely radicalism and conservatism, and was in a political sense a lost soul. Emerson had asked him to come to America and live by lecturing; but Carlyle said he could not give serious thought to it. He felt he would be no happier there, from a spiritual point of view, than in England (and, given his emotional dependence upon his family, would have been unhappier); but he did tell Emerson he fancied himself as a lecturer.

As he pressed on with the second volume, 'toiling along like a *Nigger*, but with the heart of a free Roman',[36] his spirits seemed to lift. Concerned that, as he had often done in his youth, he had alarmed his family by piling on his miseries, he wrote to Jack in mid-February to protest that he was not unhappy, but that his depression sprang from physical causes of ill-health. The harder he worked, the sicker he felt. There were consolations, though. Jane had read the first volume, and derived 'great satisfaction'[37] from it; and now Mill had the manuscript, busily annotating it with observations Carlyle might include as footnotes, and was equally impressed.

III

It was now, though, that one of the landmark events of Carlyle's life – and, indeed, of literary legend – occurred, and wrecked all his plans. The story is best told by Carlyle himself, from his journal entry of 7 March 1835:

Mill's rap was heard at the door: he entered pale, unable to speak; gasped out to my wife to go down and speak with Mrs Taylor; and came forward (led by my hand, and astonished looks) the very picture of desperation. After various inarticulate and articulate utterances to merely the same effect, he informs me that my *First Volume* (left out by him in too careless a manner, after or while reading it) was, except for four or five bits of leaves, *irrevocably* ANNIHILATED! I remember and still can remember less of it than anything I ever wrote with such toil: *it* is gone, the whole world and myself backed by it could not bring that back: nay the old spirit too is fled. I find that it took five months of steadfast occasionally excessive and always sickly and painful toil. *It is gone*; and will not return.[38]

From Carlyle's account Mill was even more distraught than he was: he had come 'in a state looking not unlike insanity'.[39] What Mrs Taylor explained to Jane while she waited in the carriage outside we do not know; but Mill stayed until midnight (later than Carlyle thought appropriate) attempting to atone for the burning of the manuscript by his housemaid, who had found it by a fender and lighted a fire with it. With surprising composure, Carlyle sought to put him at his ease by discussing other matters. Jane did everything she could to console him. That night Carlyle slept badly, dreaming his father and sister Margaret were alive, though disfigured, and had died again. On waking the next morning he resolved to write the book again. 'I will not quit the game,' he wrote in his journal, 'while faculty is given me to *try* playing.'

We know little of why the manuscript was left for the housemaid to burn, because the Carlyles, witnessing Mill's distress and displaying heroic decency, did not ask for an explanation. Froude claims Carlyle said to Jane, on Mill's departure that evening, that 'Mill, poor fellow, is terribly cut up; we must endeavour to hide from him how very serious this business is to us.'[40] It is not clear whether the manuscript had been burned at Mill's parents' home in Kensington Church Street, where he still lived, or whether it had been destroyed accidentally while Mrs Taylor had taken Mill off on an adulterous liaison, something he would have found hard to explain to Carlyle at the best of times, and harder still if the destruction had happened in such circumstances. By 1873, when Carlyle wrote to Mill's sister regretting that Mill's death had prompted stories in the press about this incident, he was certainly in no doubt about what he thought had happened. 'Mrs Taylor's house & some trifling neglect there, had been the cause of the catastrophe,' he told Miss Mill.[41] One can only speculate whether Mrs Taylor, downstairs with Jane, told her, woman to woman, the full nature of the event. Writing in 1892 from memories of talks with the Carlyles, Sir Charles Gavan Duffy gave this amusing sidelight on the way in which the news was brought:

Mrs Carlyle ... told me the story now sufficiently known of how the first volume of the 'French Revolution' got burnt. When Mill suddenly appeared at Cheyne Row to announce the misfortune, he looked so like the ghost of Hamlet's father, that she knew some catastrophe must have occurred, and exclaimed involuntarily, 'Gracious Providence, he has gone off with Mrs Taylor!' but happily the misfortune turned out to be a more remediable one.[42]

Whatever face Carlyle put on things, and however resolute he was to carry on, he was devastated. 'The miserablest accident ... of my whole life,'[43] he told Fraser, his publisher, explaining why (keeping Mill's name out of it) he would not be meeting the advertised deadline; Fraser had, at the end of February, announced the book was on its way. He claimed the work had 'pleased me better than anything I had ever done', a sharp change of attitude compared with his earlier disparaging remarks about it, but one which, in his grief, we must allow him. He promised Fraser to have the work finished as quickly as he could, but told him it was unlikely to be before mid-1836. He asked Fraser to mention the accident to no one, and to send him more books for research; with that, he set about the task again.

He also wrote, the morning after the news had been brought to him, to Mill, commiserating. 'Is there anything that I could do or suffer or say to alleviate you? For I feel that your sorrow must be far sharper than mine.'[44] Mill was not easily consoled, and offered Carlyle financial compensation. Given his limited resources, Carlyle took little persuading. 'You shall do the thing you so earnestly entreat for,' he wrote to Mill two days later.[45] 'It is not unreasonable; *ungigmanic* it may either be or not be.' He assured Mill that 'it has positively become a case which money can remedy,' and that 'the thought of my having got day's wages for my labour will give a new face to the whole matter ... It is likely enough this may prove the only portion of the Book I may ever get so much for. I can attack the thing again, with unabated cheerfulness; and certainly, one may hope, do it better and not worse.'

Before the financial question was settled, Mill sent further loads of books to Carlyle, and Carlyle, to prove his forgiving nature, told Mill he had almost finished the opening chapter of the redraft, and that Mill was welcome to borrow it and read it: 'I think of all men living you are henceforth the least likely to commit such an oversight again.'[46] But Mill did not take up the offer, and was not to read the work until it was published. Within a week he had sent Carlyle a banker's draft for £200, but Carlyle had already worked out that he could, in the time spent on *The French Revolution*, have earned £100; he sent the draft back and asked Mill to make out one for half the amount. Mill implored him to take £200, saying it was not adequate compensation simply to restore Carlyle to the state in which he had been before he started to write. In the *Reminiscences*, thirty years later, Carlyle regretted accepting even as much as he did, his perspective altered by the falling-out between him and Mill as Mill had become a zealous proponent of the liberalism Carlyle so reviled. Noting that, as well as the £100, Mill had made him a present of the *Biographie Universelle*, Carlyle lamented he could not 'find a way of getting the now much macerated, changed and fanaticised "John Stuart Mill" to take that £100 back; but I fear there is no way!'[47]

Carlyle went out more in literary society. A friend, Henry Taylor, invited him to meet Southey, whose irritability Carlyle marked out as 'his grand spiritual feature'. The editors of the *Collected Letters* also date to about this time his first meeting with Wordsworth, with whom he was unimpressed, and whom, in the *Reminiscences*, he claimed not to remember meeting before 1840. Going into society enhanced his confidence and self-respect. He told his mother that the circle in which he and Jane moved 'consists of really superior honest-minded men and women ... and the respect we are held in there could *not* be procured by running the brightest Gig in nature.'[48] He also renewed an important friendship when Jeffrey, now a judge in Scotland, came to London in early spring, and visited the Carlyles on 9 April. Although they buried their differences, and Jeffrey's visit seems to have been motivated by a genuine desire to ensure the Carlyles were prospering, Carlyle remained resolute that he wanted nothing more to do with Jeffrey, though wished him well.

The most significant social development for him came earlier that year. In February 1835 he met John Sterling, visiting Mill at India House. Sterling, a Church of England clergyman of some literary talent, was to be an important friend for the next nine years, and would to an extent fill the gap left in Carlyle's life by the death of Irving. Their first, brief conversation managed to turn to matters of deep controversy, Carlyle observing that Sterling's 'notions on the Slavery Question had not advanced into the stage of mine';[49] in other words, Sterling believed slavery, abolished in the British Empire two years earlier, was wrong. Carlyle walked with Sterling as far as Knightsbridge on his way to Chelsea, talking of 'moralities, theological philosophies; arguing copiously, but except in opinion not disagreeing'.[50] For Carlyle to have such a stimulating new companion was a great advantage, since his years of solitude, and difficulties in finding anyone sufficiently interesting since he came to London, had turned him into someone who unduly liked the sound of his own voice.

He ploughed on with his rewriting, though years later told George Smalley, a Suffolk clergyman whom he had met through the Sterlings, that for the three weeks after the catastrophe 'he did nothing but read novels'.[51] 'The second Chapter is done again; after a really tough battle; and the third goes along much more sweetly,'[52] he wrote to his mother on 20 April. He felt that having to apply himself in this way was the sign of great Christian virtue, though given his view of Christianity that was not necessarily a compliment. He was frequently interrupted by visits from old and new friends, so progress was not always smooth; he met Henry Wadsworth Longfellow, then a professor of modern languages, later famed as a poet. Carlyle's moods swung violently; by the end of April he was writing to Jack that his rewriting of the book was 'the most leaden, discouraging, all but intolerable task I ever had to do'.[53] Politics was by now disgusting him, and he found both the Tory Party and the King absurd (William was castigated by him as 'this poor half-daft Majesty of ours').[54] Wellington, whom he had regarded as one with heroic qualities, failed to live up to Carlyle's estimation. 'I saw him not many nights ago,' he told his mother, 'stepping across Piccadilly into his House, in the quiet dusk: a grey-whiskered, hollow-cheeked, *surprised*-looking, almost foolish-looking old gentleman; whose physiognomy surely inspired me with no terror or reverence.'[55]

The servant problem further upset him. Domestic calm was wrecked by a 'slut of sluts',[56] of whom the Carlyles had to rid themselves in May. They thought of an early summer visit to the family at Scotsbrig, but it did not happen. In later years, as the railways expanded, the journey became easier, and more frequently accomplished; but in 1835 it still required much planning, time and effort. Instead, Carlyle sought other forms of relief, still reading what he called 'the trashiest heap of novels',[57] including some by Captain Marryat. For several weeks he did very little except try to relax, and inevitably to worry about his lack of progress. He confided in his journal that he had never felt so disconsolate, and locked *The French Revolution* manuscript away and could not find the initiative to resume it. He thought about writing for Mill's new review, and Mill even sent him some books to write about, but he changed his mind and wrote nothing. He had never had such a deliberate lay-off in the middle of a project before, and tried to convince himself it was a good idea. He was buoyed, too, by news from America, whence Emerson was demanding another 100 copies of *Sartor* to satisfy demand. There were only four that Carlyle could find from Fraser, stitched together from the periodicals, and Fraser had no intention of printing any more. Neither he, nor Carlyle, could really believe that such demand as Emerson claimed there was existed. However, later in the summer Carlyle had a letter from a Unitarian minister in Boston, George Ripley, telling him of the wide circle of people in New England who had read the work, which Ripley judged to be 'a huge, mysterious, magnificent Symbol of the Time upon which we have fallen. It is the cry of the Heart & the Flesh for the living God.'[58]

During his 'holiday' Carlyle started to see much of Sterling, whom he found 'a sanguine, light, loving man; of whom to me nothing but good seems likely to come'.[59] He gave him *Sartor* to read, and was rewarded with three enormous sheets of constructive criticism once he had read it 'twice, with care'.[60] Sterling said he found the compositional style 'Rhapsodico-reflective',[61] reminding him of Rabelais, Montaigne, Sterne and Swift, though he assured Carlyle that the depth of feeling shown in his work far outweighed anything achieved by those four. He did, though, take exception to Carlyle's language, not least to words like 'environment' for which he could find no precedent. Carlyle, as the *Oxford English Dictionary* testifies, was a notable donor of words to the language. He criticised some of the trademarks of Carlyle's style, such as the compound nouns and adjectives, which Sterling blamed on the corrupting influence of the German. More important still, as a Christian clergyman he objected to the pantheistic quality of Teufelsdröckh's religion, which he felt severely misguided. But he concluded that the work was marked by its 'genius and moral energy',[62] praise of a sort Carlyle needed badly if his work in progress was to be sustained. He seems to have taken as a compliment, too, Sterling's view that 'according to him I can never be popular'.

He replied to the criticisms in robust style, noting that 'if one has thoughts not hitherto uttered in English Books, I see nothing for it but that you must use words not found there, must *make* words.'[63] On the religious point, Carlyle said he dared not name Teufelsdröckh's God his own God; and he reminded Sterling how fortunate he was to have an established creed in which he could readily believe. Taking the point personally, Carlyle said to Sterling: 'Assure yourself I am neither Pagan or Turk, nor circumcised Jew, but an unfortunate Christian individual resident in Chelsea in *this* year of Grace; neither Pantheist nor Pottheist, nor any Theist or *ist* whatsoever; having the most decided contempt for all manner of System-builders and Sectfounders.'[64] Jane wrote separately to Sterling, telling him that his critique was by far the best she had read on *Sartor*.

The French Revolution stayed locked in its drawer. Carlyle seriously thought at times of abandoning it and doing something different; he heard that an Education Commission was likely to be set up, and wrote to Mill asking advice on how to become a commissioner. He mentioned the matter to Charles Buller, who offered to put in a word with the Home Secretary, Lord John Russell. His American admirers, led by Emerson, asked him to go over later in the year and lecture them, but, like the education idea, that came to nothing. What he looked forward to most was the imminent return of Jack from his European travels with Lady Clare, a sign that his spiritual and social loneliness was too deep not just for his many visitors, but even for his wife, to assuage. But Jack's arrival, expected in July, was suddenly delayed by the

Countess's desire to linger in Switzerland (caused, Carlyle thought, by an aversion to her husband, who was in England); and he sank once more into disappointment.

None the less, in July he at last put aside 'trash' like Captain Marryat and returned to his writing. He found it easier after his rest, and felt his health picking up. He could foresee himself finishing the book. By the middle of August he was able to tell Jack that the rewriting was almost complete. 'The thing is worse, not very much worse, than it was; but anyway it will stand again on paper.'[65] Jane thought the new draft better than the first, what it lacked in stylistic verve being more than compensated for by second, deeper thoughts. Jane wrote to Jean Carlyle, her sister-in-law, claiming that once the rewriting was concluded 'we shall sing a *te deum* and get drunk.'[66] The process of writing the new draft can hardly have been more enjoyable for her than it was for Carlyle.

IV

In early September Carlyle toyed with going to Paris, not merely to research the work in hand, but to see Jack, who he hoped would be there. Jack, however, could not go there; and so, anxious for a break, he decided after all to make the first of his excursions from London to Annandale. London had been hot, dry, parched and unhealthy, and he was keen to be out of it. The climate had made Jane sick with headaches and colic, especially unfortunate since her mother was visiting at the time. Together they went out to the country, near Watford, to stay with friends, leaving Carlyle at his labours. Jane improved, only to fall sick again on the return to London, and was in such a state of weakness that any idea of travelling with her husband to Scotland was out of the question. Her mother stayed to keep her daughter company throughout September, while Carlyle was finishing the redraft, and through October, while he went north.

His task was completed on 23 September, six months and two weeks after the burning of the original manuscript. He told his journal: 'I seem to myself like a man that had nearly worn the Life out of him, accomplishing – *zero*.'[67] Yet the relief was immense. '*Zero* or not *zero*, what a deliverance!' he told Jack.[68] 'I shall never without a sacred shudder look back at the detestable state of enchantment I have worked for in these six months, and am now blessedly delivered from.' He told his brother he felt that, by comparison, the fresh work he had left to do 'shall go on quite like child's play'. The Carlyles' financial position was not healthy (not least because he, like Jack, made substantial subventions to their mother), and he found that the cheapest way of going north was to take a smack from the Port of London to Leith, which would cost £2. Then, refreshed by four or five days' sea air, he would take the mail coach to Dumfries. So delayed was his departure, though, that he had in the end to go by coach to Liverpool, and thence by sea to Scotland.

The passage was rough, and he was sea-sick. As well as visiting his mother, his main responsibility was to find a nice Scottish girl to bring back as a servant. A succession of temporary helps – mostly Irishwomen – during the summer had been disastrous, and the problem was now acute. Carlyle, not surprisingly, felt it was due to the wider deterioration in society of normal deferential relationships. He found his mother well and in good spirits, but his brother James was struggling as a farmer, and thinking of leaving for America: and Alick was doing so badly that he was contemplating emigrating to Canada the following year. He had trouble finding a decent servant, and of the girl he eventually recruited, Anne Cook, he wrote to Jane that she was 'if without manners, at least with no ill manners'.[69]

He stayed four weeks in Scotland, through almost all of October 1835 and into November, though soon found the dullness and quiet as unbearable as the noise and confusion he had left behind. Though happy among his family, the other society there was no longer what he was used to, and it pained him. Urged on by Jane, who had been angered by his failure to correspond with her regularly while he was away, he decided to go home to resume work. However bored he might have become during his visit, his health was stronger, and he estimated optimistically that the task of finishing *The French Revolution* would take him another six months. On Friday 6 November he started south with Anne Cook, arriving in London late the following Sunday evening.

He found Jane better and happy to see him, and was impressed that she had used his absence to become proficient in Italian with the help of Count Pepoli, an Italian refugee she had befriended. He felt he noticed changes in other of his friends, notably Mill, with whom things would never again be quite right. 'Mill,' he told Jack in a letter, 'is getting more and more confirmed into a Logician, and Utilitarian of *larger* growth. One esteems him exceedingly: but to love *him*? It were like loving the 47th of Euclid.'[70] Sterling, on the other hand, he and Jane came to like more and more ('an angel of heaven'[71] Jane called him); and she became a close companion of Sterling's mother. Carlyle went back to work gradually, falling into the routine of working throughout the day. Neglected by him, Jane, who had longed for his return, soon subsided into her routine of headaches and depression. Carlyle's spirits subsided too; on 4 December he reached, with apparently no celebration at all, his fortieth birthday.

His enthusiasms about returning to work turned into ennui, and before Christmas he was writing to his sister of 'that weary book'.[72] However difficult it still was, writing was easier than it had been. He soon took to doing it in the mornings only, which he found helped him relax and work to a higher standard; and it gave him time with Jane, which she much wanted. Progress was slow, and his target of a date by which to finish had to be revised. He and Jane went out relatively little that winter, his greatest enjoyment being to sit with a book for the evening. He was still hankering after salaried employment, however unsuitable, and in January 1836 wrote off to Glasgow to enquire after yet another astronomy professorship; before he could apply formally, he learned it was not well enough paid for him to consider. Basil Montagu, whom he had known for years, was also concerned about Carlyle's financial stringencies, and offered to create a post for him as a clerk in his legal and accounting practice, which would pay him £200 a year. With customary ingratitude Carlyle turned that down, and wrote to Jack that it had been as if Montagu ('the Sovereign of Quacks'[73]) had thought that 'the Polar Bear, reduced to a state of dyspeptic dejection, might be safely trusted tending rabbits'. Another more fitting, but still unacceptable, offer came from the proprietors of a new radical newspaper in Lichfield, the *Staffordshire Examiner*, who asked Carlyle to become their editor. Mill had suggested Carlyle for the post, and Carlyle rejected it out of hand, no doubt feeling he was too able even to be an editor.

So he pressed on with his task, constantly urging 'Courage!' to himself in his journal, and in his letters to others when talking of the work. It became easier, and he began to envisage the day when it would be finished, and the happiness he would feel. While at work, though, he felt often 'as if Hades itself were slight change to me, from this fearful and wonderful mystery of a world; surely no greater miracle it were, – past finding out'.[74] Whatever Carlyle's woes they were less than his neighbour Hunt's; Hunt had presided over the demise of his *London Journal*, and was deeply in debt with the sprawling family still to feed; and Carlyle would, of an evening, sit and talk with him, as Jane put it, to 'speak comfort'.[75] Along with Jeffrey and Mill (who had been ill for most of the winter) Carlyle sought to secure Hunt a Civil List pension; though it was to take until 1847 before it was granted, and then only with the help of Macaulay.

As spring came, so Carlyle's spirits fell again – 'one of the ugliest springs I ever anywhere beheld'.[76] He and Mill went to Kent, via steamer to Gravesend and thence overland, to see one of Mill's friends; and though the change of scene and country air was pleasant to Carlyle it disconcerted him, and made him restless and tired. He was further depressed by an illness of Sterling's, the first signs of the consumptive malaise that would kill him eight years later. Yet friends, who were plentiful, could not write his book for him, and that was the pressing task. Jack, now at last coming home, had written to ask whether he could bring any books for his brother. Carlyle replied that he already had 300 books on the subject, and what he most needed was 'good sense and good spirits to make use of what I have'.[77] He reported his state of mind as one of 'biliousness and fret, and palpitating haste and bewilderment'.

By the end of April he was writing to Emerson: 'Have compassion for me! It is really very miserable: but it will end ... it is like a Nessus' Shirt, burning you into madness.'[78] At that time, by which he had hoped to have the work finished, he had just completed the second of three volumes. He took a week's rest, spending much of the time travelling about with Jack; and then he, Jane and Jack spent the fortnight after that sick with heavy colds and headaches.

Emerson had organised the publication in Boston of an edition of *Sartor*, and news of this success reached Carlyle; it was the first proper edition of the work, not to be published in England for another year.

Not until early June did he resume writing. Mill was begging him for an article for his *London and Westminster Review* on some memoirs of Mirabeau; at least the work for Mill would bring some much needed money. It was more than two years since Carlyle had had an income – other than for Mill's compensation – and resources were low. Moreover, it could be considered necessary research for the greater project. The review took Carlyle most of June, but he found himself writing more fluently than for months. Mill was pleased with the piece, though he disagreed philosophically with much of it. He also criticised the style Carlyle had developed, telling him it would be 'better on the reader if what is said in an abrupt, exclamatory & interjectional manner were said in the ordinary grammatical mode of nominative and verb'.[79] Carlyle, owning up to why he used such a form, said that 'the common English mode of writing has to do with what I call the hearsays of things; and the great business for me, in which alone I feel any comfort, is recording the presence, bodily concrete coloured presence of things; – for which the Nominative-and-verb, as I find it Here and Now, refuses to stand me in due stead.'[80] It was not until the following January that the review was published, because, according to Mill's editor Thomas Falconer, its length was such that space forced it out of the next two quarterly issues. When it was eventually published, the style drew howls of complaint from readers. Mill, loyal to a fault, wrote to one saying that 'those who have disliked the article Mirabeau are those who cannot endure *any peculiarities* of style.'[81]

Jane was still low, and considering going to her mother at Templand for a few weeks; the Sterlings then invited her to go with them in August to Paris, and she initially accepted. However, the summer heat in London had debilitated her, and she realised Paris would be even worse; so in early July, she went to Templand after all, via Manchester, travelling by rail for the first time between there and Liverpool. In her absence, Carlyle pressed on with Volume III of his work. Mill, whose father had just died, asked Carlyle to go with him away for a weekend to his cottage at Mickleham, near Dorking in the Surrey hills. At first Carlyle wavered, claiming he was irritable, depressed by his work and sleeping badly, but in the end he went. Jane, writing from Scotland, had been anxious lest Carlyle in his solitude work himself into illness, and had implored him to 'go to bed in time and take your meals regularly'. Signifying the awareness of the neglect that she felt while he obsessed himself with his work, she added: 'and think of me as kindly as you can'.[82]

He spent two nights with Mill, waking at three on the first morning and five on the second. Seeing at close quarters for two days the dry, unemotional side of his host, Carlyle began to wonder how it was they attracted each other as friends; it was a premonition of the breach between them. On returning to London he plunged himself once more into solitude. Mill was going

abroad, and the Sterlings were off to Bordeaux; only a long visit from Jack
on his way to rejoin Lady Clare distracted Carlyle, but Jack spent much of
his time reading, or out of doors, and did not interfere with his brother's
work. After three weeks in Scotland Jane wrote that she had stayed as long as
she had only because she imagined it might make her well, but she was no
longer sure of that, and wanted to return to London as soon as she felt well
enough to cope with the journey. The wish to come home seems to have been
prompted as much by concern about her husband's feelings for her as
anything else. 'You do not say,' she wrote on 30 July, 'that you miss me – but
I hope it is out of self-denial not indifference.'[83] In his reply he told her to
come home as soon as she could. 'I wish to heaven I were better, cheerfuller
... In any case, what refuge is there but here? Here is the place for my poor
Goody; let us sink or swim together.'[84] On 1 September, wishing she had
never gone, Jane was home again, two days after Jack had set off to Rome
with the Countess. Carlyle went to meet her coach in Fleet Street, spotting it
not by seeing her, but by seeing her trunk on the top; which Jane decided was
a mark of his great genius.

Shortly after Jane had settled in, Carlyle wrote to Sterling in France to say
that he was halfway through the last volume of his book. He had no expectations
of success ('the sole blessedness I expect or desire from it is that of being done
with it'),[85] and he was beginning to fret about his next project – 'No man in
Europe perhaps has a blanker future', he added. Ironically, in a later letter, he
told Sterling that 'my habitual conviction about the work is that it ought to be
burnt, that it will never be worth a farthing to any man or woman.'[86] None the
less, the word from America was that the first edition of *Sartor*–500 copies–had
sold out, which should have encouraged him; the more radical temperament of
his American audience had helped him to a success the more conservative
London publishers would not have dreamt of. Yet his health had deteriorated,
which made writing hard, though there were consolations of amusement in
what he was doing. *The French Revolution* is as much a statement of Carlyle's
own developing political beliefs as it is an account of historical events, and he
made this point directly in a letter of 9 October 1836 to Mill:

On the whole I am sick of the Girondins. To confess a truth, I find them extremely
like our present set of respectable Radical members. There is the same cold clean-
washed patronising talk about 'the masses' (a word, expressive of a thing, which I
greatly hate); the same Formalism, hidebound pedantry, superficiality, narrowness,
barrenness. I find that Mountain was perfectly under the necessity of flinging such a
set of men to the Devil; whither also I doubt not *our* set will go.[87]

An end was now definitely in sight; the printer was expecting the manuscript
on New Year's Day 1837. Fraser had now agreed to publish 'The Diamond
Necklace' at about the same time in his *Magazine,* so, after nearly three years
of silence, Carlyle was about to re-emerge to the reading public. Fraser also
offered to publish the whole of *The French Revolution* in successive numbers of

his *Magazine*, an offer Carlyle wisely refused. Through the autumn he proceeded relentlessly. Many of the Carlyles' friends were out of town, either abroad or in the country for the autumn while parliament was not sitting, so there were few interruptions. He did, though, sit for a painter called Lewis, who was from Dumfries but now settled in London. Of the likeness, he told his mother: 'It is glaringly recognisable; has a distinct likeness of *you* in it ... I do not like it myself.'[88] It was also a sign of Carlyle's distinction that Lewis had asked to paint him as it might boost his own career to have portrayed such a subject.

In November the Carlyles made a new acquaintance who was to have far-reaching effects on them. Harriet Martineau was a thirty-four-year-old proto-feminist from a liberal nonconformist background, strongly at odds with Carlyle on certain great issues of the day – such as the abolition of slavery – but a disciple of his none the less, and a 'notable literary woman'[89] in her own right. She had acquired the Carlyle habit in America, where she had been travelling, and had just returned home to write a book (*Society in America*) on her travels. 'She pleased us far beyond expectation,' Carlyle recorded. 'She is very intelligent-looking, really of pleasant countenance; was full of talk, tho' unhappily deaf almost as a post, so that you have to speak to her thro' an ear-trumpet.'[90] She was to be a remarkable social catalyst for the Carlyles, introducing them to, among others, the Darwins. She asked Carlyle to dinner, but he had a cold and did not go; but he and Jane decided that they would be friends with Miss Martineau. In her autobiography she recalls how, having met the Carlyles through a mutual friend, she would be driven over to Chelsea once a fortnight for tea and conversation.[91]

As Christmas approached, so did the end of Carlyle's labours, and, it seemed, the end of his reasonable recent health. He took himself out for long walks in the fog and frost, which only worsened his 'inflammatory, catarrhal, atrabiliar state'.[92] It had been a year of bad weather, and the climate was having political consequences. A bad harvest had forced up the price of bread and potatoes, and beggars were more in evidence on the streets than Carlyle had ever seen. Heavy snows restricted his movements, but allowed him time to look again at his work. He restructured his nearly completed manuscript into shorter chapters (his original chapters being denominated 'books' in the final draft), and just after Christmas, with only one short chapter to write, he sent the beginning of the book to the printer. 'Mirabeau' at last came out in the *London Review* at the very beginning of the new year. It drew heavily on material recycled in *The French Revolution*; and, like 'The Diamond Necklace' (a pleasant narrative, in spite of its stylistic difficulties, with amusing descriptions of the moral sink of French life in the 1780s), it made an ideal *hors d'oeuvre* for *The French Revolution*. Carlyle was back on the map.

The problem of what to do next looked to have been solved. Harriet Martineau, together with some friends, had decided Carlyle should give some lectures on German literature at the Royal Institution in Albemarle Street.

Carlyle was willing in principle, though could not make up his mind whether he was one of nature's lecturers. Miss Martineau had marvelled at his private harangues and his ability to hold forth, colourfully, in his Chelsea drawing-room. She urged him to put on such performances in public. On 11 January 1837 he wrote to an acquaintance, Abraham Hayward, who he knew was a member of this institution, to ask about the feasibility of such a project. Two days later, at ten o'clock in the evening, he finished *The French Revolution*: 'I could almost have returned thanks audibly to Heaven with tears.'[93] He recalled that Jane was in the room when he finished it, and that he had probably given the manuscript to her to read with a 'Thank God it is done, Jeannie!'[94] before going for a walk towards Kensington to clear his head. To celebrate, Jane cooked a bread pudding the next day, while he went for a walk of, he estimated, twenty miles about London. He then settled back to await the arrival of the first proof-sheets, which themselves would be followed by the ecstatic day when 'I can hope to wash my hands of it forever and a day.'[95]

V

The aftermath, while he corrected his proofs, was a time of anticlimax. For much of January London was wreathed in black mist – not unlike smog – and Jane, predictably, was one of thousands of sufferers in a flu epidemic, whose victims' funerals distracted Carlyle as, liberated from his writing-desk, he walked about Chelsea. His own health, now the burden of composition was lifted, was, he felt, better than ever. He even started to feel optimistic about his newly completed work. 'It is not altogether a bad Book,' he told his mother. 'I consider it to be perhaps the sincerest Book this Nation has got offered it for a good few years; or is like to get for a good few.'[96] He was cheered by news from America that a second edition of *Sartor*, of 1,000 copies, was being printed. Suddenly his reputation was blossoming. Jane, writing to Sterling, said that 'I might happen to get myself torn in pieces, by the host of my Husband's lady-admirers, who already I suspect, think me too happy in not knowing my happiness.'[97] The last remark was ironic; noting the sufferings that accompanied the composition of *The French Revolution*, Jane had observed: 'Let no woman who values peace of soul ever dream of marrying an Author!' But she added:

You cannot fancy what way he is making with the fair Intellectuals here! There is Harriet Martineau presents him her ear-trumpet with a pretty blushing air of coquetry which would almost convince one out of belief in her indentity [*sic*]! And Mrs Pierce Butler, bolts in upon his studies (out of the atmosphere as it were) in riding-habit cap and whip ... And then there is a young American Beauty – such a Beauty ... and this charming creature publicly declares herself his 'ardent admirer'; and I heard her with my own ears call out quite passionately at parting with him 'Oh Mr Carlyle I want to see you – to talk a long long time about – *Sartor*'!! Sartor of all things in this world! what *could* such a young Lady have got to say about Sartor, can you imagine?[98]

After more remarks about Carlyle corrupting young women, Jane mused: 'is it not curious that my Husbands [*sic*] own writings should be only completely understood and adequately appreciated by women and mad people?' But none the less, it was fame.

Correcting his proofs, Carlyle found his book 'one of the *savagest* written for several centuries: it is a book written by a *wild man*, a man disunited from the fellowship of the world he lives in.'[99] To speed up the book's publication, Fraser had engaged a second printer to produce the third volume. The author was also starting to consider his course of lectures, due to begin on 1 May. He had decided, sensibly, to save himself work and base them on his own, unpublished *History of German Literature*. Along with Harriet Martineau another of his women admirers, Jane Wilson, a friend of Miss Martineau's who had known the Carlyles since 1835, was involved in helping with the arrangements. They had still not managed to secure the Royal Institution, and Miss Wilson and he discussed approaching one of its luminaries, Michael Faraday, the scientist, for help. However, the Institution was booked up, so the search began for somewhere else; Miss Wilson eventually settled on Willis's Rooms in King Street, St James's, though not before Carlyle had convinced himself the lectures would not reach fruition. For the first three weeks of May they were to be held every Monday and Friday afternoon between three and four: and Carlyle was to deliver them extempore. He had no choice in the matter of delivery; the urgency with which Fraser was addressing the publication of his book meant Carlyle was fully occupied on proofs, and had no time to prepare texts of lectures. It was as well the work he had done on German literature had given him all the expertise he needed; but because he did deliver the talks off the cuff, there is no surviving note of what he said.

He prepared a short piece for Mill on 'The Parliamentary History of the French Revolution', for the April number of his *Review*: but otherwise the proofs took up all his time. Jane spent much of February and March in bed ill, and so required some attention from him. He began to feel nervous about the lectures. Miss Wilson put about a prospectus for them, and a group of fine ladies, led by the Marchioness of Lansdowne, indicated support. Carlyle sent Mill some of the prospectuses, to distribute among friends. The course looked demanding for lectured and lecturer alike:

1. On the Teutonic People, the German Language, Ulfilas, the Northern Immigration, and the Nibelungen Lied.
2. On the Minnesinger, Tauler, Reineke Fuchs, the Legend of Faust, the Reformation, Luther, Ulrich von Hutten.
3. On the Master Singers, Hans Sachs, Jacob Bohme, Decay of German Literature, Anton Ulrich Duke of Brunswick, Opitz, Leibnitz.
4. On the Resuscitation of German Literature, Lessing, Klopstock, Gellert, Lavater, Efflorescence of German Literature, Werther, Goetz.
5. On the Characteristics of New-German Literature, Growth and Decay of Opinion, Faust, Philosophy, Kant, Fichte, Schelling, Art and Belief, Goethe.

6. On the Drama, Schiller. Pseudo-Drama, Klinger, Kotzebue, Werner: Romance, Tieck, Novalis, Pseudo-Romance, Hofman: Poetry and German Literature, Herder, Wieland, the Schlegels, Jean Paul: Results, Anticipations.[100]

'I tremble to the very bone to think of it,' he wrote to Mill, three weeks before the start of the course, imploring his friend to pray for him.[101] Yet he admitted the challenge of lecturing had long appealed to him, so his apprehension was not entirely negative.

As he made final preparations, political events that were to influence his work in the years ahead diverted him. Large-scale unemployment of the working classes and civil unrest were occurring in the industrial areas, on the back of collapse in commercial confidence. The Poor Law Amendment Act of 1834 failed the unemployed, because the workhouses were too small to cope with the destitute; the aim of the Act had been to stop 'outdoor relief', payment of a dole to families living other than in a workhouse. The workhouses themselves were unpopular because they divided husbands, wives and children, and it was a principal aim of Chartism to do away with them.

In the last week of April the printing of his book was finished, leaving him a few precious days to think about his lectures. However, Jane had still not recovered from flu, and indeed had taken such a turn for the worse that her mother was sent for to nurse her. Carlyle and her doctor feared she might have consumption, but as soon as her mother arrived she started to recover. Mrs Welsh prepared for a long stay, as Carlyle intended to go to his family in Scotland as soon as his lectures were over, that he might have a proper, silent rest. He also needed to talk things over with Alick, whose agricultural enterprises had been so disastrous that he could see no alternative but to emigrate. Luckily for Carlyle, money was now starting to come in again from his writing, and he was not unduly stretched by Alick's inability to repay the £140 loan he had made to him four years earlier. But for the moment professional considerations had to precede all else.

'I have got my first lecture over,' Carlyle told James Fraser on the evening of 1 May 1837. 'I had a pretty audience; mostly of quality. It was not a *break-down*; this is all that can be said of it: the next will be better we hope.'[102] Of watching him lecture, Harriet Martineau recalled that 'whenever I went, my pleasure was a good deal spoiled by his unconcealable nervousness.' Carlyle had been 'yellow as a guinea'.[103] A correspondent from *The Times* said he detected 'incidental streaks of light from a vivid and fine imagination, which relieved while they contrasted with the unpretending simplicity and untrained but touching homeliness of his style and manner'.[104] *The Spectator*'s correspondent, writing of the lecture given by a 'Mr Carlisle', said the event had attracted 'a very crowded and yet a select audience of both sexes'. He continued that 'Mr Carlisle may be deficient in the mere mechanism of oratory; but this minor defect is far more than counterbalanced by his perfect mastery of his subject, the originality of his manner, the perspicuity of his language, his simple but genuine eloquence, and his vigorous grasp of a large and difficult question.'[105] The report said Carlyle had spent much of the lecture on the character of the German people, a term he used to embrace most of northern Europe and to include the population of much of Britain, conquered and peopled as it had been by Germanic tribes. There are retrospectively unpleasant harbingers of Nazi doctrine in what *The Spectator* reports Carlyle as having said: 'He described them as the only genuine European people, unmixed with strangers. They have in fact never been subdued; and considering the great, open, and fertile country which they inhabit, this fact at once demonstrates the masculine and indomitable character of the race. They have not only not been subdued, but been themselves by far the greatest conquerors in the world.' The report added that, according to Carlyle, 'it is pretty clear that, in progress of time, they must either occupy or hold rule over the greater portion of the earth.' Bismarck's triumphs were still thirty years away; Hitler more than fifty years unborn: but Carlyle had unerringly struck upon the dominant theme of conflict in the next century and more of European history.

Fanny Wedgwood, one of the 'quality', claimed Erasmus Darwin had told her Carlyle believed he would earn £150 from his lectures (in fact, he made £135); so they were a great success. Between two and three hundred people attended each of them. Carlyle told his mother after his fifth lecture: 'I found myself in an awful flurry at first; but gradually recovered; and can go on now with comparative comfort.'[106] So happy had he been with them, indeed, that he decided to give an extra lecture, making seven in all; though one critic, Empson, said they had been inferior to Carlyle's conversation, and he suspected (not wrongly) that Carlyle had not taken enough trouble over them. In any case, Carlyle was already thinking of repeating the experiment. Jane was immensely impressed by her husband's performance. 'Nothing that he has ever tried seems to me to have carried such conviction to the public heart that he is a real man of genius,' she told her brother-in-law.[107]

In the middle of the lecture programme a still greater event occurred: *The French Revolution* was published on 9 May. 'What the critics say of the work I take no pains to know, or rather would take pains not to know,' he told his mother.[108] Mill was busily writing a review of it, and had indicated privately to Carlyle his satisfaction with the work. Carlyle, as an important part of the cathartic process of finishing the book, had sent back all the books Mill had lent him, including the *Biographie Universelle*; but, as a token of esteem, Mill presented Carlyle with a set of that work once Carlyle's book was published. They were perhaps never closer friends than at this time, though politics and philosophy were soon to start driving them apart.

VI

The French Revolution demonstrates how Carlyle would use a work of history as a vehicle for theocratic didacticism, prophecy and as a sustained political pronouncement. It also displays his immense passion, and the energy with which he approached both history and his ideology. The work's message must not be over-simplified: but it does seem a clear statement of Carlyle's belief in the effects of the destruction of God's natural order. When the leaders of French society neglected their duties, they found the political order challenged, and feudalism, then monarchy, abandoned. As faithlessness broke out and society broke down, the duty of ruling was passed to those unfitted for it, and finally to a mob. Anarchy, which Carlyle regarded as the manifestation of divine punishment, continued more and more violently until (as personified by Danton and Robespierre) exhausted with its own excesses; in the absence of a natural order came, too, rampant injustice. Humanity and civilisation were wrecked, and the effects spread far beyond France. Carlyle explained this with unrestrained passion.

He saw history as a continuum, and what had driven him on was the belief that the lessons of half a century earlier with which he lectured his readers were, like all experience, still vital today. This, like so much else of Carlyle's thought, had German roots. Talking to his friend William Allingham in 1871, Carlyle said: 'I often think of Kant's notion – no real Time or Space, these are only appearances – and think it is true.'[109] This is the 'natural supernaturalism' of *Sartor*. To make the proper didactic point, he communicates facts with, as in *Oliver* eight years later, 'elucidations' that reflect his own prejudices. Like most of Carlyle's works, it is self-centred because it is more about Carlyle than about its notional subject.

The style of the book is its greatest challenge. The story is rarely told simply, but in the abrupt, explosive, conversational, tangential way that came to typify Carlylese, with its strings of breathless clauses interrupted by semicolons. For Carlyle, as well as for his readers, the style was experimental. It may have echoed *Sartor*, but *Sartor* was a novel; no history had ever looked like this. The experiment of the style was still being conducted two decades later, when Carlyle wrote *Frederick*, though by then it had subtly affected the prose of other innovative writers, not least Dickens. Carlyle assumes much knowledge on the part of his readers, legitimately so since the events of which he wrote had happened so recently. However, for his occasional vagueness he was severely reprimanded by at least one critic. The *Literary Gazette* reviewer complained that 'there is nothing like a history of the events that took place; but, instead, there is a series of rhapsodical snatches, which may remind readers acquainted with the facts from previous histories and memoirs, what it is that the author is really writing about.' He added that 'by itself, his book is unintelligible.'[110]

Carlyle's heavy allusiveness will not help comprehension today; and the frequent weakness of his characterisations, with notable exceptions, will not help the complexly constructed story come much to life. Yet in large parts the book is stunning, energetic, and, above all, historically accurate. The principal stylistic aim of the author, to represent history in a vibrant, living and exciting way without cheapening it, is achieved. Mark Cumming suggested that 'the epic novel exemplifies for Carlyle the transformation of traditional poetic kinds into modern prose counterparts',[111] and one can see how the epic prose structure of this great work of history is meant as the counterpart to a great historical poem.

Early on, Carlyle defines the ideal of kingship. The definition serves well not just for *The French Revolution*, but for several succeeding works in which ideas of leadership are central; and like much else in this work, it serves an allegorical function in regard to England in the 1830s, plagued by calls for further reform:

Neither was that an inconsiderable moment when wild armed men first raised their Strongest aloft on the buckler-throne, and with clanging armour and hearts, said solemnly: Be thou our Acknowledged Strongest! In such Acknowledged Strongest (well-named King, *Kon-ning*, Canning, or man that was able) what a Symbol now shone for them ... a Symbol of true Guidance in return for loving Obedience; properly, if he knew it, the prime want of man ... It was well said there lay in the Acknowledged Strongest a divine right; as surely there might in the Strongest, whether Acknowledged or not, – considering who it was that made him strong.[112]

Carlyle explains how this principle was violated; a monarchy and aristocracy more interested in sensual pleasures than governing, become ornaments rather than guides. Royalty was 'decrepit, moribund',[113] and incapable of fighting off a challenge to its authority once one was mounted. Divine right was attacked by Sansculottism, promising a new 'age of miracles',[114] an alternative theology; and Sansculottism won, because of the inherent weaknesses of its corrupted opponent. 'Government is a thing that governs, that guides; and if need be, compels. Visible in France there is not such a thing.'[115] Also blamed for the decline are the clergy, who endured similar moral and spiritual decline to the aristocracy, but with the greater, spiritual responsibilities to discharge were able to cause even more damage. The clergy had the power to deceive the people, to propagate the cant of religion, and to steer further away from a true faith. This waste of power infuriated Carlyle. 'If the dead echo of it still did so much, what could not the living voice of it once do?'[116] The final result of atheism in this context is the Terror. There is a structural trait familiar from other of Carlyle's writings, and already seen in *Sartor*; an opening period of decline and loss of faith is followed by a time of doubt and destruction, and then of rebuilding.

Carlyle also condemns what he would christen the 'cash-nexus', which violates the feudal relation of man with man, with its attendant vice of *laissez-faire*, expounded by Rousseau; and, as he explained in 'Diderot', the atheistic ideas of the *philosophes*. Then there are the journalists, able editors, pamphleteers, 'the fourth estate', busy 'opening its abysmal throat wider and wider; never to close more'.[117] The people, meanwhile, are ignored except when needed for exploitation, or when being savagely punished for protesting about their lot. Once Sansculottism has won its initial victory, the King, his divine right lost, is no longer the voice of God; the people have assumed that role, and their voice is expressed through journalism, the pulpit of a secular – or secularising – society. An able editor becomes president of the tribunal that tries Louis for his life. A new order is proclaimed:

Great is Journalism. Is not every able Editor a Ruler of the World, being a persuader of it; though self-elected, yet sanctioned, by the sale of his Numbers? Whom indeed the world has the readiest method of deposing, should need be: that of merely doing *nothing* to him; which ends in starvation.[118]

This satirist's touch is seldom lacking as Carlyle details the catastrophe; it often appears in passages of ridiculously high-flown style, such as when Robespierre is consecrating his new religion, or simply in irreverence for whatever Carlyle is describing (note, for example, his translations of the French names of months of the new calendar).[119] Of all his works, this brings out best the historian as humorist. His sense of the political and philosophical significance of the events he describes is clear too. He rues the opening of the States-General as 'the baptism day of Democracy . . . the extreme-unction day of Feudalism!', and lists the results of the change:

Battles and bloodshed, September Massacres, Bridges of Lodi, retreats of Moscow, Waterloos, Peterloos, Tenpound Franchises, Tar-barrels and Guillotines; – and from this present date, if one might prophesy, some two centuries of it still to fight! Two centuries; hardly less; before Democracy go through its due, most baleful, stages of *Quack*ocracy; and a pestilential World be burnt up, and have begun to grow green and young again.[120]

Such editorial or philosophical comments pepper the book, fitting in with the rhythm of apostrophic history as Carlyle tells it. A central philosophical passage outlines not just the effects of the betrayal of feudal principles, but also sets out Carlyle's own agenda for the next fifteen years. It is strong meat, too, for those who believe that Carlyle was some sort of proto-fascist who made a rule of siding with the oppressor:

Fancy, then, some Five full-grown Millions of such gaunt figures, with their haggard faces (*figures hâves*); in woollen jupes, with copper-studded leather girths, and high sabots, – starting up to ask, as in forest-roarings, their washed Upper Classes, after long unreviewed centuries, virtually this question: How have ye treated us; how have ye taught us, fed us, and led us, while we toiled for you? The answer can be read in flames, over the nightly summer-sky. *This* is the feeding and leading we have had of you; EMPTINESS, – of pocket, of stomach, of head and of heart. Behold there is *nothing in us*; nothing but what Nature gives her wild children in the desert: Ferocity and Appetite: Strength grounded on Hunger. Did ye mark among your Rights of Man, that man was not to die of starvation, while there was bread reaped by him? It is among the Mights of Man.[121]

There are peerless insights, such as when he rounds on Marat, 'the People's

Friend', for his phrase 'no power on Earth can prevent me from seeing into traitors, and unmasking them.'[122] 'By my superior originality of mind?' interposes Carlyle. 'An honourable member like this Friend of the People few terrestrial Parliaments have had.' However, most characterisations are poor, as are descriptions of action; but some are stunning. His portrait of Mirabeau is one of the finest in the book, not least because Carlyle viewed him as one of the few people in the story with heroic qualities:

A king or leader they, as all bodies of men, must have: be their work what it may, there is one man there who, by character, faculty, position, is fittest of all to do it; that man, as future not yet elected king, walks there among the rest. He with the thick black locks, will it be? With the *hure*, as himself calls it, or black *boar's head*, fit to be 'shaken' as a senatorial portent? Through whose shaggy beetle-brows, and rough-hewn, seamed, carbuncled face, there look natural ugliness, smallpox, incontinence, bankruptcy – and burning fire of genius; like comet-fire glaring fuliginous through murkiest confusions? It is *Gabriel Honoré Riquetti de Mirabeau*, the world-compeller; man-ruling Deputy of Aix.[123]

'His death is Titanic,' says Carlyle, when he dies, 'as his life as been.'[124] But no other character – not Danton, Marat, Robespierre ('Sea-green Incorruptible!'), not Marie-Antoinette and certainly not Louis XVI – is given a chance to assume a strong, identifiable character. Part of his method of portraying history interestingly is to pluck minor figures from the drama and give them centre-stage for a chapter or two, and then to move on; it is difficult, within such a structure, to develop character properly; but at least the work has the benefit of being unpredictable, even to those familiar with the story Carlyle is telling. Suddenly, he will turn from the narrative, and give vent to his own feelings, as when we see Marie-Antoinette at the States-General:

With a most mixed feeling, wherein joy has no part, she resigns herself to a day she hoped never to have seen. Poor Marie Antoinette; with thy quick noble instincts; vehement glancings, vision all-too fitful narrow for the work thou hast to do! O there are tears in store for thee; bitterest wailings, soft womanly meltings, though thou hast the heart of an imperial Theresa's Daughter. Thou doomed one, shut thy eyes on the future![125]

Describing events, Carlyle is sometimes brilliant. His account of the execution of Louis is of this order, not least because he keeps his prose simple, his sentences short and free from allusion:

As the clocks strike ten, behold the Place de la Révolution, once Place de Louis Quinze: the Guillotine, mounted near the old pedestal where once stood the Statue of that Louis! Far round, all bristles with cannons and armed men: spectators crowding in the rear; D'Orléans Egalité there in cabriolet. Swift Messengers, *hoquetons*, speed to the Townhall, every three minutes: near by is the Convention sitting, – vengeful for Lepelletier. Heedless of all, Louis reads his Prayers of the Dying; not till five minutes yet has he finished; then the Carriage opens. What temper is he in? Ten different witnesses will give ten different accounts of it. He is in the collision of all tempers; arrived now at the black Mahlstrom and descent of Death: in sorrow, in indignation, in resignation struggling to be resigned. 'Take care of M. Edgeworth,' he straitly charges the Lieutenant who is sitting with them: then they two descend.

The drums are beating: '*Taisez-vous*, Silence!' he cries 'in a terrible voice, *d'une voix terrible*.' He mounts the scaffold, not without delay; he is in puce coat, breeches of grey, white stockings. He strips off the coat; stands disclosed in a sleeve-waistcoat of white flannel. The Executioners approach to bind him: he spurns, resists; Abbé Edgeworth has to remind him how the Saviour, in whom men trust, submitted to be bound. His hands are tied, his head bare; the fatal moment is come. He advances to the edge of the Scaffold, 'his face very red,' and says: 'Frenchmen, I die innocent: it is from the Scaffold and near appearing before God that I tell you so. I pardon my enemies; I desire that France –' A general on horseback, Santerre or another, prances out, with uplifted hand: '*Tambours!*' The drums drown the voice. 'Executioners, do your duty!' The Executioners, desperate lest themselves be murdered (for Santerre and his Armed Ranks will strike, if they do not), seize the hapless Louis: six of them desperate, him singly desperate, struggling there; and bind him to their plank. Abbé Edgeworth, stooping, bespeaks him: 'Son of Saint Louis, ascend to Heaven.' The Axe clanks down; a King's Life is shorn away.[126]

There is a radical, innovative tone to such prose that makes it like a screenplay; the same is true of the account of Charlotte Corday's murder of Marat.[127] In contrast to the serious tone of that passage, Carlyle also uses ridicule to great effect, as in the description of 'Mahomet' Robespierre, the 'seagreen Pontiff' in 'sky-blue coat, made for the occasion; white silk waistcoat broidered with silver, black silk breeches, white stockings, shoe-buckles of gold' presiding over the first act of worship in the 'Republican Religion', having decreed that a 'Supreme Being' was needed after all.[128] But much of his description is ponderous and unclear, whether because he could not properly visualise the events, or because of the rush in which he wrote the book. Nor, because of his style, does he very often tell the story as clearly as he might; one has to work very hard at his meaning.

But the ultimate message points ahead, from England in 1837 when Carlyle finished writing: 'Out of a world of Unwise nothing but an Unwisdom can be made. Arrange it, constitution-build it, sift it through ballot-boxes as thou wilt, it is and remains an Unwisdom.'[129] This belief was to dominate his thinking, producing within him a pessimism that alternated between comedy and ferocity.

VII

Once the lectures were over Carlyle started to make arrangements for a trip to Scotland, passing the weeks until leaving rooting about in his garden, digging and pruning, and going for walks. He seemed to show, in his newly found leisure time, no particular desire for Jane's company, though she was still weak from flu, and still had her mother with her. Her physical weakness, and his neglect, set patterns for the rest of their life together. He tried to avoid reviews of his book, though, as he told Sterling, he was aware that there was much to-do about the style. 'These poor people seem to think a style can be put off or put on not like a *skin* but like a coat!'[130] The dramatic style of the narrative affected and underpinned Dickens's own in the great novels he would write in the years immediately ahead. So impressed was he by the work that he carried one volume or other around with him wherever he went for a time after it was published. The good reviews helped sales, and his fame. Mill was in no doubt about his part in the success. In a smugly self-congratulatory tone he noted in his *Autobiography* that 'I believe that the early success and reputation of Carlyle's French Revolution were considerably accelerated by what I wrote about it in the Review.'[131] This was not least because he had written about the book before 'the commonplace critics' had had their chance, and they, and the public, were therefore guided by what he had to say. Considering his role in the book's production, it was the least he could do.

Throughout the composition of the first, destroyed volume Mill had warned Carlyle that his style would be too radical for some tastes; and it was this that he found himself defending in his review. An unsigned critique by Lady Sydney Morgan in the *Athenaeum* of 20 May 1837 screeched at Carlyle for his barbarities, 'neologism' and 'whimsical coxcombry'. The work was, in her view, 'three volumes of misplaced persiflage and flippant pseudo-philosophy'; it has stood the test of time, though, somewhat better than Lady Sydney. Thackeray, writing three months after the book appeared, was kinder. He noted that Carlyle's detractors had denounced him as a madman, but his supporters had acclaimed him as a genius. He tended to the latter view, though again took up the stylistic point. 'Never did ... a man's style so mar his subject and dim his genius. It is stiff, short, and rugged, it abounds with Germanisms and Latinisms, strange epithets, and choking double words,' he wrote, accurately.[132] Yet Thackeray added that the reader soon became used to the strangeness. He proved in his review that he had seen and understood Carlyle's message about the nature of liberty, and the warning it held for radicals in England. What will have pleased Carlyle most, though, was Thackeray's starkest recommendation: 'It has no CANT.'

Mill's review was, as he recognised, the most lavishly praising of all. 'This is not so much a history,' he began, 'as an epic poem; and notwithstanding, or even in consequence of this, the truest of histories ... no work of greater genius, either historical or poetical, has been produced in this country for many years.' The style, of which he had been so worried, he pronounced 'not only good, but surpassing excellence'.[133] Vindicating Carlyle's methods, Mill said that the reader could imagine himself among human beings in the story.

Carlyle left the reviewers to it, and departed for Scotland.

8

The Condition of England

1837–40

RECALLING HIS SUMMER EXCURSION, once back at Chelsea in the autumn, Carlyle commented that he had gone to Scotland where 'I lay like one buried alive till the middle of September, when I returned hither, in a kind of dead-alive state.'[1] He had been weakened by the effort of the last three years. Thirty years later, he could still remember being met by Alick off the steamer and being in a 'a wild excitation of nerves' that was 'something strange'.[2] It was the release from stress that made him feel so strange. They walked together through Annandale, and paused at a stone on the road he had walked from Ecclefechan to Annan Academy over thirty years before. 'Words cannot utter the wild and ghastly expressiveness of that scene to me,' he wrote. 'It seemed as if Hades itself and the gloomy realms of Death and Eternity were looking out on me through those poor old familiar objects; as if no miracle could be more miraculous than this same bit of Space and bit of Time spread out before me. I felt withal how wretchedly unwell I must be.'[3]

He did not improve. He felt 'utter grimness, and fixed contemptuous disbelief in the future'.[4] Having hoped he had escaped from his work, a tactless neighbour sent him Lady Sydney Morgan's offensive review of *The French Revolution*, which he read 'without pain' before, appropriately, lighting a fire with it. He was grateful for what Mill had done, telling him 'no man, I think, need wish to be better reviewed.'[5] But even Thackeray's review, which could not have its kindnesses explained away in terms of the duties of friendship, and which Jane sent him in a spirit of exultation, did little to cheer him. He could not believe anyone would agree with the reviewer. The success of the work had further stimulated interest in *Sartor*. Harriet Martineau had imported what Jane said had been termed 'a *houseful* of copies',[6] and was selling them on. Fraser, Carlyle's publisher, soon realised the commercial advantages of printing some himself. Miss Martineau embarrassed Carlyle by bringing him the profits from these sales and pressing the money into his hand. He overcame his embarrassment by buying both Harriet and Jane signet rings with the proceeds, his wife's marked '*Point de faiblesse*' his friend's '*Frisch zu!*'. When Harriet realised more money from her imports, she gave

Carlyle bottles of his favourite French brandy rather than the cash.[7]

Alick was still thinking about emigrating, though was preparing to open a shop in Annandale. Old Mrs Carlyle, not surprisingly, was against emigration. Carlyle began to miss Jane, who had not come because she was not well enough to stand the journey. He hoped that, with the coming of the railways, this would not happen again, and raved to Jane about the prospect of travelling from Birmingham to Liverpool in four and a half hours on the new line. Meanwhile, she engaged in entertaining, and being entertained by, the group of distinguished Italian refugees whom she had befriended, and sent reports to Carlyle. In August, her mother went back to Scotland, and the Sterlings took her to Malvern.

Carlyle occupied his time walking and swimming, and, when he could not avoid it, seeing old acquaintances. He read *The Pickwick Papers*, which he judged a 'dud', and therefore quite appropriate for his mental state. His mother, heroic in the lengths to which she went to show pride in her son, spent the weeks while he was with her reading *The French Revolution*, struggling with unfamiliar French names, but otherwise, according to Carlyle, reading 'not without considerable understanding of it'.[8] No other member of the family in Scotland made such progress. In August he broke his idleness by travelling to Templand to see his mother-in-law. Once he met other people the conversation inevitably turned to the economic and political problems from which he had escaped. 'Some hundreds of thousands in this country this year, as I learn too indubitably,' he wrote to Jane, 'have not known for ten months past what it is to be satisfied with food. The condition of the lower classes is frightful.'[9]

He planned to return to the realities of London in mid-September, and took his mother with him as far as Manchester, where she visited her married daughter, Jenny. After a tolerable coach journey south he was relieved to be back in Chelsea after 'the longest period of absolute idleness I can remember to have had'.[10] However, he found Jane ill and coughing again, appearing consumptive. He laid down rules for her winter regime to try to stop her deteriorating further, as in the previous year, to semi-permanent invalidity. She was to go out only in the middle of the day, and then driving rather than walking. Otherwise, she stayed in to sew, read and write letters. Her cough soon waned, but she was badly troubled by the insomnia that was to shatter her health for the rest of her life.

Optimistic about himself for the first time ('I shall be able to do better now. I am better known now,' he told his mother)[11] he decided there was no hurry about writing articles, though Mill (whose *Review* Carlyle regarded as a poor payer) was pressing him to review Lockhart's life of Sir Walter Scott. Talking of himself in a letter to his mother, he said that 'the grand improvement I trace is that of being far *calmer* than I was; the immense *fuff* having subsided into composure.'[12] After a couple of months in this new, relaxed, frame of mind he confided to Jack that 'my life is full of sadness, streaked with wild gleamings of a very strange joy.'[13] He said he could trace in himself 'such a devilish disposition on many sides, such abysses of self-conceit, disgust and insatiability, I think many times it were better and safer I were kept always sunk, pinched in the ice of poverty and obscurity, till death quietly received me, and I were at rest.' Carlyle did, however, stir from self-pity sufficiently to write to Miss Wilson advertising his availability to give more lectures the next spring. He was alarmed by the paradox that his great fame still left him with only enough money just to see out the winter. One thought was to lecture on the French Revolution, which would have stimulated sales of his book; but before long he turned instead to a broader subject, a series of lectures on varied literary figures. This, indeed, is what he ended up doing, the series being entitled *On the History of Literature*. He had deduced, cor-rectly, that in terms of money for effort, lecturing was better than writing books; the more so now he was 'considered as a kind of successful man',[14] because of the acclaim given to his book. To his delight William Macready, who had become manager of the Covent Garden theatre, sent him a free ticket for the season, as a mark of his distinction. About once a week Carlyle went to watch Shakespeare, but took care not to attend any farces.

Not until mid-October did Carlyle address himself, after all, to Lockhart. Yet, worried still about money, he sought to negotiate with Mill whether the amount he was likely to earn from reviewing would make the effort worth while, and whether he could have a year's contract to give him some security. He wanted, effectively, to be the star writer on Mill's *Review*, with an article in at least every other number; he hoped for an offer of, say, £200. Otherwise he did not want to return to reviewing, unless the books concerned were of unnatural interest to him, but would rather continue to make his name as a man of letters. 'There is,' he told Jack, 'better stuff in me still than a *French Revolution*, if I have life to bring it out.'[15] Mill had to point out to him that the financial position of his enterprise would not allow him to enter into a definite contract; sensing that an act of friendship on his part towards Mill was required in these difficult times, Carlyle pressed on with Lockhart, starting to write his review in mid-November despite being laid low by dyspepsia.

Once he finished Scott in December, he looked back upon it as 'a long, occasionally rather stupid Article', his feelings about it relieved only by the £50 he earned for writing it. Though he told his mother the article showed his 'sincere love and pity for' Scott,[16] he did admit that he had had to take Scott down a peg or two; and in the piece there are occasional signs that Carlyle had not forgotten, nor perhaps forgiven, the snub Scott had dealt him in 1828, when Carlyle had sought to present him with a medal of Goethe.[17] Carlyle does not mince words about Scott ('to write with never such rapidity in a passable manner, is indicative not of a man's genius, but of his habits'),[18] and gives vent to the view, which Froude would later call in his defence, that Lockhart did not err in being indiscreet about his father-in-law either. 'How delicate, decent is English Biography,' sneers the reviewer, 'bless its mealy mouth! A Damocles' sword of *Respectability* hangs forever over the poor English Life-writer (as it does over poor English Life in general) and reduces him to the verge of paralysis.'[19]

He soon had reason to feel happier. Convinced at last about his client's abilities, thanks to the success of *The French Revolution*, Fraser offered to bring out not merely the first British edition of *Sartor*, but also a collection of Carlyle's articles. Grudging about this too – for he had not forgotten the unwillingness of Fraser to publish *Sartor* when its author was less famous – Carlyle determined that his publisher would only have this honour if the right amount of money were forthcoming. He suggested to Fraser that the lot would fill five volumes, and that he should receive an advance of £50 a volume. He expected Fraser to bridle at this, as indeed he did. Carlyle responded that he could not take a penny less, and left Fraser to think about it.

Another result of Carlyle's new fame was that he was invited more into society, though he claimed only to go when there was no easy way of declining an invitation; but his burgeoning self-confidence, which put no restraints on his expressions of opinion, did not always endear him to those whom he met. At John Crawfurd's house at the end of November 1837 Carlyle gravely upset Henry Crabb Robinson, who had been foreign editor of *The Times* and had known both Schiller and Goethe. Carlyle's fault was to express his 'avowed approbation of the annexation of Texas and of the holding the negroes in slavery. It is a natural aristocracy, that of colour, and quite right that the stronger and better race should have dominion!'[20] So offended was Robinson by these views (which were to do much damage, even in those unenlightened times, to Carlyle's reputation) that he recorded: 'I found Carlyle so very outrageous in his opinions that I have no wish to see him again, and I avoided saying anything that looked like a desire to renew my acquaintance with him.' Carlyle's apparently crude racialism was simply the extension of his views, already clear from his lectures of the previous spring, about the domination of the Germanic tribes, and his inherent belief in those with abilities to govern to do just that, by absolute means if necessary.

II

In the peace of the Christmas season, he turned his attentions to the need to prepare the lectures he hoped to give the next spring. By January 1838 he had still not finally resolved what the subject was to be, though continued to read widely (notably Dante) in the hope of inspiration. He had no urge to write, though was feeling more and more attracted by the idea, suggested by Mill, of dilating on the condition of the working classes. Carlyle was dismayed by the failure of radicalism, the reformed parliament having done nothing to alleviate the poverty endemic in a country where the population was rising by 1,200 a day. However, he became diverted by the need to compose his lectures and by domestic difficulties. The winter cold became severe and, although he made a two-day excursion to Windsor in early February with Francis Edgworth, a friend of Sterling's, he hardly ventured out. He said the streets were so slippery that one could not walk quickly, and without walking quickly one became intensely cold. Everything in the house that could freeze froze, except in the rooms that were heated. In the morning Carlyle's towel was stiff on his wash-stand, his bedside water-jug frozen over too. He and Jane sat indoors swathed in cloaks and shawls.

Thomas Spring Rice, the Chancellor of the Exchequer, curious to meet Carlyle following a recommendation from one of his daughters who had been at the lectures in 1837, tempted Carlyle to dine with him. Not usually well disposed to politicians, Carlyle found the Chancellor 'goodhumoured',[21] and above all his house was warm; he stayed out until one in the morning, after which he had a headache for the whole of the next day; but Jane believed in moving in such circles would help drum up new subscribers for his lectures, so it was not in vain. He was not easily seduced, though, by society: 'soirées in general are a nullity and mockery to me.'[22]

Such visitors as the Carlyles had that winter came in the afternoons, the evenings being too cold to venture out in. Harriet Martineau came often, usually with gifts, such as supplies of brandy to keep out the cold. She was greatly drawn to Carlyle, though not to Jane; however, Carlyle confided in his journal, with his customary grace, that he found her a bore with little intelligent to say, especially on the subject of religion. The winter's grip did not slacken. In his journal of 14 February he described how the frost, having lasted then for five weeks, had turned the Thames into 'an Arctic river; all full of tumbling ice-masses' which men could cross on foot.[23] He worried about the effect the cold was having on the poor, and on his elderly mother, to whom he wrote extolling the virtues of hot-water bottles. One victim of the cold was James Fraser, who became so sick that his life was thought to be in danger; the negotiations about publishing more of Carlyle's works had therefore to be suspended. Emerson, however, acting as Carlyle's agent in America, published an edition of *The French Revolution*, and prepared to publish the review articles as a compilation.

On 16 February Carlyle at last started to draw up the plan of his lectures on the history of literature. He decided against holding them in Willis's rooms again, and Erasmus Darwin found him a hall in Portman Square, Marylebone, which could be hired for twenty guineas for the whole programme; Carlyle was charging his subscribers two guineas each for the course. There were to be twelve lectures, starting on 30 April and happening twice weekly, tracing literature from the Greeks onward. 'It means,' Carlyle told Jack, 'the most remarkable Books, Persons, Opinions of our Western world, from the time of Homer downwards, so far as a poor ignorant man can endeavour to get up some sincere utterances about them in Twelve most limited discourses.'[24]

Just as the weather relented Jane, who had kept in remarkable health throughout the winter, fell ill in the same way she had the previous year: a lingering cold that degenerated into flu, with consumptive symptoms. Carlyle thought seriously about taking her to Italy, to see Jack and for some badly needed warm sunshine. However, the demands of his lectures, and other financial considerations, made it impossible, even if Jane's strength had been equal to it. So, just as London started to go out of doors again, the Carlyles stayed in, she ill, he writing his lectures. Mill, once more, was a great source of books from which to cobble together facts; though Carlyle found the process tedious and difficult, as he was so lacking in inspiration. 'It is a sad business,' he told Mill, asking whether he could bear to distribute some prospectuses for the course, as he had the previous year.[25]

As the lectures neared Jane's health temporarily picked up, and the virtual house-arrest of the winter ended. They saw the Jeffreys, who were in London, and Carlyle went to a dinner where he met Gladstone (then a young Tory MP of twenty-nine), whom he liked, and Henry Hallam, the historian best remembered for his *Constitutional History* and for fathering Tennyson's friend whose death provoked *In Memoriam*. Carlyle stuck to his anti-social tenets, claiming to go out only 'once in ten days', and that 'far too much'. Once, venturing out, he saw the 'poor little Queen', who had yet to be crowned, being driven along in her carriage, looking 'timid, anxious, almost frightened'. 'I felt heartily sorry for the poor bairn,' he told his mother.[26]

Just before the lectures were due to begin on 30 April, Jane's flu finally arrived. It left quickly, and she was able to accompany Carlyle to his first outing, a lecture entitled 'Of Literature in General', which concentrated mainly upon the Greeks. Carlyle was seized by nerves, and told his sister Jean that his performance 'was not so bad as last year; nor perhaps so good'.[27] He complained that his mind felt 'half lame'. The audience was amenable, but slightly smaller than he had hoped for, which he blamed upon Messrs Wilson and Erasmus Darwin, 'two idle friends of mine' to whom he had entrusted publicity. He revised downwards the estimate of the money he would make from £300 to £200, and re-entered negotiations with Fraser.

The only series of his lectures that Carlyle prepared for publication were those *On Heroes, Hero-Worship and the Heroic in History*, given in the spring of 1840. However, a barrister called Thomas Anstey, who later became the MP for Youghal in Ireland, attended all except the ninth lecture and took a full shorthand note. After his death, and Carlyle's, the lectures were published in 1892.[28] The record is exceptionally valuable for what it tells us of Carlyle's intellectual development in these first months of his new, fame-flushed confidence. We see the consolidation of his beliefs in leadership and might. In his discussion of Rome in his first lecture, Carlyle took the unfashionable course of seeing the benefits of the downfall of the republic, saying that

Caesar, as 'the wisest, cleanest and most judicious man', deserved to take over.[29] He also pointed out that during successful ages for a nation there was not much literature, since energies were being diverted to the more important matter of conquest and expansion. 'It is not,' he said, 'till a nation is ready to decline that its literature makes itself remarkable.'[30] For this reason he expressed in the lectures his belief that English literature was at its weakest in the eighteenth century, just as England was leading the industrial revolution and beginning its period of overseas conquest. Swift he excepted from the general opprobrium, because he had had a 'genuine Saxon mind' and had, rather like Carlyle, arranged 'a little religion to himself';[31] and, of course, Dr Johnson. Gibbon, who might have hoped for praise, was condemned as having given the most futile account imaginable of the collapse of Rome, diseased as Carlyle felt he had been with scepticism. The intellectual scope of the lectures was breathtaking, not just in the range of literature that they covered, but also in the philosophical and theological views Carlyle included. Literature could act as a mirror for his theories about the decline of faith, and with it the decline of the social order. Atheism and utilitarianism were attacked as well as scepticism, which he considered a French invention finally wrecked by the revolution it caused, and buried by the spiritually supercharged writings of the Germans, especially Goethe and Schiller.

Carlyle makes clear the sentiments that would inform *Past and Present* five years later. He discounted the idea that the Middle Ages had been a time of darkness, arguing instead that it was 'universally apparent' that the age of feudalism was 'a great and fertile period'.[32] Not least was this due to the predominance of belief, the principles of which underpinned the system of duties and responsibilities that operated, for example, in the orbit of the Abbot of St Edmundsbury, as outlined in *Past and Present*; the Middle Ages had witnessed 'the great phenomenon of belief gaining the victory over unbelief'.[33] Carlyle gave an idiosyncratic view of Christianity in this context, suggesting that the Middle Ages understood the creed more clearly than any other: 'We may regard it as the revelation of eternity existing in the middle of time to man. He stands here between the conflux of two elements, the Past and the Future; the thing that we are at this moment speaking or doing comes to us from the beginning of days.'[34] This, again, is the continuum theory of history, already seen in *Sartor* and *The French Revolution*, and to be seen in *Past and Present*. Familiar, too, are his views on social loyalty, the 'attachment of man to man . . . as old as the existence of man himself'.[35] Loyalty is vital to this interpretation of Christianity, the love of men for each other; in the Middle Ages under feudalism, he adds, loyalty was 'the foundation of the state'.[36]

Carlyle defined the year 1070, in the time of Pope Hildebrand, as the time of the highest perfection of Christianity, when Europe was 'unshaken in faith' and full of teachers and preachers, absolutely sure in their own faith, converting the heathen.[37] The decline of the Church, he continued, came when material considerations overcame spiritual ones; a very Burgher Seceder point. And it was, he added, with this decline that great literature was once more created, not least by great men protesting at the decay around them; and Dante, 'a serious man, always meditating on some religious or moral subject'[38] in a Florence where the battles of faction supplanted considerations of faith, was foremost among them. Carlyle's views on the heroic qualities of Dante and the *Divine Comedy* were specifically developed in the lectures on *Heroes* two years later.

He also looked at Spain, and at Cervantes as a Spanish Dante; he lectured on French literature too, and though this was not recorded by Anstey we know Carlyle discussed the philosophical decline that preceded the revolution. Once more, inevitably, Germany formed a central part of the lectures. Contrary to 'might is right', he talks warmly of the German love of justice and says:

Strength, one may say, is justice itself. The strong man is he that can be just; that sets everything in its own rightful place, one above the other. It is the only way to do anything great and strong; and it is always the boast, and a legitimate one, of this people that they are a just people, framing all their institutions for ends of justice.[39]

He discussed Luther, another subject to be dealt with more satisfactorily in *Heroes*. He dealt with Erasmus under the heading of great Germans: for although a Dutchman 'the Dutch are in fact the same as the Germans.'[40] The English, as he had said in his earlier lectures, were German too, peopled as England had been in the Dark Ages by Saxons.

The lectures went partly into the question of how literature had shown evidence of the great or heroic mind. For all his reverence of the Germans, Carlyle saw that no greater literary mind had been demonstrated than Shakespeare's (Milton coming a long way second). He gave special praise to him for having 'arrived at more of the meaning of history than many books written on history could have done'.[41] Presaging what he would say about Cromwell, he noted of Shakespeare that 'the greatest man is always a quiet man by nature, we are sure not to find greatness in a prurient noisy man.'[42] In his tenth lecture he expanded on this:

'Speech is silvern, silence is golden!' After speech has done its best, silence has to include all that speech has forgotten or cannot express. Speech is of time, of today; eternity is silent. All great things are silent. Whenever they get to be debated on by logic, they are as good as lost.[43]

For someone who believed in a strong natural order as much as Carlyle did, the loathing of logic, which might attempt to question the natural basis that was rooted in faith, is quite understandable, though not perhaps intellectually defensible. Geraldine Jewsbury, writing to him in July 1840, sought to have him define his doctrine of silence, which she justifiably thought was 'vague'. He was hard put to explain it; it would become clearer in *Oliver*, where a reflective man of action is clearly shown as preferable to an inactive man of words. In his great anti-democratic tracts it is the talking-shop of parliament, rather than the popular choice of those who constitute it, to which he most seems to object, and on the grounds that the natural governor will decide for himself how to proceed without debate with others. It was somewhat odd for Carlyle, who loved the sound of his own voice, to take this view, though he did not see the contradiction. He simply told Geraldine: 'Really, I have in my hopelessness no other *word*: I do mean by it a great world of things; which are unknown unheeded by this generation; – which you probably do not know, and, I can assure you, ought to know! ... But I mean to indicate withal, when our words are all over, the secret of the things is not yet over; nay properly the secret may be said to be beginning just then.'[44]

III

Carlyle felt the course was going well, though he worked himself into a nervous state before each lecture, doing little good to his constitution. Sometimes he would wake at four in the morning with anxiety; he had to seek medical help to calm him down so he could sleep. There was little, in fact, for him to worry about. Thackeray had two favourable notices published in *The Times*, and Leigh Hunt reviewed all but the fourth lecture for the *Examiner*. Hunt's notices began well, though Carlyle thought he noticed bitterness creeping into the tone after a few weeks, bred, he suspected, of jealousy. He wrote to his mother that 'he, finding me this year a man whom he cannot pat on the back, and say "well done" to, is grieved in mind to see it so.'[45] Thackeray had said at the start that 'Mr Carlyle's first lecture on the history of literature appears to us both in its defects and its merits a very remarkable exhibition of a description of mind not common in our age and country, and which a period of busy and luminous refinement is not perhaps the most likely to produce.'[46] Struck by Carlyle's physical presence, Thackeray described the discourse as 'rough, broken, wavering and sometimes almost weak and abortive: but full throughout of earnest purpose, abundant knowledge, and a half-suppressed struggling fire of zeal and conviction.' Thackeray found Carlyle 'urged by an insatiable thirst for truth' that would be familiar to those who had read the lecturer's 'soul-fraught writings'. The audience grew as the weeks passed, though Carlyle still believed the Portman Square location and the publicity had conspired against bringing in even larger crowds. After his seventh lecture, in late May, he wrote to his mother that 'on the whole it goes beyond expectation, and is what they call "very successful".'[47] By that stage the audience had, by his estimate, doubled since the first lecture, and *The Times*, in another notice by Thackeray, announced that new subscribers could follow the second half of the course for half price. Thackeray's view by this time was that 'there has been a marked improvement in the ease and consequent force of the lecturer's manner and expressions, and as his subject has widened and gained vigour and vitality, he has appeared to exercise over it a freer and more serene command.'[48]

Although for the period of his lectures Carlyle declined all invitations and absorbed himself mainly in his work and his hypochondria, he did find room for one other interest. For years one of his great expenses had been the receipt of letters, paid for then by the recipient, which had deterred him from communicating with his impoverished family as often as he would have liked. When parliament was sitting his political friends, such as Jeffrey and Buller, could supply him with franks to defray the postage; indeed, many of his remarks about Jeffrey suggest that the Advocate's greatest value to Carlyle was the supply of free postage. Carlyle needed little persuasion to become involved in a campaign for the introduction of a penny post, as had been suggested by Rowland Hill. He drafted a petition to send to parliament from 'fifty men of letters' in support of the plan. It was one of Carlyle's more successful campaigns, the post being introduced only two years almost to the day from his taking up the fight.

He gave his last lecture on 11 June, having made about £260 from them. He was greatly relieved, though faced as always with the problem of what to do next. He confided in his journal on 31 May: 'For me, the cry of my soul is, For the love of God, let me alone!'[49] He was depressed that Jane's health was so poor, depressed that he could get no mental ease. His fame brought him new friends – or at least, new people who wanted to know him – and his main new admirer was John Marshall, a septuagenarian flax millionaire from the West Riding of Yorkshire, who became so devoted to Carlyle that he bought him a horse. He and Jane dined with Marshall and his family in London at the end of May, despite Carlyle's professed anti-social feelings, and in early June Carlyle went again and dined with Spring Rice. Later that month he was sent a ticket for Queen Victoria's coronation, but gave it away, watching the procession instead from a window in the house of his friend Basil Montagu. In the words of one there with him, Carlyle 'thinks kings and queens rather superfluous'.[50]

The problem of finding a generous publisher was solved that summer. A firm called Saunders and Otley offered to print both his collected articles and *Sartor* on terms no better than Fraser's, but which Carlyle accepted because he was so fed up with Fraser's attitude. They started at once to print *Sartor*, including the hostile opinion of Murray's reader in 1831. Gavan Duffy claimed the reader had been Lockhart. However, this was repudiated by Espinasse; it was in fact a friend of Murray's called Henry Hart Milman,[51] who asked balefully 'is the work a translation?', having said that the author reminded him 'of the German Baron who took to leaping on tables, and answered that he was learning to be lively'.[52] There was the critic of *The Sun*, dazzled by phrases like 'baphometic fire-baptism'; a 'North American Reviewer' claiming, humourlessly, that Teufelsdröckh clearly did not exist; but, to round it all off, there was Emerson's anonymous preface, which described the book as 'a Criticism on the Spirit of our Age' and claimed that 'the philanthropy and the purity of moral sentiment, which inspire the work, will find their way to the heart of every lover of virtue.'[53]

It was, though, Fraser who published the first edition of the *Critical and Miscellaneous Essays* the following year, since he came back to Carlyle with improved terms. There was the promise of money to come from Emerson for the American sales, and Carlyle told Jack he had '£300 to front the year with ... a great blessing for a man that has been hunted by the squalid spectre of Beggary these long periods of time, and seldom for many months could see how by uttermost exertion and uttermost thrift, bread and water were to be made sure to him!'[54]

Carlyle thought about a holiday; either going north to his family, or waiting and taking Jane to Rome for the winter to stay with Jack, and, he hoped, improve her health. But Templand and Scotsbrig were both full with other visitors, and Jack was threatening a return home in September. For the moment, he contented himself with shorter excursions, though not always with the best results. With his friend Frederick Elliott, the Agent-General for Emigration, he travelled to Gravesend at the end of June to see a ship of people leaving for New South Wales. Carlyle was late to catch the steamer for Gravesend and stumbled off a kerb, falling flat towards the pavement. He thrust out his arms to break his fall and sprained both his wrists; for a couple of weeks he could hardly write. He had a period of sustained sleeplessness, in which he would sit in the back garden in his nightshirt, smoking.

He sat during July for Samuel Laurence, the painter, and saw his friends when he could command the energy. John Sterling tried to persuade him to come away for the summer. However, in mid-August he could stand London no longer, and, since Jack showed no immediate sign of coming back to London, went to Leith by steamer and thence to Kirkcaldy. He had been invited to stay with the family of Elizabeth Fergus, who had stayed with the Carlyles at the time of the coronation in June. She, her brother and sister were children of the late Provost of Kirkcaldy, whom Carlyle had known when he taught there. He was feted and looked after lavishly, even though, with typical ingratitude, he found much in their 'solemn ironspring gig-manity'[55] to complain about when he wrote to Jane.

On 4 September he made for Edinburgh, where he renewed his friendship with Jeffrey; he felt each went to such lengths to be polite to the other that no proper conversation was possible. Thence he went south to the manse at Minto, near Hawick, where he stayed a few days with Sam Aitken, a partner in Bradfute's bookshop in Edinburgh, and his wife. He found the people dull and the weather awful, so left as quickly as he decently could for Scotsbrig. However, his mother had gone to see his sister in Manchester, and did not return for several days. He stayed at her house until early October, by which time Jack had joined them. Carlyle by then was longing to find something to work on. He felt he could give another course of lectures the following spring, but that required an idea. Emerson had started to send reasonably healthy cheques – for £50 in August 1838 – in lieu of Carlyle's American royalties, so some financial pressure was off, and both *Sartor* and the *Miscellanies* promised some sort of income from England. When he went back to London he had nothing to prove, but a reputation to sustain.

IV

He went south by steamer to Liverpool, and thence by train. The trip 'was one of the strangest in character that I ever made', he told Alick.[56] The railway was 'so new, so enchanted-looking', with no houses yet near it. Carlyle marvelled at travelling at thirty miles an hour, though his rapture ended when the engine broke down, stranding him and his fellow passengers in a deep cutting. He found Jane better, and there was a project waiting for him. Robertson, the editor of the *London and Westminster Review*, asked him to review various volumes of the memoirs of Varnhagen von Ense, a prominent German writer of the generation after Goethe.

The intellectual refreshment Carlyle gained from his travels within Britain extended beyond a readiness to take up his pen. Edward Strachey recalled that, when Carlyle and Jane dined with him on 11 October, Carlyle had talked extensively of the deteriorating conditions in the industrial north – he had visited family in Liverpool and Manchester on his way south – and their threatened political consequences. Strachey recorded that Carlyle had heard 'a loom at work till twelve o'clock at night and . . . before seven in the morning . . . he was told there was a weaver next door – a man with a wife and six children – earning six shillings a week by his seventeen hours of daily work.'[57] Carlyle felt these were desperate men who, sooner or later, would launch insurrection, as their fellow sufferers had in France half a century earlier, since the aristocracy took no notice of their misery.

His piece on von Ense was published in the December number of the *Review*; but Carlyle's overwhelming concern was now no longer Germany, but 'the Condition of England question', as he would term it. His next project – the lectures for the following spring – would not deal with the subject, but it was one he could not avoid for much longer. The harvest was bad, a victim of it his own brother, Alick. Carlyle realised the Corn Laws would have to be repealed, but resigned himself to watching yet another winter of suffering. The Anti-Corn Law League had been founded that September, led by the prominent radicals Richard Cobden and John Bright, both of whom were to enjoy distinguished careers as Liberal MPs. Its programme of demonstrations and petitions helped concentrate Carlyle's attention on the problem for most of the next year, until he wrote *Chartism*. The Anti-Corn Law movement was mainly middle class, and as such Carlyle fitted into it well. He also believed, though, that giving the poor cheaper bread would distract them from desire for further reform. A sentiment of Cobden's, in a speech of January 1845, showed precisely how close he and Carlyle were on the question of the abrogation of responsibility by the so-called governing class: 'The sooner the power in this country is transferred from the landed oligarchy, which has so misused it, and is placed absolutely – mind I say absolutely – in the hands of the intelligent middle and industrious classes, the better for the condition and destinies of this country.'[58] By 1845 Carlyle himself was calling for 'Captains of Industry' to step in and provide help, in the form of work, for the poor where the aristocracy had failed.

As he looked for inspiration for his 1839 lectures, he sought permission to read in the British Museum Library, frustrated that there should be so great a collection of invaluable books nearby to which neither he nor most other scholars had access. He had been talking with friends about the project that was to become the London Library, a subscription lending library open to all, and had sought the right to borrow books from the University Library at Cambridge through a barrister friend, Douglas Heath, a fellow of Trinity. Before long a trunkful of books arrived on loan.

Carlyle soon found a subject that was to interest him to the point of obsession, and take far longer, as a project, to execute than he imagined: Oliver Cromwell. Over Christmas 1838 and in early 1839 he devoted almost all his reading to books on the English Civil War and, in particular, to books about Cromwell. John Forster, who was to become a close friend, had just published the first volume of a biography of Cromwell, which Carlyle planned to write about for the *Westminster Review*. This project came to nothing, largely because Carlyle and Robertson, the editor, seemed unable to communicate. Instead, Carlyle began to consider writing his own life of Cromwell. John Morley, many years later, claimed this life-absorbing interest of Carlyle's was awakened by Mill.[59]

For so long Carlyle had lost the will to write, but his growing interest in Cromwell brought back some of his former creative feelings. 'I am getting into heart again,' he told his mother in January 1839, 'and not so utterly bewildered and beaten down as I was on the conclusion of my "Revolution" struggle.'[60] Although he was determined to learn more about English history, his Cromwellian studies drew him back to Scottish themes, notably Montrose and the Covenanters. In his reading of history, as in his writing of it, great men attracted him. He drafted notes on Montrose during February, but the project came to nothing. While he had little to do (another £100 in royalties from *The French Revolution* arriving from America helped sustain this idleness) he and Jane went out more into society, either with new friends attracted by Carlyle's fame, or with old ones such as Charles Buller. He used his widening connections to recruit support for the London Library; through this he and John Forster became friends, Forster using the pages of the *Examiner* to gather wider endorsement for the idea. Together with some work on drafting a petition for a new Copyright Bill, Carlyle was to have more than his share of successful campaigning.

As the worry of what he would lecture about grew greater, so Carlyle's dyspepsia and insomnia returned. Jane bore up well until February, and then went down with a heavy cold, just as her mother arrived for a long visit; she too went down with a cold for three weeks. Aggravating matters, Fraser admitted that all but seventy-five copies of the English edition of *The French Revolution* had been sold, bringing in £1,000, but because of the contractual small print that Carlyle had paid too little attention to, none of this money appeared to belong to him. 'The sharks!' was how he felt forced to describe Fraser to his sister Jean as a result.[61] Yet Carlyle was not facing penury. He thought of using his American earnings partly to buy a horse, to get him out for some exercise when the stressful time of lecturing came. He was angry that Fraser seemed to take, for a start, forty per cent of the cover price of the book purely for selling it, and made a better bargain for the second edition.

Despite her uncertain health, Jane decided to give her first – and only – soirée towards the end of February, asking (as Carlyle put it) 'between 20 and 30 entirely brilliant bits of figures; and really it all went off in the most successful manner: at midnight I smoked a peaceable pipe, praying that it might be long before we saw the like again.'[62] What Carlyle did not know was that the preparations for the event had caused a rift between Jane and her mother. With the best of intentions, Mrs Welsh had bought sweets, cakes and fine candles to adorn the proceedings. Jane, seeing her mother put out these things, became angry. As Geraldine Jewsbury recalled, 'she said people would say she was extravagant, and would ruin her husband.'[63] Jane removed some of the cakes and two of the candles, much to her mother's hurt, and Mrs Welsh started to cry. Jane, realising she had reacted improperly to this well-intentioned gesture of her mother's, tried to make amends.

Before Mrs Welsh returned to Scotland at the end of March the breach was healed; but Jane's guilt was profound. The two candles were put away safely, and Jane, during her prolonged final illness, asked for them to be brought out by a friend and lighted after her death; which they were. Carlyle, on hearing of this event after Jane's death, reflected: 'What a strange, beautiful, sublime and almost terrible little action; silently resolved on, and kept silent from all the Earth, for perhaps twenty-four years! I never heard a whisper of it, and yet see it to be true.'[64] In the thirteenth year of their marriage, the Carlyles were already sufficiently estranged from each other for Jane to have made her own secret world into which she could not admit her husband. He had pursued his writing with a single-mindedness that excluded Jane, causing her great loneliness and a feeling of neglect, fuelled by her instinctively neurotic personality. It would become worse.

Carlyle now made an acquaintance that was, in the years ahead, to put the most severe strain of all on his marriage. On 25 February he attended a dinner that he told his mother was 'one of the most elevated things I have ever seen; Lords, Ladyships and other the like high personnages [sic] ...'[65] He added that 'the Lady of the House, one Lady Harriet Baring, I had to sit and talk with specially for a long long while; one of the cleverest creatures I have met with, full of mirth and spirit – not very beautiful to look upon.' Lady Harriet's husband was William Baring, a member of the banking family, and heir to the Ashburton barony created for his father in 1835; she, the daughter of the 6th Earl of Sandwich, was ten years younger than Carlyle, though the portraits of her show her to have a matronly bearing from an early age. She ran a salon at the Barings' London home, Bath House in Piccadilly, into which the Carlyles were drawn during the 1840s. Carlyle, ironically, told his mother that the effort of going to the dinner brought him 'only a small proportion of good rather expensively purchased'.

Although he had still not settled on a subject for his lectures, he had decided to give a programme of six, twice weekly, starting on 23 April (though the start was in fact put back to 1 May). He turned down an offer to translate the *Life of Napoleon* by the Frenchman Paul Mathieu Laurent, but persisted with reading about Cromwell and the Commonwealth period, even though he knew he would never to able to gain sufficient grasp of the subject in time to lecture upon it alone that spring. He was distracted by reports of civil unrest in the north; the winter remained severely cold well into March. 'The whole country seems to be in great dearth, poverty and distress,' he wrote to Jack, who was in Naples as travelling physician to the Duke of Buccleuch.[66] He retailed rumours of disaffected artisans and starving farmers arming with pikes and muskets, preparing to revolt. That winter meetings of Chartists had been held throughout the country, drumming up support for the People's Charter, launched in May 1838 to call for democratic rights for all. Some Chartists were militant, regarding the Anti-Corn Law League as hopeless in its moderation. Carlyle's fears were not entirely groundless.

With barely six weeks to go, and forced by the need to bring out a prospectus, he decided to lecture on 'modern revolutions'. The first lecture would be on Europe to the sixteenth century; the second on Protestantism; the third and fourth on the English Commonwealth period, and the last two on the French Revolution. His book on that subject, about to go to a second edition, suddenly brought him a cheque for £110 from Fraser; and it brought him too a visit from Count D'Orsay, whom he described to his mother as 'the Emperor of the Dandies'.[67] D'Orsay came specifically to pay homage to Carlyle, and Carlyle also told his mother that 'Jane laughed for two days after at the contrast of me in my plaid dressing-gown, with my grim Presbyterian look, and this beautifullest of tall men, with his velvets, jewels and ambrosial loveliness.'

As he prepared his lectures he sent the Commons a formal petition to have the Copyright Bill enacted, citing the unacceptable pirating of the works of authors by literary entrepreneurs. His petition contains a succinct expression of his belief in the importance of reward for labour, and of the state's role in ensuring this contract is kept: 'the giving and assuring to each man what recompense his labour has actually merited may be said to be the business of all Legislation, Polity, Government and Social Arrangement whatsoever among men.'[68] Carlyle himself, through his labours, was 'no longer driven by poverty, nay I am richer than I have been for ten years'.[69] It made him more relaxed about his lecturing, and caused him to tell Emerson that he was at the end of the second chapter in his autobiography: 'we shall see what the *third* is, third there be.'[70] With a dose of familiar self-pity, he elaborated these sentiments to his Jack: 'My life passes in considerable pain, yet I do believe I am getting irresistibly into better health; my temper is far quieter, my view clearer, tho' as yet a view into mere vacancy and silence ... I thank God I am no longer hurried on by a panting necessity to speak; I prefer entire silence to any kind of speech offered me at present, and by Heaven's great blessing can indulge in silence.'

As the Chartists continued to riot in the industrial areas, Carlyle's necessity to speak in print would return soon enough.

V

The lectures, 'extempore effusions'[71] on European revolutions, started on 1 May, and continued twice weekly, on Wednesdays and Saturdays, for three weeks. No record of them survives. He once more attracted a large audience – bigger than in 1838 – of 'the quality', who received him rapturously. The publicity surrounding the lectures was much less than previously; Carlyle had built a following on reputation alone, rather than on puffery. On 10 May 1839 *The Times* said Carlyle had begun by warning that change, however undesirable, was inevitable. As well as touching on the French Revolution, he looked forward to work he was yet to do, mentioning Luther, Dante and Dr Johnson, all subjects of the following year's lectures on heroes. He used Dante as proof of the speciousness of Catholicism, saying that, in the words of the *Times*'s correspondent, 'he had placed his purgatories in the Antipodes; but since then men had sailed round the world, and had seen the Antipodes, and that there was no purgatory there; hinting thus that the reign of Catholicism was over and the fabric of Papacy a ruin.'[72]

Despite the success of his lectures, Jane was keen for him to stop this way of earning his living. 'No gain or éclat that it can yield is compensation enough for the martyrdom it is to himself, and thro' him to me,' she told her mother just before the last of the six lectures. 'In defect of the usual measure of agitation *beforehand*, he has taken to the new and curious crotchet of being ready to hang himself *after*, in the idea that he has made "a horrible *pluister* [mess] of it".'[73] However, far from abandoning lecturing, Carlyle was talking (at Emerson's suggestion) of undertaking a lecture tour to America, where his books were selling lucratively, a four-volume edition of *Miscellanies* the latest among them. To purge the feelings of failure he felt compelled to have after each lecture, he would hire a horse (until Marshall of Leeds bought him one) and ride for miles, wearing himself out; it was a routine that was to become pathological during the composition of *Frederick*. Whatever his feelings about the lectures, their financial success was tangible: they made £200 profit. Carlyle could have taken life easy, but chose instead to start writing immediately the series was over.

He was beginning to turn his mind to what, at the end of the year, would end up as the long essay *Chartism*. He wrote to Lockhart, editor of the *Quarterly Review*, on 20 May proposing a piece on '*the condition of the lower classes* in this country'. He had suggested such a piece to Mill the previous year, though Mill had refused to entertain the idea on the grounds that Carlyle, quite rightly, would not conclude in the work that the condition of the lower classes was improving. Carlyle promised Lockhart that 'my notions on this subject differ intensely from those of the speculating radicals, intensely from those of the Whigs: it seems to me the better class of the Conservatives were on the whole the persons to whom it were hopefullest and in many ways fittest to address myself.'[74] He had discerned, therefore, that the *Quarterly* was the most fitting publication for such thoughts. Lockhart saw Carlyle a few days later and gave him a little encouragement, as well as lending him books for research. In the end, however, he decided that Carlyle's piece would not be quite right for him. But Carlyle had found his next project. Unlike most of what he had previously written, his subject matter was still developing around him. Any disappointment felt at Lockhart's lack of interest in Chartism was tempered by his awareness that what he had to say would run probably to the length of a pamphlet – as it did – and therefore be unsuitable for the *Quarterly*.

Whether he received a commission or not, he planned to take Jane to Scotland for the summer, for plenty of exercise on horseback, to make a final decision on whether to go to America, and to write *Chartism*. He was anxious to go as soon as he could, and even turned down invitations to visit Jack in Germany (for the purposes of which Jack had sent him £30 expenses), and to spend a summer with Sterling at Clifton. First, though, he had to find the raw materials for *Chartism*; and he had to write a short piece for Fraser on the sinking of the French ship *Vengeur* during the revolution, about which he had been engaged in correspondence for most of the previous winter. While he waited to leave he enjoyed himself on Marshall's horse, which Marshall had kindly offered to have put out to grass in London while the Carlyles were away. Therefore, Carlyle was not in his usual state of distressed health when he went on holiday, and had a better chance of enjoying himself.

The last week of June was spent packing, and on 2 July the Carlyles went by train to Liverpool, where they broke their journey with Jane's uncle before taking the steamer to Annan. After two days at Scotsbrig they made for Templand, and Jane's mother. Later in July Carlyle went back to Scotsbrig, where happy news arrived that Jack was returning from his continental excursion. Carlyle was happy to be home, but Jane, who felt better in the hotter, drier atmosphere of London and who missed the social life she had cultivated in the preceding five years, could not wait to go back to Chelsea. Jack Carlyle had sent money for Alick to buy a gig for his brother and sister-in-law to use during their stay, so Carlyle was able to take Jane out for drives to alleviate the boredom. Carlyle was deeply touched: 'our chief secular comfort',[75] this new gigman called it, and the contraption could be put to use by the rest of the family at Scotsbrig once he returned to London.

Carlyle read desultorily through some Poor Law reports, and through his translation of *Wilhelm Meister*, which Fraser proposed reprinting. After a month or so of laziness his conscience began to spur him into addressing *Chartism* properly. In a letter to his friend Thomas Spedding, a Cumberland landowner, in early August he gave, by agreeing with a sentiment of Spedding's, a clear insight into how his thinking was developing: 'What you say of Chartism is the very truth: revenge begotten of ignorance and hunger.'[76] Here is the feudal impulse in Carlyle, the desire to rectify the problem not by giving in to the demands of the Chartists, but by reimposing authority and aristocratic obligations. There were even minor Chartist disturbances in Ecclefechan, and throughout that summer greater riots in many towns, not just industrial ones but in agricultural centres too. 'Unless gentry, clergy and all manner of washed articulate-speaking men will learn that their position towards the unwashed is contrary to the Law of God, and change it soon, the Law of Man, one has reason to discern, will change it before long, and that in no soft manner.'[77] These ideas form the substance of the introductory paragraphs of *Chartism*. The spectre of 1789 hung over Carlyle. He suspected Chartism itself would pass, but the problem it represented would not.

He had started to write down his thoughts by early August, though did not find Templand the most congenial working environment. After such a long break from composition he did not find writing easy, and his grasp of his subject made logical thought about it difficult. Although her mother took her away for a week to Ayr, Jane became intensely restless. Carlyle realised he would get no proper work done until back in Chelsea. In early September they went by coach to Carlisle and Preston (where the railway had now reached, bringing London within ten hours' travel) and thence home. He slowly carried on with his work, concentrating for the rest of the month on proofs of the new edition of *Wilhelm Meister* – Fraser reported that the *Miscellanies* were selling extremely well, and he wanted more of Carlyle's work to be available to the public quickly. As Carlyle sought the inspiration to press on with new work, he could draw comfort from an article written by Sterling for Mill's *London and Westminster Review* about his earlier achievements. Mill also sounded him out, on the request of Nichol, the Professor of Astronomy at Glasgow, about whether the chair of moral philosophy there would interest him. Carlyle was unwilling to be a candidate for anything, even if it carried a salary of £700 a year. He told Mill that if he were offered the post specifically, however, he could decide soon enough. No offer materialised.

Though Carlyle claimed to be unaffected by praise or censure, he wrote in his journal on 9 October that Sterling's article was 'magnanimous wonderful eulogistic',[78] and in a letter thanked his friend profusely for what he had written. Carlyle did not, by any means, agree with all Sterling's conclusions about him; he not only told him so then, especially in relation to Sterling's disapproval of Carlyle's belief in the wisdom of silence, but he also picked up the points twelve years later when he wrote his *Life* of Sterling.

Sterling's magisterial account of Carlyle's work is packed with insight, and is still a valuable introduction to Carlyle for anyone concerned specifically with the early works. He claims Carlyle as a visionary with 'a genuine coherent view of life', and sets out thirteen principles that summed up Carlyle's teaching.[79] These included the universe demanding reverence as a condition of insight and understanding of the nature of being; religion being the highest bond between man and the universe; the view that 'at best we are immensely ignorant', but with reverence we could awaken that 'sense of divinity' that men used to call 'prophetic'; that poetry was 'the highest Form of the Godlike in Man's being', with a 'Poetic Light dormant in all things'; that work is what God calls forth man to do; that while all work is worthy, knowledge and strength 'are the reward only of the noblest effort'; that tracing these workings in and of men – writing history – was noble work indeed; that life is earnest, and 'a cutting sorrow, a weary indignation, will not be far from him who duly weighs the world.'

This is a brilliant, and utterly accurate, analysis. In a premonitory note, Sterling added that 'to Mr Carlyle the objects of chief interest are memorable persons – men who have fought strongly the good fight.'[80] He talked too, in a detailed description of most of Carlyle's major writings, of Carlyle's passion for the truth, and his willingness to use a radical style better to convey that truth. Without question both Sterling and Mill were partisans for Carlyle, but none the less such critical attention was a sign that Carlyle was placing himself in the first rank of contemporary writers and thinkers.

Carlyle worked at *Chartism* sporadically, unsure whether it would be article, pamphlet or even book. He thought he would have a better notion of what form it would take if he could decide on who would publish it, and wrote to Mill asking whether his *Review* would, after all, now be interested in such jottings. 'I write it, comparatively speaking, half asleep,' he told his journal on 23 October.[81] He worked in between excursions on horseback, having been reunited with his horse on his return from Scotland. Daily at two an ostler would bring the mare, which Carlyle had named Citoyenne, to his door, and he would spend the afternoon in contemplation while galloping around. Open countryside was just over the river; or he could ride into the parks, or the City. His riding meant he saw fewer friends, and came to enjoy solitude more; a trait taken to an extreme in the years of *Frederick*. Jane, increasingly the victim of Carlyle's melancholy and isolation, did not allow herself to be sidelined by society; and towards the end of 1839 she formed what was to be one of the closest friendships of her life, with Giuseppe Mazzini, the Italian revolutionary, whose political views were the mirror-image of her husband's.

Throughout October and November Carlyle worked at, and eventually completed, *Chartism*, working faster now that he called on, and received calls from, nobody. Lockhart kept the piece for a week before deciding he could not take it. Mill, however, agreed to run it in what he decided would be the last number of his *Review*, calling it 'a glorious piece of work'.[82] However, both Jack Carlyle (who was staying at Cheyne Row) and Jane advised Carlyle he could secure a better platform for his work than that. 'Such an article,' he told Sterling, 'equally astonishing to Girondin Radicals, Donothing Aristocrat Conservatives, and Unbelieving Dilettante Whigs, can hope for no harbour in any review.'[83] He was about to print it at his own expense, but reached an agreement by which Fraser would publish it as a pamphlet. Its production was delayed by the Christmas holiday, but Carlyle had the first copies before the new year. Thus he started the 1840s with the distinctive tone of a political prophet that would, by the decade's end, make him one of the most admired, and criticised, men in England.

VI

The lessons imparted allegorically in *The French Revolution* are given directly in *Chartism*; and would be given more directly still, three years later, in *Past and Present*. *Chartism* is the essence of Carlyle's political thought, the clearest statement of his beliefs, attractively written in a comparatively clear, robust style that avoids the hectoring and the oppressive sarcasm of some later works. His social view was already formed, and developed little (except that it was expressed with increasing anger and intolerance) in the next quarter-century. The essay shows clearly his authoritarianism, often expressed with an apparent callous brutality that would scar his reputation. Carlyle does not really write about Chartism, but about the increasingly Godless and materialistic society that gave rise to it, and how to improve it. Chartism was 'a new name for a thing which has had many names, which will yet have many'.[84]

The work reflects, and appears largely to be motivated by, the spectre of widespread violence and insurrection that Carlyle, like other middle-class observers, feared. Displaying his contempt for the elected, reformed par-liament, he accuses it – justifiably – of not having bothered to find out what had caused all the discontent; not that his own analysis in *Chartism* would leave many much the wiser. Like most of his polemics, it is stronger on destructive than constructive criticism, a safety valve for his own passions rather than the description of a means to solve problems.

As in France in 1789, those problems had been caused by the traditional ruling class neglecting its duty. Instead of providing leadership, the aristocracy were seeking, pathetically, to ameliorate difficulties by running 'Charity-Balls and Soup-Kitchens'.[85] Missing from the reformed parliament (and, though Carlyle does not explicitly say so, missing from the unreformed one too since 1658) was 'a strong man, an original, clear-sighted, great-hearted, patient and valiant man'[86] who could take the problem and solve it by force of will and action. Carlyle does not envisage how such a man would have fitted into or been tolerated by the already fractious country he would have had to rule. The strong man of 1839, had one existed, would not have given in to the Chartists; he would simply have altered their view by governing them properly. The parliament's ignoring them showed they were not being governed at all. The aristocracy's only concern was to pass thirty-nine Acts of Parliament protecting their game; and the Church did not care at all.

Carlyle felt the working man needed not just enough money to live without starving (and in the debate about what constitutes enough he ridicules statisticians, economists, and others who confine their considerations of the problem to the purely material sphere), but also justice rather than injustice. To describe the changed relations of men with men, the removal of spiritual and social obligations and their replacement by economic and financial ones, he coined the phrase 'cash-nexus'. It was implicit in *laissez-faire*, which Carlyle defined as the need to regulate everything by economic necessity rather than by any principles of governance. He mocked the notion that the problem could be seen in economic terms. The real engine of change and improvement, man's soul, was given him by God.

In one respect the pamphlet is a belated, and hopeless, cry against the industrial revolution. Society had been changed irrevocably by the invention of the machinery of mass-production – which threw hundreds of thousands out of work – and by a rising birth rate. In the first census after Carlyle was born – 1801 – 10.5 million people lived in Great Britain. In the census after he wrote *Chartism* – 1841 – the population had almost doubled to 18.5 million. As Carlyle rightly supposed, no amount of democracy would do anything to improve that; all it might do was to repeal the Corn Laws to allow the growing multitudes to buy bread, and to change the nature of the parliament so that it was no longer full of those with an interest in not attending to the plight of the lowest classes.

The relationship between a man and his superiors would be better conducted, as Carlyle saw it, on principles drawn from 'the most perfect Feudal Ages'.[87] 'How,' asks Carlyle of the working man, 'is he related to his employer; by bonds of friendliness and mutual help; or by hostility, opposition, and chains of mutual necessity alone?'[88] He noted the struggles not just of Chartism, but of the poor throughout his adulthood, from the oppressive years of Liverpool and the Six Acts onwards; and he articulated them in his own way:

What is the meaning of the 'five points'[89] if we will understand them? What are all popular commotions and maddest bellowings, from Peterloo to the Place-de-Grève itself? Bellowings, *in*articulate cries as of a dumb creature in rage and pain; to the ear of wisdom they are inarticulate prayers: 'Guide me, Govern me! I am mad and miserable, and cannot guide myself!' Surely of all 'rights of man,' this right of the ignorant man to be guided by the wiser, to be, gently or forcibly, held in the true course by him, is the indisputablest. Nature ordains it from the first; society struggles towards perfection by enforcing and accomplishing it more and more. If Freedom have any meaning, it means enjoyment of this right, wherein all other rights are enjoyed. It is a sacred right and duty, on both sides; and the summary of all social duties whatsoever between the two.[90]

This passage is not only the intellectual heart of *Chartism*, it is also the intellectual heart of Carlyle's social philosophy right up to *Shooting Niagara*, where it is seen in its most extreme form. In *Heroes, Past and Present, Oliver Cromwell* and the *Latter-Day Pamphlets* there is always a voice, explicit or inexplicit, crying 'Guide me, Govern me!' Carlyle was leading the search for stability in a world of change, and he had no doubt that such stability could be found only where it had always been found, in the eternal verities. It would have been unlikely that those whose feelings Carlyle expressed in this way would have recognised what they were really calling for, though that would not necessarily have meant that Carlyle was wrong. Arthur Hugh Clough, the future poet, reading the pamphlet at Oxford, was deeply affected by it.

Also at the heart of *Chartism* is Carlyle's loathing of democracy, the other and closely related *Leitmotif* of the years ahead. In his pursuit of justice, he argues that fairness can be better achieved by the imposition of a wise ruler than by every man using his vote 'to send one's "twenty-thousandth part of a master of tongue-fence to National Palaver"'.[91] He defines democracy as 'a self-cancelling business; and gives in the long run a net result of *zero*';[92] he ridicules it with the jibe 'let the suffrage be still extended, *then* all will be well.'[93] It might work, he mused, in America, where no government was really needed, and each man could establish himself and survive on the resources of that great, empty and unregulated country; but it would not work in England, or any other polity with established institutions. The French had tried it, and it had failed. Neither Napoleon nor Cromwell had been able to restore order using democratic institutions. When people voted, Carlyle believed, the 'clattering of ballot-boxes' was merely a way of articulating 'the wish and prayer of all human hearts, everywhere and at all times: "Give me a leader; a true leader, not a false sham-leader; a true leader, that he may guide me on the true way, that I may be loyal to him, that I may swear fealty to him and follow him, and feel that it is well with me!"'[94]

The fundamental duty of the ruling class, in return for all this loyalty, was to ensure there was work enough for their subordinates to do; the fundamental duty of the subordinates was to do it, and expect no compassion or charity if they did not. Chartism marks the change in Carlyle from the vague desire to improve the conditions of the lower orders to a more specific desire to improve their conditions without allowing them the scope to upset the natural order. This creeping authoritarianism is, again, the result of Carlyle's growing understanding of how a 1789 in Britain could be followed by a 1792–93.

One of the evils to which the Chartists had specifically responded was the institutionalising of the poor in workhouses under the Poor Law Amendment Act, and Carlyle addressed this too. He saw the workhouses as 'an indispensable element, harsh but salutary, in the progress of things'.[95] They would make the people realise that something could not be had for nothing. He described the old Poor Law as 'a bounty on unthrift, idleness, bastardy and beer drinking', adding that 'for the idle man there is no place in this England of ours.'[96] It was a fact that, in seeking to be compassionate, those who had administered the old Poor Law had doled out so much to starving agricultural labourers in particular that they had pauperised them, and left them with no incentive but to live off the parish. Carlyle defined the amended law as a 'protection of the thrifty labourer against the thriftless and dissolute'.[97] However, the next step was for the rulers to understand that the poor, having learned that lesson, deserved better. The improvement on this 'harsh' law would come when the toiling inferior can find 'a superior that should lovingly and wisely govern'.[98] Happiness will consist in being given work, and being compliantly grateful for it; but Carlyle did regard work as a liberator of the spirit, and he himself was proof of that.

The essay is punctuated with humour, which many will interpret as brutality, but which both reflects Carlyle's robust character and, in occasionally Swiftian tone, helps him to make his point:

That this Poor-law Amendment Act meanwhile should be, as we sometimes hear it named, the 'chief glory' of a Reform Cabinet, betokens, one would imagine, rather a scarcity of glory there. To say to the poor, Ye shall eat the bread of affliction and drink the water of affliction, and be very miserable while here, required not so much a stretch of heroic faculty in any sense, as due toughness of bowels. If paupers are made miserable, paupers will needs decline in multitude. It is a secret known to all rat-catchers: stop up the granary-crevices, afflict with continual mewing, alarm, and going off of traps, your 'chargeable labourers' disappear, and cease from the establishment. A still briefer method is that of arsenic; perhaps even a milder, where otherwise permissible. Rats and paupers can be abolished; the human faculty was from of old adequate to grind them down, slowly or at once, and needed no ghost or reform ministry to teach it.[99]

As an example of where bad and thoughtless governance leads, Carlyle cites the problems in Ireland, then in the early stages of the potato famine. Again, he is seldom tactful ('"A finer people never lived," as the Irish lady said to us; "only they have two faults, they do generally lie and steal: barring these" – !'),[100] but his anger at the stupid way the English had run that country and alienated its people won him friends there. 'All men, we must repeat, were made by God, and have immortal souls in them. The Sanspotato is of the selfsame stuff as the superfinest Lord Lieutenant.'[101] The Irish destitute were arriving in their thousands on the west coast of England, where they would live in a way no English peasant would demean himself to do, and take whatever work they could get, all through the desperate need to earn money for food.

Carlyle had no grasp of economics, as is shown not just in his clever ridiculing of statisticians, but also in his *reductio ad absurdum* of the principle of *laissez-faire*. Left to fend for themselves, a savage, starving peasantry would, he felt, run riot across England, much as they had done in France half a century earlier. To prevent this there would need to be not only a discarding of modern economic nostrums, but also the reassertion of authority. He looked back to the Norman Conquest as an example of the proper reimposition of order. He saw the Frankish Normans, 'entering with a strong man', as having acted 'as an immense volunteer police force, stationed everywhere, united, disciplined, feudally regimented, ready for action; strong Teutonic men; who ... drilled this wild Teutonic people into unity'.[102] The lesson he drew from this was 'how *can-do*, if we will well interpret it, unites itself with *shall-do* among mortals; how strength acts ever as the right-arm of justice; how might and right, so frightfully discrepant at first, are ever in the long run one and the same.' This 'might is right' argument presupposes ultimately benevolent and uncorrupt aims behind the might; those reading Carlyle now find it hard to share such assumptions, as indeed many of his contemporaries did. He justified his view by saying that a purely brutal conquest would never last, but would be flung out; in modern times, the fate of Nazism and Stalinism supports his view, and the Terror in France had proved it to him. The true strong man, for that reason, was always wise; his strength lay in the soul rather than the body, and was drawn from God.

Carlyle uses the device of quoting the fictional Professor Sauerteig to present his own, romanticised interpretation of English history, and of the 'two grand tasks' that faced the nation, of conquering and then teaching the world how rule after conquest could be conducted beneficently. He recalls (and this theme would be greatly expanded in *Past and Present*) how huge the achievements were of England in the late Middle Ages, the prosperity of the country and the skill of its workmen; he contrasts these with the decline that had coincided with the democratic movement. Abandoning Sauerteig, in his own voice he lays down this creed: 'No man is justified in resisting by word or deed the Authority he lives under, for a light cause, be such Authority what it may.'[103] He adds: 'Recognised or not recognised, a man has his superiors, a regular hierarchy above him; extending up, degree above degree, to heaven itself and God the Maker, who made His world not for anarchy but for rule and order.'[104] That, according to Carlyle, is the worst thing about democracy: it interferes with the natural order.

Though compellingly written, the pamphlet suggests Carlyle still improperly understood what had caused those horrors, as opposed to what he had convinced himself had caused them. In his last chapter, appropriately entitled 'Impossible', he tries to address the question of what to do. He intended the chapter-heading to be ironic; Mirabeau, just the type of strong man for whom he longed, had cried out to his secretary, who had just said 'impossible', 'never name to me that blockhead of a word'.[105] Carlyle claims to have provided the ways out of misery, but they need a man resolute enough to execute them. 'Universal Education is the first great thing we mean; general Emigration is the second.'[106] Ordinary intellects needed to be awakened to make possible 'the discovery of the will of Nature, of God's will';[107] educate men, thought Carlyle, and they will no longer be so stupid as to cry for the panacea of universal suffrage. The education must be religious; not, as he had written years before, in the mechanistic sense, but by finding men with faith to impart faith to others.

The emigration question appealed to Carlyle's sense of logic; there was plenty of rich, fertile, empty earth in North America waiting for able Englishmen from an overcrowded island to exploit it. He despised the Malthusian view that human nature could be tempered to reduce the population by other means: 'Smart Sally in our alley proves all too fascinating to brisk Tom in yours: can Tom be called on to make pause, and calculate the demand for labour in the British Empire first?'[108] He was more humane than Malthus, who had concluded that the poor should not be stopped from starving, for only when there were fewer of them would the value of their labour rise to a level where they could earn a living. There was work in the world for as many Englishmen and women as could be produced, Carlyle argued, provided the surplus population went abroad. At the time he wrote fewer than 70,000 a year were emigrating; within twenty years that figure had trebled, with Britons populating not just North America, but Australasia too. His own brother Alick would soon take this advice, and try to make his fortune in America. Carlyle ends with another self-quoting attack (from *Sartor*) on the aristocracy for not giving a lead in this matter either:

Alas, where now are the Hengsts and Alarics of our still-glowing, still expanding Europe; who, when their home is grown too narrow, will enlist and, like fire-pillars, guide onwards those superfluous masses of indomitable living Valour; equipped, not now with the battle-axe and war-chariot, but with the steam-engine and ploughshare? Where are they? – Preserving their Game![109]

9

The Hero as Prophet

1840–43

CHARTISM CHANGED public perceptions of Carlyle. It was as if petrol had been poured on the fire of his fame. Despite its eccentricities, the pamphlet was sympathetically received, not least because in his advocacy of education for the masses and help to the poor to emigrate Carlyle tapped two main social movements of the time.

In the first month 850 copies were sold, a second edition being needed by the following April. The impact of the pamphlet made some politicians argue that the condition of the poor had to be dealt with. There was, though, no immediate action. 'A very remarkable Essay,' said the reviewer in *Tait's Edinburgh Magazine*, 'and one which, by leading men to think, must do good.'[1] The reviewer termed Carlyle 'a Tory-Radical',[2] as good a guess as any. Another Tory-Radical, Gladstone, found the work hard to put down.[3] At the other pole Disraeli and his 'Young England' group were deeply impressed by Carlyle. Disraeli's biographer says Carlyle taught them 'to deplore the excessive worship of mere wealth and machinery that prevailed to the neglect of all the higher interests of man'.[4] Unfortunately, the Young England Group saw in this influence only what they wanted to see, a common problem with politicians down the ages; Carlyle, as he became steadily more morally authoritarian, would come to revile Disraeli. It was through literature, not parliament, that the problem would be addressed; in the next decade Dickens, Kingsley, Mrs Gaskell and Mrs Trollope were just four of the better-known novelists who would write on the subject.

The Spectator was so struck by the pamphlet that it made it the subject of a long leading article, claiming that *Chartism* (from which it published several long extracts) 'institutes ... a searching, unsparing investigation into the question of popular rights, [and] unmasks with ease some of the most flourishing lies of the time'.[5] The following week the magazine defended Carlyle against the criticism that, because he wrote regularly for and was published by Fraser, he was simply a Tory mouthpiece against the Whig administration. The power of *Chartism*, as *The Spectator* recognised, was that its author wrote it without any party considerations whatever.

For others, it was not Carlyle's views so much as his expression of them that was confusing. Many were simply baffled by the originalities of style. Emma Darwin, in a letter to her aunt early in 1840, said: 'I have been reading Carlyle, like all the rest of the world. He fascinates one and puts one out of patience. He has been writing a sort of pamphlet on the state of England called "Chartism". It is full of compassion and good feeling but utterly unreasonable. Charles [Darwin] keeps on reading and abusing him.'[6] By contrast, Arthur Penrhyn Stanley, who would pronounce obsequies over Carlyle forty years later, wrote to his aunt in February 1840 expressing his belief that Carlyle 'may become the means of reviving a true Christian feeling, or at least of preparing the way for it in those branches of literature and of action, from which Englishmen latterly seem almost to have banished it.'[7] Carlyle started to become an idol to aspiring writers. In the first few months of 1840 those who wrote to him seeking advice on such a career included Geraldine Jewsbury, who was to become one of Jane's closest confidantes, and James Hutchison Stirling. However preoccupied he was, Carlyle always found the time to write back.

The work's reception gave him greater confidence, and with it greater stimulus to creativity. David Masson, writing over half a century later, said of this period:

In and from 1840 Carlyle's name was running like wildfire through the British Islands and through English-speaking America; there was the utmost avidity for his books wherever they were accessible, especially among the young men; phrases from them were in all young men's mouths and were affecting the public speech; and, though he was living frugally in his small house in Chelsea on an income of not more yet than £200 a year, that house was already looked at by many Londoners, and thought of by many at a distance, as the home of the real king of British Letters.[8]

Carlyle sought solitude to consider his next project. '*To be let alone* is the utmost ambition of my soul in these times and circumstances,' he told Sterling on 6 January 1840, nine days after *Chartism*'s publication.[9] But fame meant the chances of his being left alone were diminishing, and he began to attract the attention of the greatest in the land. Thomas Ballantyne, a prominent anti-Corn Laws agitator and sometime editor of the *Manchester Guardian*, wrote complaining that Carlyle had ignored that important subject in his pamphlet. Carlyle told him the Corn Laws would certainly be repealed, but that even when they were it would make little odds to the condition of the working people; which was why he had not written about them. Dr Arnold, the headmaster of Rugby, was particularly in tune with his views on education and emigration. Arnold had been taken with Carlyle ever since reading *The French Revolution* two years earlier. He wrote to Carlyle in January 1840 to praise the views expressed in *Chartism* (which Arnold had not then read). Carlyle replied emphasising the pessimism of his view, and declining an invitation to visit Rugby; though he would go there two years later, shortly before Arnold's death, on researches for *Oliver*.

He was already thinking of a fourth series of lectures in the spring. Pre-empting these, a group of workers in the City sent a representative to Cheyne Row to invite Carlyle to lecture to them. He saw a chance to provide some of the leadership whose lack he had lamented, by going out among the less fashionable classes and expounding his doctrines; but after some thought decided not to go tub-thumping, even in so good a cause, despite the promise of a large audience. Instead, turning down most invitations to socialise, he shut himself away from Jane in the downstairs room that Jack had used when he stayed with them, and started to correct proofs of the English edition of the *Miscellanies* – all English sales hitherto had been of American imports. He began to read widely in Norse mythology, sending for a Danish grammar that he might try to penetrate some of the sagas in the original. The idea of the lectures on heroes, of which Odin is the first, was being formed. Not unrelated to this was the time spent, in January and February, reading Forster's work on the Commonwealth period. He protested that Forster had depicted Cromwell as 'such a knave',[10] a view that would be amply corrected in his lectures. Ironically, in lending him not just books but unpublished papers, Forster was to be his greatest help in undertaking this task.

At the end of February Fraser promised him £217, mainly the proceeds of sales of *The French Revolution*, which would have alleviated the mild financial pressure Carlyle was beginning to feel were it not that Fraser paid him with bills redeemable ten months later. In his reading he progressed from the Norse to the Koran, a book which, in his second lecture, he said was 'as toilsome reading as I ever undertook ... Nothing but a sense of duty could carry any European through the Koran.'[11] By 2 March he was prepared to let Jack into the secret of this year's subject: 'I am to talk about gods, prophets, priests, kings, poets, teachers (*six* sorts of them); and may probably call it "On the Heroic".'[12] He could not give the work his undivided attention. The London Library project was at a crucial stage, with a public meeting arranged, and Carlyle was busy trying to recruit any influential acquaintance he could to support the plan. He hoped Lord Morpeth would chair the meeting, but he was not available, so he went in search of another grandee: 'Lord Northampton were my favourite too, I think – but any Lord will do.'[13] As a result of this activity, he reported in mid-March that his lectures, just six weeks off, 'remain dim and horrible'.[14]

Carlyle was in increasing demand to grace the dinner tables of the aris-tocracy, or the simply well-heeled. He was, for all his susceptibility to the likes of Lady Harriet Baring, no snob, and in the *Reminiscences* announced that of all the grand people he had met 'there was nothing of charm in any of them'.[15] He did grudgingly concede that some aristocrats he met were quite 'noble'.[16] The Edward Stanleys, who had taken Carlyle up, had him to dinner in March. His main objection to such events was that rich food, drink and late hours – to none of which he was used – debilitated him for a week afterwards. However, at the dinner Carlyle met Charles Dickens, 'a fine little fellow ... clear blue intelligent eyes, eyebrows that he arches amazingly, large protrusive rather loose mouth, – a face of the most extreme mobility, which he shuttles about, eyebrows, eyes, mouth and all, in a very singular manner while speaking ... a quiet shrewd-looking little fellow, who seems to guess pretty well what he is, and what others are.'[17] To improve his health after such excursions, and to put himself in the right mind for lecturing, he resumed his ferocious gallops into the countryside on his horse. He felt that riding for two or three hours daily helped stir up 'a great increase of movement in the inner man of me', important for someone for whom well-regulated bowels meant much. He liked to smoke a pipe, but pipes sent him from Scotland (he could not be satisfied with English ones) tended to break in the post; in the end he had to ask friends going to Edinburgh, where his favourite pipes were made, to bring them back for him. Nor was the tobacco in London very impressive, so supplies had to be sent from Scotsbrig. Jane, having remained fit all winter, went down with flu as spring arrived.

Carlyle began to think of writing down his lectures, rather than delivering them extempore. Having decided to begin with Odin, he settled that he should end with Robert Burns – though in fact that was the case only chronologically, as he ended the course with 'The Hero as King'. As April came he was seized with dyspepsia, and confided in Jack that he hoped to be well off enough not to have to lecture in 1841. Of his friends and patrons the Wilsons he sought approval of the subject matter, and the usual help in making the arrangements. The London Library project was now taking off, with advertisements asking for subscribers set to appear in *The Times* in May. Along with Edward Fitzgerald, Carlyle had become joint honorary secretary of the committee setting up the library; the committee itself included Dickens, Bulwer, Spedding and Forster, and contained five Members of Parliament among its eighteen men.

By mid-April he had stopped accepting social invitations, and had decided he would instead spend the time writing his lectures down. He had an offer from the *Westminster Review* to pay him £50 if a shorthand writer could come and take down the lectures as he delivered them, so that they could be published. Sensing that he might want to publish them himself, he rejected the offer. Instead he made sure his own texts were comprehensive, writing from eight or nine each morning until two in the afternoon, before his ride, to complete his work. He professed, though, that his texts would merely guide him, and he would not simply read them out on the day. For his own purposes, and not for any other publication, an experienced parliamentary reporter, David Keane, was hired at a guinea a lecture to take a note for Carlyle to turn into a book. It was as well Carlyle had such full notes, for a mis-understanding meant the first lecture was only taken down in shorthand by an inadequate reporter sent by Fraser. Keane, once he started, was a great improvement.

The lectures were scheduled to start on 5 May. He was reunited with

Sterling shortly before they started, and went riding with him; he found his friend 'in the worst spirits I recollect him in',[18] not least because his health was so broken down that he could not even write. Such distractions were good for Carlyle, reducing the time he had to worry about his lectures. As before, there was nothing to worry about, though that did not prevent him from waking at 4.30 a.m. on the day of the first. The next day he wrote to his sister that his audience for 'The Hero as Divinity' 'sat silent, as if it had been gospel.'[19] By the time of the second, 'The Hero as Prophet', on 8 May the audience had swelled to nearly 300, and Carlyle was expecting a profit of 200 guineas on the season. Typically, its success – Carlyle's regulars said it was his best ever lecture – so unnerved him that he hardly slept before the third, 'The Hero as Poet', which had Browning among its audience. He was relieved the newspapers had not much noticed his lectures, and professed irritation once they started to do so halfway through the course.

After lecturing on 'The Hero as Priest', he discoursed on 'The Hero as Man of Letters', which Caroline Fox, twenty-one-year-old daughter of a prominent Cornish Quaker family, attended. She noted in her *Journal* that 'his manner is very quiet, but he speaks like one tremendously convinced of what he utters, and who had much – very much – in him that was quite unutterable, quite unfit to be uttered to the uninitiated ear; and when the Englishman's sense of beauty or truth exhibited itself in vociferous cheers, he would impatiently, almost contemptuously, wave his hand, as if that were not the sort of homage which Truth demanded.'[20] Carlyle concluded the series on 22 May with 'The Hero as King', in which he sought to convince his audience that Cromwell had been 'a great and true man'.[21] It was the last time he lectured until he gave the Rectorial address at Edinburgh twenty-six years later. In a letter to his mother the following day he stated, simply, what attracted him to Cromwell; he had been 'the valiant soldier in England of what John Knox had preached in Scotland'.[22]

He resolved, after the lectures, to relax for a week: however, the recruitment of great names for the library still had to be done, and he went down with a heavy cold. There was no rest before he began writing up his lectures in early June. One relief was that Hunt and his family moved to Kensington. 'We are decidedly rather glad of it,' he told Jack. 'Our intercourse lately had reduced itself altogether to the *lending of sovereigns*.'[23] Despite his anti-social tendencies, the Carlyles were making new friends all the time. As well as Dickens, Tennyson became known to them during 1840. 'A fine large-featured, dim-eyed, bronze-coloured, shaggy headed man is Alfred,' he told Jack. 'Dusty, smoky, free-and-easy: who swims, outwardly and inwardly, with great composure in an inarticulate element as of tranquil chaos and tobacco-smoke; great now and then when he does emerge.'[24]

Once he started on the lectures he was dissatisfied, and unsure whether he would write up all six; the main problem was stylistic, conveying the manner of a lecture without deterring readers. This led him into 'fits of bilious depression'.[25] It took him the whole of June to write the first two, though work on the library distracted him still. The great public meeting, at which he made a speech, took place on 24 June. In his address, which was received and punctuated with loud cheers, he illustrated the advantages the library would have over that at the British Museum, to which most were denied access, and how it would further public education. He was also called up yet again for jury service, but at least during the delays he resolved to press on with the complete series of lectures; he was motivated, too, by the distant thought that he might go and give them again in America.

Progress remained slow. He wrote to Sterling, wondering whether his friend would ride across England from Clifton and meet him at Stonehenge, where he would have ridden to from London. Sterling, however, came to London, arriving as Carlyle finished the third lecture in mid-July. Sterling had just seen Caroline Fox, confiding in her that Carlyle had a 'low view of the world proceeding partly from a bad stomach'.[26] Carlyle was keen to have a riding holiday, and tried to persuade Godefroi de Cavaignac, a refugee from the 1830 revolution in France who had been a friend of Jane's and his for some years, to join him on a journey to Cambridgeshire, in search of relics of Cromwell. He resolved to finish the fourth lecture and then, at the end of July, be away. However, Cavaignac changed his mind, and Carlyle therefore changed his plan. He decided to ride to Leatherhead to visit the Bullers, and thence to Herstmonceux to see the Reverend Julius Hare, for whom Sterling had some years earlier been curate, and whom Carlyle described to Sterling later as 'a good man, tho' an Archdeacon'.[27] It was to be the last fling for Carlyle's horse; he felt he could no longer afford the 26s a week it cost to keep her, and asked William Marshall, the son of his benefactor, whether he would like to have her. Marshall would not take her, but instead promised to sell her and give Carlyle the money. Carlyle felt it wrong to accept it – £17 – and asked instead that it be donated to the Anti-Corn Law League; but Marshall would not do this, keeping the money instead to provide Carlyle with more riding when he was ready.

He stayed a couple of days with the Bullers before going to Herstmonceux. The weather was hot, but he felt better for the exercise; however, he told Sterling that he spent the time on horseback 'in unfathomable mournful meditation'.[28] He was away from Chelsea barely a week, and returned determined to make short work of his last two lectures. However, he was plagued by insomnia, which slowed him down. Within a fortnight he was writing to his mother of his dream to buy a house by the sea, where he could go to be cool – and quiet – in the summer. So exhausted was he by writing up the fifth lecture that he began to think of going out of London again once he had done the sixth and last. He completed his task on 4 September, regarding what he had done, with his usual optimism, as 'a sorry job'.[29] On the morning he planned to catch a steamer north, he looked at the rain falling outside and decided he had not the heart to go. Much as he had wanted to make his annual visit to his family, he resolved instead to conserve his resources for a whole summer away in 1841; he even thought of taking Jane to spend it at Craigenputtock, a sign he was really tired of London. Sending his mother, as a consolation, money for some clothes and a keg of beer, he settled in for the winter.

II

It is from the lectures *On Heroes, Hero-Worship and the Heroic in History* that Carlyle's reputation as an admirer of strong men, however distasteful they might seem to others, was founded. It was also a further, clear statement of his view of the inadequacy of the Christian religion. If *Chartism* was an analysis of the practical problems that faced England, *Heroes* analyses the spiritual ones. Notionally, it describes modes of heroic behaviour throughout history, but all the heroes and forms of heroism have features in common – faith, sincerity, righting wrongs and, as a result, leadership – that by an allegorical process (and, sometimes, by a process not so allegorical) are shown to be absent from the England of the early 1840s. For Carlyle, recognition of the hero and his correct evaluation by historians is the right way to tell history; as he says several times in his first lecture 'The Hero as Divinity', 'the History of the world is but the Biography of great men'.[30]

The stylistic problem with the work – that in trying to convey the atmosphere of the lecture-room Carlyle did not always make himself comfortable to the reader – is not too much of a handicap; though in the earlier lectures particularly there is much verbosity and circumlocution. Important points are made throughout, though it is only really in the last lecture, 'The Hero as King', that Carlyle gives us a clear sight of his meaning. The hero as King is 'practically the summary for us of all the various figures of Heroism', and the failure of the British to find such a man has been their undoing:

The finding of your *Ableman* and getting him invested with the *symbols of ability*, with dignity, worship, (*worthship*), royalty, kinghood, or whatever we call it, so that he may actually have room to guide according to his faculty of doing it, – is the business, well or ill accomplished, of all social procedure whatsoever in this world! Hustings-speeches, Parliamentary motions, Reform Bills, French Revolutions, all mean at heart this; or else nothing. Find in any country the Ablest Man that exists there; raise him to the supreme place, and loyally reverence him: you have a perfect government for that country; no ballot-box, parliamentary eloquence, voting, constitution-building, or other machinery whatsoever can improve it a whit. It is in the perfect state; an ideal country. The Ablest Man; he means also the truest-hearted, justest, the Noblest Man: what he tells us to do must be precisely the wisest, fittest, that we could anywhere or anyhow learn; – the thing which it will in all ways behove us, with right loyal thankfulness, and nothing doubting, to do![31]

Having spewed out this rhetoric, and neatly summed up in a few moments what he filled hours of lecturing trying to say, Carlyle, without shame, adds:

'alas, we know very well that Ideals can never be completely embodied in practice.' But it is a fine polemic, as strong as anything in *Latter-Day Pamphlets* but lacking their manic rage. All the 'insincere, unbelieving world'[32] can come up with are quacks, whose figure can be altered by ballot-boxes, but whose substance continues. 'Not a Hero only is needed, but a world fit for him; a world not of *valets* ... The Valet-World *has* to be governed by the Sham-Hero, by the King merely *dressed* in King-gear,' he moans. 'We shall either learn to know a Hero, a true Governor and Captain, somewhat better, when we see him; or else go on to be forever governed by the Unheroic; had we ballot boxes clattering at every street-corner, there were no remedy in these.'[33]

Lest this be interpreted nakedly as might is right Carlyle reminds us that God is watching both the ruler and the ruled, and His sanction is being applied to the 'moral acts' of ruling and being ruled. 'There is no act more moral between men than that of rule and obedience,' he writes. 'Woe to him that claims obedience when it is not due; woe to him that refuses it when it is! God's law is in that, I say, however the Parchment-laws may run: there is a Divine Right or else a Diabolic Wrong at the heart of every claim that one man makes upon another.'[34] But the mark of the hero is that he is sent by God to do God's work; and since God is not a pluralist, there is no call for democracy. The perfect example of this is, in Carlyle's view, Cromwell, whose success showed the evil of democracy as an impertinent, temporal interference with God's natural order. The hero's 'mission is Order; every man's is', says Carlyle. 'He is here to make what was disorderly, chaotic, into a thing ruled, regular.'[35] There is no equivocation about the duty of the ruled to submit to the proper ruler: 'I say, Find me the true *Könning*, King, or Able-man, and he *has* a divine right over me.'[36] However, that right exists only if exercised scrupulously. 'All power is moral ... the grand point is the distinction ... of Good and Evil, of *Thou shalt* and *Thou shalt not*.'[37]

An essential part of this creation of order is truth, the winning of the constant battle between belief and unbelief. The Puritans, such as Cromwell, saw cant and shams in religious worship, and rooted them out. Echoing the symbology of *Sartor*, Carlyle talks of the clothes in which the old religion was dressed up, obscuring its true meaning. The 'garnitures'[38] of these institutions, and of Stuart Kingship, were removed by Cromwell, whom Carlyle adoringly depicts as the last strong man to govern England, and the last just one. He berates other historians for not seeing this, for painting the Lord Protector as a cruel, ambitious man when in fact he was inspired, quietly, by God.

Neither will we blame greatly that word of Cromwell's to them; which was so blamed: 'If the King should meet me in battle, I would kill the King.' Why not? These words were spoken to men who stood as before a Higher than Kings. They had set more than their own lives on the cast. The Parliament may call it, in official language, a fighting '*for* the King'; but we, for our share, cannot understand that. To us it is no dilettante work, no sleek officiality; it is sheer rough death and earnest. They have brought it to the calling-forth of *War*; horrid internecine fight, man grappling with man in fire-eyed rage, – the *infernal* element in man called forth, to try it by that! Do that therefore; since that is the thing to be done. – The successes of Cromwell seem to me a very natural thing! Since he was not shot in battle, they were an inevitable thing. That such a man, with the eye to see, with the heart to dare, should advance, from post to post, from victory to victory, till the Huntingdon Farmer became, by whatever name you might call him, the acknowledged Strongest Man in England, virtually the King of England, requires no magic to explain it! – [39]

Passages such as this not only demonstrate the individual force and originality of Carlyle's prose style; they also show how much he had set himself apart, in tone, style, method and outlook, from the established school of historians of which he was so contemptuous.

Common, too, to all the heroes is a heroic intellect. Shakespeare, Dr Johnson, Burns, Luther, had it, and all (coincidentally) came from humble backgrounds like Carlyle's. The element of implicit self-reference in the lectures is unmissable. None of his subjects was born into the normal ruling classes; like their author, they had to make their way to positions of leadership, whether political, philosophical, theological or literary. On the way many of them, like Carlyle, had to form their own understanding of the 'open secret', their own definition of God and religion. Carlyle's own native Calvinism is shared by Luther, Knox and Cromwell; and from the way he writes of Mahomet one might think the prophet, too, an honorary Calvinist. Like Carlyle, Cromwell was a hypochondriac. He exercised his heroic intellect in periods of inarticulate silence, so beloved of Carlyle. Just as Carlyle hoped he was doing, his heroes used their intellects to see the truth, and to communicate truth to the people. Unheroic intellects – whether Charles I, or Luther's opponents at the Diet of Worms – are routinely defeated. Sincerity was all. As a joke – one presumes – he includes his *bête noire* Rousseau, as if to prove that even the heroic intellect can go wrong at times, in Rousseau's case through egotism; and the slavish adherence to such misguided heroism led, of course, to the French Revolution. Bertrand Russell, curiously, felt that Carlyle's 'cult of the hero' was a natural extension of Rousseau's philosophy.[40]

The lectures contain their share of anti-idealism, and not just in the presence of Rousseau. The printed word, Carlyle argued, had changed everything. No longer did men have to gather round a teacher at a university and learn from him: 'The true University of these days is a Collection of Books.'[41] The evil of democracy had led on from this. 'Invent Writing, Democracy is inevitable,' he said, because 'whoever can speak, speaking now to the whole nation, becomes a power, a branch of government, with inalienable weight in law-making, in all acts of authority.'[42] In the Reporters' Gallery of the House of Commons was the '*Fourth Estate*, more important far than they all', and a theme to which Carlyle would return, with greater venom, in *Latter-Day Pamphlets*. The press was the great secularising agent of the time, 'superseding the pulpit',[43] and was communicating beliefs far more effectively than conventional men of God. At their head, and more powerful than any aristocracies or governments or clergy was 'the Priesthood of the Writers of Books'.[44]

Carlyle's lectures were based on the belief that all society was founded on hero-worship. They found favour with an audience who largely expected deference from others, and who would seek themselves to emulate the best. Carlyle sought to prick consciences when he talked of the bankruptcy of an age that denied the existence of great men; for only such men could save a society in moral decline. 'No sadder proof,' he said, 'can be given by a man of his own littleness than disbelief in great men.'[45] He had led the way, himself, with his reverence for Goethe, too great a hero even to take his place among pygmies like Johnson, Burns and Rousseau in the lecture 'The Hero as Man of Letters'. Shakespeare, Dante, Burns and Johnson were heroic because as poets they were seers and prophets, and saw the 'open secret' of the God-like in everything. Mrs Gaskell, noting what would later be seen as the germ of the Nietzschean superman, was less dewy-eyed: 'A poor, unchristian heroism, whose manifestation consists in injury to others!'[46]

The work upholds all Carlyle's views of what is necessary for the correctly ordered society. It shows him as a 'moral desperado', a frame of mind nowhere seen more clearly than in Carlyle's support of John Knox's attempt to establish a theocracy in which 'Kings and Prime Ministers, and all manner of persons, in public or private, diplomatising or whatever else they might be doing, should walk according to the Gospel of Christ, and understand that this was their Law, supreme over all laws';[47] the creation of God's Kingdom on earth. However dressed up as a history of ideas, *Heroes* is a reflection of Carlyle's own nature and prejudices, and his implicit manifesto for the world in which he lived.

III

With the lectures finished he settled on his next work more decisively than was his habit: a book on Cromwell, though for the moment he kept the subject to himself in case he lost the will to proceed. He casually asked Forster to lend him some books on Cromwell, but other than that gave no clues that he would be returning at length to a man whose moral strength in governorship had fascinated him compulsively since he read widely about him in preparation for the lectures *On Heroes*. 'It is a great blessing to me that some kind of book does begin to dawn as a possibility again in my head,' he wrote to Alick on 10 September 1840. 'There is no other use in living that I can find except *working wisely*.'[48] Another controversy in which he was to become involved also had its roots at about this time. He was visited by American women delegates to a world anti-slavery convention being held in London, who were disappointed to find him against abolition. He referred them to problems of slavery nearer home, notably in the oppressed working people of England; and that, as far as he was concerned, slavery was nothing to do with him. It would, though, contribute to his construction as a hate-figure, not least in the eyes of Mill. Exeter Hall, the venue for these radical meetings then and throughout the 1840s, was to become a focus for Carlyle's antipathy.

He continued to drum up support for the library, which, in return for a £5 entrance fee and £2 annual subscription, was now inviting members. Five hundred subscribers were needed to get the venture under way, and by late September more than 400 had been found. A handful of women were among them, but the rest were lawyers, doctors, clergymen, MPs, academics and other professional people. Carlyle was already taking a leading role in deciding what stock should be purchased, and would become one of the library's heaviest users in its early years, particularly in his researches for *Oliver*. He admitted to Sterling in late September that he was deep in Puritan history. 'There is no great epoch known at all so buried under rubbish as this of Cromwell and his Puritans. I fancy I have got to see into Cromwell, for the first time very lately, as one [of] the *greatest* amorphous souls we ever had in this land.'[49] He did not enjoy his reading, confessing to Emerson that 'books equal in dullness were at no epoch of the world penned by unassisted man.'[50] A 'magnificent hamper'[51] of books arrived from Forster, prompting Carlyle not just to express gratitude, but to ask for more on every aspect of parliamentary and theological history of the period.

Forster, though distinguished in his own right, looked up and was keen to be of service to Carlyle, and Carlyle made ruthless use of him. Carlyle knew he had resigned himself to months, possibly years, of reading. However unpalatable he found the research, the subject began to obsess him; a letter from Jack, with a patient called Ogilvy in Scotland, prompted a reply from his brother telling him which battlefields were in the area. He had not even the spare mental energy to negotiate with Fraser for the publishing of *Heroes*; that was delegated to Jane, who was to become something of an expert in handling the family's financial affairs. Fraser's first offer was £150, which she felt poor. As well as neglect by her husband, she had other tribulations. Staff had always been a problem, and in October their then maid, a Kirkcaldy girl called Helen Mitchell who stayed with them longer than any other servant, became incapable after drinking a bottle of whisky. Her drink problem had been apparent for over a year, and Jane had only just forgiven her for an earlier offence. She celebrated this forgiveness by getting more drunk than ever. Carlyle had to go to eat at a tavern while Helen herself lay drunk on the kitchen floor in a pile of broken crockery and upturned furniture.

Jane had to manage with little help from Carlyle, who merely complained that the inconveniences of London and the servant problem meant he could do only a quarter of the reading in any time that he could have managed at Craigenputtock. 'Why do women marry?' Jane asked Forster, who was becoming a closer friend of hers than of her husband's. 'God knows; unless it be that like the great Wallenstein they do not find scope enough for their

Genius and qualities in an easy life.'[52] A few days later, in another letter to Forster, she complained that 'this man of mine will absolutely do nothing but write books and be sick', explaining why he had refused Forster's invitation to go the theatre. She was not to be disadvantaged, and asked Forster to take her instead, having dined at Cheyne Row first.

The longer Carlyle spent in his dull books, the worse his literal and metaphorical biliousness became. Jane chided him for having sold Citoyenne, since she was convinced a horse would have improved his spirits and health, and distracted him from his monomaniacal pursuit. As it was he turned down all invitations, and when taking himself out for walks went over Battersea Bridge and into the country rather than towards the town. 'I get far more profit silently communing with myself than from the gabble of most I could meet,' he told his mother.[53] One day, despite the persistent rain and gales of that autumn, he walked the twenty miles to Hampton Court and back. It did little good. 'My reading goes on,' he lamented to Jack in mid-November, 'my stupidity seems to increase with it.'[54] What dispirited him most was that, even after two months of solid reading, he had no idea what book he would get out of it. Nor was his last project bringing him any comfort. Jane and Fraser abandoned their negotiation about *Heroes*, and another publisher offered a mere £50 for it, prompting Carlyle to wish the thing could be burnt.

Just when he had become accustomed to his routine, he was summoned yet again to sit for a week on a jury – about a patent fraud – which disrupted him in body and soul. 'Poor Oliver lies like grains of gold dust scattered under continents of cinders and rubbish,' he lamented.[55] He soon regained his zeal for tedious reading, searching for *The History of Covenanting* by the seventeenth-century Scots divine Robert Baillie as the next important step in his studies; and there were important works to be done for the library. It had been settled at the end of November that the library would open on 1 May 1841, and Carlyle and W.D. Christie, his fellow joint honorary secretary, wrote to members asking for their £5 joining fees. A librarian had to be appointed, and Carlyle and his committee were having trouble finding the right man. Carlyle was a strong upholder of the principles of libraries even when he himself could not benefit. Hearing at this time from Alick that the library in Ecclefechan was trying to raise 45s to buy a set of his *Miscellanies*, he wrote to his brother urging them to stop, for he would present them with copies.

Domestic life was miserable. 'We have never had here so ugly a winter,'[56] Carlyle pronounced in mid-January 1841, after weeks of frost and fog had metamorphosed into snow, ice and even more bitter cold. Apart from a brief respite in late January, the freeze lasted the best part of two months. However bad the Carlyles felt, they were aware too of how badly this harshest winter for twenty years was afflicting the poor. In the coldest weather Carlyle, on rare journeys out of doors, saw half-naked beggars in the streets. It reconfirmed his fears that revolution would follow if nothing were done.

Jane wrote to her friend Susan Stirling that 'my Husband ... is as usual, never healthy, never absolutely ill – protesting against "things in general" with the old emphasis – with an increased vehemence just at present.'[57] Carlyle had formed the idea of writing a life of Cromwell – the history of the world, after all, being the biography of great men – but was in despair because he could see no way of doing it. He carried on with his requests to friends to find obscure volumes of mid-seventeenth-century history for him, in the hope that the more he studied, the more likely it was that inspiration would come. He was still depressed by his failure to find a publisher for *Heroes*, and it was a sign of his desperation that negotiations were reopened with Fraser. By the end of January they had agreed £75 for the lectures, sweetened with another £75 for a new edition of *Sartor*. Temporarily, Carlyle broke off from Cromwell, and revised *Heroes* one last time before printing started.

As well as revising proofs, and yet again having to sit on a civil jury, Carlyle had to devote much of his time to the election of the librarian for the London Library. The library committee finally settled on John Cochrane in February 1841. Cochrane, who was sixty, had been Carlyle's candidate, and Carlyle was pleased when the matter was settled as he had wished. He wanted above all to resign the joint secretaryship, and Cochrane's appointment would allow those duties to be transferred to the librarian. As it turned out, he could not divest himself of these responsibilities quickly enough, for at the end of February he went down with a vicious attack of flu, which persisted into March. He became an epic of self-pity. 'I have,' he wrote to Sterling, 'serious thoughts of getting out of London altogether this season, to witness one other Summer before I die. No words can do justice to the abhorrence I feel of this place sometimes.'[58] There was, however, a new friend to console them both. Geraldine Jewsbury, with whom Carlyle had conducted a warm correspondence for more than a year, at last came from Lancashire to London with her brother, and visited the Carlyles. 'Our fair Pilgrimess', was how Carlyle described her. 'She is one of the most interesting young women I have seen for years. Clear delicate sense and courage looking out of her small sylph figure; – a most heroic-looking damsel.'[59] After her visit, she and Jane began their prodigious correspondence, for which even one as broad-minded as Jane was unprepared. She received from Geraldine 'a philosophical desertation [*sic*] on the passion of Love as it differs in Men from Women! She is far too anatomical for me.'[60] Their correspondence was maintained in this intimate vein, and it was from this mostly destroyed set of letters that Geraldine supposedly learned of the deficiencies in the Carlyles' marriage.

In mid-March, once Carlyle was well, and Jane (who had caught his flu as usual) was recovering by drinking Guinness, he became restless, and wanted to exploit the good weather by travelling. Jack was on the Isle of Wight with Ogilvy, and Carlyle intended to take a train there and stay for ten days. However, Jack suddenly returned to London, so Carlyle's plans were changed. They went out to Hampton Court together, and made other trips to Kingston and by train to see Windsor and Eton. But he needed a longer break, and started to enquire of his family in Scotland whether they could find a place for him and Jane for the summer. Jane hated Craigenputtock so much that she simply refused to go there, thus dashing Carlyle's previous plan.

Before that could be settled Richard Monckton Milnes, an MP friend of Carlyle's who had been with him on the library committee, asked him to travel up to his seat at Fryston, near Pontefract in Yorkshire, to spend part of the Easter holiday. Milnes had been introduced to Carlyle by Charles Buller, having admired *The French Revolution* and having attended many of the lectures, and was now one of Carlyle's main admirers. He said that 'Carlyle's writings make on me the impression of the sound of a single hatchet in the aboriginal forests of North America.'[61] On 5 April Carlyle and Milnes made the first leg of the journey to Derby on the Great Central Railway, and then on to Yorkshire the next day. Milnes's parents and aged aunts were there to welcome them, and Carlyle was put in an apartment 'furnished as for Prince Albert and Queen Victory; the most absurd place I ever lived in'.[62] The grandeur of the place and the people, the curious way of squirearchical life, the liveried flunkeys and constant rounds of dinners and visitors amused him, but also so disrupted his routine that he could not sleep. He was also expected, he realised, to provide entertainment as a great literary figure; but since he liked nothing more than having a select post-prandial audience to whom to deliver monologues about the loathsomeness of modern life, that was not too distressing for him.

He was out of London as the reviews of *Heroes* started to appear, including one in the *Weekly Dispatch* that said: 'Mr Carlyle is the very worst lecturer and writer in the English language amongst men, at least, who pretend to any station in literary society.'[63] Other reviews were good, and Jane felt the *Dispatch*'s so absurd that she hardly wanted her husband to bother to read it. Since he was staying in a high Tory household and the *Dispatch* was a paper of foaming radicals, she sent it to him under plain cover. He read it out loud at the breakfast table when it arrived, to gales of laughter, though Milnes's aged aunts (who had clearly not got the measure of Carlyle) felt it most heartless of Jane to send it. *The Spectator* said Carlyle was 'distinguished by great homeliness, and great earnestness',[64] which he would have taken as the highest compliment, and praised his 'half rustic, half Germanic' style as 'provocative to reflection'.

After ten days, which Carlyle grudgingly enjoyed, he headed off to Leeds to visit his friends the Marshalls. Though he claimed he would rather dig ditches than have to live permanently at the pitch of the Milneses he was not reluctant to pay another visit, and was minded the following winter to spend a week fox-hunting with Lord and Lady Galway, Milnes's brother-in-law and sister. At Leeds he felt more comfortable, surrounded as by the fruits of labour rather than those of inherited wealth. He had then planned to return to London, but on an impulse, not quite knowing what to do next, went instead to Liverpool and by steamer to Ecclefechan, to stay with Alick. Unknown to him, his mother had been ill for a fortnight, so it was a good time to visit. Jane was not surprised, but not pleased either, that he had gone to Annandale. She urged him to come home quickly, not least because she feared it would undermine his health. However, she confessed to Sterling that his neurotics before he went away with Milnes had actually made her enjoy the rest for the four weeks he was away.

In early May he went back to Liverpool on the steamer, and thence to London by train. He had thought of going across country to Newcastle to visit Harriet Martineau, and sailing from there to London; but his letter inviting himself to see Harriet was much delayed, and her agreement did not reach him until he was about to leave on the boat south. When he reached home the doubts about what use he would make of his Cromwell studies returned, and he knew almost upon returning that he could not spend the summer in Chelsea. A large present of fine books from Varnhagen von Ense cheered him up, but he was slow to improve. He could hardly bring himself to go into London, but instead took his daily walk westwards, into the fields past Fulham. Jack was at Kingston-upon-Thames, and came to dine with the Carlyles every Sunday. There was political ferment as the Whig administration of Melbourne attempted to ameliorate the Corn Laws; the process that would lead first to a general election, and then to the premiership of Peel later that summer, had begun. Carlyle, while wanting to write history, was feeling seduced by the idea of himself as prophet – pursuing that same 'vaticination' he had derided a decade before. 'Is not *Prophecy* the grand thing?' he asked Sterling, hoping for an affirmative answer.[65]

Browning sent him his new *Sordello* and *Pippa Passes*, which Carlyle praised lavishly, urging Browning to persist with a poetic career. They, and a book on Luther, were refreshing alternatives to his Cromwellian diet. As he limped on with that reading he tried to find somewhere for a summer retreat. To avoid even this minor difficulty he thought of buying a house in the country and moving permanently from Chelsea, and to this end went out to explore Epping Forest. That came to nothing; and Alick tried to secure them a short let of Newington Lodge near Annan. So anxious was Carlyle to leave London that before Alick had done the deal he left, on 30 June, to go north. Jane, who preferred London, stayed until Carlyle had secured them a holiday home. Having visited Harriet Martineau, who found Carlyle in the best of spirits, at Newcastle, he put up at Scotsbrig while looking for somewhere to rent. Newington Lodge he did not like, preferring instead a furnished cottage on the Dumfriesshire coast at Newby. With Jane's approval he formally hired it, with a lease until 26 August. On 16 July Jane went by train to Liverpool, to see her family before catching the Annan steamer.

Carlyle, though on holiday, was still concerned about his next work. Napier wrote to solicit a piece for the *Edinburgh Review*. Carlyle pondered an article on French poetic literature, but wrote back to Napier saying that he could not do it. The good spirits Harriet Martineau detected persisted. 'I live in a silence unequalled for many years,' he wrote to Jane at Liverpool. 'I grow daily better, am really very considerably recovered now.'[66] On 20 July he met her and her maid off the steamer, and they went to Templand to see her mother, driving forty miles in the rain in an open gig. Jane was already ill from lack of sleep, and the problem was scarcely solved by this trek. 'My mother cried at the sight of me,' she wrote to John Forster. Carlyle could not sleep at Templand either, because the bed was six inches too short. So he rose at dawn – just after three o'clock – and went on ahead to Newby via Scotsbrig, where Jane joined him on the 26th.

IV

The holiday was not a success. Carlyle at once had a bilious attack, and the weather was wet and windy. He did a little writing, a preface for an English edition of Emerson's essays, returning the compliment to a man who had done more than any other to secure success for Carlyle. There were excursions to and visits from his family, and the opportunity to bathe in the sea most days. When the month was up they went briefly to Scotsbrig; then Jane went to her mother, while Carlyle (to Jane's irritation) went via Scotsbrig to spend a week at Keswick with Thomas Spedding, a Cumberland landowner who had visited the Carlyles in London in 1838. Once away from Newby, Jane described it to Fanny Wedgwood as 'that grotesque location', and hoped 'never to have to look upon its like again! never!'[67] Carlyle felt the same.

Carlyle restored his spirits at Keswick, thanks to better sleep and much exercise, riding about the fells with Spedding. After a week he returned to Scotsbrig. On 13 September Jane came over from Templand, and three days later they went by train from Carlisle to Newcastle, where they saw Harriet Martineau, before travelling south again. Taking a coach from Newcastle to Darlington they picked up a railway, and went down overnight through York to London. They had been away more than two and a half months, and Carlyle computed the expedition had cost them £70, leaving him £145 in the bank. He felt his health and temper to be only a little improved by it. But at least, among the pile of books that awaited him, were some that would help him forward again. A new edition, by David Laing, of Baillie's *Letters and Journals*, which he had been longing for, had come in his absence. He was motivated – not least by financial concerns – to write an article on them for the *London and Westminster Review*.

But otherwise, he found it no easier to address his next big work. He still had not settled the question of form, not least because he still had not mastered his material. Fraser died within days of Carlyle's return from the north, so even when he had settled on what the work on Cromwell would be he would need to find a man to publish it. One of the many reasons why Carlyle could not apply himself was the spectacle of England declining into another winter of freezing starvation and unrest. He wrote to James Marshall at the end of October of the need for a new radicalism, unlike the 'black, Atheistic, unsympathising radicalism'[68] which he sensed was coming to an end, to take on the Tory government. He suggested a new review ought to be founded to pursue these aims, which Carlyle, by chance, was available to edit, if Marshall wanted to put up the money. When Marshall showed an interest, Carlyle seemed shocked. He felt it a 'grave matter' which required more thought.[69]

For weeks he saw nobody, and so had plenty of time for thought. He gave orders to Jane that no one, including her, was to bother him before two o'clock any day. It distressed him when he emerged from this self-inflicted isolation one afternoon to find that Browning had come all the way to Chelsea, but had not been admitted; so he was shamed into a relaxation of his regime, and Browning came to dine with him and Jane on 29 December. 'It is absolutely indispensable for me to be a good-deal alone, with my own ugly self,' he told Milnes in November, shortly before declining an invitation for them to pass part of the winter at Fryston.[70] Carlyle's introspection and obsessions were becoming increasingly painful for his wife. 'My husband is writing an article with such a vengeance that I hardly get twenty words of him thro'out the day,' she told her sister-in-law, Isabella.[71] 'It is a wonder he has not put himself off sleeping with it.' As the editors of the *Collected Letters* note, she also wrote to Geraldine Jewsbury at this time (in a letter destroyed after her death by Geraldine, on Jane's orders) in so depressed a tone that it elicited a reply (which has survived) in which Geraldine assured her: 'You have neither failed nor fallen short in anything you have proposed to yourself ... I love you, my darling, more than I can express, more than I am conscious of myself.'[72]

In November Carlyle finished the piece on Baillie, and it was published just after Christmas in the *London and Westminster Review*. A by-product of his seventeenth-century studies, it reflects his belief that the best history is told simply, with much personal anecdote about events, as he had used in *The French Revolution*. He quotes extensively and approvingly in the piece from Baillie's *Letters and Journals*, but also implicitly reflects the troubles he was having with *Cromwell*: 'Everywhere the student of history has to pass his probation, his apprenticeship; must first, with painful perseverance, read himself into the century studies ... he as yet knows nobody, can yet care for nobody, completely understand nobody. He must read himself into it, we say; make himself at home and acquainted, in that repulsive foreign century.'[73]

For all his isolation, Carlyle was developing an acute political insight. He told Milnes, in December 1841, that:

In late months I have taken up a prophecy, I know not how, which all my radical friends laugh to scorn, That Peel will perhaps try to *abrogate* these insane Corn Laws (if the people do but agitate sufficiently), to institute Emigration-arrangements, Education-arrangements, &c &c; in one word, actually try to *do* something, and *be* in verity a Governor to this country which is fast falling mad and moribund for want of being governed! Truly I will confess, of all the as yet articulate and speaking classes or parties of this Country, Conservatism blind and lazy as it is does embody most of the religion, of the loyalty, humanity and available worth that exists among us. Conservatism, rallied under a truly brave and seeing man, who could understand that great black inevitable fast-swelling tide of Democracy; could *interpret* it, wisely yield to it, wisely resist it, in fact wisely accomplish what of just and right it inarticulately means: were not this a government! You told me once with great seriousness, 'Peel was a man of *real talent*,' a great man. Pray Heaven it prove so. If he be a man of really great talent, it seems clear to me he will endeavour somewhat as I say; – and may be, at such an epoch, the blessedest minister this country ever had.[74]

Five years later Peel fulfilled Carlyle's prophecy, though without receiving the gratitude of his party. Though Carlyle's view of Peel vacillated, and he even at one point thought there might be more hope in Gladstone,[75] Peel was the only senior politician Carlyle ever respected. 'What is the importance of modes of electing,' he wrote later that month to James Marshall, criticising him for his belief in democracy, 'till there be a man here and there worthy of being elected?'[76]

The diversion of 'Baillie the Covenanter' having passed, Carlyle was faced with his main work again. He wrote in his journal on 13 December that 'It is amazing how little I *learn*, read as I may.'[77] A couple of days later a letter came from some students at Edinburgh saying that more than 100 of them wanted to put his name forward for the chair of universal history at the university. The ringleader was Francis Espinasse, who had earlier written to Carlyle (provoking a stimulating reply) enquiring about the secrets of existence, and who would later become a part of Carlyle's circle.[78] Carlyle quickly decided against pursuing this idea. 'Ten years ago such an invitation might have been decisive of much for me; but it is too late now,' he replied.[79] Forster, who had been asked by Chapman and Hall to edit and find new contributors for their recently acquired *Foreign Quarterly Review*, asked Carlyle to write something, but Carlyle refused, suggesting that if he stopped on Cromwell now he might never get started again. In keeping with his anti-Dryasdust views, he realised he needed a better grasp of Cromwell's surroundings. He wrote to ask Browning whether he had Dugdale's book of 1662 on the draining of the Fens, to have an idea how the Huntingdonshire and Cambridgeshire landscape was in Oliver's time; the plan of visiting the Fenland, which was to have unexpected conse-quences for Carlyle's literary output in that it provided the spur for *Past and Present*, was being conceived.

Forster was also to bring Carlyle to Chapman and Hall's attention now that Fraser was dead. Carlyle was beginning to feel the need for someone to consult professionally, to help him make up his mind how to handle Cromwell, and Forster was building up an impressive reputation as a talent-spotter. He was to attract Trollope, Thackeray, Browning, Mrs Gaskell and Kingsley, to name but a few, to Chapman's stable. Early in 1842 Carlyle wrote to the publisher John Murray, with whom he had a slight acquaintance, asking to meet him for advice on his project. Forster's first act was to see whether Chapman's would bring out a second edition of *Heroes*, and he put them in touch with Carlyle. Carlyle was impressed with them, not least because they offered £100 for a second edition when Fraser had given him just £75 for the first. Within a few months a new, and lasting, relationship had been negotiated that was greatly to Carlyle's financial advantage; and it would not be the last time that Forster would act as Carlyle's unpaid literary agent.

He tried to start writing about Cromwell in January 1842, but it came to nothing. 'It was too soon yet,' he told his mother.[80] 'My studies in the Civil War threaten to be bottomless,' he told Sterling.[81] 'The character of O. Crl comes before me clearer and clearer, as of a great man, almost of a kind of god: but the means of representing it?' Most of what he wrote was burnt, and he saw few people in whom he could confide about his problems, or with whom he could seek distraction from them. He made a rare trip out on 29 January with Jack to the home of Baron Bunsen, the Prussian ambassador, where (along with Archdeacon Hare and Dr Arnold) he was presented to King Frederick William IV of Prussia, in London for the christening of Prince Albert Edward, the future Edward VII.

Although the winter was not so harsh as its predecessor, Carlyle noted that palings from garden fences in Chelsea were being stolen to provide fuel; and he himself realised that he was worse off than he had thought, and that there were now economic reasons to press on with Cromwell, even if the intellectual arguments were not all they could be. In February what peace they had at Cheyne Row was shattered by their neighbour's buying a cockerel, which decided to screech all night. The Carlyles, not good sleepers at the best of times, were kept permanently awake. Jane lay in her bed in the room below Carlyle, dreading that she would hear him get up in the night, woken by the bird, because she knew that would put him in a foul humour for the day ahead.

They wrote to the woman who owned the cockerel, but she would not even open the letter. 'I would give them guineas for quiet,' Jane wrote to her mother, 'but they prefer tormenting us. In the law there is no resource in such cases. They may keep wild beasts in their back yard if they choose to do so. Carlyle swears he will shoot them, and orders me to borrow Mazzini's gun.'[82] However, crowing cocks, Carlyle's despair with his book, his difficulties in wrestling with Fraser's estate to regain control of his writings so that they could be passed to Chapman and Hall, and the irritation for him of Jane having her customary winter cough and cold were quickly put into perspective by a far more shattering event.

V

On 25 February 1842 Jane's mother had a stroke. Her doctor wrote immediately to the Carlyles, but the letter was not received until Monday 28th. Mrs Welsh died at 10 p.m. on the day of her stroke, aged fifty-nine. There had been hints her health was fading, but no indication her life was in danger. Hearing of the illness, Jane took a mail train from Euston to Liverpool overnight on 28 February; she arrived at her cousin's to learn that her mother was dead. Carlyle also received this news on the Tuesday, and, having written to Jane first, made for Liverpool after a curious delay of two days. Waiting to see whether she sent for him, he was thrown into utter confusion about what he should do. When he went, it was on his own initiative, and only after he had finished the second edition of *Heroes* for the printer. He found his wife paralysed with grief. In his letter he had told her: 'Weep, my Darling, for it is altogether sad and stern; the consummation of sorrows; the greatest, as I hope, that awaits thee in this world. I join my tears with thine: I cry from the bottom of my *dumb* heart.'[83]

Carlyle had never seen Jane in such a state, and was shocked out of his usual self-obsessiveness; most of the unhappiness she had felt before had not been shared with him. She was in no state to travel anywhere. Carlyle left her in Liverpool, and went by mail coach to Carlisle, and thence to Templand, where he arrived at noon on the Saturday, eight days after his mother-in-law's death. It had been his aim to attend the funeral, which he had guessed would be on that day, but he was too late. His brother James had attended, and Carlyle sent Jane a list of the other mourners. He then started going through Grace Welsh's papers, and prepared to settle her affairs. He had no news from Jane, but reports from her cousins that she was gaining strength; for once aware of his obligations to her, he wrote to Jane almost daily while at Templand, trying to console her, but also to report on the ordering of her mother's estate.

He proved, for the first few months, a good husband to her in her grief. But by the following December Jane was writing to her cousin Jeannie that Carlyle was wont to 'lecture' her when she became sad about her mother, 'which shuts up all my sorrow in my own heart for weeks after'.[84] He wrote to Sterling and Forster, urging them to write to Jane to cheer her up, and prepared to stay at Templand well into April, to ensure the property was let out and the furniture disposed of. It was agreed that once Jane was well enough she and her cousin Jeannie would return to Chelsea, where Jeannie would nurse her back to health.

Jane's letters to Carlyle at this time have not survived, though he recalled 'their tone of mournful tenderness'.[85] The earliest in the *Collected Letters* after her bereavement is dated 23 March, to Forster, and shows Jane still struck down with a sentimental mournfulness of the sort that had scarred her for years after the death of her father. Forster had been to Chelsea to see her on her first day back, but she had given orders that no one was to be admitted. Yet she wrote to Forster, hearing he had called at Cheyne Row to see her, saying that, had she foreseen that he might have come, she would have wanted to see him 'because you once gave her a little pleasure – you took her to the play do you remember and she was so pleased with her evening – and so pleased with you.'[86]

Although Carlyle welcomed the solitude his stay at Templand afforded, he was perplexed by the financial matters he had to sort out, particularly in view of the legacy tax, of which he had never heard. He saw much of his own family, and found time to think of other matters, such as assisting in Milnes's campaign to secure a state pension for Robert Burns's aged sister, and writing to Dickens about the question of copyright and the need for it to apply internationally. Although Carlyle had been lucky to find a legitimate American publisher, Dickens's books were being pirated there. But his main concern was finding a tenant for Templand, and worrying about what he rightly detected was his wife's poor health and spirits. He did not help by suggesting that much of the furniture at Templand could be sent to Craigenputtock, to save the bother of selling it, just in case the Carlyles ever wanted to go back there. Jane was horrified at the thought of ever having to set eyes on the place again, and wrote forcefully to tell Carlyle so.

The unwanted effects of his mother-in-law were not auctioned until mid-April, after which Carlyle went to Scotsbrig. He did no serious work during his two months' absence from London; all his Cromwell books were in Chelsea. As his stay in Scotland drew to a close, black doubts returned. Writing to Jane on 19 April 1842 he said that 'Cromwell sometimes rises upon me here; but as a thing lost in abysses; a thing sunk beyond the horizon, and only throwing up a sad twilight of remembrance!'[87] He claimed he was minded to pack up the books Forster had lent him, when he returned to London, send them back, and abandon the project. However, he knew he had to do it, though no longer for economic reasons. Mrs Welsh's death had left the Carlyles relatively financially independent, because of Jane's inheritance. Later, he recalled: 'We were a little richer, easier in circumstances; and the *pinch* of Poverty, which had been relaxing latterly, changed itself into a gentle *pressure* . . . the grim collar round my neck was sensibly slackened.'[88]

It was the first week of May before Carlyle was able to take the steamer south. He broke his journey at Liverpool, where he saw Jane's uncle and cousins, and then at Manchester, where he saw Geraldine Jewsbury, who had been showering Jane with letters of affection since Mrs Welsh's death. He was depressed by the lack of smoke in Manchester, for he knew it signified lack of work and potential unrest. His fears were compounded when, not long after he returned to London, a youth tried to shoot the Queen in her carriage on Constitution Hill. Writing to his mother of that incident he noted that 'this young blackguard, it seems, is *not* mad at all; was in great want, and so forth; it is said they will hang him. Such facts indicate that even among the lowest classes of the people, Queenship and Kingship are fast growing out of date.'[89]

From Manchester he took a train to Rugby, taking up an invitation to visit Dr Arnold. He dined and stayed the night, and then with Arnold and two schoolboys went on an expedition to Naseby field, scene of Cromwell's and Fairfax's slaughtering of the royalist army under Prince Rupert in 1645, for which Carlyle, in stopping at Rugby, had made 'a desperate effort of consciencious [*sic*] martyrdom.'[90] However, his visit was not too uncongenial, for as he left he told Arnold he hoped the school would 'long continue to be what was to him one of the rarest sights in the world – a temple of industrious peace'.[91] Six weeks later, on the day before his forty-seventh birthday, Arnold died of heart failure. Recalling to Spedding his visit to Naseby ('equal to Marathon or better'),[92] Carlyle admitted that 'I pray daily for a new Oliver.' He began to see it as his mission to help people see the power of the old Oliver, that they might want another such able man to govern them. His view that, as yet, he had no way of doing so deepened his despair.

Carlyle reached Chelsea on the evening of his visit to Naseby, 7 May 1842. He found Jane 'thinner and paler than I ever saw her before',[93] though she protested she was feeling better. He set about the tasks that had been interrupted two and a half months earlier. The first was to meet William Hall, of Chapman and Hall, and settle his future arrangements with that firm. Forster had looked after him well, and £400 was paid to him immediately in return for the copyrights on earlier works. Then he went back to Cromwell. Having been absent for so long, and knowing work was his only salvation, he had to accept that there could be no long escape from the hated summer heat of London this year. Against this discomfort, he rigged himself up a shower-bath, in those days an astonishing and precarious mechanical contraption.

That spring Caroline Fox visited the Carlyles regularly, and left accounts of Carlyle's opinions at an interesting stage in their development. She claimed, for example, to find him opposed to capital punishment, a view which, if accurately reflected, was to change within a year, by the time of the essay on Dr Francia, the hangman of Paraguay.[94] His other reactionary views were being shaped. He went to the House of Commons on 15 June, hoping to hear Charles Buller speak in a debate on patronage in the Church of Scotland, but the debate was ruled out of order. This rare sight of the 'National Palaver' did not impress him, though he thought Peel 'a clever looking man'.[95] On a trip to Hampton Court with Sterling Carlyle was miserable, finding fault with everything, and Sterling set about trying to convince him that the world was not so black as he saw it. 'Woe to them that are at ease in Zion,' replied Carlyle, neatly fitting the prophet's clothes.[96] In July he went to a meeting of the Anti-Corn Law League, and continued to fret about misgovernment as another attempt was made on the Queen's life by a youth. He tried to go out only in the evenings for his exercise, that way avoiding the worst of the heat. But, partly as Jane and he were still in mourning, and partly because of his preoccupations with Cromwell, he saw hardly anyone. He told Emerson that Cromwell was 'like to drive me mad', because the idea of him was 'sunk under two hundred years of Cant, Oblivion, Unbelief and Triviality of every kind' from which Carlyle could not find the means to raise him.[97] He confessed to Emerson that he was still likely to abandon the project; his mood was swinging one way, and then the other, from one week to the next.

Jane lamented in July, as her birthday approached, that there would be no gifts for her this year, as her mother had always remembered but Carlyle never marked the occasion. To her shock he gave her a bottle of scent, 'the first thing of the kind he ever gave me in his life', she told her cousin Maggie. 'In *great* matters he is always kind and considerate, but all these *little* attentions which we women attach so much importance to he was never in the habit of rendering to anyone.'[98] She was touched by his 'desire to replace to me the irreplaceable'; he never forgot her birthday again.

VI

Carlyle did leave Chelsea that summer after all. From mid-August to mid-September Jane went to stay at Troston, near Bury St Edmunds in Suffolk, where Charles Buller's brother Reginald was rector. Shortly before she went Carlyle, on an impulse, accepted an invitation from Stephen Spring Rice, a Commissioner of Customs and younger brother of Thomas, to sail on an admiralty yacht from Margate to Ostend, thence to explore Belgium. He wrote an account of his trip, which Froude quoted, but which was not published until 1922. The party dined while the ship lay at anchor off Margate, and after Carlyle had had a poor night's sleep it sailed across the Channel and along the French coast, reaching Ostend at ten in the evening. He swam from a bathing-machine the next day, and thinking he was on an all-male beach did not wear a costume. Only when the outraged cries of a woman alerted him did he realise his mistake, and retreated back into his machine.

He went with his friends by train to Bruges, which captivated him, particularly its church architecture. He went to Ghent and admired the cathedral, but found a slum area that reminded him of England. After only four days away they returned, landing at Deptford on 9 August. Jane was still packing for her trip to Suffolk when Carlyle reached Chelsea, and left the next day. As she went a letter arrived from Lady Harriet Baring asking Carlyle to visit her and her husband at their Surrey home, Addiscombe. Carlyle knew he really had to do some work, so refused; but expressed the hope that her letter 'is not the last Note you will ever write to my poor address'.[99]

Jane benefited immediately from her rest. The Bullers – Reginald's parents, who had been Carlyle's employers, were staying there too – made her superlatively welcome, and her spirits rose. Stimulated by kindness and by the eccentricities of the rural world in which Parson Buller lived, she wrote letters to Carlyle of the deepest good humour. He, meanwhile, was repelling the advances of the Inland Revenue. Peel's most recent act of firm government had been to impose an income tax at 7d in the £ – just under three per cent – and Carlyle was being pursued for money. Like most authors before and since, he protested he made no money from writing books.

The civil disobedience he had long expected flared up, riots in Manchester necessitating the movement of troops there by train from London. Other northern towns had similar disturbances, and together they took on the nature of an insurrection. It made Carlyle feel his seventeenth-century work was irrelevant; the passionate and, as he saw them, pointless cries for reform were all that seemed to matter now. He tried to resist the temptation to join Jane at Troston; but by the end of August, having done no useful work, he capitulated, and wrote to Mrs Buller asking whether he could come. He wanted fresh air, and the chance to explore new countryside; but it had also occurred to him that he could hire a horse and ride over to Ely, Huntingdon, and other places associated with Cromwell. He left on 2 September in a 'villainous little saltbox of a coach' on a wet day for Bury, and was met by Jane, whom he found looking better, but still suffering from insomnia. He embarked immediately on explorations, first on foot (getting lost on the way back from Thetford) and then on a borrowed horse. With the horse, before the autumn weather set in, he left again on 6 September for Ely, watching the cathedral rise out of the fen as he rode at dusk through the yellow fields; 'one of the most impressive buildings I have ever in my life seen,'[100] he told Sterling, 'but I recoil everywhere from treating these things as a dilletantism at all; the impressions they give me are too deep and sad to have anything to do with the shape of stones.' It was not a religious feeling that he had, but a feeling gained from standing in a place where Cromwell, in 1643, commanded the Dean 'in a voice still audible to this Editor' to 'leave off your fooling, and come down, Sir!'[101] when he refused to stop holding his choir service.

Carlyle, from what he told Sterling, was engaging in his own form of hero-worship. He visited the house where 'my Friend Oliver dwelt and boiled his kettle some two hundred and two years ago', and sat on Cromwell's horse-block to smoke his pipe. The next day he rode through the flat, dark country-side, which he found tedious, to Huntingdon, Cromwell's birthplace, and St Ives, where he had had a farm, sitting in one of Cromwell's fields to smoke his cigar. It was here that the event occurred that was to detach him from Cromwell and almost fatally break his momentum with the work. As he writes in *Past and Present*:

Passing by the Workhouse of St Ives in Huntingdonshire on a bright day last autumn ... I saw sitting on wooden benches, in front of their Bastille and within their ring-wall and its railings, some half-hundred or more of these men. Tall robust figures, young mostly or of middle age; of honest countenance, many of them thoughtful and even intelligent-looking men. They sat there, near by one another; but in a kind of torpor, especially in a silence, which was very striking. In silence: for, alas, what word was to be said? An Earth all lying round, crying, Come and till me, come and reap me; – yet we here sit enchanted! In the eyes and brows of these men hung the gloomiest expression, not of anger, but of grief and shame and manifold inarticulate distress and weariness; they returned my glance with a glance that seemed to say, 'Do not look at us. We sit enchanted here, we know not why. The Sun shines and the Earth calls; and by the governing Powers and Impotences of this England, we are forbidden to obey. It is impossible, they tell us!' There was something that reminded me of Dante's Hell in the look of all this; and I rode swiftly away.[102]

'With a thunderstorm chasing me on the horizon', as he later recalled, he rode hard to Cambridge.[103] He spent a night there, inspecting Sidney Sussex, Cromwell's college, and then returned to Troston, arriving late on the third day 'drenched with rain but other wise in good condition',[104] as Jane told her cousin Jeannie, who was in Chelsea, minding the house. Reginald Buller was keen for them to stay another fortnight, but Carlyle was all for leaving within days; the ride had stimulated him to press on, so a creative blockage had been cleared. Also, burglars had entered their house in Chelsea, but were surprised by the maid before they could steal anything; so the building had to be made more secure.

The St Ives workhouse haunted him. On his return to Troston he wrote to Thomas Ballantyne, with whom he had been conducting a sporadic correspondence on the 'condition of England question'. 'The general condition of the Farm labourers, though not offensive to the mere cursory eye, is I fear full of misery,' he told him.[105] There was no milk for the people to drink; they lived on bread soaked in hot water mixed with salt and pepper. He felt a deep longing to write again on how the poor needed work. Once home he borrowed from the London Library the *Chronicle of Jocelin de Brakelond*, a medieval monk at the abbey at Bury St Edmunds, which recounted how the feudal structure of society had provided for the needs of the poor in an earlier age. The *Chronicle* had just been republished, and the reading of it absorbed Carlyle throughout the rest of September and October; that book, and the sight of the St Ives poor, had sown the seed of *Past and Present*.

On returning to London in mid-September Carlyle set to work at once. He wrote a long letter to his collaborator on the London Library project, Edward Fitzgerald, the poet and Cambridge contemporary of Milnes, who had just acquired the estate that included Naseby field. Enlisting him as a *de facto* researcher, Carlyle sent him notes on the battle made after his visit there with Thomas Arnold, and gave him a list of further questions he wanted answering. He made similar enquiries to a Scots antiquary, David Laing, about the battle of Dunbar, at which in September 1650 Cromwell inflicted four thousand casualties on the Scots and took ten thousand prisoners, in his efforts to break the covenanters' support for Charles II. Fitzgerald sent Carlyle a plan of the field, and some teeth in a jaw-bone one of his farmhands had dug up near the site; and told of military buttons and other relics, which quite set Carlyle's imagination racing. 'To think,' he wrote back to Fitzgerald, 'that this grinder chewed its breakfast on the 14th of June 1645, and had no more eating to do in the world, or service farther there – till now, to lie in my drawer, and by a horror!'[106] His interest in Cromwell, only weeks earlier waning, blazed again. He wrote to Milnes to ask what he knew of Marston Moor, the battlefield near his Yorkshire home where, in July 1644, the Parliamentary Army had defeated the Royalists for supremacy of the north of England.

But enthusiasm for study would not necessarily be translated into work. Never forgetting how earlier historians had failed properly to represent Cromwell, Carlyle had still not overcome his own doubts. 'Some hundreds of times,' he confided in his journal on 25 October, 'I have felt, and scores of times I have said and written, that *Oliver* is an *impossibility*.'[107] He stuck to his solitude, seeing a little of the Darwins and Thackeray, with whom he had become friends, but otherwise brooding on how to motivate himself, at last, to put his work on Cromwell to some use. He even considered writing a drama in twelve acts as the best way to tell the story.[108] He and Jane had many visitors, but it was only she who received them. During November he started to write sporadically, though much of it ended up in the fire. He made some diversions from history, whether to some of the new German books sent him by von Ense, or Tennyson's *Poems*, which elicited from him the praise that the poet clearly had 'a real man's heart ... a right valiant, true fighting, victorious heart; strong as a lion's, yet gentle, loving and full of music'.[109] His work, usually conducted between nine and two, now dragged on until three, four or even later, and after that he would walk in silence for an hour or two in the foggy autumn evening. He soon compensated for his longer hours by starting to write later and later in the mornings, a sign that interest was wearing off once more. Jane started to complain to her friends and family of Carlyle's neglect, acts of thoughtlessness like his not buying her a comfortable chair for the winter adding up until her resentment could not be suppressed.

Judging from a letter to his former patroness Jane Wilson on 9 December 1842, he seems by then to have decided a biography of Cromwell would not do. 'The means of ever in this world bringing him rightly before another heart remains invisible, impossible. There is no use writing another dreary vacuity of a "History of Cromwell".'[110] His antipathy was extreme, and by Christmas he had effectively written off the work of the last two years, and was working on another project altogether. He asked Jane to look at Jocelin de Brakelond's *Chronicle*, and see what she thought of it as a basis for a work he was beginning. The writing of *Past and Present* had started.

VII

'My own health keeps good; better than it used to do,' Carlyle wrote to his mother on 6 January 1843. 'I am fast getting ready something for publication too, – tho' it is not *Cromwell* yet; it is something more immediately acceptable to the times in hand.'[111] From the complaints he made about this composition he was finding it no easier than he had found the aborted drafts of *Cromwell*; but at least Carlyle was genuinely inspired about *Past and Present*, whereas the inspiration about Cromwell – to rehabilitate the Lord Protector in the eyes of the contemporary public and to convince them that he had been a moral giant – seemed exhausted by Carlyle's attempt to do just that three years earlier, in the lectures on *Heroes*.

However, he was soon writing at a furious pace, and told Jane the book would be ready for publishing in the spring – as indeed it was. A representative from Chapman and Hall called at Chelsea in early January to discuss the terms of publication, which were to be £200 for an edition of 2,000. But as Jane sardonically noted, there was time for distractions, namely 'Lady Harriet Baring's love-making to my husband' – she would not find it funny for much longer. In a letter to her cousin, she continued:

Lady Harriet writes to my husband that she is ill – that she dines at four o'clock and is allowed to go nowhere in the evenings – to do nothing but speak – that 'there is nobody – (she may really say almost nobody in the world) she likes so well to speak with as him' – Pray mark the fine truth-giving effect of the modifying parenthesis! – 'So he sees what a work of *charity* and *piety* is cut out for him'! When a handsome, clever and reputedly *most haughty* woman appeals to the *charity* and *piety* of a simple man like Carlyle you may be sure she will not appeal in vain – So he writes to her engaging to visit her on Thursday evening – and *forgets* to tell *me* he has done so.[112]

Jane had an exquisite revenge, however. She and Carlyle were invited for that same Thursday evening to hear a lecture on the Corn Laws by William Fox, and she gave her spare ticket to Mazzini, one of her friends for whom Carlyle did not have a high regard. Jane detected no sexual motivation in Carlyle's response to the future Lady Ashburton. Later in the same letter to Jeannie Welsh, she referred to a suggestion by Carlyle that she should invite Geraldine Jewsbury to stay with them, mainly to keep Jane company while Carlyle was busy with *Past and Present*. Jane had doubts, because she found Geraldine's state of permanent over-emotionalism exhausting and embarrassing. But she did not question Carlyle's motivation in wanting in his house this attractive woman of thirty of whom he was palpably fond – 'I have not only his habit of preference for me over all other women (and habits are much stronger in him than passions) but also his indifference to *all* women *as women* to secure me against jealousy.'[113] Jane instructed Jeannie to burn the letter, an instruction she disregarded. Such sentiments do nothing to suppress the Jewsbury-Froude speculation about Carlyle's sexuality, or lack of it, and the real reasons for the discontent in his and Jane's marriage. Jane was lonely, and so asked Geraldine to come for two or three weeks – taking care not to tell her the idea was Carlyle's, for that would have gone straight to her head.

For all his complaining, Carlyle was finding his new task easier than almost any other he had attempted. It was a mild winter, so his health and Jane's had stood up better than usual, though he was afflicted with lumbago; he was now in his forty-eighth year. 'It goes rather in a fiery strain, about the present condition of men in general, and the strange pass they are coming to,' he told his mother about his book on 20 January.[114] 'And, I calculate, it may awaken here and there a slumbering blockhead to rub his eyes and consider what he is about in God's Creation.' He admitted to his mother that he simply could not have continued with *Oliver* until he had spoken out on the condition of England question again; although how far he had convinced himself of this as a euphemism for failing to find a suitable form of book to write on Cromwell, we can only guess. The more he wrote of *Past and Present* the more his spirits rose, though he was not planning an immediate return to *Oliver* even after finishing this new work; the life of the late dictator of Paraguay, Dr Francia, had recently come to his attention, and with *Past and Present* not half written he was already seeking books on that subject, as a possible future project for Forster's *Foreign Quarterly Review.*

It is rare to find any enthusiasm by Carlyle for a work that he is composing; but *Past and Present* was different. 'The time is come for it, I think,' he told his mother on 28 January. 'When men are dying round you of want of bread, and two millions of them sitting in workhouses or living otherwise on Parish Alms, and the Governors busy only with their partridge-shooting, I think one ought to speak.'[115] In letters he leaked out parts of his new thinking. 'A real Aristocracy,' he told James Marshall, 'in place of a false imaginary Aristocracy, is becoming and already become indispensable for English Society, – and the Captains of Industry, not the Captains of Idleness whatever array and honours they may for the present hold, are the men for that.'[116] He wanted 'not Arms and the man' but 'Tools and the man', that England should work its way back to salvation. He exhorted Marshall, a Captain of Industry, to be such a guide to his employees, and not to be afraid of setting an example. 'All good fellows I have ever heard of were oftentimes in that same "minority of *one*",' Carlyle told him. 'They stood there, worked there, and it gradually became a minority of *two*, of many; gradually a *majority*, and at length a *universality!*'[117] Carlyle added in 'dead secret' that his book developed these thoughts, and he thought of calling it 'Past and Present'. It would be 'A "Tract for the Times" full of the most portentous Speculative-radicalism ever uttered in Governess English, or even in *Carlylese* as they call it!'[118] The spectacle of the starving poor was still on London's streets; and, closer to home, Alick had finally given up trying to make a living on the land in Ecclefechan, and asked Carlyle to find out for him how best to emigrate to North America.

On 22 February, after just two months of relentless industry, Carlyle was able to send the first part of his new work to the printer; another fortnight saw it finished. Writing to Sterling, he said he had been motivated by the spectre of the unemployed in their 'Poor Law Bastilles' seeming 'to ask of every English soul, "Hast thou no word to say for us?" '[119] He characterised the work as 'moral, political, historical' and added: 'It was John Sterling, I think, that first told me my nature was political; it is strange enough how, beyond expectation, that oracle is verifying itself.' Jane was longing for him to finish, not least because by this stage Geraldine had already spent 'three most uncomfortable weeks'[120] at Cheyne Row and Jane was desperate to have more of her husband's attention, that Geraldine's reasons for staying might be reduced. Carlyle took to shutting himself away not just in the mornings but also in the evenings while Geraldine was there; Jane found Geraldine's speech so 'insincere'[121] that she could hardly bear to converse with her; so Geraldine spent most of her evenings asleep on the sofa while Jane sat in grim silence.

But as he drew to the end of his work Carlyle simply wanted to get out and have some exercise. He took himself off for a day-long walk to Croydon and back, a round trip of more than twenty miles. Ironically, he was not keen to see Jane other than at meal-times while Geraldine, whom he had had the idea of inviting to stay, was in the house. He finished *Past and Present* on 8 March, by which time he was feeling shattered, and relaxed by going the next day to the House of Lords to hear Wellington speak in a debate on India, and then to sit for John Linnell, who painted his portrait. Geraldine took the hint, and left three days later. Jane was the first to admit she had been far from an ideal hostess, having been disobliging to Geraldine from the start; but she joked that Carlyle, the night Geraldine left, commented to her 'what a blessing it is to be able to sit here in peace without having that dreadful young woman *gazing* at me!'[122]

By the middle of April the proof-reading of *Past and Present* was complete. In an effort to stop pirates profiting from his work in America, Carlyle had the manuscript copied in haste and sent out on a steamer to Boston, where Emerson could arrange for its legitimate publication. Carlyle had a finished copy sent to him on 20 April, and told Chapman and Hall it looked 'very beautiful'.[123] He arranged for his two editor friends, Thomas Ballantyne of the *Manchester Guardian* and Thomas Aird of the *Dumfries Courier*, to be sent review copies at once. To have completed the work so quickly, and to feel as contented about it as Carlyle did, was a great achievement. Yet hanging over it all was the unfinished business of *Cromwell*, not abandoned, but postponed.

10

Oliver:

'Last Glimpse of the Godlike'

1843–45

DESPITE ITS EXCESSES of rhetoric and its prolixities, *Past and Present* is a masterpiece that shows Carlyle at his creative peak. It contains some originality of thought and much originality of form; it is a consummation of the diverse practical and spiritual ideas of both *Chartism* and *Heroes*. It is in a way the last wholly rational development of Carlyle's political philosophy. In his next political work, the *Latter-Day Pamphlets*, the only developments visible are those of emotion rather than of intellect. What *Past and Present* lacks in harshness it makes up for in sentimentality, however. Carlyle's idealised picture of medieval life is, to say the least, one-dimensional, but it is a tribute to his powers of expression that so many readers found it so convincing.

Much of what he has to say about the creation of a Knoxian theocracy, coupled with schemes to find work for the poor, is familiar. What gives this work its force, though, is his use of history to tell the story. Having, in the first of its four books, outlined the problems facing an England without proper – that is, divinely inspired – leadership, he uses the second book to show what government inspired by God can achieve. Drawing on Jocelin de Brakelond, he tells how an ordinary monk, from a humble background, was chosen by the Abbey of St Edmundsbury at the end of the twelfth century as its Abbot; and how by force of will, and reliance on spiritual truth, Abbot Samson stood up to all challenges to his authority, offered to him by everyone from his fellow monks right up to Richard the Lionheart himself. Samson governed with recourse to God, not the Corn Laws. This may be a merely microcosmic example of what Carlyle wanted for England, but his use of history is so persuasive that such practical considerations are pushed aside. However anachronistic and unpractical much of the thought of this work may be, it is remarkable still for the brilliance with which Carlyle, adhering to anti-Dryasdust principles, tells the story of this fragment of medieval life.

In the third book Carlyle depicts the moral shortcomings of contemporary England, showing how far the spirit of the country is from the moral ideal outlined in the first book, or the practical application of it detailed in the second. The fourth and final book, 'Horoscope', looks forward to how England might develop. It is Carlyle's personal manifesto, presenting ideas for helping the poor of which we have already heard; but a note of desperation can be detected in the text. Carlyle has washed his hands of the landed aristocracy, still interested only in shooting their partridges, and is relying on Captains of Industry, the aristocracy of labour, to provide work and, as such, take over the feudal role of the landed classes. When, at the very end, he draws a parallel with the Duke of Weimar's patronage of Goethe, Schiller and others, it is with no real hope of the English aristocracy following suit. Lord Ashley, the social reformer, is the only member of that class whom Carlyle can bring himself to identify as behaving in a manner appropriate to his position. There is never any hint that Carlyle has faith in state machinery to carry out the necessary reform; he was never a socialist. It would be up to individuals to achieve it, a point he would develop further in *Oliver*, where it would become clear that one individual in particular was needed – the strong man – to change England for the better.

Past and Present is replete with satire, vivid characterisation and much cynicism. 'The Heroic, *independent* of bed and board, is found in Drury-Lane Theatre only,' says Carlyle, solemnly. 'To avoid disappointments, let us bear this in mind.'[1] To illustrate the cash-obsessed modern businessman ('a Hell in England – the Hell of not making money')[2] Carlyle invents Plugson of Undershot; to characterise the self-interested, atheistical, aimless politician incapable of governing according to the needs of his people, he creates Sir Jabesh Windbag. Perhaps most entertaining is the non-partisan attack Carlyle launches on parliamentarians: 'Windbag, weak in the faith of a God, which he believes only at Church on Sundays, if even then; strong only in the faith that Paragraphs and Plausibilities bring votes; that Force of Public Opinion, as he calls it, is the primal Necessity of Things, and highest God we have.'[3] Whatever else may be said of this work, there is nothing anachronistic or idealistic about such writing.

The message of the book is of the nobility, and God-given necessity, of work. Carlyle holds up England, still then standing on medieval foundations of a King in parliament and a feudal system stretching down from him, as an example of what divinely inspired heroes can create if allowed to do so. There is a sub-text about the importance of confronting problems in order to solve them, rather than pursuing compromise: 'Double, double toil and trouble; that is the life of all governors that really govern; not the spoil of victory, only the glorious toil of battle can be theirs.'[4] This cannot be achieved with 'democracy, which means despair of finding any Heroes to govern you',[5] but rather 'despotism is essential in most enterprises.'[6] Carlyle advises, however:

Make your Despotism just. Rigorous as Destiny; but just too, as Destiny and its Laws. The Laws of God: all men obey these, and have no 'Freedom' at all but in obeying them. The way is already known, part of the way; – and courage and some qualities are needed for walking on it!

The only liberty worth having is the liberty to work, of securing 'a fair day's wages for a fair day's work';[7] other liberties would be protected because the leaders, or despots, would always remain the servants of God, who would hold them to account. Carlyle did not bother with economics. Those who had resources, whether landed or enriched by the industrial revolution, had an obligation to provide work with that money; it was everyone's responsibility. This proto-socialism sits uneasily with Carlyle's current reputation, but it – almost Saint-Simonian in its force – yells out of the pages of *Past and Present*. Just as the Abbot of St Edmundsbury emerged as leader because he was the best fitted to lead, and just as he, with much effort and grief, provided for all in his charge, so should a modern governor. Necessary for this was the rediscovery of God after 'these last two centuries of Atheistic Government';[8] then a government could proceed not on the greatest happiness principle – a liberal doctrine abhorred by Carlyle for its associations with atheism, and one of the causes of his growing estrangement from Mill – but on the 'Greatest-Nobleness Principle'.[9] Happiness was neither here nor there: 'Our highest religion is named the "Worship of Sorrow".'[10] As in earlier writings, he attacks the economic imperative for its effect on human loyalties and faith: 'We have profoundly forgotten everywhere that cash-payment is not the sole relation of human beings; we think, nothing doubting, that it absolves and liquidates all engagements of man.'[11]

'Might is right' is explicitly raised. In his second chapter, Carlyle claims that all the 'confusion' he detected in the world would, thanks to 'the Maker's first Plan of the World', arrive ultimately at a 'centre of right and nobleness'.[12] He then argues:

Await the issue. In all battles, if you await the issue, each fighter has prospered according to his right. His right and his might, at the close of the account, were one and the same. He has fought with all his might, and in exact proportion to all his right he has prevailed. His very death is no victory over him. He dies indeed; but his work lives, very truly lives. A heroic Wallace, quartered on the scaffold, cannot hinder that his Scotland become, one day, a part of England: but it does hinder that it become, on tyrannous unfair terms, a part of it; commands still, as with a god's voice, from his old Valhalla and Temple of the Brave, that there be a just real union as of brother and of brother, not a false and merely semblant one as of slave and master ... fight on, thou brave true heart, and falter not, through dark fortune and through bright. The cause thou fightest for, so far as it is true, no farther, yet precisely so far, is very sure of victory. The falsehood alone of it will be conquered, will be abolished, as it ought to be: but the truth of it is part of Nature's own Laws, co-operates with the World's eternal Tendencies, and cannot be conquered.

It is clear that he is talking only about the might of those motivated by strictly religious principles; that the principled use of force, even if it do not succeed at first, will ultimately be seen to have succeeded once its principles can be examined objectively. Thus it would be with Cromwell, and with Frederick, the idea becoming more and more strained as Carlyle went on. It is an entirely subjective assessment; Carlyle's own heroes are inevitably (in his view) so underpinned by religious and moral justification in their exercise of 'might' that they inevitably fulfil his criteria of what constitutes 'right'. Wrong, as in the case of Wallace that he cites, may get the better of right, only ultimately to be exposed as fraud. God, he believed, would find a way of rewarding sincerity, honesty and earnestness. All that remained was for Carlyle to convince himself that those qualities occurred in the acts of his heroes. Later on, particularly in *Frederick*, he goes to lengths to justify even the most morally dubious acts of aggression and conquest as 'right', simply because of the hero who perpetrated them.

II

The success of this polemic owed much to the widespread concern for the poor, and for the religious tone of his solution to their plight. This was in keeping with the increasingly moralistic, earnest early 1840s: for all the humour of the work, it has as its superscription *Ernst ist das Leben*, leaving no doubt of the gravity of the problem as seen by the author. The sheer impracticability of much of what Carlyle advocated was no hindrance to his work's success. It can be seen – indeed, from some of his own cynicism, one might conclude that he had seen this himself – that in being so extreme he had merely set up a bargaining position. The satire in the work also helped its popularity, and it had little of the bitterness that would impede Carlyle's reputation after *Latter-Day Pamphlets*. However, not everyone on Carlyle's side was entranced by his latest work; '*Toujours la même et toujours naive*' was how Milnes saw it, echoing a sentiment of Harriet Martineau's; as a politician, though, Milnes may just have been expressing pique at Carlyle's accurate illustration of politicians' failures.[13]

Although *The Spectator* chided Carlyle for his 'mystical verboseness' it did find the work 'excellent in a high degree'.[14] It took issue with his judgment, singling out his desire for a national teaching service as a scheme for which he offered no plan of execution; and suggested that his link of the twelfth century with the nineteenth might cause 'the critics, whom Mr Carlyle so cordially hates' to 'detect some flaws in the logic'. But it praised the book as literature, especially in the depiction of the past, almost without reservation. *Blackwood's* said, wrongly, that 'this work will have less popularity than its predecessors',[15] feeling it so full of allusions to Carlyle's previous works that most would find it unintelligible. The reviewer also complained that Carlyle thought there was no religious spirit in his own age because he was out of tune with it; which would, no doubt, have prompted Carlyle to observe that it all depended upon what one meant by 'religious'. Emerson, who had an interest to declare, described the work as a 'poem' and an 'Iliad of English woes', and a political tract unparalleled since Milton. To those who viewed Carlyle as a rhapsodist, practicalities were irrelevant; the inspiration of the soul, the preliminary to any practicalities, was what he was about.

The rapid and successful production of *Past and Present* had cheered Carlyle, but did not contribute to greater domestic happiness. He had less time for Jane than Jane thought she merited. Jack was irritating Jane too, because he would insist on staying for great lengths of time with them. Jane, who had realised Jack's main interest in life was money, felt he was selfish, disruptive to her household, and (having left Ogilvy, who had paid him £1,000 a year) showing insufficient interest in finding new work. There was also distress at Alick's imminent departure for Canada, for Carlyle had no hope ever of seeing him again once he sailed. For all Jack's supposed selfishness, he and Carlyle were prepared to put up between them the £500 Alick would need to get started across the Atlantic; and Carlyle, through his London contacts, was able to find people in Canada who would help Alick and his family on arrival. Both Carlyles were saddened, too, because of tragedy affecting John Sterling. His mother, and then his wife, had died within two days of each other in April, and Sterling's own health had been perilous since he burst a blood vessel the previous winter. This atmosphere did not help Carlyle to apply himself properly to his work.

Although he tried to revive his interest in Cromwell, his first work after *Past and Present* was to start reading Norse sagas. His finances having improved but his health having deteriorated, he thought once more of buying a horse. Fitzgerald, in early May, tried to arrange for Carlyle and Spedding to go with him to Naseby, but it took only a bad weather forecast to put Carlyle off the expedition. By mid-May Carlyle was soliciting Forster's help in finding more material on Dr Francia, the history of whose dictatorship in Paraguay was becoming more and more interesting to him, and which would be the basis of an article for Forster's *Foreign Quarterly Review.*

The essay on Francia is one of Carlyle's most significant shorter works. It foreshadows the stern authoritarianism of the era after *Cromwell*, while couching those feelings in a tone of spiteful humour already seen in *Chartism.* Carlyle was attracted to Francia because he was a modern Cromwell (the dictator had died only three years earlier). 'He did hate injustice . . . a rigorous correct man,' writes Carlyle of his new hero.[16] No doubt he also warmed to the dictator because he was 'subject to the terriblest fits of hypochondria, as your adust "men of genius" too frequently are'.[17] In the manner of Cromwell, Francia was 'the deliverer whom the Lord raised up to deliver Paraguay from its enemies',[18] and so alluring to the hero-worshipper that Carlyle writes that 'one would rather wish to know Dr Francia'.[19] To keep alien influences from interfering with his rule of goodness, Francia simply sealed off Paraguay from the outside world. To show his authority, he made frequent use of the gallows. 'The "reign of terror",' Carlyle reflects, 'was properly a reign of rigour.'[20] Those who obeyed their deliverer, and who did not interfere with God's will, had nothing to fear. Above all, Francia believed in the importance of work, the ultimate appeal to Carlyle; and seldom in his writing is there greater relish than when he describes how those who would not work were taken for a stroll under the 'workman's gallows',[21] for a hint of what might happen if they did not improve their attitude. Carlyle's *alter ego*, Professor Sauerteig, is adduced to provide evidence of Francia's rectitude, which was either an act of massive self-delusion by Carlyle or a grand exhibition of his famous sense of humour. There is a sense in this piece of Carlyle being mischievous, though for the most serious of reasons; he had taken to his subject without any of the strains that had made *The French Revolution*, and which were still making *Oliver*, so difficult to compose: as a result, the piece is perhaps the most invigorating history he ever wrote.

While writing 'Dr Francia', Carlyle was much distracted by his more important task of helping Alick with the arrangements for his emigration. From this exertion he developed 'a sort of half-mad appetite for being left alone, in green places, within sound of the sea'[22] and at the beginning of July went off without Jane to Glamorgan, on his first trip through the West Country, to stay with Charles Redwood. His host, a Welsh solicitor who had been corresponding with him since the publication of *Chartism*, was secretary of the Society for the Improvement of the Working Population, and a benefactor to the Carlyles, to whom he would send a Christmas hamper. He had been begging Carlyle to visit him for three years, and at last the invitation was accepted. Jane was delighted to have the opportunity to have Cheyne Row painted and decorated, a task impossible while he was there demanding silence and order. He had set her a budget for the renovations of £10, but she wanted to spend £15. In the interests of preserving what marital harmony there was, she paid the extra out of her own savings.

On his way to Wales Carlyle stayed with Julia Strachey at Clifton, and explored Bristol and the surrounding countryside, which enchanted him. He made a last stop at Chepstow before reaching his host, who marked his arrival with a splendid dish of veal; Carlyle could not stand veal. Gratitude was still not something that came naturally to him. 'The simplicity of my kind hosts verges also a little on the inane,' he told Jane.[23] He told Redwood that what he desired most was silence, so at least Redwood knew where he stood with his guest; and heavy rain at the start of the visit limited any other activities. While Redwood was at his office during the day Carlyle went sea-bathing and rambling; when Redwood was not at his office he, 'kindest and most wearisome of men',[24] was boring Carlyle. Within a week of his visit Llandough, the Redwoods' home, had become 'this Temple of Inanity';[25] worst of all, Redwood did not seem to take offence at his guest's continued antisocial behaviour.

After a stay of less than a fortnight Carlyle moved on. He went first to Carmarthen to spend a few days as the guest of Bishop Thirwall of St David's, whom he had met through Milnes. Then he went back east to Gloucester, where he searched for memorials of the Civil War siege. He took a train to Worcester for similar reasons, inspecting the battlefield there, and told

Fitzgerald that he had met an old man, who acted as his guide, and told him he 'wished to God we had another Oliver, Sir, times is so cruel bad'.[26] He travelled on by Birmingham to Liverpool, where he stayed with Jane's uncle and cousins and met up with Jack. His next plan was to make for Annandale, but first he and Jack had a steamer excursion along the north Welsh coast to Bangor, from where he visited Snowdon, climbing to the summit. After returning to Liverpool he left on the Annan steamer on 4 August, and went to Scotsbrig.

Once there, with an Icelandic grammar for intellectual refreshment, he lapsed into melancholy, and his bowels began to play up. He was, at least, able to indulge his passion for solitude, taking himself off most days for long walks. His mind, to judge from a letter sent to Fitzgerald ten days into his stay at Scotsbrig, was returning to Cromwell. He professed a desire to make the postponed trip to Naseby, and indicated that, while in Scotland, he might even attempt to go to the field at Dunbar. Carlyle visited such sites for research on his book, but it was also indicative of his longing for the past, a fruitless search for a tangible relic of the spirit of those times which, he had decided, were England's most glorious hour. On 1 September he left, at dawn, on the mail coach from Dumfries to Edinburgh; the driver stopped specially at Crawford, that Carlyle could visit his mother-in-law's grave. In Edinburgh he met the antiquarian David Laing, with whom he refreshed his memory about Dunbar. He then went out to Haddington and on the next day, a Sunday, there being no coach to Dunbar, walked to the battlefield and back again, a journey of twenty miles, the way littered with itinerant Irish farm-labourers getting in the harvest. He was pleased to find the field recognisable, 193 years after the event, and felt closer to Oliver as a result.

He went back to Edinburgh, then to see friends in Kirkcaldy, and finally caught a steamer from Dundee to London on 13 September. He had been away from Jane for over two months, and wrote fondly to her just before he came home: 'O Goody, Goody: I have seen many things, but a thing half so good as my Goody, my own Goody?'[27] It was a happy homecoming; Jane was reasonably well, the house was decorated, Alick had written from Canada to tell of his successful voyage and arrival (and of his plan to meet up with his and Carlyle's half-brother, John, who had emigrated some years earlier), and Jack had settled himself in lodgings nearby. Moreover, Carlyle at last felt some motivation to continue with *Oliver*.

III

But within a few days of his return, his old irritations, and some new ones, distracted him. The redecoration – which had included a certain amount of refurnishing – had limited places to store his papers, and he felt cramped. The girl next door, with whom he had earlier quarrels about her piano-playing, once more took up her instrument. A distant cock started crowing in the early morning, provoking Carlyle to tell Jane his bedroom was 'uninhabitable', and wondering whether they might move to the Isle of Wight, where she had been briefly during his absence to visit the now terminally ill Sterling. Alarmed at such apocalyptic talk, Jane had a man rig up some rudimentary soundproofing. She wrote to her sister-in-law Jean that Carlyle was in a state of deep biliousness, but that 'even thro that deteriorating medium ... he could not but be struck with "a certain" admiration at the immensity of needlework I had accomplished in his absence in the shape of chaircovers, sofacovers, windowcurtains &c &c and all the other manifest improvements into which I had put my whole genius and industry and so little money as was hardly to be conceived!'[28] But at the best of times Carlyle was oblivious to good housewifery, and this was not the best of times. To create an environment in which he could work, he shut himself in a small room off his bedroom, eight feet square, overlooking the garden, with a fireplace, to which he would admit no visitors. He fixed a copy of Cromwell's death-mask to the wall, and hoped.

Carlyle had his first approach from an aspiring biographer. A delicate enquiry from Richard Henry Horne wanting help with a biographical essay on Carlyle provoked him to write in his journal on 10 October: 'the world has no business with my Life. The world will never know my Life, if it should write and read a hundred "biographies" of me: the main facts of it are known, and are like to be known, to myself alone of all created men.'[29] To Horne he wrote curtly: 'I regret to answer that it will not in any way suit me to accept the Proposal you honour me with.'[30]

By mid-October he had settled down to reading on the Long Parliament. He also started making enquiries at the Public Record Office for details of the period. He asked Mill to lend him books on Puritanism. But still a form eluded him. 'I must write a Book on Cromwell,' he told Emerson. 'There is no rest for me till I do it.'[31] To Sterling he wrote:

My only consolation is that I am struggling to be the most conservative man in England, or one of the most conservative. If the Past Time, only two centuries back, lie wholly as a torpedo Darkness and Dulness, freezing as with Medusa-glance all souls of men that look on it, where are our foundations gone? If the Past Time cannot become *melodious*, it must be forgotten, as good as annihilated; and we rove like aimless exiles who *have* no ancestors, – whose world began only yesterday! That must be my consolation, such as it is.[32]

By December he was trying to trace Cromwell's ancestry, pausing only to read and enjoy a copy of *A Christmas Carol*, then just published, and sent to him by Dickens; he sent it on, once read, to Jane's uncle John in Liverpool. Not long before Christmas, despite all his good intentions, Carlyle accumulated most of the fruits of his latest surge of activity on Cromwell and burned them on his study fire, while Jane sat downstairs darning his socks. He consoled himself with the thought that, before the first stone of St Petersburg could be laid, 170,000 men had to die completing Peter the Great's scheme to drain the Neva Bog.

'In my whole life,' he wrote to Fitzgerald on 9 January 1844, 'I have found myself in no such hideous situation.'[33] He blamed his failings, as always, on the spirit of the times, and its disregard for the heroism of Cromwell; but knew it was his job to change those perceptions. But, at last, the form was becoming clear. He continued: 'One of the things I have at length got to discern as doable is the gathering of all Oliver's Letters and Speeches, and stringing them together according to the order of time: a series of fixed *rock-summits*, in the infinite ocean of froth, confusion, lies and stupidity, which hitherto constitutes the "History" of Cromwell, as Dryasdust has printed and read it.'

This was not to be easy, but at least it was well defined. It required much editorial and scholarly work. Unlike the modern biographer of Carlyle, the mid-nineteenth-century biographer of Cromwell had no vast, easily accessible stock of letters to go to. Carlyle began to write to Oliver's descendants, to scour museums, and to ask friends such as Laing, Milnes and Fitzgerald to search for original material. Lord Monteagle, who had been involved with Carlyle on the London Library project, was approached to help gain Carlyle access to Cromwell's state papers. For Jane, though, there was no relief; her tribulations were merely an *hors d'oeuvre* for what she would suffer in the near-interminable composition of *Frederick*. She told her cousin Jeannie she was tempted to run away to Liverpool 'for to be here in the present state of Cromwell is almost more than flesh and blood can bear ... Cromwell *must* come to an end or *he* and I will come to an end – and in either case there will be – an end!'[34] Carlyle, writing a couple of days later to his mother and reporting that all was well in Chelsea was, as so often, oblivious to Jane's feelings of neglect, and to her anger at having to put up with his self-centredness. Throughout the winter she suffered from insomnia. One night when she did manage to sleep Carlyle kicked his stone water bottle out of bed in the room above, sending it crashing on the floor and waking her up.

Anna Jameson, who spent a day with the Carlyles at Cheyne Row at the end of January, wrote to Lady Byron that Carlyle had been 'thundering away about Oliver Cromwell – of whom he thinks "as of a man sent from God" – Even his horrible Butcheries in Ireland he called "doing his appointed work" which he "could not but do" – as an instrument of God's Justice'. As well as illustrating Carlyle's developing monologic propensities when faced with any sort of audience, this remark also shows what he was up against in trying to disinter, and then rehabilitate, Cromwell. Mrs Jameson also reported that, at breakfast the next morning, Carlyle launched a strong defence of slavery, described the abolitionist movement as 'twaddle', and all in 'such grandiloquent phrases of Scorn mingled with grim laughter that I stood aghast'.[35] Her empathy with Jane extended to feeling that 'it must be something next worse to being married to Satan himself.'

Carlyle's many requests for letters and other writings of Cromwell soon started to bear fruit. His isolation continued through the winter, Jane regarding it, wretchedly, as her duty to entertain the bores who tried to call on him. Not until March did Carlyle grudgingly admit to a correspondent – his mother – that his hitherto awful work 'goes indeed, or now promises to go, a little better with me'.[36] A month later he went to the lengths of telling her that his writing was 'a little livelier',[37] and reflected on the beauty of the spring and Jane's good health. This rare burst of contentment was tempered by news that Sterling had suffered another haemorrhage, and had almost died. Despite his continued hypochondria, Carlyle's own health was good, though he still hankered after a horse for exercise. He turned down almost all invitations to go out, leaving Jane more and more to accept them on her own. 'I keep out of the way of all men and things, so far as possible, except this one thing,' he wrote to Alick.[38] He confided in his journal on 8 May 1844 that he still wished he had never taken up the task, claiming that 'my heart was never rightly in it; my conscience it rather was that drove me on.'[39] He felt the years catching up with him, though he was still only forty-eight; such reflections, and such trials, make it all the more astonishing that he took on the even greater horrors of *Frederick*.

As his work slowly moved on he relaxed a little, going out in May to a meeting organised by Lord Ashley – later Lord Shaftesbury, the great philanthropist – who was pushing through a bill to limit work to ten hours a day; an 'improvement' Carlyle fully supported. He also went out to the American Embassy; but at other times he felt the pressure of his work so intensely that he could not leave it, and wrote castigating people he really wanted to see for inviting him. He told Milnes: 'Alas, why tempt me to forbidden fruit? I ought not to come. I am in the heart of Chaos, and cannot come!'[40] He greatly regretted his behaviour when he heard that Henry Field, a descendant of Cromwell's, had called at Chelsea one May morning and been refused admittance. He hurriedly asked Field to call again, but this only complicated the problem. Field launched on a protracted correspondence with Carlyle about what exactly it was that Carlyle wanted to know from him. All Carlyle wanted was a copy of a letter from Cromwell that Field had, but could not face going to see him to get it; so he asked Browning, who lived nearby, to try to get the copy for him. 'This Mr Field, Oliver's descendent, seems to be a kind of fool,' he told the poet, encouragingly.[41]

Other materials came in; Carlyle told his sister Jean on 24 May that work was going 'not so badly, everything considered'.[42] The improvement continued despite weather in London – drought and heat – that Carlyle found inimical; but he could see no prospect of escaping for the summer, just as *Oliver* was beginning to gather momentum. He emerged into public life through the letters column of *The Times* on 19 June, writing in outrage at the revelation that his and Jane's friend Mazzini's mail was being opened at the post office on the orders of the Home Secretary, with the details, it was thought, being passed on to the Austrian government. *The Times* had already called this 'unconstitutional, un-English and ungenerous',[43] and Carlyle added that the act was particularly foul given that Mazzini, 'whatever I may think of his practical insight and skill in worldly affairs' was 'a man of sterling veracity, humanity and nobleness of mind, one of those rare men, numerable unfortunately but as units in this world, who are worthy to be called martyr-souls'.[44] Mazzini did not solicit Carlyle to do this; Mazzini was an opponent of the Neapolitan government, which was backed by the man he called in his letter the 'miserable old chimera of a Pope', and Carlyle's own feelings about the Catholic Church might not have been coincidental to his tone; he had certainly never felt that strongly about Jane's friend. The matter blew up into a minor ministerial scandal, with a debate being forced on the question in the House of Commons; Carlyle certainly had an incendiary effect.

At the end of June Jane went to Liverpool, leaving Carlyle to his work, and (best of all from his point of view) himself. Even he felt the need to get out of the house at times, and would stroll in the evenings to call on friends; however, the weekend after Jane left, after much changing of his mind, he went with Charles Buller to Addiscombe to visit the Barings. 'Much better have staid at home,' he wrote to Jane afterwards. 'We were a party of great quality, more lords and elegant my-ladies as thick as blackberries; but, in result, the state of my inner man continued of the same and worse, and, in brief, I found myself awake this morning at four, in *that* biliary predicament, and no prospect of breakfast until 10!'[45] Carlyle's routine was so self-centred, built around hypochondria and his bizarre working habits, that he made a bad guest. His stay at Addiscombe he made as short as he could; his host took no offence, and implored him to return the following Sunday – which he did, though only for lunch. Back home, he found the weather too hot to work effectively, and his books bored him; he would go out in the evenings to smoke cigars with Erasmus Darwin, or chat with Milnes, or simply walk in the twilight. He turned down an invitation to visit Redwood, protesting that work was his only option, otherwise it would take 'a deep bath of twelve months in the Silences and Solitudes, to do me any good'.[46]

However little time he had for Jane when she was with him, Carlyle started to pine for her once she went away. His letters to her are full of jests – his new nickname for her at the time was 'Necessary Evil' – and after three weeks he is begging her to tell him when she is coming home. After an absence of a little under four weeks she was back, and writing to her cousin Jeannie that 'Carlyle looked very pleased to have me back at first but he is already relapsed into his usual indifference.'[47] Refusing an invitation to visit Fitzgerald in Suffolk – Carlyle claimed his conscience would not let him leave his work – he none the less confessed to much progress, at last: 'I am fast gathering Oliver's letters together; have a big sheath [*sic*] of them copied in my own hand, and tolerably elucidated ... the ground grows always a little firmer.'[48] He gave an unidentified Scotchman, who was, he told Fitzgerald, 'near starved' a guinea for copying out the details of an election at Ipswich in 1640, and was thinking of turning this into a review article; which he did the following October, when *Fraser's* published 'An Election to the Long Parliament'.

It soon became apparent that John Sterling, racked with consumption, was deteriorating to a point where recovery was impossible. He had given up hope of surviving; so had his doctor, and so too now had his friends. Carlyle offered to go to the Isle of Wight to see him, but he refused to see anybody. On 11 August Carlyle received a letter from him which he said was 'a few words . . . for Remembrance & Farewell'. Sterling told Carlyle that 'It is all very strange but not one hundredth part so sad as it seems to the standers by.'[49] It was not his last letter to Carlyle; that came a fortnight later. Carlyle was deeply saddened by what he now realised was Sterling's inevitable end. 'My Friend, my brave Sterling!' he wrote to him. 'A right valiant man; very beautiful, very dear to me; whose like I shall not see again in this world!'[50] Sterling called the letter Carlyle sent him 'the noblest and tenderest thing that ever came from human pen', but still could not bear to see him.[51]

IV

Throughout the summer Carlyle was regularly visiting the Barings in Surrey, and in early September, once he had written his article for *Fraser's*, he went to the Ashburton estate near Alresford in Hampshire, the Grange, taking the proofs with him. He stayed about a week, greatly enjoying the silence when he lay in bed at night, the house sitting in 700 acres of parkland; though that did not mean he could sleep. He rode when he could and was careful about his diet, and came close to enjoying himself. Jane was unimpressed by her husband's visit. 'As the Lady Harriet,' she told her cousin Jeannie, 'like the Queen must have her Court about her wherever she goes or stays she has summoned Carlyle down to the Grange for a week.'[52] She added, caustically, that Carlyle '*never* by any chance refuses a wish of *hers*'. There were other attractions. Charles Buller was also staying, and Carlyle was charmed by old Lord Ashburton, Lady Harriet's father-in-law. One cannot tell how far Carlyle was susceptible to the sexual attraction of women; but he himself described Lady Harriet as 'far from regularly *beautiful*'.[53]

On 19 September he returned home, pleased to find Jane had undertaken some small renovations in his absence to brighten up the house. She, though, found him exhausted, and thought 'plainly he had been straining his nerves quite preposterously to please the Lady Harriet'.[54] The next morning a letter from Sterling's brother reported that Sterling had died on the evening of 18 September. A few days later some verses he had written just before his death, dedicated to Carlyle, were sent. They showed, had Carlyle any cause to doubt it, the deep trust and intimacy Sterling had felt for him. Fortunately, Carlyle had been prepared for the blow.

He returned to the letters of Cromwell, his by-product article on the 1640

Ipswich election being published at the end of September. Jane bought herself a piano, and would play for him in the evenings, but they were not especially happy. 'I swear to you I am almost quite sick of being alive,' she wrote to her cousin Helen in early October. 'It is such a perpetual strain upon the spirits.' The following month she told Helen she had been driven almost to the point of taking arsenic. To complicate matters further Charlotte Sterling, wife of John's brother Anthony, became convinced her husband was having an affair with Jane; and the wife of one of Carlyle's friends, Arthur Helps, believed her husband to be Jane's lover. Carlyle found this deeply amusing, and described Jane as 'the destroyer of the peace of families'.[55]

Jane also suffered a painful attack of rheumatism in the head and neck, which lasted five days, a variant of the neuralgia that was to plague her to the grave. Carlyle did little to cheer her up. She did observe, though, that 'if Carlyle thinks of nothing else but his *book* whilst he is *writing* it, one has always this consolation that he is the first to forget it once it is *written*.'[56] He was holding fast to the first part of this apophthegm. By this time he had transcribed most of Cromwell's letters, though claimed it could take as much as a week to write the commentary on each. He had not even begun work on the speeches – that began later in October – and was minded to hire a copyist for six months to help him. Moreover, he had not told his publishers they were not yet getting the biography they were expecting. Carlyle intended to write it, but the *Letters and Speeches* would be a necessary preliminary.

His calm was also a little affected by the suburbanisation of Chelsea, bringing noise and other disturbances. He told Jack the place was 'growing like a Wen',[57] and that he would not recognise the King's Road, which was now suddenly full of shops; Carlyle was pleased, though, that a pavement had been laid all the way from Sloane Square. He had overcome what Jane called his 'sacred horror of shopping'[58] two or three years before, when he started to buy Jane birthday presents. He also gave her new year's presents, but Jane, so dismayed at the torture his shopping expeditions caused him, made him promise not to buy her any more. He promised, but instead gave her a cloak for Christmas 1844. She was horrified by it, partly by the shock of his generosity and effort, partly by the colour – 'a *brownish colour* with *orange spots* and a brown velvet collar!'[59] Noting her shock, he explained he had bought it by gas-light. 'Poor Carlyle,' she told her cousin, 'his gift deserved to have excited gladder feelings – however I did my best to look glad over it before him – and he was much consoled by my insistence that *it would be worn*.' That December they saw hardly anyone: Jane had a permanent cold, Carlyle was at his books. Redwood sent his usual hamper and the Ashburtons sent a brace of hares and a brace of pheasants.

Until mid-1845, when *Oliver* was completed, the Carlyles continued to follow the routine the necessities of its composition had established. Isolation was the key; visitors to Cheyne Row would be entertained by Jane, though occasionally Carlyle would venture out for an evening, more often than not at the whim of Lady Harriet Baring. Occasionally a sense of duty would take Carlyle out to less well-regarded friends; one such dinner in January 1845, at the home of Edwin Chadwick, the sanitary reformer, led to Carlyle being out when one of the few people whose company he did crave, Tennyson, came to see him. 'I was overwhelmed with the sense of Carlyle's misfortune,' wrote Jane, 'in having missed the man he likes best.'[60] She put Tennyson – 'dreadfully embarrassed with women alone' – at his ease by doing what Carlyle would have done, and having him smoke his pipe and drink brandy. 'When Carlyle came home at twelve and found me all alone in an atmosphere of tobacco so thick that you might have cut it with a knife his astonishment was considerable.'

On 3 February Carlyle wrote to Alick that he was 'sunk deeper and deeper into my bottomless Task here, and feel quite often disconsolate and almost desperate about it'.[61] He told Emerson he was 'broken hearted', though he chose to blame not himself but the 'wretched fleering, sneering, twaddling godforgetting generation'[62] for whom he was trying to write. Jane felt he 'is now got about as deep in this Hell of his Cromwell as he is likely to get – there is a certain point of irritability, and gloom which when attained I say to myself "now soul take thy ease – such ease as thou canst get – for nothing worse can well be!" '[63] In early January he had apprised Chapman and Hall of what they were to expect; they were unhappy to be denied the biography and given, instead, what amounted to companion volumes. They underestimated Carlyle's achievement in collecting and publishing these letters for the first time, opening up a valuable historical resource. The long isolation and stress weakened his health, and he started to think again of buying a horse. Jane was ill too, so much so that she did not get up but took her breakfast in bed, and claimed only to have gone out of doors four times between late November 1844 and early February 1845; and she stayed in such seclusion until March. However her coterie of men friends, despite the anger of their wives, continued to call on her. Yet she felt Carlyle's neglect keenly: 'I do not think he has the smallest idea how ill I am.'[64]

Carlyle was no longer driven by poverty to engage decisively on his book. He did, though, pursue fragments about Cromwell furiously throughout the winter, relying especially on Fitzgerald to help, and also occasionally on Browning and Francis Espinasse, now in London and keen to be of service. Jane felt Carlyle was taking so much time that the book would never be finished, because he would suffer nervous collapse first; however, Chapmans were expecting the first part for printing by April. The royalties on previous works – not just in England, but in America, where Emerson was still negotiating for him – together with Mrs Welsh's legacy left them comfortably off, though he claimed not to make more than £200 a year from writing. *Past and Present* had been so successful that a second edition was out that summer. But the eremitic life caused few expenses. Carlyle had returned Emerson's kindness by writing the preface to the English edition of his essays, and by ensuring they were well distributed by Chapman and Hall.

In Carlyle's letters of this period, one can detect a harshening of view even since *Past and Present*, the product of his isolation and concentration on the period of dictatorship. 'I do not wonder,' he wrote to von Ense on 7 April, as he was hurriedly getting his first part ready for the printer, 'your King is in a great hesitation about setting up Parliaments in Prussia. I would advise a wise man, in love with *things*, and not in love with empty talk *about* things, to come here and look first!'[65] That same month Jane, cured of a long-standing cough and venturing out into the spring sunshine, found a small boy lost in the King's Road, and took him home. She attempted to pacify Carlyle, who was horrified to see the boy when he emerged for his dinner, by begging him to think what a state 'the poor mother' must be in. 'How do you know,' asked Carlyle, 'that the poor mother did not put it down there in the King's Road for some such simpleton as you to pick up, and saddle yourself with it for life?'[66] The boy's mother was indeed so hysterical that his elder sister called to collect him later that day, Jane having advertised that she had found him.

By mid-April a quarter of what Carlyle intended to be his book was printed, and another quarter ready for the printer; he had spent the early part of that month writing about Naseby. He hoped to be finished by July. A final period of intense activity, throughout those three months, followed. There was disruption in the form of a visit from Jane's cousin John Welsh, a law student, who stayed for three weeks in May and June 'turning the house, at least all one's regularity and quietness, upside down'.[67] He was never prepared to eat at the same time as the Carlyles, which prompted Jane to observe that 'Carlyle could almost kill him', and his worst offence was to barge into a tea-party being given in honour of Lady Harriet Baring, whom he proceeded to contradict and interrupt. Lady Harriet was doing her best to get to know Jane well, and later that summer took her and Carlyle to the opera.

A more stimulating visit was from a deputation of three Irishmen, brought by Frederick Lucas, the editor of *The Tablet*, to talk to Carlyle, five years after the event, about *Chartism*. Jane recorded that Carlyle had taxed their senses of humour by his reference in that work to the Irish having just two faults, that 'they do lie and steal',[68] and noted: 'Pity but my husband would pay some regard to the sensibilities of others, and exaggerate less.'[69] This was not advice Carlyle was prepared to take; indeed, the years ahead would see worse excesses. Having detected that Carlyle, for all his rhetorical cruelty, cared about the plight of the Irish, his visitors were minded to move the subject on to the question of Presbyterian Scots' intolerance of Catholics. This prompted Carlyle to tell them that 'if one sees one's fellow creature following a damnable error, by continuing in which the devil is sure to get him at last, and roast him in eternal fire and brimstone, are you to let him go towards such consummation? or are you not rather to use all means to save him?'[70] One of the visitors was Charles Gavan Duffy, who immediately began to correspond with Carlyle, and who helped organise his visit to Ireland in 1846.

As his task neared completion, after a gestation of nearly six years, Carlyle evaluated it as 'very torpid, after all that I can do for it; but it is authentic, indisputable; and earnest men may by patience spell out for themselves the lineaments of a very grand and now obsolete kind of man there!'[71] He reflected that he had never been busier in his life, and towards the end, in June, was slowed up so much in the final stages by unnaturally hot weather that he thought he might not finish until August or September. As a reward to himself, though with work still to do, he bought the horse he had long wanted, calling it first Black Duncan, but then Bobus, after one of the demons of *Past and Present*. It was a six-year-old black gelding, and cost him £35. He started to ride for two hours a day, though so out of condition was he that he reported 'rather an increase of biliousness'[72] when he began this regime. By early July, though, he announced that the horse was doing him good, though it was a little wild for him. Most of all, he was looking forward to retreating to Scotsbrig, to see his mother. 'The back of this sorrowful Book is now broken,' he told her on 12 July. 'I think another month of stiff labour will see it through.'[73] Just as it was the world's fault that it had been so hard to write, it would be their fault if they did not like it; he did not care a jot.

Jane preceded him out of London, going to her family in Liverpool in the third week of July. 'The fact is,' she told her cousin, 'I have been in a sad way for a long while, and was not saying anything about it to anyone – indeed I was ashamed to talk of illness which had taken the form chiefly of frightful depression of spirits – giving me occasionally apprehension that I was going out of my sane mind.'[74] This was not all Carlyle's doing. Jane was forty-four on 14 July, and becoming menopausal. 'I knew that the thing was physical,' she added, 'but that consciousness did not make it the less painful and alarming to me.' However, she was at the end of her tether, and early in July threw a tantrum that horrified Carlyle; as she suspected, he had no idea, and he immediately suggested she should go away to recuperate. But first she was committed to four agonising days and sleepless nights at Addiscombe with the Barings, for which Carlyle joined her on the Sunday, as had become his routine ('he has established a small permanent wardrobe there,' Jane sneered; 'He is going to Scotland ... not for any long time – Lady Harriet will need him at the Grange').[75] Carlyle would go to any lengths for Lady Harriet. In August he wrote to von Ense imploring him to find an illustrated life of Frederick the Great for her, and have it embossed with her initials and the name 'Addiscombe'.[76]

He had never gone to such lengths for his wife. Her awareness of his devotion to Lady Harriet ate at her like a cancer. From what we know of Carlyle it was hardly likely to have been inspired by sexual feelings, but Jane would not necessarily have seen that. She felt her life was a misery: 'my Husband always *writing*, I always *ailing*'.[77] She could not enjoy herself. Carlyle admitted defeat with Jane; he could not see how he as a husband could improve her spirits. 'She is not very strong,' he told his mother, 'and has many sorrows of her own, poor little thing, being very solitary in the world now.' Instead of trying to communicate with her, he went off in his spare time on his horse. The seeds of the self-flagellatory, self-pitying guilt that would follow her death were well and truly sown.

V

At Liverpool Jane could sleep no better, and wrote exhaustedly to Carlyle of cats outside keeping her awake all night. His conscience stirred, he took care to write in reply to Jane's complaints that her 'bits of letters' were 'a great comfort in my solitude'.[78] All he achieved was offending her with the phrase 'bits of letters', especially since his were hardly literary triumphs. But as he saw no one, except his horse, he had little to say. 'Rubbish, rubbish, day after day, I sit here solitary, annihilating rubbish, like to be annihilated by it; and have no human news left in me.'[79] His rides became longer and longer, out to Harrow one day, to Kew and back round by Acton another, watching men getting the harvest in. Although he complained about his solitude, it enabled him to race on with his work; and when visitors called unexpectedly, as Erasmus Darwin took to doing, he was irritated at the interruption to his routine.

The only news that would matter he sent to Jane on 26 August, just as she was preparing to return home. 'I have this very moment ended Oliver: hang it, he is ended thrums and all! I have nothing more to write on the subject; only mountains of wreck to burn.'[80] It would be published in October, and, despite his earlier reservations, he now regarded it as 'a kind of Life of Oliver, the best that circumstances would permit me to do'.[81] He told Emerson in the same letter that 'the book is very dull'. Jane was keen for him to come quickly and join her at Seaforth, where she had moved on to with her friends Paulets, and was infuriated when he told her it would be some days yet until he had caught up with his correspondence, given his horse to Fitzgerald for the winter, and made all the other arrangements necessary before he could leave London. Another incentive for him to linger was the return to London, unexpectedly early, of the Barings, whom he saw just after finishing *Oliver*. He eventually swore to take a train north on 3 September, dining on lobster and drinking fine wines with Forster as a rare indulgence before he left London.

They spent a week by the sea together, Carlyle relaxing by swimming but otherwise seeming to Jane 'in a highly reactionary state'[82] – and not just, of course, in the political sense. The shock to Carlyle of not having his book to write was profound. Jane returned to London and he went north to Scotsbrig by steamer. Once there he could relax totally, finding 'silence' at last. His mother, now in her seventies, claimed to be in excellent health, though her hand was shaking, Carlyle noticed, more than usual. His sister Jenny was living with her two children, her husband, Robert Hanning, having gone alone to America where he was trying to make a living. Carlyle's younger brother Jamie was also at Scotsbrig, his wife Isabella having contracted a nervous disease that prevented her from speaking. These family difficulties depressed Carlyle. 'Old Annandale is all grown strange to me; a mournful hull of the past,' he told Jane.[83] He knew hardly anybody; his old friends had died or moved on. Such people as he spoke to were immersed in gloom at the failure of the potato crop which, though not so severe as the famine in Ireland, had none the less caused severe economic problems to the region. He took his mother for walks, and drove her about in his gig, and waited for proofs of his book to be sent from London. When they arrived he found things immediately not to his liking, which stressed him further.

Shortly before Carlyle came home, after a stay of more than a month at Scotsbrig, Jane had had Lady Harriet Baring's carriage sent round for her, and had been taken to see her; and Lady Harriet had insisted that Jane (and, one supposes, Carlyle) went to winter with her at Alverstoke, on the Hampshire coast. 'And yet,' Jane wrote to her cousin, 'I have an unconquerable persuasion that she does not and never can like me.'[84] Jane said she and Carlyle would consider the matter, but was deeply reluctant to go. 'I can see,' Jane told Carlyle, 'that the Lady has a genius for *ruling*, whilst I have a genius for – not being ruled!'[85]

However, what Carlyle was up to at Scotsbrig was to prove far more damaging for Jane in the long run than any attentions of Lady Harriet's. He had started to read Preuss's *Life of Frederick the Great*, sent to him some years before by von Ense, which he was enjoying greatly, Frederick not lacking in those qualities that had so endeared Carlyle to Cromwell. He finished reading it in early October; and, having learned nothing from his struggle with *Oliver*, told Jane that 'I ... mean to inquire yet farther about the man. *Der Grosse Fritz*: if I had any turn for travelling, I should hold it very interesting indeed to go to Berlin, and try to make more acquaintance with him and his people.'[86] 'Certainly,' he told von Ense, 'there is a Hero for an Epic in these ages.' It was the same language he had used about Cromwell; and, as with Cromwell, he still found Frederick 'very dark', and asked von Ense to send him a reading list on the subject that it might be illuminated.[87] Von Ense obliged almost by return of post.

Carlyle was home by the third week in October. Because of a delay in producing a portrait of Cromwell to illustrate the book, publication was held up until December; Carlyle, though angered by the delay to accommodate a portrait he did not much care for, no longer gave it much thought. He immediately caught a cold – the autumn was unusually damp and foggy – and, both work and economics making it possible, decided with Jane (with whom, to her annoyance, he now spent so much time that she rarely had enough to write letters) that they should take up Lady Harriet's invitation. Jack was lodging with them at Cheyne Row, not practising medicine, but translating Dante's *Inferno*. Relations between Jane and her brother-in-law were again strained, so she was not entirely sorry to leave. Carlyle was positively excited by the prospect: 'great folks, very kind to us, and extremely rational, worthy people; – they promise me "a horse", and all manner of nice things; and the winter climate, I believe, is the best or one of the best in England.'[88] His devotion to Lady Harriet was carried on by practical means that autumn. He arranged for her to join the London Library and, as he had done with Jane a quarter-century earlier, started to find German books for her and direct her in her German studies.

Although he was nearly four years from *The Nigger Question*, the cast of mind that would produce it was hardening. He complained to Emerson in November of 'the sugary twaddle one gets the offer of in Exeter-Hall and other Spouting-places',[89] of the kind of liberalism that he would characterise as 'the Universal Abolition of Pain Association'.[90] He admitted to Emerson that he was getting 'more and more weary; sometimes really impatient' of this attitude. 'It seems to be the reign of Cant and Spoonyism has lasted long enough, 'he added. 'Alas, in many respects, in this England I too often feel myself sorrowfully in a "minority of one".'

On 15 November the Carlyles went to Alverstoke. Bay House, where they stayed, belonged to Lord Ashburton, Baring's father, and had only recently been built. Although the weather was bleak, the house was warm with no comfort spared, a luxury for Jane after the parsimonious, sickly winters of Cheyne Row. It was not settled how long they should stay, though Carlyle intended two or three weeks. Lady Harriet, by contrast, wanted them until the Parliamentary recess ended in February, but Jane, writing the day after their arrival, surmised that 'Carlyle's need to be ugly and stupid and dis-agreeable without restraint (never to speak of my own) will send us back to London in a month or so.'[91] In the end, it was settled they would stay for Christmas and leave on Boxing Day.

Lady Harriet went to the greatest lengths to put Jane at her ease, so the ordeal was less than she had expected. She developed a grudging respect for her hostess, realising she bestowed her affections according to the strength of character of her friends, not their social standing – hence her regard for Carlyle. Also, Lady Harriet and Jane would sit and read German together. Jane was able to forget the pressures of Chelsea; whatever the wearisome demands of socialising, she was in no hurry to return to the privations of London. *Oliver* appeared while she and Carlyle were at Alverstoke, and the reaction to it was immediately favourable. One of Carlyle's correspondents, the Reverend Alexander Scott, marvelled at the work Carlyle must have put in to it; with all honesty, Carlyle replied that 'the great thing is, Not to stop and break down'.[92] There was, though, a moment of anxiety immediately after the book was published. Another Cromwell scholar, John Sanford, wrote to him suggesting there were seventy letters, which Sanford had seen, that Carlyle did not appear to have taken note of. Carlyle replied that he was sure he had seen them; but would be grateful for a list of exactly which seventy

A Chelsea Interior by Robert Tait, 1857: another cosy evening for Tom and Jane at home, or proof of how appearances are deceptive.

Carlyle working in the soundproofed room, in the valley of the shadow of Frederick, 1857.

James Anthony Froude, Carlyle's greatest biographer, friend, disciple and, ultimately, family scapegoat.

Carlyle and the dog Nero sitting in the sun in the back garden at Cheyne Row, 1857.

Frederick the Great of Prussia, portrait by Anton Graff.

BELOW William Edward Hartpole Lecky, historian, pictured at about the time of Carlyle's death.

LEFT Carlyle pictured by H & W Greaves outside 5 Cheyne Row, 1859.

Alfred Tennyson, smoking companion of
Jane Welsh Carlyle.

John Ruskin, who turned from art to
politics under Carlyle's influence.

Ralph Waldo Emerson in old age, by which
time he and Carlyle found they had little
in common with each other.

Professor John Tyndall, who accompanied
Carlyle on his triumphant, and fateful,
journey to Edinburgh in April 1866.

Carlyle in 1865.

Carlyle, delivering his inaugural address on being installed as Lord Rector of Edinburgh University, 2 April 1866.

Jane Carlyle, not long before her death, ravaged by illness, sleeplessness, drink and drugs: on this picture Carlyle wrote 'The worst'.

RIGHT 'The Diogenes of the Modern Corinthians without his Tub': *Vanity Fair*, 22 October 1870.

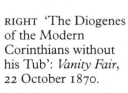

Carlyle (second left) pictured in the autumn of 1874 with his brother Jack (far left), niece Mary Aitken (second right) and Mr P. Swan (far right).

The Irish poet William Allingham, who knew Carlyle well in the last decade of his life, painted by his wife, Helen.

Carlyle in his last years, painted in watercolours by Helen Allingham.

Sanford had in mind, just to be sure. It turned out Sanford was right, and some of the appendices to later editions include the fruits of his rather than of Carlyle's researches.

The weeks of 'reactionary' idleness ('one continual course of *Handsomely doing nothing*')[93] he had experienced since finishing *Oliver* were now leaving him thirsty for another task; tempting though it was to linger at Alverstoke, he realised it would be 'suicidal'.[94] On 4 December he celebrated his fiftieth birthday. Shortly before Christmas great news reached them; as Carlyle put it, 'all hands are here rejoicing since yesternight that Peel has decided to abolish the Corn Laws: total and immediate! There is really something brave in poor Peel.'[95] Carlyle had played a small but significant part in the campaign to repeal the laws, their iniquity having been central to the theses of *Chartism* and *Past and Present*; so he could take a small share in the triumph at their demise, and hope the opportunity this afforded the country would be put to the use he had advised in *Past and Present* – to found schemes for emigration, education and the organisation of labour, all of which were contingent on proper leadership. Part of the process of demoralisation that was to reduce him to the blind anger of *Latter-Day Pamphlets*, however, was that the only use most of the country wished to make of this liberalisation was as a spur for the extension of the franchise.

Carlyle returned to London to find himself a victim of *Oliver*'s astonishing success. Within a month of publication the first edition of 1,200 copies had been sold out, and the publishers wanted a second. 'A new edition,' said Jane, 'will bring him in some three hundred pounds – but he abhors the trouble of new correcting of proofs. There is no satisfying of that man.'[96] Worse, publication had caused other letters besides Sanford's haul to be brought to light. His travails, from which he thought he had escaped, were about to reopen.

VI

Oliver Cromwell's Letters and Speeches: with Elucidations is a vivid work of history, though is more a basis for other, less emotionally involved biographers to build upon rather than a complete life in itself. As in *The French Revolution*, and particularly in *Frederick*, Carlyle sees it his duty to rescue valuable examples of human behaviour from dead piles of historical documents, and to present them for contemporary enlightenment. Appropriately enough for a man writing on a seventeenth-century subject, Carlyle follows the seventeenth-century idea of history as a mirror, held up for his con-temporaries to peer into. Carlyle succeeds in dragging Cromwell out of his words and making him real, which was what he struggled to do; not for nothing is the very first chapter entitled 'Anti-Dryasdust'. Almost incidentally, he uses Cromwell's life to demonstrate the Lord Protector's superiority over any other governor since, and the superior moral tone of the times is compared with the age in which Carlyle was writing. 'We have wandered far away from the ideas which guided us in that Century, and indeed which had guided us in all preceding Centuries, but of which that Century was the ultimate manifestation,' he says in his introduction.[97] Oliver (Carlyle more often than not uses the Christian name) had been 'the last glimpse of the Godlike vanishing from this England; conviction and veracity giving place to hollow cant and formulism'.[98]

As with many of the individuals Carlyle admires, he finds characteristics in them that he shares, or through experience can understand. Cromwell, like Carlyle, had a religious conversion, though his was to 'Calvinistic Christianity ... his deliverance from the jaws of Eternal Death'.[99] He rejected the superstitions of the cant-filled Church, and relied instead on 'the Silences ... the Eternities'.[100] Carlyle states, in his biographical introduction, that Cromwell was inspired by God, and by no temporal events. The harsh execution of God's justice throughout is depicted as inevitable and unquestionably right; its morality lies in the fact that God sent Cromwell to do it as a judgment on the moral tone of others. The victory of the Parliamentary Army over the Royalists that brought the act of regicide Carlyle describes as 'punishment of Delinquents ... abolition of Cobwebs ... a Government of Heroism and Veracity; at lowest, of Anti-Flunkyism, Anti-Cant, and the endeavour after Heroism and Veracity'.[101] But he was also the Hero as Prophet, 'the largest soul in England looking at this God's World with prophet's earnestness through that Hebrew Word'.[102] Carlyle was, effectively, celebrating the secularisation of the Calvinist idea of the elect, and would look for its continuance in contemporary England.

He makes free with such editorial comments throughout; early on, he dismisses Richard Cromwell, who succeeded his father as Protector, in the phrase 'poor idle triviality'.[103] The oppression of non-Calvinist religious practices invites equally short shrift, saying that Dryasdust, tearing out his hair over such intolerance, should 'reflect that Conviction in an earnest age means, not lengthy Spouting in Exeter-Hall, but rapid silent Practice on the face of the Earth'.[104] Cromwell's savageries in Ireland attract equal understanding. 'To those who think a land overrun with Sanguinary Quacks can be healed by sprinkling it with rose-water, these letters must be very horrible,' he writes of Cromwell's reports from there.[105] Carlyle felt that those who complained were simply 'shutting men's minds against the God's Fact'.[106] He adds that 'in Oliver's time ... there was still belief in the Judgments of God ... there was yet no distracted jargon of "abolishing Capital Punishments", of Jean-Jacques philanthropy, and universal rose-water in this world still so full of sin.'[107]

The 'universal patent treacle ... of Rousseau Sentimentalism' was 'very ominous twaddle' of which Cromwell, luckily, 'had not yet heard the slightest intimation even in dreams'.[108] He was concerned only, Carlyle adds, with being 'a Soldier of God the Just ... armed Soldier, terrible as Death, relentless as Doom; doing God's Judgments on the Enemies of God!' Such sentiments explain why, to Carlyle, might could not but be right, and why Cromwell was right to do what he did in Ireland. As Catholics, the Irish were almost beyond hope; even the Scots, who sought to implement God's law by means of Calvinism, were failing because they could find no one heroic enough to enforce the creed; they had become 'a bigoted Theocracy *without* the Inspiration', which is why Cromwell had to fight them too.[109]

As in *The French Revolution* and *Past and Present*, Carlyle's historical narrative is always vivid and immediate; his battle descriptions, weak in *The French Revolution*, are almost always brilliant in this work, helped no doubt by his visits to most of the fields about which he wrote. Dramatic, too, are his portrayals of political events, such as Cromwell, in 1653, castigating the Rump Parliament:

'You call yourselves a Parliament,' continues my Lord General in clear blaze of conflagration: 'You are no Parliament; I say you are no Parliament! Some of you are drunkards,' and his eye flashes on poor Mr Chaloner, an official man of some value, addicted to the bottle; 'some of you are – ' and he glares into Harry Marten, and the poor Sir Peter who rose to order, lewd livers both; 'living in open contempt of God's Commandments. Following your own greedy appetites, and the Devil's Commandments ... how can you be a Parliament for God's People? Depart, I say; and let us have done with you. In the name of God – go!'[110]

Carlyle always writes as though he is at Cromwell's side, a subordinate but confidential friend; and often writes as though he is a dramatist relaying events. This tone, coupled with the quality of the material he edited, sealed the work's success. Occasionally, bored with being so subtle, Carlyle resorts to quoting himself as 'a certain critic'[111] to ensure his personality can be properly impressed upon proceedings, and to praise Cromwell more highly.

Carlyle's imagination of himself as one of Cromwell's audience, interpolating 'yes!' and 'hear, hear!' into the speeches is eccentric, but endearing. When the Protector is flagging, Carlyle is there with words of encouragement: 'His Highness's utterance is terribly rusty hitherto; creaky, uncertain, difficult! He will gather strength by going. Wait till the axles get warm a little!'[112] As his narrative approaches the end of Cromwell's life, Carlyle becomes almost tender:

Courage, my brave one! Thou hast but some Seven Months more of it, and then the ugly coil is all over; and thy part in it manfully done ... England, with immense expenditure of liquor and tar-barrels, can call in its Nell-Gwynn Defender of the Faith – and make out a very notable Two-hundred Years under his guidance; and, finding itself now nearly *got* to the devil, may perhaps pause, and recoil, and remember: who knows?[113]

Throughout the agonies of composition, Carlyle recognised he was writing an allegory, a lesson for contemporary Britain. That is the note upon which he concludes, and, as so often, cannot resist a note of humour:

The Genius of England no longer soars sunward, world-defiant, like an Eagle through the storms, 'mewing her mighty youth' as John Milton saw her do: the Genius of England, much liker a greedy Ostrich intent on provender and a whole skin mainly, stands with its other extremity Sunward ... No Ostrich ... but will be awakened one day, – in a terrible a-posteriori manner, if not otherwise! – Awake before it come to that; gods and men bid us awake! The Voices of our Fathers, with thousand fold stern monition to one and all, bid us awake.[114]

The reviews were laudatory, *The Spectator*'s was typical: 'We never met so vast a mass of matter which was so readable, so real, and of so sustained an interest.'[115] However, this reviewer also pointed out the 'most extraordinary style of Carlyleism' that characterised the work, and poked fun at the chapter 'Dryasdust', 'chiefly distinguished for an unmitigated censure of all the historians and original chroniclers or recorders of the seventeenth century, and an overweening confidence in himself'.[116] But the confidence Carlyle had in himself was far less than this reviewer could imagine. Harried by personal and intellectual anxieties and pressures, the period of deepest doubt was about to begin.

11

'Deep Gloom and Bottomless Dubitation'

1846–49

THE YEARS leading up to *Latter-Day Pamphlets* in 1850 saw an acceleration of Carlyle's moral authoritarianism. His preoccupation with history was supplanted by an obsessive, and angry, compulsion to preach about contemporary problems, and to argue that a properly moral tone of governance and duty would help solve them. This belief was fuelled by the final loss of his confidence in the ability of England to reform as he felt desirable, and by his need to let out the resulting anger. He was provoked, too, by the complacent emerging liberal consensus, which he felt irrelevant to the true needs of Britain and to be rooted entirely in theory rather than in reality. When the reaction to *Latter-Day Pamphlets* told him he had failed to break this consensus, he retreated into the past again, and stayed there. Since the publication of *Chartism* his brutal sense of humour, and unrestrained expression of even then unfashionable views on slavery and the deliberately idle, had been visible in most of his works; and much more so in his private speech and letters. As early as 1833 he had written to Mill, from Edinburgh, that 'we have two blustering Turkey-cocks lecturing here at present on the Negroes: one an Anti-Slaver; the other a Slaver that follows him Ibis-like to destroy his Crocodile-eggs ... While we, under soft names, have not only Slavery but the fiercest Maroon War going on under our very noses, it seems to me Philanthropy and Eleutheromany might find work nearer home.'[1] The root of his disdain for the anti-slavery movement was that it should, instead, be using its energy to attend to problems on its own doorstep; but before long Carlyle was driven to an almost irrational hatred of it for what it symbolised of a certain section of liberal society that he believed to be shot through with atheism, decadence and self-indulgence.

Carlyle's interest in Cromwell was stimulated further by the new letters that had turned up, and he set to work in January 1846 transcribing and 'elucidating' them. There were more than fifty, 'not *all* insignificant',[2] though it meant 'I am obliged to duck into those horrid quagmires from which I had fancied myself forever escaped.'[3] He felt guilty that he had overlooked so many, and stipulated to Chapman's that a supplementary volume containing them be produced and sold for the lowest possible price, without profit to him, so that those who had bought the inadequate first edition could append it without much cost. Chapman's were anxious to have the supplement out as soon as possible, and Carlyle spent the winter in frantic correspondence with antiquaries, chasing up new submissions.

He was distressed to note a worsening in poverty after he returned to London from the unrealities of Alverstoke; the effects of the bad potato harvest had reached London, and near-inedible potatoes were selling in Chelsea at four for three-half pence. Carlyle knew such prices would mean starvation for the Irish; he could already see the English poor 'with a look of pinching hunger in their faces' on the London streets.[4] He much enjoyed the sight of the aristocracy 'struck almost with a kind of horror at sight of that terrible Millocracy, rising like a huge hideous Frankenstein up in Lancashire, – seemingly with boundless ready-money in its pocket, and a very fierce humour in its stomach' following the notice that the Corn Laws would be repealed.[5] The Commons, and then eventually the Lords, passed the bill of repeal; though in truth he was too busy with *Oliver* to pay much attention. Jane, as usual, he had little time for; his only indulgence outside work remained Lady Harriet – 'my beneficent ... my sovereign Lady ... yours to command'[6] – to whom he was becoming positively treacly.

Before long Carlyle was as worried about the second edition of *Oliver* as he had been about the first. The supplement notwithstanding, he decided that about twenty of the new letters would have to be fitted in the existing structure. He arranged to send a copy of the revisions to Emerson, who was handling publication in America. The old restlessness, held at bay by the visit to the Barings, began to return. He told Jane he thought of visiting Prussia, leaving her to wonder what was to become of her; or that he might like to go back and live in Annandale, which horrified her.

She pined when Carlyle, 'gloomy and disconsolate',[7] shut himself away to deal with *Oliver* again; but found a legacy of her stay at Alverstoke was that Lady Harriet, who returned to London in early February, was keen for her company, and would send her carriage for her of an evening so that she and Jane could read German or play chess together. As domestic stresses returned so too did Jane's insomnia, driving her almost mad with exhaustion. 'I have for a long while back been dreadfully haunted with the apprehension of going *mad* some day,' she told her cousin on 10 March.[8] Carlyle's work took longer than expected; by early March only the changes needed to the first volume had been accomplished, with the second still to do. He expected it would take him until the beginning of May; four months of additional, unlooked-for work. To console Jane, Lady Harriet asked her to Addiscombe for a month, from 20 March, and Jane accepted. Though Carlyle felt she did not encourage him enough, she was more sympathetic than he knew: 'this rewriting of Cromwell has been very hard on him,' she said.[9]

It was not the book itself that troubled Carlyle so much as the 'writing innumerable notes to stupid people' who had, kindly, sent him more material. One such person was the Duke of Manchester whose ancestor, the Earl of Manchester, had been a parliamentary general in the Civil War. The Duke found some unpublished letters and 'brought them on foot to Chelsea, and delivered them to the servant as if he were any ordinary messenger'.[10] Carlyle was gratified his interpretation of Cromwell had proved so attractive to so many that they had bought his book in large numbers; it was a rare note of optimism for him, having despaired of England as he had. 'In all probability,' he told his mother, 'this is the usefullest business I shall ever get to do in the world.' He continued to toil away at proofs when Jane was away, though would visit Addiscombe weekly from Saturday to Monday, and she came back every Wednesday to attend to domestic tasks while Lady Harriet was in town for her drawing lesson. With relief Carlyle wrote to Jane on 8 April that 'the Cromwell rubbish ... is fast disappearing before me.'[11]

As the spring came Carlyle retrieved his horse from its winter quarters, and resumed his hard riding each afternoon. He also took to having a cold bath three times a week, which he felt improved his health. Once he had almost completed *Oliver* he also found the time to have his daguerreotype taken. The picture, sent to Emerson at his request on 30 April 1846, shows Carlyle looking well and young for a man of fifty, his face unlined (and still unbearded), and jaw set determinedly; in his hair there is a touch of grey. Writing to Emerson in April, to prepare him for the shock of seeing the picture, Carlyle said that 'on me there are "grey hairs here and there" – and I do "know it". I have lived half a century in this world, fifty years complete on 4th of December last: that is a solemn fact for me! Few and evil have been the days of the years of thy servant, few for any good that was ever done in them. *Ay de mi!*'[12]

He spent an evening with Richard Cobden, whose Corn Law League could take the real credit for repeal. 'I found,' Carlyle told Thomas Ballantyne, 'a most distinct, ingenuous, energetic well conditioned man.'[13] A few days later, in early May, Fitzgerald came across Carlyle at Tennyson's lodgings, and found he was becoming 'more wild, savage and unreasonable every day'.[14] Carlyle had not yet fixed on his next task, but wanted to travel, and talked vaguely about where he and Jane might spend the summer. In early June the weather became exceedingly hot, intensifying thoughts of escape. He wanted to go to Scotland – indeed, when he was particularly depressed, insisted to Jane that he really did want to return to live there; but Jane had not been able to bring herself to go there since her mother's death four years earlier. They started to ask about possible houses they could rent, but with little success.

At the cost of his own leadership, Peel finally secured the repeal of the Corn Laws in June 1846. The second edition of *Oliver* was to be published a few days later, and Carlyle sent him a copy. In his covering letter, Carlyle asked Peel to 'let this poor labour of mine be a small testimony ... to a late great and valiant labour of yours.' He made it clear to Peel that there were lessons in *Oliver* that might help him in 'yet other labours which England, in a voiceless but most impressive manner, still expects and demands of you'. Peel thanked him 'not out of mere courtesy, but very sincerely'.[15] Peel was the closest Carlyle came to having a contemporary hero; the sage would watch the statesman closely in the few remaining years of Peel's life, but be disappointed. The disappointment started ten days after Carlyle sent him *Oliver*. Peel's protectionist opponents in his own party had their revenge on him on 29 June, when they voted him down on an Irish Coercion measure, and he was out.

Jane's relief at Carlyle's finally finishing with *Oliver* was undisguised. The final corrections of the revisions had seen him at his most contumacious. 'If he [Cromwell] had been my husband's own Father he could not have gone thro' more hardship for him,' she told her cousin Helen. 'We have lived "in the valley of the shadow" of Cromwell now, as of Death, for some three years.'[16] But it was not Cromwell that was the problem with Jane; it was her conviction that Lady Harriet was trying to seduce her husband. Her difficult mental health, which had been ameliorated by the ending of *Oliver* and the visits to Liverpool and the Barings the previous year, now flared up into a crisis again, principally because of her jealousy and insecurity, but aggravated by Carlyle's restlessness and talk of moving. By the end of June, as usual unnoticed by Carlyle, she had embarked on a full-scale nervous breakdown. Arrangements were quickly made for her to go to her friend Mrs Paulet at Seaforth again, and she left on 4 July. Carlyle, shocked by what he saw, promised to follow once he had finished checking the revisions of the index. However, he made Jane still unhappier in the process by continually suggesting she travel on to Scotland with him once they were done at Seaforth.

Carlyle's letters to her at this time show genuine concern, and not a little guilt, at her condition. He told her that when he came home after seeing her off he had felt 'the saddest I think I have been ... for ten years'.[17] He continued, mournfully:

I directly got out my work, and sat down to *it* as to the one remedy I had. All day I toiled at Christie's *Index* (a very ugly burbly job indeed), and all next day; and have just finished it, five minutes ago. These two Notes were lying for me, Redwood's with a breath of something like comfort in it: I thought of sending them off to you for your Sunday Morning; but delayed till too long, felt indeed that I could *write* little along with them that would be comfortable. I was in fact in very bad health too ... Yesterday I suppose you fancied me very happy at Addiscombe; alas, I was in no humour for anything of that laughing nature ... It was a day of resurrection of all sad and great and tender things within me; sad as very death, yet not unprofitable.

His guilt was worsened by the failure of the post office to deliver the newspaper she had promised to send him from Liverpool as a sign she had arrived safely; he thought she was punishing him for his courtship of Lady Harriet. He dutifully went to Addiscombe the weekend after Jane left but, aware that his attentiveness to Lady Harriet was not unconnected with Jane's mental state, made a point of testifying to his wife that he had not enjoyed the weekend at all. He shows desperate keenness to patch things up between them. 'Adieu my Dearest,' he ends a letter to her on 6 July 1846, '(for that *is*, and if madmen prevail not, may forever be, your authentic title).'[18] When her first letter came from Seaforth the next day, he wrote back with almost pathetic gratitude for it. He went to lengths not to forget her birthday on the 14th, but a mistake at the Seaforth post office meant the letter was not delivered. Jane, grasping the wrong end of the stick as her husband had done, felt he was angry with her for her behaviour before she left London. She became distraught, and shut herself away in her room to be miserable alone, and went into a panic attack for a couple of hours, wondering whether simply to take a train back to London to him. 'And just when I was at my wits' end,' she wrote to him that evening, 'I heard Julia crying out through the house: "Mrs Carlyle, Mrs Carlyle! Are you there? Here is a letter for you." '[19] Jane kissed the card and wrote to thank Carlyle immediately; she was still wildly unstable:

I wonder what love-letter was ever received with such thankfulness! Oh, my dear! I am not fit for living in the world with this organisation. I am as much broken to pieces by that little accident as if I had come through an attack of cholera or typhus fever. I cannot even steady my hand to write decently. But I felt an irresistible need of thanking you, by return of post. Yes, I have kissed the dear little card-case; and now I will lie down awhile, and try to get some sleep. At least, to quiet myself, I will try to believe – oh, why cannot I believe it, once for all – that, with all my faults and follies, I am 'dearer to you than any earthly creature'.

Before he went north, Carlyle had to signal to Lady Harriet that their intimacy was not reconcilable with his marriage. He went to Addiscombe in mid-July and tried to do this. He told Lady Harriet that Jane was 'very unwell'. He added, though, that 'she seems to have discerned pretty clearly for herself that our intercourse is to be carried on under different conditions henceforth, or probably to cease altogether before long; to which arrangement she gives signs of being ready to conform with fully more indifference than I expected, with no unkindness at all – but with no discernible regret either.'[20] Relations were not to be broken between the Carlyles and the Barings; just made less frequent. Conscious that Lady Harriet had been very kind to them, Carlyle begged Jane to write to her with some news: 'Her intents towards you and towards me, so far as I can read them, *are* charitable and *not* wicked,' he assured his wife.[21]

In the last week of July, slightly relieved by the happier tone of some of Jane's recent letters, he finally went to Seaforth to spend ten days with her. He remembered this time for her as 'dismal weeks' of 'ill spirits, ill health'.[22] When they came to part – he for Scotland, where she would not go, and thence to Ireland to visit Duffy and his friends, she for Manchester to stay with Geraldine Jewsbury – he still, by his own later admission, had no idea how ill she was; only his later discovery of her letters of this time brought it home to him. Her visit to Geraldine, about whom she had hitherto been rather caustic, changed much; it established Geraldine as her close confidante, and improved her spirits dramatically, perhaps – though one can only conjecture – because, in her deep unhappiness, Jane was able to pour out to Geraldine the cumulative unhappiness of twenty years' marriage to Carlyle.

II

Even while at Seaforth Carlyle was writing to Lady Harriet. After much of the usual oiling, he mentioned that 'the essential thing is to tell you that my Wife is considerably better ... we have talked of you: do not suppose that she does other, or ever did other, than respect or love you, – tho' with some degree of terror. Baseless, I do believe.'[23] To judge from Carlyle's first letter to Jane after his arrival at Scotsbrig, written on 8 August 1846, their time together at Seaforth solved little. Carlyle complained of insomnia even in the silence of Annandale, and attributed it to his anxieties at being estranged from Jane again. 'Oh, my Dearest,' he wrote, 'how little I can make thee know of me! In what a black baleful cloud for myself and thee are all our affairs involved to thy eyes, at this moment threatening shipwreck if we do not mind!'[24] Jack was at his mother's house, and the place was crowded; Carlyle could not see himself staying more than a few days. Instead, with his usual resolution, he could think of nowhere better to go before Duffy was ready to receive him in Ireland, and ended up staying for almost a month.

Part of that time, to Jane's chagrin, he spent showing the Barings, who were staying at Carlisle, around Dumfriesshire ('the queenship of our motions is naturally yours,'[25] he told Lady Harriet when making the arrangements). Jane did not write to him for several days from Manchester, mainly because she was ill, and partly because Geraldine had deliberately been keeping her busy; but Carlyle interpreted her silence as punishment for his continued contact with Lady Harriet. He wrote, hysterically, on 14 August: 'O, my Jeannie! my own true Jeannie! bravest little life-companion, hitherto, into what courses are we tending?'[26] A letter explaining her delay at writing arrived within a couple of days, and he exclaimed 'O Goody I am awfully stupid!'[27]

Once done with the Barings Carlyle, who had had his horse shipped up to Scotland for him, rode to Craigenputtock to visit the tenant, his sentiments stirred by sight of the place where he and Jane had spent so much of the early part of their marriage. He went to Dumfries to see his sister Jean; as he rode round the countryside he saw formerly distressed Yorkshire labourers now employed digging the railway from Carlisle to Glasgow, and spending the money they now earned on whisky. He went to Ayr, and from Ardrossan took a boat over to Ireland on 4 September. Landing at Belfast he made immediately for Dublin, surveying on the way a badly farmed land where the potatoes had rotted again from blight and there was 'nothing but sheer famine and death by hunger for millions'.[28] He hoped a new era would dawn for Ireland, as the government had implemented a programme of relief works to provide employment for hundreds of thousands of destitute Irishmen. In fact, the mass emigration he had advocated in England was about to take place from Ireland, and the deep anti-English feeling that was to have such a catastrophic effect on relations between the two countries was beginning to grow out of control.

He had been meant to find Duffy in Drogheda, a site of Cromwellian notoriety on the way to Dublin where the Protector had had the defeated Irish garrison of 3,000 or so men almost entirely put to the sword, but they had missed each other because of the inefficiencies of the post office. Instead, he met his guide in the Irish capital. Duffy was highly hospitable, and took Carlyle into the 'Young Ireland' circle of militant nationalists. With him he went one day to Conciliation Hall and heard a harangue by the nationalist Daniel O'Connell, 'perhaps the *most* disgusting sight to me in that side of the water'.[29] He felt O'Connell was 'the chief quack of the then world', a 'lying scoundrel' and 'this Demosthenes of blarney'; his meeting attracted 'not one that you would call a gentleman'.[30] By contrast, Carlyle had much sympathy with the intellectuals of Young Ireland, and gave no hint that he suspected what trouble they would be getting themselves into (they were arraigned for treason in 1848). After some excursions into the country, Carlyle took the steamer to Liverpool, and stayed briefly with Jane's family before heading south. Ireland was no longer simply an idea to him; but when he returned, three years later, it would be very different.

Once home he found Jane in the middle of servant problems. Helen, who following her earlier drunkenness had become almost reliable and certainly much liked, had decided to go to Dublin to keep house for her brother, who had made some money. Jane was hard put to find a replacement. Carlyle, for his part, had nothing to do, and no plans – other than his growing interest in eighteenth-century Prussia – of what to do. 'My thoughts,' he told his sister Jean on 17 October, 'are very *serious*, I will not call them sorrowful or miserable; I am getting fairly *old* and do not want to be younger.'[31] Visitors still came often, and Carlyle, now in a relaxed mode, would entertain them of an evening with his fiercely authoritarian monologues. One who came in early October was Margaret Fuller, an American friend of Emerson's, who recalled that 'the worst of hearing Carlyle is that you cannot interrupt him', and what she had tried to interrupt was a harangue in which Carlyle said 'if people would not behave well, put collars round their necks. Find a hero, and let them be his slaves.'[32]

Not having work as an excuse he went out into society occasionally too; and at the end of October he and Jane went to old Lord Ashburton's house in Hampshire to spend a fortnight with the Barings. Jane was given a suite of rooms to herself and left alone as much as she wanted, though did come out of her shell in a house-party of more than a dozen people. Carlyle was bored;

none of the company was especially stimulating, and Lady Harriet was not so available to him as hitherto. In November the Carlyles returned to London, Jane relieved at having survived the ordeal, but having also pledged to spend a month at Alverstoke after Christmas. To cheer her up she asked her cousin Helen to come to stay, a fortuitous decision as it turned out, since Helen was on hand to help when the replacement maid ('indisputably the worst specimen of Scotch character I have ever seen produced,' said Carlyle[33]) turned out to be a disaster.

Although Jane went down with her customary winter cold, taking to her bed for three weeks and staying there for Christmas, Carlyle felt in the best of health. When, just before Christmas, he felt a cold coming on, he took the 'violently heroic'[34] measure of immersing himself in a bath of freezing water, which he felt warded it off. He started to read more, though the domestic upheavals made it hard for him to concentrate. But there was 'nothing in the dark chaos that it could seem *beautiful* to conquer and *do*', as he told von Ense in December.[35] Nor could he even find anything worth reading. The inadequacy of their servant meant Carlyle not only had to help out around the house, but became angry and stressed as a result of having so to do.

Although Jane was still not well, and did not feel like travelling, Carlyle took her as planned to Alverstoke in January 1847. It had been made clear to him that, following the crisis of the last summer, he could not go without her. Lady Harriet had been ill too that winter, and had become still more estranged from Carlyle as a result. This distressed him. 'Of you I think as of the beautifullest creature in all this world; divided from me by great gulphs forevermore,' he had written to Lady Harriet on 9 January.[36] Once they reached Alverstoke, on 18 January, Lady Harriet was a model of solicitude towards Jane. She told Jane that if Carlyle wanted to return to London to get on with some work she could stay on as long as she liked; Carlyle was not so indispensable to his patroness as he had been. She no longer wanted to pass the time sitting around and reading German with him. She also had the habit – which greatly amused Jane – of listening to her parrot rather than Carlyle whenever the bird interrupted him during one of his monologues, which it frequently did. The house was only full on odd days, and generally very quiet, which suited both Carlyles well.

They stayed for over a month. Whatever the new distance put between Carlyle and Lady Harriet, Jane and her hostess improved relations. None the less, Jane was often ill and always far from content, confiding in her cousin Helen that 'in my life I never felt more desolate than lying here in my exposed French bed.'[37] Carlyle was chagrined to have been 'totally idle'[38] for so much of the winter, but had had the bonus of being away from their cold house in Chelsea for the worst part of a harsh season. He had hoped to return from his rest with an idea of what to do next, but none came. He read a new volume of Emerson's poems while in Hampshire, but, of more inspirational significance, found the latest volume of von Ense's memoirs waiting for him.

'I get a view as if into the very heart of Prussia thro' them,' he told the author.[39] He revealed to von Ense that Prussian histories and memoirs were forming a growing part of his reading. Jack was back in London, and provided him with some companionship, and he would get out and see Milnes; but otherwise Carlyle's own return to the capital did not bring him much additional stimulation. He was noting with shock the famine stalking through Ireland, and the equally severe failure of the government to do anything to ameliorate its effects; he feared that the potato blight would come across into Scotland and England where, because of the reliance of the poor on potatoes in their diet, havoc would result. He was still more horrified when, in March, he learned that the Irish peasantry were so fed up with their treatment that they were taking the further destructive step of not planting any potatoes for the coming year.

He used part of his spare time to help arrange a lecture-tour for Emerson, who, to Carlyle's delight, was planning to come to England later in the year. But for most of his waking hours he sat 'silent; often enough in a very melancholic, sad and confused state', as he told Alick.[40] He added that 'I keep very solitary; my thoughts are abundantly austere, sorrowful often as death: but it is all nonsense to call that "miserable"; I have found that all *good* whatsoever has to come to one in that way.' He was pleased by the continuing high sales of *Oliver*, and not simply from the financial point of view (he earned £800 in 1847, and reckoned to make on average £200–£300 a year); he was convinced that, for all his doubts about the work, he had entirely vindicated the Lord Protector's memory. In addition, Chapman's decided on a third edition of *The French Revolution*, and a new edition of the *Miscellanies*.

The 'solitary' existence ended in early May, when once more he and Jane were the guests of the Barings, this time at Addiscombe. Jane went first, he a couple of days later. There was little for him to do except smoke and go for long walks, as Baring was at parliament, and Jane and Lady Harriet would go for walks and drives together. Once back in London there were a few excitements. The Duke of Saxe Weimar, the youthful grandson of Goethe's patron, was visiting Queen Victoria, and wanted to meet Carlyle. The Grand Duchess, the Duke's mother, invited Carlyle to Buckingham Palace so he could meet the Duke, but Carlyle – whose nerves could be shattered for a week after an ordinary dinner party – 'politely declined' the invitation.[41] However, the Duke asked whether it would be 'convenient'[42] for him to call at Cheyne Row at noon on a Sunday in late June. Jane did not want to have to condescend to the Duke (she was especially reluctant to have to wait for permission to sit down in her own home), and so went out to visit Mrs Buller at the time he was due. In fact, the Duke arrived four hours late, his aunt, Queen Adelaide, having insisted on his going to church with her. Carlyle, who because of the Duke's lateness had to throw out an American friend of Emerson's who had come to see him for tea, was impressed with the young man. The Duke talked of Goethe and Weimar, and admired Carlyle's col-

lection of Goetheana. He invited Carlyle to come to Weimar ('Do not forget
me ... come and see us yonder')[43] and promised to send him a rare book,
which may account for some of Carlyle's good opinion of his visitor. Carlyle
was asked by the Duke why German literature was not more widely studied
in England. 'I told him,' Carlyle later informed Espinasse, 'that this was due
to our sulky radical temper.'[44]

Caroline Fox went to Chelsea on 20 May, and saw Jane in a state of distress
after taking opium and tartar for her cough, on medical prescription. The
hallucinations caused by this made her feel she had turned to marble and was
lying on her own gravestone. The medical profession, which, in the person
of Sir James Crichton-Browne half a century later, would condemn Jane as a
neurotic, was certainly doing its best to help her to that state. Carlyle drifted
in, and Miss Fox found him cordial but prolix, time heavy on his hands.[45]
The income from his books, which Carlyle now regarded as a sort of 'landed
property'[46] to him, sustained him in his idleness. His bile was mounting.
'Tolerance and a rose-water world is the evil symptom of the time we are
living in,' he told Miss Fox. He told Browning that he was 'idle not for want
of work, but rather in sight of a whole universe of work, which I have to
despair of accomplishing'.[47] *Oliver* continued to occupy him; a few months
earlier he had heard from a Norfolk merchant, William Squire, of a cache of
letters in Squire's possession. Fitzgerald was holidaying in East Anglia, and
Carlyle was anxious to hear whether he had met Squire and seen the documents. They were forgeries, though Carlyle, and some of his antiquary
friends, were for a time taken in by them, and he wasted much time over
them. The episode also made him, in retrospect, look foolish, hasty and
insufficiently rigorous. When he published an article in *Fraser's* on the strength
of them he received a number of sceptical enquiries. Another Norfolk correspondent, Edward Blakely, who wrote casting doubt on their veracity, was
sharply told by Carlyle that 'I am sorry any person whatever should fancy I
would put my name, publicly or privately, to a fiction, and, giving it out as a
fact, call the operation a good "joke".'[48]

Carlyle wanted to travel north, ultimately to see his family at Scotsbrig,
but to look at some of England on the way. However, while the few people
with whom he was prepared to socialise – notably the Barings and Milnes –
were in London, Carlyle was not minded to leave. Jack was still in London,
translating Dante, and irritating Carlyle by his failure to set himself up in his
own house. Jane, approaching her forty-sixth birthday, did not recover her
health during the summer of 1847. She had what she thought to be a tumour
in her throat, but which turned out to be merely an inflammation. She still
could not sleep, had no appetite, a high fever, was prone to headaches, and
would cry a lot. 'I suppose "the fact is", as Carlyle says, "that I am very
unwell",' she wrote in early July, feeling oppressed by the hot weather.[49]
Carlyle's continued remembrance of her birthday on 14 July distressed her
more, so touched was she by the brooch he gave her; and he was so concerned

about her health that he insisted she leave London for some country air as soon as possible. So ill was she that she did not even bridle at his suggestions of her returning to Scotland for the first time since her mother's death; but that was still not to be. Carlyle took himself out on his own occasionally, dining one evening in a party with Jenny Lind, the Swedish singer, with whom he spoke in French, and by whose singing he was utterly unimpressed.

At the beginning of August the Carlyles went to Matlock Bath in Derbyshire, where the spa waters could benefit them both. It was agreed that, afterwards, he would go on to Scotland and she home. They found an apartment of three rooms for 30s a week, with a magnificent view and relative quiet. They intended to have 'a kind of *sleep*-week'[50] there, when they would not even write letters to anyone. Carlyle was excited by the scenery, entirely new to him, and set out on foot to explore it as soon as he and Jane were settled in. While there they saw W.E. Forster, a young Bradford industrialist whom Carlyle had first met in about 1842. Forster, much influenced by Carlyle's thought, would later, having entered parliament, become the minister responsible for the 1870 Education Act, which introduced compulsory education, and subsequently Chief Secretary for Ireland. Forster suggested they explore the Peak District more widely, and (much to Carlyle's relief) organised the expedition. He had long wanted the Carlyles to stay with him at Rawdon, his home near Leeds, so the expedition headed in that direction, stopping off at Buxton and other secluded Derbyshire villages as it worked its way north. The Peak District tour ended amid the grime of Sheffield, whence they took a train to Leeds.

For a change, Carlyle was delighted to be under somebody else's roof, and truly enjoyed Forster's hospitality. The silence was absolute, and Forster went out to his business each day leaving Carlyle and Jane alone. So content were they, indeed, that they spent the best part of three weeks there, until early September. Carlyle made but one excursion, over towards Pontefract to meet Milnes, with whom he spent a night at Fryston; and Milnes came over to Rawdon later the same week. For Carlyle it was his most complete relaxation for years; he forgot, as he told Emerson, 'that there was any world but that of dreams'.[51] He had discovered the knack of not being guilty at doing nothing.

III

Carlyle went to Scotsbrig via Manchester, where he had an enjoyable but exhausting short stay with Geraldine Jewsbury. He also met John Bright, 'with his squat stout body, with his cock nose and pugnacious eyes, and Barclay-Fox quaker collar, John and I discorded in our views not a little!'[52] Carlyle and Bright's adherents may have agreed on the Corn Laws, but the rest of liberalism was anathema to Carlyle. On reaching Dumfriesshire Carlyle found all well with his family, with word from Alick in Canada of increasing prosperity and success. Carlyle stayed idly there until the beginning of October. It was no longer, however, a place of complete silence. The railway was now open through Ecclefechan, and from Scotsbrig the trains could be heard squealing through. Jane, who had taken to her bed ill again soon after her return to Chelsea, found herself attended to by John Forster (no relation of their Yorkshire host) and invited to Addiscombe by Lady Harriet. Jane's hostess was in high spirits and made no allowance for her guest's poor health, leaving Jane to think Lady Harriet regarded her as a hypochondriac. She was relieved to get back to London, where she prepared the house for the return of her husband and also for the long-awaited visit of Emerson. Because the post-master at Buxton had lost Emerson's last letter to Carlyle, and Carlyle had only just received it, there was an element of panic about the visit.

Stopping off to see Spedding at Keswick on his way home, Carlyle was back by mid-October. He resumed his solitary ways, telling von Ense that 'the world here, especially the world of "Literature" so called, is not my world.' He added that 'I begin very greatly to despise the thing they call "Literature".'[53] Since Carlyle had probably had a more relaxed, unpressured and contented few months than for years, it is hard to see what had poisoned his character so; but this is the genuine tone of the misanthropy of the *Latter-Day Pamphlets*. All one can detect is the resurgence of frustration at not being able to think of what to do. 'If I were a Prussian, or even German,' he told von Ense, 'I would decidedly try *Friedrich*'.

It was early November before Emerson, who had started his lecture-tour in Manchester, made contact with Carlyle; he had already found Carlyle's friends in that city, such as Geraldine Jewsbury, Francis Espinasse and Mrs Paulet. Carlyle wrote to him in mid-November complaining that 'I am sunk deep here, in effete Manuscripts, in abstruse Meditations, in confusions old and new; sinking, as I may describe myself, thro' stratum after stratum of the Inane, – down to one knows not what depths!'[54] Espinasse remembered Emerson saying that 'Carlyle's heart is as large as the world, but he is growing morbid.'[55] As in the time of the composition of *Oliver*, Carlyle seems to have been blaming the world for his inability to get on with work. He did, briefly this autumn, return to his writing-desk, but only to work on the Squire letters for his article in *Fraser's*. When Emerson reached London he and Carlyle no longer felt the attraction they had fifteen years earlier, which had been sustained in their letters. 'Good of him I could get none,' confided Carlyle in his journal of this reunion.[56] Carlyle had become harsher, more self-centred; Emerson remained a gentle mystic. The following year he told James Marshall, a Scot who was private secretary to the Duke of Saxe Weimar and with whom Carlyle had begun to correspond, that Emerson was now 'somewhat moonshiny'.[57]

Jane wrote to Forster (who had asked them to the theatre) that Carlyle 'no longer [has] a duty to fulfil in promoting my happiness'.[58] She also told Forster that Carlyle even found fault with the fact that she had promised to read some proofs of a new novel by Geraldine Jewsbury, because (as Jane put it) he said 'I "do not know bad grammar when I see it, any better than she does".' This prompted her to conclude that 'I do think there is much truth in the Young German idea that marriage is a shockingly immoral institution, as well as what we have long known it for – an extremely disagreeable one.' The Carlyles' marriage was at an especially low point, Jane's neuroticism and Carlyle's self-centred obsessions feeding off each other almost lethally. As a result of this and of Carlyle's other unhappinesses with the world around him, they were embarking upon the period he uncompromisingly characterised in the *Reminiscences* as that of 'deep gloom and bottomless dubitation'[59] that brought forth the *Latter-Day Pamphlets*.

So antipathetic had Carlyle become to 'literature' that he started reading the *Domesday Book* 'with the commentaries of various blockheads'.[60] A new edition of *Sartor* was coming out, prompting him to observe it was 'very strange, and is indeed almost pathetic to me, that these poor bits of books should still be read'.[61] He was also aggrieved by the Bill, consequent upon Rothschild's election for the City of London, to remove Jewish parliamentary disabilities, and wrote a ferociously anti-semitic letter to Milnes complaining about it. 'A Jew is bad, but what is a Sham-Jew, a Quack-Jew? And how can a real Jew, by possibility, try to be a Senator, or even Citizen of any country, except his own wretched Palestine, whither all his thoughts and steps and efforts tend?'[62] In these views he was little different from most of his circle.

It was a bitterly cold December, with Jane, already sick and coughing constantly, complaining a fortnight before Christmas of the water in her jug being frozen over in the house. Although the season was brightened up by Sunday visits from Tennyson, then composing *The Princess*, Christmas itself was austere. Carlyle wrote to his sister of how in London there were 'huge *walls* of slain sheep and beeves; all railroads groaning with fat turkeys, capons, hares'; but he and Jane would content themselves on having, on Christmas Day, 'perhaps *nothing*, except some small pudding of ground rice or the like'.[63] They had opulence in prospect; they had been asked to visit Alverstoke from 7 January to 15 February 1848. Carlyle was not looking forward to it, but told Jean that 'kind souls, of any rank, especially of that rank, ought to have their kindness recognised, by the like of us.'[64]

Despite the luxury, and respite from cold, waiting at the other end, Jane could not bring herself to go to the Barings; so Carlyle went alone. Either he genuinely did not enjoy his visit or, fearing Jane might not like hearing of him happy in Lady Harriet's company, he exaggerated his discomforts there. He wrote complaining of sleeplessness, dyspepsia and the cold, railing against the idleness of everyone there, and wishing (despite the presence of Milnes and Buller) he had stayed at Chelsea. He begged Jane to change her mind, but she resisted. After barely a fortnight Carlyle made his excuses and left.

He returned to find Jane still confined to bed. His first act was to read Julius Hare's *Life of Sterling*, which he found unsatisfactory. Ironically in the light of Carlyle's views on the question, Baron Rothschild tried to recruit him to write a pamphlet (naming any price he liked for doing so) advocating the removal of parliamentary disabilities on Jews. Hardly surprisingly, he passed up the offer. Yet, in his journal, he castigated himself for having done no work for two years, an indolence that left him 'weary and near heartbroken'.[65] Because he felt the world was daily growing more 'unspeakable in meaning' to him he had given up trying to speak to it. It was not that he had nothing to say; he had too much, and did not know how to compose it into sense. Some readers of *Latter-Day Pamphlets* might contend he never succeeded.

Even his friends and their work disgusted him. Tennyson's *The Princess* he regarded as a 'gorgeous piece of writing' but also 'new melancholy proof of the futility of what they call "Art" '.[66] No wonder Tennyson said of Carlyle at around this time 'you would like him for one day but then get tired of him; so vehement and destructive.'[67] In the same journal entry, dated 9 February 1848, Carlyle rehearsed various plans for his next project; the *Life of Sterling* was the only one of four he specified that came to fruition. He thought of 'spiritual sketches' of Ireland, and of something called 'The Scavenger Age', saying that 'our age is really up to nothing better than the sweeping out the gutter.'[68] Most seriously occupying him, though, were thoughts of a work provisionally entitled 'Exodus from Houndsditch', the area of London then populated by second-hand clothes sellers, mostly Jews. Using his favourite metaphor, he wanted to write about the importance of people casting off the 'spiritual old clothes' of conventional Christianity, and finding a theocentric religion like his own; but, in his demoralised state, and with reality making a brief appearance in his calculations, he saw that such a work would be hopeless; nor had he forgotten his mother's horror at his question about God Almighty and the wheelbarrows, and could not bring himself to attack this most sensitive matter in the way he would have liked.[69] The stripping away of organised religious cant might be central to national revival, but he would not be undertaking the task. A similar argument was put forward at this time by Froude in his *Nemesis of Faith*, which Forster sent to Carlyle, and which drew the observation that it was just 'a wretched mortal's vomiting up all his interior crudities, dubitations, and spiritual, agonising belly-aches, into the view of the public'.[70] Carlyle and Froude, despite their subsequent closeness, never quite understood each other. Like Ruskin, Froude treated Carlyle with unmixed veneration, and attendant humourlessness. Oblivious to flattery and generally too self-absorbed to reflect at all on what others thought of him, Carlyle could not appreciate either the intensity or the danger of mis-understandings arising from such discipular attitudes.

Material about Cromwell was still trickling in to Carlyle, and his own conscientiousness and desire for the truth would not allow him to ignore it. One correspondent, the Reverend J. Edleston of Trinity College, Cambridge, communicated with Carlyle throughout 1848 and 1849, supplying additional items that Carlyle promised to incorporate 'whenever the opportunity of a new edition occurs'.[71] Carlyle, in his increasing depression about modern life, saw Cromwell as an ever-brighter beacon. 'All notices and vestiges show him to us,' he told Edleston, 'in an interesting way, consistent with himself; doing his work to the last, whoever may neglect theirs.'[72]

Further inspiration soon came, with the uprising in France that triggered similar protests against governments across Europe. He had predicted such an event in England throughout the 1840s, and, once France went up, the Chartists were reignited to pursue that aim. His friends in the Young Ireland group sought help from the French against the British, which led to their arraignment for treason. Carlyle wrote a short essay on Louis-Philippe, the deposed monarch, for *The Examiner*, the first of several such excursions into print that year. He thought he wanted to write more; he spelled out in his journal at the time a plan for a work on the themes of democracy and cant; but then, perhaps realising he had said all this before, concluded 'Shall I begin it? I am sick, lazy, and dispirited.'[73] He toyed with the idea for several weeks, though told his old friend Thomas Erskine on 24 March that he had not started writing because 'I am not yet grown sufficiently *miserable* to set about it straightaway'.[74] Earlier that week, thanks to an initiative by the Barings, he was asked to dinner and placed next to Peel, and found himself impressed most of all by the ex-Prime Minister's sense of humour. He still regarded him as the greatest figure in English public life and, as the rioting spread to Berlin, felt there might one day be a need for him to return to office.

In April Emerson returned to London, bringing with him Joseph Neuberg, a Jewish businessman from Nottingham whom he had met while lecturing, and who longed to meet Carlyle. Neuberg, who had grown up in Germany, was to become a close companion of Carlyle's during the 1850s, helping with *Frederick*. A few days later Lady Harriet at last persuaded Jane to go to Addiscombe, not least because the London middle and upper classes were beginning to worry about the prospect of insurrection in the capital. Carlyle, who had struggled with his own cough and cold ever since his return from Alverstoke, became even more miserable once his wife was away, and before long was begging her to come back. His self-pity reached new heights. He told her he was 'more like an ancient Egyptian mummy at present than a modern living British man'.[75] He amused himself on 10 April by going to Hyde Park to watch the great Chartist demonstration, which, he noted with an air of disappointment, produced no revolution.

Ireland, he knew, was different, and its problems stirred him into a prolific interlude. With an open invitation from Forster to write in *The Examiner*, Carlyle wrote a short essay on the Irish there in late April, pointing out that Ireland was vulnerable to the movements seen on the continent of Europe. Another piece appeared on 13 May, the same date as the editor of *The Spectator*, R.S. Rintoul, ran two pieces by Carlyle. The first, 'Ireland and the British Chief Governor', acknowledged that troubles in Ireland could be put down by force, but that such measures gave 'no indication how the Irish population ... is to continue living at all'.[76] Carlyle said the attitude of the Irish towards the British served the British right, because it had been fostered by 'our government of make-believe and not of truth and reality'.[77] He condemned the Lord Lieutenant, Lord Clarendon, for seeking to redress the problem simply by encouraging the registration of Irish voters: 'Extension of the electoral suffrage – good heavens, what will that do for a country which labours under the frightfullest immediate want of potatoes?'[78] He added: 'Could the chief governor, in his beneficence, extend the suffrage through municipalities and counties, through villages and parishes, so that not only all the men of Ireland, but all the women and children, and even all the oxen and asses and dogs of Ireland, should be asked their vote, and taught to give it with the exactest authenticity, and the last finish of constitutional per-fection – of what avail would that be?' He stated explicitly that the only practical reform would be 'curtailing the suffrage again', and that the auth-orities should look at what had happened to Louis-Philippe if they wanted to see where sham-government got them: 'one huge Democracy, one huge Anarchy or *Kinglessness*'. As usual with Carlyle, his analysis was more destruc-tive than constructive, and never descended into the world of the practical.

Conscious of this, perhaps, he immediately wrote a second article for *The Spectator* called 'Irish Regiments of the New Aera', which suggested organised labour forces of Irishmen to help revive the country. Many of the 'unemployed vagrant miscellaneous Irish, once dressed in proper red coats, and put under proper drill sergeants', would, he knew, make fine soldiers.[79] An extension of this talent for fighting was 'an indisputable talent for spade work'. He had seen them for the last decade digging railways in England, and knew they could work harder on fewer rations than any other race. He wanted them sent, in regiments, to cultivate Ireland. He doubted the British government could ever act so sensibly, and in his cynical dismissal of them presaged the *Latter-Day Pamphlets*. Almost incidental to this is his accidental invention of what the twentieth century would call Keynesianism, ninety years before its time.

IV

In the depths of his frustration Carlyle still had, none the less, some reserves of good humour, easily brought out by his friends. On 25 April he, Dickens and Emerson had dinner with Forster at Forster's rooms in Lincoln's Inn Fields, and the host later recalled the 'mountainous mirth' drawn out of Carlyle on this occasion.[80] To start to write again after so long a silence also improved Carlyle's spirits. The 'wild revolutionary times'[81] were provoking him towards activity. He told Alick that a set of newspaper articles was a possibility; but it was the *Latter-Day Pamphlets* he was working towards. In a fit of energy he decided to go with Emerson, in London to lecture after witnessing the excitements in Paris, to see Stonehenge on 7 July. Carlyle found it overwhelming in its mystery, and wandered round it with Emerson looking for shelter from the wind so he could light his cigar. They pottered about until twilight, after which they returned to their inn at Amesbury for a tea that was 'the worst in nature',[82] and for Carlyle to write to Jane complaining about the journey. To Emerson the trip was a great joke, 'a bringing together of extreme points, to visit the oldest religious monument in Britain, in company with their latest thinker, and one whose influence may be traced in every contemporary book'.[83] They went back the next morning with a local antiquary, driving over the Downs in a dog-cart, and Carlyle cursing the landowners who left the vast expanse of Salisbury Plain for sheep when it should have been cultivated by unemployed artisans. Before returning to London they went to see Wilton House and Winchester Cathedral, where Carlyle affectionately patted the hands of the statue of William of Wykeham, in tribute to his services to education. Having been brought out into the world himself by means of education, it was hardly surprising that his optimistic belief in its power to improve people was the only part of liberal philosophy to which Carlyle could still bring himself to subscribe.

He and Jane stayed in London that summer; but as the city emptied they became more and more isolated, seeing no one. A few weeks earlier Chopin, who was in London giving some concerts, had been to see them. Once such excitements had passed, Carlyle retreated back into himself. In his journal on 10 August he wondered whether he had reached 'the nadir of my spiritual course'.[84] Forster tried to cheer him and Jane up by taking them to the opera to hear Jenny Lind, and then out to dinner. Carlyle sat once more to Samuel Laurence for a portrait, but the artist abandoned it after four sittings, and Carlyle returned to Chelsea to sit in 'the utmost attainable silence' and wait for something to happen.

The Barings, once more, provided a diversion. Baring had succeeded to his father's peerage the previous May, and was now Lord Ashburton. The period of mourning now over, he and his wife decided to host a lengthy house-party at the Grange, now their main country house. Carlyle was not looking forward to going, so used had he become to his own company, but none the less he and Jane left for Hampshire on 1 September for a long stay. The silence at the Grange appealed to him, and his spirits quickly revived. He was also cheered up by Charles Buller, who was of the party, though found the rich food – quite unlike the plain, almost spartan diet he had at home – began to interfere with his digestion, and therefore his sleep. He was able to keep to himself for the mornings, as he did at home, and then go riding in the afternoons. By 19 September he was writing to Jack, who was back at Dumfries, that 'the inner man . . . begins to get decidedly a little weary of the affair.'[85] Jane, though, was enjoying herself, and there was no urge on her part to leave. She had made what would turn out to be a life-long friendship with Lady Ashburton's mother, the dowager Countess of Sandwich. He became bored with the company, which he characterised to Jack as a 'twaddle-deluge'; and when he remonstrated with the twaddlers passionately, through one of his monologues, they simply thought he was being amusing; unintentionally, he probably was. He took himself out for walks and explored the surrounding countryside, soaking up the solitude. Lord Ashburton had a plan of putting a farm on his estate permanently at the Carlyles' disposal, but this act of kindness (not to mention the farmyard noises) would have been too much for them, and they ensured that the matter dropped.

They eventually escaped home in early October, after a stay of five weeks. Carlyle was keenly aware of the kindness shown him and Jane, but his deep feelings of loneliness, despite the constant companionship available to him, made him miserable. All the time he had had for thought had still brought no plan of a book to him; and, although he had more than thirty-two years of life left, he wrote in his journal that 'I am grown old. My next book must be that of an old man, and I am not yet got into that dialect.' Relevant to his 'next book' was a visit he and Jane paid to the 'model prison' at Millbank with Forster soon after their return to London; a visit Forster ironically rounded off with a fine dinner at which the Carlyles 'were filled half drunk with champagne as usual'.[86] Such indulgence was not practised at home. On the advice of Emerson, the Carlyles had started eating Indian meal (the maize indigenous to America, grown there by Indians, and said to be unfit even for the rearing of poultry) with everything as potatoes were again in short supply, and Carlyle was forced to write to his friend for advice on how better to cook it to remove its bitterness. Eventually a method was discovered, and Carlyle became such a zealot for the food that he wrote a short encomium to it in *Fraser's* the following spring. He was depressed that *The Times* did not want to publish his thoughts on the subject; he felt that a means of feeding a man for a penny a day was something deserving of wider publicity.

Carlyle was thinking about Ireland. Charles Gavan Duffy had been arrested for treason allegedly arising out of his involvement with Young Ireland; Carlyle wrote to him while he awaited trial (he was acquitted). Though no friend of revolutionaries, Carlyle's distaste at the way the British ran Ireland, and his conviction that Duffy must have behaved honourably, led him to be sympathetic. 'If this bit of paper do reach you within your strait walls,' he wrote on 21 October, 'let it be an assurance that you are still dear to me; that in this sad crisis that has now arrived, we here at Chelsea do not find new cause for blame superadded to the old, but new cause for pity and respect, and loving candour, and for hope still, in spite of all!'[87]

The autumn was grim for Carlyle. To add to his creative frustration came news, at the end of November, of the unexpected death of Charles Buller at the age of forty-two. His brilliant ex-pupil, now an ebullient radical Liberal MP and popular social figure about London, had become Commissioner for the Poor Law in Lord John Russell's government. Though Buller had yet to live up to his promise, Carlyle hoped he might yet reform the system sensibly.

However, due to a mistake by a surgeon during a minor operation, Buller was never to have the chance. His family and friends were united in grief; and so catastrophic was the effect on his mother, widowed but a few months earlier, that she died the following March. Carlyle paid tribute to him as 'the cleverest of all Whig men, and indeed the only genial soul one can remember in that department of things'.[88] He wrote a eulogy to him in the *Examiner*; yet again, ironically, he was provoked to take up his pen only by sadness and upheaval. Buller had seen through Carlyle – or so he thought – some years earlier. Writing from Alverstoke when the Carlyles were staying, he had told Milnes (in tones that echoed Matthew Arnold): 'I think he is going the way of all flesh into extravagance and cant. His great business is working every truth which he ever taught into the shape of a paradox or falsehood. He is a prophet without a mission, holding no belief and promising no deliverance.'[89] Carlyle had little opportunity to dwell on Buller's death. His energies were fully occupied during the succeeding weeks consoling Lady Ashburton, who was distraught.

His fit of creativity was temporary. He told his journal on 14 December that he was 'unable to stir myself, writhing with hand and foot glued together, under a load of contemptible miseries'.[90] As usual, it was not his fault. 'Very often, I think, "Would the human species universally be so kind as to leave me altogether alone ..." the hurt that others (involuntary for the most part) do me is incalculable.' Modern philosophies drove him to deeper despair, the modes of thought he stigmatised as 'the general Bankruptcy of Humbug', 'Economics, Religions, alike declaring themselves to be *Mene, Mene*; all public arrangements among men falling as one huge *confessed* Imposture, into bottomless insolvency.'[91] It was at this time, though, that he embarked on what were to become the *Latter-Day Pamphlets*; the earliest manuscript fragments that have been traced are dated November 1848.[92] He busied himself reading, and wrote on 29 December to von Ense that 'I shall start up too, some day.' With another year about to begin he felt he had to start work; and he told von Ense that the message of the discontents across Europe in 1848 was the 'bankruptcy of imposture', from which he drew a rare piece of comfort.

Yet the only work he could attempt was another revision of *Oliver*, for a third edition Chapman wished to bring out. He could just about apply himself to it. 'The history of man,' he wrote to Marshall in Weimar, 'in all forms of it – this is alone interesting to man.' Yet he also admitted that he was feeling 'most inarticulate, chaotic wholly, and abhorrent of speech, or the vain effort to speak. This "general Bankruptcy of Humbug all over the world", one of the most scandalous sights the sons of Adam ever saw, is enough to create silence in a serious man ... on the whole I love silence more and more, and speech less and less, in this world.'[93] However silence, which appears here to be a metaphor for Carlyle's right to be morose undisturbed, was a precious commodity. Jane irritated him during January by having to stay with them the six-year-old daughter of William Macready, the impresario, to whom she was godmother. Jane, with no experience of children, was thrilled at the chance to mother the little girl for three days, though the novelty wore off when she threatened to madden Carlyle by her inclination to sing continuously.

Carlyle saw little of his wife at this time. She had devoted herself to Mrs Buller, soon to die herself, and her friendship with Lady Sandwich had opened up new opportunities for her. She and Carlyle went in February to stay for a week near Epsom with Captain Sterling, brother of their late friend, which at least allowed Carlyle some exhausting walks and rides. Unusually, he had invited himself, tempted by a good report of the place from Jack, and Anthony Sterling had acceded to the self-invitation on the condition that Carlyle brought Jane. Carlyle had no objection, because Jane would be useful to 'keep Anthony off him and let him enjoy *the perfect* silence'.[94] For Jane there was the slight difficulty of Mrs Sterling's earlier conviction that her husband was in love with Jane, and there had been a long stand-off between them. Mrs Sterling, who was slightly deranged, was living elsewhere, but Jane none the less sought her permission to visit her husband.

Their return to London brought a shock. Helen, recently returned from Dublin to keep house for them again, was discovered spectacularly drunk. She opened the door with 'a hideous smile of idiotic self-complacency', and Carlyle had to drag her downstairs and deposit her on the kitchen floor while she sobered up.[95] The house was a shambles, since Helen had been drunk daily during their absence, and had held drinking-parties there. She ran out that evening to drink more, Jane computing her intake for the day as a half-pint of rum, the same quantity of gin and a quart of ale. It was the last straw. Pressing two sovereigns in Helen's hand to tide her over, Jane sent her back to Kirkcaldy and told her never to show her face in Chelsea again. As a therapy, Jane busied herself making the print screen that can still be seen in the library on the first floor in Cheyne Row.

Slowly, Carlyle returned to writing. He was making final changes to *Oliver* for a new edition, though wearily. Having incorporated the final items sent from Cambridge by Edleston, he wrote back to say that he had at last done with 'that sorrowful book' and 'I now feel as if I might wash my hands again.'[96] He was keen to visit Ireland again, and wrote a piece *The Spectator* published on 14 April about the need to remove Russell and bring back Peel, who had recently made two impressive speeches on Ireland, to exert the correct authority over the problem. His vigorous, apostrophising style, exhorting politicians to abandon the 'bankruptcy of imposture' about Ireland, declared the identity of this piece, signed only by 'C'. 'The reader will not have needed the initial "C" to identify the author, whose signature is stamped on every line of this contribution,' added the editor.[97] He said the piece showed 'the most recluse of our philosophers coming forward to bear the testimony of perennial history in aid of the most practical statesman of our day.'

Carlyle was still determined to write about the 'revolutionary time we have got into'.[98] His spirits began to improve, his desire for society fed not just by visits to Addiscombe and the Grange to see the Ashburtons, but also by going out more in London and dining with the likes of Dickens and Forster. His circle expanded in this year; Neuberg was encouraged to call on him regularly, and noted of Carlyle at this time that 'he walks rather like a Catholic priest, his long thin body somewhat shambling.'[99] Carlyle would have hated the comparison. As he studied the Irish question he felt more and more that the country's ills were a direct result of its non-participation in the Reformation.

Having made up his mind to go to Ireland, with a view at last to writing a book, he obtained and pored over maps of the country, working out where he would most like to go; and decided the easiest way to get there was by steamer from London to Dublin. He wrote to Gavan Duffy, still on bail for his role in Young Ireland's activities the previous year, to ask for assistance. Duffy offered to be his guide, provided he was not taken into custody again. As Carlyle was making his plans he made another important acquaintance. James Spedding brought James Anthony Froude, who had just resigned his fellowship at Oxford, to Cheyne Row one evening in June. Carlyle had wanted to meet Froude, despite his disgust at the sentimentality of *The Nemesis of Faith*. They found Carlyle sitting outside his back door on the summer's evening smoking his pipe, and reading Jocelyn of Ferns *Life of St Patrick*, and trying to imagine what Ireland had been like before the Danes and Saxons reached it. Froude gives a precise description of Carlyle in middle age:

He was then fifty-four years old; tall (about five feet eleven), thin, but at that time upright, with no signs of the later stoop. His body was angular, his face beardless ... His head was extremely long, with the chin thrust forward; the neck was thin; the mouth firmly closed, the under lip slightly projecting; the hair grizzled and thick and bushy. His eyes, which grew lighter with age, were then of a deep violet, with fire burning at the bottom of them, which flashed out at the least excitement.[100]

Froude was met not rudely, but with the minimum social grace. He did not worry. 'No one need look for conventional politeness from Carlyle – he would hear the exact truth, and nothing else.' Leaving aside his hero-worship, he detected a warmer side to Carlyle in his gently mocking talk to both Jane and to Spedding. The Carlyles also asked Froude to visit them again, to his relief.

V

On 30 June Carlyle took the steamer to Dublin. Jane was glad to see him go. She had arranged to travel to Scotland for the first time since her mother's death, and was happier to do so without the accompanying emotional baggage of her husband. He arrived in Ireland on 3 July. He had asked Duffy to ensure he was taken to the famine districts, even though cholera was rife in many of them; but first he had to satisfy the demands of various prominent Irishmen to see him. He stayed at the Imperial Hotel, owned by Edward Fitzgerald's aunt, and a welcome had been prepared for him. Duffy met him that evening. The representatives of authority whom he met were shocked that Carlyle should travel with Duffy, a virtual outlaw, which amused Carlyle greatly. He declined an invitation to dine with Clarendon, the Lord Lieutenant, and most evenings found himself at a dinner table with some of Duffy's friends, debating the problem he had come to investigate.

'I am really like to be killed with "attentions" here,' he wrote to Jane on his third day in Dublin.[101] He had no time for silent reflection, and had slept badly. He was keen to get away from Dublin, and on the Monday after his arrival went off to Wicklow with Fitzgerald's cousin Peter. As they went through the expanse of uncultivated country, Carlyle noted that the silence was disturbed only by cries of beggars for alms. He remarked, in a letter to Jane on 11 July, on the wild and ragged state of the people in Kilkenny, and the large numbers of soldiers and policemen required to keep order. The next day he and Duffy went to Waterford, Carlyle becoming more and more depressed by the waste of the land and the evidence all around of bad husbandry. From Cork on 17 July he wrote he was thinking of parting from Duffy, because Duffy was a good sleeper and was grating with Carlyle, who was not. They continued to and up the west coast, often visiting the homes of the Ascendancy, with whom Carlyle had been put into contact by friends in London. Travelling to Killarney they passed through what Carlyle called '70 of the saddest miles I have seen',[102] with 'hordes of beggars' and ruined hovels everywhere. At Westport Carlyle found 'human swinery at its acme'.[103] Half the 60,000 population of the town were paupers, costing £1,100 a week to keep. It was the worst case in Ireland. As he looked round the Westport and other workhouses, and saw bailiffs going out to perform evictions, it provoked new thoughts in him of the absurdity, as he saw it, of Exeter-Hall philanthropists working for the abolition of slavery when there were such evils so near home.

Carlyle had hoped W.E. Forster (with whom Jane had stayed on her way north) would make the whole trip with him, but they did not in fact meet until Mayo. Carlyle continued with Forster north to Londonderry, which he reached in early August, and whence – after the now usual celebrity reception – they took a boat to Glasgow. Jane was in Scotland, having just paid her first visit to Haddington since their marriage twenty-three years earlier, and now staying with her cousin Walter at Auchtertool. But Carlyle decided to go straight to Scotsbrig, and parted with Forster at Ecclefechan station. He was glad to be home, not having seen his family for two years.

He had time to reflect on how he could use in a book what he had seen. Still he was undecided. 'I seem to be farther from speech on any subject than ever,'[104] he wrote to Emerson on 13 August from Scotsbrig. He was not just in despair at his own lack of creativity, but – and this was the root of it – in despair at what might be done to relieve Ireland. He stayed a week with his mother before joining Jane in Fife. He had an invitation to join the Ashburtons, in a shooting-party at Kingussie in the Highlands, and visited Jane on the way north. She was far from pleased he had accepted the Ashburtons' invitation, suspecting his motives as he did not in the least like shooting-parties. She had her revenge; his first letter to her, on 2 September, details a tedious journey and boring aristocratic company on arrival. The house, Glen Truim, he found uncomfortable and inconvenient, and he was astonished at the profligacy of Lord Ashburton, who had paid £1,200 to rent these inadequate facilities.

Carlyle's letter to Jane also begs her to 'dismiss your anger against me'; he was further dispirited during his stay by the lingering unpleasantness of their parting. Thanks to a 'too violent excursion'[105] he went down with severe colic, following on from an attack of lumbago. He wrote to Jack of the futility of his visit, and then to Jane again telling her that 'my visit prospers as *ill* as could be wished.'[106] His only relief was the arrival of Milnes, which at least gave him some intelligent company. Carlyle did not stay more than ten days with the Ashburtons. He went to Edinburgh, where he saw Jeffrey for an afternoon – for the last time, as it turned out, as 'the Advocate' died the following year. He then returned to Scotsbrig; in a self-pitying fortnight he wrote to Jane of how nobody understood the suffering he had to endure on his 'Life Pilgrimage',[107] and then came back to Chelsea.

For Jane, the shock of being back in a noisy town was sufficient to drive her to morphia. Carlyle tried to return to some sort of routine, but tension in the house was great. One evening, when they were talking to each other, Jane thought Carlyle had gone mad when he 'suddenly stamped his foot on the hearth-rug and called out furiously, "Get along sir!" ' He had, in fact, seen a mouse run by him. Jane was pleased to have seen Scotland again; but Carlyle, by contrast, was plunging to a new depth of despair. He disciplined himself to write the *Reminiscence* of the Irish journey, which took him most of the first half of October; and, to help out Duffy, who had relaunched the *Nation* newspaper in Dublin, he sent him a short article on the need to plant trees in Ireland. Duffy misunderstood the thrust of the piece; he thought Carlyle was seeking to make an economic point, when in fact he was making a symbolic one about hope and belief in the continuity of Irish life.

On 11 November 1849, Carlyle was telling his journal that he was 'lonely', and regretting, surprisingly late in the day, how 'hard' he had become.[108] He would chide Jane for being sentimental; but the warmth and cheer of sentimentality was something in which he now wanted to share, but could not. A fortnight earlier he had complained self-pityingly to his sister Jean that 'alas, in bitter earnest, I am growing an old man, and have still an immensity of things which I have never got said.'[109] However, he was coming to a view, at last, of the form of his next work, drawing on the confusion of ideas and feelings that were taunting him now he was at the depths of his 'deep gloom and bottomless dubitation'.[110] In his journal he wrote that he was 'trying to sort something out ... for magazine articles, series of pamphlets, or whatever they will promise to turn into'. He had been jotting down random thoughts on scraps of paper ever since he left for Ireland; now came the task of trying to rationalise them. He had an offer from Neuberg, who was wealthy enough to consider it, to act as a 'volunteer secretary'. Carlyle, normally too proud to accept help, unhesitatingly agreed. He could benefit not just from Neuberg's organisational skills, but also from his fine intellectual judgment.

Carlyle identified the theme running through his angry reflections. They were 'in dissent from all the world; in black contradiction, deep as the bases of my life, to all philanthropic, emancipatory, constitutional, and other anarchic revolutionary jargon'.[111] Fundamentally, he wanted to assault the priggishness and smugness of the liberal and philanthropic consensus that believed the lower orders could be reformed and improved and entrusted with greater responsibility; Carlyle believed no such thing. His first attempt to order these things was the *Occasional Discourse on the Nigger Question*, which he began in November, and which was scheduled for publication in *Fraser's* the following month. Though separate from the *Latter-Day Pamphlets*, it is effectively the first of them; identical to them in form, tone and style, and motivated by the same loathing of contemporary attitudes. 'It looks,' Carlyle told Jean on 21 November, 'as if I had a *continent* of foul liquid *glar* and scavengery to wheel away; barrow, shovels and *self* nearly buried in the vile black infinite of quagmire.'[112]

His frame of mind had become well known, even though (but for his short *Spectator* and *Examiner* essays) he had said nothing now for almost four years. Matthew Arnold, writing a rather precious letter to Arthur Hugh Clough two months earlier, complained of 'these ... damned times', and of how 'everything is against one – the height to which knowledge has come, the spread of luxury, our physical enervation, the absence of great *natures*, the unavoidable contact with millions of small ones, newspapers, cities, light profligate friends, moral desperadoes like Carlyle, our own selves, and the sickening consciousness of our own difficulties.'[113] Arnold, like Clough, had been a devotee of Carlyle's as an undergraduate, but had come to detest 'that regular Carlylean strain which we all know by heart and which the clear-headed among us have utter contempt for'.[114] Not for nothing had his Oxford contemporaries nicknamed him 'Mr Kid-Gloves Cocksure'.[115] When Carlyle died Arnold condemned him for 'preaching earnestness to a nation which had plenty of it by nature, but was less abundantly supplied with several other useful things',[116] a remark Carlyle would, if he could summon sufficient politeness, have taken as indicative of the crisis of faith in intellectuals of Arnold's generation. However much Arnold may have detested Carlyle ('part man of genius, part fanatic – and part Tom-fool'[117]) for asking religious questions to which Arnold could not find the answer, his political influence on Arnold was profound. The authoritarian tone of much of the social philosophy of *Culture and Anarchy* may owe much, ostensibly, to Arnold's father, but it owes just as much to the doctrines propounded over the preceding thirty years by Carlyle.

Religion, though, was the main problem Carlyle presented to younger intellectuals in the 1840s. The previous year Clough had told Emerson that many of his fellows had been handicapped by Carlyle's implicit religious teachings because 'Carlyle led us out into the desert and he has left us there';[118] but then Carlyle never made any allowances for the failure of those who read him to have the capacity for moral stringency, self-discovery and theological radicalism needed to follow him all the way. Clough's biographer, R.K. Biswas, characterised what Clough and his contemporaries learned from Carlyle as 'essentially a pessimistic vision, turning away from a stark and unmanageable present to a heroic past and the myths of order'.[119] Emerson could offer no solution, perhaps recognising that Carlyle had invented his own world view, or even created his own world, and retreated there. Though it may not have realised it, the Oxford generation of the 1840s was changed immeasurably by its exposure to Carlyle, and was to be the main conduit of Carlyle's influence for the rest of the century. At a time when Oxford was divided in debate between Protestantism and Catholicism, a thinker – in the shape of Carlyle – who stood above Christianity and offered other options was seductive. Such radicalism brought benefits to those who partook of it. G.M. Young wrote, nearly a century later, of how 'to the new Englishman of the late forties and fifties, a travelled man bred up on Carlyle and Tennyson and the romantic classics, the world was a far more interesting place than it had been to those late Augustans ... his religion conformed to the awakening of his senses.'[120]

The moral desperado himself spent December writing *The Nigger Question*, coincidentally a perfect example of the style that so offended young cultural conservatives like Arnold, himself still nearly twenty years away from his own complaints against 'our liberal practitioners' in *Culture and Anarchy*. Carlyle's original title for his pamphlet was *The Negro Question*, and as such it was published by *Fraser's*. The anger it provoked caused him to make the title more offensive, as a gesture of his unshakeable belief in its doctrines, when it was republished three years later. Mill, who had clearly never thought sufficiently deeply about Carlyle's beliefs, was stunned by it, and used the next edition of *Fraser's* to write a fierce rebuttal. Their friendship was over.

If the succeeding pamphlets can be easily traced back to events Carlyle had seen or participated in in the preceding years, the genesis of his attack on 'nigger philanthropists' is broader. He was looking not for an issue of burning importance upon which to expatiate, but for any issue that would provide a vehicle for his loathing of liberals. The treatment of emancipated slaves in the British West Indies was an ideal subject, because emancipation was trumpeted by the Exeter Hall philanthropists, who had so disgusted him for years, as their prime achievement. Carlyle felt their idea of slavery was ignorant; its wrong-headedness, as he saw it, had been made even more

obvious by his trip to Ireland. Froude called the pamphlet 'Carlyle's declaration of war against modern Radicalism',[121] a radicalism of which many,
reading his attacks on the governing classes but not reading them closely
enough, had thought he subscribed to. The author himself was delighted to
have hit his target, boasting to Jack of how the liberals were 'in a terrible
temper about The Niggers; chaunting mournful "Ichabod!" at me. Which is
all right.'[122]

It is the form and tone, rather than the actual message, that did most of
the damage. Carlyle constructs a brilliant parody of an Exeter Hall meeting,
with an unnamed speaker spelling out unpalatable truths to an audience
driven deeper and deeper into shock. Philanthropy in general he parodies as
'the Universal Abolition of Pain Association', which is at risk of turning into
a 'Sluggard and Scoundrel Protection Society'.[123] Carlyle did not feel he was
attacking the blacks; his targets were the liberals who were destroying them.
This was not, though, how his audience saw it.

He was so open to interpretation because of the callous, heartless and
brutally sarcastic language he used. He talks of the emancipated blacks being
like the Irish, with a land of plenty they are refusing to exploit, because no
one is there to guide them to the greater happiness that exists beyond eating
pumpkins. The essay is also an attack on the 'dismal science' of economics;
the blacks were not more constructively employed because it was in no one's
economic interest at that stage to do so, just as it was not in Ireland. Carlyle
is ruthless in his description of the value of these people in their then state,
'equalling almost in number of heads one of the Ridings of Yorkshire, and in
worth . . . perhaps one of the streets of Seven Dials'.[124] Reminding his readers
of the social disasters at home, he comments: 'How pleasant to have always
this fact to fall-back upon: Our beautiful Black darlings are at last happy.'[125]
He attacks philanthropy as the 'sad product of the sceptical Eighteenth
Century', the misguided efforts of man to make up for the perceived shortfalls
of the Almighty, all tempered with his other hate, 'rosepink Sentimentalism'.[126]

Familiar from his earlier works are the demands for governors to apportion
work irrespective of the economic need for it, and his despair at democracy
and the cash-nexus. As self-defence, whenever he makes a really extreme
observation, he inserts in the text asides such as '*Here various persons, in an
agitated manner, with an air of indignation, left the room.*'[127] That will have been
hard enough for comparatively humourless, liberal souls like Mill to stomach;
but when Carlyle goes on to suggest that no black man unprepared to work
for it should be given pumpkins to eat, 'but has an indisputable and perpetual
right to be compelled, by the real proprietors of said land, to do competent
work for his living',[128] the anguish would have been unbearable. This was not
a racialist observation; Carlyle continued that 'this is the everlasting duty of
all men, black or white, who are born into this world'; and later in the
essay he execrates slavery as 'a contradiction of the laws of the universe'.[129]
However, the terms in which he suggests that the blacks might be made to

work are too reminiscent of slavery: 'Every coachman and carman knows that secret ... and applies it to his very horses as the true method.'[130] He defines it further, later on in the essay, as the 'beneficent whip';[131] but argues it was just how serfs were compelled in feudal England, a society he still considered a model. He cannot envisage the black man being born for any other purpose than to serve; and while he may abhor slavery, he wonders whether being bound for life to a master in other circumstances is not the most humane and appropriate way to deal with the 'emancipated', and ease them into civilisation. To apply the principles of *laissez-faire* to them was, he argued, cruel, as they had no means to survive on their own. Again (and the allegorical is never far away), all this was true of Ireland, as he saw it.

His strictures about what actually constitutes slavery cannot be easily dismissed, and reflect directly his Irish experiences. 'You cannot abolish slavery by act of parliament,' he claims, 'but can only abolish the *name* of it, which is very little!'[132] He claimed that the philanthropists had, instead, instituted 'the slavery of Wisdom to Folly' in the nature of the emancipation they had won; worse, for this lover of heroes, this meant 'the slavery of the strong to the weak'.[133] He is as dismissive of idle whites as of idle blacks, and of the democratic movements of 1848. Not caring what sensibilities he offended, Carlyle reminds us of another act where the will of the majority prevailed: 'Crucify him! Crucify him!'[134] Though not of the *Latter-Day Pamphlets*, in its agenda this is the essential preface to them.

Once this work was finished, he embarked on the first of these pamphlets, *The Present Time*. Jane, absorbed in the novels of the Brontës and Miss Mulock, and with a new little dog for company, left him to it, embarking for Addiscombe. The pamphlets were to be brought out singly, then published as a book by Chapman's. Carlyle thought of writing one a month throughout 1850, though he would manage only eight. The near-primitive scream of rage they articulate was to change him and his reputation for ever.

12

Primitive Pamphleteer

1849–53

WITH PUBLICATION OF the first of the *Latter-Day Pamphlets* set for 1 February 1850, Carlyle was hard at work throughout December, Neuberg helping him put his thoughts into some sort of order. At the turn of the year Chapman came to collect the drafts of the first two, *The Present Time* and *Model Prisons*. Carlyle was inspired by the outrage *The Negro Question* had provoked, telling Jack that 'alas, this is but the first sough of the storm I shall have to raise among that class of cattle, when I do fairly open my pack, and make known to them what my mind is.'[1] That seems to prove he was setting out not just to unburden his conscience, but wilfully to provoke. He felt the anonymous so-called 'man of rank' who attacked him in the next issue of *Fraser's* was 'some poor hide-bound dunce'. It was actually Mill.

Mill defined Carlyle's piece in his first sentence as 'a speech against the rights of Negroes',[2] which suggests his somewhat rigid mind caused him to miss much of Carlyle's point – though in this regard Carlyle was his own worst enemy. But he went to the heart of Carlyle's philosophy in another respect: that it was based upon 'the old law of the strongest, – a law against which the great teachers of mankind have in all ages protested.'[3] He stated that if 'the gods' will this law to be enforced, 'it is the first duty of human beings to resist such gods'.[4] He said Carlyle had misunderstood the emancipation movement (undoubtedly true) if he thought it based on sentiment; though he will have confirmed all Carlyle's prejudices by adding that what had driven the movement had been that it had been a cause 'of religion'.[5] He found the comparison with Ireland absurd, which may again have been the fault of his too logical mind, and sought to prove, with some success, that Carlyle's idea of life in the West Indies was based on hearsay rather than fact.

Yet, Mill claimed, it was not the facts that bothered him so much as the moral tone of *The Negro Question*. He dismissed the gospel of work as something 'which, to my mind, as justly deserves the name of a cant as any of those which he [Carlyle] has opposed'.[6] Here, Mill's superior understanding of economics both as a science and a philosophy helped him get the better of Carlyle. 'Work,' he wrote, 'is not a good in itself. There is nothing laudable in work for work's sake. To work voluntarily for a worthy object is laudable; but what constitutes a worthy object?'[7] Mill simply did not believe that work was the end of human existence. 'In opposition to the "gospel of work," I would assert the gospel of leisure, and maintain that human beings cannot rise to the finer attributes of their nature compatibly with a life filled with labour.'[8] He wanted the blacks to have their fair share, in accordance with the laws of supply and demand; he felt that the excesses of the 'brutal portion of the population' were the fault of the humane portion not being 'humane enough'.[9]

Most damning was the personal element of the attack on Carlyle, by one who had been so close a friend. Of Carlyle's idea that some were born simply to serve others he said 'a doctrine more damnable ... never was propounded by a professed moral reformer.'[10] Mill was looking, prophetically, across the Atlantic, to the tensions in America that would, ten years later, lead to civil war. 'Your contributor steps in, and flings this missile, loaded with the weight of his reputation, into the abolitionist camp,' he complained. 'I hardly know of an act by which one person could have done as much mischief as this may possibly do; and I hold that by thus acting, he has made himself an instrument of ... "a true work of the devil".'[11]

The proofs of his first two pamphlets came back in early January, and Carlyle busied himself with rewriting and corrections, delighted that *Model Prisons* 'runs a red-hot poker through all that nasty stuff, of "abolition" [of capital punishment]'.[12] The period of 'deep gloom and bottomless dubitation' had ended, to be replaced by an almost demonic, aggressive frenzy of loathing against the society with which Carlyle had finally lost patience. It is a mood of Germanic pessimism almost exactly reflected in Nietzsche a generation later. Carlyle wrote to Alick: 'I have decided to venture out with a set of *Reform* Discourses, "Latter-Day Pamphlets" I call them, upon the frightful aspects of human affairs ... I am minded, perilous as it looks, to tell the people somewhat of my real mind about it.'[13] By the time he wrote, on 25 January, the first two were already on the presses, and he was turning over in his mind the third, 'Downing Street'. 'A paper I published in *Fraser* about *Niggers* has raised no end of clamour,' he joyously told his sister Jean the next day. Of the forthcoming pamphlets he told her that 'it is to be expected they will occasion loud astonishment, condemnation, and a universal barking of "Whaf-thaf? Bow-wow!" from all the dogs of the Parish.'[14] Perhaps it was the rejection of his ideas by Mill that prompted a most significant comment in this letter: 'All the twaddling sects of the country, from Swedenborgians to Jesuits, have for the last ten years been laying claim to "T. Carlyle", each for itself; and now they will find that the said "T." belongs to a sect of his own, which is worthy of instant damnation.' Even someone as loyal as Forster was taken aback by the ferocity of the sentiments; Carlyle recalled that he 'soon fell away ... into terror and surprise';[15] he was not even sure that Neuberg, his main helper on the work, or indeed anyone apart from Jane approved of what he wrote. Before the first pamphlet appeared Carlyle went on his own for a short rest at the Grange with the Ashburtons. On his way by train someone in his carriage read out from *The Times* that Jeffrey was dead; it little affected Carlyle.

The Present Time got the series off to a poor start. 'Rather too much of the manner of Carlyle,' noted *The Spectator*, 'without the matter that should support it.'[16] It contains hardly any original thought, the old Carlylean ideas of the failings of democracy, the evil of philanthropists, the loathsomeness of shams and the blight on Ireland being rattled out again. He does display even more conviction than before, and the style, carried along by black humour, is not so hard to negotiate as in some earlier works. Its tone of pessimism is profound, abetted by the cloacal imagery that Carlyle invokes: 'This general well and cesspool once baled clean out today, will begin before night to fill itself anew.'[17] Carlyle had stopped caring for the sensibilities of others. Lest anyone adduce the example of America as a democracy that works, he argues that the country is still so new, and not really a nation at all, that the comparison is pointless. It did not strengthen his point that he felt compelled to add that America's achievement had been that 'they have begotten, with a rapidity beyond recorded example, Eighteen Millions of the greatest *bores* ever seen in the world before.'[18] He was saying this of a public without whose help he might never have been launched as a writer.

The main point of the pamphlet is a call for an organised regiment of the unemployed, rather as he had earlier suggested for the Irish; only this regiment is tempered with authoritarianism, and Carlyle's philosophy is tantamount to the criminalisation of poverty; there will be compulsion to work. One of Carlyle's more exhaustive biographers, David Alec Wilson, suggested Carlyle had found the idea in the writings of Andrew Fletcher of Saltoun, an MP in the last Scottish parliament before the Act of Union in 1707, whose works Carlyle was reading at this time.[19] Carlyle unhesitatingly declares that 'it is the everlasting privilege of the foolish to be governed by the wise; to be guided in the right path by those who know it better than they.' Lest anyone complain that such compulsion might not be compatible with human rights, he adds that such governance 'is the first "right of man", compared with which all other rights are as nothing'.[20] He adds that 'the whole Universe, and . . . some two hundred generations of men' would support this; and says wearily that the 'few Wise will have, by one method or another, to take command of the innumerable foolish'. He ridiculed emancipation because he sincerely felt it meant the emancipation of the governing classes from their duties towards the governed. He is explicit that such rule is God's work. A tone of Old Testament-based religious mania permeates this and the other pamphlets, justifying their religiose title.

The acme of Carlyle's apparent lack of humanity comes in the parody speech at the end, by a British Prime Minister 'to the floods of Irish and other Beggars, the able-bodied Lackalls, nomadic or stationary, and the general

assembly, outdoor and indoor, of the Pauper Populations of these Realms'.[21]
It is Carlyle at his most Swiftian, but more callous than anything Swift ever
wrote. It is good satire because it makes the point of the atrociousness of the
workhouses, and the government's failure hitherto to provide properly for
the poor; but it still takes for granted that those poor are little better than
animals, and ridicules their aspirations. Coming in such a peculiar context,
Carlyle's desire for an army of the unemployed can hardly be taken seriously.
Telling the paupers to enlist in this regiment, and saying the workhouses will
no longer be there as an alternative, the 'Chief Minister' perorates:

Refuse to strike into it; shirk the heavy labour, disobey the rules, – I will admonish
and endeavour to incite you; if in vain, I will flog you; if still in vain, I will at last shoot
you – and make God's Earth, and the forlorn-hope in God's Battle, free of you.
Understand it, I advise you![22]

Because of the form in which this threat is made – in a sarcastic fictional
address from an imaginary leader – one cannot take it literally; unfortunately
for Carlyle, some of his critics did, and still do. He summed up the critics'
view as 'Carlyle got deep into whisky', and that they had decided the work
'divided me altogether from the mob of "Progress-of-the-Species." '[23] He was
unshaken. The pamphlets were 'a great relief to my own conscience as a
faithful citizen', he added in the *Reminiscences*, written seventeen years later,
'and have been ever since'.

Model Prisons is even more ferocious, and a masterpiece of invective. He
had been disgusted to see, on his visit to the Millbank Penitentiary, that the
inmates were being better cared for than many of the innocent struggling
outside. It was a sign to Carlyle that there was 'no longer a divine sense of
Right and Wrong',[24] and of philanthropy gone mad. 'If I had a commonwealth
to reform or to govern, certainly it should not be the Devil's regiments of the
line that I would first of all concentrate my attention on.'[25] Prisoners were
'scoundrels' whose reform would be made harder by the fact that the tread-
wheel had been abolished. He described the convicts with bestial imagery:
'ape-faces, imp-faces, angry dog-faces, heavy sullen ox-faces' for whom 'love'
was the last method of redemption that should be used.[26] 'Most sick am I,'
he cries, 'of this sugary disastrous jargon of philanthropy, the reign of love,
new era of universal brotherhood, and not Paradise to the Well-deserving but
Paradise to all-and-sundry, which possesses the benighted minds of men and
women in our day.'[27]

Those who had followed the devil, he added, should have the way to the
gallows cleared for them. He could not take seriously the 'universal syllabub
of philanthropic twaddle', because its practitioners claimed to base it on
Christianity which was 'as good as extinct in all hearts'.[28] He poured out
sarcasm on these prison reformers, duped as they were being by the convicts,
and asked them: 'Does the Christian or any religion prescribe love of scoundrels then? I hope it prescribes a healthy hatred of scoundrels: otherwise what

am I, in Heaven's name, to make of it?'[29] He saw nothing wrong with revenge, believing it an important part of the discharge of God's justice, and 'intrinsically a correct, and even a divine feeling in the mind of every man'. He did not confuse it with making an 'example' of a criminal, which he thought was nothing to do with God's justice at all, but of one man judging another.[30] All the punisher was required to do was to say to the criminal: 'Caitiff, we hate thee; and discern for some six thousand years now, that we are called upon by the whole Universe to do it. Not with a diabolic but with a divine hatred.'[31]

The first pamphlet sold well, and with the second written Carlyle struggled through much of February trying to write the third, *Downing Street*. He learned at about this time, to his surprise, that Mill had been his attacker in *Fraser's*. He could not understand why Mill had forsaken him, for they had never had any sort of quarrel. Grandly, he wrote in his journal on 7 February that 'instead of reverent discipleship, which he aspired to, [Mill] seems to have taken the function of getting up to contradict whatever I say.'[32] He complained of indifference overtaking him, and of his finding humanity 'contemptible', feelings which, had he read his own writings, could scarcely have come as a surprise.

By the first week in March he realised he had too much material for his third pamphlet; therefore he divided it, the second half becoming the fourth pamphlet, *The New Downing Street*. These two do embody some original thought, which would help explain why they were not written so easily as their predecessors. The first calls for a reformed executive, whereby the sovereign could nominate half a dozen men to sit in the House of Commons and to act as ministers; this would get round Carlyle's basic objection to democracy, that the ballot-box was incapable of finding the best men to govern England. He ignores the fact that the monarch, or the Prime Minister, had long had such a facility, in the form of patronage to the House of Lords for anyone deemed necessary for inclusion in a government. He says explicitly, though, that 'Parliaments ... are not the remedy,' adding that it is not they, 'reformed or other, that will ever send Herculean men to Downing Street, to reform Downing Street for us; to diffuse therefrom a light of Heavenly Order, instead of the murk of Stygian Anarchy ... that is the function of a King'.[33] He also makes the sound point – still valid today – that just because a man can score points in a parliamentary debate, it does not make him a good administrator; as always, Carlyle has an instinctive preference for the silent and reflective. Nor does he see any need for ministers to waste time coming to parliament to answer 'frivolous' questions. In an attempt to be practical, he advocates Peel as the only man living even remotely qualified to impose 'order' on the 'twenty-seven millions, many of them fools'.[34] A new way has to be found to ensure that strong men come to the fore, for that, he argues, is the only true democracy.

The New Downing Street, out on 15 April, develops the argument about the dearth of spiritual talent in once-heroic England; it repeats earlier calls for unemployed labour to be organised, and for Peel to take charge. Carlyle digresses into colonial government, saying we should, at least, govern those lands properly even if we fail at home; but the pamphlet gives the impression the author is once more running out of steam, not least because it contains most of the few notes of optimism to be found in the pamphlets.

Carlyle, in the midst of this frenetic burst of energy, was becoming close to Neuberg, and would often ride over to his house at Hampstead to sit and smoke with him, and to discuss the evolving work. Some evenings he would go to Bath House, the London home of the Ashburtons, usually on his own. He was amused to hear he had been nominated for the Lord Rectorship of Aberdeen University. He hoped the post would go to his rival, the Duke of Argyll, as it would have meant a long round-trip to Scotland at a very busy time, and the anguish of preparing an address; he lost.

In March Jane went to Addiscombe to stay with Lady Ashburton, leaving Carlyle in London. He joined her for three days at the end of the month once he had finished *The New Downing Street*. His work continued to attract much outcry about the town. 'The noise about those Pamphlets,' he wrote to his mother at the end of March, 'is very great, and not very musical – but indeed I take great care not to hear it.'[35] Yet Chapman was now printing the fourth thousand of the first pamphlet, precisely the sort of outcry Carlyle enjoyed. He occupied himself on the fifth pamphlet, *Stump Orator*, through early April; and then by the end of the month was already writing *Parliaments*, the sixth. He had always despised journalism, but the instant increases to his fame and income, and the ability to discharge hitherto constipated views in so gratifying and lucrative a fashion kept him firmly at his task.

Carlyle called *Stump Orator*, published on 1 May, 'a command to men to hold their tongues more',[36] another plea to observe the teachings of his gospel of silence. Again, a familiar sentiment is rehearsed at length, with only one or two novel thoughts tacked on. Carlyle warned, rightly, of the dangers of confusing eloquence with wisdom, and the importance of teaching people to act rather than speak. He lamented that the highest offices, 'Premiership, woolsack, mitre and quasi-crown,' were 'attainable if you can talk with true ability ... Do not talk well, only work well, and heroically hold your peace, you have no chance whatever to get thither.'[37] Talking is one reason Carlyle found parliaments offensive, a point he laboured in the sixth pamphlet, but which he introduced here to illustrate the absurdity of parliament's proceedings being reported and read by a population he characterised again as 'twenty-seven millions mostly fools', too foolish to see how much more beneficial action would be than these mere words. He exhorted his readers to 'love silence rather than speech in these tragic days'.[38] And, lest they feel insulted by their inclusion in a population branded by their author as 'mostly fools', Carlyle took trouble at the opening of the sixth pamphlet, *Parliaments*, published on 1 June, to say that he considered his readers 'to be a select class, the true Aristocracy of England, capable of far better things'. *Parliaments* covers much the same ground as *Stump Orator*: branding parliament itself as a talking-shop that is no remedy for the ills of the world. Carlyle looks back with blind romanticism to William Rufus's Christmas gatherings at the close of the eleventh century, where the King, once the feast was over, would go round the table and ask his barons their opinion on events. That was a proper parliament, with a King in it literally, with no voting, but discussions among the great providing the leader with what knowledge he needed to take a better decision. The closest equivalent to that 'National Consult' that Carlyle could find in 1850 was the press, 'where all mortals vent their opinion, state their grievance' in the manner of a feudal court.[39]

Without a King in parliament, rendering it the adviser of the sovereign rather than the sovereign itself, Carlyle felt it was useless; it could only talk, not act. Worse, it was '*not* very much in earnest, not at all dreadfully in earnest, to do even the best it can; that in general the nation it represents is no longer an earnest nation, but a light, sceptical, epicurean one, which for a century has gone along smirking, grimacing, cutting jokes about all things, and has not been bent with dreadful earnestness on anything at all, except on making money each member of it for himself.'[40] Indeed, he concluded, only the Long Parliament and the French National Convention had ever shown, among parliaments, any appropriate signs of earnestness. But the fundamental problem with parliaments – and this is the root of Carlyle's objections to democracy – was that 'the Laws of the Universe, of which if the Laws of England are not an exact transcript, they should passionately study to become such, are fixed by the everlasting congruity of things, and not fixable or changeable by voting!'[41] The best Carlyle can say for voting is that it might give governors an idea of whether they are governing in the interests of the people: 'For example, the Chief Governor of Constantinople, having no Parliament to tell it him, knows it only by the frequency of incendiary fires in his capital, the frequency of bakers hanged at their shop-lintels; a most inferior *ex-postfacto* method!'[42] Writing to Jean at this time Carlyle gave a hint of one factor fuelling his rage, namely his bowel problems: 'the whole inside machinery is far out of order.'[43]

As he worked on *Parliaments* Carlyle began to relax a little, taking Jane one day on an excursion to Richmond, and on another dining with his hero, Peel; they met again a few days later at Lady Ashburton's, and began to become friendly. In June he was writing the seventh pamphlet, *Hudson's Statue*, an attack on the discredited railway king George Hudson, who had been exposed as a fraudster, but whom the public – in their new regard for anyone with a capacity for making a fortune – so admired that they had raised £25,000 to put up a statue to him. Carlyle cannot resist contrasting this with more proper subjects for hero-worship. Also, he attacks Hudson for the way the railways had changed British life, and had driven many local, economically uncom-petitive businesses to the wall now that other more efficient firms could expand their geographical reach. But Carlyle vented his disgust, too, at Hudson's shareholders, who had supported him so long as he was enriching them, but disowned him when he was in trouble; so it is when the cash-nexus is all that binds man to man.

He spent part of June reading Leigh Hunt's *Autobiography*, in which his former neighbour gives a precise, and flattering, picture of him. He wrote to Hunt saying it was 'an excellent good book'[44] that had had quite a 'religious' effect upon him; and were he not 'horribly sick and lonely, and beset with spectral lions' he would have made the journey to Kensington to see Hunt and tell him so personally. His moroseness did not stop him taking Jane to the Ashburtons' grand summer ball at Bath House, where he saw her kiss the Duke of Wellington. Carlyle found the old hero 'truly a beautiful old man . . . clean, clear fresh as the June evening itself'.[45]

'Hudson's Statue', he told Jack, was 'a very bad pamphlet'.[46] It is certainly not an interesting one. The novelty of the form was wearing off, and the need to be permanently splenetic was beginning to tire even Carlyle. Having, in late May, told Jean he meant to do 'three or four more' pamphlets because he was 'nothing like beaten yet',[47] it took just one more pamphlet to change all that. He found the effort of writing *Jesuitism* almost impossible. He was under a cloud of depression, as on the last Saturday in June Peel was thrown by his horse on Constitution Hill and badly hurt; three days later, on 2 July, he died. On the day of his death Carlyle walked to Whitehall to seek news, finding dozens milling around awaiting bulletins; Peel died, after appearing to be improving, at eleven that night. Ruskin, with whom Carlyle was still forming an acquaintance, was with him that night. They were well matched, despite Carlyle's aesthetic limitations. Ruskin would begin *Praeterita*, his autobiography, with the affirmation that 'I am, and my father was before me, a violent Tory of the old school; – Walter Scott's school, that is to say, and Homer's.'[48] This was a language Carlyle understood, particularly as Ruskin went on to define his Toryism as 'a most sincere love of kings, and dislike of everybody who attempted to disobey them.'[49] They were an appropriate pair to mourn Peel together. Carlyle said in his journal that 'I have now no definite hope of peaceable improvement for this country.'[50] Jane wrote to her cousin Helen that 'Mr C. is mourning over him as I never saw him mourn before – went today to look at the house where he lies dead!'[51]

Jesuitism was finished on 18 July. The thinking is confused and unoriginal, and the piece boils with religious bigotry as Carlyle seeks to erect Jesuitism as the ultimate symbol of cant, 'the most virulent form of sin which the Old Serpent has yet rejoiced in on our poor Earth,'[52] as he put it. However, its value is that in it he shows, without his usual prolixity and obscurity, his own view of religion:

A man's 'religion' consists not of the many things he is in doubt of and tries to believe, but of the few he is assured of . . . His religion, whatever it may be, is a discerned fact, and coherent system of discerned facts to him; he stands fronting the worlds and the eternities upon it: to *doubt* of it is not permissible at all! He must verify or expel his doubts, convert them into certainty of Yes or No; or they will be the death of his religion.[53]

The mistake of the followers of St Ignatius Loyola had been to convert their doubts 'into certainty of Yes *and* No; or even of Yes *though* No'. He makes the appeal for his readers to make their 'Exodus from Houndsditch',[54] using the title of the pamphlet he never wrote, to cast off the old clothes of their false religion and find a true one. This would not be a 'new religion', but one that had been there all along if only his readers could have his own good fortune to see it for themselves. Perhaps it was such a plea for humanity to redeem itself that prompted the *Examiner* to reach the astonishing conclusion that the pamphlets showed 'the still loving and generous soul'; or perhaps it had more to do with the editor of the *Examiner* being John Forster.[55]

Carlyle decided there were no more pamphlets in him. 'I have hardly had a heavier year,' he told Emerson.[56] He could not bear to stay at Chelsea, as the house had to be redecorated. Redwood in south Wales, with whom he had spent that boring holiday in 1843, invited him again, and Carlyle chose to go for want of a better idea. He was physically, but not intellectually, exhausted, protesting that 'I have much more to say'[57] – even though the pamphlets themselves seem to say very little, but to be remarkable for the way in which that little is said. Carlyle had made himself a figurehead of the idea, and practice, of reaction that was sweeping Europe (ironically led, there, by an illiberal Catholic establishment) two years after the events of 1848; but he manifestly had nothing new to say about politics.

II

At the end of July Carlyle headed west, calling on the poet Walter Savage Landor at Bath on the way, and reaching Wales on 1 August, the day *Jesuitism* was published. Landor forced quantities of claret and sherry on Carlyle to which he was not used, and exhausted his visitor with talk; yet Carlyle found him 'really stirring company'.[58] This contrasted with Redwood, who was still 'dreadfully dull'; however, Carlyle recognised the value of Redwood's devotion to him, and was less caustic in his ingratitude than he had been before.[59] He took refuge in riding and sea-bathing, though his hair was so thick he could never properly dry it afterwards, and so wrote to Jane asking her to send him a cap to wear in the sea. There were also less indulgent excursions; Redwood took him to Merthyr Tydfil to see the mines there. The '50,000 grimy mortals' Carlyle found were 'such a set of unguided, hard-worked, fierce and miserable-looking sons and daughters of Adam as I never saw before ... like a vision of *Hell*.'[60]

He stayed with Redwood for three weeks, and then went by train to Liverpool via Gloucester and Birmingham; and thence to Annan by steamer.

He mournfully recalled his departure from Redwood, whom he would never see again; he died the following year. 'I still remember him with grateful affection,' he wrote in *Letters and Memorials*, 'the thoroughly honest soul.'[61] Once he reached Annandale he wrote to Jane complaining of the discomfort he suffered after refusing to sleep in a small, smelly cabin on the steamer with sixteen other men; she told him it might make him have more sympathy in future with 'Quashee', Carlyle's term for black slaves.[62] His mother, now seventy-eight but relatively hale, was overjoyed to see him. She had lost most of her teeth since Carlyle's last visit, and her appearance had changed. Carlyle tried to persuade a dentist to make her some false ones, but the dentist said her dental health was such that any attempt he made to replace her teeth would do more harm than good.

At Scotsbrig he was under no obligation to be an entertaining guest, but could relax. The weather was uncommonly good, and he went for long rides and walks. He found time for some reading, principally Kingsley's *Alton Locke*, which he enjoyed, not least because of the frequent references to his own wisdom in it. He left for London at the end of September, stopping off in the Lake District to visit the Marshalls and the Tennysons, who had recently married, at Coniston. Carlyle, on first meeting Emily Tennyson, apparently 'surveyed her earnestly from head to foot for some moments and then shook her heartily by the hand in token of approval'. When, a little later, he went into a misanthropic rant, Emily shut him up by saying 'that is not sane, Mr Carlyle.'[63]

He found he could get no rest there, but came home at the beginning of October to an empty house. Jane was at the Grange with the Ashburtons, an invitation Carlyle had not felt minded to accept. Jane was sad not to be with him: 'the first time in all the twenty years I have lived beside you that you ever arrived at home and I away'; yet for all her longing to see him, she was not sure he would still rather prefer solitude.[64] He had no desire to substantiate this feeling of Jane's, and promised to travel to the Grange a few days later after all. He did not enjoy the trip in the least; and came back whining in his journal, not for the first time, that this was 'really the Nadir of my fortunes'.[65] As usual, he did not know what to do next. The anxiety this caused him brought on his dyspepsia, and limited his sleep.

He had an almost blank autumn. He was stung by criticism from America, where the pamphlets had reached, of his remark about the 18 million bores. He wrote, in a rare spirit of humility, to Emerson in November protesting that Britain had millions of them too. Emerson had been dismayed by Carlyle's glibness, and one of his friends, Elizur Wright, wrote a riposte entitled *Perforations in the 'Latter Day Pamphlets' by one of the 'Eighteen Millions of Bores'*. Carlyle felt chastened, although Jane stuck up for him, saying the pamphlet was fit only to be put on the fire and its author 'ill natured ... and *dully* so';[66] quite unlike her husband, who was making a career of being ill-natured in the most entertaining way, albeit often unintentionally. He claimed to Emerson that 'on those wretched Pamphlets I set no value at all, or even less than none: to me their one benefit is, my own heart is clear of them (a benefit not to be despised, I assure you).'[67] Not normally one to worry about what others thought of him, Carlyle went to unusual lengths to propitiate Emerson: 'Have tolerance for me, have sympathy with me; you know not quite (I imagine) what a burden mine is, or perhaps you would find this duty, which you always do, little easier done!'[68]

The pamphlets began to leave a bad taste in Carlyle's mouth. He realised he had made relatively little money from them, despite their sales, because of a bad bargain with Chapman; he was also bored with the continued execration of him. Even a close friend like Harriet Martineau said she could not read them.[69] He did a little work: Hunt had started a new periodical, and asked him to contribute. Not up to writing anything profound, Carlyle sent instead his elucidations of three of the historical manuscripts in his possession: an account of a duel in Nottinghamshire in the 1590s; of another at Croydon races, early in King James's reign; and a third on the beach at Calais in 1610. They were published in early December. On Christmas Eve he wrote to von Ense apologising that 'for many months past, I have been too sickly and dispirited to write to any one.'[70] He spent hours each day reading, and took to going out late at night for a walk with Jane's dog Nero to Hyde Park and back, a four-mile round-trip, from which he might not return until midnight. At least the weather was mild, so the usual winter afflictions did not trouble him or Jane.

They had had a sociable Christmas. Ballantyne of the *Manchester Guardian* and Jane's cousin John Welsh came for Christmas dinner, and Kingsley and Erasmus Darwin called before the new year. Carlyle also met Elizabeth Gaskell at a dinner with Dickens; he had been impressed by *Mary Barton*, but was less prepossessed by its author. His own problems were, as so often, all he really cared about. He complained in his journal on 30 December that 'I can get to no work … my poor days pass in the shabbiest, wastefullest manner … Good is to be got out of no creature.'[71] Such a mood was just right for his first excursion of the new year, on 2 January 1851, with Jane to visit Pentonville prison as the guests of a prison inspector named Perry, a friend of Darwin's. Perry shared Carlyle's views about the punishment of criminals and the sanctity of labour, and Carlyle felt he detected sympathy for this view much more generally than the initial outcry against *Latter-Day Pamphlets* had suggested. Labour was not something to which he could easily turn himself, however, and he spent January brooding. He went to the Grange on his own to see the Ashburtons, his brooding having more specifically been directed towards the memory of John Sterling. Julius Hare had made some patronising and, in Carlyle's view utterly wrong-headed, observations about Sterling's retreat from Christianity, which Carlyle had regarded as one of Sterling's greatest triumphs. This was a misconception he wanted to fight.

Dean Trench of Westminster and Bishop Thirwall were both at the Grange.

Talking to them about Sterling's theology, Carlyle began to realise that the record had to be put straight. He took both these churchmen on and had a fierce argument with them. No sooner was he back in Chelsea than he started to write his *Life of Sterling*, stating Sterling's attitude to religion as he had seen it. He stuck to his task single-mindedly throughout the next eight weeks, writing with astonishing speed and ease, though it meant relegating Jane to a position where he hardly had time to notice her. She was beset with servant problems – no one had been satisfactory since Helen's departure – and her insomnia and neuralgia had driven her almost into an addiction to morphine, which did not improve her temper during the day.

They both suffered from flu during March, and Carlyle was diverted by Ruskin's *Stones of Venice*, which he admired greatly. None the less Carlyle could report to Jack on the 29th that he had finished *Sterling*. He genuinely did not seem to know whether the book that Froude later called 'perhaps the most beautiful biography in the English language'[72] was up to much; but Jane read the manuscript and, he told Jack, 'warmly votes for immediate printing'.[73] 'It was one of the things,' he told Emerson, 'I felt a kind of obligation to do.'[74] He asked John Forster to read the manuscript, not something Carlyle was accustomed to do, and was relieved that Forster 'pronounced it readable'.[75] Although the writing had been the easiest since *Past and Present*, he was no better in spirit once it was finished. There were still things he wanted to write, chief among them, having written of Sterling's creed, an exposition of his own as one others could follow, having cast off the 'old clothes' of Christianity. But he judged, perhaps wisely, that such an exercise would be more trouble than it was worth.

Although Carlyle's personality at times interferes unduly, and makes the reader feel he is learning as much about the author as of the subject, *The Life of Sterling* does give a complete and well-rounded (and, what is more, well-written) portrait of his friend. He is not blind to Sterling's faults and limitations; and, indeed, wrote the sort of truthful biography of him that Froude felt it his duty to write of Carlyle thirty years later. 'How happy it comparatively is,' said Carlyle in the introductory chapter of *Sterling*, about to ignore his own advice, 'for a man of any earnestness of life, to have no biography written of him.'[76] The reader learns that Carlyle possessed a deep vein of humanity and capacity for love, not qualities that radiate from the other works of this period. Carlyle had the added incentive, in attempting this project, of venting his contempt for orthodox religion in general and the established Church in particular; and he gently, but firmly, criticises Hare for having written his book on Sterling as if his religious career were all that mattered. Carlyle sees Sterling not just as a man who (unseen by Hare) built up his own, satisfactory religious view, but also as a man of great literary and humane potential. 'Let a man be honestly forgotten when his life ends,' Carlyle said with reference to Hare's work, 'but let him not be misremembered in this way.' Carlyle felt Sterling had only emerged in his true, able character once he, like Carlyle in Leith Walk thirty years before, shook off the 'Hebrew Old Clothes'.[77] Sterling's decision to seek a calling in the Church of England Carlyle described as 'rash, false, unwise and unpermitted'.[78]

The work also gives Carlyle a chance to reflect, in tones more moral than political, on his and Sterling's own times, which he dismissed as 'this waste-weltering epoch'.[79] Sterling had been a rare heroic soul shining through the darkness, though Carlyle teases him for his occasional beliefs in emancipation, democracy and the Church of England – all diluted, we are left in no doubt, by Carlyle's influence. Carlyle, in that respect, is the hero of his own book; the man who, though he does not spell it out too clearly, saved Sterling from more malign influences; and the most malign of all was Coleridge. Carlyle's attack on Coleridge was the only feature of the book that interrupted the otherwise widespread approval it received. Again interposing his own personality, he depicts Coleridge as 'flabby and irresolute', both physically and mentally.[80] The attack is all the more damaging for being delivered in a passage of rare stylistic restraint, without the surge of hyperbole and apostrophising that Carlyle used to give weight to most of his denunciations.

He also ridicules Coleridge *ad hominem,* parodying his pronunciation of 'object' and 'subject' as 'om-m-mject' and 'sum-m-mject' – and, in the process, ridiculing Coleridge's exposition of Kant in which these two terms frequently appeared.[81] The Coleridgean disciple – and many of them were still alive and among Carlyle's audience – was described by him as 'a passive bucket' to be 'pumped into' with the poet's 'flood of utterance'; a remark made by one of the main monologuists of his day.[82] Recalling his own experience, Carlyle said he had 'heard Coleridge talk, with eager musical energy, two stricken hours, his face radiant and moist, and communicate no meaning whatsoever ... he began anywhere ... he would accumulate formidable apparatus, logical swim-bladders, transcendental life-preservers and other precautionary and vehiculatory gear, for setting out; perhaps did at last get under way, – but was swiftly solicited, turned aside by the glance of some radiant new game on this hand or that, into new courses.' As if this were not enough, Carlyle adds that 'his talk ... was distinguished, like himself, by irresolution.'[83] When he concludes the attack by proclaiming 'let me not be unjust to this memorable man', the joke is complete.[84] The attack presages the character assassinations of the *Reminiscences;* and, indeed, once Carlyle writes of the period when he knew Sterling, the mode of the *Reminiscences* is brought to mind again.

In the search for a new direction he resumed his study of Danish, hoping to be stimulated by something in Scandinavian history. The Crystal Palace, then rising in Hyde Park for the Great Exhibition, horrified him as a temple to commercial 'Blockheadism'.[85] It depressed him and he wanted to cry out against it, but he lacked the energy. The fourth meeting of the Peace Congress was being held in London at the same time, and Carlyle was invited to attend. He declined, but wrote to say that 'I altogether approve your object' and 'hold myself bound to do, by all opportunities that are open to me, whatever I can towards forwarding the same'.[86] He contemplated going to Denmark to pursue his language studies; and as the summer drew on, and London became more obsessed with the exhibition, the desire for travel that would take him away until 'the inexpressible Glass Palace with its noisy inanity'[87] had gone gripped him more fervently. The proofs of *Sterling* occupied him in May and June, and he had, at the age of fifty-five, to buy some spectacles to read, as he put it, 'small print in the twilight'.[88]

The first thoughts of travel were of going to take a water-cure. Because the printers had taken their time over *Sterling* the Carlyles could not leave England, so they availed themselves of a long-standing invitation from one of Carlyle's admirers and leading exponents of the cure, Dr J.M. Gully, to visit him at Malvern Spa in Worcestershire. They spent August there, though Carlyle felt the experience – 'a strange half-ridiculous and by no means unpleasant operation'[89] – made him no better, though the opportunity he had for walks and rides did. Jane, by contrast, he reported to be 'improving in every respect' as a result.[90] He was still deeply depressed, which it seemed nothing could cure. At the end of the month Jane went to Lancashire to see her family and Geraldine Jewsbury, and Carlyle 'full of gloom and heaviness, and totally out of health, bodily and spiritual'[91] went to Scotsbrig. He told those who asked that his misery was to do with the state of the world; but it was really to do with the fact that he had identified Frederick the Great as the next project worthy of him. He was in no doubt as to the size of it, nor of the agonies likely to be entailed in undertaking it properly. 'Prussian Friedrich, and the Pelion laid on Ossa of Prussian Dryasdust, lay crushing me with the continual question, "Dare I try it? dare I not?" '[92] His mood even at this stage of contemplation of the work was irritating enough to Jane; she cannot have imagined what was to come.

III

Scotsbrig was depressing for him. He had parted from Jane on less than civil terms, she taking offence that (as she thought – he denied it) he was about to kiss her goodbye with a cigar in his mouth. His mother was physically declining. He brooded for the whole of his stay there – nearly a fortnight, until past mid-September – whether or not to write *Frederick*. Nor could he settle down on his return to London. He had earlier promised the Ashburtons that he would visit them in Paris, whence they had travelled after a summer in Switzerland, and on 24 September he took a train with the Robert Brownings to Newhaven for the ferry to Dieppe; the price of the return journey to Paris was 32s. His record of the trip, written between 4 and 7 October once he had returned to Chelsea, was published posthumously in *Last Words of Thomas Carlyle*. Its title – 'Excursion (Futile Enough) to Paris' – sums up the satisfaction Carlyle felt he derived from it. He had not planned to travel with the Brownings, but on hearing, when he was applying for his visa, that they were going on the 24th, he postponed his journey from the 23rd to have their company.

They had a rough voyage, on which Browning was sick, and Carlyle nearly so. After a night in Dieppe they went on to Paris, where Carlyle arrived in time for an early dinner and an evening at the theatre with his hosts. He spent as much time as he could walking hard around Paris, both for the exercise and to see how much it had changed since his short visit there nearly thirty years earlier. The company the Ashburtons kept bored him, and he slept even worse than usual, which redoubled his irritability. The last straw came when Prosper Mérimée, the critic and historian, told Carlyle that Goethe had been an 'insignificant, unintelligible . . . paltry kind of scribe *manqué*'. Carlyle told Mérimée, who was Jewish, that he was an 'impertinent blasphemous blockhead', and felt he had committed 'the sin of the Jews . . . crucify him, he is naught!'; and went out into the street to have a cigar.[93] The confrontation unsettled him and he slept badly; and was so miserable the next day that, once he realised he could get home again in less than a day, he resolved to do so. A couple of days later, he and Ashburton made the journey together.

His recuperation was a mixture of sleeping and writing up his notes of the trip; and having the pleasant surprise of the critical approval of his *Life of John Sterling,* published soon after his return. 'Utterly revolting to the *Religious people* in particular,' he noted, with obvious satisfaction.[94] *The Spectator*, while admiring the book, had not been able to resist observing that 'Christianity as understood commonly, perhaps everywhere except, it may be, at Weimar and Chelsea, and church-formulas certainly as understood everywhere, he is in the habit of classing under a category which in his hands has become an extensive one – that of shams. He calls them by various . . . ugly names, – as "old clothes," "spectral inanities," "gibbering phantoms," or, with plainer meaning, "huge unveracities and unrealities." '[95]

Jane put Carlyle's early return from France down to the fact that the Ashburtons came back sooner than expected; she was entering a period of the deepest bitterness about Lady Ashburton's relations with Carlyle. Lady Ashburton had knitted a scarf for him, and a less handsome one for Jane; and Jane decided she had only knitted a scarf for her in order that she might give one to Carlyle too without causing offence. She and Carlyle had a fierce argument about it; she found it odd that he, who was unwilling to put himself out for anyone (including his wife) would walk off in pouring rain to sit with Lady Ashburton for an evening. 'And he,' she told her cousin Jeannie, ' "could not see what the devil business I had to find anything strange in that or to suppose that any slight was put on *me*".'[96] She told her cousin she was 'angry and sorrowful' at Carlyle's thoughtlessness, and his readiness always to put Harriet Ashburton's feelings before hers. It is perhaps of this time that Froude was thinking when he noted, in *My Relations With Carlyle*:

Forster ... alluded to some mysterious secret in connection with the Ashburtons. When I said I knew nothing about it he seemed greatly surprised, and proceeded to tell me that Lady Ashburton had fallen deeply in love with Carlyle, that Carlyle had behaved nobly, and that Lord Ashburton had been deeply obliged to him ... I was greatly astonished. Lady Ashburton was a great lady of the world. Carlyle, with all his genius, had the manners to the last of an Annandale peasant.[97]

Froude subsequently notes that, in fact, it had not been any affections of Lady Ashburton's for Carlyle that had offended Jane, but Carlyle's dog-like devotion to his patroness.

As the days shortened and the London fogs closed in, he settled down in between visits to Lady Ashburton to receiving the odd visitor – Thackeray called not long after Carlyle's return – and to reading, though at first French histories rather than German ones. On 29 October he wrote to von Ense that 'if I were a brave Prussian, I believe I should forthwith attempt some Picture of Friedrich the Great, the *last* real *king* that we have had in Europe.' However, he added that he did not have the qualities needed to undertake such a work, but was about to content himself reading Preuss's great history of Fritz instead. This 'terrible hulk of compilation'[98] occupied him for weeks. Jane, with great reluctance, went to the Grange at the end of November, and Carlyle stayed behind immersed in German studies, resolving to join her in mid-December, but still uncertain that his reading would lead to any writing. He told Jack that Frederick's 'being a foreigner is a grand drawback to such an enterprise',[99] since it would involve Carlyle in much travelling if he were to research a biography properly. He stayed in complete solitude, with only Nero, Jane's dog, for company.

Another barrier to his work on *Frederick* was a lingering desire to write about religion, to which end he started to write some notes about faith entitled 'Spiritual Optics'.[100] Froude found the notes in the papers Carlyle gave him over twenty years later. They cover familiar ground: man's relations with the universe, the incredibility of Christian miracles, the redundancy of the 'Hebrew old clothes'. It was Carlyle's first attempt to write *in extenso* about religion directly, rather than using another subject as a vehicle for his religious views. He could not shape the piece in a way that would make it fit to be published because of his inability to 'name the name of God'.[101] The writing is vague, highly metaphorical, incoherent, prolix. But in failing to bring himself to be precise he could not hope to communicate his ideas to others, and one wonders how much he really understood them himself. Froude does not clarify his master's voice either, perhaps for the same reason. The clearest statement in the notes is that 'divineness ... does not come from Judaea, from Olympus, Asgard, Mount Meru, but is in man himself; in the heart of everyone born of man – a grand revolution, indeed, which is altering our ideas of heaven and earth to an amazing extent in every particular whatsoever.'[102] That makes it clear that Carlyle's post-Christian vision had not changed since he formed it, with Goethe's help, thirty years earlier;

unchanged, too, was the impossibility of sharing it comprehensibly with anyone else, however much Froude might have thought that he had been allowed into the secret.

A week before Christmas Carlyle went to Hampshire as arranged, and he and Jane stayed on until new year. He had been gloomy about making the visit, telling Jack before he went that Jane had written to say 'that they are all three (Lady A, her mother and Jane) somewhat on the invalid list'.[103] There was an absurd ceremony on Christmas Day, when Lady Ashburton called out the guests' names and doled out presents; and Jane sardonically noted how pathetically happy her husband looked when his hostess had called out 'Thomas Carlyle – the *Scholar!*' and presented him with a jigsaw map of the world.[104] The house was crammed with dignitaries, including the pre-eminent Thomas Babington Macaulay for a couple of days, with whom Carlyle (to his apparent surprise) got on well. 'A man of truly wonderful historical *memory*', Carlyle told Jack, though added that not one of Macaulay's ideas 'has the least tincture of greatness or originality'.[105] As usual the opulence and organised frivolity bored Carlyle, and he was glad to get home.

He embarked upon one of his most sustained periods of reading for years – a whole winter of 'dull and dreadful books'[106] on Frederick, which made the subject even less attractive to him. He wrote to James Marshall in Weimar to tell him that, despite his German studies, 'of all the countries in the world, Russia is the one I have the most curiosity about, evidently a grand country, peer of Saxondom and Yankeedoodledom, and with a grand destiny ahead of it – to which, even without "liberty of the press" (singular to say) it is rapidly, and grandly, in the view of all men, advancing by inevitable law ... what would one give for a fit, true life of Peter the Great, of Catherine the Second.'[107] Those lives were not, though, his task. He soon diverted into Margaret Fuller's biography of Shelley, and into that poet's letters, in an edition introduced by Browning; but otherwise his application on *Frederick* was relentless, interrupted only by his duties at the court of Lady Ashburton.

By late March he was complaining to his sister that he made so little progress because 'I cannot get the *right* books here: even when I send for them, at my own charges, the *delay* is quite overpowering.' He knew he could only get the right books in Germany, and he and Jane began to talk of a six-month sojourn there. Carlyle was not sure he wanted to commit himself to such a project, because he was not sure whether he really cared about Frederick. He was encountering a philosophical paradox; reading the vast correspondence between Voltaire and Frederick, and learning just how influenced Fritz had been by the thinking of the *philosophe* from what Carlyle had always thought to be the most decadent period in modern history.

But Carlyle was, at times, tolerant and broad-minded. In April he wrote to Mill on a favour for a friend, seeking an address Mill might have; and wrote to him in such civil tones that any hurt Carlyle felt had been caused by the row over *The Negro Question* must have been repaired. Mill had disappeared from society, having married Mrs Taylor, and knowing the views of society on her. Carlyle simply told him that 'I respect your solitude; and indeed find it necessary myself to cultivate the same, as years grow upon me.'[108]

Word of Carlyle's possible project had reached America by April, for Emerson wrote saying he had heard he was engaged on *Frederick*. When Carlyle wrote back on 7 May 1852 he did not mention the subject, though in a letter the following week he said: 'About Fredk the Great and other high matters shortly.'[109] He was preoccupied that month with a campaign – successful, as it turned out – to stop an Italian protégé of Gladstone's, Lacaita, becoming the new Librarian of the London Library. Writing to Emerson the following month, once Lacaita's defeat had been secured, he announced:

I am not *writing* on Frederic [*sic*] the Great; nor at all practically contemplating to do so. But, being in a reading mood after those furious Pamphlets (which have procured me showers of abuse from all the extensive genus Stupid in this country, and not done me any other mischief, but perhaps good) and not being capable of reading except in a train and *about* some object of interest to me, – I took to reading, near a year ago, about Frederick, as I had twice in my life done before; and have, in a loose way, tumbled up an immense quantity of shot rubbish on that field, and still continue. Not with much decisive approach to Frederick's *self*, I am still afraid! The man looks brilliant and noble to me; but how *love* him, or the sad wreck he lived and worked in? I do not even yet *see* him clearly; and to try making others see him?[110]

He did confide details of his progress more willingly to Neuberg, to whom he admitted that Frederick's character was beginning to seduce him. He volunteered to von Ense on 6 June that 'all is yet vague; I may say chaotic, pathless.'[111] As usual, Carlyle was hamstrung by hypochondria, complaining of being 'unusually torpid in the bowels, and weak and lazy', and then going down with mild flu.[112] Cataloguing the boring accounts of Prussian history he had been ploughing through, Carlyle said that his 'love of the Heroic' was keeping him going, along with the absence of anything better to do. He asked von Ense for help in finding works that would provide him with a detailed chronology of Frederick's life; Preuss, with which he had been struggling, and which had pretensions to such a status, he dismissed as inadequate, since Preuss had regarded Frederick's writings as 'literature ... and not as Autobiographic Documents of a World Hero'.[113] He also wanted an almanac of the court and the peerage.

He mentioned to von Ense the possibility of his and Jane's travelling to Germany, to visit Potsdam and Berlin, and the fields of Frederick's battles, as he had with Cromwell's a decade earlier. He asked von Ense to give him an idea of what historical and other resources he might be able to draw upon if he made the trip. However, even before a reply could be sent, the trip – which he and Jane had talked of as perhaps lasting as much as a year – was postponed. Instead, they decided to take a thirty-one-year lease on Cheyne Row, and to engage in home improvements; extending and enlarging rooms on the ground and first floors, and ultimately converting the attic to provide what was to become Carlyle's soundproof room. It was an important psychological step for Carlyle. As he told Alick, in a letter written in January 1853, 'nearly every year since I came to live here, especially in late years since there was a *possibility* for me of getting elsewhither, I have madly struggled, in my thoughts, expressed or not, to be out of this horrible uproar of London, and into some place of country quiet and fresh air.'[114] Now that was buried for ever. Jane never wanted to leave London; she had never recovered from the isolation of Craigenputtock. To Carlyle Scotland was but 'a place of graves', and a remote part of England held no attraction for him. Chelsea, almost a country village when they moved here in 1834, was now part of the metropolis. But they would put down their roots and stay.

The first phase of improvements – to plans made by Jane – started in July. She had been ill with a long bout of neuralgia; however, the upheavals improved her spirits, and she was busily engaged upon superintending the workmen. Carlyle found his own work impossible, and the weather became exceedingly hot; so, on 21 July, he made for Scotland. He had arranged to stay with Thomas Erskine in Fife, taking his books with him. Jane, who saw him on to the steamer from London to Dundee, was relieved. She had not expected him to stay at all while the builders were in, and he had continually got in her way. Worse, he never stopped complaining.

At Linlathen, Erskine's house, Carlyle was left to himself as much as he wanted, and his reading progressed. He became tormented by the desire to go to Germany; he knew he could not convert his reading into something tangible if he did not go, but that he would almost certainly not enjoy himself if he did. From Scotland he could take a Leith steamer to Rotterdam; but he did not want to go without Jane. As usual, when apart from her, he worried endlessly that she had finally had enough of him, and the days that passed when a letter did not arrive drove him into depressive frenzy. He badly wanted to make up to Jane for some of his past thoughtlessness. She had never been abroad, and he wanted to take her with him. Yet as he became bored at Linlathen, she still had work to superintend at Chelsea.

He went to see his family at Scotsbrig, hoping Jane would come, as it was years since she had seen her mother-in-law; and the old lady would say to Carlyle plaintively that she would like a last look at Jane before she died. But still the workmen, and her own reluctance to travel, kept Jane away. The sight of the improvements she had designed taking shape before her gave her more satisfaction than anything else had for years. She told Carlyle that if he were unwilling to go to Germany alone, he ought to find a seaside retreat in Dumfriesshire where he could stay until Cheyne Row was finished. Eventually, she implored him to go to Germany without her; if time allowed, she would join him later. He finally made up his mind to go, prompted by 'a kind of shame, and the desire *not* to be a poor coward'.[115] On 28 August, therefore, he went to Leith and took the boat to Holland.

IV

He had a dreadful voyage to Rotterdam. Instead of the thirty-six hours scheduled, it took eighty. He stayed one night in Holland, and then made for Düsseldorf and Bonn, where he had arranged to meet Neuberg. Once it was clear Jane would not accompany him, he had accepted an offer from Neuberg to be his guide. Although bewitched by the scenery as he sailed up the Rhine to Bonn, Carlyle, who was a dreadful traveller, was relieved to see Neuberg waiting for him, 'to take me out of all that puddle of foreign things'.[116] He also found lodgings for Carlyle where he could catch up on lost sleep, and as a result of this kindness Carlyle soon felt in a more constructive mood. As soon as he had recovered he went to the university library at Bonn, where he found a trove of books on Frederick of which he had never heard, and which proved invaluable to him.

He and Neuberg ('Bless him! the good and sensible but wearisome and rather heavy man!'[117]) travelled to Frankfurt and Homburg. Carlyle was continually busy, making notes and excerpts from the books he found; he was also buying many books to bring home. While shaving in Frankfurt one morning, looking out of his window, he felt a sharp pang: 'I caught, with the corner of my eye, sight of a *face* which was evidently Goethe's,' he wrote to Jane. '*Ach Gott!* merely in *stone*, in the middle of the Platz among the trees. I had so longed to see that face alive.'[118] He toured Frankfurt and went to Goethe's house there, and after watching the cream of Europe playing at Homburg, he went on to the Goethean holy-of-holies at Weimar.

Carlyle found his reputation had preceded him. He was fêted when he reached Weimar, and Goethe's house opened specially for him. He found on the shelves there the last book he had sent his master, Taylor's *Survey of German Poetry*. Schiller's house, which he saw next, touched him deeply, as he looked at the bed where Schiller had died. The next result of his fame was an invitation to dine with the Grand Duchess, whose son he had earlier received at Cheyne Row, and who had read of Carlyle's arrival in the newspapers. He had a 'singularly empty intellectual colloquy'[119] with her, in French, English and German, made all the more difficult by her deafness. Carlyle, normally so cynical, was 'right charmed' by the honour done him, and glad too that Neuberg (whose value had now risen to the level where Carlyle deemed him worth six couriers) had been with him, and had been given a glimpse of court life he would never otherwise have had.

They moved on to Leipzig and Dresden, thereafter going to see Lobositz, where they walked over the first battlefield of the Seven Years' War. This was in Bohemia, and Carlyle found the natives quite unlike the Germans: 'half savage ... with their fleas, their dirt, and above all their noises'.[120] Carlyle had found much of value, but was exhausted after a month of touring. He wrote to von Ense from Dresden on 25 September 1852 that '*I can hardly get any sleep*, in these noisy bedrooms, in these strange beds,'[121] and begged von Ense to see if he could find quiet rooms for Carlyle's visit to Berlin, where he was planning to spend the last week or so of his expedition. He ended up, on 30 September, in the British Hotel in Unter den Linden, having come from Kunersdorf, 'where Fritz received his worst defeat'.[122] He found another haul of books in Berlin, and called on the British Ambassador, to whom Lady Ashburton had given him an introduction.

While in Berlin he met a number of distinguished historians, including Preuss, of whom he had been so disparaging. He tried to spot what relics he could of Fritz, including finding some of his clothes in a museum, and went both to Potsdam and Sans Souci. He met von Ense, who was ten years older than he, and who opened what doors he could for Carlyle in Berlin. But, as on 9 October he prepared to leave for Cologne, Ostend and home, he could not help thinking he still had not the urge to write Frederick's history. 'On the whole I made but little of Germany,' he told James Marshall the following year. 'My journey was somewhat of a failure.'[123]

Carlyle returned to find the builders had still not finished their work, and the house was full of the smell of paint. Far less tolerant than Jane, and feeling '"half dead" out of those German horrors of indigestion, insomnia, and continual chaotic wretchedness'[124] he could not bear to stay at Chelsea. He took her after a few days to the Grange, to lodge until early November with the Ashburtons. He remained in a state of 'bilious misery'[125] there, and on returning to Chelsea, with no excuse but to get on with his work, he realised that 'my heart was not in it'.[126] He was further distressed by the constant crowing of a cock in the yard next door, which prompted him to write to his neighbour, a Mr Remington, with the sad admission that 'we have the misfortune to be people of weak health in this house; bad sleepers in particular; and exceedingly sensible in the night hours to disturbances from sound.' He asked Remington, in a rare tone of mildness, if he 'would have the goodness to remove that small animal or in any way render him inaudible from midnight to breakfast time'.[127] Remington immediately obliged his distinguished neighbour.

Carlyle attempted a catharsis by pouring out his miseries into his journal on 9 November. 'My survey of the last eight or nine years of my life yields little comfort,' he wrote, complaining of a 'solitude of soul coupled with a helplessness, which are frightful to look upon, difficult to deal with in my present situation'. There follows the now-familiar litany of hypochondriacal woes about his liver, his insomnia, and his perception that 'I have become an old man.' In fact, photographs of him show him looking a good ten years younger than a man on the verge of his fifty-seventh birthday.[128]

He had to get used to the new layout of his house, which he found irritating and confusing until he knew where his books, clothes and other effects were now stored. Nor was this the only great change. Jack had, at the age of fifty-one, finally married, to Phoebe Watts, a widow in her late thirties, and they had settled in Moffat, near Carlyle's mother. Carlyle 'liked his [Jack's] Missus very much after a sort'[129] when he met her, while Jack and his bride passed through London on the way to honeymoon on the Isle of Wight. Chelsea was in a ferment as huge crowds came to the Royal Hospital for the lying in state of the Duke of Wellington: on 19 November the Carlyles went to Bath House to watch his funeral procession with the Ashburtons; the pomp nauseated Carlyle as 'vulgar and disgusting',[130] as did the sight of one of the dignitaries in a coach reading a newspaper.

As Christmas approached he continued reading, but his mind was still not made up. 'Shall I try Frederick, or not try him?' he asked his journal on 5 December, the day after his fifty-seventh birthday.[131] He spent much of that month translating a document that detailed a day in Frederick's life, which he had been working at on and off since the summer. He told his sister Jean that 'the sight of actual Germany ... has hurt poor Fritz very much in my mind.'[132] He was momentarily distracted by the collapse of Derby's ministry (brought about by Gladstone's assault on Disraeli's Budget, which had increased taxation on the less wealthy). The main legacy of that ministry for Carlyle had been to instil a loathing of Disraeli, the 'superlative Hebrew conjuror' of *Shooting Niagara*. 'This Jew,' he told his sister Jean, 'will not hang himself; no, I calculate he has a great deal more of evil work to do in the world yet ... Whatever brutish Infatuation has money in its purse, votes in its pocket, and no tongue in its head, here is the man to be a tongue for it ... and to use all his "fine intellect" to put words in its mouth.'[133] He had told Duffy, since the previous year an Irish MP and a regular visitor to Cheyne Row, that Disraeli was 'a cunning Jew ... an impostor, with no sort of purpose in all he was doing but to serve his own interests. He was a man from whom no good need be expected, a typical Jew, ostentatious, intrinsically servile, but stiffnecked in his designs.'[134] Of Disraeli's colleagues Carlyle was scarcely more charitable. 'Such a set of vilenesses,' he told Jack, 'take them for all in all, had not appeared in British history before; and it is comfortable that the general British so-called "mind" has, amid all its fearful obstructions found means to cast *them* off again. Old Lansdowne, they say, is trying to make a "coalition" ministry of some kind, – more power to his elbow! A worse ministry than we have had even he (one would think) cannot ... contrive to make.'[135]

The winter was mild, stormy and wet, and Carlyle interspersed his reading with long muddy walks, in which he further contemplated *Frederick*. Lord Ashburton, as a mark of the esteem in which he held Carlyle and as an antidote to Carlyle's tendencies to withdraw from society, asked him whether he would accept nomination for immediate election to the Athenaeum. Carlyle haltingly declined; and before he knew it he had been elected, his entrance fee and subscription paid for by Ashburton – 'so handsomely done that there was no rejecting or refusing it'.[136] When Ashburton first took his candidate there for dinner, Carlyle noted various of his friends – Erasmus Darwin, Crabbe Robinson and the like – were members too. But Carlyle was uninterested in the clubland establishment, being temperamentally unsuited to it; and used the club only rarely in the remaining twenty-eight years of his life.

It took another couple of months of agonising before he could even make the first attempts at writing, spending part of his time idly reading, and loathing, *Uncle Tom's Cabin*, and suggesting that for the work to have been such a public success must mean the public were like 'the Gaderene Swine'.[137] He told Jack on 10 March 1853 that 'I begin to *try* more seriously to get something gradually brought to paper, in this sad affair of Fritz.'[138] Fritz's Prussia was not the Germany that had originally gripped his imagination. Writing to James Marshall in Weimar on 13 March he longingly recalled Goethe's home as 'that interesting little city; if I were a painter I could put it all on canvas by help of memory.'[139] He expressed to Marshall his feelings, close to anger, that no German had taken up the duty of writing a proper life of Frederick, obliging him, therefore, to do it instead:

Of a truth, if Frederic [*sic*] the Great did injury to German literature and *Kunst*, said *Kunst* and literature have richly paid him back again. I said to myself a hundred times, ye speaking, painting, dissertating ... *vorstellungsfachig* German People, is *this* then all you can do to represent a great man and hero, when the gods send you one?[140]

He went alone to the Grange for Easter to try to make a final decision on the shape of his great project. He decided nothing, and wrote in his journal on his return that the visit had been 'a long nightmare; *folly* and *indigestion* the order of the day.'[141] Trying to work made him no better. He told Jean that he had been 'twice at the museum' reading manuscripts 'with headaches in consequence'.[142]

There were no great financial pressures on him; all his writings were in print, some, like *Heroes*, now in their fourth editions, and translations being made of them for the European market. 'I am not writing anything, at least not anything that will stand on paper,' he told Alick on 8 April.[143] He kept reading, and kept agonising. In his journal on 13 April he is 'still struggling and haggling about Frederick'. The great depression that was to consume him during the composition of the work was taking root. 'No words,' he added, 'can express the forlorn, heart-broken, silent, utterly *enchanted* kind of humour I am kept in; the worthless, empty, and painfully contemptible way in which, with no company but my own, with my *eyes* open, but as with my hands bound, I pass these days and months, and even years.'[144] He was acquiring a persecution complex, thinking others unjust to him, and seeking to criticise him destructively. At the end of this most self-pitying passage he none the less cries: 'Be not a sluggard. And so give up this and take to something like work.'[145]

Execution of this wish was not easy. He asked Neuberg how to get the work under way, and Neuberg offered whatever help he could. But the decision was Carlyle's alone. 'I am still reading, reading, most nightmare

Books abt Fritz; but as to writing – Ach Gott! Never, never,' he wrote to Emerson on 13 May. 'My difficulties with Frederick,' he wrote to Jack a week later, 'are two: first, the vague shoreless nature of the subject, which has been treated hitherto by hardly any man of superior understanding, and lies "like water spilt upon the ground" ... second, what is still worse, the want of sufficient *Love* for lean Frederick and his heroisms, on my part.' He added, forbiddingly, 'Only pain can now *drive* me through the subject; *led* and induced through it I shall never be.'[146] The decision to proceed had been taken at last, and he was to prove himself right about the method; but the pain was not to be his alone.

13

Frederick:
'A Botch and a Wreck'
1853–58

OLIVER HAD EXHAUSTED Carlyle and made him unfit for serious work for
the best part of five years; it had also helped Jane to a nervous breakdown. It
might have seemed a clear lesson for him in contemplating *Frederick*, a subject
for whom he had none of the fanatical reverence he felt for Cromwell. Yet he
was now set upon the work; and in the *Reminiscences* stated that '*Cromwell*
was by much the worst Book-time; till this of *Friedrich*; which indeed was
infinitely worse; in the dregs of our strength too; – and lasted for thirteen
years.'[1] Carlyle was fifty-seven when he started to write it and almost seventy
when he finished. He passed, in that time, from well-preserved, youthful-
looking middle age to being an old man; not yet truly infirm in body, but
with his mind set on his decay, death and oblivion. The effect on Jane was
far worse.

Having, in the late spring of 1853, started to draft his history, he decided
to forgo his annual trip to Scotland. It was a hard decision. Jack had written
at the end of June informing him of a sudden deterioration in their eighty-
two-year-old mother's health. She was not expected to live long. To Carlyle,
the news meant that 'the thing that I have feared, all my life ever since
consciousness arose in me, is now inevitably not distant.' He told Jack that
'the Past is now all that we have; in the Future there can be rationally no store
of hope', and it was not merely his mother of which he was thinking.[2] He
wrote, a couple of days later, a letter of extreme emotion to his mother,
bidding her take courage and be firm in her religion, and exclaiming: 'Oh
thank you, thank you, dear pious-hearted Mother, for the precious breeding
you gave me: things that I feel to be *wise*, to be God's *truth*, and fit to be
spoken aloud before all mortals, and even thundered in their ears in these
sad days, – how often do I find with an unspeakable tenderness of recollection,
"*That* is *thy Mother's*, now; that thou got from thy poor Mother, long ago!" '[3]

Jane did go north, to see her mother-in-law for the last time, and to stay
with Jack and his new wife. Carlyle was left on his own to sort out the way
forward on *Frederick*, as with *Oliver*; 'a dreadful job to riddle his history into
purity and consistency out of the endless rubbish of so many dullards as have

treated of it ... I cannot afford to be beaten.'[4] As he says in the opening of the work: 'it has always seemed possible ... to acquire some real understanding of him; – though, practically, here and now, I have to own, it proves difficult beyond conception ... Let the reader now forgive me; and think sometimes what probably my raw material was!'[5]

He was perplexed by painters, who still had not decorated the house to his and Jane's taste, but had visits to Lady Ashburton to divert him. He went to Addiscombe for a few days in July, where he found Milnes and several other friends, but no consolation. He was still worried about his mother, and Jane wrote of how the old lady had seemed on a visit she made to her: 'too weak and frail to be out of bed, but without pain or sickness'.[6] Jane believed her mother-in-law's natural strength would rally her for a while, and so it proved. Back in Chelsea, Carlyle decided the main obstacle now was noise; Jane and he agreed to have a soundproof room built at the top of the house. The notion was good, but Carlyle was to believe the room so created was in fact 'the noisiest in the house' and 'my first view of Satan's invisible world'.[7]

Jane came home in early August, and found him submerged to the extent even of refusing invitations from the Ashburtons. Carlyle was glad to be in London with everyone else out of it, not just to concentrate on his work, but to prepare himself for his mother's death. By mid-September the Irish labourers engaged on the construction of the soundproof room had already fallen through the ceilings five times, and Carlyle's patience expired. Leaving Jane to superintend further disasters, he went after all to Addiscombe for more than three weeks. He began, in the silence there (the Ashburtons were away), to make progress. By October, when back at Chelsea, the worst of the reconstructions were over; and Carlyle was further cheered to hear from his friend Sir James Stephen that Prince Albert had proposed him for a pension. However, the Prime Minister, Aberdeen, had demurred, thinking Carlyle's ' "heterodoxy" on some points might be objectionable'. Flattered though he was, Carlyle had been equally determined to refuse any offer that was made; and he thought he might get 'a better offer' later.[8]

The Carlyles agreed to spend December 1853 at the Grange. The sound-proofing was not protecting him from the noise of fowls next door; and, in any case, after months of hermit-like behaviour, even he was glad of some good company. The Ashburtons' party included 'a truly wondrous miscellany of Bishops, Foxhunters, Lords & Commons, not to speak of ladies great and little'.[9] While at the Grange, the Carlyles talked of renting 6 Cheyne Row as well, and leaving it empty; and just before Christmas Jane went to London to discuss the suggestion with the landlord. Notice for them to quit had to be given by Christmas. Jane bought the lease, and enforced it with a proscription against animals. The tenants complied, and stayed, thus saving the Carlyles further expense. This irritation, though, was soon put in perspective.

Jane's cousin Helen, to whom she had been close, and with whom she had corresponded regularly for years, died suddenly; and, three days before Christmas, Jack wrote from Scotsbrig to say his mother was nearing death. Jane packed Carlyle away there immediately, resolving that he should have the privilege denied her of seeing his last parent alive for the last time. He reached Scotsbrig on 23 December, and found his mother sinking. On Christmas Eve Jack, as Carlyle went into his mother, said: 'Here is Tom come to bid you good night.' She answered: 'I'm mickle obliged to thee!'[10] She did not speak to him again. On Christmas Day, at just after four in the afternoon, she died. For Carlyle there was no shock, and his grief was tempered by having found her still alive when he arrived. He stayed in the house with her body until the funeral, walking out by day on the clear hillsides, white with frost; and on 2 January 1854 took the train south. Scotland now was all ghosts to him; and his mother's death had made him aware of his own advancing years, and mortality.

II

There was nothing now to distract Carlyle from *Frederick*. Indeed, on 15 January he told von Ense that he was 'looking out more earnestly towards new labour (if that might be possible for me), as the one consolation in this and in all afflictions that can come'.[11] Through the winter, usually working under the handicap of a heavy cold, he read on, slowly and mostly fruitlessly. 'Hardly from ten tons of learned inanity is there to be riddled an old rusty nail,' he wrote to Emerson on 8 April.[12] 'The insuperable difficulty of *Frederick* is,' he added, 'that he, the genuine little ray of Veritable and Eternal that was in him, lay imbedded in the putrid Eighteenth Century, such an ocean of sordid nothingness, shams, and scandalous hypocrisies, as never weltered in the world before.'

Stuck aloft in his allegedly soundproof room he paid little regard to events outside, thinking of the prospect of war in the Crimea only to dismiss it. He and Jane went into society again in mid-April, visiting the Ashburtons at Addiscombe, and as spring advanced went out more in London. Jane enjoyed hearing the gossip about the Ruskins, who had split up, and whose marriage was shortly to be annulled on grounds of non-consummation; her sympathies were entirely with Mrs Ruskin, perhaps unsurprisingly, Wilson claims, without corroboration, that Charles Gavan Duffy had, at this time, com-plained of Ruskin's behaviour, only to have his hero Carlyle's own impotence flung at him by a colleague. Wilson says Duffy relayed this story to Carlyle, who denied it; and blames Geraldine Jewsbury for originating the rumour – she had, allegedly, made advances to Carlyle which he had ignored – and then for passing it on to Froude.[13]

Whether sexual or psychological, Carlyle's neglect of Jane was now routine. He devoted his time almost exclusively to reading, rarely seeing anybody, shut away two or three floors above his wife, who was under orders not to disturb him. By June he was telling his journal he was at 'just about the *nadir* in my affairs', and in the habit of taking himself off for long, strenuous, solitary walks around Wandsworth Common and Tooting.[14] He and Jane were hardly to leave London that year, though the Ashburtons had offered them Addiscombe for as long as they wanted it, while the owners were in Scotland. Even the epidemic of cholera in London – Jane noted six funerals during a half-mile walk one day – could not tempt them away. Carlyle became so tetchy that, needing to consult some manuscripts in the British Museum, he wrote to the librarian to beg to be given a private corner 'delivered from noise' where he might consult them, rather than have to endure the populous reading room.[15]

Jack and his wife, who was expecting, at the age of almost forty, their first child, moved to London in June; and insofar as Carlyle had contact with anyone outside, it was with his brother. Despite Phoebe's condition, she and Jack charged around looking for a house; until, when she was eight months pregnant, they were on a train that narrowly avoided a crash. According to Carlyle's account his sister-in-law went into shock, then into hysterics; a week after the incident she gave birth to a stillborn child, and died herself hours later. Jack bore the bereavement with fortitude; Carlyle, less emotionally disciplined, still found writing impossible. 'Try to get some work done,' he wrote in his journal on 16 September, 'or thou wilt go mad.'[16]

The previous year he and Ashburton had talked of growing beards; and Carlyle had said that if Ashburton grew one, he would follow. When, in early October, Ashburton returned to London sporting rather a fine one, Carlyle was kept to his promise. Jane removed all his razors from his dressing-table; he shaved for the last time on 9 October 1854, and thereafter began to acquire an appearance appropriate to a sage. It also, as he noted happily, saved him half an hour each day.

Neuberg had come back to London and was acting as unpaid research assistant – finding, and making long excerpts from, books Carlyle needed. Carlyle went to the State Paper Office to look up documents concerning Prussia, in the hope of finding inspiration; after examining much mid-eighteenth-century correspondence between British ambassadors to Berlin and Vienna and the Foreign Office, he felt he was at last seeing Frederick clearly. Having identified what he wanted, he sent Neuberg to make copies.

Bearing an introduction from Lady Ashburton, Carlyle went out to Windsor to look at the royal collection of German portraits. He also saw Prince Albert, who gave him an hour's interview and whom Carlyle found 'very good and human'.[17] They discussed Saxon genealogy and Luther, and Carlyle was charmed. Otherwise, there was no respite from the toil of *Frederick*. Carlyle summed up 1854 by saying that 'she [Jane] was in poor fluctuating health; I in dismal continual wrestle with "Friedrich", the *unexecutable* book ... my days were black and spiritually muddy.' Only later did he realise how oppressive the isolation and monomania were to Jane, who 'never did complain once of *her unc*hosen sufferings and miserable eclipse under the writing of that sad book'.[18] Jane spent the last six weeks of the year confined to the house with a heavy cold; Carlyle, varying his diet a little, wrote a short piece, 'The Prinzenraub', for *Fraser's*, which was published in January 1855. It was a by-product of his submergence in German history, being the tale of the kidnap of the two teenage sons of a fifteenth-century Elector of Saxony. His main task had stagnated. 'My book goes on ill here,' he told Jack just before Christmas, 'which is ... the fruit of my own languid inability to grapple heartily with it and crush it down under me.'[19]

Writing to Ruskin on 23 January 1855 he apologised for not having acknowledged receipt of Volumes II and III of *The Stones of Venice*. 'The truth is,' said Carlyle, 'I have been eclipsed into near utter darkness this long while, by Prussian dust and other sore sufferings hard and tender; and have done very little except diligently hold my peace, in hope of better days.'[20] Carlyle found Ruskin 'very pleasant company now and then',[21] and a man of supreme intellect. He told Ruskin he and Jane hardly ever went out, though would value a visit from him one afternoon or evening. 'If I had a horse ... I wd come to Denmark Hill myself, in a hurry, and seek you out.' But Carlyle went virtually nowhere, apart from out on his late-night constitutional, and so it remained for the rest of the winter. This did not necessarily benefit his book. 'My work,' he told his sister Jean on 16 February, 'is threatening to get into terrible stagnation again.'[22] He stopped reading the newspapers, not least because British foreign policy and the Crimean War continued to annoy him. He had no time to write for the public about his 'private sorrow and gloom'[23] at the government's handling of the war. The cult of silence gripped him; he wrote fewer and fewer letters, but did at last start writing some of *Frederick* – or so he told his journal on 4 April. The winter was harsh, Carlyle thought the harshest he could recall; so there was little incentive to do anything but work. He wallowed in thoughts of mortality. He wrote to James Marshall that 'I often look forward with longing to be ... in at least profound peace forevermore, and freedom from the unworthy wretchedness of this life, with the loved ones that I had, – all joined to me, at least so. "God is Great": I depend wholly on that fact, will take it as God orders, not complaining with my will.' His depression poured out. 'For the last year and more I have sat here in general very solitary, not too joyful by any means ... and extremely futile in my attempts at working ... ugly work too; ugliest and dispicablest, not the work I would have chosen.'[24]

In May he told Emerson that 'this last year has been a grimmer lonelier one with me than any I can recollect for a long time.' His work, he added, was 'a Task that I cannot do, that generally seems to me not worth doing, and yet must be done. These are truly the terms. I never had such a business in my life before.'[25] He complained that the other books on which he was relying, which were bad enough to start with, were made worse by their lack of indices; and he was frustrated at being so far from Berlin, and the seat of the information he needed. As usual, he was too obsessed with his own problems to notice the grimness and loneliness of his wife's existence.

Having exchanged some words with her at breakfast, he would shut himself in the soundproof room until at least 3.30 p.m. He would then have an afternoon nap, or lie on a sofa reading. Between 5.30 p.m. and 7.30 p.m. he would have a simple dinner, and then take himself off alone for his walk. Once home, usually after eleven o'clock, he would sit up on his own reading until the early hours. Occasionally a friend would come and walk with him, like Ruskin, who was himself prodigiously busy with *Modern Painters*, or Froude, deep in his *History of England,* a work suffused with a distaste for Catholicism and an admiration for authoritarian government that shows all too clearly Carlyle's influence. However engrossed Carlyle was in his own history, he had time in September 1855 to send a detailed critique to Froude of the manuscript of the *History of England.* As well as making textual suggestions, Carlyle offered some principles about the writing of history: 'The rule throughout is, that *events* should speak. Commentary ought to be sparing; clear insight, definite conviction, brought about with a *minimum* of Commentary; that is the *Art* of History.'[26]

Carlyle had had no time out of London since his mother's death, and so readily accepted an invitation to stay at Farlingay Hall in Suffolk for ten days with Fitzgerald in August 1855. He slept well there, and had some badly needed fresh air on daily drives with his host; and Fitzgerald took him for a sea-bathing excursion to Aldeburgh. To round off the trip he went to Orford to stay with Parson Crabbe, the son of the poet, and came home by steamer from Ipswich, the now relatively short train journey being, in Carlyle's imagination, 'horrible'.[27] Jane stayed at Chelsea, taking herself by train for excursions into the country. When Carlyle returned they both went to Addiscombe, offered to them again in the absence of the owners by the Ashburtons; but Jane was bored, sleepless and restless, and after a few days returned to Chelsea and left Carlyle in the country on his own for three weeks to read Voltaire, a crucial element of his work on *Frederick.* He soon became lonely, though told his sister Jean that 'I fancy I have got some real improvement by these three weeks solitude and riding'.[28] Once the hot summer ended, he came back to Chelsea.

As a mark of her deteriorating spirits, Jane began to keep a journal. This was the document Carlyle found after her death, and which proved to him his part in her wretchedness. Noting, on 22 October, Carlyle's return from a visit to Lady Ashburton at Bath House, she wrote: 'I wonder how many thousand miles Mr C. has walked between there and here, putting it all together; setting up always another milestone and another betwixt himself and me.'[29] She records her sore feelings and her continued recourse to morphia to help her sleep; and her evenings spent repairing Carlyle's clothes while he paid court to Lady Ashburton. She had taken over from Carlyle all the financial worries too, having earlier that year persuaded him beyond doubt that she was hard put to manage on the housekeeping allowance he gave her, and that she deserved more. This released Carlyle from domestic worries, and allowed him to devote himself to his research and writing. On his sixtieth birthday, 4 December 1855, he wrote a long letter to Browning in Paris listing books to which the poet might have access in France, and which could provide useful material for *Frederick*. Jane had more down-to-earth priorities. When the income tax inspectors decided Carlyle was earning more than he was declaring, it was Jane who went to Kensington to battle with them, fearing Carlyle would lose his temper. 'Mr C said "the voice of honour seemed to call on him to go himself," ' Jane recorded. 'But either it did not call loud enough, or he would not listen to that charmer.'[30] Carlyle was not a tax evader; he merely could not any longer find the energy to be concerned with such trivial, temporal matters.

Though neither she nor Carlyle ('I am in my usual dreary steadfast condition'[31]) really wanted to, both went for a brief Christmas visit to the Grange, Carlyle accepting the invitation in a letter in which he addressed his hostess as 'best of Women, best of friends'.[32] There was the usual ritual of the doling out of presents, and Jane apparently was offended at being given a silk dress by Lady Ashburton. The atmosphere was difficult; and the pull of *Frederick* was irresistible, so by mid-January they were back at Chelsea. Neuberg had been charged during their absence with sifting and sorting through Carlyle's materials. By the time Carlyle returned the work was in better shape, and an end of the first two volumes in sight. He spent much of January reading Clausewitz on warfare, better understanding Frederick's martial policies as a result, and then resumed writing. So extensive was his material that he began to realise the work was likely to be of a size and scope he had not envisaged before starting.

He found time to read *Little Dorrit* and the third volume of *Modern Painters*, and sent praises to Dickens and Ruskin. Though his work was going well he told Ruskin in March that he was 'pretty nearly brokenhearted in these Prussian Dust-whirlpools'.[33] Jane fell ill again, not leaving the house for weeks because of a cold, and dosed with morphia by night because of her insomnia. As Carlyle began to see some chinks of light in his travails he went out more, especially to Bath House, and introduced Ruskin into the Ashburtons' circle. Jane would sometimes, but not always, go with him. She had abandoned her journal the previous December, but resumed it the following March with tales of her ill-health and lowness of spirits. Geraldine Jewsbury had moved to London and would visit her frequently, providing the ideal sounding-board for Jane's anguish against Carlyle. Geraldine later told Froude that Jane 'was miserable: more abidingly and intensely miserable than words can utter. The misery was a reality, no matter whether her imagination made it or not.'[34]

Nor did Geraldine doubt that Lady Ashburton was the source of it, since she knew how Carlyle's interest in his patroness played on Jane's fractured nerves. And she reminded Froude: 'Bear in mind that her inmost life was solitary – no tenderness, no caresses, no loving words; nothing out of which one's heart can make the wine of life. A glacier on a mountain would have been as human a companionship.' Despite her physical weakness, she and Nero, her dog, would go out on spring days on omnibuses, so the dog could play and she could take some air.

By May Carlyle felt that 'the First Half of my wretched Book'[35] would be at the printer by the autumn; but he still had not gauged how big the work was to be. Chapman was also planning a cheap edition of his works, which would bring in some much-needed money. A barrister called Alexander Gilchrist, whom Carlyle had met the previous year, volunteered to prepare existing works for the presses while Carlyle was occupied with *Frederick*. Another young admirer, Henry Larkin, was recruited during the following winter to help index these works; and a third, less successful recruit was Frederick Martin, an East European Jew, whose excellent copying and linguistic skills were offset by his propensity to steal Carlyle's autograph manuscripts. The works published in *Last Words of Thomas Carlyle*, and the *Reminiscence* of the Irish journey of 1849 disappeared in this way.

The prospect of a printer waiting for his manuscript always improved Carlyle's industry, and if anything he was, for the rest of that year, still more single-minded about *Frederick* than hitherto. He and Jane talked for weeks about whether to go to Scotland for the summer, but the decision was made for them: 'the intolerable heats of July forced us north again.'[36] Jane had been more than usually ill, suffering a period of deepest depression, revealed in her diary as published by Froude in the *Letters and Memorials*. Froude, however, censored the most damning comment. An entry for 21 June 1856 states that 'the chief interest of today expressed in blue marks on my wrists.' It is not clear whether these were bruises as a result of a struggle between Carlyle and Jane during an argument; Paul, Froude's biographer, hints that they may have been bruises caused by a suicide attempt.[37]

The Ashburtons were going for their now traditional Scottish shooting holiday, and had rented a railway carriage, built for the Queen, to take them to Edinburgh. Lady Ashburton offered to take the Carlyles north with them, and the offer was accepted. She was ill, and all concerned had an uncomfortable journey on a blisteringly hot day. The axles caught fire at Peterborough, and at every main station thereafter had to have its axles hosed down. At Newcastle it was dispensed with altogether, and the party transferred to an ordinary vehicle, which reached Edinburgh without further incident. The Carlyles stayed a night in the capital; the next day Jane went to see her cousins at Auchtertool near Kirkcaldy, Carlyle went to see his sister Mary at the Gill on the Solway Firth. He stayed there for two months, working on corrections to *Frederick* and reading Plato, and finding 'perfect solitude, kindness, and silence'.[38]

Jane then returned to Edinburgh to see other cousins in Morningside, and made an excursion out to Haddington. Carlyle went over to see Scotsbrig, which he found depressing, but otherwise left the Gill only to travel to Ross-shire to stay with the Ashburtons in mid-September. Jane was intensely annoyed and, sensing this, he wrote making out that he was having a wretched time. She replied that she frankly did not believe him. However, he was complaining not purely for effect. The aristocratic friends shooting with the Ashburtons bored him, and the house was uncomfortable. He was also becoming aware that Harriet Ashburton was seriously ill, and this distressed him; the atmosphere was bad, and he took himself off for ten-mile walks as a respite. His only consolation was reading Emerson's *English Traits*, just published, in which he featured. He was hurt by Jane's choleric correspondence with him, though she had administered a corrective that, though unjust, was perhaps overdue.

III

As well as being conscious of getting older, Carlyle was aware how much the world was changing. He had seen it in microcosm in Chelsea, which was now a suburb; and he had seen the railways bringing everywhere closer together, and speeding up the pace of life. Other changes seemed to affect him even more. 'Jamie says,' he wrote to Alick of their brother, '*porridge* will be out of use altogether in 20 years.'[39] As soon as he and Jane had returned from Scotland in October, they each began to complain of impaired health: Jane with more reason than Carlyle. However, he did at last have something to show for *Frederick*, though alleged his hard work was conducted 'in a humour grimmer and sadder than I ever knew before'.[40] To try to keep up his health he bought a horse in November, having road-tested several. His acquisition, Fritz, was described by Jane as 'beautiful', but because it had been badly shod went lame almost immediately. Fritz altered Carlyle's routine; the late-night walks were supplemented by evening rides. The pressure from his publisher, and his sense of ageing and becoming less energetic, changed him for the worse. As he says in the *Reminiscences*:

[*Frederick* was] to me a desperate dead-lift pull at that time; my whole strength devoted to it; alone, withdrawn from all the world (except some bores would take no hint, almost nobody came to see me, nor did I wish almost anybody then left living for me), all the world withdrawing from me; I desperate of ever *getting through* (not to speak of 'succeeding'); left solitary 'with the nightmares' (as I sometimes expressed it), 'hugging unclean creatures' (Prussian Blockheadisms) 'to my bosom, trying to caress and flatter their secret out of them!' . . . She [Jane] was habitually in the feeblest health; often, for long whiles, grievously ill. Yet by an alchemy all her own, she had extracted grains as of gold out of every day, and seldom or never failed to have something bright and pleasant to tell me, when I reached home after my evening ride, the most foredone of men. In all, I rode, during that book, some 30,000 miles, much of it (all the winter part of it) under cloud of night, sun just setting when I mounted. All the rest of the day, I sat silent aloft; insisting upon work, and *such* work, *invitissima*

Minerva for that matter. Home between five and six, with mud mackintoshes off, and nightmares locked up for a while, I tried for an hour's sleep before my (solitary, *dietetic*, altogether simple, simple) bit of dinner; but first *always*, came up for half an hour to the drawing-room and Her ... that was the one bright portion of my black day.[41]

Such a time was captured by the Dumfriesshire artist Robert Tait in his *Chelsea Interior*, painted the following year, which now hangs in the room it depicts in Cheyne Row; Carlyle, tall, still spare, bearded, and looking younger than his sixty-one years, fills his pipe by the fireplace, that the smoke (which Jane detested) might go up the chimney; Jane, with a look not quite of sadness, sits in a corner looking away from her husband. At the time Carlyle did not realise the comfort Jane gave him; his guilt at not doing so explains the sentimentality of the passage quoted above, written after her death.

In late 1856 the printer started to send Carlyle proofs of the first two volumes of *Frederick*, and the whole of the succeeding year was spent in their correction and revision. Had Carlyle known then that there would have to be four more he might have lost heart altogether; there was little else to console him. Lady Ashburton's health had become so perilous that her husband decided to take her to the Riviera for the winter; so Carlyle's main London diversion, and Jane's main source of grief, were removed. There was no corresponding increase in their intimacy, however. Jane would take her main meal at two o'clock, while Carlyle was working. He ate at six, after a happy afternoon with his horse. Jane spent most of the winter as what her husband called a 'prisoner'[42] in the house with a severe cough and cold, and went out only for rides on the omnibus. Eventually she became so ill for so long that Carlyle could not ignore it, though it depressed him further and, he felt, impeded his progress with *Frederick*. She became insomniacal for days on end, developed a ghastly cough, and became 'weak and thin', refusing though to send for a doctor.[43] Carlyle's response was to escape with his horse for three hours a day, and when not writing at home to become engrossed with his assistants. He had Henry Larkin often around him, compiling indices; and he would notice manuscripts going missing, only for them to reappear once his want of them was advertised. When he did not notice something had gone, Martin, his sly copyist, sold it to autograph-hunters.

As he stuck to his task through the winter the word from Nice was that Lady Ashburton was not recovering. Dropsy was diagnosed, and her heart was affected. At Paris, on 4 May 1857, on her way back to England, she died suddenly from a heart attack. Carlyle, to whom the news was brought two days later by Milnes, was pitched into grief; only his mother's death was comparable. In his journal he noted it was 'a great and irreparable sorrow to me'.[44] Years later, as he prepared Jane's letters, he recalled that Lady Ashburton was 'the most queen-like woman I had ever known or seen'. Despite by then being aware of Jane's feelings, he added: 'The honour of her constant regard had for ten years back been among my proudest and most valued possessions.'[45] He told Jack three weeks after the event that 'I got a great blow by that death ... I have indeed lost such a friend as I never had, nor am again in the least likelihood to have.'[46] Jane, too, was 'shocked, and dispirited'.[47] But her rival, real or imagined, had been removed for ever; now only *Frederick* would compete with her for Carlyle's affections. He went to the Grange for the funeral, which Jane described as being 'conducted with a kind of royal state; and all the men, who used to compose a sort of *Court* for her, were there, in tears. I never heard of a gloomier funeral.'[48]

IV

Still not reckoning on the scope of *Frederick*, he sent the finished first two volumes to the printer just after Lady Ashburton's death, believing half the work done; in fact, only a third had been completed, and correcting that would take him another year. He was finding that, as Froude put it, the work was becoming 'the history of contemporary Europe, and even of the world'.[49] He hoped for a rest before continuing with the book, and Jane, whose winter illness had seriously debilitated her, wanted to go to Scotland. As so often in such matters, indecision reigned. For a time they thought of going together to Germany, so Carlyle could undertake more extensive research, but that idea was abandoned. With the salon at Bath House no longer calling him, his anti-social attitudes became entrenched. 'I refuse all invitations whatsoever for several reasons,' he told Jack on 11 June, 'and may be defined as a mute solitary being at present.'[50] He made slow progress in his painstaking corrections and rewritings of *Frederick*, and encouraged Jane, as her strength recovered with the warm weather, to take herself off on her own, not merely for omnibus rides, but to stay with friends in the country. Jane went to Haddington in July for a holiday on her own, while he sat in the garden at Chelsea correcting his proofs. In the house was Tait, sketching and photographing for *A Chelsea Interior*. Carlyle rode his horse in the evenings to spare it during the hot weather, and took Nero for regular walks; but otherwise did not stir.

Jane was away until September. They corresponded with their customary regularity, and Carlyle kept his wife informed of progress in his work. He broke off briefly from *Frederick* to revise the *Latter-Day Pamphlets* for Chapman's complete edition, but otherwise Fritz dominated his thoughts. 'Oh, my dear!' Jane wrote on 24 August, having been sent a pile of proofs. 'What a magnificent book this is going to be! The best of all your books. I say so, who never flatter, as you are too well aware.'[51] Not even this praise, nor the progress he was making, improved Carlyle's morale. 'The book will be a botch and a wreck,' he wrote to her, though he admitted he was encouraged by her view of it so far.[52] 'I have been working like a slave,' he had told Alick the previous week. 'I fight along, and hope fairly to finish this frightful job too; after which I contemplate taking a rest for the remainder of my life.'[53]

He told von Ense the burden was such that he thought it would kill him. He had, by now, begun to suspect the four volumes might become five; he still could not see all of it.

By the time Jane came home even Carlyle had started to feel lonely. 'A very serious man am I growing,' he told her on 19 August, as if he had never been earnest. The printer gave him no respite; but then he had written at great length, so the task was never going to be light. He was glad to see Jane. 'Mr C says I look much better,' she wrote to her friend Mary Russell, 'and never ceases to pay me compliments on my – *appetite!*'[54] But her husband's humour was variable. He complained to von Ense on 7 October that 'I should have *come to Berlin* to write this book: but I did not candidly enough *take measure* of it, before starting, or admit to myself, what I dimly felt, how *gewaltig* an affair it was sure to be!'[55]

Within weeks, Jane had gone down with her usual neuralgia, sleeplessness and general physical debilitation. She was irritated by Tait, who was still composing his picture. 'My chief impediment,' she told Mary Russell on 20 November, 'has been that weary Artist who took the bright idea last Spring that he would make a Picture of our sitting room, – to be "amazingly interesting to Posterity a hundred years hence".'[56] Tait's visits, which had started twice weekly six months earlier, were now happening every day; of which the magnificent quality of his finished work is a testament. But it irritated Jane that it would take Tait a day to paint her portfolio, and another to do her workbox. 'Not the minutest object in these three rooms, opening into one another, but what is getting itself represented with Vandyke fidelity!' Eventually Tait did his painting at his studio, borrowing objects from the Carlyles as he needed meticulously to paint them. However, he interrupted the already tense ménage one day simply to invade Carlyle's dressing-room in order to paint a likeness of his subject's shoes. What with Carlyle 'so dreadfully busy just now, and so easily disturbed that my life is spent in standing between him and the outer world', Jane was nearing the end of her tether.

'Christmas,' he recalled, 'was spent among the most refractory set of proof sheets I expect in this world.'[57] He was supposed to write to his sister Mary on Christmas Day, but when he came downstairs in mid-afternoon, making no allowances for the festival, and Jane asked him whether he had discharged this task, he cried out that he had 'fifteen hours of the most awful work of correcting proofs ahead of him, that I who have nothing to do should have written to Mary!'[58] The language of his letters is more than ever that of survival. On 30 December he wrote that 'I am holding on here; health still holding out.'[59] In January 1858 they were due to stay at the Grange with Ashburton; but Jane, in the midst again of servant problems, sent Carlyle on his own. The break from labour lasted only three days. The proofs had to be in by May if the first two volumes were to be out in September, and Carlyle was determined to keep to the schedule.

Jane caught another foul cold, and imprisoned herself in the house as she had the previous winter. When Carlyle came down to dine she would sit and watch him eat, and tell him the news of the day. She was not quite as ill as a year earlier, but Carlyle's strength was declining. He had been told by his doctor not to ride so hard, and the sheer amount of work on *Frederick*, which he was attacking still without any days of rest, was shattering. Throughout that winter Tait was still a regular visitor, putting the last touches to his painting. It was exhibited at the Royal Academy the following summer, and Ashburton bought it for £500 (equivalent to £25,000 today). The servant trouble continued, and the atmosphere at Cheyne Row became so fractious that Carlyle went with Ashburton to Addiscombe in late March to find the silence in which to correct his proofs. Until then he had refused all invitations to go anywhere.

It was the first of several visits Carlyle, either with or without Jane, paid there during this period of proof-correcting. He had shown great compassion to Ashburton in his loneliness, and would take him riding with him of an afternoon when in London. When at Addiscombe the regime was more relaxed than in Chelsea. Proofs (the worst of which were over by the spring) could be restricted to three hours a day; the rest of it was given over to riding and 'to idle reading, lounging, smoking – with perhaps a *Proofsheet* which had rather not *wait* till my return home'.[60] His letters at this time show he was at last becoming sensitive to Jane's weakness of health, and he seems to have begun to moderate his behaviour accordingly, making most of his demands on Neuberg and Larkin.

As the first two volumes neared publication he allowed himself a brief respite from self-denial, and resumed contact with some old friends. Writing to Emerson on 2 June 1858 he claimed that 'for the last 18 months I have pretty much ceased all human correspondence'.[61] At this stage he had 'one packet more of Proofs' to handle before his 'nightmare' – or at least the first part of it – was finished.[62] 'No job approaching it in ugliness was ever cut out for me; nor had I any motive to go on, except the sad negative one, "Shall we be beaten in our old days, then?"' This prospect that posterity would know only of Carlyle's unfinished *History of Frederick the Great* was to propel him relentlessly as the task became ever more arduous, and the decline in Jane's health arrested his progress. Already, he told Emerson, he was 'humbled', 'shattered and trampled down to an inhuman degree', and the book on which he had already spent six years was 'bad ... poor, misshapen, feeble, *nearly* worthless'. But he concluded: 'My poor Wife suffers sadly the last two winters; and I am much distressed by that item of our affairs.'[63]

This understanding was obviously not conveyed to Jane. She was a sounding-board for Carlyle's frustrations, miseries, and the other manifestations of his selfishness, which depressed her to the point of madness. He not only wanted, in what Jane called 'the collapse from the strain of his book, and the biliousness developed by the heat',[64] to go to Scotland to stay with his sister at the Gill, but wanted Jane to come too. He also continued to rant about his desire to leave London and settle permanently in the country. Ultimately, as Jane wrote to her friend Mrs Russell, she had had enough:

The imaginary houses, in different parts of the Kingdom, in which I have had to look round me on bare walls, and apply my fancy to furnishing with the strength I have (!) (about equal to my canary's, which, every now and then, drops off the perch on its back, and has to be lifted up), would have driven me crazy, I think, if one day I hadn't got desperate, and burst out crying. Until a woman cries men never think she can be suffering. Bless their blockheadism! However, when I cried, and declared I was not strong enough for all that any more, Mr C. opened his eyes to the fact, so far as to decide that, for the present, he would go to his sister's and let me choose my own course after.[65]

It took no change of air, but simply the absence of her husband, to feel better. They had parted with their customary misunderstanding, and Carlyle had to write to Jane on his arrival that he had not been discontented with her, but merely with himself. He was in a position to rest now – on 12 June he wrote to Jack that 'my book is at last actually done';[66] he was just going through putting dates in the margins of the proofs. However, he had more in mind than just Scotland. If the rest of *Frederick* were to be done properly, he would need to go again to Germany; he was aiming to do so after his Scottish holiday. There was no question that Jane could go too; his memories of sleeplessness and anxiety on his first trip convinced them both that she would suffer greatly from such a journey. She did not even feel equal to a train ride to Scotland.

Carlyle was at his sister's from the end of June to the middle of August. He slowly recovered his health in a climate he felt better suited him, and in a place where he could sleep. He took as much exercise as he could, started reading about Alexander the Great, and tried to put together a plan for Germany. Annandale depressed him, for he knew virtually no one there and virtually no one knew him. 'A man of 63 has a strange feeling,' he wrote later that year to Alick, 'when visiting his native country, – as of a ghost coming back to the Earth!'[67] He used the time now on his hands to wallow in remorse about his thoughtlessness towards Jane, and found it easier to express affection for her on paper than face to face. 'Oh,' he wrote on 5 July, 'if I sent you all the thoughts – sad extremely some of them – which I have about you, they would fill much paper, and perhaps you would not believe in some of them.'[68] Three days later he told her that 'we have had a sore life pilgrimage together, much bad road, poor lodging, and bad weather, little like what I could have wished or dreamt for my little woman.'[69] Such was his guilt that he panicked whenever a letter went astray in the post, fearing Jane had finally cut him off. She was improving greatly. Neuberg and Larkin kept her company, and Ashburton's sister asked her to Bay House to take the air. Carlyle need not have worried.

In his solitude at the Gill Carlyle even wrote to Mill, commending to him a young disciple who wanted guidance. Carlyle bore no grudge against Mill. He even told him, in his letter of 28 June, that 'I often think, if you were in the next cottage, half a mile off, what discoursing we should still have, in front of the ancient Selgovian Sea and the Cumberland Mountains rising dumb and grand to the rear of it, – not grown old as some others of us.' He added, though: 'Perhaps Pythagorean silence, tho' painfuller, is better.'[70] He promised, too, to go to Blackheath and renew his acquaintance with Mill; but his continuing obsession with *Frederick* once he was back home helped ensure that did not happen. Mill had further developed his critique of Carlyle in relation to German ideas, complaining that Carlyle had 'made a great mistake in presenting Goethe as the example to the modern world of the lines on which it should shape itself'.[71]

He had decided to sail across the German Ocean from Newcastle, and had, of course, forgotten to take his passport with him. Jane, charged to find it in his bureau, could not discover where he had placed the key, and wasted a whole morning looking for it. It was eventually found, and Carlyle pored over his *Continental Bradshaw* working out where he would have to go and the quickest way of covering the ground. Neuberg had gone back to Leipzig in July and was unsure whether he could spare the time to act as Carlyle's companion and courier; but another man, F. J. Foxton, was recommended to Carlyle for the task, and was anxious to be of service. Foxton came up to Edinburgh to see Carlyle, who found him 'good compared with nothing'. They sailed to Hamburg, arriving on 24 August 'after such a voyage for tumult and discomfort . . . as I have seldom made'.[72] Carlyle found Neuberg in attendance after all, and Foxton, of whom he had had doubts, was deemed 'very good'.[73] He had been asked to stay on Rugen, an island in the Baltic, by friends of Ashburton's who were there for the summer, and arrived on 27 August. His hosts, the von Usedoms, went out of their way to smooth his journey, meeting him at Rostock and conveying him the sixty-four miles to their island. Foxton was no longer required, and left for Berlin to undertake his own business. Herr von Usedom and Neuberg between them made arrangements for Carlyle to see whom and what he had to.

Forgetting his age, Carlyle celebrated his arrival on Rugen by swimming in the Baltic, and caught a ferocious cold. After three days swilling castor-oil he was well enough to travel by steamer and rail to Berlin, where Neuberg had taken him a room at the British Hotel in Unter den Linden, and was waiting to meet him. Both Neuberg and Foxton, with whom Carlyle was reunited, were ill, but none the less the progress around Fritz's battlefields went ahead: Liegnitz, Breslau, Prague and Dresden were the first stops. Carlyle was already hating the poor German food and uncomfortable beds, and promised Jane on 5 September that 'I will never leave my Goody any more.'[74]

Carlyle, Neuberg and Foxton left Berlin on 6 September, armed with a letter from the *aide-de-camp* of the Prince of Prussia instructing any Prussian officer they met to give them any assistance they needed. Having seen the field at Liegnitz they moved on to Breslau, where they stayed while looking at the sites of the battles of Leuthen and Molwitz. However much he thought he was not enjoying himself, Carlyle did grudgingly admit to Jane that 'there is a kind of comfort in doing what one intended.'[75] He found the places smellier, the food worse and the people ruder as he went deeper into Bohemia, past the battlefield of Kolin. Prague, though, Carlyle found a 'grand, picturesque town',[76] and they saw the battlefield there. The journey thence to Dresden took him and his companions through 'the beautifullest country ever seen', but left him in need of sleep and silence. From there they went to Leipzig, and by train to Weimar where (close to his spiritual roots) he at last slept soundly. So resolute for rest was he that he turned down an invitation from the Grand Duchess, and it was as well he conserved his strength. The next stage, to Aix-la-Chapelle, 'was among the hardest in my experience of physical misery', starting at four in the morning and not finishing until seven in the evening. The following day, with Neuberg violently sick, they reached Ostend and took the boat to Dover. He was back at Chelsea on 22 September. Jane having gone to Thornhill in Scotland to stay with Mary Russell, a friend of her family's, Carlyle, alone, sat down at once to write her an account of his travels.

He was back in time for the publication of the first two volumes of *Frederick.* Froude says that 'the literary success was immediate and exceptionally great',[77] the first 2,000 copies selling immediately, then another 2,000, with a third impression ready by Christmas. 'Their appearance is not only the event of the publishing season,' said *The Spectator*, 'but it is of lasting literary moment. All that Mr Carlyle writes at once takes its place among our standard English literature, without waiting for the suffrages of criticism, and is as sure to be read thoroughly and calmly studied generations hence as now.'[78] But this success was little consolation: all he could think of was the labour still to come.

14

Frederick:
'This Mother of Dead Dogs'
1858–65

CARLYLE'S TRAVELS OVER, relentless work began again. 'Mr C is home from his battlefields,' wrote Jane, shortly after her own return from Scotland, 'and as busy and private as before.' It was still hard on her. 'My evenings are now sacred to reading on his part, and mortally ennuying to myself on mine.'[1] To try to propitiate her, Carlyle sought diversions for her that did not cost him anything except money; there was plenty of that around now, since by the end of 1858 the proceeds to him from the first two volumes of *Frederick* were £2,800. Having always rejected gigmanity, Carlyle hired a brougham and made Jane go for drives in it. 'An expensive luxury,' was how she described it, 'which Mr C forces on me twice a week "now that I am old and frail, and have a right to a little indulgence".'[2] But Froude recalled that if he or any others of the circle happened to visit Cheyne Row at this time, they inevitably found Jane alone, and Carlyle either out on his late-night walk or ride, or locked away in the soundproof room refusing to be disturbed. He was not, though, finding it easy to settle down to work. He told his sister Jean that 'I shudder to engage again' on Frederick. Instead, he was 'just poking about the outskirts, timidly skirmishing.'[3]

Carlyle still thought he had just two more volumes to do, which he estimated at 'perhaps two years of hard work, if I still live'.[4] For the winter he went, as the lonely tone of Jane's letters confirms, utterly into isolation to try to get his work finished. 'I have in general lived perfectly alone,' he wrote to his sister on 7 January 1859, 'working all day with what strength remained to so grey a man, then rushing out into the dusk to ride for a couple of hours, then home again to Books, etc.'[5] This was his excuse for writing to her, and indeed to everyone else, so rarely. 'His horse gives him more satisfaction than I ever saw horse, or person or thing give him in the world before!' wrote Jane, miserably, later that month.[6] She drank whisky more than was good for her, ostensibly as a sleeping draught, and often would hardly move from her bed, staying there either to sleep or read. Her solitude was relieved by the steady stream of visitors who came to Cheyne Row, and on whom, with the brougham at her disposal, she now made visits.

Six months after his return from Germany Carlyle realised his progress was far slower than he had expected. This depressed him to greater depths than he had known before. He told Emerson, on 9 April 1859, that 'I never in my life was so near choked; swimming in this mother of Dead Dogs, and a long spell of it still ahead!' He added: 'I profoundly pity myself (if no one else does),' and claimed it was 'getting beyond a joke'.[7] Matters could, though, get worse, and did. The next week he told Ruskin that Jane 'has fallen into the worst cold I have ever seen her have', and Carlyle, taking hypochondria to spectacular lengths, complained that a sudden change in the weather after what had been an exceptionally mild winter had 'renewed' the cold he had caught in the Baltic almost eight months earlier. Jane's cold, though, genuinely distressed him, for he had never seen her so ill, and the doctors could do nothing for her. He thought, once more, of moving to the country as soon as Jane was fit enough for the upheaval, and not coming back to London. Jane, unfairly, did not think Carlyle had quite understood how frail she was, and wrote to Mrs Russell: 'There was a need of somebody who knew to explain to Mr C that if care were not taken, I should die of sheer weakness! – a thing which makes no show to inexperienced eyes, – especially to eyes blinded with excessive contemplation of Frederick the Great!'[8]

He broke from his routine for the occasional ride with Ruskin, and also to read Mill's *On Liberty*. 'In my life,' he told Jack, 'I never read a serious, ingenious, clear, logical Essay with more perfect and profound dissent from the basis it rests upon, and most of the conclusions it arrives at.'[9] The gulf between him and Mill was vast. 'As if,' Carlyle exploded, 'it were a sin to control, or coerce into better methods, human swine in any way; – as if the greater and the more universal the "liberty" of human creatures of the *Swine* genus, the more fatal all-destructive and intolerable were not the "slavery" the few human creatures of the *Man* genus are thereby thrown into, and kept groaning powerless under.' The task of answering Mill was partly, but rather ineffectually, undertaken by Carlyle in *Shooting Niagara: and After?* eight years later; but the most brilliant demolition of him was made by James Fitzjames Stephen in *Liberty, Equality, Fraternity*, perhaps the finest example of Carlyle's influence bearing fruit in a great mind.

As summer approached Carlyle realised both he and Jane would have to have a rest from Fritz. They agreed to go to Scotland, and found a house to rent at Aberdour in Fife. In the last week of June, Carlyle, his horse and their maid went by sea to Scotland. Jane followed by train, wrecking her health by travelling overnight, so she could stop off at Haddington before joining her husband. Once she arrived she was in no state to enjoy the break. 'She is very feeble, indisposed to locomotion, ankles so weak that she can walk little,' Carlyle told his brother.[10] He found a side-saddle for her and took her for slow rides, leading her through the countryside; and although she found the landscapes beautiful she felt no better for the change of pace and air; her husband found her still 'feeble and feckless'.[11] Carlyle did, though, recover his health, bathing in the sea every morning and building his strength on dairy food. After six weeks they moved three miles inland to Auchtertool to stay near Jane's cousins; Jane went back by train to London in late September, Carlyle went home via Scotsbrig to see his brother Jamie, who had recently been widowed. He was not home until 1 October.

Age was mellowing him out of old, rigorous anti-sentimentality. He recalled that when he had gone with Jamie to visit his wife's grave 'I could not forbear a kind of sob, like a child's, out of my old worn heart, at first sight of all this.'[12] More evidence of softening came when Nero, Jane's little dog, whom Carlyle would take on a walk each evening, was run over by a butcher's cart that autumn. It was not killed, but its health was so impaired that by the following February Carlyle had to take it to be put down 'with a degree of pitying sorrow even from me,' he subsequently recalled, 'which I am still surprised at'.[13] In tears, he buried the dog in the garden.

That autumn and winter of 1859–60 were the grimmest times yet for him, for his fears deepened that he was not going to contain *Frederick* in four volumes. He was well into writing the third and was starting to plan the fourth, but there would have to be more. He recalled his attitude as having been to make 'a determined onslaught ... to vanquish by sheer force the immense masses of incondite or semi-condite rubbish which had accumulated.'[14] He told Jean on 13 November 1859 that 'I hang on, like a spavined gin-horse, to my uncomparable harness.' A fortnight later he wrote to James Marshall in Weimar of 'that unutterable horror of a Prussian book; which has quite broken my heart, and indeed has often seemed as if it would kill me outright before I had done with it'.[15] Having finished reading Dickens's *A Tale of Two Cities*, he forswore diversion, and went to his task relentlessly. He attempted to meet the schedule his publisher, with an excess of hope, had forced on him, for the printing of the rest of the work in mid-1860; however, he finally abandoned that hope in February, exhausted and harried by Jane to stop his monomaniacal approach to the book. He slowed down, but only a little; the effort was still back-breaking. He had realised that what was being printed was not satisfactory, and had to devote himself to recasting the whole of the third volume, leaving the fourth for the moment untouched. He and Jane had had a period of absolute solitude, with the exception of a ten-day stay at the Grange in January 1860. Jane wrote that 'it is cheering to get out of the valley of the shadow of Frederick the Great for even eight days!'[16] Ashburton had married again in November 1858; his young wife, Louisa Stewart Mackenzie, became close to Jane in a way her predecessor could never have been. It was as well, because Carlyle simply did not have time for his wife. 'My darling must have suffered much in all this,' he recalled in the depths of regret after her death. 'I sometimes thought how cruel it was on her ... never once in her deepest misery did she hint, by word or sign, what she too was suffering.'[17] Nero's demise was a terrible blow to her, like the loss of a child; but she passed the winter in better physical health than in preceding years.

Whatever the misery of composing *Frederick*, its success made Carlyle rich. He wrote to Alick in Canada to offer him £200 to launch the career of his son, and Carlyle's namesake, Tom. Explaining his prosperity to Alick, Carlyle said that 'my late books have sold beyond common; the British public, after having tried in vain to starve me into compliance or death, now renounces the attempt, and says, "Live!" '[18] Jane's view was not so optimistic. She wrote to Mrs Russell that 'my husband is working himself to death; has no thought of going North this year.'[19] She felt she could not leave him in his present state, which meant she had no holiday either.

Carlyle had had a premonition he would never finish *Frederick*; it was his habit late at night, or when he could not sleep, to sit in the kitchen at Cheyne Row and smoke, directing his fumes up the chimney. One such night this sense of impending failure came to him; his sleeplessness, after that, became chronic, and his mood by day unbearable. It was, he recalled, 'the first real assault of fear'. His agitation affected Jane, and by July she was on the verge of a breakdown through worry and lack of sleep. Though she claimed to have woken 'twenty or thirty times every night of my life for years and years',[20] the stress this caused her was nothing compared to that caused her by the sound of Carlyle, in the room above, leaping out of his bed once or twice in the night. She had become utterly estranged from him, even afraid of him, and certainly not able to comfort him.

On medical advice from Jack, now in lodgings in Kensington, Carlyle changed his mind about an excursion. He and Jane went to Brighton for some sea air; but, of all things, crowing cocks made their stay unbearable, and they were back at Chelsea within a week. There was, happily for them both, an alternative. Sir George Sinclair, owner of Thurso Castle in the far north of Scotland, invited Carlyle to spend a month there. Carlyle went by sea in early August; Jane was immediately ordered by her doctor to go nowhere, least of all with Carlyle, but simply to rest. As before, she found that Carlyle's departure was the tonic she needed, though the doctor also gave her three tranquillising draughts of medicine a day. For his part, the voyage and change of air solved his sleeplessness, though he remained 'very sad, "soul exceeding solitary" '.[21]

Sinclair was a lavish host, though Carlyle was relatively undemanding. He went for a daily swim in the Pentland Firth, and for long solitary walks. He arranged that he should be able to work on his book until three o'clock each afternoon, which his host understood. Sinclair, an erudite and interesting man, did his best to cheer up his guest, but Carlyle was resistant. Jane had warned Sinclair about his sad demeanour, and allowances were made. The posts to the far north were slow, and both he and Jane were made anxious by what each thought was the failure of the other to correspond. None the less, he managed a substantial amount of work, and was relieved in late August to hear that Jane had recovered sufficiently to go to Cheshire and stay with her friend Lady Stanley at Alderley Park. From there she planned to go to rest with Mrs Russell in Dumfriesshire, especially valuable as Mrs Russell's husband was a physician who could watch Jane's health closely; then she would join Carlyle at the Gill with his sister. However, confusion intervened.

Sinclair suffered an invasion of grandchildren, which pushed Carlyle to the limit of boredom and irritation. He wrote to Jane, who he thought was still at Chelsea, saying he would 'sail South' imminently. He meant he would go to Leith, and hope to join her in Scotland. She, when she received the letter in Cheshire, it having been sent on from Chelsea, thought he meant he was going home. In helpless rage she panicked and left for London immediately. The house was shut up and stripped for cleaning, with no servant there to look after him; fearing his anger at finding such a situation, she felt she had to race on to prepare the place for him. Only on reaching London did she learn the truth, and her rage was now undilutedly turned on Carlyle.

Alexander Carlyle, editing the *New Letters and Memorials* in his customary anti-Jane tone, suggests on the flimsiest of evidence that Jane had, in fact, become tired of travel and welcomed the opportunity to return home, having left Cheyne Row in the care of someone whose honesty she doubted and who, subsequently, was convicted of an offence. But Jane, not known for mendacity, told Mrs Russell that all she wanted to do was have 'a good hearty cry'[22] because of her disappointment. This, and other letters to Carlyle published by Froude in *Letters and Memorials*, Alexander blatantly suggests should not have been published;[23] indeed, such honest scholarship would have undermined his campaign to paint Carlyle as a man virtually without blemish saddled with a neurotic wife, and Froude as a prevaricating monster. Froude makes no comment in his selection of letters, having them speak for themselves, along with a short note of Carlyle's regret; it is Alexander who trumps up a simple, unfortunate misunderstanding. The letters are mild in their rebuking of Carlyle; only when he himself, out of self-defence, suggested to Jane that she might have lost heart with her travel plans does she turn on him ferociously, stating categorically that 'had I lost heart I would have said so.'[24] Alexander, determined to persecute Froude, chose not to believe her.

As soon as he found out what had happened Carlyle wrote to Jane in contrition, claiming he had 'seldom in my life been so vexed by anything of that kind as by the news you sent me this afternoon'.[25] Having been soundly upbraided by her, he left Thurso on 7 September to begin a slow progress home. Jane soon forgave and forgot, though the upheaval had made her ill and sleepless again, and there was no question of her going to Scotland herself. After Carlyle had visited his family he travelled south via Alderley, and reached home on 22 September. He resolved 'not to revisit Scotland till the unutterable Frederick were done',[26] a resolution which, mainly for unhappy reasons, he kept.

II

'Mr C. doesn't seem to have benefited from his long sojourn by the sea-side so much as I had hoped, and at first thought,' Jane wrote to her sister-in-law Mary on 19 October 1860.[27] Not only was he not sleeping, sitting all night smoking up the chimney; he was also, perversely, taking cold baths to ward off insomnia. He was mindful, too, of the opportunity cost of writing *Frederick*, that he was denied the time to attack the social malaises that still irritated him. Ruskin, now emerging into fully fledged discipleship as he turned his attentions from art to politics, was publishing 'Unto This Last' in the *Cornhill Magazine*, and seemed to be doing Carlyle's work for him. 'You go down thro' those unfortunate Dismal-Science people,' Carlyle wrote to his acolyte on 29 October 1860, 'like a Treble-x of Senna, Glauber and Aloes; like a fit of British Cholera, threatening to be fatal.'[28] Carlyle and Ruskin were by now immensely close; Jane observed that:

No-one managed Carlyle so well as Ruskin ... It was quite beautiful to see him. Carlyle would say outrageous things, running counter to all Ruskin valued and cared for. Ruskin would treat Mr Carlyle like a naughty child, lay his arms round him, and say, 'Now, this is too bad!'[29]

The printing of the third volume of *Frederick*, which Carlyle was still revising, was under way; and, although going slowly, Carlyle told Jack in November that he felt he would complete the work, and that he would now 'seldom fall into the desperate view of things'.[30] The old, stark regime of work was adhered to. 'No Xmas here', he wrote to Ruskin on Christmas Eve. 'The wife is prisoner; I too in a sense.'[31] They were kept in not just by work, but by the weather, as heavy snow set in in mid-December and lingered until the new year. Lady Ashburton had offered Carlyle every facility he could have wanted at the Grange to continue his work, and Jane was keen to go both to have some companionship and a holiday from the gloom of Chelsea. They went in January 1861, but stayed for only four days before Carlyle's inability to work at the rate he wanted brought them home again. He wanted Jane to stay there – she had shown a marked improvement as soon as she left Chelsea – but she refused. On reaching home on 27 January he immediately left her, and rode over to Denmark Hill to dine at 4.30 p.m. with Ruskin, 'one of the wholesomest rides and afternoons I have had for a long time'.[32]

He acknowledged receipt of Emerson's *Conduct of Life* on 29 January, claiming that 'I literally do not write the smallest Note once in a month, or converse with anything but Prussian Nightmares of a hideous [*sic*], and with my Horse (who is human in comparison), and with my poor Wife (who is altogether human, and heroically cheerful to me, in her poor weak state).'[33] The optimism of the previous autumn had already evaporated. 'In my life I was never worn nearly so low, and seem to get weaker monthly,' he told Emerson. He did find time to write to a victualler in February 1861, revealing the alcoholic pressures his life was placing upon him:

In my present state of health and occupation, it is far more important for me that the Brandy be *right* than that it be *cheap* – very much more so indeed. And I am informed, it is now extremely difficult to get Brandy that has *not* been doctored, more or less, with that inferior stuff of the *Scotch* Distilleries.[34]

He suspected he was a year from finishing; he was, in fact, four. Forster, as a favour to Jane, tried to seduce Carlyle out into society, and when he succeeded, tempting him round one Sunday evening, Carlyle even claimed he had benefited from the occasion; but it was not easy for Forster to repeat the experiment. Carlyle still saw few visitors at Cheyne Row, though Ruskin, when he was in London, was always welcome and usually seen. Forster remained an important friend, Carlyle telling him at this time that 'the sound of your friendly voice again' would seem like a 'melody striking into the wearied heart of me'.[35] Froude also became a close companion, being invited to accompany Carlyle on his late-night walks two or three times a week. He had moved to London in 1860, and took the opportunity whenever he could to see Carlyle. He gave this insight into his personality, as revealed during this new intimacy:

I had been accustomed to hear him impatient of contradiction, extravagantly exaggerative, overbearing opposition with bursts of scornful humour. In private I found him impatient of nothing but of being bored; gentle, quiet, tolerant; sadly-humoured, but never ill-humoured; ironical, but without the savageness, and when speaking of persons always scrupulously just.[36]

Froude's biographer, Herbert Paul, says he was attracted to Carlyle by the sage's conversation, which 'dazzled him'.[37] Froude had had a loveless and often brutal childhood followed by a tormented adulthood as he wrestled with religious doubts; he was not naturally light of spirit, and it is as likely that he was attracted by the power of Carlyle's reactionary mind as by his charm. The frequently ebullient humour of Carlyle could not have been more of a contrast with Froude's understated personality. As an example of the former, Paul recalls 'a sober Scotsman, by no means addicted to frivolous merriment, telling me that he had come out of Carlyle's house in physical pain from continuous laughter at an imaginary dialogue between a missionary and a negro which Carlyle had conducted entirely himself'.[38] Froude adopted a tone of complete Carlylean earnestness, failing to observe how selectively Carlyle practised it himself.

In his haste and frustration Carlyle was often producing chunks of manuscript that his printer was unable to decipher, and which had to be sent back for Carlyle – or more to the point, Larkin – to correct before even a fair proof was possible. This, as well as the depletion of energy, slowed the process down further, and there was a further complication when Neuberg, upon whom Carlyle had come to rely hugely, fell seriously ill. Carlyle's mood continued to swing between optimism and despair. He told his sister Jean on 19 May that 'the worst half is as good as altogether off my hands'. Volume

III had almost been printed, and he was now fluently writing the fourth, which he hoped would be the last. He also said that 'the Book promises to be better, too, than I ever thought it could have been.'[39] His slowing-down also allowed him to rest more, and he got in the habit of a short sleep after riding and before dinner, which helped.

He resolved not to travel that summer, but was keen that Jane, whose health was still weakening, should have a holiday. Her plans to go to the Russells were thwarted by her cook suffering a strangulated hernia, and leaving inadequate servant-cover for the immensely demanding master of the house. She found a replacement and, in early August, went with Geraldine Jewsbury to Ramsgate for a short and unsatisfactory holiday, in range of Carlyle if he needed her. He survived better than she, in Geraldine's company, did. He at least had the achievement of seeing Volume III off his hands, 'about 100 pages too long, but not ill otherwise'. He was not, though, sanguine about the future. 'Now I stand face to face with vol 4th at last; a sufficiently hideous and impossible object now that I am close to it. But that has all along been the way. Courage.'[40] He mused to his sister on Browning, who was in London and came to see him. 'I believe he is very sad about the loss of such a wife; but I believe it may ultimately prove a great gain to him.'[41] In time, Carlyle would be forced to understand such grief differently.

Once back, Jane persuaded Carlyle to accept an invitation from Lady Sandwich, mother of the first Lady Ashburton, to spend a fortnight in September with her in a house she had rented in Windsor Forest. Jane travelled to Berkshire by train, but Carlyle rode there and back on Fritz. He found the ride 'disgusting' and was annoyed at the invasion of Windsor by 'Cockneydom'.[42] He declined further by sitting on some wet grass and developing, as a result, lumbago.

The autumn was spent in the usual routine of relentless work and little leisure. Jane weakened early on, seldom leaving the house, and sometimes not leaving her bed, but not, to Carlyle's mind, any more ill than she had been before. Throughout the winter he stuck to the book, while Jane stuck to her fireside. He made the now routine winter trip to the Grange, this time on his own, and found himself drawn into debates with other guests, including the Bishop of Oxford, about the American Civil War. The old scourge of 'nigger emancipation' found himself instinctively on the side of the South, but was unwilling to argue about it. He had been so sunk in *Frederick* that he had not had time to work out what was actually going on across the Atlantic.

In the first part of 1862 he hardly communicated with or saw anyone, and even went to the lengths of begging Jane to see that he was not asked to the wedding of one of her young friends, as it would, he claimed, have disrupted his life for three weeks. 'I feel very lonely in late years,' he wrote to Jean, 'and see more than ever what a fearful and wonderful thing this Earthly Existence of ours is. Courage, Hope; and steady to the last!'[43] Some could, though, tempt him. When the Duke of Argyll asked him to dinner in March 1862

Carlyle replied that 'it is extremely against the law for me to dine at all, in these sad *Prussian* times of mine; – but I decide to be a bad boy for once, on such temptation, and will give myself the pleasure of waiting on you.'[44] In May the third volume of *Frederick* was published, exciting almost as much praise as its two predecessors, but finding Carlyle more and more exposed to the charge that he believed 'might is right'. As *The Spectator*'s reviewer said, 'Mr Carlyle lets no opportunity pass to inculcate the doctrine that it is physical force which governs the world.'[45] Admiring the scene-painting in which Carlyle indulges when describing the Silesian war, the reviewer added that 'he is the Turner of literature, painting in colours as glowing and as graphic as the greatest of our English landscape painters. It seems a sorrowful waste that such powers should be devoted to whitewashing despot kings, advocating human bondage, and worshipping physical force.'

Carlyle was visited at this time by Charles Boner, a minor author and fellow Germanophile, who recalled the occasion in his memoirs. He found the sage in his dressing-gown and slippers, sitting with Jane by the fire, reading proofs. They talked of the decline of German art and soldiery; but it is the description of the everyday life and behaviour of the Carlyles that fascinates most:

Carlyle's long, wild, grey hair hangs over his forehead. His eye is bright and lively – his complexion healthy, and his look generally betokens a man who leads a calm life, not mixing in the struggle and rush going on around him. His wife told me she took in the Daily Telegraph, in order to know what was going on in the world. Her husband never reads the papers. He speaks slowly, and as if what he says were well weighed beforehand, as if all had been thoroughly thought over long ago. His way of stating his opinions shows that there is not a shadow of doubt in his mind as to their correctness. He makes you feel, too, he has no thought of changing his views, or allowing himself to be influenced by aught another may say. His mind is made up, once and for ever.[46]

Jane's loneliness intensified for reasons other than her husband's work. Old Lady Sandwich and Elizabeth, Countess Pepoli, two of her closest friends, both died that winter. So did one only slightly less close, Mrs Edward Twisleton. She wanted to go away as soon as the summer came, but Carlyle simply refused to leave. He had decided there would have to be a fifth volume, and the fourth was not half finished by June. Jane knew she could not leave him; but confided in Mrs Russell that 'if I go on in this way, however, I shall die.' She eventually prevailed upon him to take a break. The Ashburtons had taken rooms at Folkestone and invited them both down. Jane went for a fortnight, and Carlyle joined her for the second week, shortly after the third volume of *Frederick* was published. Noting he had survived a week at Chelsea without her, Jane suggested she might go away again later in the summer. Her plans to do so were, however, hindered by a sprain to her foot she suffered when slipping off a pavement on one of her rare walks out in late July. As soon as she recovered, though, she went by train to Mrs Russell, at last making the visit that had been aborted two years earlier, but nervously monitoring each letter from Chelsea lest she felt matters had reached a stage where she should return home.

Carlyle had to contend with the usual summer upheavals of carpet-cleaning and chimney-sweeping, but otherwise carried on, weighed down by the knowledge that the work was stretching even out of the confines of a fifth volume. He had his own clear-out of papers and other debris, and was surprised in Jane's absence by a visitor from the past. Bessy Barnet, their first maid in Chelsea from nearly thirty years earlier and now a fine lady, about to marry a doctor, turned up to seek to reacquaint herself with her former employers. Both Carlyles had heard, twenty-five years earlier, that she had died; and Jane was astonished to hear from Carlyle of his coolness in seeing her again. He was less composed when he received a letter from Jane on the envelope of which he thought (wrongly) he saw the handwriting of Dr Russell, and thought Jane must have been taken ill. She was not, indeed, especially well, and routinely still taking morphia and occasionally other tranquillisers – some prescribed, some not.

Carlyle soon became lonely, and most of those to whom he now felt close – like Ruskin – were far away. On 11 September, to his relief, Jane returned, having been to the Gill and Edinburgh after seeing the Russells. They were both convinced her health had improved, and to celebrate he took a week off from *Frederick*, of which he was just finishing the fourth volume. Many photographers had been soliciting him for years to come and have them take his portrait, and he and Jane at last accepted one of the invitations, from a photographer called Jeffray. Within days Jane was ill again, sick in her stomach and sleeping abominably, and she knew she had to have some sea air once more. Miss Davenport Bromley, a friend of the Ashburtons, asked her down to Dover; she left Carlyle behind and went at the start of October. She immediately felt better. To try to maintain her health, and to take one of the rests he was more frequently needing as the burden of *Frederick* was dragged into its tenth year, Carlyle took her to the Grange for a week soon after her return. He tried to forget one of his miseries by recalling another, driving out one day to Hursley, to see the birthplace of Cromwell's daughter-in-law. Jane was cheered by the week away, Louisa Ashburton gladly filling the gap left by the deaths of so many other close friends. Lady Ashburton's wish for that closeness was deepened by the illness of her husband, who had been ailing for months. 'We dread now that the next post will bring the news of our dear Lord Ashburton's death,' Jane wrote to her sister-in-law on 23 October. 'Carlyle will lose in him the only friend he has left in the world.'[47] Luckily, there was life in Ashburton yet; he survived the winter by spending it in the south of France.

Carlyle ploughed on with *Frederick*, maintaining remarkable composure for one who had started to write about a man but ended up writing about a whole continent. On his sixty-seventh birthday, on 4 December, he wrote to

Jack that 'I am rather pleased to feel myself shaping, according to ability, so long as I live, something cosmic and true out of the chaotic mendacious and unknown.'[48] He could sense victory, now just over two years away. Ruskin returned from Italy and Carlyle came out of isolation to see him. Otherwise, he still communicated with the world only late at night, on his traditional walk, despite Jane's fear that he would be attacked by garotters, whose crime was suddenly in vogue. Carlyle dismissed the threat as 'more a terror and a rumour than anything very practical'. But he added: 'I do generally leave my watch; carry a thick stick, and keep a sharp eye.'[49] Often of an evening Larkin would come with him on his walk once they had finished that day's business on *Frederick*. He still rode Fritz when he could, describing the horse as 'a half-rational companion, in the absence of others'.[50]

Carlyle spent the winter of 1863 at work on his fifth volume, and correcting the proofs of his fourth. To start with Jane was tolerably well, except when putting herself under strain because of conflict with and between the servants – for several years, since their prosperity had improved, Carlyle had allowed her to keep two. That autumn she noticed Carlyle becoming even fussier about his food just at a time when she could find no good cook; Carlyle was reduced to abusing one incumbent of the kitchen as a 'mooncalf', 'cow' and 'brute-beast'.[51] The strains on Jane were made worse by her having to teach any new servant she hired the way of cooking all sorts of dishes in the way Carlyle liked them. Later on she went down with severe and chronic neuralgia, so bad that she could neither eat nor talk and had to tie her pocket-handkerchief around her jaw. She longed to escape from Chelsea, and the Valley of the Shadow of Frederick, but that would not, she knew, be yet; and she could not imagine what life after *Frederick* would be like.

A dramatic change in Carlyle's routine came with the sale of Fritz to an apothecary for £9; neither the horse nor its owner was any longer up to the hard riding of the old days, and when Fritz fell on his knees and cut them badly in Regent's Park Carlyle decided to call it a day. He kept up his walking, and started, to Jane's amusement, to go for rides on omnibuses. 'He "now meets human beings to speak to",' Jane chortled to her niece on 20 March.[52]

By April 1863 Carlyle was convinced he would have the book finished by the end of the year. However, it would turn out to be just the latest of his deadlines to be breached, despite another summer of constant labour. One evening at the end of that month he heard Dickens give a public reading, and found the performance hilarious. It was a rare interruption in the remorseless earnestness of his existence. Bessy Barnet – now Mrs Blakiston – returned to Cheyne Row in May to be reunited with Jane, and was shocked by what she saw. 'I looked so ill,' Jane recalled, 'she was sure I had some disease.' Jane told her she had 'none that I could specify, except the disease of old age, general weakness and discomfort'.[53] Bessy insisted Jane come and stay with her and her husband by the sea at St Leonards, in Sussex, and would not hear of any delay. Duly, at the beginning of June, Jane left for a week of cosseting, worried only that Carlyle would sit up all night and drink too much tea. She was not yet sixty-two, but photographs of her show her looking like a ghost.

Returning in good health, she soon fell sick with stomach trouble. Carlyle sent for a doctor, but refused to contemplate going away, as *Frederick* had to be finished. 'Very bad for him,' said Jane, 'and very bad for the work.'[54] She was desperate to leave Chelsea, but lacked the courage to suggest it, given her conviction that the servants would not be up to looking after Carlyle. She hoped the imminent return home of Ashburton, still ill, would provoke an invitation to the Grange that Carlyle, even at his most obstinate, would not have the heart to refuse. When the hot days came he set up a canopy in the back garden, and worked outdoors; dined at three thirty in the afternoon, and then went for a ride on a new horse Lady Ashburton had sent him, which in his devotion to Dickens he had named Noggs, after the character in *Nicholas Nickleby;*[55] he felt it not a patch on Fritz, and even morally defective compared with that horse, in that it did not seem to want to put itself out for Carlyle.

During this summer Carlyle's reputation in America was beginning to give him an unwitting, and apparently unsought, influence on public opinion during the Civil War. *The Nigger Question* was dragged up as proof that England's greatest man of letters was on the side of the South; and Carlyle's critics used the episode to damage him. He made the mistake of publishing this short parody in *Macmillan's Magazine* that August:

Peter of the North (to Paul of the South). – 'Paul, you unaccountable scoundrel, I find you hire your servants for life, not by the month or year as I do! You are going straight to Hell, you ——!'
Paul. – 'Good words, Peter! The risk is my own; I am willing to take the risk. Hire you your servants by the month or the day, and get straight to Heaven; leave me to my own method.'
Peter. – 'No, I won't. I will beat your brains out first!' (*And is trying dreadfully ever since, but cannot yet manage it.*) – [56]

The piece was signed simply 'T.C.', and went down badly in a culture that had drunk deep of *On Liberty*, and which was alerted to attack Carlyle for his assaults on freedom. *The Spectator* doubted he was 'altogether serious', and hoped 'no Englishman will be its [slavery's] last defender in an age which believes in freedom.'[57]

Writing to his sister Jenny on 13 August, Carlyle was still sure he would be finished 'in six or eight months' – just as he had been four months earlier.[58] The expected invitation to the Grange arrived and the Carlyles spent three weeks there, but it was far from satisfactory. He spent until three o'clock each day buried in books about Poland, and such was his state of mental distraction that he started to scribble inane poetry. One such verse, written on 12 September at the end of their stay, simply reads:

Simon Brodie had a Cow
He lost his Cow & he could not find her:
When he had done what man could do, –
The Cow came home and her tail behind her.[59]

Jane's neuralgia had spread from her face to her arm, and she was in constant pain. Potions and embrocations were prepared for her, and by September were beginning to have some small effect; but her illness was so serious that it provided the greatest impediment yet to Carlyle's work, the likely completion date for which was now pushed back well into 1864. He slowly began to take more notice of her, and recalled that 'the one bright point in my day was from half an hour to twenty minutes' talking with her, after my return from those thrice dismal rides.'[60] That, though, was about the limit of time he could spare her, and he remembered, to his regret, how he would bore her with details of what he had written that day, which were the last things she wanted to spend this precious time talking about. There was, however, worse to come.

III

On the evening of 22 September 1863 Carlyle returned from his ride to find Jane had gone to visit a cousin in the City. He was relieved, for Jane's sake, as she had not been anywhere for weeks. Eventually he heard carriage-wheels outside bringing her home. He went out to find her being carried out of the vehicle by Larkin, for whom she had sent on arrival at Cheyne Row to spare Carlyle the shock. She had fallen heavily trying to avoid being run over by a cab while getting on a bus in St Martin-le-Grand, and had torn ligaments in her thigh. Larkin and Carlyle carried her upstairs and the doctor was sent for. For three days she was in dire pain, which then abated. Friends showered her with gifts and came to see her, and she seemed to make a remarkable recovery; though, typically, she worried about disrupting her husband's routine. Late one evening a month after the accident, as Carlyle was reading his Prussian books, she hobbled out of her bedroom to see him, leaning on a cane, and saying: 'Here I am come back to you my dear.' A few days later she was even well enough to receive Froude and his wife for an evening of pleasant conversation. However, as Carlyle recalled, 'this was but a gleam of sunlight, and ended swiftly in a far blacker storm of miseries than ever before.'[61]

Jane became racked with pain again, and could not sleep. 'The nights and days that followed,' Carlyle remembered, 'continued steadily to worsen, day after day, and month after month, no end visible.'[62] He told Jean that 'I have never seen her so broken ... the pain altogether horrible, not the least movement possible, no sleep, and all the sad concomitants.'[63] Her doctor could not help, and for six to eight months the pain was so intense that

Carlyle regarded it as a miracle when, eventually, it began to fade. Her cousin Maggie Welsh came and spent the winter with Jane to nurse her, and the doctors made it clear that a change of air as soon as Jane was well enough to travel was essential. Carlyle, after a brief hiatus, stuck to his work; he knew Jane would only be happy again once he had finished it, and that was what drove him on; that, and the awful thought that 'she will die, and leave thee here!'[64] At the end of November 1863 he told Jack the fifth volume would be finished by the end of January. He had already written far more than could be contained in one more volume, so there would have to be a sixth – which would see the whole work completed, he hoped, by the middle of the following year. As ever, he was optimistic about that.

In December Bessy and Dr Blakiston came to see Jane, and confirmed the diagnosis of Barnes, Jane's doctor, in every particular. To ease the neuralgia Blakiston prescribed more opiates, but Jane was still eating little and sleeping badly; Carlyle began to doubt the wisdom of 'druggings and opiate abominations',[65] and for a while ordered them to be stopped. The Blakistons resolved that Jane would go with them to St Leonards as soon as she could, but that was unlikely to be before spring. In early January 1864 Jane at last began to sleep a little, and Carlyle sensed perhaps a corner had been turned. He was able to devote himself more to *Frederick*, telling Neuberg on 9 January that the sixth volume 'threatens to be as tough *a fight with chaos* as any'.[66] Jane remained perilously low; a normally irrepressible correspondent, she wrote virtually no letters for four months. For weeks Carlyle kept one eye on her, another on his fast-completing manuscript. The fourth volume was published, the fifth finished, and the material for the sixth simply required ordering. She had one or two other low periods, which her doctor, with the aid of opiates, managed to treat; by early March she had recovered sufficiently, and the weather was mild enough, for the journey to St Leonards to be contemplated.

Now Carlyle, 'sad as the realms of Hades',[67] did not stint in his affection for and attention towards her. The effort of moving to the south coast (in a sick-carriage that reminded them both of a hearse) had been immense, and he wrote straight to her after it was over telling her she had 'behaved like a heroine', and that on his own return to Chelsea, having left her safely with the Blakistons, he had felt so lonely that he 'could have burst into a passion of tears'. It was a foretaste of the desolation to come two years later, when Jane was beyond the reach of the post office. Maggie Welsh, Jane's cousin, had gone with her, and wrote a bulletin to Carlyle daily.

Left alone, he stuck to his task. The fourth volume came out that March, the final two scheduled for publication in 1865. Once more Carlyle was chided for his devotion to his 'hero king', on whom, as *The Spectator* pointed out, 'unlimited praise' was heaped while his enemies were 'buried under mountains of obloquy and ridicule'.[68] Carlyle was also attacked for concentrating so much on Frederick's martial achievements, but so little on peace-time, and ignoring the role of ordinary Prussians in the success of their country. He paid little regard to reviews, especially ones he deemed insolent; and at this time he had too much else on his mind. He wrote daily to Jane of his concern, sadness and the zeal with which he was tackling his work. He did his best to encourage her, hoping she was feeling better as the weather became better; but then another, albeit long-expected, blow fell on them: on 25 March Ashburton died. Carlyle went to the funeral, made worse for him by the loss of a black cap Jane had made for him twenty years earlier, which he left in a cab on his way back from the station. The old enemy of sentimentality was now being vanquished by that foe almost daily. Ashburton left him £2,000 in his will – around £100,000 today – but Carlyle and Jane lamented they were past the stage where money could be of use to them. He gave it all away in small charitable bequests, the perfect expression of gratitude for all Ashburton and his family had done for him and Jane.

Carlyle was embarrassed that the Blakistons would take no fee for the attention and nursing they were providing Jane with; and so, to ease matters, Carlyle decided to rent his own house in St Leonards, to which he could remove with his work and with Jane. Jack, keen to use his own medical skills to Jane's benefit, came down too, and a place was found for them by the beginning of May; Larkin moved in to the house at Chelsea to mind it in the Carlyles' absence. Carlyle was relieved to be back with Jane, for her condition seemed to have worsened, and once she had started to write to him it was simply to report on the awfulness of her suffering. He came to her shortly after receiving the following letter, dated 25 April 1864: 'Oh, my husband! I am suffering torments! each day I suffer more horribly. Oh, I would like you beside me! I am terribly alone. But I don't want to interrupt your work. I will wait till we are in our own hired house; and then if am no better, you must come for a day'.[69] He went with a view to staying indefinitely. Shortly before leaving he rode to Denmark Hill to see Ruskin, and found the company stimulating. Ruskin had his seventeen-year-old cousin Joan Tweddale, from Wigtownshire, staying with him. Carlyle had known her family, and in a 'rapture' described how he once been to Galloway, 'where he was most hospitably entertained in the town of Wigtown by a Mr Tweddale'.[70]

Jane does not seem to have been explicit with Carlyle about her illness. She told her aged aunts, however, that the 'malady is in my womb – you may fancy. It is the nervous consequence of that unlucky fall; no disease there, the doctors say, but some nervous derangement.'[71] It was just part of what was wrong with her; a paralysis of one of her arms, weakness of her spine and legs, her body damaged by years of addiction to morphia and opiates. Even without knowing the detail, Carlyle knew enough to depress him. 'Dreary and tragic was our actual situation there,' he recalled, though they found a 'new, clean, light .. well-aired' house.[72] On his and Jack's arrival she dressed and had dinner with them, but the effort so shattered her that she did not try it again. She was able to go out for drives, mostly with Jack, though Carlyle would take her for one early in the evening, once he had finished his day's work. This experience left him so wretched that, immediately on returning to their house, he would go to a livery stable and hire a horse for a three-hour ride, often around the battlefield at Hastings, feeling mournful about Jane's illness, and disgusted by all the 'cockneys' he saw invading the region for holidays. He confided in Froude on 23 June that 'in sanguine moments I persuade myself that my poor wife is actually recovering; but at all times I have to own that the process is slow, very slow.'[73]

Various visitors, including her favourites like Forster, came to see her, but she could not see them. In June she thought of keeping the house until the end of July, but the weather became so hot (and she, once more, so sleepless) that on 12 July she decided, suddenly, to go north; not to Chelsea, of which she could not stand the prospect, but to Forster's house in Kensington, and then on an overnight train to Dumfries, in order to stay first at the Gill, and then with Dr and Mrs Russell at Thornhill. Jack accompanied her; Carlyle stayed on a week or so at St Leonards, and then took his books back to Chelsea. Slowly and uncertainly Jane recovered under Dr Russell's care and in the cooler climate; however, as she became stronger, her morale was undermined by her fears of having to make the long journey home, and by groundless worries that Geraldine Jewsbury might be interfering at Cheyne Row (in fact, Forster's wife Eliza was, with Jane's full blessing, put in charge of the redecoration of the house). The neuralgic pains returned savagely.

Carlyle was now, after many false dawns, in sight of the end of his work. Hoping to make Jane feel better, he reported his progress, and the intensity of his labour, faithfully to her. To ward off loneliness he started to venture out to visit friends, such as Ruskin one evening early in August, but told Jane that 'Ruskin has no real regard for one.'[74] He busied himself preparing the house for her return, having her room repapered and laying in supplies of her favourite foods. He wrote telling her of the redecorated house and the welcome awaiting her, and on 27 September added, best of all, that 'I shall not be long with my book now.'[75] Champagne, sent by Louisa Ashburton, was brought out on 1 October, when Jane finally, to Carlyle's unconcealed joy, returned. 'By far the gladdest sight I shall ever see,' he recalled. Worn down by his work though he was, he said that 'this again awoke me into life and hope.'[76] He wept over her with joy as he took her in, though that may have had something to do with the fact that she was an hour and a half late, and he was, according to Jane's account, imminently expecting a telegram to say she had died on the journey. It had taken him thirty-eight years of marriage to express such spontaneous affection.

Miraculously, and not least because of Carlyle sticking to his reformed husbandry, she continued to improve; and he found, from her happiness and growing health, the energy needed to finish the book. He felt the time between her return from Scotland and her death was 'a second youth'.[77] She said of him, three weeks after her return, that 'I cannot tell you how gentle and good Mr Carlyle is! He is busy as ever, but he studies my comfort and peace as he never did before.'[78] Instead of hiring a fly three times a week to take her for a drive, Carlyle bought Jane a brougham for £60, not least because he reproached himself for not having done so earlier – he had long been able to afford it, and to have had one sooner would, he thought, have avoided her street accident clambering for the omnibus, and the subsequent misery. It made Jane intensely happy.

He pressed on with his book, trying to have it finished by new year; but the time he had lavished on Jane put him a little behindhand, and the work carried over into 1865. On Sunday 15 January, though, he

went out to post-office with my last leaf of 'Frederick' MS. Evening still vivid to me. I was not joyful of mood; sad rather, mournfully thankful, but indeed half-killed, and utterly wearing out and sinking into stupefied collapse after my 'comatose' efforts to continue the long flight of thirteen years to *finis*. On her face, too, when I went out, there was a silent, faint, and pathetic smile, which I well felt at the moment, and better now![79]

In his journal he was even more concise: 'It nearly killed me.'[80]

IV

It is tragic how, after all that effort, *Frederick* remains one of the great unread books in the language; tragic, but unsurprising. Equally unsurprising is how the way Carlyle was overwhelmed by his task comes through in many parts of the book, especially towards the end. William Allingham, one of his most devout disciples, called the work 'the *reductio ad absurdum* of Carlyleism'.[81] However Allingham also observed that, if you left out the doctrinal and political questions of the King of Prussia, you found 'a supreme work of Literary Genius ... a world of wit, humour, picture, narrative, character, history, thought, wisdom, shrewdness, learning, insight'.

In *Oliver* Carlyle had sought to impose order on a mass of historical data, and had partly succeeded. In *Frederick* he sought to do the same, and unquestionably failed. For long stretches of the book, in the minute details of Frederick's battles, the book ceases to be historical writing and becomes a map of manoeuvres. Non-military historians will find it impregnable, as Carlyle knew they would; but he could not prevent himself from showing everything in the minutest detail. He jokes that it was inconvenient for him, as a biographer, to have a subject with 'fine gifts of silence', who as a result left relatively few testimonies; but, already overwhelmed by 'facts' as Carlyle was, it was as well. His book is unread because in large parts it is unreadable.

Yet Ruskin – admittedly not an independent witness – called Carlyle the 'greatest of historians since Tacitus' on the strength of *Frederick*.[82] His friends, and some of his critics, saluted the intensity of his labour rather than the quality of his product. The book is shot through with Carlyle's fundamental prejudices. It is a pursuit of a hero, one made all the more special by his self-reclamation from a degenerate, effete youth. It is a celebration of Germanism, more particularly Prussianism, and the resolute process of Germanisation. Above all, it is the text adduced, quite fairly, by Carlyle's critics to prove his belief in the 'might is right' thesis. Carlyle paints Frederick as a man of peace who, in his desire for peace, had frequently to go to war, because of the provocations of his rivals. 'He is a very demon for fighting,' says his biographer. He is also 'the stoutest King walking the Earth just now, may well be a universal one. A man better not to be meddled with, if he will be at peace, as he professes to wish being.'[83] He is a man who loves battle. At the time of the Peace of Hubertsburg, a minion says on Frederick's behalf: 'Such Reichs Princes as wish for Peace with my King can have it; those that prefer War, they too can have it!'[84] And, if he is not directly provoked, then his conquests can be portrayed as acts of deliverance. In partitioning Poland between himself and the Czar, Frederick did, in Carlyle's view, save that country from 'Anarchy, Pestilence, Famine, and Pigs eating your dead bodies', and Europe from another war – which the Prussians would have started.[85] Carlyle's characterisation of Frederick, despite being mounted at the greatest length, rarely rises above the superficial; yet occasionally, when describing the soldier-king, he leaves a clear, unforgettable impression. Never does he portray Frederick more vividly than at the Battle of Kunersdorf, the memorable occasion when he yearned to die for his country, and was reduced, as Carlyle reports, to crying out '"*N'y a-t-il donc pas un bougre de boulet qui puisse m'atteindre?*" (Is there not one b— of a ball that can reach me then)?'[86]

The need to fight to maintain peace was an excuse used by Hitler for his conquests, with less cause than in the case of Frederick. But the real example for Hitler was in Frederick's power of recovery when all seemed lost, in the penultimate winter of the Seven Years' War. That was why Goebbels read the book to his Führer in the bunker, to cheer him up; and it is the philosophical smell of the book, as much as its style and structure, that alienates modern readers. Frederick was 'the last of the kings ... he ushers in the French Revolution, and closes an epoch of World History'.[87] Froude points out that *Frederick* was a history of civilisation in the eighteenth century, but it was also a post-dated preface to *The French Revolution*; a model for a society of authoritarianism and conquest that, had the French followed it, would (in Carlyle's simplistic view) have saved them from misery. As in his earlier works, history is a continuum, part of present experience, or should be: and speaking in the person of Sauerteig, Carlyle says that 'all history is an imprisoned Epic, nay an imprisoned Psalm and Prophecy'. Despairing, Carlyle says that 'I wish ... he had disimprisoned it in this instance.'[88]

Where Sauerteig failed, Carlyle did not entirely succeed. He sought to create an epic, and in some respects did; but in his desire to present 'God's Fact as it *was*'[89] he became lost under the weight of that fact. Occasionally, he loses his temper with his sources, such as when he calls one of the German histories from which he is extracting 'one of the most hideous imbroglios ever published under the name of a book' – though he made this observation before he had finished his second volume.[90]

Yet, for the persistent, there are rewards in occasional flashes of humour, a quality that placed even Carlyle at his worst above his stern and pompous contemporaries. In a splendid passage early on, before Carlyle became too miserable, entitled 'His Prussian Majesty falls into one of his hypochondrical Fits', Carlyle describes the relationship between Frederick William, Frederick's father, and King August of Poland, 'called even "August the Great" by some persons in his own time; but now chiefly remembered by his splendour of upholstery, his enormous expenditure in drinking and otherwise, also by his Three-Hundred and Fifty-four Bastards (probably the maximum of any king's performance in that line)'.[91] Such moments of wit and humanity are essential to the morale of a reader to whom Carlyle, after passages of great tedium, habitually exhorts 'courage!'

Carlyle used Frederick and his ethos as an insulation from the increasingly unbearable world in which he felt he was living. Whatever his belief in history as a continuum, it was also, for him, an escape, a leap from reality, an antithesis to the liberalising world. Yet he is writing about a century ('a Hypocrisy worthy of being hidden and forgotten') he despised, seeking to 'extricate the man from his Century';[92] and the work contains a manifesto of his loathing:

To resuscitate the Eighteenth Century, or call into men's view, beyond what is necessary, the poor and sordid personages and transactions of an epoch so related to us, can be no purpose of mine on this occasion. The Eighteenth century, it is well known, does not figure to me as a lovely one; needing to be kept in mind, or spoken of unnecessarily. To me the Eighteenth century has nothing grand in it, except that grand universal Suicide, named French Revolution, by which it terminated its otherwise most worthless existence with at least one worthy act; – setting fire to its old home and self; and going up in flames and volcanic explosions, in a truly memorable and important manner. A very fit termination, as I thankfully feel, for such a Century. Century spendthrift, fraudulent-bankrupt; gone at length utterly insolvent, without real money of performance in its pocket, and the shops declining to take hypocrisies and speciosities any farther.[93]

The narrative starts not with the birth of Frederick, but with Henry the Fowler in 928. That in itself is an obstacle to the reader, as are the lengthy descriptions of pointless diplomatic activity in seeking to find Frederick a bride. The work only comes alive, for the non-militarist, in the descriptions of Frederick's relationship with his brute of a father, whose force Carlyle clearly admires. Notwithstanding the mental and physical savageries Frederick William inflicts on his son, he is also a man who summons in some judges (with one of whose verdicts he has disagreed) so early one morning that they are still in their dressing-gowns, and then 'smites down upon the crowns of them with the Royal Cudgel itself' when they seek to explain themselves.[94] Carlyle admires what he claims to be Frederick William's 'just-ness', and that 'there is a divine idea of fact put into him; the genus sham was never hatefuler to any man.'[95] Better still, he was the 'great Drill-sergeant of the Prussian Nation', imposing order and building up the army with which his son would expand Prussia by fire and the sword. 'Of all things,' opines Carlyle, 'a Nation needs first to be drilled; and no Nation that has not first been governed by so-called "Tyrants", and held tight to the curb till it became perfect in its paces and thoroughly amenable to rule and law, and heartily respectful of the same, ever came to much in this world.' He continues:

England itself, in foolish quarters of England, still howls and execrates lamentably over its William Conqueror, and rigorous line of Normans and Plantagenets; but without them, if you will consider well, what had it ever been? A gluttonous race of Jutes and Angles, capable of grand combinations; lumbering about in potbellied equanimity; not dreaming of heroic toil and silence and endurance, such as leads to the high places of this Universe, and the golden mountain-tops where dwell the Spirits of the Dawn.[96]

This is a symbol of Carlyle's withdrawal from reality, a measure of the moral authoritarian stance he wanted the England he lived in to adopt, as silent, unperturbed Frederick William and, later, his son had adopted it. For all his youthful delinquencies, and his mature association with Voltaire, Frederick is instinctively conservative and religious, and 'is not the man to awaken Parliamentary sleeping-dogs well settled by his ancestors'.[97] He has above all a regard for the truth: 'this man is capable of shaking [Europe] a little out of its stupid refuges of lies, and ignominious wrappages and bed-clothes, which will be its grave-clothes otherwise; and of intimating to it, afar off, that there is still a Veracity in Things, and a Mendacity in Sham-Things, and that the difference of the two is infinitely more considerable than was supposed.'[98] Carlyle never quite gives a naked message of 'might is right'; but endorses might being right when might is backed by veracity. One then has to argue with Carlyle's judgment of what constitutes veracity, a quality often con-comitant with inhumanity. Never in his whole career does Frederick do anything that Carlyle does not argue, forcefully, that he was wickedly pro-voked into. When, for example, he starts the Seven Years' War, Carlyle ridicules those who saw this as unreasonably bellicose. 'What a loud-roaring, loose and empty matter is this tornado of vociferation, which men call "public opinion".'[99] He himself seems to become Prussian. After his description of the Battle of Hochkirch, Carlyle talks of '1,000 prisoners they lost to us.'[100]

As the narrative progresses, one can detect Carlyle losing patience with himself and his seemingly endless task. When he finally concludes the Seven Years' War, he exclaims, 'Oh readers, do not at least you and I thank God to have now done with it!'[101] When the book finishes, he says, bad-temperedly, 'Adieu, good readers; bad also, adieu.'[102] His various devices of self-quotation, like Smelfungus, are wheeled on to provide some tonal contrast, or simply comic relief as Carlyle pillories the decadence of the eighteenth century. Occasionally, as if when Carlyle knew he had to press on, the style becomes crisper, more urgent, rather like the dramatic writing of *The French Revolution*. The battle descriptions themselves are often tedious, but sometimes pages and pages of sustained, breathless drama. With the descriptions of battle, so does Frederick emerge as a fully fledged hero; a man of silence, who thinks earnestly and acts swiftly and decisively; like Cromwell, an ultimate Carlylean figure. Apart from the personal example of heroism, Carlyle is motivated by his regard for the importance of the nation state. Victory in the Seven Years' War is Frederick's greatest achievement; 'Prussia has gone through its Fire-Baptism, to the satisfaction of gods and men; and is a nation henceforth.' And that it has become a nation after territorial conquest at the expense of Austria and others is of no consequence to Carlyle, for it was God's will.

Such a sentiment explains why this unmanageable epic is seen as the ultimate embodiment of Carlyle's approval of force. One suspects that the desire to communicate what the author would have regarded as this semi-religious feeling to a degenerate reading public was most of what impelled and motivated Carlyle through the years of misery spent composing it. His constantly expressed longings for the end, and the faint hopes of happy retirement that underpinned them, may also have driven him on; in which case the tragedy soon to befall him was even graver than we might imagine.

15

An End of Sorrows

1865–67

'FOR LONG MONTHS AFTER THIS,' Carlyle wrote of the period that followed *Frederick*, 'I sank and sank into ever new depths of stupefaction and dull misery of body and mind.'[1] The shock of having nothing to do was profound. It did allow him to renew neglected friendships, and even to search for new interests; such as a visit he paid to Ruskin at Denmark Hill at the end of February, to receive (at his own request) a lecture on geology. But he was sad about parcelling up the books Forster had lent him on Frederick the Great, and returning them. 'I feel,' he told Jack, 'as if I had not only got done with *Friedrich*, but with all the work I had to do on this planet. A gloomy but quiet collapse there is, in mind and body.'[2] He noticed his right hand shaking a lot; something that had started two years earlier.

With spring coming, he and Jane decided to visit Devon, now she seemed well enough to make the trip. The idea was nearly scuppered by a relapse, Jane catching a chill that inflamed her bowels; but such a problem, which merely caused the excursion to be postponed until March, was a relief to Jane compared with her sufferings of the previous year. Louisa Ashburton invited the Carlyles to stay with her at her cottage at Seaforth, and met them off the train after a cold and uncomfortable journey. They had a month of absolute rest, Jane sleeping much, Carlyle going out riding with a fellow guest, Sir Walter Trevelyan. Carlyle was as cantankerous as ever. He wrote to his sister Jean on 18 March of his rapture at being in 'the beautifullest country possible', but told Jack two days later of his 'considerable dyspepsia' and 'general misery'.[3] Jane's relations with the second Lady Ashburton were so good that, when Carlyle indicated at the end of March that he was ready for home, she was most reluctant to go. But Carlyle had promised himself a visit to Scotland when *Frederick* was finished, had not been there for five years, so would delay no further.

He did not go to Scotland immediately, but spent much of April sitting to the sculptor Thomas Woolner, who was making a bust of him, and for innumerable photographers. He also started a small reorganisation of Cheyne Row, moving his books downstairs to the first-floor library, and abandoning the soundproof room to servants for their quarters. He had resolved never to work at the scene of his miseries again, and, indeed, found it hard to imagine he would ever write another book. On 14 May, 'being about to set out for Scotland, very wearied and forlorn after my long struggle with the Book on Frederick', he made his will, leaving all to Jane.[4] On 22 May he went to Dumfries. Jane had arranged for friends to stay with her during his absence – not least the omnipresent Geraldine – which eased Carlyle's worries for her. Though her health was better, a paralysis of her right arm had set in, and was beyond treatment. He expected to be gone three months, and was.

On arrival Carlyle went to see Dr and Mrs Russell at Thornhill, and thanked them for all they had done for Jane the previous year. He then moved on to the Gill, to his sister Mary. There he wallowed in silence. He had had Noggs shipped up (at a cost of £5) and went for rides on the sands of the Solway Firth each evening. His mood was depressed when a letter from Jane arrived in the hand of a Mrs Macmillan, a new friend with whom she had been staying at Tooting. Jane's right hand was so weak that she could not hold a pen. Carlyle urged her to master writing with her left hand, not least because Geraldine took charge of drafting Jane's letters shortly afterwards. Carlyle too was finding writing difficult, his hand shaking so much that it took two hours to write a relatively short letter to Emerson.

In mid-June Jane felt strong enough to come to Scotland herself, and, because of cramped accommodation at the Gill, went to stay with the Russells. Carlyle went to see his wife for a day each week, and took her out for drives. After the first such trip he told her that 'my *day* yesterday was the only beautiful one I have had in these parts, and yet it was steeped in sadness to me.' He added that 'my very heart is sore for thee, poor little soul, worried with continual pain.'[5] On 24 July Jane returned to London, Carlyle meeting her train at Dumfries and riding with her in it for an hour as far as Annan. He found her in low spirits and tried to cheer her up, remembering afterwards that 'I felt in secret extremely miserable,' but also that 'I little thought it would be her last railway journey.'[6] However, to her surprise, Jane found she slept well on her return to Chelsea. Within a couple of days she had reverted to her old ways, however, and even a massive dose of morphia could no longer put her out. By early August her right arm had returned to use, she started to sleep, and by the middle of the month was well enough to go alone to Folkestone to stay with Miss Bromley.

Carlyle himself was uncertain what to do. He complained to Jane that the solitude he had longed for in Scotland had become 'stagnation'.[7] He sat around reading periodicals, reserving particular odium for a review Trollope had written of Ruskin's *Sesame and Lilies*. He told Jane the reviewer had shown 'considerable insolence, stupidity and vulgarity'. He added: 'A distylish little pug, that Trollope; irredeemably imbedded in commonplace, and grown fat upon it, and prosperous to an unwholesome degree … nasty gritty creature.'[8] He inspected Craigenputtock before going to Edinburgh and

Stirling with Jack, and then back to Dumfriesshire. 'Nothing could exceed my private weariness, sadness, misery and depression,' he recalled.[9]

'The truth is,' he wrote to Alick on 6 August 1865, 'I am much worn out; also very old; and ought now to know well that the *end* cannot and even should not be far off.'[10] He started to long for home, possessed by what Jane called a 'demon of impatience'. Enjoying herself in Folkestone, she sought to delay him so she did not have to truncate her holiday. She suggested he either stay where he was, or come home via their friends the Stanleys at Alderley Park in Cheshire. He obeyed her wish not to come before 28 August, the day her visit to Folkestone was due to end, and so arrived on the 29th. He found Jane 'considerably improved since I last saw her', and the house spruced up too. Once he had unpacked, and acquainted himself with the new layout of his library that Jane had arranged in his absence, he pitched once more into idleness. Ruskin, Forster (who had just had cholera) and Froude all came to see him in the days after his return. Now they were no longer sent away, or entertained by Jane downstairs, while Carlyle laboured above.

Mostly, he used his newly found leisure to become reacquainted with Jane; though when this meant taking her out for an omnibus ride she hated it, being reminded of her accident, and was paralysed with fear at the sight of carriages charging through the packed streets. However, this happy time with each other, without any distractions, sustained him after her death, though it was always to seem unbearably short.

II

Gladstone had just vacated the Rectorship of Edinburgh University. Froude had been to hear him make his last address, speaking for three hours on Homer, keeping his audience 'in a state of electric tension'.[11] Now a successor was sought; and the decision of the students was that one of their own, the author of *Frederick the Great*, should be asked to fill the post. It was not the first time Carlyle's name had been mentioned in this context; but it was the first time he had been willing to do it. Disraeli, whom Carlyle would vilify two years later as a 'superlative Hebrew Conjuror',[12] was proposed by the other camp; but lost by 657 votes to 310, helped by anti-semitic joshing from Carlyle's supporters. A handbill circulated before the contest included the advice:

The Hebrew Synagogue are most anxious that the homage to be paid to their great countryman to-morrow should be such as to be according to the Cocker of their nation.

1. Circumcision must be performed immediately on all Mr Disraeli's supporters, especially on the Members of his Committee, as otherwise they cannot be allowed to vote.

2. Every elector must be prepared to asseverate that he has not had Bacon or Ham for breakfast since he last settled with his old-clothesman.[13]

'They,' said *The Spectator* of the student electorate, 'have practically declared that Mr Carlyle's writings have stirred them much more than Mr Disraeli's, which is a very proper state of mind for University men.'[14] *The Spectator*, its writers clearly well versed in Carlylean form and thought, also suggested themes for the Rectorial address:

Not I, but the solemn fact of the universe, must warn you, at peril of drowning forever in said froth-oceans of logical jargon, to desist from long-eared hallelujahs and laudatory psalmody to middle-class education, sciences 'called pure', University extension, and the like, and retire into silences, till you can catch some audible whisper of an everlasting yea announcing, as with a clap of thunder, what sort of body-pilgrimage nature and fact have enjoined upon you, under peril of your soul, in this distracted universe, to pursue.

Even when the matter was settled – he wrote to accept the honour on 14 November 1865 – Carlyle was far from happy, particularly about the spectacle involved in performing the duties of his induction. He had not spoken on a public platform since the lectures on heroes in 1840. The ceremony was set for the following April. Carlyle was glad of the delay because he felt people would forget about it; extensive comment about his succeeding Gladstone had depressed him. He also still felt exhausted, and hoped that would have changed by the spring.

But he was almost seventy; and when his birthday came in December, his friends, led by Forster, fêted him. 'To set about rejoicing because one's seventieth year is done, would not have occurred to myself by any means,' he complained to Jack the next day, after Forster had had him, Jane and Browning round for a dinner.[15] The Froudes, too, entertained them, Tennyson visited to pay his respects on the preceding Sunday, and Carlyle found a new admirer, Professor John Tyndall, a physicist, 'a cheery thoroughgoing man' who was becoming a regular visitor to Cheyne Row. As well as tributes from his peers, he received from a cork-cutter in Sunderland and some of his fellow working men a fair edition of *Bewick's Birds*, in honour of the occasion. The same cork-cutter, Thomas Dixon, was the correspondent to whom Ruskin wrote the thoughts collected in *Time and Tide*.

No sooner were the celebrations over than Christmas came, spent with the Forsters. Carlyle passed much of his time at the end of 1865 reading Ruskin's *Ethics of the Dust*, which he found problematic. Jane was reading the serialisation of Trollope's *The Belton Estate*, something one can hardly imagine Carlyle, given his views on that particular author, enjoying. Jane went down with a cold after Christmas, and was further weakened by lack of sleep when a cock started crowing during the night. Carlyle seemed not to have heard it, and she did not tell him, but sought to find out where it was and to have it stopped. She did not mind the actual noise; but dreaded the stamp of Carlyle's foot on the bedroom floor above her, which signalled he had been woken, and (judging from her past experience) would be in a foul temper the next day. She wanted to get well, for she wanted to feel strong enough to accompany Carlyle to Edinburgh in the spring.

The date was set for Monday 2 April. That last winter they spent together was a quiet and uneventful one, though with Carlyle vexing himself on what he would say to the students. Despite her optimism, Jane would not be strong enough to go north. She had not been seriously ill, but showed no sign of shaking her cold off. Apart from during a January snowstorm, she none the less took her three hours' drive every day. Not only could she not travel, but she wished Carlyle could accept the office without having to deliver a speech. 'It will tear him to tatters,' she felt.[16] Jack stayed with them for much of the winter, and they did a little entertaining, mainly of close friends such as Ruskin and Froude; but most of the effort was being directed towards the speech. 'I am afraid,' Jane wrote to her aunt Ann at the end of March 1866, 'and he himself is certain, his address will be a sad break-down to human expectation.'[17] The effect on her nerves of her fears for Carlyle finally persuaded her against going with him, especially when she heard he planned to give the speech extempore. In the letter she wrote him that was intended to reach him after the ordeal, she admitted that 'what I have been suffering, vicariously, of late days is not to be told. If you had been to be hanged I don't see that I could have taken it more to heart.'[18] Whether the extreme strain this placed on her contributed to her death must be a matter for conjecture.

Carlyle arranged to stay in Edinburgh with his old friend Thomas Erskine of Linlathen; and John Tyndall, his newest friend, offered to escort him safely there, since he was to receive an honorary degree from the university (an honour Carlyle had been offered, but had declined). On 29 March at nine in the morning Carlyle took his leave of Jane and headed north. 'I was in the saddest, sickly mood,' he recalled, six weeks later, 'full of gloom and misery, but striving to hide it; she too looked very pale and ill, but seemed intent only on forgetting nothing that could further me.' Tyndall was waiting in the cab to take him and Carlyle to King's Cross. 'She stood with her back to the Parlour-door to bid me her good-bye. She kissed me twice (she me once, I her a second time).'[19] With that, they left.

Carlyle and Tyndall broke the journey at the Yorkshire house of Milnes, who had been created Lord Houghton. The visit unsettled Carlyle. The railway had been built near Milnes's estate since Carlyle was last there in the 1840s, and the noise of the trains, as well as his own sense of dread at having to speak in public, kept him awake and exhausted. He wanted Tyndall to take him straight away to Edinburgh. Unwilling to seem ungrateful to Milnes, who had gone to lengths to provide impeccable hospitality, Tyndall had the idea of taking Carlyle out for a long, exhausting ride; after which he slept for hours, and before leaving for Edinburgh had recovered completely. On reaching Scotland Carlyle wrote to Jane of his surprise at feeling so calm, trying to reassure her it would all go smoothly. He shut himself away in silence, refusing even to see Tyndall, and went over his notes for the address.

He and Jack, whom he met in Edinburgh, went to see David Masson, to discuss the nature of the address; but in his own mind he had settled on what he would say.

On 2 April ('gloomiest, chaotic day'),[20] he went to the ceremony, clad uncomfortably in the red and black gown of his office. Every seat in the Music Hall, where the event was held, was taken. The Principal of the University, who led the panoply of academics there, was Sir David Brewster, who forty-five years before had supplied Carlyle with his first hack-work for his encyclopaedia. Other old friends, and some of Jane's family, were in the crowd. Carlyle was introduced as 'the foremost of living Scotsmen'.[21] Masson has left his own recollection of Carlyle giving the address:

The old man stood up in the Music Hall before the assembled crowd, and threw off his Rectorial robes, and proceeded to speak, slowly, connectedly, and nobly, raising his left hand at the end of each section or paragraph to stroke the back of his head as he cogitated what he was to say next, the crowd listening as they had never listened to a speaker before, and reverent even in those parts of the hall where he was least audible.[22]

He had taken some notes with him, but cast them aside, and appeared to speak extempore, refreshed only by some sips of brandy Jane had given him. His purpose was to offer advice to young men who, like him half a century earlier, wanted to make their way in the world. It was no Gladstonian oration, more a civilised monologue, and it shows not just Carlyle's breadth of humanity, but also his sense of humour.

Modestly, but forthrightly, he told how he had developed his career, and rehearsed some of his main prejudices. He joked at the beginning that he was touched by their desire to honour him, but that 'you will modify your opinions of me and of many things else, as you go on.'[23] This brought the first outburst of cheers and laughter that were to punctuate his address. Having committed himself to serve the university, he began his remarks, observing, to general laughter, that 'I ought, I believe, according to custom, to have written all that down on paper, and had it read out. That would have been much handier for me at the present moment.'[24]

His 'advices', which he said he gave reluctantly, were the themes of his life. Fundamental was his view that 'the interest of your whole life depends on your being diligent.'[25]This was especially important while studying at university, so that the mind could harden into diligent ways as the student became older. From diligence it was a short step to honesty. 'A dishonest man cannot do anything real; he never will study with real fruit.'[26] He quoted himself, from 'The Hero as Man of Letters', saying that 'the true University of our day is a Collection of Books,'[27] to illustrate the importance of what a university education had taught him, and was teaching them: that he, and they, could spend the life after university reading fruitfully. By learning to read in a discriminating fashion, they would, as he had done, arrive at a field in which they wished to be master. His own field, history, was one he especially recommended, though his own years of submergence in the undiscriminating literature about Frederick suggested that he was giving advice he wished he had received himself.

He argued that history was especially valuable because of the way in which it led to the study of religion, which brought him inevitably to praise Cromwell and the attempts at theocracy by Knox. The Protectorate he described as 'the most salutary thing in the modern history of England' because there was 'perfect truth' in it while Cromwell was in charge.[28] Carlyle's defence of the idea of a dictatorship, because it ran in accordance with the 'laws of Heaven',[29] was received with applause, a testament to the immense influence he could exert over the intelligent classes.

The address was not all illustration of Carlyle's opinions, as already read in his works. Drawing attention to the large amounts of money coming into the university from endowments, he called for a proper library – of well-chosen books – to be established, to help fulfil the aims of his address. The workings of capitalism continued to depress him, however: 'money was never so abundant, and nothing that is good to be done with it.'[30] For all the wealth of the English universities, he noted, they had hardly produced a decent scholar. He reverted to his old criticism of supposedly educated humanity. The universities taught them to speak well, whereas the best work and thought were accomplished by the silent. The great nations, he said, had all gone off 'into wind and tongue', ignoring the precept that 'silence withal is the eternal duty of a man.' Carlyle felt the world too full with people of whom it could be said 'every one that wants to be persuaded of the thing that is not true; here is the man for you!' This caused great hilarity. 'I recommend you,' he added, 'to be very chary of that kind of excellent speech.'[31] Most necessary to be taught were 'faithful obedience, modesty, humility, and correct moral conduct'.[32] Carlyle had set the agenda for the high moral tone, with all its inherent hypocrisies when followed by souls weaker than he, of the mid-Victorian era.

More significant for those who wish to understand Carlyle, he points to the passage on education in *Wilhelm Meisters Wanderjahre*, 'a scheme of entirely mute education',[33] conducted 'with no more speech than is absolutely necessary for what the pupils have to do', on which hinges his interpretation of the Gospel of Silence. The senior of the three elders educating Wilhelm tells him there is one quality no child brings into the world, but which it is essential for every child to learn. It is *Ehrfurcht*, or reverence: 'the soul of all religion that has ever been among men, or ever will be.'[34] From this earnest, silent reverence other qualities may be developed, or educated into the young, and art may be achieved. Carlyle hoped the Goethean scheme, which he had sought to follow, would be attempted by his audience too.

He concluded with advice to them to look after their health – a tribute to his own life-long hypochondria – and with some strains of prophecy about the anarchic colour of the world, and the struggle that lay ahead in an era of revolutions. He warned the students to 'avoid what is called ambition; that is not a fine principle to go upon, – and it has in it all degrees of vulgarity, if that is a consideration.'[35] He added: 'There is a nobler ambition than the gaining of all California would be, or the getting of all the suffrages that are on the Planet just now [*Loud and prolonged cheers*].' Perhaps most surprising of all, he ended on notes of abundant optimism: 'You will rarely find anybody designedly doing you ill';[36] and he closed with some Goethean verse, and the exhortation '*Wir heissen euch hoffen*, "We bid you be of hope!"' He felt he had delivered the address 'in a mood of defiant despair', reflecting that 'some feeling that I was not speaking lies, alone sustained me.'[37]

This rare and intimate insight into Carlyle's private thoughts – for that, more than anything, is what the Rectorial Address was – was received with deafening cheers. To put Jane out of her misery, Tyndall at once sent a telegram to Cheyne Row that simply read 'a perfect triumph'. It arrived at six that evening, as Jane was dressing to go out to Forster's birthday party. She immediately suffered 'a violent fit of crying',[38] such were her shock and relief; and then took the telegram with her to Forster's, and the assembly – which included Dickens and Wilkie Collins – drank the sage's health. The success uplifted Carlyle as few things ever had. The students followed him to Jack's lodgings, where they stood outside and cheered until bidden by him to leave him in peace. When he eventually found the time to write to Jane the next day, he told her that 'there came a tone into their cheering, which for a moment actually entered my heart, with a strange feeling made up of joy and sorrow.'[39]

Kindness and honour were lavished upon him. To his amusement, he presided at the University Court, which he hoped would be the last official function his Rectorship would demand. Before he could press on to Scotsbrig, where he intended to stay with his family, there were friends longing to entertain him. Flushed with triumph, and buoyed with relief, he threw himself into social life with a vigour he had seldom had, and would never have again. Masson gave a dinner for him, and recalled:

Then too he was in the best of possible spirits, courteous in manner and in speech to all, and throwing himself heartily into whatever turned up. At the dinner-table, I remember, Lord Neaves favoured us with one or two of his humorous songs or recitatives ... No one enjoyed the thing more than Carlyle; and he surprised me by doing what I had never heard him do before – actually joining with his own voice in the chorus.[40]

The dinners and other festivities over, he left Edinburgh in the best of spirits and went to Dumfriesshire. 'I am well, wonderfully,' he wrote to Jane on his arrival there.[41] He was busily correcting the proofs of the printed version of his address, which had been taken down by shorthand-writers; however, before the official version could be published, a pirated one appeared, which Jane saw before Carlyle's proofs reached her.

He wrote almost daily to Jane from Scotsbrig, and then from Dumfries, where he moved on to see his sister Jean; he wrote to Jack on 16 April, and, noting how his hand was shaking, told his brother, 'see how my hand is going.'[42] Jane was busier than ever. Her mind unburdened, she made plans to see many of her neglected friends. On the morning of Saturday 21 April she wrote to Carlyle about how angry Chapman was at the pirating of the Rectorial Address, and about the tea-party she planned to give that afternoon for, among others, Geraldine Jewsbury, the Froudes and Mrs Oliphant, the authoress. She went out to lunch with the Forsters at Palace Gate House, driven there in her carriage with her little dog, Tiny. She was cheerful, not least because she knew Carlyle would be home two days later. At 3.20 p.m. Silvester, her coachman, drove her from Forster's house and through Kensington Gardens. She stopped and walked out to the Serpentine with Tiny; Silvester picked her up by the south side of the bridge over the lake. She took the dog inside the carriage and they rode to Marble Arch; and when nearing it she put the dog out again, only for it to be hit by a brougham. The dog was not badly hurt – merely an injury to its paw – but Jane, upset, left the carriage, put the dog back in after exchanging a word with a woman in the brougham, and ordered Silvester to drive on.

He did so, to Hyde Park Corner and back towards the Serpentine. As he passed St George's Hospital he became concerned that Jane, who would give him continual directions, had fallen silent. He looked behind through an opening and could only see her hands folded in her lap. Moments later he looked round again, and found her sat in the same position. He stopped and asked a lady to look in the carriage. Jane was dead, bolt upright. It was just after quarter past four. Geraldine Jewsbury, who interviewed Silvester, told Carlyle, 'she was leaning back in one corner of the carriage, rugs spread over her knees; her eyes were closed, and her upper lip slightly, slightly opened. Those who saw her at the hospital and when in the carriage speak of the beautiful expression upon her face.'[43] Carlyle believed that 'her last brief thought, if she had any, must have been a pang of sorrow about *me*.'[44] She had had a massive heart attack.

Her body was taken to the hospital nearby. Silvester, distressed, went to Chelsea, where the maids were preparing for the tea-party. He got word to Froude of what had happened, and from there the news spread quickly round the Carlyles' circle. Forster went to the hospital at once, and took charge. As a lunacy commissioner he had the clout to secure a death certificate and have Jane's body released without any of the usual post-mortem and inquest formalities associated with sudden death. Froude, having visited the hospital, called for Geraldine and told her what had happened. He, she and Forster met at Cheyne Row in the early evening. Not knowing quite where Carlyle was they sent telegrams to Jack Carlyle in Edinburgh, and to the Aitkens at Dumfries. It was the second that found Carlyle, where he was planning to return to his wife two days later.

III

The telegrams arrived at 9.30 on the Saturday night. 'It had a kind of stunning effect on me; not for above two days could I estimate that immeasurable depth of it, or the infinite sorrow which had peeled my life all bare, and, in one moment, shattered my poor world to universal ruin.'[45] His sister and brother took him for a walk the next day, and that afternoon Jane's last letter to him arrived; his to her would be on the sideboard at Cheyne Row, unopened, when he returned. Slowly, the horrible reality sank in. 'In all my life ... there fell on me no misfortune like it; – which has smitten my whole world into universal wreck ... and extinguished whatever light of cheerfulness, and loving hopefulness life still had in it to me.'[46]

He was fortunate to have his family with him. Jack took him to London on the Monday morning, the day of his scheduled return. The events on his arrival were burned into his memory, and recalled in the *Reminiscences*:

Never, for a thousand years, should I forget that arrival here of ours, – my first unwelcomed by her; she lay in her coffin, lovely in death; I kissed her cold brow ... pale Death and things not mine or ours had possession of our poor dwelling. Next day wander over the fatal localities in Hyde Park; Forster and Brother John settling, apart from me, everything for the morrow. Morrow, Wednesday morning we were under way with our sacred burden; John and Forster kindly did not speak to me ... I looked out upon the spring fields, the everlasting Skies, in silence.[47]

She was taken to Haddington to be buried, according to a wish made to Carlyle at the time of their marriage. On 22 April he wrote a simple note to William Dods, an old friend of Jane's at Haddington whom she had commended to him, to make the arrangements. The letter ended simply 'pity me'.[48] On arriving at Haddington Carlyle was overcome with sentimentality; remembering his first visit there with Irving in 1821, and the struggle of the years of courtship that followed. He stayed with the Dodses, who went out of their way to tend to him; but he could not sleep, had no appetite, and was simply buried in grief.

The funeral took place at one o'clock on the Thursday, attended by little more than a dozen people. She was laid in the ruined choir (now restored) of the church, next to her father. A few weeks later this epitaph, written by Carlyle, was added to the stone:

HERE LIKEWISE NOW RESTS

JANE WELSH CARLYLE

SPOUSE OF THOMAS CARLYLE, CHELSEA, LONDON

SHE WAS BORN AT HADDINGTON, 14TH JULY 1801, ONLY DAUGHTER OF
THE ABOVE JOHN WELSH, AND OF GRACE WELSH, CAPLEGILL,
DUMFRIESSHIRE, HIS WIFE. IN HER BRIGHT EXISTENCE SHE HAD MORE
SORROWS THAN ARE COMMON; BUT ALSO A SOFT INVINCIBILITY, A

CLEARNESS OF DISCERNMENT, AND A NOBLE LOYALTY OF HEART, WHICH
ARE RARE. FOR FORTY YEARS SHE WAS THE TRUE AND EVER-LOVING
HELPMATE OF HER HUSBAND, AND BY ACT AND WORD UNWEARIEDLY
FORWARDED HIM, AS NONE ELSE COULD, IN ALL OF WORTHY, THAT
HE DID OR ATTEMPTED. SHE DIED IN LONDON, 21ST APRIL 1866;
SUDDENLY SNATCHED AWAY FROM HIM, AND THE LIGHT OF HIS LIFE,
AS IF GONE OUT.

That night Carlyle, Forster and Jack went back to London, arriving at
Chelsea at ten the next morning for him to confront his widowerhood. Jane's
cousin Maggie came to look after him; but all he wanted was solitude, 'my
one solace and employment that of doing all which I can imagine she would
have liked me to do.'[49] Messages of condolence poured in, including one from
the Queen, whom at that point Carlyle had not met. He replied to her via
Lady Augusta Stanley, his friend, from whom the message had come, saying
that 'I can write to nobody. It is best for me at present when I do not even
speak to anybody.'[50] He started to search through Jane's papers, which was
when the full truth of his awfulness – real or imagined – towards her came
thundering home to him. He found the letters complaining of his thoughtlessness; he found her journals detailing her inner miseries; and in his state
of mind was incapable of distinguishing between genuine feelings of neglect
and those accelerated by neuroticism. This further deep shock propelled him
to start, in contrition and penance, to write his *Reminiscence* of his wife. He
would have done well to hear what Mrs Forster said to Sir James Crichton-
Browne when he suggested Jane had had a difficult time with Carlyle: 'Don't
you believe all that! She was rather an actress, and liked to pose as a martyr,
talking of her sufferings and getting sympathy. I assure you he was the great
sufferer.'[51] If Froude, who was already being told a version of the truth by
Geraldine, ever heard those sentiments, he chose not to act upon them.

Deep though his grief was, he set about regaining his equilibrium. 'Day by
day,' he wrote to Jean on 28 April, 'I am getting bits of order introduced into
this great overturn of my past existence; that is the only thing *she* would have
wished as a consolation to me.'[52] He kept self-obsession at bay. When he
received a letter of condolence from Ruskin, who was in Dijon, he was able
to write back and condole with Ruskin's own ill-health and unhappiness. 'You
have a great work still ahead,' Carlyle told his disciple, 'and will gradually
have to gird yourself up against the *heat of the day*, which is coming on for
you.'[53] However, he was still not ready for any society, telling Ruskin he
preferred 'to gaze steadily in silence on the blackness of the abysses that have
suddenly opened round me, and as it were swallowed up my poor little world.'
Her death had made him think of his; but it had not snuffed out his will to
work quite yet. Maggie Welsh assumed temporarily the role of mistress of
the house; so at least Carlyle did not have to bother with domestic matters
like the ordering of servants, something he was ill-equipped to do anyway.

He started to write the *Reminiscence* of Jane on Monday 7 May, but began with the end, making careful notes of the circumstances of her death. It was only when some inaccurate recollections of Jane were sent to him by Geraldine, later in the month, that he set more formally about writing the memoir, to which the notes of her death were appended. This was the document he gave Froude to publish posthumously. It looks like a rough draft, which helps fuel the arguments of those on the side of Carlyle's saintly reputation that it was never intended for publication. The *Reminiscence* has the flavour of an extended *mea culpa*, a work of homage done in an attempt to atone for what Carlyle suddenly realised had been his sins. He certainly did not seem to intend at this time that the work should be read by anyone else. In an abrupt letter to Geraldine Jewsbury on 22 May he proclaimed there was 'no need that an idle-gazing world should know my lost Darling's History, or mine; – nor will they ever, they may depend on it!' He outlined the 'one fit service . . . they can do to Her or to Me: cease speaking of us, through all Eternity, as soon as they conveniently can.'[54]

Through May and June he wrote down his memories of Jane, venturing elsewhere only rarely, despite the entreaties of friends who wished to help him. Dickens wrote to him on 30 May that 'my thoughts have been with you, for I truly love and honour you.'[55] Tyndall took him to the National Portrait Exhibition on 4 June, but late that night, on his usual solitary walk, he felt himself more bereft than ever, 'as if she had been defrauded of my thoughts every instant they had been away from her'.[56] He wrote more than ever the next day, his escapes into memory his only consolation. In his spare time he tried to motivate himself; as the weather became hotter he felt his health declining, and he urged himself to 'take new courses; form new resolutely definite plans'.[57] Yet he knew he lacked the calmness to do anything yet, and had little urge for anyone's company except his own. He wondered, in his darkest moments, whether to abandon the *Reminiscence*, but realised on further reflection that it had become not just his consolation, but a form of religious support, and as such indispensable. It was not merely about Jane that he wrote; it was a substantial fragment of autobiography, so much so that he parenthetically apologised to her at one point for 'defrauding thee' by speaking so much of others. He told Jean on 28 June that 'I walk about silent with my thousands of memories for company. Plenty of people come, too many rather. I do not, except it be to leave a card for mere civility, go to almost anyone.'[58]

By early July Jack Carlyle was writing to Alick that their brother was 'looking much better' and had 'now got over all the painful details and arrangements consequent on his wife's death'. Though Jack paid tribute to his departed sister-in-law as 'really a most true-hearted and excellent woman' he also added that 'none of the rest of us except Mary ever got on well with her.'[59] He quit London for the country that month and left Carlyle to himself in Chelsea, still writing almost daily. Carlyle had reached the stage of reading

Jane's diaries from the mid-1850s, annotating them with a mournful 'a very sad record'.[60] He and Maggie searched the house for Jane's letters, and found some as far back as 1842; Carlyle knew there must be some around from the 1830s, and wanted to find them. Having done so, he broke off writing for a while in order to try to arrange them chronologically, as many were undated. He spent 7 July reading her letters for 1857, finding them 'full of misery', his own sense of guilt deepening all the time. He began to revise his view of never publishing anything to do with Jane, so touched was he by the evidence of her brilliance even at the times of her deepest suffering. Froude, 'almost the only man I care to speak with in these weeks', interrupted him in this melancholy indulgence. He took Carlyle for walks in Battersea Park; if one sought to speculate about how and when the germ of the idea of publishing Jane to a wider audience was conceived, one could profitably start here.

By mid-July he was dealing, in the narrative, with the miserable aftermath of Jane's accident in 1863; every detail presented with such clarity as trauma can imprint upon the memory. By the time he reached the last chapter of Jane's life, on 23 July, he was crying out for 'five minutes more of your dear company, in this world; oh that I had you yet for but five minutes, to tell you all!'[61] By 28 July he had reached the end, where he had begun eleven weeks earlier. He promised himself:

I still mainly mean to *burn* this Book before my own departure; but feel that I shall always have a kind of grudge to do it, and an indolent excuse, 'Not *yet*; wait, any day that can be done!' – and it *is* possible the thing may be left behind me, legible to interested survivors, – *friends* only, I will hope, and with *worthy* curiosity, not *un*worthy!'

What follows starts the case against Froude:

In which event, I solemnly forbid them, each and all, to *publish* this Bit of Writing *as it stands here*; and warn them that *without fit editing* no *part* of it should be printed (nor so far as I can order, *shall* ever be); – and that the '*fit* editing' of perhaps nine-tenths of it will, after I am gone, have become *impossible*.[62]

IV

The comfort of the past drugged Carlyle. Once he had finished writing about Jane, his thoughts turned to Edward Irving. Before writing anything he went to stay with Miss Bromley in Kent for a fortnight. Although his bowels were plaguing him sufficiently for him to write to Jack to ask for some pills to treat them, Carlyle regained some of his strength by riding and swimming, and went back to Chelsea at the end of August, more minded to go back into his own sort of society. 'I must not give up,' he told his brother, 'if I can at all help it.'[63] George Smalley, an American friend of Emerson's, saw Carlyle shortly after his return, and left a colourful picture of the new widower.[64] Having quizzed Smalley about Emerson, Carlyle insisted on taking his visitor for a walk in pouring rain. They walked briskly, and 'the stream of talk ran not less swiftly'. Smalley made no note of what was said, but recalled that Carlyle was 'in a despairing and hostile mood with reference to the world in general'. The physical description is more interesting:

A sad, stern face . . . and I know not whether it was more sad or stern, nor whether the sadness of it was not deepest when he laughed. He had still a florid complexion, and the ruddy hue stood out strongly against the iron-gray hair which fell in shaggy clumps about his forehead, while the eyes, naturally deep-set, seemed lost beneath the thicket of eyebrow which overshadowed them. The moustache and beard he wore full; wrinkled and gnarled rather than curled. When he laughed . . . it was a portentous laugh; open-mouthed and deep-lunged, and prolonged; ending mostly in a shout of triumph, and seldom quite glad or kindly.

Smalley was also treated to a monologue. He recalled, with disappointment, that the subject matter was unoriginal; but rather familiar passages from *Sartor, Past and Present* and *Latter-Day Pamphlets*. It lasted two hours, mixed with periods of silence. Carlyle always liked the sound of his own voice, especially now he was so lonely.

William Allingham, a former Irish customs official and practising minor poet in his early forties whom Carlyle had first met in the early 1850s, became a regular visitor, and was to remain so until the end of Carlyle's life. Allingham kept a full record of his meetings with Carlyle in his *Diary*, creating one of the most personal portraits of the widower. Carlyle was trying to think of suitable projects for the future, and talked to Froude and Ruskin about establishing a periodical to carry articles of opinion against the liberalising trend of the government; but nothing came of it. A political issue had flared up to occupy his thoughts, too, by this time. Nearly a year earlier, in October 1865, Edward Eyre, the Governor of Jamaica, had put down with much force a rising by the black population in which eighteen white men had been killed and thirty-one others wounded. Martial law was imposed by Eyre, and of a final death toll of 439 there were 354 hanged after courts martial. Floggings of others, and the burning down of several settlements, were also part of the medicine Eyre ordered. Liberal opinion in England was outraged when the news reached home, just before Jane had died. She, believing whole-heartedly in the doctrines outlined in *The Nigger Question*, had enthused in support of Eyre to her husband. Now a defence committee was being formed to champion Eyre, who was under threat from a judicial enquiry, and Carlyle was keen to support it.

Typically, Carlyle felt the plaintiveness of English liberals about Eyre was hypocritical, since they were keeping so quiet about the indignities inflicted on their fellow Englishmen and women – much the same argument as in *The Nigger Question*. Moreover, he believed in Eyre's style of leadership. The defence committee had its work cut out, not least because there was a strong *prima facie* case that in some respects Eyre (who in an earlier posting to

Australia had been known as a protector of aborigines) had acted unlawfully in his application of martial law. The defence committee was a response to a Jamaica committee, under the chairmanship of Mill and including John Bright, Darwin, Huxley and Leslie Stephen, established with the purpose of having Eyre prosecuted. Mill characterised what had happened in Jamaica as 'a general display of the brutal recklessness which usually prevails when fire and the sword are let loose' and branded those who defended Eyre 'the same kind of people who had so long upheld negro slavery'.[65]

Carlyle, one such, became vice-president of the defence committee, which also included Ruskin, Tennyson, Kingsley and John Tyndall. Whatever their views of Eyre as a man with a political mandate, this group unquestionably supported him because they supported the Carlylean notion of the strong man. Carlyle was in the chair when the committee first met on 29 August 1866. The previous week Carlyle, in a letter to Hamilton Hume, the secretary of the defence committee, had described Eyre as 'a just, humane and valiant man, faithful to his trusts everywhere, and with no ordinary faculty of executing them'. As to the specific incident in question, Carlyle said that Eyre's late services in Jamaica were of great, perhaps of incalculable value, as certainly they were of perilous and appalling difficulty'.[66] He added that to prosecute Eyre would be 'a blind and disgraceful act of public injustice'. Eyre was deeply touched by what Carlyle had done 'in my defence against the prosecutions or rather I should say persecutions threatened by the self-styled "Jamaica Committee",' and wrote to tell him so. 'The cause you have so disinterestedly espoused is not an unjust or undeserving one ... I cheerfully accepted the responsibility my position entailed upon me and I should have deemed myself unworthy of the name of Englishman and undeserving of the high trust reposed in me by my Sovereign, had I hesitated or wavered at such a time.'[67]

The legal proceedings against Eyre dragged on for several years. When no criminal charges could be made to stand up against him, Mill and his friends tried civil ones, which failed too. The greatest irony in the case was that Mill's main hired lawyer was James Fitzjames Stephen, who tried to stop Mill (of whom he had been an admirer) persisting with his attacks on Eyre. Stephen grew more and more attracted to the ideas of Carlyle, and came to know him through Froude, a mutual friend. In 1873 he published *Liberty, Equality, Fraternity*, the most savage rebuttal of Mill's *On Liberty*, and owing much to Carlyle's influence. Mill, having failed to have Eyre prosecuted, consoled himself with the thought that Sir Alexander Cockburn, the Lord Chief Justice, had during the proceedings upheld Mill's view of the liberties of Jamaican subjects; and it clearly further pleased him that the letters of abuse he received for his pains came, mostly anonymously, from 'the brutal part of the population at home',[68] an idea he expressed with all the disdain available to one of his impeccable liberal credentials.

The work of the committee occupied Carlyle throughout September. Once the initial excitement subsided, Ruskin took much of the work off Carlyle's shoulders, and Carlyle set about writing the *Reminiscence* of Irving. He became reclusive again, wallowing in the memories of his earliest days. He started to break his silence, on 20 October apologising to Alick for not writing sooner. Not having communicated directly with him since Jane's death he returned to that subject, showing signs of being able to describe it with some detachment. He was also eloquent about the after-effects of *Frederick:* 'the 12 years deadly wrestle with my last Book had quite broken me of itself, not to speak of the 58 *foregoing* years, and the calamities that have followed!'[69]

He felt an urge to travel for the winter. He settled on visiting Menton in the south of France, where Lady Ashburton had a house. He needed to find a companion to escort him there as he was not up to a rigorous journey alone, and John Tyndall offered to accompany him. Having made more changes to his will, this time leaving Craigenputtock (which he had inherited from Jane) to Edinburgh University to provide scholarships in Jane's father's name, he left London with Tyndall on 22 December, and headed south. The main purpose of the trip was to gain relief from the winter cold; and, as his friends saw it, from the excesses of winter solitude. He had been making slow progress with Irving, but attacked it once he arrived at Lady Ashburton's, finishing the manuscript on 2 January 1867. The rest, the climate, the availability of silence, and the cathartic progress of nostalgic creativity all helped improve Carlyle's morale. With uncharacteristic optimism, he wrote to Jack on 25 January that 'things continue all well, and as it were at their best with me.'[70] He was sleeping well and was left alone as much as he wanted. Lady Ashburton, who had as usual gone to lengths to accommodate Carlyle, tried to arrange dinner parties for him when he first arrived; he signalled he would rather not endure them, so she arranged no more.

He took himself for walks to look at the sea, and, in the distance, at the Alpes-Maritimes, appreciating the beauty of the spectacle. He was in no hurry to go back to England; yet beneath the superficial improvement, there was a deep and abiding melancholy. 'My poor life seems as good as over,' he told his journal on 20 January. 'I have no heart or strength of hope or of interest for further work.'[71] Yet Carlyle's intellect, and the strength of his opinions, could not be turned off by a mere bereavement. Gladstone, travelling home for the opening of parliament in February, called on Lady Ashburton and dismayed Carlyle by having 'gone irrecoverably into House of Commons shape – man once of some wisdom or possibility of it, but now possessed by the Prince, or many Princes, of the Power of the Air'.[72]

Amidst the regime of walks and contemplations he continued slowly with the *Reminiscences.* His short recollection of Jeffrey was finished on 19 January; that of Southey on 8 February. He caught a cold in February, and a general depression of spirits that resulted from it meant that the next, Wordsworth, was not started until 3 March. In the meantime Carlyle had reread Shakespeare, which helped feed his mood of 'pure sadness'.[73] Caroline Fox, visiting him on 5 March, found him reading Shakespeare in 'a sort of pavilion' adjoining the house: 'He looks thin, and aged, and sad as Jeremiah.'[74] He completed the short work on Wordsworth on 8 March, and decided he had enough of reminiscing in print. 'Finished the rag on Wordsworth to the last tatter,' he wrote that day. 'Won't begin another ... it is wearisome and naught even to myself ... ETERNITY, which cannot be far off, is my one strong city.'[75] But it was still almost fourteen years off.

V

He made his way back to Chelsea in the second week of March, having declined Lady Ashburton's offer to accompany her to Rome. He had become keen to return home. Reform agitation was growing, and Carlyle could not help but have old prejudices excited by it. 'Oh! this cry for Liberty!' he had told Miss Fox. 'Liberty! which is just liberty to do the Devil's work, instead of binding him with ten thousand bands.'[76] The explosion of his great anti-reform pamphlet, *Shooting Niagara*, a few months later was no surprise after this. Yet the first thing facing him on reaching London was not of great political, but of personal, moment. Neuberg, who had spent the winter translating *Frederick* into German, had also been in fading health; and on 24 March he died. Carlyle knew what a friend he had lost; he attended the funeral in a highly emotional state and lamented in his journal that Neuberg had never sought any reward for the help he had given him, nor received any. It seems that whenever anyone close to Carlyle died, it prompted intense regret that he had not shown more appreciation of them during life. His feelings about Neuberg were a reduced version of those about Jane.

Carlyle had to make domestic plans. He had, in his grief, spurned an invitation from Jack to come and live with him; and with Jane's cousin Maggie not intending to stay in London, he needed a companion. He sought to propitiate Jack; being more reasonable than his brother, he was waiting for Carlyle on his return from France. Carlyle sought the company of the few people left who interested him. He saw Froude briefly, just before his future biographer left for Spain to undertake historical researches; and bade Ruskin call for conversation on Wednesday evenings. He prepared himself for the first anniversary of Jane's death, a day he spent suitably 'abundantly downcast, dreary, sorrowful', swimming in remorse and regrets.

He soon found himself embroiled in a public controversy with, of all people, Ruskin. His disciple was publishing *Time and Tide*, a series of letters to 'a working man of Sunderland on the laws of work'. In the last, published on 27 April, Ruskin referred to a recent meeting with Carlyle at which Carlyle had allegedly mentioned to him that he could not walk about London without being abused and insulted by the common people, who picked on him because he was elderly and well dressed; and Ruskin further alleged that Carlyle had contrasted their behaviour unfavourably with that of the peasant classes of the south of France, whom he had just had the opportunity to observe closely. It seems that, if Carlyle said anything of the sort, it was said in jest; but the disciple did not allow for jest to enter into his worship. One of Ruskin's readers, an artisan from Rochdale, wrote to Carlyle to ask whether this was true. Carlyle denied it categorically, saying that the allegation 'diverges from the fact throughout, and in essentials is curiously the reverse of the fact'.[77] The letter was picked up by the press, and on 29 May the *Pall Mall Gazette* published a letter from Carlyle in which he denounced Ruskin's claim as 'altogether erroneous, misfounded, superfluous, and even absurd'.[78]

Ruskin was apoplectic. 'My Dear Carlyle,' he wrote on 30 May (it had always been 'Mr Carlyle' hitherto, displaying the respect appropriate to a man almost twenty-five years Ruskin's senior), 'I deeply regret, for many not trivial reasons, that you have been induced to write this letter.' He added that 'it seems to me that the only thing which now in justice remains for you to do, is to furnish me with a succinct statement of what you remember yourself to have said on the occasion in question; and to permit me to substitute that statement, in the edition of collected letters, for the one which has offended you.'[79] There seems little doubt Ruskin was convinced he had quoted Carlyle correctly; and equally little doubt Carlyle thought he had not. It could be that Carlyle was unhappy at having publicly quoted what he had felt to be a private conversation. Because of Ruskin's destruction of Carlyle's reply to him, we cannot be sure. When Ruskin received that reply, it merely prompted him to say that 'I am under the sorrowful necessity of ignoring your present letter,' accusing Carlyle of having 'given the lie publicly, and in the most insulting terms possible to you, to the man who probably of all men living, most honoured you.'[80] Ruskin demanded that either Carlyle give his version, or retract his remarks about his friend; indeed, he felt so intent on having Carlyle do this that he wrote to him again later the same day, 1 June, to beg him to retract or justify himself.

While Ruskin was boiling with indignation, Carlyle was simply becoming bored with the whole issue. *The Times* published a leader on the subject on 3 June. It unhesitatingly took Carlyle's word against Ruskin's, inflaming matters somewhat by suggesting that, even though Carlyle had denied ever having made the remark, Ruskin had still proved that it was 'possible to libel a whole population as well as an individual'. It also added that Ruskin had caused the sort of problem that leads to the creation of irrational prejudices, that he should have been intelligent enough to know better, and that 'we should protest, on behalf of our fellow Londoners, against Mr RUSKIN'S very gratuitous imputations.'[81] It should further have pleased Carlyle that the leader-writer dismissed any suggestion that he was from time to time suffering abuse because of his recent exertions on behalf of Governor Eyre. 'The natural instinct of Englishmen would lead them to respect Mr CARLYLE for standing by a brave man in trouble, and this instinct is, perhaps, strongest in the working classes.'

The outburst from *The Times* did, at least, allow an opportunity for Carlyle to set the record straight. He wrote the newspaper a letter, which it published on 8 June; and before it was published he wrote to Ruskin, stressing how tedious the matter had become to him, and that he had written a letter 'after such concoction, rejecting, remodelling, nightly and daily botheration, and sheer waste of time and means as might have sufficed for a Book of the Iliad almost, instead of a note to the Newspaper!'[82] The letter referred to Ruskin as 'a much valued friend' whom Carlyle 'by no means' heavily blamed 'except for the almost inconceivable practical blunder of printing my name'. Carlyle added that he was on good terms with his two million neighbours in London, who had all been 'struck with amazement' at what Ruskin had written; however, he concluded 'that in regard to the populace or *canaille* of London, to the class distinguishable by behaviour as our non-human, or half-human neighbours, which class is considerably more extensive and miscellaneous, and much more dismal and disgusting than you seem to think, I substantially agree with all that Mr Ruskin has said of it.'[83] So honour was satisfied. Carlyle hoped it was an end to the matter ('in about 4 or 5 weeks of silence, I calculate that all this will have vanished or subsided')[84] and that Ruskin, contrite, would resume his Wednesday visits. But Ruskin was in no mood to be contrite. 'You do not yet *in the least* see into this thing,' he replied on 10 June. 'I emphatically deny its falsehood.'[85]

The next day, still in a highly emotional state, Ruskin wrote again, protesting that his shock at Carlyle's behaviour in still insisting that he had not said what Ruskin reported him to have done would force Ruskin to end his discipleship, because he would form a new estimate of Carlyle that precluded his previous respect for him. In an especially histrionic passage, Ruskin wrote: 'And I always suffer this kind of thing from those I have most cared for, and then I *cannot* forgive, just because I know I was the last person on earth they ought to have treated so. *Turner* did something of the same kind to me. I never forgave him, to his death.'[86]

Carlyle replied that 'with a Poet's temperament, you immensely exaggerate this miserable, but intrinsically small and paltry matter,'[87] and made it clear that, still burdened as he was by his own melancholy and self-pity on a far grander scale, his patience with Ruskin's trivialities had finally been exhausted. At last, he gave Ruskin the clear statement – though for private, not public, consumption – that Ruskin had been pleading for:

I never told you, nor could tell or have told any mortal, that 'Mr Carlyle' was liable to be insulted on the streets of London or Chelsea; the constant fact being that I have the natural liberty of all quiet persons to walk the streets unmolested, and if need were, protected and defended; and that in no street, lane or place of London or any other City, Town or region, did 'Mr Carlyle', when personally recognised, meet with anything hitherto but an evident respect far beyond what was his due, or what was in the least necessary to him. This is the steadfast fact; and this you have carelessly tumbled heels over head into a statement incredible to all who hear it, and monstrous to imagine.[88]

He did admit he had abandoned his ancient habit of going for a midnight walk, though on medical advice only; and he did admit to having discussed with Ruskin the problems that might be encountered on a ride through the slums; but it seemed Ruskin had got the wrong end of that stick. He advised Ruskin to cool down, and accept he had misinterpreted Carlyle; and hoped they could resume their friendship on its old terms. Carlyle had been hurt by the episode, despite his having sought to play it down in his correspondence with Ruskin. His disciple regarded this latest letter as 'ugly', though if it did nothing to cool him when he received it, after a few more days of reflection the wound was starting to heal. On 25 June he wrote to Carlyle asking to come and see him, as a son might see his father, but only on the condition that the matter of contention between them was not mentioned. The next day they met, and the breach was mended. When *Time and Tide* was published in book form, the offending paragraph was excised.

VI

Carlyle spent part of that summer sitting to George Frederic Watts, the painter, and brooding upon what he considered to be the betrayal by the Tory government of its principles as it sought to pass the Reform Bill. By fits and starts, during July, he came to write what was to be his last substantial contribution to contemporary affairs: the article *Shooting Niagara: and After?*, subsequently republished as a pamphlet. The bile that characterises this masterpiece of reaction was fed by an onset of dyspepsia ('my digestion etc etc,' he told Jack, 'has gone quite to chaos'),[89] and the need to return in his spare time to *Frederick*, which he was revising and updating for a new edition. His friend David Masson, the editor of *Macmillan's Magazine*, had invited him to write the piece, and in the end it had been written easily enough.

He had been jotting down thoughts about the Reform Bill sporadically in his journal throughout the summer – 'England getting into the *Niagara rapids* far sooner than I expected'.[90] In his journal, he continued:

Let it come when it likes, since there are Dizzies, Gladstones, Russells, &c., triumphantly prepared to bring it in. Providence truly is skilful to prepare its instrumental men. Indeed, all England, heavily though languidly *averse* to this embarking on Niagara rapids, is strangely indifferent to whatever may follow it. 'Niagara, or what you like, we will at least have a villa on the Mediterranean (such an improvement of climate to this), when Church and State have gone,' said a certain shining countess to me, yesterday. Newspaper editors, in private, I am told, and discerning people of every rank, as is partly apparent to myself, talk of approaching 'revolution', 'Common wealth,' 'Common illth,' or whatever it may be, with a singular composure.

These thoughts needed relatively little adaptation for public consumption in *Shooting Niagara*. Carlyle congratulated himself that the article was 'very fierce, exaggerative, ragged, unkempt and defective', and that the 'howling doggeries' – the entire political class, for now Liberal and Tory were indiscernible in their pursuit of popular reform – should have his 'last word on their affairs and them'.[91] Within three weeks of being published as a pamphlet, the 'last word' had sold 4,000 copies. However out of step Carlyle was with the times, what he had to say still mattered.

The essay is the perfect conclusion to Carlyle's political thought. All the great themes of his philosophy are included in it; the regard for strength, the importance of silence, the loathing of democracy, the importance of disciplining a fractious people along military lines, the spuriousness of the contemporary idea of equality, the hope that the aristocracy might stop shooting its game and instead start playing a proper feudal role of active leadership, the hypocrisy of 'nigger philanthropists', the need to bring back the proper regard for God instead of the phoney regard for the ballot-box. It was the appropriate statement for 'these ballot-boxing, Nigger-emancipating, empty, dirt-eclipsed days'.[92] Bearing in mind Carlyle's age, and the burden of grief and self-pity under which he had been struggling for the preceding fifteen months, it is also a work of extraordinary vigour and robustness; though also one likely to cause the greatest offence to a modern audience unused to meat as strong as Carlyle. Glorying in the agony that he is capable of causing his opponents, he provokes them gratuitously:

One always rather likes the Nigger; evidently a poor blockhead with good dispositions, with affections, attachments, – with a turn for Nigger Melodies, and the like: – he is the only Savage of all the coloured races that doesn't die out on sight of the White Man; but can actually live beside him, and work and increase and be merry. The Almighty Maker has appointed him to be a Servant. Under penalty of Heaven's curse, neither party to this pre-appointment shall neglect or misdo his duties therein; – and it is certain (though as yet widely unknown), Servantship on the *nomadic* principle, at the rate of so many shillings per day, *cannot* be other than misdone. The whole world rises in shrieks against you, on hearing of such a thing.[93]

The author's voice is powerful and apocalyptic; he opens the work with the contention that 'there probably never was since the Heptarchy ended, or almost since it began, so hugely critical an epoch in the history of England as this we have now entered upon.'[94] Recognising the inevitability of 'the Niagara leap of completed democracy',[95] Carlyle scorns the notion of 'liberty' that this confers. 'Liberty of conscience' threatens to erode religion, something about which he was remarkably accurate; and 'everybody shall start free, and everywhere, "under enlightened popular suffrage," the race shall be to the swift, and the high office shall fall to him who is ablest if not to do it, at least to get elected for doing it.'[96] It depressed Carlyle that this should happen at just the time when, through strength of leadership and action, Bismarck was forging the Second Reich, and showing what could be achieved by resolution. Bismarck, who used ruthless military and economic means to create a united Germany, and who was swift to take the opportunities afforded him by lax or degenerate leadership in the countries which he had lined up for conquest, was the greatest living example of Carlylean man. In Britain there was 'swarmery', a phenomenon exemplified by the philanthropists and reformers lobbying for change, and encouraging duplicity and treachery in politicians; notably the 'superlative Hebrew conjuror', Disraeli, about whom Carlyle forcibly makes the point that he was not English, and was acting against the interests of England that he, as a Tory, was notionally supposed to serve.[97] 'We are a people drowned in hypocrisy,' Carlyle lamented, 'saturated with it to the bone.'[98] The constitutional or conservative system, in his definition, was simply institutionalised mendacity; and those who were its alleged beneficiaries 'with whatever cry of "liberty" in their mouths, are inexorably marked by Destiny as slaves'.[99]

The piece is given extra vigour by topical references to the Jamaica committee, and particularly to the Lord Chief Justice, who had given Mill and his supporters reason to believe Eyre might have a case to answer since there was no allowance in law for the declaration of martial law. Carlyle treats him with the same disgust applied to the rest of the establishment:

Lordship, if you were to speak for six hundred years, instead of six hours, you would only prove the more to us that, unwritten if you will, but real and fundamental, anterior to all written laws and first making written laws *possible*, there must have been, and is, and will be, coeval with human society, from its first beginnings to its ultimate end, an actual *Martial Law*, of more validity than any other law whatever. Lordship, if there is no written law that three and three shall be six, do you wonder at the Statute-Book for that omission? You may shut those eloquent lips and go home to dinner. May your shadow never be less; greater it has little chance of being.[100]

The restoration of God to His proper eminence in the minds of the people was Carlyle's imperative. As he had so often said, this could only be achieved by a hero, ordained for that purpose; and, never mind the desire for democratic representation, that work necessitated doing what God, and not popular suffrage, wanted. But the tone of Carlyle's plea suggests he knew he was beaten, as do the defeatist comments in his letters and diaries of the time. The sentiments show his philosophy had not developed a jot in the quarter-century since *Heroes* and *Past and Present*. The entertaining roar of *Shooting Niagara*, many of whose fears about weak government and national decline have been proved grounded, none the less shaped Carlyle as a curiosity and an anachronism in the years of decline that remained to him.

16

The Pursuit of Silence

1867–81

THE FINAL PHASE of Carlyle's life began with the publication of *Shooting Niagara*, his last work of any significance. The remaining thirteen and a half years were in some ways abundantly full – he had the companionship of his disciples, and received (in differing humours) a constant stream of visitors – but his failing health, his lack of motivation, and above all the absence of Jane made his last years seem profoundly empty. As he approached his seventy-second birthday he was, dyspepsia aside, astonishingly healthy. He took up riding again in the autumn of 1867, and had the strength to see a new edition of his collected works through the press. But, hereafter, his influence on life and thought was as a presence merely, living off what he had called his 'landed property'; but through the discipleship of some of the leading literary figures in the land he was still penetrating and shaping the minds of a new generation without having to raise his pen. Mill's tangential condemnations aside, society was polite enough to this elderly sage to wait until he was dead – though only just – before taking apart his reputation and achievements.

Although he had to spend part of every day dealing with a mountain of mail, and the 'incipient authors, beggars, blockheads and canaille of various kinds'[1] that stopped by his front door, loneliness ate at him. He occasionally thought he wanted to go out into society, and had no shortage of friends; but once there he felt miserable, at sea, and merely wanted to retreat to Chelsea, where he would fight to repress the wish to 'rejoin her there in the Land of Silence'.[2] His old friend Thomas Spring Rice wrote to him in August 1867 to invite him to dine and meet other old acquaintances. Sixteen months after Jane's death, Carlyle mournfully replied on black-edged paper that 'I go out nowither to dinner, for the last twelve months or more.'[3] As he continued to revise *Frederick* for the complete works the very scale of it, and (more to the point) the scale of the sacrifice he had had to make and the pain he had had to inflict to write it, began to disgust him. It was small consolation when, at the end of October, Forster told him that *Shooting Niagara* had sold 7,000 copies. His journal became a sporadic outpouring of memories of Jane, his visits to friends were occupied with thoughts of her grave at Haddington. He began to be much troubled at the prospect that God did not order the universe in such a way that, after his own death, he would see Jane again. He continued to ponder whether he should collect her letters and publish them, and whether the *Reminiscence* should have a wider audience.

He became even less predictable in temper than before. William Allingham, calling in October 1867, was told abruptly: 'Go away, Sir! I can do nothing with you.' Allingham, shaken by this gratuitous rebuff from a man he idolised, mentioned it to Froude, and received the next day a letter from Carlyle telling him how welcome his company always was, and how the earlier outburst had been a problem of mistaken identity. Certainly, such petulance was never repeated, however miserable Carlyle was.[4] Invited to Belton in Lincolnshire to stay with Lord Brownlow, Carlyle on arrival reported that 'seldom in my life have I felt so entirely wretched, body and mind.'[5]

Inevitably, his health began to fail. Most significant was the shaking in his right hand that, by the early 1870s, was so serious that he could not write, but had instead to dictate. In February 1868 he is already complaining to his sister Jenny that 'I am dreadfully indisposed to writing, and even my poor shaking right hand makes continual protest.'[6] He felt 'excessively languid, dispirited, weary, sad and idle', but his experience as a hypochondriac allowed him, when Jack complained of excessive flatulence, to be able to recommend to the doctor that he take charcoal for it.[7] W.H. White ('Mark Rutherford') went to see him on 22 March, recording the event in his journal. He found Carlyle rereading *Frederick* to make corrections for a new edition, glad of some company and quite loquacious. Most of all, though, White was struck by how 'infinitely tender' the sage was.[8]

Carlyle's main recreation had become walks with the historian and moralist William Lecky, Allingham and Froude (the conversations he had with him heavily inform the biography written fifteen years later). Allingham reports in his diaries on the predominantly melancholic nature of these events, though they had their entertaining moments. In June 1868 he was with Carlyle when the MP for Chelsea, Sir Charles Dilke, called to canvass him for his vote in the forthcoming election. 'I never gave a vote in my life,' said England's supreme anti-democrat, with which Dilke left. It gave Carlyle an excuse for an anti-parliamentary rant at Allingham, which seems to have cheered them both up; but Carlyle took his leave of his friend by solemnly announcing: 'You won't walk many more times with me.'[9] To Lecky, Carlyle would philosophise. 'The chief meaning of fame,' he told him one day, 'seems to be that you have all the owls of the community beating at your windows.'[10] Lecky, who was captivated by the sage, recalled that he had 'a singularly musical voice, a voice peculiarly fitted for pathos, and this (to me, at least) quite took away anything grotesque in the very strong Scotch accent'.

Occasionally, he was tempted out of London. In the spring of 1868 he went down to Hampshire to stay with Lord Northbrook, a future Viceroy of

India, whom he had met through the Ashburtons; and they went over to the Grange, and to the church on the estate, where Carlyle, who had not visited there for many years, 'sat in silence looking and remembering', and felt 'as though in a dream'.[11] The past was made more remote for him by the absence from his life of many with whom he had shared it, and some friends who were left were fading; on 11 April he walked over to see Forster, whom he found 'in a very coughing, struggling, ailing condition'.[12] Back in London, he brooded in his journals about increasing Godlessness, and empowering the mob through democracy; but the urge to write more on this had deserted him. At the end of the summer he went to Scotland, to visit Professor James Syme, a surgeon, in Edinburgh for treatment of a minor intestinal problem, and stayed with the professor for a fortnight. He went on to Dumfriesshire, where he collected his niece, Mary Carlyle Aitken, and brought her back to London with him as his long-term companion. Allingham says that this 'Scotch lassie' had never been to London before, but spoke 'gravely and sensibly'.[13] Once in London, he set about trying to put Jane's letters into some sort of order, though still felt at this time that they should not be published until perhaps twenty years after his death.

He had had his riding to occupy him, but that stopped in the autumn of 1868. Comet, a horse lent him by Miss Bromley, threw him. He fell gently with the horse and was not injured; but he realised he was becoming too old for such larks. He became more valetudinarian, and without hesitation turned down an invitation from the students of Edinburgh to make a valedictory address as he stepped down from the post of Rector; but he did send a letter advising his disciples there to 'consult the Eternal Oracles (not yet inaudible, nor ever to become so, when worthily inquired of); and to disregard, nearly altogether, in comparison, the temporary noises, menacings and deliriums'.[14]

He concentrated all efforts on Jane's papers. They occupied him throughout the winter of 1868–69, though took second place to the correction of proofs of the Library Edition. Mary, as well as being companion, became a literary assistant and, eventually, as his hand became more and more unsteady, his amanuensis. He had no financial worries. Forster had secured a generous settlement from Chapman's for the new edition, which would support Carlyle throughout his old age. It had, though, also been Forster's idea to have Watts paint him; soon, Carlyle found the sittings tedious and the portrait ghastly – 'so distracted a monster of Painting I have never seen before: cross between a Lunatic and an Imposter: no feature of me recognisable in it.'[15]

On 4 March 1869 there was a splendid interruption. The Queen had expressed a wish to see Carlyle, and a meeting was arranged through her lady-in-waiting, Lady Augusta Stanley, at the Westminster Deanery where she lived with her husband. Carlyle wrote to Jack, displaying his customary sense of priorities, about his 'interview with Sacred Majesty ... Sacred Majesty was very good; thing altogether decidedly insignificant, ditto tiresome; and *worsened* a kind of cold I had (and am still dropping with).'[16] A few days later, he elaborated on the event to his sister Jean:

Walking up at the set time, I was there ushered into a long Drawingroom in their monastic edifice ... Grote and Wife, Sir Charles Lyell and ditto, Browning and myself, these I saw were to be our party ... Her Majesty, punctual to the minute, glided softly in, escorted by her Dame in waiting (a Dowager Duchess of Athol), and by Princess Louise, decidedly a very pretty young lady, and *clever* too, as I found in speaking to her afterwards. The Queen came softly forward, a kindly little smile on her face; gently shook hands with all three women, gently acknowledged with a nod the silent deep bow of us male monsters; and directly in her presence everybody was as if at ease again. She is a comely little lady, with a pair of kind clear and intelligent grey eyes; still looks plump and almost young (in spite of one broad wrinkle that shows in each cheek occasionally); has a fine soft low voice; soft indeed her whole manner is and melodiously perfect; it is impossible to imagine a politer little woman. Nothing the least imperious; all gentle, all sincere-looking, unembarrassing, rather attractive even; – makes you feel too (if you have sense in you) that she is Queen.[17]

She then said a few words to each of the literary men in turn. 'To me it was, "Sorry you did not see my Daughter," Princess of Prussia (or "she sorry," perhaps?), which led us into Potsdam, Berlin, etc., for an instant or two.' Once they had drunk some 'very black and muddy coffee' Carlyle was bidden over to talk again to the Queen; being 'an old infirmish man' he asked, and was given, permission to sit. The conversation was routine; she asked where Carlyle had come from in Scotland, before Mrs Grote, anxious for her husband (a celebrated historian) to have some more royal attention, diverted the Queen away from Carlyle. It was perhaps as well someone did for, as Ruskin later recounted, Carlyle allegedly became so intent in telling the Queen a story of the beauties of Galloway that he did not notice he had pinned her dress to the floor with his chair, and she could not move.[18] 'By the underground railway I was home before seven, and out of the adventure, with only a headache of little moment.'[19] He claimed the event had been worth nothing to him, but that is hardly the impression one gets from his loving recollection of the sovereign. The Queen, recording the event in her journal, noted Carlyle as 'a strange-looking eccentric old Scotchman, who holds forth, in a drawling melancholy voice, with a broad Scotch accent, upon Scotland and upon the utter degeneration of everything'.[20]

His gentle regime protected his health, though he suffered badly from insomnia. He heard with shock from Forster that Dickens, seventeen years his junior, had almost died of exhaustion, rushing around earning money by reading out his novels 'in chase of still other thousands of pounds, which he needed so little!'[21] With Mary's help, there was no rush to compile the *Letters and Memorials*, a task they stuck to throughout the year; though he attributed his sleeplessness to the constant reminder of Jane that the work gave him. By July 1869 the insomnia had eased, and his health was further helped by visits to Lady Ashburton at Addiscombe: 'London and its empty broiling tumult are becoming quite intolerable to me.'[22]

His relations with Ruskin, who had been abroad for some time, had steadily improved since the contretemps two years earlier. In August Carlyle wrote to him lamenting that his weak right hand prohibited him from being a better correspondent, and professing a longing to see him. He had read *The Queen of the Air*, a study of Greek storm-myths, and poured praise on his disciple for it. They met in early September, directly Ruskin arrived from the continent. Carlyle found Ruskin 'much improved',[23] and was happy to see him. He tried to establish a routine in which Ruskin would visit him at a regular time each week, as other friends did. Carlyle went off again to Addiscombe, and Lady Ashburton, in October, in search of rest, having finished with his preparations of the *Letters and Memorials*. He put them away until the time was right to publish them. His right hand was failing fast, and when he wrote the following month to Emerson, the letter was largely in his niece Mary's hand. Yet he told Emerson that 'in bodily health I am not to be called ill, for a man who will be 74 next month.'[24]

He no longer had the energy for politics, but the loss of religious faith troubled him deeply. In his journal on 13 November he laments that 'the quantities of potential and even consciously increasing Atheism, sprouting out everywhere in these days, is enormous. In every scientific or quasi-scientific periodical one meets it ... there is clear prophecy to me that in another fifty years it will be the new religion to the whole tribe of hard-hearted and hard-headed men in this world.'[25] His faith did not shake. On his seventy-fourth birthday he looked, as he did every day, at the photograph of Jane's tomb, and told his journal that he totally disbelieved the atheist analysis.

II

He and Mary went out occasionally, usually to dine with the Froudes or Ruskin; on Christmas Day 1869 he ate with Browning at Forster's. None the less, his life became more solitary, and he more depressed. The difficulty of writing letters was a further isolating factor. When Alick wrote in January 1870, he was spurred to write back quickly by a sense of guilt that he had neglected his brother; but reassured him that 'in our silence, we think of each other, almost every day of our lives, with a sad and solemn tenderness, with wishes, hopes and memories, that only deepen as the end draws nigh.'[26] 'No joy' was 'now possible' for him, he reminded Alick. 'I am far sadder and gloomier of mind than I used to be.' He painted a desperate picture of his existence. 'This wretched blockhead and beggar of a world can now do nothing for me, nothing against me: I look upon it (if at all, which is not often) with authentic and nearly complete contempt; sometimes (what I hope may become more frequent) with a great deal of pity. All is going ... into unspeakable downbreak.'[27] But, as Carlyle contemplated extinction, he had positive thoughts. His now considerable wealth was offered as a resource for Alick's family if needed to secure an education, or a start in business. The following June he sent Alick's two children £800, a fortune in those days. There is a sense that Carlyle was making his final dispositions, ironically so since more than ten years remained to him.

In February Lady Ashburton took him and Mary down to Hampshire, and the change of air and the silence suited him. He went back on a horse for the first time in ages, and rode fourteen miles, but still he could not conquer his insomnia. They stayed for ten days before Carlyle returned to Chelsea. 'I have as it were fairly ceased all working of the old sort,' he wrote to Jack on 19 March 1870. 'Without and within all seems to say to me: Be content to cease; thy work is done, and thou art done; cease!'[28] He saw Tennyson again; he was up in London briefly from the Isle of Wight, and called on Carlyle, who took the poet out on a walk. Carlyle felt that the rules of society obliged him to pay a reciprocal visit to Tennyson at his lodgings a few days later; but he was relieved to find Tennyson out, and to have to do nothing more strenuous than leave his card. Yet he missed his regular friends when they were away, as Froude was that spring, doing researches in Vienna, and Allingham too, in Dublin.

Another friend went still further. On 8 June Dickens, busy writing *The Mystery of Edwin Drood*, had a stroke and died the next day. Carlyle, who had known him since the late 1830s, was deeply distressed. He wrote to Forster, who was to be Dickens's biographer, that 'It is an event world-wide; a *unique* of talents suddenly extinct . . . no death since 1866 has fallen on me with such a stroke. No literary man's hitherto ever did.'[29] Although privately he had disparaged some of the more sentimental and hack-work elements of Dickens's novels, Carlyle had always revered him as a friend. He wrote to Dickens's daughters that 'it is almost thirty years since my acquaintance with him began; and on my side I may say every new meeting ripened it into more and more clear discernment (quite apart from his unique *talent*) of his rare and great worth as a brother man. A most correct, precise, clear-sighted, quietly decisive, just and loving man; till at length he had grown to such recognition with me as I have rarely had for any man of my time.'[30]

Carlyle went away to Scotland, at the end of June, taking Mary with him. She was now his amanuensis, and therefore indispensable. Emerson, with whom he now more frequently corresponded, had been trying to persuade him to go to America. Although Carlyle admitted that 'I do sometimes talk dreamily of a long Sea-Voyage', the idea of crossing the Atlantic was 'pure Moonshine'.[31] Dumfries, instead, was his destination. He and Mary stayed there until mid-September at the house of his sister Jean, the solitude, clean air and silence spoilt only by the intermittent piercing whistles from express trains on the railway that would wake him up at night, on the occasions he could get to sleep. The noise eventually drove him to the seclusion of

Craigenputtock for a few days, which he described to Alick as the most 'heavy-laden' of his life.[32] Masochistic indulgences in nostalgia became a habit on the trip. He went to Ecclefechan, and made the journey across country to Jane's grave at Haddington. The first he felt did him good; the second entailed three sleepless nights at Edinburgh, and was therefore less useful. He stayed with David Masson, and used the opportunity of being in Edinburgh to visit the Philosophical Institution, of which he had agreed to become President on surrendering the Rectorship of the university in 1868. One evening he and Masson took a walk together, and, passing the Institution, Masson persuaded Carlyle to go inside. He made a point of examining the library for three or four minutes, and then they left.

At least Carlyle's visit to Dumfries reassured him he need have no worries of a family nature. His sisters Jean and Mary were both well enough; his brother Jamie, like Carlyle, was lonely, sleeping badly, and suffering from digestive problems, but otherwise surviving. He went back to London in September not necessarily better in body, but healthier in spirit. The Franco-Prussian War had started, and Carlyle found himself on the winning, but less popular, side. He teased Ruskin for not sharing his convictions. 'Bismarck knows very well what he is aiming at; & I find withal that it is a perfectly just thing.' Bismarck had the 'power to cut France into thongs, and, in a few days, to convert Paris, if he liked, into a red hot Cinder.'[33] A few days later Carlyle mused in his journal that the reclamation of Alsace and Lorraine by the Germans was a long-overdue lesson for France. The French had not yet, he felt, restored proper order after the upheavals of 1789; Lecky recalled Carlyle telling him at this time that the Prussian action was 'the most beneficent thing that had happened in the universe since he had been in it'.[34]

It was hardly surprising, as he listened for the next few weeks to what he regarded as cant and hypocrisy about the Germans' behaviour, that he should feel the urge to relay his robust views to a wider public. He lacked the energy for a philippic of the scope of *Shooting Niagara*, but instead dictated Mary an article-length letter to *The Times*, published on 18 November. He rebuked his fellow Englishmen for their historical ignorance in imagining that France was the wronged party in the war. 'The question for the Germans,' he asserted, 'is not one of "magnanimity", of "heroic pity and forgiveness to a fallen foe", but of solid prudence, and practical consideration what the fallen foe will, in all likelihood, do when once on his feet again.'[35] France had, he said, a distinguished record of perfidy and bad neighbourliness towards Germany, the most recent of which, perpetrated by Napoleon, was still within his living memory. And as for Alsace and Lorraine, 'there is no law of Nature that I know of, no Heaven's Act of Parliament, whereby France, alone of terrestrial beings, shall not restore any portion of her plundered goods when the owners they were wrenched from have an opportunity upon them.'[36] These territories were French only by dint of 'the cunning of Richelieu [and] the grandiose long-sword of Louis XIV'. If France was in a mess now it was because it was badly and immorally led, 'scattered into anarchic ruin, without recognisable head'.[37] This compared with the divinely inspired strength of Bismarck, who had administered, with Carlyle's approval, 'a terribly drastic dose of physic to sick France'. He hoped France was now recovering and that, if not, more physic would be given until she was. In the battle between 'noble, patient, deep, pious and solid Germany'[38] and 'vapouring, vain-glorious, gesticulating, quarrelsome, restless and over-sensitive France' there could be only one possible just victor.

Carlyle was deluged with mail, much of it offensive, but which he dismissed as 'a much a-do about nothing'.[39] His post included, however, letters of support from German soldiers in the trenches, and Bismarck too saw a translation of his words and was cheered by them. The spat seems to have improved Carlyle's spirits, for three weeks later, on 9 December, he went out for his first grand dinner since before Jane's death. The Duke of Argyll called personally on him to invite him to it; and was admitted after Carlyle's housekeeper had mistaken him for a canvasser in a local election, and berated him. Carlyle felt, after this unintentional rudeness had been suffered by the Duke, that he had to attend. After his evening with the aristocracy, at which he dined on venison and grouse, he had to confess that he was 'astonished to find I had been so cheerful'.[40] As the year drew to a close he philosophised, in his journal, on a question of perennial interest to his students, the con-clusions about which reflected this sudden burst of comparative contentment. 'I wish I had the strength to elucidate and write down intelligibly to my fellow-creatures what my outline of belief about God essentially is,' he wrote. 'It might be useful to a poor protoplasm generation, all seemingly determined on those poor terms to try Atheism for a while . . . I find lying deep in me withal some confused but ineradicable flicker of belief that there is a "particular providence".'[41] He told Allingham, who bumped into him in the King's Road on a frosty day in late January 1871, that a recently deceased friend of theirs had escaped from 'this confused puddle that we must still go floundering in a while longer', and that 'Europe seems determined to try the experiment of doing without a God.'[42]

Carlyle's next task was to revise his translations of *Wilhelm Meister*, done almost half a century earlier. A popular edition of his works was coming out, at 2s a volume, but he was spared proof-reading. His charitable instincts were exploited in trying to secure a pension for Geraldine Jewsbury. A petition was being raised in her support, 'which,' he told Jack, 'in the sickness of Forster and the laziness of Froude, Mary has had to undertake and is managing with great vigour and success'.[43] Now seventy-five, Carlyle's own health held up well despite a fierce winter. He still managed to walk every day; and complained of nothing except the uselessness of his right hand and his bad digestion. He told Alick in a letter on 28 February 1871 that he did not want for companions, but 'I find the company of my own thoughts and recollections, what may be called conversing with the Dead, a more salutary, though far mournfuller, employment.'[44] He told his brother, too, of his depression at the explosion of wealth at one end of society and poverty at the other, sounding almost like a proto-socialist as he contemplated revolution. In April, though, he was reading Ruskin's *Fors Clavigera*, and congratulating him on the non-socialist message of that work; a letter that spoke of 'no equality ... but recognition of every betterness that we can find', Carlyle claimed it made him so happy that it almost brought tears to his eyes.[45] While both Carlyle and Ruskin loathed concentrations of wealth on the one hand and the proliferation of 'cheap and nasty' on the other, they sought a levelling-up, not a levelling-down. Ruskin's 1862 essays on political economy were collected and published this spring as *Munera Pulveris*, and dedicated to Carlyle, 'who has urged me to all chief labour'.[46] He paid tribute in the essays to *Past and Present* and the *Latter-Day Pamphlets*, observing that 'for these twenty – now twenty-six – years, this one voice of Carlyle's has been the only faithful and useful utterance in all England, and has sounded through all these years in vain.'[47]

Yet the sage was not so unheeded as Ruskin might have thought, at least not by the people. Though Carlyle himself was declining, his fame was never greater than now; as the large royalty cheques, the bulging post-bag, and the stream of visitors at Cheyne Row continued to prove. One such was Henry Nevinson, a classics master at Westminster School, who explained his admiration thus:

It was not so much Carlyle's impulse to social revolution that made us his disciples. Rather it was his rebellion against the so-called 'materialism' of the period – his insistence upon spiritual realities as truths still possible of belief, though the forms of time-honoured religion were fading fast ... and Carlyle was so beloved a master that I accepted all he said; so beloved that, hearing how Froude used to take him for a drive in his brougham every afternoon, I ... took my stand nearly opposite the familiar house in Cheyne Row ... Supported by Froude, a small and slightly bent old figure came down the steps. A loose cloak, a large, broad-brimmed hat, a fringe of white beard and white hair, a grave and worn face, deeply wrinkled and reddish brown, aged grey eyes turned for a moment to the racing clouds – that was all. What was to me incomparably the greatest spirit of the living world entered the carriage.[48]

Carlyle felt much the worse for the winter that year, and as soon as spring came he went, with Mary, to convalesce at Melchet Court in Hampshire, the country home of Lady Ashburton. While there he was visited by the Russian novelist Ivan Turgenev, whom he had met in London and liked and whose conversation he particularly enjoyed. His spirits were low because he had none of the energy needed to get down to some work, and he shunned obligations; an invitation from the Glasgow University Liberal Association to be their candidate for the Rectorship was rejected. His health declined too; he noted on 17 June 1871 that 'for ten days past I have been in such a state of health as I never knew in my life.'[49] He went, with Jack, to the Highlands

of Scotland for the summer to stay at another Ashburton house. He communicated with no one since Mary was with her mother in Dumfries. Once
back in London he fell for months into the usual routine of being paid court
to by various younger and middle-aged disciples. From Ruskin, though, he
had once more become cut off, not hearing from him for most of 1871, 'a
fact that has become not only surprising to me, but distressing, and the
source latterly of continual anxieties both about myself and you.' Ruskin had
told Carlyle earlier in the year that he was weighed down with work on *Fors
Clavigera*; this was true, and the main explanation for his silence. But he
had also been seriously ill that summer, a chill caught in the Peak District
deteriorating until it endangered his life. His mind, too, was showing signs of
strain; he had been tormented by vivid dreams, such as of the bronze horses
at St Mark's in Venice putting on their harnesses.

Feeling no better for his summer's rest, Carlyle was anxious for the stimulation of friends in a way he had not been in the past. Ruskin came to see
him immediately he was asked, and their relationship deepened, helped,
ironically, by the death of Ruskin's mother in December. 'To all of us,' Carlyle
told him, 'the loss of our mother is a new epoch in our Life-pilgrimage, now
fallen lonelier and sterner than it ever seemed before.'[50] So concerned was
Carlyle about his friend in his bereavement that he borrowed Lady Ashburton's brougham to drive out to Denmark Hill to see him, and was distressed to find him out. He was even more distressed to hear that his friend,
in his grief, might even contemplate leaving London altogether and going to
live in Oxford or, worse, the Lake District. He was spending much time
reading Ruskin, claiming to derive 'spiritual comfort' from him.[51]

Froude recalled that it was in the summer of 1871 that Carlyle visited him
and pressed into his hands 'a large parcel of papers' that were the *Letters and
Memorials of Jane Welsh Carlyle* and the *Reminiscences*.[52] In a passage that was
to constitute Froude's defence in the aftermath of Carlyle's death, he wrote:

He told me to take it simply and absolutely as my own, without reference to any other
person or persons, and to do with it as I pleased after he was gone. He explained,
when he saw me surprised, that it was incomplete, that he could himself form no
opinion whether it ought to be published or not, that he could do no more to it, and
must pass it over to me. He wished never to hear of it again. I must judge. I must
publish it, the whole, or part – or else destroy it all, if I thought that this would be the
wiser thing to do.

Froude adds that Carlyle specified no biography of him should be written,
but that the papers he had given him should be the record of his life. Froude
said he could not immediately accept this responsibility, but would think
about it. Reading through the papers once Carlyle had gone, he was stunned
by the intimate details, and saw Carlyle's repeated protestations of regret
since Jane's death in their true light. Yet Froude felt Carlyle exaggerated his
guilt, but believed too that Carlyle wanted publication as an 'expiation of

his own conduct ... which removed the shadow between himself and her memory'.[53] Froude judged it was up to him whether Carlyle should be allowed to complete his act of atonement; and he did not feel able to deny him the right, with the consequences we now know. Later in the year he informed Carlyle of his decision, and Carlyle agreed. He wanted a delay of twenty years from then before they were published; but Froude, though more than twenty years Carlyle's junior, pointed out that he might be dead himself twenty years later. Carlyle agreed they could be published ten years later; as they were, though with the unhappy coincidence that they seemed to come an indecently short time after Carlyle's own death. Ironically, it was in this year that Carlyle first met Alick's son Alexander, his twenty-eight-year-old nephew, who was to be Froude's great adversary, critic and, eventually, persecutor.

Carlyle formalised his 'bequest' to Froude in his will of 1873; and later that year gave Froude more materials connected with his own life, signifying that another of his wishes, that his own biography should not be written, had been altered. In the will Carlyle said that 'the manuscript [of the *Letters and Memorials*] is by no means ready for publication; nay, the questions how, when (after what delay, seven, ten years) it, or any portion of it, should be published are still dark to me; but on all such points James Anthony Froude's practical summing up and decision is to be taken as mine.'[54] These were words his family, particularly the vindictive Alexander, would choose to ignore. Carlyle had heard that various people were at work on lives of him; and, as Froude saw it, he preferred an authentic record should be written by someone intimate with him, and with access to the facts contained in private papers. Long before Carlyle's last illness, therefore, Froude was at work on his masterpiece. The popular view was that Carlyle was blind to Froude's failings, chief among them a lack of judgment, because of the flattery Froude heaped on him. But Carlyle was not that stupid, despite the contention of Charles Eliot Norton, later an editor of Carlyle's letters, at this time that Froude's face 'exhibits the cynical insincerity of his disposition'[55] and Carlyle could not see it. When, the following year, Froude upset audiences in America by his extreme views on Ireland, Carlyle was intensely critical of him. To a generation determined for reasons of prudishness and hypocrisy to attack Froude, however, all evidence, whether or not relevant to the question of the handling of Carlyle's papers, was useful.

III

The year 1871 had been a mixed one for Carlyle. Alick's two sons, whom he had never met, came over from Canada and saw him, much to his joy; but Mary's brother John was killed in a bus accident in London that autumn. Whether meeting his younger relations or learning of their deaths, it all further concentrated Carlyle's already obsessive thoughts about his own mortality. On 23 December, though, he wrote to James Marshall that 'except weakness I have no special complaint, no bodily organ gone diseased at all.' His intellect and opinions were robust as ever: 'Very hateful to me are the anarchies, the platitudes and baseness of these poor times that are come. Detestable, contemptible, altogether damnable seem to me the Darwinisms and other philosophic balderdashes.'[56] He at last got down to some work, reading heavily in Norse mythology for what was to be *The Early Kings of Norway*. Writing to Jack in January 1872 he laments that '*if* I knew Icelandic like you ... I feel as if I could still write a rather bright and useful little book about them.'[57] By mid-February he had finished the first draft of the little book, though on reading back what he had dictated he was depressed at how difficult it was to compose to his usual high standards by that method. He had lost none of his old cynicism about his endeavours. 'Seldom did I undertake a more totally worthless thing, never anything at all which so bothered me in getting executed or came so near the impossible in this my fatal want of a right hand.'[58] By early March a fair draft was finished, and sent to Jack to read.

He worked, that spring, at a critique of the portraits of John Knox, which was not completed until 1874; and then on an appendix to his *Life of Schiller*; but there was little more left in him. He revived his interest in Ireland, but found much of what he read on the subject uncongenial. Allingham felt that 'he cares to hear nothing about Ireland save what feeds his prejudices. His is the least judicial of minds.'[59] He spent much of his time reading Browning, but could not understand Browning's meaning; Carlyle was one of the least poetic of minds, so this was not too surprising. The letters he dictated became rarer and rarer too, and the entries in his journal more and more sporadic, as they could be written only by the most Herculean effort when his hand permitted; Mary could not come between him and his most private thoughts. He grew to spend days, weeks and months in sad recollection, though friends, notably Lady Ashburton, sought to prise him away from Chelsea as often as they could.

There were still occasional great events. In May 1872 he met the Empress of Germany when she visited London, and she told him he was a 'hero'.[60] Emerson came to England in the autumn of 1872, while his house, which had burned down earlier in the year, was being rebuilt. He stayed until the following spring; but Carlyle was no longer able to be inspired even by the arrival of so close and old a friend. He became less and less aware of his surroundings, or bothered by them. 'Were not the fountain of tears quite dried in me,' he told Forster in September 1872, 'I could feel it a consolation to sit and weep.'[61] It was a lonely autumn, as both Froude and Tyndall, his two most frequent visitors, were in America. He saw more of James Fitzjames Stephen, with whom he had much in common intellectually and who would take him for conversational walks on Sunday afternoons, chewing over ideas that were to be the basis of *Liberty, Equality, Fraternity*. Allingham was frequently in attendance, and there were dinners with the Forsters; but other than that only his rereading of Schiller, and other works on him, kept his interest. He did, though, become godfather to the child of a friend, Sir Baldwyn Leighton; a bizarre thing for a man of Carlyle's religious view to do. 'I didn't like it,' he told Allingham, 'but was told it was only a form. I don't think it was right. I have an unfortunate difficulty in saying *No*.'[62]

Early in 1873 he learned from Alick of the death of their half-brother John, who had preceded Alick to Canada and to whom Carlyle had never been close. None the less, it was a further chipping away of the edifice of Carlyle's existence. Forster, too, was ill, but despite his own problems assisted in the drawing-up of Carlyle's will; Forster, along with Jack, was one of those Carlyle had bidden Froude consult if in doubt about the publication of the papers Carlyle had given him. By the time Froude came to act, neither was available for comment. The will divided Carlyle's wealth among his five poorer siblings, excluding Jack, who had made a large fortune himself; and directed he be buried with his parents at Ecclefechan. Another link with the past was severed that spring when Mill died; 'a great black sheet of mournful more or less tragic memories, not about Mill alone, rushed down upon me,' Carlyle recalled of the moment he heard the news.[63] Later in the year he was disappointed by Mill's *Autobiography*, published posthumously. He told Jack it was 'wholly the life of a logic-chopping machine, little more of human in it than if it had been done by a thing of mechanised iron. Autobiography of a steam-engine . . .'[64] He claimed that 'I have never read a more uninteresting book; nor should I say a sillier, by a man of sense, integrity and seriousness of mind.'[65] Mill had retained some affection for Carlyle to the end. In 1869 he wrote that 'it is only at a particular stage in one's mental development that one benefits much by him (to me he was of great use at that stage), but one continues to read his best things with little, if any, diminution of pleasure after one has ceased to learn anything from him.'[66]

Mill's death reopened the old wound of the burned manuscript. Reading the story in *The Daily Telegraph* (a 'purely imaginary' report, he thought it), Carlyle wrote to Mill's bereaved sister to regret that 'the babbling newspapers should have brought it home to your sad heart in these solemn moments' when he, the victim of the accident, had long since forgotten any hurt done by it.[67]

His literary bequests were not all that concerned Carlyle. He was now fairly wealthy, and Jack warned him of the foolishness of having money gaining only one per cent interest at the bank when a far better return could be had on the stock market. Carlyle admitted to having 'several thousands'[68] lying idle in such a fashion, when a pound would buy approximately fifty times what it can today.

After spending part of his summer sitting for a portrait by Whistler, Carlyle went to Scotland, this time to Annandale, and filled his time rereading Goethe. He had just, with Allingham's encouragement, had a course of reading in

English poets, which left him unsatisfied. Back in London he sat down with, of all things, Tom Paine's *Rights of Man*, and told Allingham Paine had been 'entirely misrepresented ... I found I agreed with him.'[69] On 6 December 1873, two days after his seventy-eighth birthday, barely able to write now, he made his last legible entry in his journal, complaining of the worthlessness of his existence now that his flesh was weak, however willing his spirit. There were occasional signs that some of the flavour of the old days could still be recaptured, such as when he dined at Forster's with Tennyson and James Spedding. Forster was in failing health, and causing concern to Carlyle. He himself was no worse than usual. 'If the poor Digestive Apparatus,' he told Jack, 'could be persuaded (which it can't) to behave with any propriety at all, I might follow my idle existence all day without any special complaint.'[70] His interest in aspects of his life other than his bowels picked up too, despite his frequently expressed pessimism; he devoted much of the winter of 1873–74 campaigning that the 'disgrace' of Scotland's failure to erect a statue to John Knox be rectified; and then, too, was an honour done him by his beloved Germany.

In February 1874 the Prussian ambassador told him he had been made a member of the Prussian Order of Merit. Whether for *Frederick*, or for his help during the late war, was not specified. The bureaucracy attached to this was enormous; Carlyle had to fill in a form indicating not just his name, place of birth and occupation, but also his residence and religion. Carlyle thought the Star of the Order 'really very pretty'[71] but had no intention of displaying it; it was given to Mary to fold up and put away, and Carlyle told Jack he would rather the Prussians had sent him a quarter-pound of tobacco. Allingham recorded what good spirits Carlyle was in at this time, even though 'the scandalous enemy within me' – as Carlyle referred to his bowel problems – was plaguing him.[72] On 30 March he 'spoke of the first Nigger Minstrels in this country; some one took him to a theatre to hear them. He was extremely tickled by their "tempest of enthusiasm about nothing at all"; and imitated "Who's dat knocking at the door" with energy.'[73] Allingham was with him, too, on the anniversary of Jane's death. As usual, he and Carlyle walked to Hyde Park, but this time to the spot where he believed she had died, where he removed his hat and stood for a while silently.

Ruskin, who now addressed his letters to Carlyle to 'dearest Papa', had gone still further away, to Naples. Carlyle begged him to write often; Ruskin was a good correspondent through the summer of 1874, but Carlyle had less and less to say. Eventually Carlyle and Mary went up to Scotland, first to stay on Skye with Lady Ashburton, and then on to Fife. Carlyle was quite uplifted. 'I feel myself better today,' he wrote to Jack on 1 September, 'than I have been, not only since leaving Chelsea, but for many months before that.'[74] Shortly after he returned to London he saw Ruskin again, who started to come regularly after lunch on Saturdays. Carlyle found, to his regret, that Ruskin's 'sensitive, flighty nature disqualifies him for earnest conversation and frank communication of his secret thoughts'. The better spirits he felt as a result of his visit to Scotland were used to complete his work on Knox's portrait. Froude had gone away on a government commission to South Africa; Carlyle worried that he might die before Froude's return – scheduled for ten months hence – and, with an eye to the papers he had given him, told Jack that 'there are various, to me, important little things that have to be settled with him in case we meet no more.'[75]

Though honoured by Prussia, Carlyle had had no official recognition from his own country. Disraeli, who had been abused by Carlyle viciously, had come into office that year, and now sought to do something about this. The Order of Merit did not then exist – it was created by Edward VII in 1902 – but Disraeli had talked to Lord Derby about the need to create some such honour. In the short term, though, it was good for Disraeli's public relations to honour those perceived as having contributed to society. He began with scientific matters, by giving financial help to Sir George Nares's Arctic expedition. Lord Derby then suggested to Disraeli that something should be done for literature, and that Carlyle and Tennyson were the two obvious candidates. Derby, in commending Carlyle, reminded Disraeli that the sage had been 'for whatever reason, most vehement against Gladstone'.[76]

Disraeli put these arguments to the Queen. 'Mr Carlyle is old, and childless, and poor; but he is very popular and respected by the nation. There is no KCB vacant. Would a GCB be too much?' The Grand Cross of the Order of the Bath is one of the highest orders of chivalry, conferring a knighthood, and would have been a great honour to Carlyle. The Queen agreed with Disraeli, who wrote to Carlyle on 27 December 1874. He said the government was determined to recognise intellect, and that the GCB had never been granted before except for direct services to the state. Moreover, Disraeli also told Carlyle that 'I see no reason why a great author should not receive from the nation a pension as well as a lawyer and a statesman.'[77] Carlyle replied on 29 December that he had received Disraeli's letter to his 'great surprise' and that it was a 'magnificent proposal ... unexampled ... in the history of governing persons towards men of letters'. But he could not accept. 'Titles of honour are, in all degrees of them, out of keeping with the tenour of my own poor existence hitherto in this epoch of the world, and would be encumbrance, not a furtherance, to me.'[78] He also admitted he was not, as Disraeli had said, poor.

Carlyle was sure that Lady Derby, with whom he was acquainted, had been the originator of the idea, and the next day wrote to her with a copy of Disraeli's letter to him, and his to Disraeli, with his deep gratitude. He also sent copies on New Year's Day 1875 to Jack, telling him that 'I do however truly admire the magnanimity of Dizzy in regard to me,' adding, with a note of guilt, that 'he is the only man I almost never spoke of except with contempt, and if there is anything of scurrility anywhere chargeable against me, I am sorry to own he is the subject of it; and yet see, here he comes with a pan of hot coals for my guilty head!'[79] It did not fit in with Disraeli's political plans for Carlyle to refuse; but he was unpersuadable. Allingham felt it was not so much magnanimity on Disraeli's part as a desire to be seen to be magnanimous towards his critics.

IV

What little work Carlyle had set himself in the preceding years he had done slowly. His writings on the Knox portraits and the Kings of Norway were not published until the spring of 1875, and he had no inclination to do any more. Allingham, who had become editor of *Fraser's*, had asked to publish these last writings. 'Except for the encouragement and benefit it may give poor Allingham,' Carlyle told Jack on 30 January 1875, 'nothing could have induced me to bother with it further; but the poor man was so passionately anxious, I could not find it in my heart to say No.'[80]

Though he had abandoned hope of working again, Carlyle was still hale in his eightieth year. He received many visitors and, if Wilson's accounts are to be believed, was still as argumentative as ever.[81] His public fame, which Disraeli had tried to commemorate, was marked in other ways. Sir Edgar Boehm, the sculptor, was making a statue of him, which now sits in the gardens at the end of Cheyne Row, on the Embankment. Wilson quotes a new acquaintance of Carlyle's, a Mrs A.A. Anstruther, finding him that summer 'a wonderful talker ... he says he is too old to pay visits. But he is very active, walks out every day. Except that his hand shakes very much and he cannot write, one would not observe anything very aged about him.'[82] Froude returned early from South Africa as he had a daughter gravely ill with consumption, and the two men resumed their routine of walks and rides. Carlyle went out for part of the summer to stay with Lady Derby in her house near the Crystal Palace, and there met Charles Darwin, whose brother Erasmus he had known well since he came to London forty years earlier. Carlyle, not entirely convinced by evolutionary theory, asked Darwin whether there was a possibility of men turning back into apes.

Wherever Carlyle turned he was met with evidence of the esteem in which he was held not just by ordinary men and women, but by his peers. In April 1875 he went out to call on J.L. Motley, the American historian famed for his *Rise of the Dutch Republic,* now living in London and just widowed; it was his bereavement that prompted the call from Carlyle, who knew what Motley must be suffering. Motley had gone to his daughter's house in Dorset, but was distressed to miss Carlyle, whom he had never met. 'There is hardly a living man that I could have so much liked to converse with as yourself at this time.'[83] Fanny Kingsley, widow of Charles Kingsley, wrote to Carlyle later that year to ask for any letters from her husband to him, as she was collecting an edition of them. She told Carlyle that 'you can never know what you and your books were to him.'[84]

As his eightieth birthday approached, honours and tributes began to pour in. Harvard University sent him a doctorate, which he accepted, though refused to use the title since he feared God would confuse him with his brother. Allingham's wife Helen painted his portrait. Boehm engraved a gold medal with which Carlyle was presented on his birthday, the funds raised by admirers who also signed an address composed by David Masson and John Morley, a young man on the fringe of Carlyle's circle who was to sit in the Liberal cabinet after 1906. The framed encomium can still be seen on the wall of the staircase in Carlyle's house, and is signed by almost every literary figure of the day – obvious friends such as Browning and Tennyson, Lecky and Harriet Martineau, Fitzgerald and Tyndall – but also some with noted antipathies to Carlyle such as Trollope, who was to turn on him within a few years in his *Autobiography*, principally out of intellectual jealousy. Part of the address read: 'A whole generation has elapsed since you described for us the Hero as a Man of Letters. We congratulate you and ourselves on the spacious fullness of years which has enabled you to sustain this rare dignity among mankind in all its possible splendour and completeness.'[85] Bismarck, too, wrote to him and described him as a hero for having 'placed before the Germans our great Prussian King in his full figure, like a living statue', though he congratulated him on reaching his seventieth ('*siebzigsten*')[86] rather than eightieth birthday. The mistake, he told Jack, was 'enough to quench any vanity one might have on a Missive from such a man'.[87]

Having passed eighty he would walk along the Chelsea Embankment, or over the bridge and through Battersea Park, most days, and if he became tired he could catch a bus home. However, his longevity brought with it the grief of frequent bereavements, each of which intensified his sense of isolation. A particularly fierce blow fell on 1 February 1876, when Forster, who had been badly ill since the previous autumn, died. Though he had been ill for some time, no one had expected him to die so soon; he was just sixty-four. Carlyle was taken by Froude to Forster's funeral on a bleak February morning at Kensal Green cemetery, where he found himself effectively chief mourner, leading the procession with Forster's widow. 'It is the end of a chapter in my life,' he wrote, 'which had lasted, with unwearied kindness and helpfulness wherever possible on Forster's part, for above forty years.' One of the last kindnesses of Forster's is to be seen in the first-floor library at Cheyne Row: a chair with a swivelling book-rest fixed on the arm, which was of great help to Carlyle once his right hand became weak. In his will, too, Forster bequeathed Carlyle a gold repeater watch left him by Dickens.

Another old friend, Lady Augusta Stanley, died shortly afterwards, and Carlyle found himself sat with the Archbishop of Canterbury at her funeral in Westminster Abbey, where her husband was Dean. Carlyle was prompted to write to Jack of how he was 'mournfully musing in my own mind of the chaos of immensities and eternities with which one is surrounded in his closing years in this world'.[88] Worse grief, however, was to come. Within a few weeks he received news from Canada of the death of Alick on 30 March, at the age of seventy-eight. Carlyle had been aware of his brother's illness, so was prepared for the worst, 'but the shock was heavy and sore'.[89] Two years Carlyle's junior, and four years older than Jack, Alick had always had a very close relationship with his brother. Although physically Carlyle was closer to Jack, and had not seen Alick since 1843, Jack's self-centred, intellectually competitive personality had (especially while Jane was alive) always put a little distance between him and Carlyle. Carlyle and Alick had corresponded frequently, and in terms of simple, familial affection and compassion rather unlike the businesslike tone of the correspondence with Jack. Writing to his nephew and namesake Thomas after Alick's death, Carlyle recalled that his brother had been 'the first human being I ever came to friendship and familiarity with in this world; and our hearts were knit together by a thousand ties.' Alick's devotion to Carlyle was unquestioned. On his death-bed he repeatedly asked 'if Brother Tom were not coming from Edinburgh tomorrow'.[90] Carlyle recalled how, more than sixty years before, Alick would walk out to meet him on his return from Edinburgh University. His sadness at the loss of this lifetime's companion was intense.

Carlyle was still in demand for occasions that wanted celebrity. In April 1876 the Lord Mayor of London wanted him to be guest of honour at a banquet he was giving for authors. Carlyle refused, which prompted the Lord Mayor, 'in considerable state' to turn up one Sunday at Chelsea to seek a personal interview. 'I at length answered – well I will not say no; but we will keep it open.' The Lord Mayor then, however, made the mistake of telling the newspapers that Carlyle had conditionally accepted, and further guests were being invited on the strength of this. Carlyle was determined to have his revenge. 'On Friday next,' he told Jack, 'we will therefore write to his Civic Highness that I am *not* coming.'

His intellect remained sharp, and in need of food. Lecky found him, in the autumn of 1876, 'deep in Swift … much pleased with some more books I had got him about Swift'.[91] He read Trevelyan's life of Macaulay during 1876 and wrote to the author that the week's reading he had had was 'by far the best I have had for a long while … I have nowhere found in any biography, not even in Boswell's Johnson, a human life and character more clearly, credibly and completely brought home to the conception of every intelligent reader.'[92] However, soon even intellectual energy began to be threatened. Early in 1877 Carlyle had a serious bout of illness, attributable to the weakening of his heart, and was indisposed for several weeks. He had long had trouble sleeping, telling Jack that 'I generally get three or two hours sleep at the beginning of each night.'[93] Froude had tried to persuade him to go to Madeira for the climate, but Carlyle could not be shifted. As soon as he could, though, he re-established his old routines: walks along the Chelsea Embankment with friends, and streams of young visitors to Cheyne Row, among whom was Joe Chamberlain, brought along by John Morley. Chamberlain wanted to canvass Carlyle's opinion on his idea of, effectively, nationalising public houses and brewing, restricting the times when drink could be sold and ploughing the profits from it into the state. Carlyle, who never understood the profit motive properly, was pleased at the notion; Chamberlain then asked him about what compensation should be paid to the publicans. Carlyle found the idea of compensating such people iniquitous. Summoning, as Morley recalled, an imaginary landlord before him, Carlyle cried out 'Compensation! You dare come to me for compensation! I'll tell you where to go for compensation! Go to your father the devil, let him compensate you!' Chamberlain listened in stunned silence.[94] Morley, with proper liberal disdain, described Carlyle in Chelsea as 'a poor, soured, wise old genius coiling himself up in his own virtue where one might expect to find one's washerwoman'.[95]

His last two missives to the outside world were both letters in *The Times*; one on 'The Eastern Question', published on 28 November 1876, and one on the Russo-Turkish War, published on 5 May 1877. The first was written to a George Howard, who sent it on to *The Times* for publication. Carlyle reaffirmed that the Russians were 'a good and even noble element in Europe' who had done 'a signal service to God and man in drilling into order and peace anarchic populations all over their side of the world'. To assist the Turk in a war against them would, he said, be 'insanity', as that 'mass of the most hideous and tragic stupidity', the Crimean War, had been twenty years earlier. He advocated as the only realistic policy 'immediate and summary expulsion of the Turk from Europe'.[96]

Carlyle saw Disraeli (who had just been created Earl of Beaconsfield and whom, despite the offer of the GCB, he still loathed) trying to drag Britain into the war on the side of the Turks, having learned nothing from the bloodshed in the Crimea. The 'superlative Hebrew conjuror' had now become 'a cursed old Jew, not worth his weight in cold bacon'.[97] Carlyle felt Disraeli was playing with England, its reputation and the lives of its soldiers, for party political purposes. He, Froude and Ruskin put themselves on the same side as Gladstone; an almost unprecedented occurrence, and one which Gladstone, according to Morley, found hard to fathom ('Mr G could not understand how it was that Carlyle was anti-jingo').[98] It was not, though, a political question for Carlyle, but one of right and wrong. Politicians had ceased to matter to him. When Lord Wolseley, a senior army officer, was taken to meet Carlyle, Carlyle told him to 'lock the doors of the parliamentary palaver, and walk off with the key'.[99]

In the letter of 5 May 1877, Carlyle sneered at 'our miraculous Premier' for dressing up his own hoped-for advantage in the clothes of 'care for British interests'. Carlyle feared that if Britain declared war on Russia to help the Turks, she would find she was taking on instead 'all Europe', which would be 'the maddest and most criminal thing that a British Government could do'. He claimed not just to feel this, but to know it 'as an indisputable fact'. He could see no British interest, and stated quite baldly that 'it should be felt by England as a real ignominy to be connected with such a Turk at all.' He added that 'the newspaper outcry against Russia is no more respectable to me than the howling of Bedlam, proceeding, as it does, from the deepest ignorance, egoism, and paltry national jealousy.'[100] Carlyle had never equivo-cated, and to the last he maintained his fervour of tone. In this matter, his view prevailed. 'There is no chance,' he wrote to Jack of Disraeli, 'of his ever trying to become a Chatham in this world to which he has long been a disgrace.'[101] Why Carlyle termed his knowledge 'an indisputable fact' is significant. Derby was opposed to what he believed to be Disraeli's plan to send a force into Constantinople. The conclusion can be drawn that this plan had, via Derby or his wife, been communicated to Carlyle, whose view was identical to Derby's. The following year, while visiting a mutual friend, Carlyle met Disraeli for the first and only time, and exchanged civilities to the point where Carlyle regretted some of his previous harshnesses.

As Carlyle's health picked up that summer, Froude managed to persuade him to sit to Millais, whose famous portrait of Carlyle hangs in the National Portrait Gallery in London. It shows him gaunt, and with beard white and shaggy, but the hair thick and the eyes intense. Carlyle found the painter 'evidently a worthy man'[102] whom 'I did not at all dislike'. 'The picture I think does not please Mary,' he told Jack, 'nor in fact myself altogether, but it is surely strikingly like in every feature & the fundamental condition was that Millais should paint what he himself was able to see there.'[103]

Though he had stopped writing, Carlyle was determined to keep his mind active. He not only reread the Bible, Goethe and Shakespeare, but also Gibbon ('very disappointing'),[104] several of his favourite Latin authors, and the *Lives of the Saints*, lent to him by Lecky. Though by his own admission 'idle' and 'solitary', he complemented the reading and walking with afternoon rides 'in a Brompton omnibus',[105] where he became a tourist-attraction in his broad-brimmed hat and was treasured by the conductors who had him as a passenger. In the autumn of 1877 he took to going further afield, taking a bus to Portland Place and walking round Regent's Park. Froude was his most frequent companion on these rides; apart from Mary, no one was closer to Carlyle in these last years.

The journalist W.T. Stead was introduced to Carlyle in Cheyne Row in October 1877, and has left a brilliant picture of him: 'His eyes were bright, brilliantly bright, and blue as the azure lochs which gem the hills between St Mary's Loch and Hawick ... beneath the blue eyes were ruddy cheeks, almost hectic in their colouring ... his lips were rather fallen in owing to the lack of teeth.' He had been taken by Madame Novikoff, a Russian émigrée who had become friendly with Carlyle following his pro-Russian pronouncements of the preceding year. 'She had emphasised,' Stead recalled, 'her admiration for his "darling little face". It *is* a little face. But in place of the infinite sadness which I had believed ever brooded over the face of the author of *Sartor Resartus* there was nothing but kindly mirth and ready sympathy.'[106]

Allingham found Carlyle 'very weary and depressed' but also reported him as saying 'I am better off than many a one. I am free of an irritability of nerves that tortured me a year ago.'[107]

In May 1877 he and Jack were corresponding about the choice of Carlyle's burial-place, which he affirms to be with his mother and father at Ecclefechan. He hoped, though, to discharge one last duty before he came to rest there, and that was to write a memoir of Forster, in recognition of Forster's kindnesses to him. However, he simply could not find the energy. By late 1878, as he approached his eighty-third birthday, even reading was becoming too much, and frailty was conquering him. Jack, though six years his junior, was in even worse health, and by the end of 1878 Carlyle was expecting this closest remaining link with the past to be severed. Carlyle, too, was preparing for his own end. 'I feel I may die at any time,' he told Allingham on 14 November.[108] Jack had gone back to die in Dumfries. Froude recalls that the winter of 1878–79 was intensely cold, and that Carlyle became convinced his brother had died but the news was being kept from him by Froude and other friends. It was not so; Jack survived until September 1879, dying after a summer's visit from Carlyle and Mary. The two brothers' mood was inevitably bleak. 'About you, dear brother, I think daily,' Carlyle wrote to Jack on 14 December 1878, 'with a tender sorrow for your sake, and surely have to own with you that there is no good news to be expected on either side. God's will be done.'[109]

Through that winter it was always a relief to hear from Dumfries that his brother still lived. Carlyle had become passive as his own strength faded away, and the weather became severe. Helen Allingham came and painted him again, sitting in the reading chair Forster had had made for him. The occasional 'poor cripply walk half way down the Embankment'[110] was still just about possible, but he was aware his legs were giving up. Instead of walking with him, his court of Lecky, Froude and Allingham would come separately and take him for drives. Carlyle wrote to Jack of his sadness at his brother's 'imprisonment'[111] with illness, but knew his own could not be far off. His tenderness towards Jack never waned, the weekly letter being composed every Friday or Saturday morning even when, as usual, there was no news to report, and the talk was simply of the weather.

Though no religious conversion took place as his own death neared, Carlyle did take to travelling on the omnibus to St Paul's Cathedral (whose magnificence had gripped him ever since he glimpsed it on his first visit to London in 1824), and sitting far away from the East End, simply listening to the beauties of the Anglican service. Now mellowed by infirmity, he became susceptible to the 'exquisite music from the organ and *vox humana*'.[112] It was a painful contrast with the news from Dumfries, where Jack's eyes had weakened so that he could no longer even read. In his very last letter to his brother, before Carlyle too became too weak to correspond, he mused that 'the final mercy of God, it in late years always appears to me, is that He delivers us from a life which has become a task too hard for us.'[113]

V

The final stage of decline began before Jack's death on 15 September 1879, which accelerated it. Though numerous visitors still called (including Ruskin, who would, in the continental manner, kiss his 'papa' on arrival), Carlyle saw fewer and fewer of them for shorter and shorter interviews. Where he used to walk, he now went for rides in the carriages of friends. By March 1879 he had become too weak even for that, and spent most of his time asleep; by May he had recovered sufficiently to go on omnibus-rides again. His strength held up for him to go to Scotland in the late summer. He was visited there by the Allinghams, who were also on holiday, and was well enough to take them on tours of his birthplace. He had a slight falling-out with Froude, whose limited sense of humour was unequal to some trenchant criticism of Carlyle's of his new work on Caesar; Froude ceased to call at Cheyne Row until Mary begged him to resume his visits. On his eighty-fourth birthday, 4 December 1879, Carlyle received a stream of visitors, including Browning, Ruskin, the Allinghams and the Leckys. The Prince of Wales, later King Edward VII, sought an interview, but Carlyle refused him. He no longer had the energy to meet new people, princes or not. 'I am too old,' Carlyle told his nephew Alexander, who replied to the Prince's private secretary. 'He might as well come and see my poor old dead body.'[114] Remarks like these caused Ruskin, when contemplating old age a few years later, to promise that 'I'll never mew about it like Carlyle.'[115]

Allingham said of Carlyle in March 1880 that he was 'noticing nothing of the outer world'. Shortly afterwards, according to Froude, he confirmed his desire for Froude to publish all the *Reminiscences*, including the memoir of Jane, separately from the *Letters and Memorials*. Mary, who became Mrs Carlyle by marrying her cousin Alexander, Alick's son, told her aunt Janet in Canada on 18 July 1880 that her uncle was 'exceedingly weak, hardly able to walk fifty yards without help, and yet until about ten days ago, when he had a very severe attack of diarrhoea which has left him very much below par, he was what one might call for him very well.'[116] She sketched out Carlyle's day: he would lie on a sofa or sit in an easy chair until 2.30 p.m., after which he would go out for a drive until five o'clock. He would then lie on the sofa and read until 6.30 p.m., when he would have his dinner, and then sleep again until his tea at nine. Then he would read until bed-time, which was about midnight. She concluded:

He looks very well in the face, has a fine, fresh, ruddy complexion and an immense quantity of white hair, his voice is clear and strong, he sees and hears quite well; but for the rest, as I have said, he is not good at moving about. In general he is wonderfully good-humoured and contented; and on the whole carries his eighty-four years well. He desires me to send you his kind love and his good wishes: as you know, he writes to nobody at all. I do not think he has written a single letter, even dictated one, for over a year.

Jack's death had removed from him his main medical adviser. However, by October 1880 his health was such that a doctor had to visit constantly. In November he suddenly asked Froude, who he knew was writing his biography, what he intended to do with the manuscript of the *Letters and Memorials*; Froude told him he intended to publish them, a decision which Carlyle did not dissent from. The Allinghams went to see him on his eighty-fifth birthday, and found him looking 'better and easier; more himself'.[117] By Christmas, though, Allingham felt Carlyle hardly knew him. Yet, he still managed to get out most days, taking his last drive on New Year's Day 1881.

In mid-January, a fortnight before the end, his condition became serious. Though Carlyle had long desired death, he fought instinctively against it. His nephew John, Mary's brother, recalled that 'the Doctor declared he had never met such tenacity of life and vitality in the whole course of his varied London and other experience.'[118] The public took a huge interest in the sage's health. Reporters from newspapers would ring the doorbell at all hours, forcing young Alick to post bulletins on the door. Lecky, in a letter to a friend on 17 January 1881, wrote that 'Carlyle has got very much weaker, both in body and mind, during the last few months. He has lately given up going out and almost wholly given up reading. It is painful to see the extreme dregs of life.'[119] Four days later Lecky found the sage surviving on a diet of brandy and water 'in a state of extreme weakness and prostration. I saw him yesterday for a few minutes, and he was just able to say three or four sentences.'[120]

Carlyle suffered no pain, but just slipped away on 5 February in 'little more than a gentle flickering sleep, ending in a scarcely heard last sigh of sound'. His death had been expected for the week before it came; he was hardly breathing, and his heart hardly beating, for some of that time. He was unconscious for much of the last few days, though he asked for his father, his mother, for 'Sandy' (Alick, whose son he confused him with), and for Jack; and he threw his arms around Mary's neck, thinking she was his mother. The afternoon before his death he uttered his last word, 'Alick'. Froude came to see him, but Carlyle was unconscious. 'Ours has been a long friendship,' Froude said to him. 'I will try to do what you wish.'[121]

Mary and young Alick were with him at the end:

At half-past eight the breathing quietly ceased (as it had done often before); she [Mary] ran to him and listened and the lungs moved once or twice again very gently and then stopped – forever. A slight tremor seemed to run through the body and a faint flutter or gurgling sound was heard inside and then all was still. And so passed away calmly and peacefully the noblest, greatest and best spirit that ever lived on earth![122]

NOTES

INTRODUCTION: DEATH
AND ASSASSINATION
[1] Clubbe, 182.
[2] Hutton, 1.
[3] Seigel, 456ff.
[4] Ibid, 513–20.
[5] 'Signs of the Times', CME II, 56.
[6] LDP, 23.
[7] John Stuart Mill, 'The Negro
Question', *Fraser's Magazine*, January
1850, 25–31.
[8] The two main Reform Acts had been
in 1832 and 1867; another was to come
in 1885. The first meeting of the Trades
Union Congress in 1868 had been the
first establishment of an organised
Labour movement. The Independent
Labour Party was formed in 1893,
becoming the Labour Party in 1906.
[9] Bullock, 780–1.
[10] In conversation with the author,
February 1992.
[11] *Daily Telegraph*, Monday 7 February
1881, 5.
[12] *The Times*, Monday 7 February 1881,
4.
[13] Sir John MacDonnell (1847–1921),
book reviewer, leader-writer and writer
on legal and philosophical topics for *The
Times* from 1870 to 1910.
[14] *The Times*, Friday 11 February 1881,
5.
[15] *The Times*, ibid. *The Times*'s archivist,
to whom I am indebted, tells me that
those of the paper's records that would
have contained the key to the identity of
'Common Sense' were destroyed when
Printing House Square was hit in the
Blitz of 1940–41. It may not be too
fanciful to detect similarities between the
style of this letter and that of the attack
by Trollope on Carlyle in his
Autobiography.
[16] *Spectator*, 12 February 1881, 214–15.
[17] Seigel, 456ff.
[18] *Spectator*, 12 February 1881, 209–10.
[19] Austria and Prussia occupied the
duchies of Schleswig and Holstein on 1
February 1864, following the death of
Frederick VII of Denmark on 15
November 1863. Bismarck dared Europe
to take action against him, but it did not.
See Marriott, 341–6.
[20] *Athenaeum*, 9 April 1881, 488.
[21] *Saturday Review*, 12 February 1881,
199.
[22] *Fraser's Magazine*, April 1881, 515–28.
[23] *Spectator*, 12 March 1881, 341–3.
[24] Rem, 258.
[25] Froude I, v.
[26] Froude V, 11.
[27] CME IV, 29.
[28] Letter of 10 March 1883, quoted in
Cook II, 562.
[29] Wilson VII, 247 (n).
[30] Froude V, 16.
[31] Ibid, 32–3.
[32] Ibid, 34.
[33] They were: *Thomas Carlyle, the Man
and his Books*, by William Howie Wylie
(Marshall Japp); *Thomas Carlyle*, by
Henry J. Nicol (Macniven and Wallace);
Thomas Carlyle, by M.D. Conway
(Chatto and Windus); *Memoirs of the Life*

and Writings of Thomas Carlyle, by R.H.
Shepherd (WH Allen); and *Thomas
Carlyle, Ein Lebensbild und Goldkorner
aus seinen Werken*. Dargestellt durch
Eugen Oswald (Trubner).
34 *Spectator*, 12 November 1881, 1435–8.
35 *Spectator*, 8 April 1882, 468–9.
36 *Spectator*, 22 April 1882, 530–2.
37 *Spectator*, 8 April 1882, 462–3.
38 Sadleir, 157–8.
39 Ibid, 169.
40 Trollope I, 182.
41 Trollope II, 323.
42 John Tyndall was a leading scientist of
the period. He was close to Carlyle in
the last twenty years of his life, and
accompanied him on the journey to
Edinburgh in 1866, when Carlyle was
inaugurated as Rector of the university.
43 *Spectator*, 5 Ma 1883, 573–4.
44 Masson I, 41.
45 This religious process began for
Froude after he had read, but before he
had met, Carlyle. See Wilson VII,
Chapters V and VI. Wilson's book,
which preceded his monumental
biography, is (rather like his biography)
devoted to illustrating Froude's
inaccuracies, though attributes these to
haste rather than malevolence.
46 Elliott, II, 373.
47 Froude III, 293.
48 Heroes, 2.
49 Masson I, 71–2.
50 Chadwick, 70.
51 NL II, 189–91.
52 Froude IV, 260.
53 Ibid, 261.
54 Johnson, 39–40.
55 Tennyson, 94–5.
56 Harrold, 27.
57 See Stephen, passim.
58 *Spectator*, 31 January 1874, 138.
59 There is nothing in Carlyle to match,
for example, the literary command of
the first paragraph of *The Stones of Venice*;
but this judgment is made in aesthetic
terms, terms irrelevant to Carlyle.
60 *Spectator*, 7 December 1895, 810–11.
61 *The Times*, 4 December 1895, 9.
62 Lectures given in the spring of 1840.
63 Paul, 45.
64 Nemesis, viii.

65 Ibid, 81.
66 Dunn, 3
67 Morley I, 56–7.
68 Quiller-Couch, 212.
69 Young, 331.
70 Russell, 667.
71 Grierson, 11.
72 Masson I, 96–7.
73 Grierson, 28.
74 Ibid, 47.
75 Ford, 13.
76 Turner, 200.
77 Maurice Cowling, 'Author as Mirror
to the Soul', *Times Higher Education
Supplement*, 27 March 1992.
78 Kenyon, 103.
79 Peter Quennell, 'Noble Savage',
Spectator, 10 February 1956, 188–9.

I EDUCATING TOM
1 The *Oxford English Dictionary* points
out that the common use of this Lowland
Scots word to mean 'superior thane' was
erroneous. Its correct meaning is an
abbacy of the early Scottish Church.
2 Wylie, 34–41.
3 Rem, 15–16.
4 Ibid, 27.
5 Quoted in a note by Carlyle on a letter
of 23 December 1835 from Jane Carlyle
to her mother-in-law; see *Collected Letters*
VIII, 273.
6 Apart from Thomas these were:
Alexander (1797–1876); Janet (1799–
1801); John Aitken (1801–79); Margaret
(1803–30); James (1805–90); Mary
(1808–88); Jean (1810–88); and Janet
(1813–97).
7 Rem, 3.
8 Ibid, 6.
9 Ibid, 177.
10 Ibid, 27.
11 Ibid, 29.
12 Tennyson, 10.
13 Rem, 29.
14 Ibid, 12.
15 Two Rem, 30.
16 Rem, 178.
17 Ibid, 30.
18 Two Rem, 28.
19 Sartor, 84–5.
20 Rem, 174.
21 Ibid, 17.

[22] Ibid, 173.
[23] Ibid, 179 (n).
[24] Sartor, 82–3.
[25] Collected Letters VI, 193.
[26] Rem, 180.
[27] Sartor, 70.
[28] Rem, 308. The bilious tone is typical of many of the personal reflections in the *Reminiscences*, and helps explain why the author's reputation was so damaged when the work was published.
[29] Ibid, 310. Carlyle adds that Smail 'became, with success, an insignificant Burgher Minister (somewhere in Galloway)'.
[30] Ibid, 309.
[31] Wylie, 93.
[32] Campbell, 17.
[33] For the full list of Carlyle's early reading see Masson II, 231–3.
[34] Rem, 185.
[35] Sartor, 88.
[36] Ibid, 92.
[37] Allingham, 253.
[38] Sartor, 90–1.
[39] Collected Letters I, 3–6.
[40] Masson II, 239.
[41] Two Rem, 36.
[42] Collected Letters I, 6–7.

2 'MY CONDUCT IS ABSURD'
[1] Collected Letters I, 88.
[2] Ibid, 290–1.
[3] Rem, 180–1.
[4] Ibid, 182.
[5] Masson II, 249.
[6] Rem, 31.
[7] Ibid, 181.
[8] Ibid, 314.
[9] Ibid, 184.
[10] Collected Letters I, 15 (n).
[11] Ibid, 22.
[12] Ibid, 35.
[13] Rem, 181.
[14] Collected Letters I, 30.
[15] Masson I, 95–6.
[16] Collected Letters I, 53.
[17] Ibid, 57.
[18] Ibid, 65.
[19] Ibid, 65 (n).
[20] Rem, 182.
[21] Collected Letters I, 69.
[22] Ibid, 70.

[23] A village on the main road from Moffat to Edinburgh, about thirty-five miles from the city.
[24] A hamlet in north Peeblesshire, about twenty miles south of Edinburgh.
[25] Collected Letters I, 71.
[26] Rem, 183–4.
[27] Collected Letters I, 77.
[28] Burdett, 54.
[29] Collected Letters I, 80.
[30] Rem, 185.
[31] Two Rem, 38.
[32] Froude I, 396.
[33] Allingham, 232.
[34] Masson II, 264.
[35] Collected Letters I, 90.
[36] Ibid, 96.
[37] Two Rem, 35.
[38] Collected Letters I, 98.
[39] Ibid, 98–9.
[40] Two Rem, 39.
[41] Collected Letters I, 103.
[42] Rem, 10.
[43] Ibid, 191–2.
[44] Collected Letters I, 125.
[45] Ibid, 119.
[46] Ibid, 127.
[47] Ibid, 135–6.
[48] Ibid, 140–1.
[49] Rem, 206.
[50] Collected Letters I, 141–2.
[51] Rem, 206.
[52] Ibid, 315.
[53] Ibid, 206.
[54] Collected Letters I, 148.
[55] Ibid, 150.
[56] Ibid, 148.
[57] Halliday, passim.
[58] Ibid, ix.
[59] Collected Letters I, 157.
[60] Rem, 205.
[61] Ibid, 206.
[62] Collected Letters I, 159.
[63] Ibid, 166.
[64] Ibid, 174.
[65] Ibid, 179.
[66] Ibid, 184.
[67] Two Rem, 35.
[68] Collected Letters I, 213.
[69] Ibid, 217 (n).
[70] Ibid, 230.
[71] CME V, 65–167.
[72] Collected Letters I, 229.

[73] Ibid, 231–2.
[74] Ibid, 245.
[75] Rem, 225.
[76] Ibid, 226.
[77] Collected Letters I, 251.
[78] Ibid, 255.
[79] Rem, 227.
[80] Collected Letters I, 282. A sooterkin is defined by the *Oxford English Dictionary* as 'a supplementary or imperfect character'.
[81] Ibid, 292.
[82] Ibid, 293.
[83] See his letter to William Graham, 28 January 1821, ibid, 315.
[84] Ibid, 300 and 304.
[85] Ibid, 313.
[86] Ibid, 325.
[87] See, for example, Masson I, 44–6.
[88] Rem, 224.

3 COURTING JANE
[1] Rem, 38–9.
[2] Ibid, 98–9.
[3] Collected Letters I, 359.
[4] Masson II, 299.
[5] Two Rem, 49 (n).
[6] Ibid, 51.
[7] Ibid, 49.
[8] Sartor, 134–5.
[9] Collected Letters VII, 349 (n).
[10] Collected Letters I, 366.
[11] Ibid, 367.
[12] Ibid, 368.
[13] Ibid, 383–4.
[14] Ibid, 398.
[15] Ibid, 408 (n).
[16] Ibid, 404.
[17] Ibid, 420.
[18] Collected Letters II, 7.
[19] Ibid, 18.
[20] Rem, 234.
[21] Collected Letters II, 25.
[22] Ibid, 20.
[23] Ibid, 26.
[24] Ibid, 38.
[25] Ibid, 285.
[26] Ibid, 41.
[27] Ibid, 51.
[28] Ibid, 58.
[29] Ibid, 62.
[30] Ibid, 72.
[31] Ibid, 74.

[32] Ibid, 107.
[33] Ibid, 141.
[34] Rem, 222.
[35] Collected Letters II, 158.
[36] Ibid, 191.
[37] Ibid, 180.
[38] Ibid, 184.
[39] Ibid, 226.
[40] Ibid, 255.
[41] CME V, 196.
[42] Collected Letters II, 285.
[43] Ibid, 289.
[44] Ibid, 291.
[45] Ibid, 336–7.
[46] Ibid, 326.
[47] Ibid, 338.
[48] Rem, 241.
[49] Collected Letters II, 343.
[50] Ibid, 350.
[51] Ibid, 353.
[52] Ibid, 362 (n).
[53] Ibid, 390.
[54] Ibid, 406.
[55] Ibid, 434.
[56] Rem, 241.
[57] Harrold, 7.
[58] Collected Letters II, 422.
[59] Ibid, 427.
[60] Ibid, 432.
[61] Ibid, 442.
[62] Ibid, 446.
[63] Ibid, 456.
[64] Ibid, 450.
[65] Ibid, 458.
[66] Ibid, 459–60.
[67] Ibid, 474.
[68] Ibid, 475.
[69] Rem, 241.
[70] Collected Letters III, 12.
[71] Schiller, 123.
[72] Ibid, 28–9.
[73] Ibid, 41.
[74] Ibid, 101.
[75] Ibid, 108.
[76] Ibid, 191.
[77] Collected Letters III, 36.
[78] Ibid, 69.
[79] Ibid, 81.
[80] Ibid, 87.
[81] Ibid, 90.
[82] See p. 290 infra.
[83] *Examiner*, 13 June 1824.
[84] Collected Letters III, 93.

[85] Ibid.
[86] Rem, 242.
[87] Collected Letters III, 104.
[88] Rem, 258.
[89] Collected Letters III, 121.
[90] Ibid, 131.
[91] Ibid, 161.
[92] Rem, 268.
[93] Ibid, 269.
[94] Ibid, 271.
[95] Ibid.
[96] Collected Letters III, 181.
[97] Ibid, 195.
[98] Ibid, 219–20.
[99] Ibid, 235.
[100] Ibid, 240.
[101] Ibid, 241–2.
[102] Ibid, 244.
[103] Ibid, 249.
[104] Ibid, 266.
[105] Ibid, 268.
[106] Ibid, 334.
[107] Ibid, 339.
[108] Ibid, 349.
[109] Ibid, 378.
[110] Ibid, 394.
[111] Ibid, 405.
[112] Collected Letters IV, 13.
[113] Ibid, 59–60.
[114] Ibid, 62.
[115] Ibid, 68–9.
[116] Ibid, 71.
[117] Ibid, 89.
[118] Collected Letters VII, 375.
[119] Collected Letters IV, 103.
[120] Ibid, 111.
[121] Ibid, 143.
[122] Ibid, 137.
[123] Ibid, 141.
[124] Ibid, 142.

4 MARRIAGE AND RETREAT
[1] Froude V, 17.
[2] Ibid, 21.
[3] Ibid, 22.
[4] Ibid, 23.
[5] Ibid, 25.
[6] Kingsmill, 50.
[7] Collected Letters V, 433.
[8] Wilson VII, 194–5.
[9] Collected Letters IV, 152.
[10] Rem, 43.
[11] Collected Letters IV, 154.

[12] Ibid, 156.
[13] Last Words, 13–14.
[14] Ibid, 185.
[15] Rem, 55.
[16] Ibid, 317.
[17] Collected Letters IV, 190.
[18] Rem, 318.
[19] Collected Letters IV, 214.
[20] Ibid, 218.
[21] Ibid, 210.
[22] Ibid, 253.
[23] Norton, 22.
[24] Masson I, 65–6.
[25] Norton, 26.
[26] Collected Letters IV, 248.
[27] Ibid, 245.
[28] CME I, 22.
[29] Ibid, 22–3.
[30] Harrold, 17.
[31] Collected Letters IV, 256 (n).
[32] CME I, 27.
[33] Ibid, 43.
[34] Ibid, 58.
[35] Collected Letters IV, 310.
[36] Norton, 78.
[37] Collected Letters IV, 354.
[38] Masson II, 351.
[39] Rem, 56.
[40] CME I, 203.
[41] Ibid, 216.
[42] Rem, 56.
[43] Quoted in Collected Letters VII, 103 (n).
[44] Collected Letters IV, 385.
[45] Ibid, 408.
[46] Rem, 320.
[47] Collected Letters IV, 417.
[48] Ibid, 433.
[49] Ibid.
[50] CME I, 357.
[51] Ibid, 393.
[52] Ibid, 396.
[53] Ibid, 456.
[54] Ibid.
[55] Ibid, 461.
[56] Rem, 57.
[57] Ibid, 58.
[58] CME II, 26.
[59] Ibid, 6.
[60] Ibid, 58.
[61] Heroes, 31.
[62] CME II, 67.
[63] Ibid, 70.

[64] Ibid, 74.
[65] Ibid, 76.
[66] Ibid, 77.
[67] Ibid, 78.

5 *Sartor*: 'THAT DIVINE ME'
[1] Collected Letters V, 70.
[2] Rem, 329.
[3] Collected Letters V, 87.
[4] Ibid, 109.
[5] Rem, 291.
[6] Collected Letters V, 127.
[7] Pankhurst, vii.
[8] Ibid, 30.
[9] Collected Letters V, 136.
[10] Zeldin, 431.
[11] Collected Letters V, 171.
[12] Ibid, 175.
[13] Ibid.
[14] Ibid, 185.
[15] Ibid, 207.
[16] Ibid, 211.
[17] Ibid, 215.
[18] Ibid, 243.
[19] Ibid, 247.
[20] Ibid, 283.
[21] Ibid, 297.
[22] Ibid, 303.
[23] Collected Letters VI, 396.
[24] Tennyson, 5.
[25] Holloway, 24–5.
[26] Sartor, 24.
[27] Harrold, 104 and 111.
[28] Sartor, 57.
[29] Larkin, Chapters 1–5 passim.
[30] Sartor, 47–8.
[31] Ibid, 52–3.
[32] Ibid, 35.
[33] Ibid, 52.
[34] Ibid, 92.
[35] Ibid.
[36] Ibid, 129.
[37] Ibid, 133.
[38] Ibid, 153.
[39] Ibid.
[40] Ibid, 177.
[41] Ibid, 208.
[42] Ibid, 186.
[43] Ibid.
[44] Ibid, 215.
[45] Collected Letters V, 319.
[46] Ibid, 330.
[47] Ibid, 351.

[48] Rem, 297.
[49] Ibid, 293.
[50] Collected Letters V, 340.
[51] LDP, 209.
[52] Collected Letters V, 341.
[53] Ibid, 354.
[54] Ibid.
[55] Ibid, 375.
[56] Ibid, 378.
[57] Ibid, 398.
[58] Mill, 147–8.
[59] Ibid, 137.
[60] Collected Letters V, 406.
[61] Ibid, 399.
[62] Rem, 295.
[63] Ibid, 34.
[64] Collected Letters VI, 31 (n).
[65] Ibid, 18.
[66] Ibid, 38.

6 OUT OF EXILE
[1] Collected Letters VI, 58.
[2] CME III, 12.
[3] Ibid, 20.
[4] Ibid, 23.
[5] Collected Letters VI, 61.
[6] Ibid, 85.
[7] Ibid, 70.
[8] Ibid, 102.
[9] Ibid, 105.
[10] Ibid, 107.
[11] Rem, 297.
[12] Collected Letters VI, 111.
[13] CME III, 71 (n).
[14] Ibid, 79–80.
[15] Ibid, 80–1.
[16] Collected Letters VI, 143.
[17] CME II, 376.
[18] Ibid, 377.
[19] CME III, 145.
[20] Ibid, 158–9.
[21] Ibid, 160. 'Tares' are weeds.
[22] Collected Letters VI, 355.
[23] CME II, 395; and see also the passage on Goethe as reconciler on 434.
[24] Collected Letters VI, 269.
[25] Ibid, 440.
[26] Collected Letters VI, 240 (n).
[27] Ibid, 174.
[28] Ibid, 209 (n).
[29] Ibid, 172.
[30] Ibid, 210.
[31] Ibid, 235.

[32] Ibid, 267.
[33] Ibid, 243 (n).
[34] Ibid, 246.
[35] Ibid, 290.
[36] Ibid, 292.
[37] Ibid, 299 (n).
[38] CME III, 177.
[39] Ibid, 180.
[40] Ibid, 223.
[41] Ibid, 230.
[42] Ibid, 231.
[43] Ibid, 233.
[44] Collected Letters VII, 23.
[45] Collected Letters VI, 302.
[46] Ibid, 328 (n).
[47] Ibid, 349.
[48] Ibid, 362.
[49] Ibid, 335.
[50] Rem, 67.
[51] Collected Letters VI, 388.
[52] Ibid, 395.
[53] Ibid, 396.
[54] Ibid, 414.
[55] Collected Letters IX, 395.
[56] Collected Letters VI, 425.
[57] Ibid (n).
[58] Emerson, 1.
[59] Ibid, 9.
[60] Ibid, 11.
[61] Collected Letters VI, 427.
[62] Ibid, 432.
[63] Ibid, 446.
[64] Collected Letters VII, 138.
[65] Ibid, 78.
[66] Rem, 336.
[67] Collected Letters VII, 79.
[68] Ibid.
[69] Ibid, 101.
[70] Ibid, 104.
[71] Ibid, 151.
[72] Ibid, 153.
[73] Ibid, 172.

7 REVOLUTION IN CHELSEA
[1] Collected Letters VII, 193.
[2] Ibid, 172–3.
[3] I am indebted to the account given by Dr Alexander Carlyle, Carlyle's nephew, to be found in the National Trust Guide, available from Carlyle's House.
[4] Rem, 69.
[5] Collected Letters VII, 207.

[6] Ibid, 214.
[7] Ibid, 247.
[8] Ibid, 216.
[9] Ibid, 211.
[10] Hunt, 505–6.
[11] Rem, 71.
[12] Ibid, 304.
[13] Ibid, 305.
[14] CME III, 323.
[15] Collected Letters VII, 266.
[16] See a letter to Alick, ibid, 281.
[17] Ibid, 280.
[18] Ibid, 288.
[19] Ibid, 306.
[20] Ibid, 319.
[21] Ibid, 339.
[22] Ibid, 343.
[23] Ibid, 333.
[24] CME III, 322.
[25] Ibid, 321.
[26] Collected Letters VIII, 3 (n).
[27] Ibid, 9.
[28] Ibid, 19.
[29] Ibid, 9.
[30] Ibid, 11.
[31] Ibid, 31.
[32] Ibid, 32.
[33] Ibid, 35.
[34] Ibid, 36.
[35] Ibid, 41.
[36] Ibid, 75.
[37] Ibid, 53.
[38] Ibid, 67 (n).
[39] Ibid, 84.
[40] Froude III, 28.
[41] NLS MS 1778.
[42] Duffy, 169.
[43] Ibid, 66.
[44] Ibid, 70.
[45] Ibid, 71.
[46] Ibid, 72.
[47] Rem, 73.
[48] Collected Letters VIII, 85.
[49] Sterling, 106.
[50] Ibid.
[51] Smalley, 301.
[52] Collected Letters VIII, 96.
[53] Ibid, 102.
[54] Ibid, 111.
[55] Ibid.
[56] Ibid, 110.
[57] Ibid, 113.
[58] Ibid, 186 (n).

59 Ibid, 125 (n).
60 Sterling, 108.
61 Ibid, 109.
62 Ibid, 117.
63 Collected Letters VIII, 135.
64 Ibid, 137.
65 Ibid, 184.
66 Ibid, 194.
67 Ibid, 208 (n).
68 Ibid, 209.
69 Ibid, 228.
70 Ibid, 263.
71 Ibid, 314.
72 Ibid, 271.
73 Ibid, 288.
74 Ibid, 307.
75 Ibid, 308.
76 Ibid, 342.
77 Ibid, 326.
78 Ibid, 335.
79 Collected Letters IX, 15 (n).
80 Ibid, 15.
81 Ibid, 145 (n).
82 Ibid, 13.
83 Ibid, 32.
84 Ibid, 33.
85 Ibid, 53.
86 Ibid, 67.
87 Ibid, 70.
88 Ibid, 87.
89 Ibid, 88.
90 Ibid.
91 Martineau, 377.
92 Collected Letters IX, 107.
93 Ibid, 115.
94 Ibid, 161.
95 Ibid, 116.
96 Ibid, 125.
97 Ibid, 134.
98 Ibid. Mrs Pierce Butler was Fanny Kemble, the well-known actress.
99 Ibid, 145.
100 Froude III, 98–9.
101 Collected Letters IX, 185.
102 Ibid, 201–2.
103 Martineau, 384.
104 Collected Letters IX, 201 (n).
105 Anonymous notice (by John Crawfurd), Spectator, 6 May 1837.
106 Collected Letters IX, 205.
107 Ibid, 217.
108 Ibid, 206.
109 Allingham, 203.

110 Literary Gazette, 27 May 1837, 330–2.
111 Cumming, 22.
112 FR I, 9.
113 Ibid II, 1.
114 Ibid I, 213.
115 Ibid I, 40.
116 Ibid II, 10.
117 Ibid I, 235.
118 Ibid II, 28.
119 Ibid III, 184.
120 Ibid I, 133.
121 Ibid I, 227.
122 Ibid III, 75.
123 Ibid I, 137.
124 Ibid II, 141.
125 Ibid I, 148.
126 Ibid III, 110–11.
127 Ibid III, 164–72.
128 Ibid III, 266.
129 Ibid, 'The Whiff of Grapeshot', III, 315.
130 Collected Letters IX, 228.
131 Mill, 183–4.
132 The Times, 3 August 1837, 6.
133 Seigel, 52–68.

8 THE CONDITION OF ENGLAND

1 Rem, 75 (n).
2 Ibid, 350.
3 Ibid.
4 Ibid, 351.
5 Collected Letters IX, 255.
6 Ibid, 247.
7 Martineau, 383–4.
8 Collected Letters IX, 284.
9 Ibid, 294.
10 Ibid, 307.
11 Ibid, 328.
12 Ibid.
13 Ibid, 342.
14 Ibid, 311.
15 Ibid, 343.
16 Ibid, 357.
17 Vide supra.
18 CME IV, 81.
19 Ibid, 29.
20 Collected Letters IX, 368 (n).
21 Collected Letters X, 28.
22 Ibid, 29 (n).
23 Ibid, 17 (n).
24 Ibid, 43.
25 Ibid, 62.

26 Ibid, 69.
27 Ibid, 71.
28 The edition from which I have worked is *Lectures on the History of Literature*, delivered by Thomas Carlyle, edited by Professor J. Reay Greene, published by Ellis and Elvey, London, 1892. I am grateful to Mr Cowling for lending me his copy, with annotations, of this work.
29 Ibid, 46.
30 Ibid, 48.
31 Ibid, 169.
32 Ibid, 59.
33 Ibid, 60.
34 Ibid, 63–4.
35 Ibid, 66.
36 Ibid, 67.
37 Ibid, 69.
38 Ibid, 84.
39 Ibid, 120–1.
40 Ibid, 131.
41 Ibid, 149.
42 Ibid, 151.
43 Ibid, 165.
44 Collected Letters XII, 200–1.
45 Collected Letters X, 84.
46 *The Times*, 'Mr Carlyle's Lectures', 1 May, 1838.
47 Collected Letters X, 84.
48 *The Times*, 'Mr Carlyle's Lectures', 22 May 1838.
49 Collected Letters X, 94 (n).
50 Ibid, 114 (n).
51 Duffy, 90; Espinasse, 230. See also the *Carlyle Newsletter*, 1985, 38–41, 'John Murray's Reader and the Rejection of *Sartor Resartus*', by Thomas C. Richardson.
52 Sartor, 241.
53 Ibid, 246.
54 Collected Letters X, 120.
55 Ibid, 164.
56 Ibid, 201.
57 Ibid, 203 (n).
58 Woodward, 120.
59 Morley, I, 54.
60 Collected Letters XI, 4.
61 Ibid, 28.
62 Ibid, 39.
63 Rem, 167.
64 Ibid, 168.
65 Collected Letters XI, 40.
66 Ibid, 43.
67 Ibid, 75.
68 CME IV, 205.
69 Collected Letters XI, 81.
70 Ibid.
71 Ibid, 93 (n).
72 *The Times* 10 May, 1839.
73 Collected Letters XI, 98.
74 Ibid, 104.
75 Ibid, 155.
76 Ibid, 160.
77 Ibid, 161.
78 Ibid, 191 (n).
79 Reprinted in Seigel. The thirteen points are given on 104–6.
80 Collected Letters XI, 107.
81 Ibid, 206 (n).
82 Ibid, 225 (n).
83 Ibid, 218.
84 CME IV, 119.
85 Ibid, 162.
86 Ibid, 122.
87 Ibid, 165.
88 Ibid, 127.
89 Carlyle actually means the six points of the People's Charter: annual parliaments, universal male suffrage, equal electoral districts, abolition of the property qualification for MPs, secret ballot and payment of MPs.
90 CME IV, 157–8.
91 Ibid, 187.
92 Ibid, 158.
93 Ibid, 190.
94 Ibid, 159–60.
95 Ibid, 129–30.
96 Ibid, 132.
97 Ibid, 133.
98 Ibid, 134.
99 Ibid, 130.
100 Ibid, 137.
101 Ibid, 136.
102 Ibid, 147.
103 Ibid, 189.
104 Ibid.
105 Ibid, 191.
106 Ibid, 192.
107 Ibid, 194.
108 Ibid, 201.
109 Ibid, 204.

9 THE HERO AS PROPHET
1 Seigel, 164.
2 Ibid, 165.

3 Morley III, 219.
4 Monypenny, 164.
5 *Spectator*, 4 January 1840.
6 Bowlby, 240.
7 Stanley I, 48.
8 Masson I, 67–8.
9 Collected Letters XII, 6.
10 Ibid, 51.
11 Heroes, 65.
12 Collected Letters XII, 67.
13 Ibid, 69.
14 Ibid, 79.
15 Rem, 79.
16 Ibid, 80.
17 Collected Letters XII, 80–1.
18 Ibid, 128.
19 Ibid, 134.
20 Fox, 91.
21 Collected Letters XII, 150.
22 Ibid.
23 Ibid, 171.
24 Ibid, 239.
25 Ibid, 169.
26 Fox, 99.
27 Collected Letters XIII, 185.
28 Collected Letters XII, 220.
29 Ibid, 238.
30 Heroes, 29.
31 Ibid, 196–7.
32 Ibid, 216–17.
33 Ibid.
34 Ibid, 199.
35 Ibid, 203.
36 Ibid, 199.
37 Ibid, 31.
38 Ibid, 208.
39 Ibid, 215.
40 Russell, 623–4.
41 Heroes, 162.
42 Ibid, 164.
43 Ibid, 165.
44 Ibid, 168.
45 Ibid, 13.
46 Uglow, 147.
47 Heroes, 152.
48 Collected Letters XII, 247.
49 Ibid, 264.
50 Ibid, 267.
51 Ibid, 269.
52 Ibid, 288.
53 Ibid, 325.
54 Ibid, 326.
55 Ibid, 345.
56 Collected Letters XIII, 19.
57 Ibid, 11.
58 Ibid, 48.
59 Ibid, 50.
60 Ibid, 101.
61 Pope-Hennessy, 113.
62 Collected Letters XIII, 82.
63 Ibid, 84 (n).
64 *Spectator*, 20 March 1841, 280.
65 Collected Letters XIII, 131.
66 Ibid, 190.
67 Ibid, 224.
68 Ibid, 289.
69 Ibid, 299.
70 Ibid, 304.
71 Ibid, 296.
72 Ibid, (n).
73 CME IV, 237–8.
74 Collected Letters XIII, 311.
75 Collected Letters XIV, 42.
76 Collected Letters XIII, 317.
77 Ibid, 313 (n).
78 For the background to Espinasse's original letter, and Carlyle's reply to it, see Espinasse, 58–60.
79 Collected Letters XIII, 319.
80 Collected Letters XIV, 8.
81 Ibid, 11.
82 Ibid, 49.
83 Ibid, 52.
84 Collected Letters XV, 221.
85 Collected Letters XIV, 31.
86 Ibid, 85.
87 Ibid, 154.
88 Rem, 84.
89 Collected Letters XIV, 198.
90 Ibid, 181.
91 Stanley II, 455.
92 Collected Letters XIV, 184.
93 Ibid, 185.
94 Fox, 124.
95 Collected Letters XIV, 206.
96 Fox, 136–7.
97 Collected Letters XIV, 228.
98 Ibid, 226.
99 Collected Letters XV, 7.
100 Ibid, 68.
101 Oliver I, 179.
102 PP, 2.
103 Trinity MS letter, 25.2.1848.
104 Collected Letters XV, 80.
105 Ibid, 83.
106 Ibid, 108.

[107] Ibid, 139 (n).

[108] See article by K.J. Fielding, the *Carlyle Annual* 1980, 7–8.

[109] Collected Letters XV, 216.

[110] Ibid, 223.

[111] Collected Letters XVI, 5.

[112] Ibid, 21.

[113] Ibid, 22.

[114] Ibid, 26.

[115] Ibid, 38.

[116] Ibid, 39.

[117] Ibid, 40.

[118] The *Oxford English Dictionary* cites the first use of 'Carlylese' as being in the *Saturday Review* in 1858, fifteen years after this letter. The *OED* also credits Carlyle with the coinage of the phrase 'Captains of Industry', attributing it to *Past and Present* later this year.

[119] Collected Letters XVI, 56.

[120] Ibid, 59.

[121] Ibid, 60.

[122] Ibid, 79.

[123] Ibid, 133.

10 *Oliver.* 'LAST GLIMPSE OF THE
        GODLIKE'

[1] PP, 57.

[2] Ibid, 169.

[3] Ibid, 223.

[4] Ibid, 99.

[5] Ibid, 215.

[6] Ibid, 282.

[7] Ibid, 18.

[8] Ibid, 147.

[9] Ibid, 153–4.

[10] Ibid, 153.

[11] Ibid, 146.

[12] Ibid, 12–13.

[13] Pope-Hennessy, 184.

[14] *Spectator*, 29 April 1843, 398.

[15] Seigel, 214.

[16] CME IV, 292–3.

[17] Ibid, 282. 'Adust' means dried up or dusty.

[18] Ibid, 310.

[19] Ibid, 271.

[20] Ibid, 302.

[21] Ibid, 313–14.

[22] Collected Letters XVI, 222.

[23] Ibid, 236.

[24] Ibid, 254.

[25] Ibid, 258.

[26] Collected Letters XVII, 50.

[27] Ibid, 120.

[28] Ibid, 148.

[29] Ibid, 153 (n).

[30] Ibid.

[31] Ibid, 164.

[32] Ibid, 199.

[33] Ibid, 233.

[34] Ibid, 239.

[35] Ibid, 251 (n).

[36] Ibid, 301.

[37] Collected Letters XVIII, 18.

[38] Ibid, 32.

[39] Ibid, 32 (n).

[40] Ibid, 47.

[41] Ibid, 48.

[42] Ibid, 50.

[43] *The Times*, leading article, 17 June 1844.

[44] Ibid, 19 June 1844, and in Collected Letters XVIII, 72–4.

[45] Collected Letters XVIII, 97.

[46] Ibid, 122.

[47] Ibid, 155.

[48] Ibid, 157.

[49] Sterling, 260–1.

[50] Collected Letters XVIII, 193.

[51] Ibid (n).

[52] Ibid, 202.

[53] Rem, 80.

[54] Collected Letters XVIII, 221.

[55] Ibid, 268.

[56] Ibid, 261.

[57] Ibid, 255.

[58] Ibid, 299.

[59] Ibid, 300.

[60] Huxley, 230.

[61] Marrs, 607.

[62] Slater, 377.

[63] Huxley, 235.

[64] Ibid.

[65] Last Words, 234.

[66] LM I, 307.

[67] Huxley, 242.

[68] CME IV, 137.

[69] LM I, 308.

[70] Ibid, 308–9.

[71] Last Words, 236.

[72] Marrs, 615.

[73] Copeland, 178.

[74] Huxley, 248.

[75] Ibid, 249.

[76] Last Words, 238–9.

[77] NLM I, 159.
[78] Bliss I, 207.
[79] Ibid, 208.
[80] Ibid, 210–11. 'Thrums' are odds and ends in weaving.
[81] Slater, 380.
[82] LM I, 333.
[83] Bliss I, 217.
[84] Huxley, 254.
[85] Bliss II, 170.
[86] NL II, 7.
[87] Last Words, 242.
[88] NL II, 9.
[89] Slater, 384.
[90] CME IV, 349.
[91] Huxley, 256–7.
[92] NL II, 11.
[93] Collected Letters XX, 62.
[94] Ibid, 12.
[95] Ibid.
[96] Huxley, 260.
[97] Oliver I, 1.
[98] Ibid.
[99] Ibid, 51.
[100] Ibid.
[101] Ibid, 414.
[102] Oliver II, 174.
[103] Oliver I, 70 (n).
[104] Oliver II, 33.
[105] Ibid, 51.
[106] Ibid.
[107] Ibid.
[108] Ibid, 52.
[109] Ibid, 170.
[110] Oliver III, 35.
[111] See for example the passage at III, 71–2.
[112] Oliver III, 270.
[113] Oliver IV, 171.
[114] Ibid, 207.
[115] *Spectator*, 6 December 1845, 1167.
[116] Ibid, 1166.

11 'DEEP GLOOM AND
        BOTTOMLESS DUBITATION'

[1] Collected Letters VI, 351.
[2] Slater, 390.
[3] NL II, 13.
[4] Ibid, 14.
[5] Slater, 391.
[6] Collected Letters XX, 125.
[7] Huxley, 264.
[8] Ibid, 268.
[9] Ibid, 269.
[10] Espinasse, 81.
[11] Froude III, 374.
[12] Slater, 394.
[13] NL II, 20.
[14] Wilson III, 325.
[15] Ibid, 330–1.
[16] Huxley, 277–8.
[17] Bliss I, 222.
[18] Ibid, 223.
[19] LM I, 368.
[20] Bliss I, 225.
[21] Ibid, 227.
[22] LM I, 370.
[23] Collected Letters XX, 261.
[24] Bliss I, 229.
[25] Collected Letters XXI, 9.
[26] Bliss I, 231.
[27] Ibid, 233.
[28] Marrs, 636.
[29] Ibid, 637.
[30] LM I, 373.
[31] Copeland, 190.
[32] Froude III, 402.
[33] LM I, 380.
[34] Collected Letters XXI, 115.
[35] Last Words, 246.
[36] Collected Letters XXI, 130–1.
[37] Ibid, 154.
[38] Slater, 416.
[39] Last Words, 248.
[40] Marrs, 646.
[41] NL II, 37.
[42] Huxley, 301.
[43] NL II, 37.
[44] Espinasse, 220.
[45] Fox, 171–4.
[46] NL II, 34.
[47] MSB, 282.
[48] Shepherd II, 17.
[49] LM I, 390.
[50] Marrs, 653.
[51] Slater, 427.
[52] Bliss I, 236.
[53] Last Words, 253.
[54] Slater, 434.
[55] Espinasse, 156–7.
[56] Froude III, 422.
[57] BM MS (Egerton 3032).
[58] LM II, 19.
[59] Rem, 85.
[60] Slater, 435.
[61] NL II, 53.

[62] Pope-Hennessy, 268.
[63] Ibid, 54.
[64] Ibid, 55.
[65] Froude III, 421.
[66] Ibid, 422.
[67] AT, 231.
[68] Froude III, 423.
[69] Ruth apRoberts, in her specialised study of Carlyle's religion, claims that after his mother's death his attacks on Christianity became less guarded. However, he never wrote *Exodus from Houndsditch*. See apRoberts, 58–72.
[70] NL II, 59.
[71] Trinity MS letter, 4.3.1848.
[72] Ibid, 8.4.1848.
[73] Froude III, 429.
[74] Ibid, 431.
[75] Ibid, 435.
[76] Thomas, 174.
[77] Ibid, 175.
[78] Ibid, 176.
[79] Ibid, 179.
[80] Davies, 188.
[81] Marrs, 665.
[82] Bliss I, 247.
[83] Emerson, 207.
[84] Froude III, 443.
[85] NL II, 66.
[86] Huxley, 313.
[87] Duffy, 31–2.
[88] Slater, 446.
[89] Pope-Hennessy, 157.
[90] Froude III, 450.
[91] Shepherd, 35.
[92] Goldberg, xxxix.
[93] BM MS (Egerton 3032).
[94] Huxley, 322.
[95] Ibid, 323.
[96] Trinity MS letter, 2.4.49.
[97] *Spectator*, 14 April 1849, 344.
[98] Marrs, 671,
[99] Wilson IV, 91.
[100] Froude III, 459.
[101] Bliss I, 248.
[102] Ibid, 252.
[103] Froude IV, 5. He quotes from Carlyle's own *Reminiscence* of his journey to Ireland, published without the authority of his executors after his death.
[104] Slater, 455.
[105] LM II, 80.
[106] Bliss I, 259.
[107] Froude IV, 15.
[108] Ibid, 21.
[109] NLS MS 513.
[110] Rem, 85.
[111] Froude IV, 22.
[112] NL II, 83.
[113] Arnold, 111.
[114] Willey, 267.
[115] I am indebted to Mr Hywel Williams for this piece of information.
[116] Ibid.
[117] Trilling, 202.
[118] Ford, 84.
[119] Biswas, 152.
[120] Portrait, 72.
[121] Froude IV, 23.
[122] NLS MS 513.
[123] CME IV, 349.
[124] Ibid, 350. Seven Dials, in Covent Garden, was then the most depressed area of central London, full of thieves and prostitutes.
[125] Ibid.
[126] Ibid, 351.
[127] Ibid, 354.
[128] Ibid, 355.
[129] Ibid, 381.
[130] Ibid, 356.
[131] Ibid, 376.
[132] Ibid, 359.
[133] Ibid, 360.
[134] Ibid.

12 PRIMITIVE PAMPHLETEER

[1] NL II, 85.
[2] *Fraser's Magazine*, January 1850, 25.
[3] Ibid.
[4] Ibid.
[5] Ibid, 26.
[6] Ibid, 27.
[7] Ibid.
[8] Ibid, 28.
[9] Ibid, 30.
[10] Ibid, 29.
[11] Ibid, 31.
[12] NL II, 85.
[13] Marrs, 677.
[14] NL II, 86.
[15] Rem, 126.
[16] *The Spectator*, 2 February 1850.
[17] LDP, 28.

[18] Ibid, 21.
[19] Wilson IV, 254.
[20] LDP, 23.
[21] Ibid, 38.
[22] Ibid, 46.
[23] Rem, 85.
[24] LDP, 51.
[25] Ibid, 58.
[26] Ibid, 55.
[27] Ibid. 66.
[28] Ibid. 68.
[29] Ibid, 70.
[30] Ibid, 73.
[31] Ibid, 77.
[32] Froude IV, 28.
[33] LDP, 10.
[34] Ibid, 115–16.
[35] NL II, 92.
[36] Ibid, 93.
[37] LDP, 187.
[38] Ibid, 213.
[39] Ibid, 221.
[40] Ibid, 226.
[41] Ibid, 234.
[42] Ibid, 241.
[43] NLS MS 513.
[44] NL II, 94.
[45] Rem, 87.
[46] NL II, 97.
[47] NLS MS 513.
[48] Ruskin, 5.
[49] Ibid, 6.
[50] Froude IV, 48.
[51] Huxley, 344.
[52] LDP, 311.
[53] Ibid, 313.
[54] Ibid, 329–30.
[55] Davies, 200.
[56] Slater, 459.
[57] Ibid, 460.
[58] Bliss I, 261.
[59] Ibid, 262.
[60] Ibid, 264.
[61] LM II, 122.
[62] Ibid.
[63] AT, 245.
[64] Ibid, 136.
[65] Froude IV, 62.
[66] NLM II, 21.
[67] Slater, 465.
[68] Ibid, 466.
[69] Martineau I, 387.
[70] Last Words, 257.

[71] Froude IV, 67.
[72] Ibid, 68.
[73] NL II, 107.
[74] Slater, 467.
[75] Davies, 191.
[76] Sterling, 4.
[77] Ibid, 3.
[78] Ibid, 97.
[79] Ibid, 39.
[80] Ibid, 54.
[81] Ibid, 55.
[82] Ibid.
[83] Ibid, 56.
[84] Ibid, 60.
[85] NL II, 110.
[86] Wilson IV, 345.
[87] Slater, 473.
[88] Ibid, 469.
[89] MSB, 286.
[90] NLS MS 514.
[91] LM II, 150.
[92] Ibid.
[93] Last Words, 182.
[94] Rem, 127.
[95] The Spectator, 25 October 1851.
[96] Huxley, 352.
[97] Froude V, 15–16.
[98] NL II, 117.
[99] Ibid, 118.
[100] Froude II, 8–18.
[101] Ibid, 17.
[102] Ibid, 11.
[103] NLS MS 514.
[104] Huxley, 356.
[105] Ibid, 120.
[106] NL II, 124.
[107] BM MS (Egerton 3032).
[108] MSB, 183.
[109] Slater, 481.
[110] Ibid, 484.
[111] Last Words, 265.
[112] NLS MS 514.
[113] Ibid, 267.
[114] Marrs, 693.
[115] Bliss I, 280.
[116] Ibid, 287.
[117] Ibid, 291.
[118] Ibid, 292.
[119] Ibid, 297.
[120] Ibid, 298.
[121] Last Words, 273.
[122] Bliss I, 299.
[123] BM MS (Egerton 3032).

[124] LM II, 208.
[125] Huxley, 366.
[126] LM II, 209.
[127] NL II, 139–40.
[128] Froude IV 122–3.
[129] Marrs, 695.
[130] Rem, 88.
[131] Froude IV, 126.
[132] NL II, 142.
[133] Ibid, 143.
[134] Duffy, 180.
[135] NLS MS 514.
[136] NL II, 146.
[137] NLS MS 515.
[138] NL II, 145.
[139] BM MS (Egerton 3032).
[140] Ibid.
[141] Froude IV, 127.
[142] NLS MS 515.
[143] Marrs, 697.
[144] Froude IV, 128–9.
[145] Ibid, 130.
[146] NL II, 149.

13 *Frederick*: 'A BOTCH AND A
      WRECK'

[1] Rem, 125.
[2] NL II, 151.
[3] Ibid, 153.
[4] Bliss I, 306.
[5] Frederick I, 10–11.
[6] LM II, 223.
[7] Ibid, 230 (n).
[8] NL II, 157.
[9] BM MS (Egerton 3032).
[10] Bliss I, 308.
[11] Last Words, 275.
[12] Slater, 501.
[13] Wilson, V, 117–18.
[14] Froude IV, 159.
[15] BM MS (Egerton 2845).
[16] Froude IV, 172.
[17] LM II, 249.
[18] Ibid.
[19] NLS MS 515.
[20] Cate, 64–5.
[21] Cook I, 476.
[22] NLS MS 516.
[23] Ibid.
[24] BM MS (Egerton 3032).
[25] Slater, 505.
[26] Paul, 86.
[27] Trinity MS.
[28] NLS MS 516.
[29] LM II, 258.
[30] Ibid, 263.
[31] NLS MS 516.
[32] Wilson V, 189.
[33] Cate, 75.
[34] LM II, 273.
[35] NL II, 178.
[36] LM II, 278.
[37] Paul, 293–4.
[38] LM II, 278.
[39] Marrs, 721.
[40] NL II, 184.
[41] Rem, 133–4.
[42] NLS MS 516.
[43] Ibid.
[44] Rem, 81 (n).
[45] LM II, 310.
[46] Froude IV, 186–7.
[47] NLM II, 135.
[48] Ibid, 136.
[49] Froude IV, 189.
[50] Ibid, 188.
[51] LM II, 332.
[52] Bliss I, 327.
[53] Marrs, 724.
[54] NLM II, 158.
[55] Last Words, 281. '*Gewaltig*' is German for 'enormous' or 'vast'.
[56] NLM II, 165–6.
[57] LM II, 342.
[58] Ibid, 343.
[59] NLS MS 516.
[60] NL II, 191.
[61] Slater, 521.
[62] Ibid, 522.
[63] Ibid, 523.
[64] LM II, 350.
[65] Ibid, 351.
[66] NL II, 192.
[67] Marrs, 730.
[68] Bliss I, 329.
[69] Froude IV, 210.
[70] MSB, 184–5.
[71] Morley I, 61.
[72] Bliss I, 336.
[73] Ibid, 337.
[74] Ibid, 341.
[75] Ibid, 342.
[76] Ibid, 344.
[77] Froude IV, 228.
[78] *The Spectator*, 2 October 1858.

14 *Frederick*: 'THIS MOTHER OF DEAD DOGS'

[1] LM II, 388.
[2] Ibid, 393.
[3] NLS MS 516.
[4] Marrs, 730.
[5] Copeland, 221.
[6] NLM II, 200.
[7] Slater, 526.
[8] NLM II, 211.
[9] NL II, 196.
[10] Ibid, 197.
[11] NLS MS 516.
[12] Marrs, 733.
[13] LM III, 11.
[14] Ibid, 17.
[15] BM MS (Egerton 3032).
[16] NLM II, 222.
[17] LM III, 18.
[18] Marrs, 736.
[19] NLM II, 226.
[20] LM III, 63.
[21] Ibid, 26.
[22] Ibid, 42.
[23] NLM II, 229 (n).
[24] LM III, 53.
[25] Bliss I, 352.
[26] LM III, 62.
[27] Ibid.
[28] Cate, 89.
[29] Cook II, 561.
[30] NL II, 209.
[31] Cate, 90.
[32] NLS MS 517.
[33] Slater, 533.
[34] TJ, 77–8.
[35] Davies, 188.
[36] Froude IV, 257.
[37] Paul, 291.
[38] Ibid, 425.
[39] NL II, 210.
[40] NLS MS 517.
[41] Ibid.
[42] LM III, 88.
[43] NLS MS 517.
[44] NLS MS 7197.
[45] *Spectator*, 17 May 1862.
[46] Shepherd II, 185.
[47] LM III, 135.
[48] NL II, 215.
[49] Ibid.
[50] NLS MS 517.
[51] LM III, 140.
[52] NLM II, 287.
[53] LM III, 168.
[54] Ibid, 170.
[55] It was a kind of reverse compliment; a decade earlier, Dickens had dedicated *Hard Times* to Carlyle.
[56] Wilson V, 524.
[57] *Spectator*, 8 August 1863.
[58] Copeland, 230.
[59] Advertised for sale in Catalogue 62 of Wilder Books, Illinois, 1993; I am indebted to Mr Giles Gordon for bringing this to my attention.
[60] LM III, 174–5.
[61] Ibid, 178.
[62] Ibid.
[63] NLS MS 517.
[64] LM III, 181.
[65] Froude IV, 274.
[66] Wilson V, 539.
[67] LM III, 193.
[68] *Spectator*, 12 March 1864.
[69] LM III, 197.
[70] Ruskin, 504.
[71] LM III, 197.
[72] Ibid, 198.
[73] TJ, 74.
[74] Bliss I, 370.
[75] NL II, 224.
[76] LM III, 215.
[77] Ibid.
[78] Ibid, 228.
[79] Ibid, 243.
[80] Froude IV, 283.
[81] Allingham, 230.
[82] Olive, 242.
[83] Frederick V, 195.
[84] Frederick VII, 480.
[85] Frederick VIII, 115.
[86] Frederick VII, 80.
[87] Frederick I, 6.
[88] Ibid, 17.
[89] Ibid, 20.
[90] Frederick II, 245 (n).
[91] Ibid, 107.
[92] Frederick I, 8.
[93] Ibid.
[94] Frederick II, 365.
[95] Frederick I, 339.
[96] Ibid, 346.
[97] Frederick III, 312.
[98] Frederick IV, 132.
[99] Frederick VI, 2.

[100] Ibid, 420.
[101] Frederick VII, 490.
[102] Frederick VIII, 300.

15 AN END OF SORROWS
[1] LM III, 243.
[2] NL II, 226.
[3] NLS MS 517.
[4] See 'Carlyle makes his will (1865–1871): new documents discovered', by K.J. Fielding, *Carlyle Annual* 1989, 56–63.
[5] Bliss I, 379–80.
[6] LM III, 273.
[7] Cate, 112.
[8] Bliss I, 381.
[9] LM III, 280.
[10] Marrs, 741–2.
[11] Froude IV 295.
[12] CME V, 11.
[13] TJ, opp. 49.
[14] *The Spectator*, 18 November 1865, 1281.
[15] NL, 232.
[16] LM III, 309.
[17] Ibid, 312.
[18] Ibid, 316.
[19] Rem, 161–2.
[20] Ibid, 162.
[21] Wilson VI, 50.
[22] Masson I, 27–8.
[23] CME IV, 449.
[24] Ibid, 451.
[25] Ibid.
[26] Ibid, 453.
[27] Ibid.
[28] Ibid, 459.
[29] Ibid, 460.
[30] Ibid, 467.
[31] Ibid, 472.
[32] Ibid, 470.
[33] Ibid, 473.
[34] Ibid, 474.
[35] Ibid, 478.
[36] Ibid, 480.
[37] Rem, 162.
[38] LM III, 328.
[39] Bliss I, 386.
[40] Masson I, 28.
[41] Bliss I, 388.
[42] NLS MS 518.
[43] LM III, 340.
[44] Rem, 164.
[45] Ibid, 165.
[46] Ibid.
[47] Ibid, 166.
[48] NLS MS 526.
[49] Rem, 167.
[50] Froude IV, 321.
[51] Wilson VI, 78.
[52] NL II, 236.
[53] Cate, 117.
[54] Rem, 49.
[55] NLS MS 666.
[56] Rem, 69.
[57] Ibid, 89.
[58] NLS MS 518.
[59] Marrs, 754.
[60] Rem, 135.
[61] Ibid, 155.
[62] Wilson VI, 88.
[63] NLS MS 526.
[64] Smalley, 291–307.
[65] Mill, 251.
[66] Shepherd II, 239.
[67] NLS MS 666.
[68] Mill, 254.
[69] Marrs, 758.
[70] NL, 241.
[71] Froude IV, 334.
[72] Ibid, 335.
[73] Rem, 357.
[74] Fox, 238.
[75] Rem, 364–5.
[76] Fox, 239.
[77] Wilson VI, 128.
[78] Ibid, 129.
[79] Cate, 131.
[80] Ibid, 132.
[81] *The Times*, Monday 3 June 1867.
[82] Cate, 133.
[83] Ibid.
[84] Ibid, 134.
[85] Ibid, 135.
[86] Ibid, 136.
[87] Ibid, 137.
[88] Ibid.
[89] NLS MS 526.
[90] Froude IV, 350.
[91] Ibid, 353.
[92] CME V, 30.
[93] Ibid, 5.
[94] Ibid, 1.
[95] Ibid, 3.
[96] Ibid, 2.
[97] Ibid, 11.

[98] Ibid, 13.
[99] Ibid, 21.
[100] Ibid, 12.

16 THE PURSUIT OF SILENCE
[1] Froude IV, 353.
[2] Ibid, 355.
[3] Trinity MS letter, 23.8.67.
[4] Allingham, 165–6.
[5] NLS MS 526.
[6] Copeland, 236.
[7] Ibid, 237.
[8] Rutherford, 9.
[9] Allingham, 182.
[10] Lecky, 58.
[11] Froude IV, 368.
[12] NLS MS 518.
[13] Allingham, 196.
[14] NL II, 251.
[15] Davies, 284.
[16] NL II, 252.
[17] Ibid, 254.
[18] Ruskin, 505.
[19] NL II, 255.
[20] LL, 113 (n).
[21] NL II, 257.
[22] Ibid, 258.
[23] Cate, 147 (n).
[24] Slater, 556.
[25] Froude IV, 386.
[26] Marrs, 760.
[27] Ibid, 761.
[28] NL II, 266.
[29] Forster II, 396.
[30] FT, 124.
[31] Slater, 573.
[32] Marrs, 768.
[33] Cate, 155.
[34] Lecky, 74–5.
[35] CME V, 49.
[36] Ibid, 52.
[37] Ibid, 54.
[38] Ibid, 59.
[39] NL II, 272.
[40] Ibid, 274.
[41] Froude IV, 395.
[42] Allingham, 203.
[43] NL II, 274.
[44] Marrs, 771.
[45] Cate, 159–60.
[46] Munera, 162.
[47] Ibid, 304 (n).
[48] Nevinson, 57–8.

[49] NLS MS 527.
[50] Cate, 165.
[51] NL II, 284.
[52] Froude IV, 408.
[53] Ibid, 410.
[54] Paul, 297.
[55] Wilson VI, 276.
[56] BM MS (Egerton 3032).
[57] NL II, 283.
[58] Ibid, 284.
[59] Allingham, 209.
[60] NL II, 286.
[61] Ibid, 288.
[62] Allingham, 217.
[63] NL II, 298.
[64] Froude IV, 420.
[65] NLS MS 527.
[66] Elliott II, 221.
[67] NLS MS 1778.
[68] NLS MS 527.
[69] Allingham, 227.
[70] NLS MS 527.
[71] NL II, 305.
[72] NLS MS 528.
[73] Allingham, 232.
[74] NL II, 307.
[75] NLS MS 528.
[76] Buckle, 355.
[77] Ibid, 357.
[78] Froude IV, 430.
[79] NL II, 310–11.
[80] Ibid, 313.
[81] Wilson VI, 352ff.
[82] Ibid, 355.
[83] NLS MS 666.
[84] Ibid.
[85] Wilson VI, 373.
[86] NL II, 319.
[87] Froude IV, 435.
[88] NLS MS 528.
[89] Marrs, 788.
[90] Ibid.
[91] Lecky, 113.
[92] Trinity MS letter (transcription) 3.4.76.
[93] NLS MS 528.
[94] Morley I, 154.
[95] Robertson Scott, 26.
[96] The Times, 28 November 1876.
[97] Wilson VI, 392.
[98] Gladstone I, 292.
[99] Gladstone II, 49.
[100] The Times, 5 May 1877.

[101] NL II, 332.
[102] Ibid, 333.
[103] NLS MS 528.
[104] Allingham, 256.
[105] NL II, 334.
[106] Robertson Scott, 169.
[107] Allingham, 259.
[108] Ibid, 267.
[109] NLS MS 528.
[110] NL II, 339.
[111] Ibid, 336.
[112] Ibid, 341.
[113] Ibid, 342.
[114] Wilson VI, 458.
[115] Cook II, 483.
[116] Copeland, 254.
[117] Allingham, 306.
[118] Copeland, 257.
[119] Lecky, 148.
[120] Ibid, 149.
[121] Froude IV, 469.
[122] Marrs, 792.

BIBLIOGRAPHY

1. CARLYLE'S WORKS

Schiller: *The Life of Friedrich Schiller, Comprehending an Examination of his Works*, by Thomas Carlyle (Chapman and Hall, 1899) (Vol XXV of the Centenary Edition).

CME: *Critical and Miscellaneous Essays*, by Thomas Carlyle (Chapman and Hall, 1899) (5 vols: XXVI–XXX of the Centenary Edition).

Sartor: *Sartor Resartus, The Life and Opinions of Herr Teufelsdröckh*, by Thomas Carlyle (Chapman and Hall, 1901) (Vol I of the Centenary Edition).

FR: *The French Revolution, a History*, by Thomas Carlyle (Chapman and Hall, 1898) (3 vols: Vols II–IV of the Centenary Edition).

Heroes: *On Heroes, Hero-Worship, and the Heroic in History*, by Thomas Carlyle (Chapman and Hall, 1901) (Vol V of the Centenary Edition).

PP: *Past and Present*, by Thomas Carlyle (Chapman and Hall, 1899) (Vol X of the Centenary Edition).

Oliver: *Oliver Cromwell's Letters and Speeches: with Elucidations*, by Thomas Carlyle (Chapman and Hall, 1897–1902) (4 vols: Vols VI–IX of the Centenary Edition).

LDP: *Latter-Day Pamphlets*, edited by Thomas Carlyle (Chapman and Hall, 1898) (Vol XX of the Centenary Edition).

Sterling: *The Life of John Sterling*, by Thomas Carlyle (Chapman and Hall, 1897) (Vol XI of the Centenary Edition).

Frederick: *History of Friedrich II of Prussia, called Frederick the Great*, by Thomas Carlyle (Chapman and Hall, 1897–98) (8 vols: Vols XII–XIX of the Centenary Edition).

Rem: *Reminiscences*, by Thomas Carlyle, edited by C.E. Norton (Everyman, 1932).

Two Rem: *Two Reminiscences of Thomas Carlyle*, edited by John Clubbe (Duke University Press, 1974).

Last Words: *Last Words of Thomas Carlyle* (Longmans, 1892).

2. LETTERS

Bliss I: *Thomas Carlyle: Letters to his Wife*, edited by Trudy Bliss (Gollancz, 1953).

Bliss II: *Jane Welsh Carlyle, a New Selection of her Letters*, edited by Trudy Bliss (Gollancz, 1950).

Cate: *The Correspondence of Thomas Carlyle and John Ruskin*, edited by George Allan Cate (Stanford University Press, 1982).

Collected Letters: *The Collected Letters of Thomas and Jane Welsh Carlyle*, edited by Charles Richard Sanders, Kenneth J. Fielding and Clyde de L. Ryals (Duke University Press, 1970–1995) (24 vols so far).

Copeland: *The Letters of Thomas Carlyle to his Youngest Sister*, edited by C.T. Copeland (Chapman and Hall, 1899).

Huxley: *Jane Welsh Carlyle: Letters to her Family*, edited by Leonard Huxley (John Murray, 1924).

LM: *Letters and Memorials of Jane Welsh Carlyle*, edited by James Anthony Froude (Longmans, 1883) (3 vols).

Marrs: *The Letters of Thomas Carlyle to his Brother Alexander: with Related Family Letters*, edited by Edwin W. Marrs Jnr (Harvard University Press, 1968).

MSB: *Letters of Thomas Carlyle to John Stuart Mill, John Sterling and Robert Browning*, edited by Alexander Carlyle (Unwin, 1923).

NL: *New Letters of Thomas Carlyle*, edited by Alexander Carlyle (Bodley Head, 1904) (2 vols).

NLM: *New Letters and Memorials of Jane Welsh Carlyle*, edited by Alexander Carlyle (Bodley Head, 1903) (2 vols).

Norton: *The Correspondence between Goethe and Carlyle*, edited by C.E. Norton (Macmillan, 1887).

Slater: *The Correspondence of Emerson and Carlyle*, edited by Joseph Slater (Columbia University Press, 1964).

TJ: *Thomas and Jane: Selected Letters from the Edinburgh University Library Collection*, edited by Ian Campbell (Friends of the EUL, 1980).

3 OTHER WORKS

Allingham: *William Allingham's Diary*, with an introduction by Geoffrey Grigson (Centaur, 1967).

apRoberts: *The Ancient Dialect: Thomas Carlyle and Comparative Religion*, by Ruth apRoberts (University of California Press, 1988).

Arnold: *The Letters of Matthew Arnold to Arthur Hugh Clough*, edited by Howard Foster Lowry (OUP, 1932).

AT: *Alfred Tennyson*, by Charles Tennyson (Macmillan, 1950).

Biswas: *Arthur Hugh Clough, Towards a Reconsideration*, by Robindra Kumar Biswas (OUP, 1972).

Bowlby: *Charles Darwin, a New Biography*, by John Bowlby (Hutchinson, 1990).

Buckle: *The Life of Benjamin Disraeli, Earl of Beaconsfield*, Vol V, by G.E. Buckle (John Murray, 1920).

Bullock: *Hitler, a Study in Tyranny*, by Alan Bullock (Odhams, 1952).

Burdett: *The Two Carlyles*, by Osbert Burdett (Faber, 1930).

Campbell: *Thomas Carlyle*, by Ian Campbell (Hamish Hamilton, 1974).

Chadwick: *The Secularization of the European Mind in the 19th Century*, by Owen Chadwick (Canto, 1990).

Clubbe: *Carlyle and his Contemporaries: Essays in Honor of Charles Richard Saunders*, edited by John Clubbe (Durham, North Carolina, 1976).

Cook: *The Life of Ruskin*, by E.T. Cook (George Allen, 1911) (2 vols).

Cumming: *A Disimprisoned Epic – Form and Vision in Carlyle's French Revolution*, by Mark Cumming (University of Pennsylvania Press, 1988).

Davies: *John Forster, a Literary Life*, by James A. Davies (Leicester University Press, 1983).

Duffy: *Conversations with Carlyle*, by Sir Charles Gavan Duffy (Sampson Low, 1892).

Elliott: *Letters of John Stuart Mill*, edited by Hugh Elliott (Longmans, 1910) (2 vols).

Emerson: *English Traits*, by Ralph Waldo Emerson (Harrap Library Edition, undated).

Espinasse: *Literary Recollections and Sketches*, by Francis Espinasse (Hodder and Stoughton, 1893).

Ford: *The Pelican Guide to English Literature*, Vol VI, edited by Boris Ford (Pelican, revised edition, 1969).

Forster: *The Life of Dickens*, by John Forster (2 vols, Everyman, 1927).

Fox: *The Journals of Caroline Fox 1835–1871*, edited by Wendy Monk (Elek, 1972).

Froude I: *Thomas Carlyle, A History of the First Forty Years of His Life 1795–1835*, by James Anthony Froude (Longmans, 1882).

Froude II: Ibid, Vol II.

Froude III: *Thomas Carlyle, A History of his Life in London 1834–1881*, by James Anthony Froude (Longmans, 1884).

Froude IV: Ibid, Vol II.

Froude V: *My Relations with Carlyle*, by James Anthony Froude (Longmans, 1903).

FT: *Carlyle Past and Present, A Collection of New Essays*, edited by K.J. Fielding and Rodger L. Tarr (Vision Press, 1976).

Gladstone: *The Life of W.E. Gladstone*, by John Morley (Macmillan, 1905) (2 vols).

Goldberg: *Carlyle's Latter Day Pamphlets*, edited by M.K. Goldberg and J.P. Seigel (Canadian Federation for the Humanities, 1983).

Grierson: *Carlyle and Hitler*, by H.J.C. Grierson (CUP, 1933).

Halliday: *Mr Carlyle – My Patient*, by James L. Halliday (Heinemann, 1949).

Harrold: *Carlyle and German Thought*, by C.F. Harrold (Yale University Press, 1934).

Holloway: *The Victorian Sage*, by John Holloway (Macmillan, 1953).

Hunt: *Autobiography*, by Leigh Hunt (OUP World's Classics, 1928).

Hutton: *Modern Guides of English Thought*, by R.H. Hutton (1887).

Johnson: *Thomas Carlyle 1814–1831*, by W.S. Johnson (Yale University Press, 1911).

Kenyon: *The History Men*, by John Kenyon (Weidenfeld and Nicolson, 1993) (Revised Edition).

Kingsmill: *Frank Harris*, by Hugh Kingsmill (Cape, 1932).

Larkin: *Carlyle and the Open Secret of his Life*, by Henry Larkin (Kegan Paul, 1886).

Lecky: *Memoir of the Rt Hon W.E.H. Lecky*, by his Wife (Longmans, 1909).

LL: *The Later Letters of Lady Augusta Stanley*, edited by the Dean of Windsor and Hector Bolitho (Cape, 1929).

Marriott: *The Evolution of Prussia*, by Sir J.A.R. Marriott and Sir Charles Grant Robertson (OUP, 1946) (Revised Edition).

Martineau: *Autobiography*, Vol I, by Harriet Martineau (Smith, Elder, 1877).

Masson I: *Carlyle Personally*, by David Masson (Macmillan, 1885).

Masson II: *Edinburgh Sketches and Memories*, by David Masson (A&C Black, 1892).

Mill: *Autobiography*, by John Stuart Mill (OUP World's Classics, 1924).

Monypenny: *The Life of Benjamin Disraeli, Earl of Beaconsfield*, Vol II, by W.F. Monypenny (John Murray, 1912).

Morley: *Recollections*, by Viscount Morley (Macmillan, 1917) (2 vols).

Munera: *Munera Pulveris*, by John Ruskin (OUP World's Classics, 1923).

Nemesis: *The Nemesis of Froude – A Rejoinder to J.A. Froude's 'My Relations with Carlyle'*, by Sir James Crichton-Browne, MD, and Alexander Carlyle (Bodley Head, 1903).

Nevinson: *Changes and Chances*, by Henry W. Nevinson (Nisbet, 1923).

Olive: *The Crown of Wild Olive*, by John Ruskin (George Allen, 1902).

Pankhurst: *The Saint-Simonians, Mill and Carlyle – a Preface to Modern Thought*, by Richard K.P. Pankhurst (Sidgwick and Jackson, 1967).

Paul: *The Life of Froude*, by Herbert Paul (Pitman, 1905).

Pope-Hennessy: *Monckton Milnes – The Years of Promise*, by James Pope-Hennessy (Constable, 1949).

Portrait: *Victorian England: Portrait of an Age*, by G.M. Young (OUP, 1953) (Revised Edition).

Quiller-Couch: *On the Art of Writing*, by Sir Arthur Quiller-Couch (CUP, 1923).

Robertson Scott: *The Life and Death of a Newspaper*, by J.W. Robertson Scott (Methuen, 1952).

Ruskin: *Praeterita*, by John Ruskin (OUP, 1978).

Russell: *The History of Western Philosophy*, by Bertrand Russell (George Allen and Unwin, 1946).

Rutherford: *Pages from a Journal, with other papers*, by Mark Rutherford (OUP World's Classics, 1930).

Sadleir: *Trollope, a Commentary*, by Michael Sadleir (Constable, 1945) (New Edition).

Seigel: *Thomas Carlyle: The Critical Heritage*, edited by Jules Paul Seigel (RKP, 1971).

Shepherd: *Memoirs of the Life and Writings of Thomas Carlyle*, edited by R.H. Shepherd (WH Allen, 1881) (2 vols).

Smalley: *London Letters*, Vol I, by George W. Smalley (Macmillan, 1890).

Stanley I: *Letters and Verses of Arthur Penrhyn Stanley, DD*, edited by Rowland E. Prothero (John Murray, 1895).

Stanley II: *The Life of Dr Arnold*, by Arthur Penrhyn Stanley (Ward Lock edition, undated).

Stephen: *Liberty, Equality, Fraternity*, by James Fitzjames Stephen, with a new foreword by R.A. Posner (University of Chicago Press, 1991).

Tennyson: *Sartor Called Resartus*, by G.B. Tennyson (Princeton University Press, 1965).

Thomas: *The Story of 'The Spectator'*, by W. Beach Thomas (Methuen, 1928).

Trilling: *Matthew Arnold*, by Lionel Trilling (George Allen and Unwin, 1949) (Revised Edition).

Trollope I: *The Warden*, by Anthony Trollope (OUP World's Classics, 1918).

Trollope II: *Autobiography*, by Anthony Trollope (OUP World's Classics, 1923).

Turner: *The Oxford History of English Literature*, Vol IX Part I, edited by Paul Turner (Clarendon Press, 1989).

Uglow: *Elizabeth Gaskell: A Habit of Stories*, by Jenny Uglow (Faber, 1993).

Willey: *Nineteenth Century Studies*, by Basil Willey (Penguin, 1949).

Wilson I: *Carlyle till Marriage (1795–1826)*, by David Alec Wilson (Kegan Paul, 1913).

Wilson II: *Carlyle to 'The French Revolution' (1826–1837)*, by David Alec Wilson (Kegan Paul, 1924).

Wilson III: *Carlyle on Cromwell and Others (1837–1848)*, by David Alec Wilson (Kegan Paul, 1925).

Wilson IV: *Carlyle at his Zenith (1848–1853)*, by David Alec Wilson (Kegan Paul, 1927).

Wilson V: *Carlyle to Threescore and Ten (1853–1865)*, by David Alec Wilson (Kegan Paul, 1929).

Wilson VI: *Carlyle in Old Age (1865–1881)*, by David Alec Wilson and D. Wilson MacArthur (Kegan Paul, 1934).

Wilson VII: *Mr Froude and Carlyle*, by David Alec Wilson (Heinemann, 1898).

Woodward: *The Age of Reform*, by Sir Llewellyn Woodward (OUP, 1962) (2nd Edition).

Wylie: *Thomas Carlyle, the Man and his Books*, by William Howie Wylie (Unwin, 1909).

Young: *Carlyle, His Rise and Fall*, by Norwood Young (Duckworth, 1927).

Zeldin: *France 1848–1945*, Vol I: *Ambition, Love and Politics*, by Theodore Zeldin (OUP, 1973).

4 UNPUBLISHED SOURCES

Trinity MS: Manuscripts in the library of Trinity College, Cambridge.

BM MS: Manuscripts in the British Library, British Museum, London.

NLS MS: Manuscripts in the National Library of Scotland, Edinburgh.

Northampton MS: Manuscripts in the collection of the Marquess of Northampton.

INDEX